American Casebook Series
Hornbook Series and Basic Legal Texts
Nutshell Series

of

WEST PUBLISHING COMPANY
P.O. Box 3526
St. Paul, Minnesota 55165
June, 1980

ACCOUNTING

Fiflis and Kripke's Teaching Materials on Accounting for Business Lawyers, 2nd Ed., 684 pages, 1977 (Casebook)

ADMINISTRATIVE LAW

Davis' Cases, Text and Problems on Administrative Law, 6th Ed., 683 pages, 1977 (Casebook)

Davis' Basic Text on Administrative Law, 3rd Ed., 617 pages, 1972 (Text)

Davis' Police Discretion, 176 pages, 1975 (Text)

Gellhorn's Administrative Law and Process in a Nutshell, 336 pages, 1972 (Text)

Mashaw and Merrill's Introduction to the American Public Law System, 1095 pages, 1975, with 1980 Supplement (Casebook)

Robinson, Gellhorn and Bruff's The Administrative Process, 2nd Ed., 959 pages, 1980 (Casebook)

ADMIRALTY

Healy and Sharpe's Cases and Materials on Admiralty, 875 pages, 1974 (Casebook)

AGENCY—PARTNERSHIP

Crane and Bromberg's Hornbook on Partnership, 695 pages, 1968 (Text)

Fessler's Alternatives to Incorporation for Persons in Quest of Profit, approximately 290 pages, 1980 (Casebook)

Henn's Cases and Materials on Agency, Partnership and Other Unincorporated Business Enterprises, 396 pages, 1972 (Casebook)

AGENCY—PARTNERSHIP—Continued

Reuschlein and Gregory's Hornbook on the Law of Agency and Partnership, 625 pages, 1979 (Text)

Seavey's Hornbook on Agency, 329 pages, 1964 (Text)

Seavey and Hall's Cases on Agency, 431 pages, 1956 (Casebook)

Seavey, Reuschlein and Hall's Cases on Agency and Partnership, 599 pages, 1962 (Casebook)

Selected Corporation and Partnership Statutes and Forms, approximately 885 pages, 1980

Steffen and Kerr's Cases and Materials on Agency-Partnership, 4th Ed., 859 pages, 1980 (Casebook)

Steffen's Agency-Partnership in a Nutshell, 364 pages, 1977 (Text)

ANTITRUST LAW

Gellhorn's Antitrust Law and Economics in a Nutshell, 406 pages, 1976 (Text)

Oppenheim and Weston's Cases and Comments on Federal Antitrust Laws, 3rd Ed., 952 pages, 1968, with 1975 Supplement (Casebook)

Oppenheim and Weston's Price and Service Discrimination under the Robinson-Patman Act, 3rd Ed., 258 pages, 1974 (Casebook—reprint from Oppenheim and Weston's Cases and Comments on Federal Antitrust Laws, 3rd Ed., 1968)

Posner and Easterbrook's Cases and Economic Notes on Antitrust, 2nd Ed., approximately 1100 pages, 1980 (Casebook)

Sullivan's Handbook of the Law of Antitrust, 886 pages, 1977 (Text)

ANTITRUST LAW—Continued

See also Regulated Industries, Trade Regulation

BANKING LAW

See Regulated Industries

BUSINESS PLANNING

Epstein and Scheinfeld's Teaching Materials on Business Reorganization Under the Bankruptcy Code, 216 pages, 1980 (Casebook)

Painter's Problems and Materials in Business Planning, 791 pages, 1975, with 1980 Supplement (Casebook)

CIVIL PROCEDURE

Casad's Res Judicata in a Nutshell, 310 pages, 1976 (Text)

Cound, Friedenthal and Miller's Cases and Materials on Civil Procedure, 3rd Ed., approximately 1120 pages, 1980 with 1980 Supplement (Casebook)

Cound, Friedenthal and Miller's Cases on Pleading, Discovery and Joinder, 643 pages, 1968 (Casebook)

Ehrenzweig, Louisell and Hazard's Jurisdiction in a Nutshell, 4th Ed., 232 pages, 1980 (Text)

Federal Rules of Civil-Appellate-Criminal Procedure—West Law School Edition, 344 pages, 1980

Hodges, Jones and Elliott's Cases and Materials on Texas Trial and Appellate Procedure, 2nd Ed., 745 pages, 1974 (Casebook)

Hodges, Jones and Elliott's Cases and Materials on the Judicial Process Prior to Trial in Texas, 2nd Ed., 871 pages, 1977 (Casebook)

Kane's Civil Procedure in a Nutshell, 271 pages, 1979 (Text)

Karlen's Procedure Before Trial in a Nutshell, 258 pages, 1972 (Text)

Karlen and Joiner's Cases and Materials on Trials and Appeals, 536 pages, 1971 (Casebook)

Karlen, Meisenholder, Stevens and Vestal's Cases on Civil Procedure, 923 pages, 1975 (Casebook)

Koffler and Reppy's Hornbook on Common Law Pleading, 663 pages, 1969 (Text)

McBaine's Cases on Introduction to Civil Procedure, 399 pages, 1950 (Casebook)

McCoid's Cases on Civil Procedure, 823 pages, 1974 (Casebook)

Park's Computer-Aided Exercises on Civil Procedure, 118 pages, 1976 (Coursebook)

CIVIL PROCEDURE—Continued

Shipman's Hornbook on Common-Law Pleading, 3rd Ed., 644 pages, 1923 (Text)

Siegel's Hornbook on New York Practice, 1011 pages, 1978 with 1979–80 Pocket Part (Text)

See also Federal Jurisdiction and Procedure

CIVIL RIGHTS

Abernathy's Cases and Materials on Civil Rights, 660 pages, 1980 (Casebook)

Cohen's Cases on the Law of Deprivation of Liberty: A Study in Social Control, 755 pages, 1980 (Casebook)

Lockhart, Kamisar and Choper's Cases on Constitutional Rights and Liberties, 5th Ed., approximately 1244 pages plus Appendix, 1980 (Casebook)—reprint from Lockhart, et al. Cases on Constitutional Law, 5th Ed., 1980

Vieira's Civil Rights in a Nutshell, 279 pages, 1978 (Text)

COMMERCIAL LAW

Bailey's Secured Transactions in a Nutshell, 377 pages, 1976 (Text)

Epstein and Martin's Basic Uniform Commercial Code Teaching Materials, 599 pages, 1977 (Casebook)

Henson's Hornbook on Secured Transactions under the U.C.C., 2nd Ed., 504 pages, 1979 with 1979 P.P. (Text)

Murray's Commercial Law, Problems and Materials, 366 pages, 1975 (Coursebook)

Nordstrom and Clovis' Problems and Materials on Commercial Paper, 458 pages, 1972 (Casebook)

Nordstrom and Lattin's Problems and Materials on Sales and Secured Transactions, 809 pages, 1968 (Casebook)

Nordstrom's Hornbook on Sales, 600 pages, 1970 (Text)

Selected Commercial Statutes, 1277 pages, 1979

Speidel, Summers and White's Teaching Materials on Commercial and Consumer Law, 2nd Ed., 1475 pages, 1974 (Casebook)

Stone's Uniform Commercial Code in a Nutshell, 507 pages, 1975 (Text)

Uniform Commercial Code, Official Text with Comments, 994 pages, 1978

UCC Article Nine Reprint, 128 pages, 1976

Weber's Commercial Paper in a Nutshell, 2nd Ed., 361 pages, 1975 (Text)

COMMERCIAL LAW—Continued

White and Summers' Hornbook on the Uniform Commercial Code, 2nd Ed., 1250 pages, 1980 (Text)

COMMUNITY PROPERTY

Huie's Texas Cases and Materials on Marital Property Rights, 681 pages, 1966 (Casebook)

Verrall's Cases and Materials on California Community Property, 3rd Ed., 547 pages, 1977 (Casebook)

COMPARATIVE LAW

Langbein's Comparative Criminal Procedure: Germany, 172 pages, 1977 (Casebook)

CONFLICT OF LAWS

Cramton, Currie and Kay's Cases-Comments-Questions on Conflict of Laws, 2nd Ed., 1021 pages, 1975 (Casebook)

Ehrenzweig's Conflicts in a Nutshell, 3rd Ed., 432 pages, 1974 (Text)

Goodrich and Scoles' Hornbook on Conflict of Laws, 4th Ed., 483 pages, 1964 (Text)

Scoles and Weintraub's Cases and Materials on Conflict of Laws, 2nd Ed., 966 pages, 1972, with 1978 Supplement (Casebook)

CONSTITUTIONAL LAW

Engdahl's Constitutional Power in a Nutshell: Federal and State, 411 pages, 1974 (Text)

Ginsburg's Constitutional Aspects of Sex-Based Discrimination, 129 pages, 1974 (Casebook)—reprint from Davidson, Ginsburg and Kay's Cases on Sex-Based Discrimination, 1974

Lockhart, Kamisar and Choper's Cases-Comments-Questions on Constitutional Law, 5th Ed., approximately 1664 pages plus Appendix, 1980 (Casebook)

Lockhart, Kamisar and Choper's Cases-Comments-Questions on the American Constitution, 5th Ed., approximately 1249 pages plus Appendix, 1980 (Casebook)—reprint from Lockhart, et al. Cases on Constitutional Law, 5th Ed., 1980

Lockhart, Kamisar and Choper's Cases and Materials on Constitutional Rights and Liberties, 5th Ed., approximately 1244 pages plus Appendix, 1980 (Casebook)—reprint from Lockhart, et al. Cases on Constitutional Law, 5th Ed., 1980

CONSTITUTIONAL LAW—Continued

Miller's Presidential Power in a Nutshell, 328 pages, 1977 (Text)

Nowak, Rotunda and Young's Hornbook on Constitutional Law, 974 pages, 1978, with 1979 pocket part (Text)

Vieira's Civil Rights in a Nutshell, 279 pages, 1978 (Text)

William's Constitutional Analysis in a Nutshell, 388 pages, 1979 (Text)

CONSUMER LAW

Epstein's Consumer Protection in a Nutshell, 322 pages, 1976 (Text)

McCall's Consumer Protection, Cases, Notes and Materials, 594 pages, 1977, with 1977 Statutory Supplement (Casebook)

Schrag's Cases and Materials on Consumer Protection, 2nd Ed., 197 pages, 1973 (Casebook)—reprint from Cooper, et al. Cases on Law and Poverty, 2nd Ed., 1973

Selected Commercial Statutes, 1277 pages, 1979

Spanogle and Rohner's Cases and Materials on Consumer Law, 693 pages, 1979 (Casebook)

Uniform Consumer Credit Code, Official Text with Comments, 218 pages, 1974

CONTRACTS

Calamari & Perillo's Cases and Problems on Contracts, 1061 pages, 1978 (Casebook)

Calamari and Perillo's Hornbook on Contracts, 2nd Ed., 878 pages, 1977 (Text)

Corbin's Text on Contracts, One Volume Student Edition, 1224 pages, 1952 (Text)

Freedman's Cases and Materials on Contracts, 658 pages, 1973 (Casebook)

Fuller and Eisenberg's Cases on Basic Contract Law, 3rd Ed., 1043 pages, 1972 (Casebook)

Jackson and Bollinger's Cases on Contract Law in Modern Society, 2nd Ed., approximately 1200 pages, 1980 (Casebook)

Keyes' Government Contracts in a Nutshell, 423 pages, 1979 (Text)

Reitz's Cases on Contracts as Basic Commercial Law, 763 pages, 1975 (Casebook)

Schaber and Rohwer's Contracts in a Nutshell, 307 pages, 1975 (Text)

Simpson's Hornbook on Contracts, 2nd Ed., 510 pages, 1965 (Text)

COPYRIGHT

Nimmer's Cases and Materials on Copyright and Other Aspects of Law Pertaining to Literary, Musical and Artistic Works, Illustrated, 2nd Ed., 1023 pages, 1979 (Casebook)

See also Patent Law

CORPORATIONS

Hamilton's Cases on Corporations—Including Partnerships and Limited Partnerships, 998 pages, 1976, with 1979 Case and Statutory Supplement (Casebook)

Hamilton's Law of Corporations in a Nutshell, approximately 350 pages, 1980 (Text)

Henn's Cases on Corporations, 1279 pages, 1974, with 1974 Statutes, Forms and Case Study Supplement (Casebook)

Henn's Hornbook on Corporations, 2nd Ed., 956 pages, 1970 (Text)

Jennings and Buxbaum's Cases and Materials on Corporations, 5th Ed., 1156 pages, 1979 (Casebook)

Selected Corporation and Partnership Statutes, Regulations and Forms, approximately 785 pages, 1980

CORRECTIONS

Krantz's Cases and Materials on the Law of Corrections and Prisoners' Rights, 1130 pages, 1973, with 1977 Supplement (Casebook)

Krantz's Law of Corrections and Prisoners' Rights in a Nutshell, 353 pages, 1976 (Text)

Model Rules and Regulations on Prisoners' Rights and Responsibilities, 212 pages, 1973

Popper's Post-Conviction Remedies in a Nutshell, 360 pages, 1978 (Text)

CREDITOR'S RIGHTS

Epstein's Debtor-Creditor Law in a Nutshell, 2nd Ed., 324 pages, 1980 (Text)

Epstein and Landers' Debtors and Creditors: Cases and Materials, 722 pages, 1978, with 1979 Supplement (Casebook)

Riesenfeld's Cases and Materials on Creditors' Remedies and Debtors' Protection, 3rd Ed., 795 pages, 1979 with 1979 Statutory Supplement (Casebook)

Selected Bankruptcy Statutes, 351 pages, 1979

CRIMINAL LAW AND CRIMINAL PROCEDURE

Cohen and Gobert's Problems in Criminal Law, 297 pages, 1976 (Problem book)

CRIMINAL LAW AND CRIMINAL PROCEDURE—Continued

Davis' Police Discretion, 176 pages, 1975 (Text)

Dix and Sharlot's Cases and Materials on Criminal Law, 2nd Ed., 756 pages, 1979 (Casebook)

Federal Rules of Civil-Appellate-Criminal Procedure—West Law School Edition, 344 pages, 1980

Grano's Problems in Criminal Procedure, 171 pages, 1974 (Problem book)

Heymann and Kenety's The Murder Trial of Wilbur Jackson: A Homicide in the Family, 340 pages, 1975 (Case Study)

Israel and LaFave's Criminal Procedure in a Nutshell, 2nd Ed., 404 pages, 1975 (Text)

Johnson's Criminal Law: Cases, Materials and Text on Substantive Criminal Law in its Procedural Context, 2nd Ed., 956 pages, 1980 (Casebook)

Kamisar, LaFave and Israel's Cases, Comments and Questions on Modern Criminal Procedure, 5th ed., approximately 1572 pages, plus Appendix, 1980 (Casebook)

Kamisar, LaFave and Israel's Cases, Comments and Questions on Basic Criminal Procedure, 5th Ed., approximately 790 pages, 1980 (Casebook)— reprint from Kasimar, et al. Modern Criminal Procedure, 5th ed., 1980

LaFave's Modern Criminal Law: Cases, Comments and Questions, 789 pages, 1978 (Casebook)

LaFave and Scott's Hornbook on Criminal Law, 763 pages, 1972 (Text)

Loewy's Criminal Law in a Nutshell, 302 pages, 1975 (Text)

Saltzburg's American Criminal Procedure, Cases and Commentary, 1253 pages, 1980 (Casebook)

Uniform Rules of Criminal Procedure—Approved Draft, 407 pages, 1974

Uviller's The Processes of Criminal Justice: Adjudication, 2nd Ed., 700 pages, 1979. Soft-cover reprint from Uviller's The Processes of Criminal Justice: Investigation and Adjudication, 2nd Ed. (Casebook)

Uviller's The Processes of Criminal Justice: Investigation and Adjudication, 2nd Ed., 1320 pages, 1979 with 1979 Statutory Supplement (Casebook)

Uviller's The Processes of Criminal Justice: Investigation, 2nd Ed., 650 pages, 1979. Soft-cover reprint from Uviller's The Processes of Criminal Justice: Investigation and Adjudication, 2nd Ed. (Casebook)

CRIMINAL LAW AND CRIMINAL PROCEDURE—Continued

Vorenberg's Cases on Criminal Law and Procedure, 1044 pages, 1975, with 1979 Supplement (Casebook)
See also Corrections, Juvenile Justice

DECEDENTS ESTATES

See Wills, Trusts and Estates

DOMESTIC RELATIONS

Clark's Cases and Problems on Domestic Relations, 3rd Ed., approximately 1100 pages, 1980 (Casebook)
Clark's Hornbook on Domestic Relations, 754 pages, 1968 (Text)
Kay's Sex-Based Discrimination in Family Law, 305 pages, 1974 (Casebook) —reprint from Davidson, Ginsburg and Kay's Cases on Sex-Based Discrimination, 1974
Krause's Cases and Materials on Family Law, 1132 pages, 1976, with 1978 Supplement (Casebook)
Krause's Family Law in a Nutshell, 400 pages, 1977 (Text)
Paulsen's Cases and Selected Problems on Family Law and Poverty, 2nd Ed., 200 pages, 1973 (Casebook)—reprint from Cooper, et al. Cases on Law and Poverty, 2nd Ed., 1973

EDUCATION LAW

Morris' The Constitution and American Education, 2nd Ed., 992 pages, 1980 (Casebook)

EMPLOYMENT DISCRIMINATION

Cooper, Rabb and Rubin's Fair Employment Litigation: Text and Materials for Student and Practitioner, 590 pages, 1975 (Coursebook)
Player's Cases and Materials on Employment Discrimination Law, 878 pages, 1980 (Casebook)
Player's Federal Law of Employment Discrimination in a Nutshell, 336 pages, 1976 (Text)
Sovern's Cases and Materials on Racial Discrimination in Employment, 2nd Ed., 167 pages, 1973 (Casebook)—reprint from Cooper et al. Cases on Law and Poverty, 2nd Ed., 1973
See also Women and the Law

ENVIRONMENTAL LAW

Currie's Cases and Materials on Pollution, 715 pages, 1975 (Casebook)
Federal Environmental Law, 1600 pages, 1974 (Text)

ENVIRONMENTAL LAW—Continued

Hanks, Tarlock and Hanks' Cases on Environmental Law and Policy, 1242 pages, 1974, with 1976 Supplement (Casebook)
Rodgers' Hornbook on Environmental Law, 956 pages, 1977 (Text)
Selected Environmental Law Statutes, approximately 800 pages, 1980
See also Natural Resources and Water Law

EQUITY

See Remedies

ESTATE PLANNING

Casner and Stein's Estate Planning under the Tax Reform Act of 1976, 456 pages, 1978 (Coursebook)
Lynn's Introduction to Estate Planning, in a Nutshell, 2nd Ed., 378 pages, 1978 (Text)

EVIDENCE

Broun and Meisenholder's Problems in Evidence, 130 pages, 1973 (Problem book)
Cleary and Strong's Cases, Materials and Problems on Evidence, 2nd Ed., 1124 pages, 1975 (Casebook)
Federal Rules of Evidence for United States Courts and Magistrates, 325 pages, 1979
Kimball's Programmed Materials on Problems in Evidence, 380 pages, 1978 (Problem book)
Lempert and Saltzburg's A Modern Approach to Evidence: Text, Problems, Transcripts and Cases, 1231 pages, 1977 (Casebook)
Lilly's Introduction to the Law of Evidence, 486 pages, 1978 (Text)
McCormick, Elliott and Sutton's Cases and Materials on Evidence, 5th Ed., approximately 1100 pages, 1980 (Casebook)
McCormick's Hornbook on Evidence, 2nd Ed., 938 pages, 1972, with 1978 pocket part (Text)
Rothstein's Evidence in a Nutshell, 406 pages, 1970 (Text)

FEDERAL JURISDICTION AND PROCEDURE

Currie's Cases and Materials on Federal Courts, 2nd Ed., 1040 pages, 1975, with 1978 Supplement (Casebook)
Currie's Federal Jurisdiction in a Nutshell, 228 pages, 1976 (Text)

FEDERAL JURISDICTION AND PROCEDURE—Continued

Federal Rules of Civil-Appellate-Criminal Procedure—West Law School Edition, 344 pages, 1980

Forrester and Moye's Cases and Materials on Federal Jurisdiction and Procedure, 3rd Ed., 917 pages, 1977 (Casebook)

Merrill and Vetri's Problems on Federal Courts and Civil Procedure, 460 pages, 1974 (Problem book)

Wright's Hornbook on Federal Courts, 3rd Ed., 818 pages, 1976 (Text)

FUTURE INTERESTS

See Wills, Trusts, and Estates

HOUSING AND URBAN DEVELOPMENT

Berger's Cases and Materials on Housing, 2nd Ed., 254 pages, 1973 (Casebook)—reprint from Cooper et al. Cases on Law and Poverty, 2nd Ed., 1973

See also Land Use

INDIAN LAW

Getches, Rosenfelt and Wilkinson's Cases on Federal Indian Law, 660 pages, 1979 (Casebook)

INSURANCE

Keeton's Cases on Basic Insurance Law, 2nd Ed., 1086 pages, 1977

Keeton's Basic Text on Insurance Law, 712 pages, 1971 (Text)

Keeton's Case Supplement to Keeton's Basic Text on Insurance Law, 334 pages, 1978 (Casebook)

Keeton's Programmed Problems in Insurance Law, 243 pages, 1972 (Text Supplement)

INTERNATIONAL LAW

Henkin, Pugh, Schachter and Smit's Cases and Materials on International Law, approximately 1200 pages, 1980, with Documents Supplement (Casebook)

Jackson's Legal Problems of International Economic Relations, 1097 pages, 1977, with Statutory Supplement (Casebook)

Kirgis' International Organizations in Their Legal Setting, 1016 pages, 1977 (Casebook)

Weston, Falk and D'Amato's International Law and World Order—A Problem Oriented Coursebook approximately 1250 pages, 1980, with Documents Supplement (Casebook)

INTRODUCTION TO LAW

Dobbyn's So You Want to go to Law School, Revised First Edition, 206 pages, 1976 (Text)

Kinyon's Introduction to Law Study and Law Examinations in a Nutshell, 389 pages, 1971 (Text)

See also Legal Method and Legal System

JUDICIAL ADMINISTRATION

Carrington, Meador and Rosenberg's Justice on Appeal, 263 pages, 1976 (Casebook)

Nelson's Cases and Materials on Judicial Administration and the Administration of Justice, 1032 pages, 1974 (Casebook)

JURISPRUDENCE

Christie's Text and Readings on Jurisprudence—The Philosophy of Law, 1056 pages, 1973 (Casebook)

JUVENILE JUSTICE

Fox's Cases and Materials on Modern Juvenile Justice, 1012 pages, 1972 (Casebook)

Fox's Juvenile Courts in a Nutshell, 2nd Ed., 275 pages, 1977 (Text)

LABOR LAW

Gorman's Labor Law-Unionization and Collective Bargaining, 914 pages, 1976 (Text)

Leslie's Labor Law in a Nutshell, 403 pages, 1979 (Text)

Nolan's Labor Arbitration Law and Practice in a Nutshell, 358 pages, 1979 (Text)

Oberer, Hanslowe and Anderson's Cases and Materials on Labor Law—Collective Bargaining in a Free Society, 2nd Ed., 1168 pages, 1979, with 1979 Statutory Supplement (Casebook)

See also Employment Discrimination, Social Legislation

LAND FINANCE—PROPERTY SECURITY

Bruce's Real Estate Finance in a Nutshell, 292 pages, 1979 (Text)

Maxwell, Riesenfeld, Hetland and Warren's Cases on California Security Transactions in Land, 2nd Ed., 584 pages, 1975 (Casebook)

Nelson and Whitman's Cases on Real Estate Finance and Development, 1064 pages, 1976 (Casebook)

Osborne's Cases and Materials on Secured Transactions, 559 pages, 1967 (Casebook)

LAND FINANCE—PROPERTY SECURITY—Continued

Osborne, Nelson and Whitman's Hornbook on Real Estate Finance Law, 3rd Ed., 885 pages, 1979 (Text)

LAND USE

Beuscher, Wright and Gitelman's Cases and Materials on Land Use, 2nd Ed., 1133 pages, 1976 (Casebook)

Hagman's Cases on Public Planning and Control of Urban and Land Development, 2nd Ed., approximately 1200 pages, 1980 (Casebook)

Hagman's Hornbook on Urban Planning and Land Development Control Law, 706 pages, 1971 (Text)

Wright and Webber's Land Use in a Nutshell, 316 pages, 1978 (Text)

See also Housing and Urban Development

LAW AND ECONOMICS

Manne's The Economics of Legal Relationships—Readings in the Theory of Property Rights, 660 pages, 1975 (Text)

See also Regulated Industries

LAW AND MEDICINE—PSYCHIATRY

King's The Law of Medical Malpractice in a Nutshell, 340 pages, 1977 (Text)

Sharpe, Fiscina and Head's Cases on Law and Medicine, 882 pages, 1978 (Casebook)

LEGAL RESEARCH AND WRITING

Cohen's Legal Research in a Nutshell, 3rd Ed., 415 pages, 1978 (Text)

How to Find the Law With Special Chapters on Legal Writing, 7th Ed., 542 pages, 1976. Problem book available (Coursebook)

Rombauer's Legal Problem Solving—Analysis, Research and Writing, 3rd Ed., 352 pages, 1978 (Casebook)

Statsky's Legal Research, Writing and Analysis: Some Starting Points, 180 pages, 1974 (Text)—reprint from Statsky's Introduction to Paralegalism, 1974

Statsky and Wernet's Case Analysis and Fundamentals of Legal Writing, 576 pages, 1977 (Text)

Weihofen's Legal Writing Style, 2nd Ed., 332 pages, 1980 (Text)

LEGAL CLINICS

Freeman and Weihofen's Cases and Text on Clinical Law Training—Interviewing and Counseling, 506 pages, 1972 (Casebook)

LEGAL PROFESSION

Aronson's Problems in Professional Responsibility, 280 pages, 1978 (Problem book)

Aronson and Weckstein's Professional Responsibility in a Nutshell, approximately 400 pages, 1980 (Text)

Mallen and Levit's Legal Malpractice, 727 pages, 1977 (Coursebook)

Mellinkoff's The Conscience of a Lawyer, 304 pages, 1973 (Text)

Mellinkoff's Lawyers and the System of Justice, 983 pages, 1976 (Casebook)

Pirsig and Kirwin's Cases and Materials on Professional Responsibility, 3rd Ed., 667 pages, 1976, with 1977 Supplement (Casebook)

LEGAL HISTORY

Presser and Zainaldin's Cases on Law and American History, approximately 850 pages, 1980 (Casebook)

LEGAL METHOD AND LEGAL SYSTEM

Aldisert's Readings, Materials and Cases in the Judicial Process, 948 pages, 1976 (Casebook)

Bodenheimer, Oakley and Love's Readings and Cases on an Introduction to the Anglo-American Legal System, approximately 170 pages, 1980 (Casebook)

Fryer and Orentlicher's Cases and Materials on Legal Method and Legal System, 1043 pages, 1967 (Casebook)

Greenberg's Judicial Process and Social Change, 666 pages, 1977 (Coursebook)

Kempin's Historical Introduction to Anglo-American Law in a Nutshell, 2nd Ed., 280 pages, 1973 (Text)

Kimball's Historical Introduction to the Legal System, 610 pages, 1966 (Casebook)

Leflar's Appellate Judicial Opinions, 343 pages, 1974 (Text)

Mashaw and Merrill's Introduction to the American Public Law System, 1095 pages, 1975, with 1980 Supplement (Casebook)

Murphy's Cases and Materials on Introduction to Law—Legal Process and Procedure, 772 pages, 1977 (Casebook)

Reynold's Judicial Process in a Nutshell, 292 pages 1980 (Text)

Statsky's Legislative Analysis: How to Use Statutes and Regulations, 216 pages, 1975 (Text)

LEGISLATION

Davies' Legislative Law and Process in a Nutshell, 279 pages, 1975 (Text)

LEGISLATION—Continued

Nutting and Dickerson's Cases and Materials on Legislation, 5th Ed., 744 pages, 1978 (Casebook)

Statsky's Legislative Analysis: How to Use Statutes and Regulations, 216 pages, 1975 (Text)

LOCAL GOVERNMENT

McCarthy's Local Government Law in a Nutshell, 386 pages, 1975 (Text)

Michelman and Sandalow's Cases-Comments-Questions on Government in Urban Areas, 1216 pages, 1970, with 1972 Supplement (Casebook)

Stason and Kauper's Cases and Materials on Municipal Corporations, 3rd Ed., 692 pages, 1959 (Casebook)

Valente's Cases and Materials on Local Government Law, 2nd Ed., 980 pages, 1980 (Casebook)

MASS COMMUNICATION LAW

Gillmor and Barron's Cases and Comment on Mass Communication Law, 3rd Ed., 988 pages, 1979 (Casebook)

Ginsburg's Regulation of Broadcasting: Law and Policy Towards Radio, Television and Cable Communications, 741 pages, 1979 (Casebook)

Zuckman and Gayne's Mass Communications Law in a Nutshell, 431 pages, 1977 (Text)

MILITARY LAW

Shanor and Terrell's Military Law in a Nutshell, 378 pages, 1980 (Text)

MORTGAGES

See Land Finance—Property Security

NATURAL RESOURCES LAW

Rodger's Cases on Energy and Natural Resources Law, 995 pages, 1979 (Casebook)

See also Environmental Law & Water Law

OFFICE PRACTICE

Binder and Price's Legal Interviewing and Counseling: A Client-Centered Approach, 232 pages, 1977 (Text)

Edwards and White's Problems, Readings and Materials on the Lawyer as a Negotiator, 484 pages, 1977 (Casebook)

Freeman and Weihofen's Cases and Text on Clinical Law Training—Interviewing and Counseling, 506 pages, 1972 (Casebook)

Shaffer's Legal Interviewing and Counseling in a Nutshell, 353 pages, 1976 (Text)

Strong and Clark's Law Office Management, 424 pages, 1974 (Casebook)

OIL AND GAS

Hemingway's Hornbook on Oil and Gas, 486 pages, 1971, with 1978 pocket part (Text)

Huie, Woodward and Smith's Cases and Materials on Oil and Gas, 2nd Ed., 955 pages, 1972 (Casebook)

See also Natural Resources

PARTNERSHIP

See Agency—Partnership

PATENT LAW

Choate's Cases and Materials on Patent Law, 1060 pages, 1973 (Casebook)

See also Copyright

POVERTY LAW

Brudno's Poverty, Inequality, and the Law: Cases-Commentary-Analysis, 934 pages, 1976 (Casebook)

Brudno's Cases on Income Redistribution Theories and Programs, 480 pages, 1977 (Casebook)—reprint from Brudno's Cases on Poverty, Inequality and the Law, 1976

Cooper, Dodyk, Berger, Paulsen, Schrag and Sovern's Cases and Materials on Law and Poverty, 2nd Ed., 1208 pages, 1973 (Casebook)

LaFrance, Schroeder, Bennett and Boyd's Hornbook on Law of the Poor, 558 pages, 1973 (Text)

See also Social Legislation

PRODUCTS LIABILITY

Noel and Phillips' Cases on Products Liability, 836 pages, 1976 (Casebook)

Noel and Phillips' Products Liability in a Nutshell, 365 pages, 1974 (Text)

PROPERTY

Aigler, Smith and Tefft's Cases on Property, 2 volumes, 1339 pages, 1960 (Casebook)

Bernhardt's Real Property in a Nutshell, 425 pages, 1975 (Text)

Browder, Cunningham, Julin and Smith's Cases on Basic Property Law, 3rd Ed., 1447 pages, 1979 (Casebook)

Burby's Hornbook on Real Property, 3rd Ed., 490 pages, 1965 (Text)

Chused's A Modern Approach to Property: Cases-Notes-Materials, 1069 pages, 1978 (Casebook)

Cohen's Materials for a Basic Course in Property, 526 pages, 1978 (Casebook)

Donahue, Kauper and Martin's Cases on Property, 1501 pages, 1974 (Casebook)

Hill's Landlord and Tenant Law in a Nutshell, 319 pages, 1979 (Text)

PROPERTY—Continued

Moynihan's Introduction to Real Property, 254 pages, 1962 (Text)
Phipps' Titles in a Nutshell, 277 pages, 1968 (Text)
Smith and Boyer's Survey of the Law of Property, 2nd Ed., 510 pages, 1971 (Text)
Uniform Land Transactions Act, Uniform Simplification of Land Transfers Act, Uniform Condominium Act, 1978 Official Text with Comments, 462 pages, 1978
See also Housing and Urban Development, Land Finance, Land Use

REAL ESTATE

See Land Finance

REGULATED INDUSTRIES

Morgan's Cases and Materials on Economic Regulation of Business, 830 pages, 1976, with 1978 Supplement (Casebook)
Pozen's Financial Institutions: Cases, Materials and Problems on Investment Management, 844 pages, 1978 (Casebook)
White's Teaching Materials on Banking Law, 1058 pages, 1976, with 1980 Case and Statutory Supplement (Casebook)
See also Mass Communication Law

REMEDIES

Cribbet's Cases and Materials on Judicial Remedies, 762 pages, 1954 (Casebook)
Dobbs' Hornbook on Remedies, 1067 pages, 1973 (Text)
Dobbs' Problems in Remedies, 137 pages, 1974 (Problem book)
Dobbyn's Injunctions in a Nutshell, 264 pages, 1974 (Text)
McClintock's Hornbook on Equity, 2nd Ed., 643 pages, 1948 (Text)
McCormick's Hornbook on Damages, 811 pages, 1935 (Text)
O'Connell's Remedies in a Nutshell, 364 pages, 1977 (Text)
Leavell, Love and Nelson's Cases and Materials on Equitable Remedies and Restitution, 3rd Ed., 704 pages, 1980 (Casebook)
York and Bauman's Cases and Materials on Remedies, 3rd Ed., 1250 pages, 1979 (Casebook)

REVIEW MATERIALS

Ballantine's Problems
Smith's Review
West's Review Covering Multistate Subjects

SECURITIES REGULATION

Ratner's Securities Regulation: Materials for a Basic Course, 2nd Ed., 1050 pages, 1980 with 1980 Supplement (Casebook)
Ratner's Securities Regulation in a Nutshell, 300 pages, 1978 (Text)

SOCIAL LEGISLATION

Brudno's Income Redistribution Theories and Programs: Cases-Commentary-Analysis, 480 pages, 1977 (Casebook) —reprint from Brudno's Poverty, Inequality and the Law, 1976
Cooper and Dodyk's Cases and Materials on Income Maintenance, 2nd Ed., 449 pages, 1973 (Casebook)—reprint from Cooper et al. Cases on Law and Poverty, 2nd Ed., 1973
LaFrance's Welfare Law: Structure and Entitlement in a Nutshell, 455 pages, 1979 (Text)
Malone, Plant and Little's Cases on Workers' Compensation and Employment Rights, 2nd Ed., 951 pages, 1980 (Casebook)
See also Poverty Law

SURETYSHIP

Simpson's Hornbook on Suretyship, 569 pages, 1950 (Text)

TAXATION

Chommie's Hornbook on Federal Income Taxation, 2nd Ed., 1051 pages, 1973 (Text)
Hellerstein and Hellerstein's Cases on State and Local Taxation, 4th Ed., 1041 pages, 1978 (Casebook)
Kahn's Hornbook on Basic Corporate Taxation, 3rd Ed., approximately 550 pages, 1980 (Text)
Kahn and Gann's Corporate Taxation and Taxation of Partnerships and Partners, 1107 pages, 1979 (Casebook)
Kragen and McNulty's Cases and Materials on Federal Income Taxation, 3rd Ed., Vol. 1, 1270 pages, 1979 (Casebook)
Kramer and McCord's Problems for Federal Estate and Gift Taxes, 206 pages, 1976 (Problem book)
Lowndes, Kramer and McCord's Hornbook on Federal Estate and Gift Taxes, 3rd Ed., 1099 pages, 1974 (Text)
McCord's 1976 Estate and Gift Tax Reform-Analysis, Explanation and Commentary, 377 pages, 1977 (Text)
McNulty's Federal Estate and Gift Taxation in a Nutshell, 2nd Ed., 488 pages, 1979 (Text)

TAXATION—Continued

McNulty's Federal Income Taxation of Individuals in a Nutshell, 2nd Ed., 422 pages, 1978 (Text)

Rice's Problems and Materials in Federal Estate and Gift Taxation, 3rd Ed., 474 pages, 1978 (Casebook)

Rice and Solomon's Problems and Materials in Federal Income Taxation, 3rd Ed., 675 pages, 1979 (Casebook)

Rose and Raskind's Advanced Federal Income Taxation: Corporate Transactions-Cases, Materials and Problems, 955 pages, 1978 (Casebook)

Selected Federal Taxation Statutes and Regulations, 1415 pages, 1979

Sobeloff's Federal Income Taxation of Corporations and Stockholders in a Nutshell, 374 pages, 1978 (Text)

TORTS

Green, Pedrick, Rahl, Thode, Hawkins, Smith and Treece's Cases and Materials on Torts, 2nd Ed., 1360 pages, 1977 (Casebook)

Green, Pedrick, Rahl, Thode, Hawkins, Smith, and Treece's Advanced Torts: Injuries to Business, Political and Family Interests, 544 pages, 1977 (Casebook)—reprint from Green, et al. Cases and Materials on Torts, 2nd Ed., 1977

Keeton's Computer-Aided and Workbook Exercises on Tort Law, 164 pages, 1976 (Coursebook)

Keeton and Keeton's Cases and Materials on Torts, 2nd Ed., 1200 pages, 1977 (Casebook)

Kionka's Torts in a Nutshell: Injuries to Persons and Property, 434 pages, 1977 (Text)

Malone's Torts in a Nutshell: Injuries to Family, Social and Trade Relations, 340 pages, 1979 (Text)

Prosser's Hornbook on Torts, 4th Ed., 1208 pages, 1971 (Text)

Shapo's Cases on Tort and Compensation Law, 1244 pages, 1976 (Casebook)

See also Products Liability

TRADE REGULATION

Oppenheim and Weston's Cases and Materials on Unfair Trade Practices and Consumer Protection, 3rd Ed., 1065 pages, 1974, with 1977 Supplement (Casebook)

See also Antitrust, Regulated Industries

TRIAL AND APPELLATE ADVOCACY

Appellate Advocacy, Handbook of, 249 pages, 1980 (Text)

Bergman's Trial Advocacy in a Nutshell, 402 pages, 1979 (Text)

Hegland's Trial and Practice Skills in a Nutshell, 346 pages, 1978 (Text)

Jean's Trial Advocacy (Student Edition), 473 pages, 1975 (Text)

McElhaney's Effective Litigation, 457 pages, 1974 (Casebook)

TRUSTS

See Wills, Trusts and Estates

WATER LAW

Trelease's Cases and Materials on Water Law, 3rd Ed., 828 pages, 1979 (Casebook)

See also Natural Resources & Environmental Law

WILL, TRUSTS AND ESTATES

Atkinson's Hornbook on Wills, 2nd Ed., 975 pages, 1953 (Text)

Averill's Uniform Probate Code in a Nutshell, 425 pages, 1978 (Text)

Bogert's Hornbook on Trusts, 5th Ed., 726 pages, 1973 (Text)

Clark, Lusky and Murphy's Cases and Materials on Gratuitous Transfers, 2nd Ed., 1102 pages, 1977 (Casebook)

Gulliver's Cases and Materials on Future Interests, 624 pages, 1959 (Casebook)

Gulliver's Introduction to the Law of Future Interests, 87 pages, 1959 (Casebook)

Halbach (Editor)—Death, Taxes, and Family Property: Essays and American Assembly Report, 189 pages, 1977 (Text)

Mennell's Cases and Materials on California Decedent's Estates, 566 pages, 1973 (Casebook)

Mennell's Wills and Trusts in a Nutshell, 392 pages, 1979 (Text)

Powell's The Law of Future Interests in California, 91 pages, 1980 (Text)

Simes' Hornbook on Future Interests, 2nd Ed., 355 pages, 1966 (Text)

Turrentine's Cases and Text on Wills and Administration, 2nd Ed., 483 pages, 1962 (Casebook)

Uniform Probate Code, 5th Ed., Official Text With Comments, 384 pages, 1977

Waggoner's Future Interests in a Nutshell, approximately 330 pages, 1980 (Text)

WOMEN AND THE LAW

Davidson, Ginsburg and Kay's Text, Cases and Materials on Sex-Based Discrimination, 1031 pages, 1974, with 1978 Supplement (Casebook)

WOMEN AND THE LAW—Continued

See also Employment Discrimination

WORKMEN'S COMPENSATION

See Social Legislation

TRIAL PRACTICE

CASES AND MATERIALS

JOSEPH R. NOLAN
Associate Justice
Massachusetts Appeals Court

AMERICAN CASEBOOK SERIES

ST. PAUL, MINN.
WEST PUBLISHING CO.
1981

Printed in the United States of America

Library of Congress Cataloging in Publication Data

Nolan, Joseph R
Cases and materials on trial practice.

(American casebook series)
Includes index.
1. Trial practice—United States. I. Title.
II. Series.
KF8914.N64 347.73'7 80-29182

ISBN 0-8299-2129-X

Nolan Cs.Trial Prac.ACB

To Peggy whose devotion is boundless, and
To Molly who makes it all worthwhile.

*

PREFACE

The training of a trial lawyer is not entirely dissimilar to the training of a surgeon. A knowledge of anatomy is essential before the surgical tyro learns to tie off blood vessels. The trial lawyer must bring to his specialty a thorough grasp of substantive and adjectival law. Scoring high in the field of evidence is no substitute for knowing the elements of a contract and tort and the types of equitable restrictions which may be placed on Pinkacre.

This work is designed to permit the professor to lecture, to illustrate and to organize teams or law firms to argue motions and to try civil and criminal cases. Clearly, there is more material than can be conveniently used, but this is as it should be. The professor should be free to select those assignments and cases which appear to be most profitable to his students. To provide some uniformity, citations have been made to the Federal Rules of Evidence, Federal Rules of Criminal Procedure and Federal Rules of Civil Procedure. The Disciplinary Rules and Ethical Considerations of the Code of Professional Responsibility of the American Bar Association have been invoked where appropriate.

To the following people I owe a debt of gratitude but I hope that they and the readers will not apply that canon of construction so useful in statutory hermeneutics, but which may lead to embarrassment in this context—inclusio unius est exclusio alterius, because I may have forgotten some benefactors.

My sincere gratitude is extended to Thomas F. Reardon, Assistant District Attorney in the office of District Attorney Newman Austin Flanagan of Suffolk County, Massachusetts; James F. Meehan, Esquire, of the firm of Parker, Coulter, Daley & White, of Boston; Joseph I. Mulligan, Esquire, of the firm of Reed and Mulligan of Boston. They made available to me certain case files for use in the book after all names and places were changed to protect the guilty and the negligent defendants and the privacy of the aggrieved plaintiffs. The Honorable John J. McNaught, Judge of the United States District Court for the District of Massachusetts made available to me on an "as is" basis most, if not all, of his classroom assignments. He gave me an unrestricted right to use them as I saw fit. I have used every scrap of this material but I have changed the names of the dramatis personae only out of a desire for creativity because he had already made changes necessary to protect professional confidences.

Simple justice makes it necessary for me to single out Jill Ryan who acted as my faithful law school research assistant long after she had fulfilled her requirements for credits at Suffolk University Law School. Her attention to detail and editorial assistance were invaluable.

Finally, nearest home and heart is my wife, Peggy Kelly Nolan, who has maintained a generous attitude in the face of a husband who has turned her home into a working cell to the utter neglect of tasks which most wives have come to expect even from mediocre husbands. To her, my eternal gratitude.

JOSEPH R. NOLAN

Belmont, MA
January, 1981

SUMMARY OF CONTENTS

*

TABLE OF CONTENTS

CHAPTER III. PRE-TRIAL MOTIONS AND PRELIMINARY INJUNCTIONS

CHAPTER IV. DISCOVERY

CHAPTER V. READY FOR TRIAL—IMPANELING JURY

CHAPTER VI. OPENING STATEMENT—ADVICE TO WITNESS

CHAPTER VII. DIRECT EXAMINATION

CHAPTER VIII. CROSS AND RECROSS EXAMINATION

CHAPTER IX. OBJECTIONS AND MOTIONS AT TRIAL

CHAPTER XII. POST-TRIAL PROCEDURES

TABLE OF RULES

References are to Pages

FEDERAL RULES OF CIVIL PROCEDURE

TABLE OF RULES

CASES AND MATERIALS ON TRIAL PRACTICE

Chapter One

ADVOCACY

A. NATURE OF ADVOCACY

An advocate is one who speaks for another. The older brother who intercedes with mother on behalf of his younger sister who wants a favor is an advocate. Our attention in this work is focused on legal advocacy, more particularly, trial advocacy. Appellate advocacy is beyond the scope of this book.

Altogether too many lawyers act as if the case were theirs. They seldom consult their client. They treat the client as a stranger looking through a shop window at a demonstration. They deem it unnecessary to transmit offers of settlements unless the offer corresponds with their own evaluation of the merits of the case. They tell their client nothing of the negotiations between themselves and opposing counsel. In a word, these lawyers pretend that they own the litigation. This pretension is a serious mistake. The trial lawyer is an advocate, whose commitment is to represent his client.

On the other side of the coin is the obligation of the lawyer to make preliminary determinations that what the client says is true. For example, the Federal Rules of Civil Procedure provide that the ". . . signature of an attorney constitutes a certificate by him that he has read the pleadings; that to the best of his knowledge, information, and belief there is good ground to support it; and that it is not interposed for delay." [1] While it is true that some papers filed in court must bear the signature of the client, i. e. answers to interrogatories,[2] answers in response to requests for admission,[3] the bulk

1. Fed.R.Civ.P. 11.

2. Fed.R.Civ.P. 33(a).

3. Fed.R.Civ.P. 36(a).

of documents filed in connection with a law suit are signed by the attorney. Accordingly, there is an obligation on the trial lawyer to make a preliminary determination as to the truth of the allegations which he sets forth. A client is bound by what his trial attorney does in court. This sobering consideration makes the subject of trial advocacy all the more important.

B. NEED FOR ADVOCACY

The triteness of the expression that one who represents himself has a fool for a client does not diminish its stark truth. It is difficult to speak for oneself, to urge belief in one's own testimony, to press one's own rights. Though the right to represent oneself is of constitutional stature, the practice of it offends the virtue of prudence.

Moreover, the complexity of litigation makes it almost impossible for the untrained to conduct it with any measure of success. The rules of evidence are perplexing to the lay person. The drawing of pleadings is an art which even some professionals never master. The need for objective judgment divorced from emotion and passion is obvious. The client who can be coldly objective is handicapped by a lack of expertise in the law.

In sum, there is a continuing need for good trial lawyers who will bring to their cases seasoned judgment, a mastery of the law of evidence and the command of the rules of advocacy.

C. QUALITIES OF AN ADVOCATE

It is difficult, if not impossible, to establish a pecking order for the attributes and virtues required of a good trial lawyer. Some of these qualities are set forth here in no particular hierarchical order.

1. *Sincerity*

Juries are capable of detecting a mountebank. The lawyer must persuade the jury that he means what he says; else, he should not say it. He need not adopt a park bench familiarity, but he should not betray his client by talking and acting as if he were in a school play. Though the trial lawyer is not permitted to reveal his own private opinion about the merits of the case,[4] he is under an obligation not to indicate a disbelief in his cause.

2. *Honesty*

Rather akin to sincerity is fresh air honesty. The lawyer who impresses the jury with his deviousness has lost the case regardless of its merits. Honesty does not require the advocate to reveal a grocery

4. DR7–106(4).

list of defects in his client's case. However, on occasion, it is the better part of practical prudence to admit candidly a weak sector in the client's armor. Jurors do not expect perfect cases. A frank avowal of some weakness in your case, while pointing out all the strong points, can work wonders with the jury.

3. *Attraction to Combat*

In every good trial lawyer there is a substantial measure of combativeness. If he lacks the warrior's thirst for action, he will not succeed in the litigation department. He should enjoy the intellectual dueling which is the grist mill of a trial. He cannot afford to hide from hand to hand combat because he will soon find himself locked in close range fighting with a devious witness.

4. *Good Memory*

A good memory may not be essential but it makes the work of a trial lawyer easier. The ability to effectuate instant recall of the testimony of a witness who left the stand a week earlier or whose direct examination lasted for a considerable period of time is a great gift. Use of notes is important but it is so much more effective if you can summon the recall of the testimony of the witness. A good memory can be cultivated. It has been compared to a muscle which must be exercised in order to function properly. It will become atrophied if left unused.

5. *Patience in Preparation*

Trials are won or lost, in the main, before counsel steps inside a courtroom. A lawyer who has thoroughly investigated the facts, drawn good pleadings, made a judicious use of discovery and conducted the necessary legal research has more than a leg up on an adversary who thinks that he will win by spellbinding the jury with histrionics.

A practice still honored by seasoned trial lawyers is the preparation of the opponent's case. Your own case will look differently to you if you put yourself into the shoes of your opponent. You will be in a position to steal his thunder if you have prepared his case as well as your own. You will learn the weaknesses of your own case and the vulnerability of your adversary.

6. *Ability to Speak Extemporaneously*

There are no telepromptors in a courtroom. Too many lawyers depend on the yellow note pad. Notes should merely suggest ideas. A trial lawyer must develop the ability to clothe his ideas with articulation. In the trial of a case, more often than not, you will not have time to sit down and compose your remarks. Accordingly, develop the ability to speak extemporaneously.

In the opening and in the closing argument to the jury, avoid like the plague a physical attachment to the yellow note pad. Speak forcefully, using those figures and tropes that make the speeches of

Cicero and Churchill good reading even today. If you have discarded the text on rhetoric which you used in college, buy another one and consult it.

Draw on other branches of learning when speaking to the court and to the jury. If your reading habits are confined to lawbooks, you will find it difficult. Broaden your reading pastures. Don't neglect the classics which you can now read without the compulsion which in school days made them disagreeable.

D. DIFFERENT TYPES OF ADVOCATES

A successful trial lawyer does not need the velvet voice of Daniel Webster nor the genius of Demosthenes' spoken word. However, he should cultivate a voice with a pleasant sound. It should ring with sincerity.

God has endowed some lawyers with a mellifluous voice. Others must work hard to acquire rhetorical talent. Though imitation may be the highest form of flattery, one lawyer should not strive to imitate another lawyer in every detail of delivery. He must be himself. His style is himself. However, every lawyer should make a constant effort to improve. He should strive to soften a harsh voice, smile instead of frown when addressing the judge or jury and treat witnesses courteously. You can learn to be politely aggressive. In a word, make the most of the talents which you have.

E. ETHICS OF ADVOCACY

1. *In General*

A lawyer is bound to exercise zeal within the bounds of law on behalf of his client.[5] He must act competently.[6] He has no right to undertake litigation which is beyond his professional capabilities.[7]

From the initial contact with his client, the lawyer is bound to act ethically. In drawing pleadings, he should be careful to allege only what appears to be accurate.[8] He may never assert what he knows is false though his client insists on its truth. If the case has no merit whatsoever, a lawyer may not accept employment.[9] If he has already accepted, he should withdraw.[10] It is unethical for a lawyer to file suit solely for delay or harassment.[11] It is highly improper to subvert the criminal process to enforce a civil claim.[12]

5. DR7–101.

6. DR6–101.

7. DR6–101(A)(1).

8. Fed.R.Civ.P. 11; EC7–25.

9. DR2–109.

10. DR2–110.

11. DR7–102(A)(1).

12. EC7–21; DR7–105.

2. *In Court*

Courtesy and politeness are enjoined on the advocate.[13] It is unethical to assert as fact what is not admissible in evidence.[14] Equally blameworthy is the lawyer who puts to a witness a question which implies a fact not in evidence. An example is the old saw: "When did you stop beating your wife?" There is no evidence that the witness ever beat his wife. In fact, he never hit his wife in anger.

A lawyer who knows that a witness whom he is going to produce is prepared to offer perjured testimony should refuse to allow him to perjure himself.[15] If a lawyer should discover that there is a misstatement of fact in pleadings which he has signed, he has the obligation to call it to the court's attention without delay. He should not have made the statement in the first place, but having made it, he now is bound to correct it.[16]

In arguing to the court and jury, a lawyer should not inject his personal beliefs about the case and the credibility of witnesses.[17] He may point out weaknesses in the opponent's case and the unlikelihood of the testimony of witnesses who testified against his client.

A public prosecutor's task is not merely to seek a conviction. First and foremost, he must seek justice. Justice is served by his disclosure of exculpatory evidence.[18]

It is unethical for a lawyer to communicate in person with the judge or hearing officer without informing his opponent and giving him an opportunity to be present. Copies of all written communications to the court should be sent to opposing counsel.[19]

In a word, whether in court, in the office or in public, a good lawyer will avoid even the appearance of professional impropriety.[20]

ASSIGNMENT #1

KARL NORMAN, ADMINISTRATOR

Estate of Peter Bendt

v.

MILDRED BENDT

PRELIMINARY FACTS

Geoffrey Bendt, a widower with one son Peter, married Mildred in Yr.-25. Geoffrey and Mildred dabbled in real estate, although

13. EC7–36.

14. EC7–25.

15. EC7–26; DR7–102(A)(4).

16. Fed.R.Civ.P. 11.

17. DR7–106(4).

18. DR7–103(B).

19. EC7–35.

20. Canon 9.

Geoffrey had a steady job on the railroad. Geoffrey died in Yr.-15. Peter, a mailman, continued to live with his stepmother, always referring to her as "Mother."

At the time of Geoffrey's death, Geoffrey and Mildred had owned two houses as tenants by the entirety. One of these they had used as their residence, and the other as income producing property. Mildred sold the income producing house and turned the proceeds over to Peter, stating that it was principally through his father's efforts that the house was originally purchased. Peter, who apparently lived frugally, invested the money in the stock market, as he had done with most of his savings through his lifetime.

Peter was a diabetic. He had only two friends, a fellow worker at the Post Office named Dick, and his stockbroker, Doug.

Last year Peter became very ill. He was hospitalized with an ulceration of the left leg. The leg had to be amputated.

The day after the surgery, Dick visited Peter and Peter said to him: "Dick, I want you to go directly to my house. In the living room, under my rocker, you'll find a yellow metal box with two elastics around it. Hand the box to 'Mother' and tell her that I want her to keep it. What's inside is hers. Then, on Monday, I want you and Doug to come here with a lawyer. I want to take whatever steps are necessary to transfer all my property to 'Mother.' " Dick promised that he would do as directed.

Dick left the hospital and went to Peter's home. He found the box, handed it to Mildred without opening it, and told her that Peter had said that the contents were hers. Mildred responded: "God bless my boy for whatever he's given to me." Dick then called Doug, the stockbroker, and his own family lawyer, Mr. Thompson, and made an appointment to meet them at Peter's bedside at 10:00 A.M. on Monday. Peter died Sunday night at 11:00 P.M.

Mr. Thompson was asked by Mildred to administer whatever estate Peter might have left. She gave him the key to Peter's room. Peter had customarily left his door locked when he was not in his room.

Mr. Thompson entered the room to make an inventory of any assets he might find. He found stock certificates in old shirtboxes and dresser drawers. Current value of the stock was about $250,000. He also found roughly twenty pounds of paper-covered sugar cubes, balls of string and twine, hundreds of small bars of soap bearing the names of many hotels, dozens of swizzle sticks, bubble gum baseball cards, dividend checks from corporations in the total amount of Fifty-Two Thousand Dollars, and many religious pamphlets.

Investigation disclosed that Mildred had never adopted Peter. She had no idea that Peter had been successful in the stock market.

Peter hadn't seen a relative in at least fifteen years, although he had a second cousin who lived only five miles away.

Mr. Thompson knew that Mildred could not take any part of Peter's estate under the laws of intestacy; that the sole living relative, the second cousin, would inherit whatever Peter did not dispose of in his lifetime. He so notified Mildred.

Mildred now brought out the metal box and recited the actual facts concerning how she came into possession of it. Mr. Thompson, with her permission, opened the box and found therein bankbooks with deposits amounting to $54,000 and about $6,000 in cash. He advised Mildred that in his opinion (which was correct) if Peter was capable of making a gift the day after the surgery, the funds in these banks and the cash were hers, but that all the remainder belonged to the cousin.

Mr. Thompson, with Mildred's consent, called the cousin on the telephone and notified him of Peter's death, and the fact that Peter had left assets. The cousin did not attend Peter's funeral, but shortly thereafter the cousin's attorney contacted Mr. Thompson. This attorney took the necessary steps to have the cousin appointed administrator of Peter's estate. He also asked that Peter's assets be turned over to him. Mr. Thompson complied, although he did not relinquish the yellow metal box and its contents. He told the attorney the facts concerning them.

The Administrator seeks, in the Probate Court, an order requiring Mildred to turn over the contents of the box as part of the assets of the estate. Mr. Thompson seeks a judgment to the effect that a valid gift was effected by Peter. The matter has not yet been set down for hearing.

PROBLEM

Any member of the class may be called upon by the Instructor to perform this assignment or any part of it.

A. Each of you is a member of Mr. Thompson's law firm and you have been assigned by him to prepare and try the action. Ethically, may you do so, as matters now stand? Mr. Thompson expects that he will appear as a witness, and the opposition does not yet know anything about the sugar cubes, string, soap, swizzle sticks, or baseball cards.

Be prepared to explain your decision.

B. You are an independent practitioner. Mr. Thompson has withdrawn his appearance and Mildred has asked you to prepare and try the action. Up to the present only you, Mr. Thompson, Mildred and Dick know about the bubble gum cards, swizzle sticks, soap, string and sugar. Mildred and Dick are in your office and you are preparing them to testify.

Advise them concerning their testimony, if any, concerning these items.

Be prepared to give the reasons for your advice to Mildred and Dick.

C. Each of you is a member of the firm representing the cousin, and you have been assigned to try this action.

You intend to call Doctor Stone, Peter's attending physician during his final hospital admission, as a witness. Doctor Stone, as coincidence would have it, is a brother-in-law of the cousin. On Peter's hospital record, the doctor noted that Peter submitted a request that he be treated as a "charity" patient. The record also reveals that Doctor Stone ordered that Peter be given large quantities of medication for pain, particularly after the surgery.

You hope to prove that Peter was incapable of making a valid gift. You know that the doctor pleaded guilty to income tax evasion last year, that he was given a ten year sentence (suspended, with a probationary period) and had to pay a hefty fine.

You are worried about the criminal record and the relationship of the doctor to the cousin.

You are preparing Doctor Stone to testify. Discuss these matters with him. Be prepared to give the reasons behind your advice to him.

F. RULES OF COURT AND A FEW SUGGESTIONS FOR CLASSROOM TRIALS

NOTE: All of the following rules are subject to deletion and amendment in the unfettered discretion of the instructor.

1. The Federal Rules of Civil Procedure (Fed.R.Civ.P.), the Federal Rules of Criminal Procedure (Fed.R.Crim.P.) and the Federal Rules of Evidence (Fed.R.Evid.) will be used. Questions of substantive law will be resolved by the law of the forum or treated as questions of first impression to be ruled on by the instructor or judge.

2. Those students who are not participating as counsel will serve as clerk, court officer, bailiff, jurors and witnesses. The instructor will appoint the clerk and court officer. Counsel will select the witnesses.

3. The students will form "law firms" consisting of two members selected by the instructor or chosen by themselves. Each member of a law firm is a "full partner" with an equal right of control over the litigation. The division of labor is within the joint authority of the partners. The right to divide the labor does not permit two attorneys to conduct direct examination or cross examination of one witness or make an opening statement. Only one partner may conduct an

examination though the partner who conducts the direct examination is not required to conduct the redirect examination of the same witness.

4. Persons who have not been designated as witnesses in advance of trial may not be "found" and presented as "surprises" to the opponents.

5. Bench conferences should be conducted in such manner that the class is able to hear the remarks of counsel and the judge.

6. If a motion is to be presented to the court, notice of it shall be given before the trial begins. No "surprise" motion should be permitted unless it is dictated by the exigency of the moment (e. g. motion for mistrial).

7. All doubts and difficulties with trial procedure should be expressed to the instructor *before* the trial. He will institute special rules for special problems.

G. FORMS FOR COURT OFFICER AND CLERK

1. OPENING OF COURT

All rise, please. Hear ye—All persons having anything to do before the justices of the (Superior Court), draw near, give your attention and you shall be heard. Judge Jones is presiding. You may be seated.

2. OATH FOR VENIREMEN

Do you solemnly swear or affirm that you will fully and truthfully answer all the questions put to you concerning your qualifications to serve as a juror?

3. OATH FOR JURORS SELECTED

Do you all, individually and collectively, solemnly swear or affirm that you will faithfully perform your duties as jurors in the case that you are about to hear?

4. OATH FOR WITNESSES

Do you solemnly swear or affirm to tell the truth, the whole truth and nothing but the truth?

Chapter Two

INVESTIGATION—DRAWING OF PLEADINGS

A. INITIAL INTERVIEW WITH CLIENT

The first meeting with your client is very important for lawyer and client. It sets the stage for future contacts. You should be candid with the client about the amount of the fee, the arrangement for payment of the fee, whether it is contingent, on an hourly basis, or a flat amount regardless of the outcome. If it is to be a contingent fee, your state may require the preparation and signing of a contingent fee agreement.

Generally at this early juncture, the lawyer is in no position to evaluate the merits of the case. The client is anxious to secure an early reading of his case from his lawyer, but you should not be hasty. Until your investigation is complete, you are in no position to assess the value of the client's grievance or his defense. Tell the client that as soon as your investigation of the facts and your research of the law are completed, you will sit down for a frank discussion of his case.

The first meeting is not too early to secure from your client all the data which he has concerning the case. His diaries may be crucially important. His books and records and correspondence should be preserved. The client's own narrative of the events of the case should be given to you at this meeting. The client should be warned about the hazards of failing to tell the whole truth. Whether the client thinks it is harmful or helpful, he should not hesitate to tell his lawyer all the facts.

The client should furnish you with a list of all witnesses. While the client is describing the facts of his case, stop him when necessary, make him back up and concentrate on what you know is essential to the case.

While it may seem awkward, you must ask the client whether he has a criminal record. The existence of a record and its content may play a large part in your trial strategy and even in your settlement negotiations.

B. INTERVIEWING WITNESSES

A decision as to whether a professional investigator should be retained must be made early in the case. If the case is of modest proportion in terms of complexity and money you may decide to conduct the investigation without the aid of a private investigator. In this event, be careful in interviewing witnesses. Under no guise can you afford to make the witness think that you are trying to make him say something because it is helpful to your client's case. When this happens, the witness becomes hazardous on the witness stand. Tell the witness that all you want from him or her is a description of what was seen or heard, good or bad, favorable or unfavorable.

A witness may be helpful in revealing other witnesses. In asking a witness to tell you what occurred, be frank when asked whether he will be called as a witness at trial. Don't deceive the witness and permit him or her to think that at the close of the interview, his work is completed.

If you plan to record the statement of the witness on tape, tell him so ahead of time. He may object. Honor his objection. If possible, secure a statement in writing from the witness. You will undoubtedly write down what he tells you while he narrates the events from memory. When completed, let him read the statement and then ask him to sign it.

Ask the witness whether he took any pictures of the scene or whether he observed anyone else taking pictures. You should arrange for photographs of the scene.

Never pay the witness or offer to pay him. The devastating effect of this is all too obvious. However, if the witness has lost time from work to accommodate you or your investigator or if he has incurred some expense, there is nothing improper about reimbursing the witness.

C. PHYSICAL INVESTIGATION

If the case is a motor vehicle accident or a crime, it is crucially important to visit and examine in detail the area where the events took place. Measure the street's width, curbing and distance from the nearest light post. At this juncture, it is advantageous to interview people who live in the immediate neighborhood. What they saw and heard is important. There is no substitute for first-hand knowledge of the scene when you are examining or cross-examining a witness.

The weather conditions at the time of the occurrence may be important. It is possible to secure an official weather report for that day.

If it is a product liability case, there is no equivalent to an intimate knowledge of the machine or product which caused the harm. The fact that you will hire an expert is no excuse for failing to learn all about the product.

D. PRELIMINARY HEARING IN CRIMINAL COURT

If you have been retained to represent a person who has been injured in a motor vehicle accident, check to see whether there has been a criminal proceeding commenced as a result of the accident. The driver of the other car may have been cited by the police for driving under the influence of liquor or driving so as to endanger the lives and safety of the public. In this connection, there may be a preliminary hearing to determine whether probable cause exists for the issuance of criminal process or a trial to determine whether the operator was guilty of the crimes.

As counsel for the injured party, you should attend the hearing and with the court's prior permission, you may hire a stenographer to take the testimony in this proceeding. This can be a very valuable discovery device. The operator's conviction may also bring about an advantageous settlement of the case.

E. LEGAL RESEARCH

After you have completed the investigation and digested the statements of your client and the witnesses, you should be in a good position to know what actually happened. This knowledge should prepare you to evaluate the case. This knowledge should also direct the course of your law search. If it is a motor vehicle accident in which your client was a pedestrian, all cases in your jurisdiction under this caption should be examined. The "holes" in your case, so much a part of almost all cases in everyday life, must be recognized.

If you are defending, all possible defenses should be explored. Cases touching every possible defense should be read with care and "run out" to determine whether they remain good law. All cognate statutes should be explored.

If your client is the plaintiff, it is good strategy to anticipate every viable defense. "Prepare the other fellow's case" is an admonition from older lawyers which is sound. If your case involves a tort, make a laundry list of the elements of this tort. Similarly, prepare a list of the elements of every defense which may be implicated.

F. CONTINUING CONTACT WITH CLIENT

There is probably no more common ground for client dissatisfaction than failure of the lawyer to stay in contact. Let the client know at *regular* intervals precisely what you are doing and what the opposition is doing. Tell the client what the next step is in the conduct of the case. For example, if you contemplate noticing the deposition of the defendant, write to your client and inform him of this step. Afterwards, let him read it.

A workable rule of thumb is that at least once a month, you should write to the client and advise him of the status of the case. Clients become disenchanted when they are ignored. Clients are lost and complaints are filed because lawyers fail to keep the client informed. Some lawyers telephone the client every other month and write in the odd month.

Once you have investigated the case sufficiently to give the client an evaluation, be honest with him. If the case is weak, tell him so. Tell him where the weakness lies. He has a right to know the hazards of his case. This candor may be helpful when the subject of settlement is first suggested.

G. TIME TO SETTLE

At this point in the progress of the case, you should explore thoroughly the option of settling the case. You have completed your investigation of the facts and the legal research. You know the strength and weakness of the case. If you represent the plaintiff, it may be the ideal time to initiate a discussion of settlement. The case has not been entered in court. You have not yet retained an expert witness. Costs of discovery are still to be incurred. The time is ripe for an overture.

Be realistic in your demand. Don't frighten away the defendant with a figure which bears no relation to the value of the case. Be forthright as to what your investigation reveals.

If you are defense counsel, you will probably find this juncture —after investigation and before the action has been commenced—a propitious time to evaluate the case and to advise your client about the desirability of settling the case. It is true that not all cases can or should be settled because there are some cases which are open and shut in your favor or against you. A client's attitude can make settlement impossible if he or she insists on a trial "out of principle." On the whole, however, most cases can be settled at the "right time." Immediately before a case is entered is commonly the "right time."

H. TIME TO ENGAGE IN PLEA BARGAINING

Criminal dockets are so crowded throughout the country that plea bargaining has become an enforced way of life in most jurisdictions. If you are defense counsel, always keep an open mind and a ready ear for an offer from the prosecution. Unless you have an airtight defense or a client who thinks that he has an air-tight defense, listen carefully to what the government is offering. For a plea of guilty to a lesser included offense, your client may be able "to stay on the street." For a substantial measure of cooperation with the authorities in the prosecution of an accomplice, your client may be able to enjoy his freedom.

Timing is important in plea bargaining. Don't wait too long after an offer is made. It may be withdrawn. The prosecutor may discover a witness who will make your client's cooperation unnecessary.

You should be in a position to advise your client after you have completed the investigation and discovery. Always keep in mind that the decision is the client's, not yours. He or she is entitled to your advice, but it is the client's future which is at stake, not yours.

I. CHOOSING THE FORUM

If you represent the plaintiff, you will control the choice of forum. The first choice is as between the state and the federal court. You must reckon with the amount in controversy if it is a case which lends itself to the diversity jurisdiction of the federal court. Within the state, there may be two or more courts with subject matter jurisdiction of your case. The following factors should be considered by you in choosing the forum.

1. *Trial Before Judge or Jury*

Not all cases are best tried before a jury. While the defendant may thwart your choice to try the case jury-waived because of his statutory or constitutional right to a jury trial, you should not plan on the defendant's claim of jury trial in the first instance. Cases implicating more questions of law than of fact, cases which involve complex fact patterns and criminal cases in which public fury is running high—these cases may better be tried to a judge. It may be safer in the initial stages of a case to claim a jury and later waive it when it becomes clear that the case does not lend itself to adjudication by a jury.

Cases which are founded entirely upon equitable principles may not permit a jury trial. You may be guided in the selection of a forum in this case by the reputation of the judges in the various courts which possess the necessary equity jurisdiction and by the condition of the dockets.

2. *Jurisdiction of the Defendant*

There is no point to considering the merits of a particular forum unless you are satisfied that you can acquire personal jurisdiction over the defendant in that forum.

3. *Convenience*

The choice of a forum may be dictated in part, at least, by convenience of counsel. Though jurisdiction over subject matter may not be waived nor supplied by the parties, venue is waivable. It is not uncommon for plaintiff's counsel to enter a case in a forum which is not a court of proper venue. Defense counsel, finding this forum more convenient than the proper court, may file an answer to the merits without raising the issue of venue.

4. *Court Calendar*

Plaintiffs generally want a speedy trial. If there are two or more courts in which an action may be brought, the condition of the trial calendars may dictate the forum. Those courts which suffer a severe backlog will generally not be the plaintiff's choice.

5. *Difference in Laws*

Before a case is entered, care should be taken to research the prevailing laws in the various courts in which the case could be entered. These courts may be located in different states or in one state and the U. S. District Court in that state. It may be important to know whether one forum honors contributory negligence while another has comparative negligence. The law as to the effect of a statutory violation in terms of whether it constitutes negligence may be important. You may even be able to escape the draconian effect of a short statute of limitations by the prudent choice of a forum.

You should explore both the procedural and substantive law of the jurisdictions implicated in your case.

J. JOINDER OF PARTIES

The decision as to who shall be joined as parties defendants must be made early in the case,[1] although amendments allowing joinder of new parties are generally allowed without too much trouble if made before the case grows old.[2] If the tortfeasor is an employee of a corporation, the employer should be joined. Of course, it is the plaintiff's burden to prove that the employee was acting within the scope of his employment when he ran down the plaintiff with the company truck. Employers generally are in a better position to pay a judgment than an employee.

If the defendant is a minor, some thought should be given to joining his parent or guardian or guardian ad litem.

The scope of discovery is governed to a great extent by the parties who are joined as defendants. Although a deposition may be taken of any person,[3] interrogatories,[4] a motion for production of documents and things [5] as well as requests for admissions [6] may be directed only to a party to the action.

1. Fed.R.Civ.P. 19, 20.
2. Fed.R.Civ.P. 15.
3. Fed.R.Civ.P. 30.
4. Fed.R.Civ.P. 33.
5. Fed.R.Civ.P. 34.
6. Fed.R.Civ.P. 36.

K. CHOOSING THEORY OF CASE

Your investigation reveals that your client has been injured in his person and in his property by the defendant's conduct. Before drawing the declaration or complaint in the case, you should reflect on the theories of the case. There may be an action for common law negligence, a statutory cause of action based on a violation of a consumer protection law, a breach of warranty and an action founded on contract. You may join them all in different counts of the complaint.[7]

Your client may be entitled to only one recovery but the burden of proof may be substantially lighter in the action for breach of warranty than in the count for common law negligence.

L. THE COMPLAINT

If you represent the plaintiff, the first pleading to be drawn is the complaint. Draw it with great care. Avoid uncommon words and repetitious phrases. Legal jargon has no place in the complaint. Words used in ordinary, day to day conversation are better. Remember that you will read the complaint to the jury some day when the trial is commencing. In some jurisdictions, the trial judge may ask you to summarize the complaint and answer when you make your opening to the jury. However, the complaint will probably go to the jury room and be read by the jurors. Accordingly, write simply but clearly.

The Federal Rules mandate a ". . . short and plain statement of the claim showing that the pleader is entitled to relief, and . . . a demand for judgment for the relief . . . ."[8] The facts on which the claim for relief is founded are important, not the legal theory or conclusion. The pleading should be ". . . simple, concise and direct."[9]

Alternate and hypothetical pleading is permissible, although care should be taken to separate the different claims into discrete counts.[10] A claim in tort founded on malpractice should not be joined in the same count with a claim for malpractice predicated on contract. Claims which are inconsistent with each other may be joined in the one complaint, although in separate counts. When a complaint is attacked, it is to be so interpreted as to do substantial justice.[11]

Your client's circumstances may require quick action by way of interlocutory relief in equity. A mortgage foreclosure which ap-

7. Fed.R.Civ.P. 18(a).

8. Fed.R.Civ.P. 8(a).

9. Fed.R.Civ.P. 8(e)(1).

10. Fed.R.Civ.P. 8(e)(2).

11. Fed.R.Civ.P. 8(f).

pears improper may have to be enjoined, a sale of property may require a temporary restraining order—these actions are all possible if you include in the complaint a demand for a temporary restraining order and present it to the court without delay in order to keep the status quo while the case is being litigated on the merits.[12]

Take pains to draw your complaint in such form that you demand the type of relief that you need. You must fashion the complaint in such a mode that if equitable relief is sought in addition to damages, the prayer or demand is set forth in tailored form. For the most part, the plaintiff is bound by his complaint in his quest for relief.

Apart from the requirements after a counterclaim and cross-claim are interposed, the plaintiff is not required in most jurisdictions to respond to the allegations of the defendant's answer, even as to affirmative defenses raised by the defendant, unless ordered to do so by the court.[13] The former pleading denominated replication, has gone the way of the automobile hand crank.

M. THE ANSWER

The hoary form of general denial ("Now comes the defendant and denies each and every allegation in the plaintiff's declaration contained") has gone the way of the rumble seat. In most jurisdictions and in all states which have adopted rules of civil procedure, a party shall state "in short and plain terms" [14] his defenses to each claim asserted by the plaintiff. He will admit, deny or state that he is without sufficient knowledge to admit or deny (this amounts to a denial). The failure to deny is an admission.[15]

Affirmative defenses such as accord and satisfaction, contributory negligence and the like shall be specially pleaded. If you are in doubt as to the viability of an affirmative defense, better to plead it. You can graciously waive it down the road. However, if you fail to plead it, you must rely on the discretion of the judge at a later time to permit you to amend your answer to include it.[16]

Draw your answer with a view towards its effect on the jury when it is read to them. Avoid technical nomenclature whenever possible.

N. COUNTERCLAIM—CROSS-CLAIM

A defendant who has a claim against the plaintiff *may*,[17] and in some circumstances, *must* [18] assert it by way of counterclaim within

12. Fed.R.Civ.P. 65.

13. Fed.R.Civ.P. 7(a).

14. Fed.R.Civ.P. 8(b).

15. Fed.R.Civ.P. 8(d).

16. Fed.R.Civ.P. 15(a).

17. Fed.R.Civ.P. 13(b).

18. Fed.R.Civ.P. 13(a).

the framework of the action commenced by the plaintiff. If he files a counterclaim, the plaintiff is required to file a reply to it in a form similar to the answer required of the defendant in response to the complaint.[19]

If there are two or more plaintiffs or two or more defendants, a claim asserted by one defendant against a codefendant and a claim advanced by one plaintiff against another plaintiff is called a cross-claim. They are claims asserted by and against parties on the same side of the lawsuit.[20] The party against whom such a cross-claim is raised shall file an answer to it in the form required of answers to a complaint.[21]

O. THIRD PARTY PRACTICE

In most jurisdictions, a person who is sued may cause an action to be commenced against one "who is or may be liable to him for all or part of the plaintiff's claim against him." [22] The defendant in this instance becomes the third party plaintiff and the new party becomes the third party defendant.

A plaintiff may implead a third party defendant when a counterclaim is asserted against him under circumstances which would permit a defendant to implead.[23]

The third party defendant has available all the rights of first party defendants to assert a counterclaim, cross-claim or implead under third party practice against another who is or may be liable to him for all or part of the claim asserted against him.[24]

P. INTERPLEADER

A defendant against whom a claim is asserted may admit to his liability for the claim but allege that he does not know to whom the money is owed. Similarly, a plaintiff may be exposed to double liability if all persons asserting a claim against him are not joined. The remedy for a party, plaintiff or defendant, who owes a debt or admits to liability for a claim but is unable to determine to whom the liability runs is the device of interpleader by which all claimants are brought before the court and the claims are adjudicated.[25]

19. Fed.R.Civ.P. 7(a), 8(b).

20. Fed.R.Civ.P. 13(g).

21. Fed.R.Civ.P. 7(a).

22. Fed.R.Civ.P. 14(a).

23. Fed.R.Civ.P. 14(b).

24. Fed.R.Civ.P. 14(a).

25. Fed.R.Civ.P. 22.

FORMS

COMPLAINT ON A PROMISSORY NOTE

1. Allegation of jurisdiction.

2. Defendant on or about June 1, Yr.-2, executed and delivered to plaintiff a promissory note [in the following words and figures: (here set out the note verbatim)]; [a copy of which is hereto annexed as Exhibit A]; whereby defendant promised to pay to plaintiff or order on June 1, Yr.-1 the sum of ______ dollars with interest thereon at the rate of ______ percent per annum.

3. Defendant owes to plaintiff the amount of said note and interest.

Wherefore plaintiff demands judgment against defendant for the sum of ______ dollars, interest, and costs.

Signed: ______________________
Attorney for Plaintiff
Address: ______________________

COMPLAINT FOR NEGLIGENCE

1. Allegation of jurisdiction.

2. On June 1, Yr.-2, in a public highway called ______ Street in [*City*], [*State*], defendant negligently drove a motor vehicle against plaintiff who was then crossing said highway.

3. As a result plaintiff was thrown down and had his leg broken and was otherwise injured, was prevented from transacting his business, suffered great pain of body and mind, and incurred expenses for medical attention and hospitalization in the sum of one thousand dollars.

Wherefore plaintiff demands judgment against defendant in the sum of ______ dollars and costs.

COMPLAINT FOR SPECIFIC PERFORMANCE OF CONTRACT TO CONVEY LAND

1. Allegation of jurisdiction.

2. On or about December 1, Yr.-2, plaintiff and defendant entered into an agreement in writing a copy of which is hereto annexed as Exhibit A.

3. In accord with the provisions of said agreement plaintiff tendered to defendant the purchase price and requested a conveyance of the land, but defendant refused to accept the tender and refused to make the conveyance.

4. Plaintiff now offers to pay the purchase price.

Wherefore plaintiff demands (1) that defendant be required specifically to perform said agreement, (2) damages in the sum of one thousand dollars, and (3) that if specific performance is not granted plaintiff have judgment against defendant in the sum of ______ dollars.

ANSWER PRESENTING DEFENSES UNDER RULE 12(b)

First Defense

The complaint fails to state a claim against defendant upon which relief can be granted.

Second Defense

If defendant is indebted to plaintiffs for the goods mentioned in the complaint, he is indebted to them jointly with G. H. G. H. is alive; is a citizen of the State of ______ and a resident of this district; is subject to the jurisdiction of this court, as to both service of process and venue; can be made a party without depriving this court of jurisdiction of the present parties; and has not been made a party.

Third Defense

Defendant admits the allegation contained in paragraphs 1 and 4 of the complaint; alleges that he is without knowledge or information sufficient to form a belief as to the truth of the allegations contained in paragraph 2 of the complaint; and denies each and every other allegation contained in this complaint.

Fourth Defense

The right of action set forth in the complaint did not accrue within six years next before the commencement of this action.

Counterclaim

(Here set forth any claim as a counterclaim in the manner in which a claim is pleaded in a complaint. No statement of the grounds on which the court's jurisdiction depends need be made unless the counterclaim requires independent grounds of jurisdiction.)

Cross-Claim Against Defendant M. N.

(Here set forth the claim constituting a cross-claim against defendant M. N. in the manner in which a claim is pleaded in a complaint. The statement of grounds upon which the court's jurisdiction depends need not be made unless the cross-claim requires independent grounds of jurisdiction.)

ANSWER TO COMPLAINT WITH COUNTERCLAIM FOR INTERPLEADER

Defense

Defendant admits the allegations stated in paragraph 1 of the complaint; and denies the allegations stated in paragraph 2 to the extent set forth in the counterclaim herein.

Counterclaim for Interpleader

1. Defendant received the sum of ______ dollars as a deposit from E. F.

2. Plaintiff has demanded the payment of such deposit to him by virtue of an assignment of it which he claims to have received from E. F.

3. E. F. has notified the defendant that he claims such deposit, that the purported assignment is not valid, and that he holds the defendant responsible for the deposit.

Wherefore defendant demands:

(1) That the court order E. F. to be made a party defendant to respond to the complaint and to this counterclaim.

(2) That the court order the plaintiff and E. F. to interplead their respective claims.

(3) That the court adjudge whether the plaintiff or E. F. is entitled to the sum of money.

(4) That the court discharge defendant from all liability in the premises except to the person it shall adjudge entitled to the sum of money.

(5) That the court award to the defendant its cost and attorney's fees.

Chapter Three

PRE–TRIAL MOTIONS AND PRELIMINARY INJUNCTIONS

A. TEMPORARY RESTRAINING ORDER

A temporary restraining order may be issued without prior written or oral notice to the adverse party if the moving party by affidavit or by verified complaint satisfies the court that ". . . immediate and irreparable injury, loss or damage will result to the applicant before the adverse party or his attorney can be heard in opposition . . ."[1] and if the applicant's attorney certifies in writing the efforts which have been made to give appropriate notice to the adverse party. The order expires by its terms on the date fixed by the court. Notice of its issuance may be transmitted to the adverse party and his attorney by telephone before the officer has had an opportunity to serve the order.

A court should be particularly careful in granting this type of relief. It should be given only when it is clear that without it, great harm will come to the party seeking it. As a matter of strategy, a victory at this point may spell a victory on the merits for all practical purposes. The time constraints may be such that if the defendant is restrained from taking certain action at this juncture, the plaintiff has won the entire fight and not just the first round. The court should be on guard against this opportunity for abuse.

B. PRELIMINARY INJUNCTION

A preliminary injunction shall not be issued without notice to the adverse party.[2] It commonly follows the temporary restraining order after the adverse party has had an opportunity to be heard. If the court is satisfied that an order should continue until the case is adjudicated on the merits, the court will issue a preliminary injunction.

C. CRITERIA FOR ISSUANCE OF TEMPORARY RESTRAINING ORDER AND PRELIMINARY INJUNCTION

There are four conditions which must be met before the court will grant a temporary restraining order or a preliminary injunction.

1. Fed.R.Civ.P. 65(b).

2. Fed.R.Civ.P. 65(a)(1).

1. *Irreparable Harm*

If a trial on the merits can be completed before any injury occurs to the applicant, the interlocutory relief is denied. It is not enough for the applicant to prove harm; it must be irreparable harm.[3] If damage beyond relief will follow from the failure to grant the restraining order, it should be allowed. If the foreclosure of the mortgage will take place, leaving the applicant homeless or at least displaced, such harm is irreparable. If the former employee is on the verge of improperly disclosing trade secrets of his former employer, irreparable harm will follow. Interlocutory relief in the form of a preliminary injunction is in order to keep the status quo between the parties until there is a trial on the merits.

2. *Balancing of Harm to Both Parties*

The equities of the situation must be measured. If the balance of harm tips in favor of the adverse party, denial of a preliminary injunction is in order.[4] At least, the applicant should be required to post security from which the adverse party may be made whole if he prevails on the merits after suffering harm as a result of the interlocutory relief. In this connection, a mandatory injunction which has the effect of ordering the adverse party to do or to perform an act as contrasted with a prohibitory injunction by which the adverse party is ordered *not* to perform a certain act, is more likely to harm the adverse party.

3. *Likelihood of Success on the Merits*

In most jurisdictions, the applicant for a preliminary injunction must present a prima facie case. He should persuade the court that he will prevail on the merits, though he is not required to prove certainty of success.[5]

4. *Public Interest*

If the public interest would be severely and adversely affected, injunctive relief should be denied.[6] Conversely, an application for injunctive relief which would curb the adverse party from violating a statute should, other things being equal, be granted.

D. ARRAIGNMENT

After a person has been arrested, his first appearance in court is generally for purpose of arraignment.[7] At this proceeding, the clerk reads the complaint or indictment and asks the defendant how he pleads. His options are three. He may plead not guilty, guilty or nolo

3. Fed.R.Civ.P. 65(b).

4. Wright & Miller, Federal Practice and Procedure: Civil, § 2948 (hereinafter cited as Wright & Miller).

5. Wright & Miller, § 2948.

6. Id.

7. Fed.R.Crim.P. 10.

contendere.[8] The consent of the court is required for acceptance of a plea of nolo.[9]

The arraignment day is important because in most jurisdictions it starts the running of time for pre-trial motions.

E. PLEA OF GUILTY

It is generally better practice to persuade your client to plead not guilty at arraignment because time for investigation is required before you are in a position to advise him as to the merits of changing his plea to guilty. After you have satisfied yourself that there is no viable defense to the indictment and that the prosecutor has the evidence to prove your client guilty, it is appropriate to discuss a change of plea.[10] It is not amiss to inquire of the prosecutor whether a plea bargain may be struck by a plea to a lesser included offense or to the offense as charged in return for some consideration in his recommendation of sentence at this early stage of the case.

Once the client has indicated a desire to plead guilty, it is your solemn obligation to explain every facet of the criminal process which might affect him as a result of his plea. Point out to your client the length of the possible sentence, the probable place of incarceration, parole terms, the precise nature of the crime to which he is pleading in terms of its elements, the fact that the court is not bound by the prosecutor's recommendation and may impose a more severe sentence up to the maximum provided in the statute, the surrender of his right to a jury trial, his right of confrontation, his privilege against self-incrimination and other rights which are waived on a plea of guilty.

The court will undoubtedly propound questions to your client with a view to determining that his offer to plead is intelligently and voluntarily made. The court will very probably inquire whether he committed the crime as alleged by the state. In a word, your client must be prepared to tell the court that he understands the elements of the crime and the consequences of his plea.[11]

QUESTIONS TO BE ASKED OF DEFENDANT WHO OFFERS TO CHANGE HIS PLEA TO GUILTY

1. What is your name and age?

2. How far have you gone in school?

3. Have you ever been treated for a mental condition? Are you aware of any mental condition that you now have?

4. Have you taken any medication today? Any drug? Any intoxicating liquor?

8. Fed.R.Crim.P. 11(a).

9. Fed.R.Crim.P. 11(b).

10. Fed.R.Crim.P. 11(c).

11. Fed.R.Crim.P. 11(d).

5. Are you aware that you have been charged with the crime of ______?

6. (At this point either the judge or the prosecutor or defense counsel reads a police report as to what the government alleges the facts of the crime to be.) Did you do what has just been read to you?

7. Did you commit the crime of ______ with which you are charged?

8. Do you understand that by pleading guilty you admit the facts which have just been read?

9. Are you pleading guilty freely and willingly?

10. Do you know that by pleading guilty you give up the following constitutional rights:

(1) The right to a fair and impartial trial before a jury or a judge who would determine whether you are guilty;

(2) The right to confront your accusers, to cross-examine them and to present a defense if you wish;

(3) The privilege against self incrimination which is the right that you have to require the state to prove all the elements of the crime with which you have been charged beyond a reasonable doubt without any help from you and without the necessity of your taking the witness stand. In other words, you cannot be compelled to be a witness against yourself.

11. Do you know that the maximum penalty for this offense is ______ years?

12. (If there is more than one offense) Are you aware that this court may give you consecutive sentences, sometimes called from and after sentences?

13. By pleading guilty, you leave it to this court to impose such sentence as the judge deems appropriate consistent with the law. Do you understand this?

14. Do you understand that regardless of any agreement which your attorney and the prosecutor may have about the prosecutor's recommendation, the court is not bound by such agreement? In fact, the court may disregard it entirely and impose the maximum sentence.

15. Have any promises been made to you to induce you to plead guilty?

16. Have any threats been made to you? Have you been forced in any way to offer to change your plea to guilty?

17. Have you been given sufficient time to discuss the case and the change of plea with your lawyer?

18. Do you believe that your lawyer has acted in your best interests and represented you in a manner satisfactory to you?

19. If you are an alien, you may be deported for conviction of this offense.

20. Are you confused in any way by the questions which I have asked you?

21. Am I correct in concluding that you are pleading guilty because you are guilty and for no other reason?

F. NEED FOR PRE–TRIAL MOTIONS IN CRIMINAL AND CIVIL CASES

It may come to your attention after being retained by one accused of crime that the government has illegally seized material which it will use as evidence at trial against him. This discovery is generally made early in the case when you interrogate your client as to what the police seized and what he said when arrested and brought to the police station.

A motion to suppress should be filed immediately on learning what the police seized and what your client said. Most jurisdictions require such motions to be filed within two or three weeks after arraignment.[12]

On the civil side, you may find it necessary to ask for immediate equitable relief to stave off an impending mortgage foreclosure which appears to be irregular or the sale of property to an innocent third party, leaving your client in a position wherein he may recover only money damages, losing the house which he contracted to buy. All that you seek by the invocation of immediate interlocutory equitable relief is the preservation of the status quo until the case can be heard on the merits.[13] Speed is of the essence in these crises.

G. MOTION TO SUPPRESS

In criminal cases, it is important to determine as early as possible what evidence the prosecution is going to use against your client. If you are satisfied that such evidence was obtained illegally in violation of your client's rights under the 4th and 6th Amendments to the U. S. Constitution or under State Statutes, a motion to suppress such evidence will lie.[14] It must be timely filed and the time frame is governed by local law and rules of court. Of course, it can be filed at any time, however late, on a showing that it was not apparent that the prosecution had seized such evidence.

12. Fed.R.Crim.P. 12(b).

13. Fed.R.Civ.P. 65.

14. Fed.R.Crim.P. 12(b)(3); see sample motion infra.

In a hearing on a motion to suppress, bear in mind that testimony which would be totally inadmissible at the trial on the merits, may be perfectly competent at the hearing because the object of the hearing is different from the object of the trial. For example, to determine whether a police officer had probable cause to arrest without a warrant, the officer's state of mind is important. It is quite correct to elicit from the officer what he knew at the time of the arrest. At trial, however, such evidence is inadmissible on the merits of the defendant's guilt.

A defendant may also want to suppress statements which he allegedly made to the police officer before the Miranda warnings were given. A show-up or lineup identification may be defective and its admissibility may be challenged by a motion to suppress.

The defendant's motion should be accompanied by an affidavit of the defendant. This should set forth the facts which form the basis for the motion and for the relief sought. It is the defendant's affidavit, not the lawyer's. A motion without an accompanying affidavit signed by the defendant is defective and should not be entertained.

H. MOTION TO DISMISS—CRIMINAL

In many jurisdictions, the catalogue of pre-trial motions which seek to attack the indictment or complaint carries names different from those of yesterday. No longer are there demurrers and motions in abatement. Under the one umbrella of a motion to dismiss are those pleas which formerly carried different monikers.[15]

A motion to dismiss is the appropriate weapon by which to raise the legal sufficiency of the indictment. A defendant who feels aggrieved by a denial of speedy trial should invoke a motion to dismiss. Under the aegis of a motion to dismiss are those defects exposed in the process by which the complaint or indictment issued.

The motion to dismiss must be timely filed. Every jurisdiction has its own time schedule for filing pre-trial motions. If you fail to meet these time constraints, your client's case may be severely damaged. An attack on the court's subject matter jurisdiction, however, may be raised at any time and by the court, sua sponte.

I. MOTION TO DISMISS—CIVIL

In those jurisdictions which have adopted some form of rules practice, pleadings formerly denominated demurrer, plea in abatement, plea in bar and answer in abatement have been supplanted by a single motion to dismiss or a motion for judgment on the pleadings.[16]

15. Fed.R.Crim.P. 12(a); see sample motion, infra.

16. Fed.R.Civ.P. 7(c); see sample motion to dismiss, infra.

A motion to dismiss shall be used to reach the following defects: lack of jurisdiction over the subject matter, lack of personal jurisdiction, improper venue, insufficiency of process, insufficiency of service of process, failure to state a claim on which relief may be granted and failure to join a necessary party. These defects may also be raised in the defendant's answer.[17]

The time restriction must be met or you will be deemed to have waived most of these defects. Clearly, there can be no effective waiver of an absence of subject matter jurisdiction.

J. MOTION FOR SUMMARY JUDGMENT—MOTION FOR JUDGMENT ON THE PLEADINGS

After the pleadings are completed, they should be examined to determine whether they reveal a genuine issue of material fact. In a motion for summary judgment,[18] the court will examine all relevant documents filed in the case-pleadings, depositions, answers to interrogatories and affidavits—to determine whether there is a genuine issue of material fact and whether the moving party is entitled to a judgment as a matter of law.

A motion for judgment on the pleadings raises the same issues but the court is confined to the pleadings for a resolution of the problem. If the court is required to examine matters outside the pleadings on a motion for judgment on the pleadings, such motion will be considered a motion for summary judgment.[19]

Note carefully, if you are resisting a motion for summary judgment, that it is not sufficient for you *to have* a genuine issue of material fact. It is essential that you *demonstrate* it. Ordinarily, this is best accomplished by an affidavit which may make reference to other documents such as statements in response to requests for admissions, answers to interrogatories and depositions. In a word, you cannot afford to sit on your case. You must satisfy the court that there is a genuine issue of material fact to be tried.

If you are the moving party, your burden is twofold. You are required to demonstrate that there is no genuine issue of material fact *and* that you are entitled to a judgment as a matter of law.[20] A judgment may be rendered in favor of the party against whom a claim is made.[21] A partial summary judgment may be rendered as to liability, leaving the issue of damages open for adjudication.[22] Although no judgment may be rendered, the court may enter an order specifying those facts about which there is no controversy, thereby reducing trial

17. Fed.R.Civ.P. 12(b).

18. Fed.R.Civ.P. 56.

19. Fed.R.Civ.P. 12(c).

20. Fed.R.Civ.P. 56(c).

21. Fed.R.Civ.P. 56(b).

22. Fed.R.Civ.P. 56(c).

time to hearing evidence on matters which are genuinely controverted.[23]

There is no substitute for the filing of a detailed brief on motions for summary judgment and for motions for judgment on the pleadings. Oral argument should not be waived. There may be reasonable inferences to be drawn from the documents and pleadings which will create the genuine issue of material fact.

K. OTHER PRE-TRIAL MOTIONS

MOTION TO STRIKE

If your opponent has filed a pleading which contains matter which is redundant, immaterial, impertinent or scandalous, a motion to strike lies.[24] If this material is left unchallenged, it will probably be read to the jury to the detriment of your client's case. It is good strategy to eliminate this matter early in the proceeding.

MOTION FOR MORE DEFINITE STATEMENT

If your opponent's complaint is so vague or ambiguous that you are unable to file a responsive pleading to it, a motion for more definite statement is in order.[25] However, this device is not a proper substitute for discovery. This motion is seldom granted but it is available in extreme cases.

MOTION TO CONSOLIDATE

The court may order two or more pending actions which involve common questions of law or fact tried together.[26] Such consolidation may be beneficial to your case or detrimental. You don't want to try your case with a companion case which may prejudice your client by reason of the joinder. You should avoid any move which may permit a jury to paint your client with the same brush as another whose case is not as strong as yours. You must avoid being tarnished by association which comes about as a result of an order of consolidation for trial.

MOTION TO SEVER

Claims which are asserted through a complaint, a cross-claim or a counterclaim may appear to be so related that a trial in joinder is indicated. However, it may be to your advantage to try the case in chief before the other claims are adjudicated. There may be prejudice in a joint trial of all claims. A consolidated trial may result in oppressive delay or inconvenience. These are the factors which you should urge in arguing the motion to sever.[27]

23. Fed.R.Civ.P. 56(d).

24. Fed.R.Civ.P. 12(f).

25. Fed.R.Civ.P. 12(e).

26. Fed.R.Civ.P. 42(a).

27. Fed.R.Civ.P. 13(i), 20(b).

In criminal cases, it is commonly argued that defendant A should not be tried with defendant B because of the prejudice resulting to one or the other.[28] Although the allowance of such a motion is almost entirely discretionary with the court, you should not, on this account, be dissuaded from arguing the prejudice to your client. It may also be to your client's advantage to sever an indictment for a serious crime from a complaint for a misdemeanor.[29]

You may satisfy your burden of demonstrating prejudice by indicating the nature of the evidence as to each defendant. If A has made damaging admissions implicating B, and if you represent B, argue the difficulty of the jury in following the court's instructions limiting the admissions to A.

MOTION FOR TRANSFER OF CASE—CHANGE OF VENUE

If your case has received an inordinate amount of recent publicity, it may be difficult, if not impossible, to impanel an indifferent jury. Unless the jury is sequestered, they will be exposed to daily newspaper copy which will render a just verdict impossible. Under these circumstances, file a motion to transfer the case to a distant county. A change of venue may be the only way in which your client will receive a fair trial.[30]

(FORM OF MOTION TO SUPPRESS)

STATE OF ______

Tricolor, ss. Superior Court #12345

STATE v. JABIS

MOTION TO SUPPRESS

Now comes the defendant, John Jabis, and moves that certain material, to wit: fingernail clippings, cut from the fingernails of the defendant while he was under arrest and now in possession of the State, be suppressed.

As grounds for suppression, the defendant says that he never consented to the surgical process by which his nails were cut, that they were seized without a warrant and not as an incident to a lawful arrest and that the circumstances were not exigent.

28. Fed.R.Crim.P. 14.

29. Fed.R.Crim.P. 13.

30. Fed.R.Crim.P. 21, 22.

The facts on which this motion is founded are fully set forth in an affidavit dated December 1, Yr.-0.

John Jabis,
By his attorney,

/s/ Clarence Darrow

December 1, Yr.-0.

(FORM OF MOTION TO DISMISS—CRIMINAL)

STATE OF ______

Ambush, ss.

Superior Court
#12345

STATE v. MAGEE

MOTION TO DISMISS

Now comes the defendant, Jason Magee, and moves that the indictment be dismissed on the ground that it fails to set forth facts which constituted a crime at the time at which the defendant allegedly committed the acts.

Jason Magee,
By his attorney,

/s/ Rufus Choate

December 2, Yr.-0.

(FORM OF MOTION TO DISMISS—CIVIL)

STATE OF ______

Sunlight, ss.

Superior Court
#12345

JONES v. SILVER

MOTION TO DISMISS

The defendant moves the court to dismiss the complaint in the above entitled action on the ground that it fails to state a claim upon which relief may be granted.

John Silver,
By his attorney,

/s/ Mary Connors

July 1, Yr.-0.

ASSIGNMENT #2

STATE OF ______

______, ss.

Superior Court
Criminal 377 689

STATE v. GARY CUMMINGS

DEFENDANT'S MOTION TO SUPPRESS EVIDENCE AND FOR THE RETURN OF PROPERTY

Now comes the Defendant and complains that he was illegally arrested, and was unlawfully searched, and that certain property was seized from him, and moves this Honorable Court to order that certain property, to wit:

> Seventeen (17) cases of Kleer beer, each case containing twenty-four (24) 10 oz. cans of beer and one (1) five gallon keg of said beer be returned to him.

Said unlawful arrest occurred on January 26, Yr.-0 in the basement apartment of the premises known as and numbered 12–J Plantation Ave., Middle City at 12:00 o'clock noon, and the unlawful search occurred at the same time and place.

The arrest was illegal and the search and seizure were illegal because:

1. There was no probable cause for the arrest.
2. The search of the defendant's premises was illegal because it preceded the arrest.
3. The search was illegal because it was not made incident to a valid arrest.
4. The search, conducted without a warrant, was not made "upon probable cause."
5. The officers who conducted the search were not lawfully admitted to the premises in which the defendant has a possessory interest.
6. There were no exceptional circumstances sufficient to by-pass the constitutional requirement of obtaining a search warrant.

The defendant says there has been a violation of his right to be secure from an unreasonable search and seizure guaranteed by the Fourth Amendment to the Constitution of the United States.

By his Attorney,

/s/ Francis X. Moody

OFFICER TERRY FLEMING, WHEN CALLED BY THE DEFENDANT, MUST TESTIFY IN ACCORDANCE WITH THE FOLLOWING

I am Officer Terry Fleming of the Middle City Police Department. I have been with the department for 15 years.

During the month of January I was assigned to the "Property Theft" Division. On January 25th I received information in the form of a report filed by Officer Martin Pelletier that at 3:00 A.M. that morning two men aged about 25, had been observed in the railroad yards in the East end of the city. They had a Jeep station wagon, and were in the process of filling the wagon with cases of beer from the open door of a railroad car. The people who observed them lived in a house adjoining the railroad yard. These people called the department.

Officers were dispatched to the scene, but, on arrival, found no trace of the Jeep or the men. The officers interrogated the neighbors and were given descriptions of the alleged thieves. Investigation turned up the information that the contents of the railroad car had been consigned to the local warehouse of the Kleer Beer Company; that the car had contained 200 cases of the company's beer in 10 ounce cans, and fifty five-gallon kegs of beer. Subsequent to the incident an inventory was taken, and it was found that twenty-five cases and two five-gallon kegs were missing. On the evening of January 24th the car had been checked, and the seal on the door was unbroken at that time.

The people who had 'phoned the station lived at 6 Plantation Avenue in this city.

At 8:00 A.M. on January 26th I got a phone call from Tony Hart, manager of the Kleer Beer Company's warehouse. He said that he had received a call at his place of business from the residents at 6 Plantation Avenue. They had just told him that while they were passing the premises at 12 Plantation Avenue, going for the morning paper, they heard loud noise from the basement apartment, as though someone was playing a stereo set at full volume. They saw a young man come out from the cement sidewalk along the left side of the house. This young man resembled one of the men whom they had seen loading the Jeep with beer. He got into a sedan-type car and drove off.

I was busy with other matters until about 11:30 to 12:00 noon. At that time, with another officer I went to the premises at 12 Plantation Avenue. I had called the owner of this apartment house before going there. He told me that the basement apartment had been rented for some months to the defendant Gary Cummings, but that Cummings had failed to pay his rent in time last December, and he had notified Cummings in writing there was cause for him to be evicted.

The landlord said he accepted the January rent only for "use and occupation" on his lawyer's advice, making Cummings a "Tenant at Sufferance." He also told me that the Cummings tenant had allowed other persons to live in the basement apartment with him, without notifying the landlord.

When I and the other officer arrived at the scene, looking from the street at the apartment house, there was a cement walk along the left side. It led to the rear of the building. We walked along this walk, until we came to a casement window in the foundation. By squatting down I was able to look in the window, and I saw cases of Kleer beer stacked up along the opposite wall. It appeared that I was looking into a living room. I could hear music. It was loud.

We went to the back of the building. There was a door leading into the basement apartment. This was open about an inch or two. I pushed on the door. It resisted, but by keeping up pushing, I was able to open it so we could enter. What had been holding the door was a "tremendous number" of beer cans. We stepped into the basement apartment.

The first room was a kitchen. From the kitchen we went into a living room, which could be "shut off" from the kitchen by an "accordion" type of folding door. We opened this door. In the living room there were empty beer cans all over the floor. Against the wall were 17 unopened cases of canned Kleer beer, and one five gallon keg, unopened. There was a sleeping bag on the floor. We picked up a wallet which was lying on the sleeping bag. There was nothing in the wallet except for a social security card bearing Mr. Cummings' name and the social security number assigned to him.

We opened another "pleated" type of folding door. This enabled us to gain entrance to the bed room. There we found Mr. Cummings asleep in bed. He reeked of the odor of beer. We told him that he was under arrest and read him his Miranda rights. We had other officers take him to the station.

We marked each case of beer, and the keg, and had Mr. Hart come to the apartment and check the numbers on each case to see that they were a part of the consignment that had been taken from the railroad car. They checked out correctly. We then took the property to the station where it remained until it was produced before the Grand Jury.

The location of 12 Plantation Avenue is approximately one and a quarter miles from the nearest court house—the Middle City Municipal Court. Yes, I did know that the court was in session the morning of January 26th, but I was afraid that if I took the time to get a search warrant Mr. Cummings might wake up and leave the apartment.

COMMONWEALTH v. GARY CUMMINGS

PROCEDURE

I. Opening Statement by defendant's counsel.

II. Direct Examination of Officer Fleming by defendant's counsel.

III. Examination of Officer Fleming by Prosecutor.

IV. Argument by prosecutor.

V. Argument by defendant's counsel.

VI. Ruling by the Court on admissibility of the evidence at trial. The Court will make preliminary Findings of Fact.

ASSIGNMENT #3

FORSYTHE, INC. v. BARNABY INCORPORATED, et al.

The plaintiff has filed a Complaint in the Superior Court, alleging that:

1. The plaintiff Forsythe, Inc., is a corporation organized under and existing by virtue of the laws of this State with a principal place of business at 107 Brown St., Blueville, in the County of Grand, conducting a wholesale florist operation therefrom.

2. The defendant Barnaby Incorporated is a corporation organized under and existing by virtue of the laws of this State, with a principal place of business at 27 Bonnie Lane, Summit in the County of Larin. It too conducts a wholesale florist operation, within fifteen miles of the city of Blueville.

3. The defendant Tiffany Stockler is a citizen of the State, residing at One Hill Road, Blueville, in the County of Grand.

4. On January 1, Yr.-3, the defendant Stockler entered into a written contract of employment with the plaintiff. A copy of the contract is attached to the Complaint, marked "A." By its terms, the defendant Stockler agreed to enter and remain in the employ of the plaintiff for a period of five years from the date of execution of the contract. Also by its terms, the defendant Stockler agreed that, during the period of her employment by plaintiff, and for two years subsequent thereto, she would not accept employment from a competitor of the plaintiff in the wholesale florist business, nor would she "perform any act to the detriment of the plaintiff's business." This restriction on the defendant Stockler's activities was to be in force in a geographical area encompassing all cities and towns within fifty miles of the city of Blueville.

5. By the terms of the contract, the plaintiff agreed to pay the defendant Stockler a base salary of $15,000 per year, payable in

weekly installments plus (at the end of each full year in which she had been so employed) a sum equal to 10% of the gross sales of the plaintiff each year. It was agreed that the defendant Stockler should assume and perform all of the duties of general manager of the corporate business during the period of her employment; that she would be in sole charge of the purchase of seed, flowers, floral tools and supplies, the renting of premises for the carrying on of business activities, the hiring and firing of employees (including sales personnel), customer accounts, and pricing of products.

6. The plaintiff alleges that it was at all times material willing and able to perform its obligations under the contract, and did so perform for a period of one year.

7. Plaintiff alleges that the defendant Stockler breached her contract with the plaintiff. In January, Yr.-2, after serving but one year of her five year contract, the defendant Stockler accepted employment as the general manager of the defendant Barnaby Incorporated, a competitor of the plaintiff. The defendant Stockler, in exchange for accepting employment with the defendant Barnaby, was guaranteed by the defendant Barnaby, a salary of $25,000 per year, and one third of the stock of that corporation, with a proportionate share of its net profits achieved during her period of employment with Barnaby.

8. Plaintiff alleges on information and belief that the defendant Barnaby was fully aware of the existence of the employment contract between the plaintiff and the defendant Stockler. As reason for its belief, plaintiff appends to the Complaint a document marked "B," entitled "Articles of Incorporation" of the defendant Barnaby Incorporated, filed with the Secretary of State on May 20, Yr.-10, listing as its incorporators and principal officers the husband of the defendant Stockler, her mother and her father.

9. Plaintiff alleges further that the defendant Stockler, during the last month in which she served as general manager of the plaintiff's business, photostated all of the index cards on which plaintiff's customers were listed; all of the records of the plaintiff identifying the sources of supply of seeds, flowers, floral tools and supplies; all records of the plaintiff containing quotations of price lists offered to plaintiff's customers, and that she took the photostated materials with her.

10. Many of its customers have informed the plaintiff that they will no longer do business with the plaintiff, but have become customers of the plaintiff's competitor, Barnaby Incorporated.

The plaintiff asserts that the defendant Stockler is liable for breach of contract in damages; that defendant Barnaby is liable in damages for intentional interference with a contract relationship; and that irreparable harm is being done to plaintiff and will continue to be done unless defendant Stockler is restrained from employment by any competitor of the plaintiff in any community within fifty miles of Blueville, and unless defendant Barnaby is restrained from employing the defendant Stockler in any capacity, pending a hearing on the merits of the Complaint.

Defendant Stockler has filed an Answer, with a Counterclaim. She admits the allegations contained in paragraphs 1 through 5 above. She denies essentially all of the other allegations contained in the Complaint. She alleges that the plaintiff corporation did not perform its part of the bargain; that she was hired because the plaintiff had been "running in the red" for two years; that by reason of her ability, business education and background, and her business contacts she was able to obtain flowers and floral supplies at "excellent" prices; that by reason of her efforts the sales of the plaintiff were increased; that she selected and hired talented sales personnel; that she put on "outstanding" floral shows and exhibits for potential customers in the retail end of the business; that she alone was responsible for bringing the plaintiff business "into the black" in a period of ten months; that the plaintiff's officers and directors knew that, with the new life that she had "pumped" into the failing business, plaintiff could now prosper without her aid. She claims that the plaintiff wanted to save the 10% of the gross profits they would have to pay her on future profits and that the plaintiff's officers and directors embarked on a planned campaign to make it impossible for her to act fully in her capacity as general manager. She specifies that the president-treasurer of the plaintiff, Mr. E. L. Forsythe, wilfully interfered with the performance of her duties; that he cancelled orders for supplies that she wanted and needed; that he changed prices when lists were ready for mailing to customers; that he arbitrarily cancelled two "shows" which she had planned, and otherwise interfered with the performance of her duties. By reason of these activities, says Mrs. Stockler, she was no longer the "general manager" of the business; the plaintiff breached the contract, and she was entitled to leave the plaintiff's employ, no longer bound by the "negative" covenant with respect to competition. She alleges that Mr. Forsythe intentionally spread the false rumor among plaintiff's employees that she was carrying on an adulterous relationship with a male sales employee of plaintiff.

By way of counterclaim, Mrs. Stockler seeks damages for the alleged breach of contract, and for defamation by Forsythe.

The defendant Barnaby has also filed an Answer, conceding that the corporation has hired Tiffany Stockler, but denying interference with the previous contract relationship between Forsythe and Mrs. Stockler.

PROBLEM

Counsel for the plaintiff Forsythe will prepare and present to the Court a "Motion for the Issuance of a Preliminary Injunction," and argue for its issuance.

Counsel for the defendant Stockler and the defendant Barnaby will argue against the issuance of such an injunction.

Chapter Four

DISCOVERY

A. DISCOVERY IN GENERAL

Discovery is not limited to those devices which historically have provided the parties with means for ferreting out the opponent's case —interrogatories, depositions, etc. From the first interview with your client, you should have a nose for discovery. Ask questions of all those who can contribute any information about the case. Discovery in the broadest sense embraces just about every approach to the case by which lawyer and client learn the facts and the events which actually occurred.

The lawyer who alerts his client to every step in the discovery process has a contented client and one who is impressed with his attorney's energy and acumen. Don't ignore your client. Tell him when you propound interrogatories, notice a deposition and request the admission of facts from the adversary. It is *his* or *her* case, not yours; you are the advocate working in behalf of the client.

B. INTERROGATORIES

A party to an action may propound questions to any other party to the litigation.[1] The interrogatories are to be answered under oath by the party interrogated within a time frame established by statute or rule in the forum. The scope of inquiry is delimited by the matters which are material to the case. One rule of thumb which may be helpful, though its admits of some exceptions, is that a party may propound any interrogatory which he could ask as a question if the party interrogated were on the witness stand at trial. The Federal rule is broader. Under this rule, it is "not ground for objection that the information sought will be inadmissible at trial if the information sought appears reasonably calculated to lead to the discovery of admissible evidence." [2]

If the party to whom the interrogatories are propounded objects to a question, he may refuse to answer until ordered by the court. If he is unable to answer the interrogatory at the time that it is propounded, he will be required to supplement his answers when such information becomes available to him.[3]

In most jurisdictions there is a limit to the number of interrogatories which may be propounded to one party without leave of court.

1. Fed.R.Civ.P. 33(a).

2. Fed.R.Civ.P. 33(a).

3. Fed.R.Civ.P. 26(e).

Each question should be carefully drawn to elicit from the party interrogated the information which you consider important to your case. Better still, you may try to evoke an admission from the adverse party. The next best achievement is an answer or series of answers which will lead to an admission if artfully approached when the party takes the witness stand.[4] In a word, don't waste interrogatories on matters which are of little or no moment to your case.

C. DEPOSITIONS

After an action has been commenced, a decision must be made as to the desirability, vel non, of taking depositions. In some jurisdictions, a deposition may not be taken if there is no reasonable likelihood that the plaintiff will recover in excess of some specified amount such as $5,000.00. Taking a deposition may also be costly. It may prove harmful to your case if you alert your sleeping opponent to matters which are advantageous to his case.

A deposition may be taken of any person.[5] There is no limit as in the case of interrogatories which may be propounded only to parties to the action. The attendance of witnesses may be compelled by subpoena. If your client's deposition has been noticed, prepare him for it by reviewing the matters germane to the case. Run him through a series of questions, simulating as best you can the conditions under which the deposition will be taken.

The time of a deposition may be important. You may want to depose eye witnesses early in the process before their memories fade. An early deposition may expedite a settlement. It fixes the testimony of a witness so that you need not fear a "new" version of the facts when the witness is called to the witness stand at trial.

A witness of advanced age or impaired health should be deposed soon after the commencement of the action to preserve his testimony in the event of his death.[6]

Videotaped depositions may be helpful. Experts who reside outside of the forum state can be deposed on videotape and no further worry need be expended as to the expert's availability for trial. In most jurisdictions, a special order of the court is required to depose a person by videotape. The order should contain the safeguards necessary for fairness.[7]

The party deposed is entitled to have counsel with him during the taking of the deposition. After a witness has been examined, the other parties have the right to cross-examine him. Objections

4. As to the use of interrogatories in cross examination, see infra.

5. Fed.R.Civ.P. 30; as to depositions in criminal cases, see Fed.R.Crim.P. 15.

6. Fed.R.Civ.P. 32.

7. Fed.R.Civ.P. 30(b)(4).

interposed to evidence shall be noted, but the evidence shall be taken.[8] If a party does not wish to attend the deposition, he may serve written questions on the party taking the deposition. These questions shall be propounded to the deponent and his answers recorded verbatim.

D. REQUEST FOR ADMISSION

Most jurisdictions have a device which permits a party to serve on any other party a series of statements with a request that the party to whom they are addressed either deny or admit them.[9] The party to whom they are addressed may admit, deny or state that he can neither admit nor deny them with accompanying reasons. He may also object to the request for admission, leaving it to the court to order him to respond.

This discovery device is most valuable for saving time at trial. If the case involves a quantity of documentary evidence, the request for admission is valuable in securing admissions as to the genuineness of the signatures as well as to the genuineness of the documents themselves. Further, matters about which there should be no dispute can be admitted, saving time which would be required to prove these matters.

The admission is conclusively binding, though for good cause shown, the court may relieve the party.[10] If not relieved, the admitting party may not explain his admission as he is permitted to do in the case of an answer to an interrogatory.

If the matter denied or not admitted is such that it should have been admitted, the requesting party may, on motion, recover the costs incurred in proving the matter at trial.

E. PRODUCTION OF DOCUMENTS

Under common law restraints, if a party wished to examine real estate or personal property in possession of the adversary he was required to bring a separate action in the form of a bill in equity for discovery or, as it was popularly known, a bill of discovery. This was an equitable device in aid of a lawsuit.

Today, in most jurisdictions, either by motion, petition or request, a party may demand to see, examine and copy documents, test or sample tangible things which are otherwise discoverable and to enter upon land and buildings in possession or control of the adverse party for purposes of measuring, photographing, testing or sampling objects thereon.[11]

8. Fed.R.Civ.P. 30(c).

9. Fed.R.Civ.P. 36.

10. Fed.R.Civ.P. 36(b).

11. Fed.R.Civ.P. 34.

Under the Federal Rules provision is made for an independent action against a person not a party for production of documents and things and permission to enter upon land.[12]

This discovery device can be most helpful when you wish your expert to examine the product or machine which allegedly caused your client's injuries. It probably reposes within the control of the adversary and is thereby subject to this discovery weapon.

F. PROTECTIVE ORDERS

Discovery may not be used to harass a person. A party or one from whom discovery is sought may ask the court on motion to terminate discovery or to regulate it in such a way that the moving party is protected "from annoyance, embarrassment, oppression, or undue burden or expense . . . ." [13] The scope of discovery may be limited by the court. Trade secrets and confidential information may be protected from disclosure by a court order. The court may direct that discovery proceed on a course directed by its order to the effect that only certain discovery devices be used before other methods are undertaken. For example, a party may be ordered to use interrogatories before a deposition may be noticed.

G. SANCTIONS

Discovery will not bear all its fruits unless the party seeking it carries it to its conclusion. If an answer to an interrogatory is incomplete or if no answer is supplied, a motion to compel the answer and to strike the incomplete answer should be filed without a delay. If the responding party persists, a motion for sanctions is in order.[14] Attorney's fees and expenses, an order that the disobedient party may not introduce evidence of facts which are the subject matter of the questions left unanswered, an order establishing as true for purpose of the trial the facts of the disputed question, an order staying further proceedings until there is compliance—these are some of the sanctions which may be imposed upon the errant party or person. An order treating as contempt of court the failure to obey may be entered in addition to the sanctions already enumerated.[15]

H. CRIMINAL CASE—DEFENDANT'S DISCOVERY

In all jurisdictions there are statutory and rule provisions which permit the defendant to make discovery of the prosecution.[16] Mo-

12. Fed.R.Civ.P. 34(c).

13. Fed.R.Civ.P. 26(c).

14. Fed.R.Civ.P. 37.

15. Fed.R.Civ.P. 37(b)(1).

16. Fed.R.Crim.P. 16.

tions for particulars permit the defendant to call on the government to specify the time, place, manner and means by which the government alleges the commission of the crime.[17] Other motions which may be filed are: motion for exculpatory evidence; motion for production of statements of the defendant and witnesses; motion for names of all witnesses whom the prosecution intends to call at trial; motion for inculpatory evidence. A good trial lawyer uses one or all of these devices to prepare the defense of his criminal case. They may reveal information which will persuade your client to plead guilty because of the strength of the prosecution's case.

I. CRIMINAL CASE—PROSECUTION'S DISCOVERY

Historically, only the defendant sought discovery in a criminal case. Recently courts have recognized the reciprocal right of the government to discover some of the defenses which the defendant intends to interpose. By motion, the prosecution may compel the defendant to disclose whether he will use an alibi.[18] In return, the government is required to disclose the names and addresses of those witnesses whom the prosecution will call to testify as to the defendant's presence at the scene of the crime. Similarly, the government can compel the defendant to reveal whether he intends to interpose the defense of insanity.[19]

FORMS

REQUEST FOR ADMISSION UNDER RULE 36

Plaintiff A. B. requests defendant C. D. within ______ days after service of this request to make the following admissions for the purpose of this action only and subject to all pertinent objections to admissibility which may be interposed at the trial:

1. That each of the following documents, exhibited with this request, is genuine.

[*Here list the documents and describe each document.*]

2. That each of the following statements is true.

[*Here list the statements.*]

Signed: ______________________,
Attorney for Plaintiff

Address: ______________________

17. Fed.R.Crim.P. 7(f).

18. Fed.R.Crim.P. 12.1.

19. Fed.R.Crim.P. 12.2.

REQUEST FOR PRODUCTION OF DOCUMENTS, ETC., UNDER RULE 34

Plaintiff A. B. requests defendant C. D. to respond within ______ days to the following requests:

1. That defendant produce and permit plaintiff to inspect and to copy each of the following documents:

[*Here list the documents either individually or by category and describe each of them.*]

2. That defendant produce and permit plaintiff to inspect and to copy, test, or sample each of the following objects:

[*Here list the object either individually or by category and describe each of them.*]

[*Here state the time, place, and manner of making the inspection and performance of any related acts.*]

3. That defendant permit plaintiff to enter [*here describe property to be entered*] and to inspect and to photograph, test or sample [*here describe the portion of the real property and the objects to be inspected*].

[*Here state the time, place, and manner of making the inspection and performance of any related acts.*]

Signed: ______________________
Attorney for Plaintiff

Address: ______________________

ASSIGNMENT #4

HARPER, ADMINISTRATRIX v. ADAM HIGHFILL, et al.

CERTAIN OF THE MATERIALS IN THE POSSESSION OF ATTORNEY PINE, COUNSEL FOR ADAM HIGHFILL AND HIGHFILL JEWELRY CORPORATION:

I. Excerpt from the Report of Officer Keith Norwood of the Tripoli Police Department:

. . . May 3, Yr.-1. At 9:00 A.M., Adam Highfill, President of Highfill Jewelry Corp., was operating a De Novo convertible northbound on Route 8, this City. Weather clear. Roadway dry.

Car registered in the name of Highfill Jewelry, purchased April 2 this year from Avery Motors, this City.

The De Novo was in collision, in the southbound lane, with a car travelling southbound, operated by one Jonathan Harper of Andover.

On my arrival at the scene at 9:15 A.M., the Highfill vehicle was on its roof on the roadway and the Harper car was up against a tree 300 feet south of the apparent point of impact off the right side of the highway. Both parties had been removed to nearby City Hospital.

Both cars legally registered. Both operators legally licensed. Cars towed to Tripoli Auto Body.

On arrival of State Police, who assisted with traffic, I interviewed Attorney Leonard Courcy, 126 Toby Road, this City, who stated as follows: He was operating behind Harper car, on way to Superior Court. Harper and he were both doing about 55 mph (the posted speed limit). He saw the Highfill car travelling northbound, about 75 miles per hour, create a cloud of dust as it left the northbound lanes onto the median strip. It nosed down into a depression in the median strip, struck a cement drainage ditch at the bottom, then, its rear first, it flew up into the air flipped, went about 37 feet, and came down on the roof of the Harper car. It then bounced to the pavement, roof down. Courcy pulled to the right, off the road. He saw the Harper car, its roof crushed, going about 5 mph after impact, travel about 300 feet, then off the road to its right, and it came to a stop against a tree. He saw Highfill crawl out of the wreckage of his car. He assisted other bystanders in removing Harper, unconscious, from his vehicle. . . .

II. Excerpt from Supplementary Report of Officer Norwood:

. . . 11:00 A.M., May 3, Yr.-1. Interviewed Adam Highfill at City Hospital. He told me that he was travelling 55 mph northbound in the lane nearest the center strip; that the traffic ahead of him slowed; that he applied his brake; that his steering wheel suddenly pulled sharp left; that the car went on to the median; that the next thing he knew he was upside down in the De Novo and scrambled out of the wreckage in the southbound lanes, fearing the car would catch fire. Injuries: Fracture, left lower arm, contusions and abrasions.

I asked to speak to Mr. Harper at 11:40 A.M., and was informed that he had just passed away from injuries received in the accident. . . .

III. Letter to Attorney Pine, dated June 2, Yr.-1.

Dear Mr(s) Ms. Pine:

On receipt of your telephone request on May 4, on behalf of the collision carrier which covered the Highfill Corp.'s new De Novo car, I visited Tripoli Auto Body late that afternoon.

There was no doubt that the car had been "totalled." While at Tripoli Auto Body, I called Mr. Highfill, who was still recuperating at City Hospital. I explained that I had been commissioned to investigate the possibility that the car he was operating had a defect in it, and that I was a designer of brake systems, employed by De Novo Motors until last year, when I left as a result of their refusal to seek a patent on one of my concepts.

Mr. Highfill stated that one week after the car was delivered by Avery Motors he was driving on Route 128 and felt a peculiar "wobbling." He said he brought the car back to Avery Motors and verbally informed the service manager of the problem. The car was returned to him the next day and he had a similar "wobbling" experience with the steering two days later. He turned the car back in again and complained to the service manager. When the vehicle was delivered to his place of business by the service manager the following day, he was assured that everything has been fixed.

At my request, the mechanic on duty at Tripoli Auto Body started disassembling the De Novo—to ascertain the cause of the car pulling to the left on the application of brakes. We found differential fluid on the brake shoe of the left rear wheel.

I have observed personally that the seal which was designed to keep differential fluid from travelling out the length of the rear axle was manufactured with a channel in it. The same is true on both sides. Supposedly, air could enter and help keep the axle cooler, but I am of opinion that very little, if any benefit, is derived therefrom. I believe that the channel permits fluid to escape (and did in this case). The fluid escaped when the car tilted to the left in the ordinary course of travel, then dropped on the brake drum cover, found its way to the inside, and thence on to the brake shoe. Its presence caused a "grabbing" when the four wheel brakes were applied, locked the left rear, and made the vehicle swerve.

I am most pleased that you represent not only the collision carrier, but, I am informed, Adam Highfill and the Highfill company. We have worked together well in the past. I hope that my telephone conversation with Mr. Highfill may have played a part in your being retained by him and his company.

For my usual fee, I will be willing to testify in accordance with the above, if you bring an action against De Novo Motors Corporation.

Very truly yours,

Moto Research Ltd.,
By: Chet Haas, President and
Chief Design Engineer.

STATE OF THE LITIGATION

On November 1, Yr.-1, Christine Harper, Administratrix of the Estate of Jonathan Harper, brought an action in Superior Court, Brandon County to recover compensatory and other damages on behalf of herself (widow to Jonathan) and her minor son. The defendants were Adam Highfill and the Highfill Jewelry Corp. Highfill and his corporation impleaded Avery Motors, the dealer, and De Novo Motors Corporation, the manufacturer of the Highfill car. Adam Highfill also stated a claim against Avery Motors and De Novo Corporation for his personal injury.

Highfill and his company have pleaded that (1) the dealer negligently inspected the vehicle before delivering it as a new car, and negligently failed to remedy a defect of which it had knowledge; (2) the dealer breached an implied warranty of merchantability in the sale of the vehicle to Highfill Jewelry Corp.; (3) the manufacturer negligently designed the seal which should have kept the differential fluid from exiting out the length of the rear axle.

The third party defendants have filed their Answers.

Harper's administratrix has NOT amended her Complaint to state claims against Avery or De Novo.

PROBLEM

LAW FIRM # 1. You are members of Attorney Pine's firm, You represent the third party plaintiffs, Adam Highfill and the Highfill Jewelry Corp. Two months ago you served upon the third party defendant De Novo Motors Corporation a Request for Production of Documents under the Rules of Civil Procedure. No response has been received, and you have filed a Motion under the Rules for the production of the documents described in the Request. The body of the request contains (inter alia) the following:

1. Copies of all advertisements published within 100 miles of the city of Tripoli, relating to the De Novo convertible, Model GR 100, by De Novo Motors Corporation, between October 1, Yr.-6 and April 2, Yr.-1 (the latter being the date on which such a vehicle was purchased by Highfill Jewelry Corp. from Avery Motors). Please include all advertisements which appeared in daily or Sunday newspapers, and/or magazines.

2. Copies of all "advertising" material distributed by De Novo Motors Corp., to dealers of De Novo motor vehicles, containing references to, pictures of, and information of any type concerning the De Novo convertible, Model GR 100, and all similar vehicles manufactured and sold within 5 years prior to April 2, Yr.-1.

3. Copy of the "Owner's Manual" published by De Novo Motors Corp., for delivery by its authorized dealers to purchasers of the De Novo Convertible, Model GR 100.

4. Copies of all correspondence between De Novo Motors Corporation and Avery Motors between May 3, Yr.-1 and the present date concerning the De Novo convertible, Model GR 100, the car purchased by Highfill Jewelry Corp. from Avery Motors.

5. Copies of all materials in the possession of De Novo Motors Corporation and obtained by said corporation, its agents, attorneys and employees in the course of investigating the accident of May 3, Yr.-1, including written and verbal statements, reports, photographs, and reports of examinations (if any) of the vehicle involved in the accident which is the subject of this action.

6. Written reports of all tests conducted on De Novo convertibles since the accident of May 3, Yr.-1.

7. Reports of all experts hired by De Novo Motors Corporation (a) who are expected to testify at the trial of this action, and (b) who are not expected to testify, but have been used to prepare for trial.

LAW FIRM # 2. Argue for the allowance of the Motion.

LAW FIRM # 3. You are the attorneys for De Novo Motors Corporation. Argue against the allowance of the motion for production of these documents.

Chapter Five

READY FOR TRIAL—IMPANELING JURY

A. READY FOR TRIAL

The long awaited moment has arrived. If you represent the plaintiff, you have perfunctorily moved for trial. The defendant does not oppose. Your client is present because you deem it important for him or her to consult with you as to those on the jury venire who will sit as jurors in his or her case whether he or she is plaintiff or defendant and whether the case is criminal or civil. If it is a criminal case, the government is the moving party.

From the first moment of your arrival in the courtroom, you have started to try your case. Your demeanor, attire and speech are all part of your case.

B. DEMEANOR IN COURTROOM

There is a fine but important line between self assurance and cocksureness. At all costs avoid the latter. Be friendly with the staff of the courthouse—the court reporter, the clerk, the court officers and bailiffs. Your attitude toward the judge should be one of respect but not subservience. Your speech should be clear and unaffected, forceful but not brassy.

Unless you are suffering from a physical handicap, you should always stand while addressing the court and jury. The judge may excuse you from this requirement, but you have no right to presume such a dispensation. Ask him or her for permission to stay seated while speaking to the court or examining a witness if you find it necessary in the light of your physical condition; otherwise, always stand.

In some courtrooms, a lecturn is provided and the trial judge requires counsel to remain at the lecturn while examining a witness unless a document or exhibit is shown to the witness. In this case, permission to approach the witness should be sought from the judge. Some lawyers enjoy roaming around the courtroom while examining a witness. Be careful not to distract the jury by these perambulations. Some lawyers face the jury and not the witness while asking questions. You will develop your own style as you try cases.

Avoid sarcasm. It seldoms wins friends for you and commonly it creates sympathy for the witness. The jury is very much aware that you have a captive audience and that the witness is under your control. Don't browbeat the witness. Honey is generally more effective than vinegar and much less dangerous than vitriol.

If the witness is a know-it-all, don't discourage him. He will bury himself and the party who has called him. Let the witness appear to "score" if he or she is fatheaded. Your deferential attitude will heighten the witness's folly.

C. IDENTIFYING PARTIES, LAWYERS AND WITNESSES BEFORE IMPANELING

With the court's permission and in many jurisdictions at the direction of the court, the attorneys introduce themselves to the entire panel of jurors before impaneling starts. Then each lawyer identifies his client by revealing his or her name and address, either orally or by use of a blackboard. The jurors should be told the names and addresses of those whom the parties intend to call as witnesses. Care should be taken to point out that perhaps not all of them will be called and no adverse inference should be drawn by reason of the decision not to call a particular person as a witness though he or she was introduced as a potential witness.

The court will describe briefly the bare allegations of the case, such as the thrust of the plaintiff's complaint, the time, place and date of the occurrence which is the heart of the case.

These efforts are all directed to the end that no juror who is related or very friendly with a party, lawyer or witness will serve as juror. Much time is saved in avoiding a mistrial after two weeks of trial because juror number 5 discovers that the last witness is his brother-in-law.

In a criminal case, a defendant probably cannot be forced to disclose the identities of his witnesses unless they are alibi witnesses or psychiatric experts. In these instances, on motion of the government and with a right to reciprocity, the defendant may be compelled to disclose these witnesses.

D. IMPANELING JURY—SOURCE OF JURORS

Jurors are selected at random from a voting list or street listing which is sometimes called a police listing. They are drawn mechanically or by computer and finally they are served a summons ordering them to appear at the courthouse on a particular morning ready to serve as jurors for a period of one day or for one case, whichever is longer or for a period of one month. Jurisdictions differ as to the method of selecting persons to serve as jurors and they differ as to the time period for service. Not every person ordered to appear considers it a duty imposed by basic notions of patriotism. It is not uncommon for a line to form at the courthouse door, composed of people who have "grave reasons" for not serving on the jury. At the point that these jurors arrive in the courtroom where your case is to be tried, many, though not all, reluctant jurors have been either excused or pacified. However, if you sense that a member of the venire is impatient to be excused, exercise some restraint in allowing him or her to serve. You might even ask the judge to excuse such a one so as not to require you to use a challenge.

Theoretically, the jury represent a cross-action of the community. In reality, the jury in your case may be heavy with older people who are retired, Irish, Italians, Germans or Polish, depending upon the district in which the case is being tried.

In most jurisdictions, there is provision for extra jurors in a protracted case. The judge may direct that 14 or 16 jurors be seated instead of the customary 12, or 7 jurors instead of 6.[1] Ultimately, only the statutory number of 12 or 6 jurors will decide the case but the extra jurors are available to fill the void if sickness or death should deplete the ranks.

E. VOIR DIRE QUESTIONS TO JURY PANEL

Your goal as an advocate is to select a jury who will be most sympathetic to your case. At bar association meetings and at patriotic gatherings, lawyers speak of the great jury system as the bulwark of freedom and justice. However, you are ever an advocate and the justice which you seek is a victory for your client who has been wronged or who has been sued but is free of any wrongdoing. Your case is not for moot court competition or for a trial advocacy course. Your case is in real life and your client wants to win.

First and foremost, you want to discover any hidden prejudices among the venire from which the jurors in your case will be chosen. If your client is the victim of a taxi driver's negligence, you probably want to know whether the jurors are related to a taxi driver. The jury list will disclose whether the juror himself is a taxi driver and may reveal the occupation of his or her spouse. However, such a one may have been a taxi driver a few years earlier.

If your client is indicted for a crime of violence, you will want to know whether any of the jurors or members of their family have been the victims of violent crime.

The goal is a jury who will not allow their prejudices to control the outcome of this case. Don't expect to select 12 people who have no prejudices. Such people probably don't exist. You don't want people who have no idea of the real world. A tabula rasa is not desirable in a juror. All that you should expect is a juror who will decide the

1. Fed.R.Civ.P. 47(b); Fed.R.Crim.P. 23 (b), 24(c).

case on the basis of the evidence and the law with as little interference from his prejudices as the fallen state of humankind permits.

With all this in mind, draw the voir dire questions with a view toward ferreting out pockets of prejudice and passion. Put them on the table, as it were, and make your judgment with your client by your side as to the juror's capability of rendering a just verdict.

Veteran lawyers can be helpful in advising you about the pitfalls to be avoided. However, they, too, are victims of totally unfounded and unproved theories. One lawyer with years of trial experience routinely challenges a pharmacist if he is representing a personal injury plaintiff. Pharmacists (according to him, *all* pharmacists) "think small" like the pills with which they deal daily. In a prosecution for rape, some defense lawyers are more comfortable with two or more women on the jury because they will hold the victim to exemplary conduct and, therefore, they will more readily find consent. This theory has never been proved but it is in vogue among some trial lawyers.

Some prospective jurors will answer questions in a manner that almost requires them to be excused. Accordingly, they are quick to point out their prejudices against blacks, Italians, Irish, motorcycle drivers, policemen, and divorcees. Ask the court to excuse them because they will not be good jurors, not because of their feigned prejudices, but because of their reluctance to sit as jurors.

The observant lawyer will note the *manner* in which the prospective juror responds. Are his eyes shifty? How is she dressed? Does he have difficulty in hearing your questions? Not every young man with long hair is flirting with anarchy as a way of life. Not every man with a West Point coiffure believes that your client must be guilty because he was arrested. However, a dirty and unkempt appearance may tell a story which deserves your attention.

In a word, while asking your well drawn voir dire questions, keep a close eye on the prospective juror. If her answer suggests a question which is not on your "approved list" ask the court for permission to pursue the particular subject matter. In some states, it is the custom for the judge to ask the questions.[2]

Questions should be tailored to your case. Don't slavishly follow a form book. Some questions are appropriate for all criminal cases, but there are more questions which are suitable only for your case.

An important inquiry in a criminal case concerns the burden of proof beyond a reasonable doubt. It is generally productive to frame a question as to whether the prospective juror would find a defendant not guilty if not convinced of his guilt beyond a reasonable doubt. Follow this by asking whether his vote would be not guilty if he had

2. Fed.R.Civ.P. 47(a); Fed.R.Crim.P. 24(a).

only strong suspicion of guilt and would feel uneasy leaving the courthouse after voting not guilty.

A juror takes an oath to follow the law as it is presented to him by the judge. This mandate may be difficult in certain cases. For example, unless the law of joint enterprise in criminal law is explained with care, a juror may convict on a guilt by association principle. On the other hand, the prosecutor should inquire of prospective jurors whether they are prepared to follow the instructions of the court in this area of the law and in the sector of the felony murder rule. Voir dire questions should pose short hypothetical cases to make it possible for you to determine as best you can whether the juror will follow the law.

F. PEREMPTORY CHALLENGE—ITS USE AND ABUSE

There are statutory provisions in most jurisdictions which permit both sides to challenge a certain number of prospective jurors without assigning a reason for the challenge.[3] Your client should be consulted before a challenge is made. Though no reason need be given for the challenge, the trend in criminal cases is in the direction of prohibiting challenges solely on a basis which is outlawed by statutes on discrimination, i. e. color, national origin, sex, etc. If the trial judge is satisfied that there is a developing pattern of peremptory challenges based on one of the prohibited bases, he will warn the party. If it continues, a mistrial will be declared.

The number of challenges without cause is limited; hence, be sparing in their use. Try to induce the judge to excuse a juror before exercising your challenge.

In most jurisdictions, a challenge is not made until the entire panel of twelve or six is seated. Then, you should approach the clerk's bench and furnish him or her the numbers of the jurors challenged. He will announce their numbers and request that they leave the jury box because they have been challenged.

Among the legitimate considerations which should occupy your mind when the opportunity to challenge is at hand are the juror's occupation, and the occupation of his or her spouse and members of the immediate family, any history of crime in the family, his knowledge of the case from radio, television and newspaper accounts of the case, and his prior experience in a courtroom as a witness or victim of a crime or accident.

If you and your client think that a juror should be challenged but you don't feel too strongly about it, ask yourselves whether your

3. See, e. g., Fed.R.Crim.P. 24(b)(1).

opponent may challenge him. It may be wise to gamble on his challenge.

G. CHALLENGE FOR CAUSE

If you can demonstrate that a prospective juror should not serve because of some problem uncovered in your voir dire examination, first ask that he or she be excused. Failing in this move, interpose a challenge for cause.[4] Be prepared to demonstrate to the court solid ground on which your challenge rests. The juror may have been a client of your opponent's law partner many years ago. The juror may have indicated a desire, in fact, a need, to return to his business within three days and you know that the case will require two weeks for trial.

4. Fed.R.Crim.P. 24(b)(2)(a).

Chapter Six

OPENING STATEMENT—ADVICE TO WITNESS

A. OPENING STATEMENT—ITS PURPOSE

The first time that the jury will hear about your case is at the time of your opening statement. It is your opportunity to set the stage for what will follow. You will outline the case, furnishing a scenario to the jurors. You will narrow the issues. You can showcase your client's case. If you represent the plaintiff, you will open first. If the defendant is your client, in most jurisdictions, you have the choice as to whether you will make an opening statement immediately after the plaintiff's opening or wait until the plaintiff rests and before you start the presentation of your evidence. In some jurisdictions, the court will direct you to make the opening immediately after the plaintiff's.

First impressions are often lasting. Although your opening is not evidence, it is important. It should rarely, if ever, be waived. In jury-waived cases, the court may suggest that you omit the opening. If the judge does not raise this question, make a brief opening. It will help him follow the evidence and alert him to the issues of the case.

B. OPENING STATEMENT—ITS CONTENT

In some jurisdictions, you will be required to read the pleadings. At least the complaint and answer will be required reading if you represent the plaintiff. In most states, you will be encouraged to summarize the pleadings. You should be cautious in delivering your summary. Don't omit an allegation because it may have a strong flavor against your case. Generally, you are not permitted to read the ad damnum or amount of money damages claimed by the plaintiff.

Obviously, if you represent the defendant, you are spared the burden of summarizing the pleadings, although you may find it useful to refer to them, especially to your answer and its allegations.

As counsel for the plaintiff, you will be anxious to reach that point in time when you can preview your case. Don't hesitate to use the names of the witnesses whom you are sure to call. Be careful of overblown familiarity in the use of first names. Some people are offended and consider it demeaning to be called by his or her first name by one who is not all that familiar to them.

The jury is waiting for you to tell them what happened, or at least, what the plaintiff says happened. Launch into the facts which you intend to prove without delay. "Ladies and Gentlemen of the jury, probably the first witness to take the stand will be Mrs. Mary Johnson who will tell you in her own words what she saw as she waited for the bus at the corner of Elm and Central Streets, in Sleepy Hollow. Tom Plaintiff had never met or even seen Mrs. Johnson until she came to the hospital to reveal to Tom that she had seen the accident and would gladly be a witness for him. She will tell you that it was a clear night about 6:30 P.M. when she left work and walked to the bus stop. Her attention was attracted by the speed of a Ford Mustang driven by the defendant down Central Street when the traffic was quite heavy. The light had been red for a few seconds when the defendant approached it. He just never stopped. Tom was walking across Central Street at the time within a cross walk. It was over in seconds when the defendant failed to brake in time to avoid hitting Tom. The police and hospital ambulance arrived in a few moments. The defendant kept hollering, 'I'm sorry. I'm sorry. When will I learn to slow down and watch for traffic lights? Here goes my license.' Mrs. Johnson will have more information for you but I'll leave that for her."

You will leave for Mrs. Johnson all the minutiae but after you have told the jury this much about her testimony, they will be waiting for her to take the witness stand. You have told them just enough and let them know that there is more to come from the lips of the witness.

Don't gild the lily more than is necessary to excite the interest of the jury in what the witness will say when called to the stand.

After you have outlined the case to the jury in terms of what the various witnesses will say, add that important epilogue which prevents directed verdicts on the opening. "I haven't told you what every witness will testify to, but I assure you that you will hear an abundance of evidence on all the essential elements of Tom Plaintiff's case."

All that has been said about the opening in a civil case may be applied to a criminal case. The prosecutor is representing the moving party, the plaintiff-state, as it were. It is essential for him to outline the case and what he expects to prove to the jury. Defense counsel commonly will open by reminding the jury that they should keep an open mind until all the evidence has been admitted. "There are two sides to every case. Just wait until you hear the defendant's side of this sordid story of intrigue."

With the court's permission, you may find it helpful to use diagrams and chalks in your opening to prepare the jury for what they will see and hear during trial. A diagram of the intersecting streets where the accident occurred is always helpful. In no event should a chalk or diagram be produced until the court has granted permission for its use.

C. OPENING STATEMENT—A FEW SUGGESTIONS

Your opening statement should be prepared in advance of the trial. You might find it helpful to write out the opening and commit it to memory. Don't read it to the jury.

It should be long enough to touch the salient points of your case and short enough to keep the interest of the jurors.

Tell the jury that your statement is not evidence but a preview of the case. Don't assure them that John Dome is going to testify unless you are certain that he will testify. If you fall into this trap of promising to deliver a witness and then fail to deliver, you are fair game for comment by your adversary in his final argument. Similarly, don't exaggerate your case. Better that your case go to the jury in a stronger posture than you have described than to suffer the embarrassment of falling short of the dazzling performance promised in your opening.[1]

When you represent the defendant, listen carefully to the opening of your brother, take notes and at the close of the case before you argue to the jury, compare notes of what he said he would prove and what evidence he introduced in actuality. This discrepancy can furnish you a forceful argument.

Unless he is outrageous, don't interrupt your brother's opening to object. It will appear rude to the jury who have not been instructed in the manner of a trial. When he has completed his opening statement, ask to approach the bench and at the side bar you can record your objections and ask the court to instruct the jury as to the errors of your adversary in his opening. Of course, if he is scandalously out of order, spring to your feet and object. Ask the court to instruct the jury to disregard the offensive remarks and to warn your opponent not to repeat the performance.

There is a fine line between outlining a case properly in an opening and arguing the same case. Arguments must be left until final summation. They have no place in an opening. They are offensively premature. Exercise restraint and avoid characterizations of the evidence and estimates of the value of your case and the shoddiness of your opponent's case.

Another trap to avoid is the law lecture masquerading as an opening. It falls to the trial judge to instruct the jury on the law of the case, on burden of proof, presumption of innocence in a criminal case and on all the legal facets of the case. It is improper for counsel to tell the jury about the law except ever so tangentially when arguing the facts. However, in no event is there justification for a lecture on the law of the case in the opening.

1. See EC7–25.

The style of delivery must be yours, not that of a television lawyer who never loses a case. It has been said that style is you and nobody else. This aphorism is not an excuse to perpetuate old errors, sloppy delivery, insipid rhetoric and embarrassing solecisms. You are talking to people who have had no special training in the law. Don't deliver an argument fit for an appellate court, but don't become too folksy. You don't want to appear insincere. Don't talk down to the jury, but be equally careful not to fly above the jurors in flights of legal fancy. In medio stat virtus.

Don't "sweet talk" the judge in referring to him as "the brilliant jurist who presides at our trial," or "the learned judge" or similarly flattering language. You will not promote the fortunes of your client by appearing to be a sycophant.

D. THE VIEW

In some cases there is no substitute for taking the jury or the judge to the scene of the crime or to the building which the state has taken by eminent domain or to the railroad grade crossing at which the deceased was killed. A motion for a view is addressed to the sound discretion of the trial judge. If he grants your motion, ask for the opportunity to make an opening to the jury on the subject of the view. In this statement, which is not a substitute for the regular opening statement in the case, you will give the jury advance notice of what they will see. The importance of the place to be seen can be demonstrated.

At the view, you and your opponent will be permitted to point out things including distances which may be material in the case. No further critique or comment may be made at the view beyond those remarks necessary to point out to the jury the items of importance.

E. IN LIMINE MOTION

If you are satisfied that your opponent is going to speak of a matter in his opening which may be prejudicial or inadmissible in evidence, don't wait for him to say it and then ask that it be struck. It is too late. The jury has heard it. The judge will dutifully demand that the jury disregard the statement, but they are human and it may be almost impossible for them to purge their memory of the offensive statement.

You represent a plaintiff who has a serious criminal record, but in all the cases which resulted in conviction he was neither represented by counsel nor does the record indicate a waiver of his right to counsel. You have a right to keep those records out of evidence and no mention should be made of them. In another vein, at the time of the accident which is the subject of the action, your client was in the company of a woman not his wife. In fact, the injury occurred in her apartment at midnight under circumstances which indicate that he was not the most faithful husband. This evidence of the time and place and attendant circumstances may be enough to sink your client.

In both of these situations, you should bring a motion in limine which the judge will hear outside the presence of the jury. He will make his ruling and you will have an opportunity to argue the merits of your position without risk. You may not always succeed. For example, the court may rule that the importance to the jury of learning the time, place and attendant circumstances outweighs the prejudice to your client in the disclosure of these compromising details. In the case of photographs which depict gruesome scenes or human anatomical details, the court will decide where the balance must be struck as between the need for relevant evidence on a material matter on the one hand and the right of the parties to try their case free of inflammatory evidence, on the other.

F. ADVICE TO WITNESSES

At some point not too far in advance of their taking the witness stand, the witnesses whom you will call should be given a few instructions. Unless they are experts who have testified regularly in the past, the experience of being a witness is new and frightening. They will be sworn to tell the truth and be asked a series of questions by you and more questions perhaps by a hostile cross-examiner. The following suggestions should be helpful.

1. You should furnish the questions which you are going to propound to them in advance, or at least advise them orally of the nature of your questions. It is foolhardy to put them on the stand if you don't know exactly how they will respond to your questions. You are entitled to know what their testimony will be *before* they take the stand. Ask them.

2. Warn them about the question which so many cross-examiners ask as to whether they have spoken to you or your client about the case before taking the witness stand. Assure them that it is quite proper and even necessary for counsel to discuss a witness's testimony with him or her before the witness is called to the stand. Hence, the answer should be a resounding, "Of course I have discussed the case with Attorney Murphy and with the plaintiff."

3. Don't volunteer information which is not solicited by the question. Just answer the question. A witness who tends to be garrulous is dangerous. Warn him of the danger of going beyond the question which is asked.

4. A witness should be reminded that he is not an information machine or a computer. He may be asked questions and he will not

know the answer. Let him say so. There is no shame in not knowing the answer to every question asked. A candid answer, "I don't know" is not shameful.

5. If the witness is asked a question about a matter which he may have once known but which he has forgotten, he should frankly say that he cannot remember. The only occasion when this answer may be harmful is when the witness has exhibited a good memory about matters which are favorable to him and then claims a faulty memory as to all details which are adverse to him or her. Much hay can be made of this selective memory in your opponent's argument. Your witness should be warned about this failing.

6. The muffle-voiced witness is almost worthless to your case. If a witness does not speak with sufficient volume for the judge and jury to hear the testimony, the whole enterprise is dead. One way to insure an audible witness is to stand at the end of the jury box. If you have difficulty hearing, then the jurors will share your difficulty. You are then positioned to request the witness to keep his voice up.

7. Warn the witness of the dangers of becoming sarcastic. There is no room in the trial for the surly witness. If the cross-examiner should make the mistake of being sullen or flippant, the witness's soft answer will redound to the cross-examiner's embarrassment.

8. On occasion a witness will become so caught up in the question and answer form of interrogation, that he will ask the examiner a question. Then the judge will intervene and remind the witness that he, and not the attorney, is on the witness stand, and that it is the function of the lawyer to ask the question and the function of the witness to answer. This is generally embarrassing to the witness. Warn him or her in advance of his appearance.

9. Remind the witness that he should think before he answers. Nobody will fault the witness who pauses to consider the question before giving an answer. This is proper and quite necessary for all but the most obvious answers.

10. Occasionally, a witness will make answer to a question and then realize that his answer is not accurate. This will occur commonly after the witness has had an opportunity at recess to examine a document or to talk with the attorney who called him. It may occur within minutes after the first answer has been given. Whenever it is evident to the witness that he has responded to a question inaccurately, he must retract his answer and make a truthful answer. The contretemps is not necessarily fatal to the credibility of the witness because his candor in admitting his mistake generally will evoke the sympathy of the jury.

11. A favorite device of cross-examiners is to attempt to demonstrate that a witness who had testified at an earlier hearing or deposition failed to testify in the same manner at trial. The question is,

"Well, you didn't say that at the probable cause hearing, did you?" The shortest rescue route is the response: "I wasn't asked that question at the probable cause hearing." Fair enough, if that is so. One way in which to close off that escape is to ask at the preliminary hearing or deposition whether the witness can recall anything else happening at this point in time. If the answer is "No," a later arousal of memory may be suspect.

12. Although you cannot give the witness a course in evidence, he or she should be made familiar with the basic rules of hearsay. Warn the witness not to testify as to what a third person told him or her because, generally although not always, this testimony violates the hearsay rule. Similarly, a witness should not tell the jury what he believed, thought, had a feeling about or surmised, unless such testimony comes within an exception to the opinion rule.

13. The personal appearance of the witness is important. A witness should not chew gum on the witness stand. He or she should look directly at the examining lawyer when the question is asked and then turn slightly to the jury when making answer. There is no substitute for sincerity. Good grooming means that the witness should not wear flashy clothes and display an unusual coiffure or model exotic jewelry while on the witness stand. These have the effect of at least distracting the jury, if not worse.

14. Jokes and calculated humor have no place in the trial of a case. The best humor is that which falls out without planning. There are occasions when funny things happen in a courtroom without the intentional intervention of anybody. Innocently, a question or answer may be of the double meaning variety. A witness who tries to be humorous always fails.

15. A witness should be warned that the cross-examiner may try to antagonize him. He will be pleased if the witness becomes visibly upset or angry. There is very little room for righteous anger in a courtroom. Most anger is unpleasant and unprofitable. Warn the witness that the other lawyer will try to induce him "to blow his top." If he succeeds, the witness's testimony is generally discredited. There is no substitute for self-control when under the ordeal of cross-examination.

16. A witness should be told a few things about the reasons for rules of evidence. Tell the witness to stop talking once an objection has been presented. This admonition may save the witness the embarrassment of being scolded by the judge for not holding his fire until a ruling has been made on the objection.

G. MOTION TO SEQUESTER WITNESSES

The motion to sequester witnesses is used more often on the criminal side than on the civil side of the court.[2] In effect, you ask the court to separate the witnesses and prohibit them from listening to other witnesses testify at least before they have taken the witness stand. In a criminal case, the trial judge will generally exempt from the sweep of his sequestration order the police officers who have actively managed the case and helped prepare it with the prosecutor. Those officers and detectives who fall into this category are permitted to remain in the courtroom at the prosecutor's table to continue to help him. The other witnesses are ordered to remain outside the courtroom and to respond to the bailiff's call when they are wanted as witnesses. A most important facet of this motion is a request that the judge's order include the admonition to witnesses not to speak about their testimony or about the case with other witnesses until the close of the case. A violation of this order subjects the miscreant to punishment for contempt.

The purpose of the motion is clear. It is your hope that the witness will testify consistently with what he saw, heard or experienced at the time in question and not be influenced by what another saw, heard or experienced. You want the answers of *this* witness, not the answers of another witness after they have been laundered.

In defending an action or a criminal case, you are more apt to be able to demonstrate inconsistency in the testimony of a number of eye witnesses if they have not had the benefit of discussing their impressions with one another and of listening to each other testify. If you can elicit inconsistent narratives from three or four different eye witnesses, you can make hay of it in your final argument.

FORM

State of Rest

Sunlight, ss. Superior Court #4657

STATE v. DEFENDANT

MOTION IN LIMINE

The defendant moves that the court exclude from evidence all the photographs of Jane Smith because they are purely inflammatory and lacking in probative value. The prejudice to the defendant

2. Fed.R.Evid. 615.

outweighs by far the value which they might possibly have for the jury.

John Defendant
By his attorney,
/s/ William B. Barrister
____
William B. Barrister

FORM

STATE OF ______

Brunswick, ss. Court of General Sessions

PEOPLE v. JOHNSON

MOTION TO SEQUESTER WITNESSES

The defendant moves the court to order all the witnesses who will testify in the instant case to be separated and to be barred from the courtroom until they are called to testify. Further, the defendant moves the court for an order to all witnesses that upon completion of their testimony they leave the courtroom and not communicate with other witnesses regardless of whether these other witnesses have already testified or not.

John Johnson
By his attorney,
/s/ Robert Barrister
____
Robert Barrister

ASSIGNMENT #5

THEODORE BLAISDELL, p.p.a., et al. v. WARREN DE LURIO, PERRY DE LURIO and TURCOTTE SPORTING GOODS STORE, INC.

PROBLEM

LAW FIRM # __1__. will make an opening statement on behalf of Theodore Blaisdell and his father Jarrod Blaisdell, both of whom are from the city of Tullytown, Grey County, ______. This opening will be directed to all defendants in the action.

LAW FIRM # __2__. will be required by the Court to make an opening on behalf of the defendants Warren De Lurio and Perry De Lurio immediately thereafter.

LAW FIRM # __3__. will be required by the Court to make an opening on behalf of the defendant Turcotte Sporting Goods Store, Inc.

(1) There will be no reference to any ad damnum.

(2) Pleadings may NOT be read.

(3) Opening for a party may not exceed 15 minutes.

(4) The opening shall be a "statement of expected evidence," not an argument.

PRE-TRIAL STIPULATION

It is stipulated by the parties through counsel:

I. This action of tort was brought on behalf of Theodore Blaisdell, by his father Jarrod. Theodore was age 12 on July 1, Yr.-2 when the incident which is the subject matter of this action occurred. He is now age 14. He seeks damages for personal injuries. His father and next friend seeks consequential damages in the form of reasonable value of medical services rendered to his son.

II. The defendant Warren De Lurio was age 15 on the date of the incident. He is now 17. A guardian ad litem has been appointed to protect his interest at the trial of this case.

III. Perry De Lurio is the father of the defendant Warren De Lurio. They reside at 2101 Susan Road, Tullytown. To the rear of the De Lurio property is land owned by the Blaisdell family.

IV. On March 16, Yr.-2, Warren De Lurio, and his father visited the Turcotte Sporting Goods Store. One of them bought and paid for a .22 caliber rifle and two boxes of ammunition. One Simon Spencer, an employee of Turcotte Sporting Goods Store, Inc., was on duty and sold the rifle and ammunition. No stipulation is made with respect to whether the father or the son purchased the weapon and ammunition.

V. On July 1 of the same year, while Warren De Lurio was sitting on the back porch steps of his home, holding the rifle, the weapon discharged a bullet. The bullet struck Theodore Blaisdell who was, at that time, riding a horse on the Blaisdell property.

VI. Theodore Blaisdell was taken to Central Hospital where he remained as an inpatient for 35 days. Upon discharge, he returned to his home. He was scheduled to enter the seventh grade class at the Tullytown Junior High School on September 9 of that year, but remained at home (with the exception of two additional hospital admissions) for the remainder of the school year. He was tutored at home 5 days a week and received a grade average of "B" for his work. The second and third hospital admissions occurred December 2 the year of the incident and March 4 of the following year. Each admission was of 3 weeks' duration.

VII. Medical bills incurred to the date of trial, which are agreed to be fair and reasonable, are:

Central Hospital	
First admission	$4,200.00
Second admission	3,150.00
Third admission	3,362.00
Dr. Xavier Hall, orthopedic surgeon	
3 procedures	4,100.00
Hospital visits	930.00
Dr. A. Lawrence Jones, gen. pract.	
Home visits	650.00
Rentals—wheelchair, walker, crutches	481.00

VIII. This action has been tried to a Master, Attorney Percy McNamara. His Report may be read into evidence.

/s/ ____________________
Attorney for the plaintiffs

/s/ ____________________
Attorney for defendants and Perry De Lurio

/s/ ____________________
Attorney for Turcotte Sporting Goods Store, Inc.

EXCERPTS FROM DEFENDANT TURCOTTE SPORTING GOODS STORE, INC.'S ANSWERS TO REQUESTS FOR ADMISSIONS OF FACT BY THE PLAINTIFFS:

. . . Req. No. 8. That there was in effect in the City of Tullytown on July 1, Yr.-2 and on March 15 of the same year, an ordinance (Rev.Ord. & By Laws, c. VII, § 17) forbidding the sale by any person, firm or corporation, his, her or its agents, servants or employees, of any firearm and/or ammunition to a minor. (Copy attested by City Clerk attached hereto, with Certificate of said Clerk that city records disclose that said Ordinance was adopted by the Council, and signed by the Mayor, on January 17, Yr.–10, and that said section 17 had not been repealed or amended to July 1, Yr.–2.)

Answer: Admitted.

Req. No. 9. That on March 15, Yr.-2, Simon Spencer sold a .22 caliber rifle and 2 boxes of ammunition to Warren De Lurio of 2101 Susan Road, Tullytown.

Answer: Denied.

Req. No. 11. That the weapon referred to in the preceding request had a defective "safety."

Answer: See answer to request numbered 10, wherein it is denied that Simon Spencer sold a weapon to Warren De Lurio.

EXCERPTS FROM INVESTIGATIVE REPORT OF TULLYTOWN POLICE CHIEF, MARK CAINE

. . . On this date, July 1, Yr.-2 I investigated a report telephoned in by Perry De Lurio, that his son, Warren, age 15, was cleaning a 22 caliber rifle at their home at 2101 Susan Road; that while the boy was sitting on the back porch steps, the weapon discharged, and that the bullet struck Theodore Blaisdell, age 12, while the victim was riding a horse on the adjoining property.

Officers Vandermark and Tracey in the East Car were assigned by radio to respond, and had already moved the victim from the scene, suffering from a gunshot wound of the left hip, when I arrived at the De Lurio residence.

I was finally able to interrogate the De Lurio boy in the presence of his father, his mother and his family doctor, two hours after the incident. The boy was reported to have been hysterical immediately after the shooting, but he calmed down after the doctor gave his something to quiet his nerves, and he appeared to answer rationally the questions I put to him.

He said that he was allowed by his father to buy the weapon and two boxes of ammo for it on March 15th at Turcotte Sporting Goods; that his father placed no restrictions on the use of it. At that point the father interrupted and said: "Dammit, Warren. You know I said you shouldn't touch the thing unless I was with you!" The boy started to wail, but was calmed again by his mother. He then said "All right, Dad." The boy reported further that he had used the weapon twice for target practice; that on this date, July 1, he took the gun from his bedroom closet, went to the back porch steps, checked to make sure the safety was on, and was cleaning the trigger guard with a cloth when it went off. He said he heard a scream, put the gun down on the steps, and rushed to the spot where the scream came from. He saw Theodore Blaisdell lying on the ground with a wound in the left hip; that Theodore said "Help me," and closed his eyes, and Warren thought he was dead. Warren said his father then came rushing out of their house, and that he, Warren, told his father what had happened. Mr. De Lurio telephoned this station after rendering first aid to the victim.

I confiscated the weapon and ammo on the spot. I checked the gun quickly. It did not appear to have been fired. There was nothing in the chamber, where I expected to find a spent casing, nor did the bore have the appearance of a weapon that had been fired. I asked the father who had cleaned it. He denied that it had been cleaned. I went and searched around the back porch steps for a spent casing, but found none.

Officers Vandermark and Tracey stated to me that the victim did not regain consciousness enroute to the hospital. I telephoned there and was informed that the Blaisdell boy was in surgery for two hours; that the bullet had entered the head of the left femur and had been lodged between it and the "acetabulum," the bony cup in which the head turns when one walks.

I turned the weapon and remaining ammunition over to Amy Freeman, our ballistician and firearms expert who, on examination this date, reported to me that the safety on the weapon is defective; that when the safety is "on," if the weapon is tilted so that the barrel points downward, the safety will go "off" and the gun can be fired subsequently.

EXCERPT FROM REPORT OF ARTHUR NEWEY, DESIGNER OF THE WEAPON, RETAINED BY DEFENDANT TURCOTTE SPORTING GOODS, INC., TO TESTIFY AS EXPERT AT TRIAL.

Note: The identity of the expert, his opinion, and the bases for the opinion, have been given to the plaintiffs in answers to interrogatories. See Rules of Civil Procedure.

. . . After the allowance of your motion for an order permitting inspection and testing of the weapon, I took the weapon to my laboratory.

I examined it and ten others identical to it which I obtained from the manufacturer. I placed each of them in the hands of an assistant. Their identities are noted on the attached Certificates, executed by each under oath.

In my presence and at my direction, each of the weapons, with the safety "on," was pointed to the floor, and was kept pointed in that direction, for ten seconds. The barrels were then raised and the triggers pulled. Not one of the weapons could be "fired." The weapons were pointed toward the floor and raised again fifty times before attempting to pull the triggers a second time. When the triggers were pulled a second time, no weapon "fired."

I am of the opinion that none of the safeties was defective, including that on the subject weapon.

I returned the weapon to the custody of the Chief of Police.

In response to your specific inquiry: Yes, I am aware of the fact that of the 7,500 weapons of this design that were manufactured, there were 37 claims of "defective safeties" received by the manufacturer. In not one instance, however, was a person injured. In each and every case, I personally examined the weapons and found no defect in the safety. The purchasers were satisfied with a cash refund from the manufacturer. It is my personal belief that those persons simply decided that they had made an investment beyond their means, and were seeking some method of obtaining their money back. I was opposed to the manufacturer advertising the weapon "Satisfaction guaranteed, or your money back." . . .

EXCERPTS FROM REPORT OF MASTER PERCY McNAMARA, ESQUIRE

FINDINGS OF FACT

. . . 24. I find that Turcotte Sporting Goods Store issued instructions to its employees prior to March 15, Yr.-2 (by posting a letter signed by its president Samuel Turcotte in a conspicuous place in the store, and by including a copy of the same letter in a paycheck envelope for each employee) never to sell weapons or ammunition to minors.

25. I find that on March 15, Yr.-2 Simon Spencer, employed by the defendant Turcotte Sporting Goods Store as a salesman on a salary plus commission basis, sold the weapon in question to Warren De Lurio, who paid $129.35 plus a sales tax of 5% for it. This was money which the boy had saved. The bill of sale was made out to his father, Perry De Lurio.

. . . 36. From the evidence at the hearing and from reasonable inferences which I draw therefrom, I find that the minor plaintiff suffered a bullet wound in the left hip. The bullet caused a fracture of the head of the left femur, and a comminuted fracture of the left acetabulum. It has interfered with, and will continue to interfere for the remainder of the minor plaintiff's life with, the blood supply to the head of the femur. It has disrupted the normal "lubrication of the joint," causing a form of traumatic arthritis. I find that it is reasonably probable, on the basis of expert medical testimony, that at some time in the future, this young man will require surgery in the form of an amputation of the head of the femur, and the insertion of a prosthesis—a metallic "head" to substitute for his own. While the reasonable cost of such surgery and the hospitalization required thereby cannot be estimated with any degree of accuracy, it is safe to say that the cost will be many thousands of dollars.

CONCLUSIONS OF LAW

. . . 7. The defendant Warren De Lurio was negligent in that he failed to check his rifle to determine whether it was loaded, before cleaning it.

8. The defendant Perry De Lurio was negligent in entrusting the weapon and ammunition to his son and particularly in failing to supervise a 15 yr. old boy in the care and handling of a dangerous weapon.

9. The defendant Turcotte Sporting Goods, Inc., is liable for the conduct of its employee in selling a weapon and ammunition to a minor

in violation of an ordinance; and in failing to inspect the weapon and discover its defective safety before offering it for sale.

10. The minor plaintiff is entitled to recover damages for personal injury: for pain and suffering, past, present and future, and for future diminution of earning capacity. His damages are in the sum of $121,122.50.

11. The plaintiff Theodore Blaisdell is entitled to recover damages for the reasonable value of medical services rendered to his son, in the amount of $16,873.00 to the time of trial, and in the amount of $20,000.00 for medical bills reasonably expected to be incurred in the future.

Note: The Master has committed an error, in award of damages. Future medicals should be awarded to the minor plaintiff. To this point, neither party has filed any motion.

Chapter Seven

DIRECT EXAMINATION

A. PURPOSE

The purpose of direct examination is to present your case in the most favorable light to the judge or jury. It represents the unveiling of your suit or defense. You will call witnesses who will help you present your best case. The direct examination of each witness should be undertaken with great care. There is never an excuse for presenting a witness whose testimony you have not discussed before the witness takes the stand.

Many lawyers are convinced that the conduct of direct examination is far more difficult than that of cross-examination. If you represent the plaintiff you should have near you at all times the "laundry list" of elements of your case. Once you have introduced some evidence as to each required element, check it off. Directed verdicts can be avoided by this simple device.

It is in direct examination in a negligence action that you will elicit evidence of the duty of care, the breach of this duty, the damage to your client and the causal connection between the breach and the damage. If it falls to you to prosecute a criminal case, it is from direct examination of the witnesses for the government that evidence of the various elements of the crime emerges.

B. LEADING QUESTIONS

The vice of a leading question is that the answer is suggested by the lawyer interrogating the witness instead of by the witness who is under oath. It is a vice which should be avoided, though it is tolerated under certain circumstances.[1] If the witness is old and feeble, or very young, or mentally slow or otherwise mentally handicapped, the court will indulge counsel and permit a measure of leading. If the witness has difficulty with the language, counsel will be permitted to help him by leading.

If your opponent appears to be heading in the direction of leading his witness, act early because it may be too late after the witness has given important testimony. The judge will tell the jury to disregard the answer but the damage may already have been done. On the other hand, it is customary to permit leading questions which are merely introductory or foundation-laying. "Now, you are a New York policeman and you were on duty in the Bronx on Saturday, March 17, at

1. Fed.R.Evid. 611(c).

11 p. m. . . ."—this is perfectly proper as far as it goes. However, it should not go much further.

C. NARRATIVE ANSWER

You should neither permit your own witness nor tolerate a witness called by your opponent to answer by way of a narrative. The question and answer form of presenting evidence has been tried in the fire and is the best. If you allow your own witness to testify for a considerable period of time without accompanying questions, the witness will stray all over the lot. He may not cover all that is essential to your case and when you direct him back to the reservation, you may have problems in eliciting what you need, or it may seem repetitious or wooden to the jury.

It is even more important not to permit your opponent's witness to give a narrative answer. He may "bury you" somewhere in the middle of his long story. It is desirable at times to ask the judge to caution the witness at the start to answer only the question asked and even to caution opposing counsel who seems to be heading in the direction of permitting or encouraging narrative answers by the type of question asked. For example, "Tell us in detail everything that you saw, heard, said and did from 7:30 a. m. to 11:00 p. m. on March 1, Yr.–1 while you were at the plaintiff's apartment" . . . this is bound to bring forth a narrative answer. Better to break it up into time segments.

D. DOCUMENTARY EVIDENCE

Commonly in the course of a trial you will find it necessary to introduce a document into evidence. Before the contract or deed or letter is entitled to admissibility, it must be qualified.[2] It is rare when a document speaks for itself and requires no identification. If it is a letter sent to the witness, it falls to you to ask the witness whether he received it from the other party. If the document bears the signature of the witness, ask him or her whether it is his or her signature.

Even after identifying the document, you may be required to satisfy the trial judge that it is relevant if an objection is interposed. In qualifying and identifying the document, *don't* permit the witness to read it aloud. Ask him pointed questions: "Is this your signature"? —"Did you receive this document from the plaintiff?" Then permit your opponent to examine it while you tell the court that you will offer it into evidence. Common courtesy demands that you offer it to opposing counsel before offering it to the court through the clerk.

2. As to authentication of public documents, see Fed.R.Evid. 901(7)(8), 902.

Once the court allows it to be marked as an exhibit, pause and permit the court reporter to mark it with an appropriate number. Don't continue to ask questions during this time because the reporter cannot mark and record your interrogation at the same time. Wait until the reporter indicates that she or he has completed the marking or until it is obvious to you.

After an exhibit has been marked, refer to it as the numbered exhibit. For example, "Mrs. Witness, I show you Exhibit Number 14 which has been described as an agreement between your husband, the plaintiff, and Mr. Sparrow, the defendant."

E. PRESENT RECOLLECTION REVIVED

Trials are held years after the events which are their subject matter have occurred. Human memories are feeble. It is not unusual for a witness (even one whom you have rehearsed diligently) to forget. When this lapse of memory occurs, you have the right to jog his memory. You are permitted to use anything which will refresh his memory. Commonly, the memory is revived by a document. The witness reads the document and he is then able to testify as to the events about which you are examining him. The paper used to jog his memory does not become an evidential exhibit because it is his testimony which is the evidence. Opposing counsel when he cross-examines this witness has the right to examine whatever document the witness used to refresh his recollection. In most jurisdictions, the opponent may introduce into evidence those portions of the document which relate to his testimony.[3]

The item used to refresh the witness's memory is generally a document but it need not be. An apple, a paper clip or a blank piece of pink paper may do the trick of refreshing his memory.

F. RECORDED RECOLLECTION

The memory of every witness cannot be refreshed. The witness may have made a record of what he saw at the scene of the accident or the crime. If the witness made such a memorandum when the events were fresh in his mind or if he dictated a report and approved its accuracy when his memory was still fresh, such memorandum or report is entitled to admissibility in most jurisdictions. The federal rule[4] is a squeamish approach because it permits it to be read to the jury but not introduced as an exhibit except by the opposing party. In most jurisdictions, the report is simply admitted after it is qualified as reflecting the witness's perception of events and after the best evidence rule is satisfied. In these instances, unlike

3. Fed.R.Evid. 612.

4. Fed.R.Evid. 803(5).

the rule of refreshing recollection, the document itself becomes the evidence.

G. BUSINESS ENTRIES—HOSPITAL RECORDS

Part of your case may require proof that your opponent made payment or failed to pay or performed some act which was recorded by a business entry. Records which are kept in the ordinary course of business may qualify under this heading and be admissible.[5] Preliminary findings must be made by the court. These findings, though varying from state to state, generally include the following: that the entry was made in the ordinary course of business; that it was the ordinary course of business to make such entries; that it was made in good faith; that it was made before the action was commenced. If you offer such entry, it is your burden to elicit from the custodian of the records such evidence as will permit the judge to make these preliminary findings. Generally, it is not necessary to produce the person who made the entry.

In just about all jurisdictions, there are statutory provisions which govern the admissibility of hospital records. Generally, material in the record which deals with history, treatment and prognosis is admissible. Whatever touches liability, criminal or civil, is not admissible.

H. PHOTOGRAPHS—RECORDINGS

One good picture is worth more than a thousand words. Photographs may play an important role in your case. If a witness testifies that the photograph fairly depicts that which it purports to depict, the trial judge will generally permit it to be marked as an evidential exhibit in the case.[6] It should be an aid to the trier of fact unless it is a distortion or "trick photography." It is not necessary generally to produce the photographer.

Pictures of persons who have been stabbed, shot or burned may accurately represent the features of the person depicted at the time of the picture but the court may not allow them to be admitted because of their tendency to inflame or prejudice the jury. The resolution of this issue is almost entirely discretionary with the court. The party offering the photograph should, in this instance, select the least prejudicial of the batch in his possession. The original should be produced.[7]

The recording of a person's voice may be admissible if the message is relevant and if the recording was secured in accordance with

5. Fed.R.Evid. 803(6); Cf. Fed.R.Evid. 803(8).

6. Fed.R.Evid. 1001(2).

7. Fed.R.Evid. 1002, 403.

applicable statutes.[8] The test is whether it is a recording of the person's voice. One familiar with this voice may testify on this issue. It is open to the cross-examiner to demonstrate any distortion which the mechanical device for recording may cause. Here, too, the original should be produced.

I. AUTHORITY OF AN AGENT

Agents acting within the scope of their authority and employment may bind their principals. It may be important for you to introduce the statement of an agent in an action against his principal. The agent may have made a devastating admission which is all that you need to recover against the principal. Before a statement of an agent is admitted, it is essential to prove the scope of the agent's authority. An unsupported statement by one that he is an agent of another is generally insufficient to prove agency, and much less does it prove the parameters of his authority to bind his principal.[9]

Once there is evidence of the agent's authority to bind, a statement by him concerning a matter within the scope of his agency and made during the existence of the relationship is admissible and it is not hearsay.

J. BEST EVIDENCE RULE

The best evidence of the content of a written document is the original of that document. Accordingly, unless he is excused, the party offering the document must produce the original. Under the Federal Rules of Evidence,[10] a duplicate is admissible to the same extent as an original unless there is a genuine question of authenticity or unless it would be unfair to admit it. The rule is preferential rather than exclusionary.

Secondary evidence is admissible if the trial judge rules that the absence of the original has been satisfactorily explained.[11] For example, the original may be in the hands of one who is beyond the reach of a subpoena or it might have been destroyed. These are issues for the court. However, whether there ever was such a document is a jury question.

K-1. EXPERT WITNESS—QUALIFICATION

There are some matters beyond the competence of a jury or judge.[12] You will need an expert opinion to connect the defendant's

8. Fed.R.Evid. 901(5).

9. Fed.R.Evid. 801(d)(2).

10. Fed.R.Evid. 1002, 1003.

11. Fed.R.Evid. 1004.

12. Fed.R.Evid. 701, 702, 703, 704, 705.

negligence with the plaintiff's injury in many cases. Generally, a lay person is not permitted to give his opinion though there are instances in which such an opinion is competent.[13]

When you find it necessary or desirable to produce an expert witness, you must first qualify him on the witness stand. You are required to satisfy the judge before anything else transpires that he is qualified to give his opinion. This process of qualifying the witness requires you to elicit from the witness his educational and academic attainments together with his professional experience.

After you have completed your examination of the expert's qualifications, the court will permit your opponent to cross-examine the witness on his qualifications. Frequently, the opponent will waive his right to cross-examine at this time and reserve it until he is ready to cross-examine on the substance of his testimony. It is his choice. If he thinks that your expert has weak qualifications, he may cross-examine early in order to persuade the judge that he should not be qualified. On the other hand, if your expert's credentials are irreproachable, he may suggest that you "not waste the court's time in qualifying" him. You should not fall into this trap. Take all the time required to display your expert's impressive qualifications and attributes. This helps his credibility. "Thanks but no thanks" to this "generous" offer of your opponent to pass up the opportunity to help your case is your rejoinder.

K–2. EXPERT WITNESS—HYPOTHETICAL QUESTION

You have retained an expert to render an opinion on a matter which is important in your case. This opinion may be the causal link between the defective condition of the product and the ultimate injury to your client. You may seek an opinion that the operative technique of the defendant physician was negligent. The foundation for this opinion is the collocation of assumptions which constitute the hypothetical question. When you propose the hypothetical question, there should be already introduced some evidence as to each assumption. If there are eight assumptions of fact and only seven have any foundation in the evidence, the question should be struck, on objection, as defective. Occasionally, you will have a witness who is delayed. He will supply evidence necessary as a foundation of the hypothetical. This factor should be brought to the court's attention before the hypothetical is propounded. If this witness fails to supply this evidence when he arrives, your opponent will move to strike both the hypothetical question and the expert's answer.

There is never an excuse for a trial lawyer to produce an expert witness without having first explored his expected testimony. The hypothetical question should have been prepared with the expert's ad-

13. Fed.R.Evid. 701.

vice and reduced to writing. Both the examiner and the expert should have a copy of the question during the examination.

It is always safer to ask your expert witness to set forth the financial arrangements that you have made for his appearance. Don't allow your opponent to make hay out of the fact that the witness is to be paid or has been paid. It will not shock the jury to learn that an expert is not donating his time. However, it is unethical to agree to pay a contingent fee to any witness, and this prohibition includes an expert witness.[14]

L-1. STEALING OPPONENT'S THUNDER—YOUR WITNESS'S CRIMINAL RECORD

If an important witness for you has a criminal record of which your opponent is aware, don't permit him to demolish the witness's credibility by introducing it.[15] You can take much of the sting out of the record by asking the witness on direct examination about his past criminal involvement. It is much less dramatic and clearly less prejudicial when the witness is asked on direct examination. In some jurisdictions, you will not be permitted to steal your opponent's thunder in this way because such a procedure appears to violate the maxim that you may not impeach your own witness. This latter rule has many exceptions.[16]

L-2. STEALING OPPONENT'S THUNDER—PRIOR CONTRADICTORY STATEMENT OF YOUR WITNESS

It makes little sense to allow your opponent to expose your witness by demonstrating his prior contradictory statements if you know ahead of time the circumstances surrounding their utterance. If, in your preparation of the witness, you learn that he has made statements which contradict what he will say on the witness stand, your first obligation is to determine which statement is true. After you are satisfied that his earlier statement is false, tell him that you will be required to demonstrate that he told this earlier story in order to prevent the opponent from demolishing his credibility.[17] If care is used, you may be able to satisfy the jury that he was mistaken in his earlier statement and that he intended no harm. At a minimum, you should be able to steal your opponent's thunder and make the blow easier to accept.

14. EC7-28.

15. Fed.R.Evid. 609.

16. Fed.R.Evid. 607.

17. Fed.R.Evid. 613(b).

L–3. STEALING OPPONENT'S THUNDER— CONCEDE BIAS OF YOUR WITNESS

If you detect that your witness and the opponent are not on the best terms of friendship, bring this factor out as early in the examination of the witness as possible. Structure your questions in such a way as to persuade the judge or jury that in spite of the enmity between the parties, your witness knows the meaning of an oath and will tell the whole truth regardless of the consequences to him and the opponent. Display to the jury a witness who, though he dislikes the opponent, will not color his testimony to hurt him. Personal disaffection is one thing, but perjury is something else.

M–1. JUDICIAL NOTICE OF FACTS

If a fact which is essential to your case can be proved by judicial notice, do not waste time in trying to prove it by evidence. Ask the court to take judicial notice. The fact must be of sufficient notoriety and acceptance to qualify for judicial notice.[18] If the court acquiesces, tell the jury about judicial notice and its effect on the burden of proof. It is a valuable shortcut. Don't make the common mistake of buttressing a fact which has been judicially noticed by testimony and proof. This is not only unnecessary but wholly improper. In your closing argument to the jury, you may again allude to this fact.

M–2. JUDICIAL NOTICE OF LAW

A statute of your state or of another may be important to your case. For example, the burden of proof on the issue of comparative negligence may be governed by the law of a sister state because of the cognate rules of conflicts of law. It is sufficient if you call to the judge's attention the law and its citation. Proof in the evidential sense is not required. A certified copy of the law of the other state is not required. However, a good trial lawyer will not fail to point out the foreign law to the judge with particularity.[19]

N–1. NEGATIVE EVIDENCE—CONDITIONS FOR ADMISSIBILITY

That something did *not* happen may be terribly important. The absence of a sign or sound of warning may be crucial to your case in proving negligence. It will avail you nothing to produce a blind person to testify that he saw no sign. A person with impaired hearing will not help you prove that the engineer failed to sound a warning

18. Fed.R.Evid. 201.

19. Fed.R.Civ.P. 44.1.

as the train approached the grade crossing. You must first demonstrate the witness's ability to see and hear. This will require testimony as to his perceptive faculties and his proximity to the scene or place at which the occurrence should have taken place. He may have been near the grade crossing, equipped with reliable hearing, but he may have been listening to the ball game on radio, paying no auditory attention to whether the whistle or bell sounded. If so, he should not be permitted to testify as to the failure of the engineer to sound the whistle. In a close case, the judge may allow the evidence and permit extensive cross-examination of the issue of the witness's ability to hear the sound.

N–2. NEGATIVE EVIDENCE—PUBLIC AND PRIVATE RECORDS

1. *Public Records*

The birth or death of a person in a particular town may be important to your case. You may prove that a person was not born in a certain city by demonstrating the absence of a public record of his birth.[20] This may be accomplished by calling a witness who examined the records and found no entry. In some jurisdictions, such a witness must be shown to be an official of the registry whose records were examined. In others, you may qualify any person who has examined the records.

2. *Private Records*

It may be important to your case that a business record fails to show a transaction. The absence of an entry that a car was rented by a leasing company may be evidence that it was stolen. In most jurisdictions, such negative evidence is admissible though clearly it does not have the force of positive evidence and it is subject to abuse.

O. USE OF DEPOSITION

A deposition may be an important instrument at trial. A witness deposed shortly after the entry of the case at a time when the events were fresh in his mind may become unavailable at the time of trial. His deposition, however, may be admissible for all purposes. If it is ruled admissible because of the deponent's death, illness or general unavailability, you may read it to the jury.[21] A convenient procedure for reading it is the use of another lawyer who takes the witness stand (with the court's prior permission) and plays the role of the deponent while you read the questions to him.

20. Fed.R.Evid. 803(7).

21. Fed.R.Civ.P. 32(a)(3); Fed.R.Crim. P. 15(e); Fed.R.Evid. 1007.

If you learn that your adversary intends to use a deposition, you should examine it with care *before* it is used. The trial judge should be asked to rule on objections to questions and answers in the deposition *before* they are read to the jury.

P. STIPULATIONS

Every effort should be made by trial counsel to enter into stipulations which will save the time required in producing evidence. If you are satisfied that your adversary can prove some fact which is necessary to his case, you are not sacrificing your client's cause if you stipulate. For example, if one issue in the case is the fact that a street is a public way, no harm is done to your case if you stipulate to this fact.

A warning is in order after you have agreed on a stipulation. Write the stipulation on paper. Allow your opponent time to read it. Then, ask the judge for permission to read it to the jury. It is the court's function to tell the jury the effect of the stipulation, not counsel's.

Q. DEMONSTRATIVE EVIDENCE

The term "demonstrative evidence" includes not only items which qualify as real or "thing" evidence, but also photographs, X-rays, and "live" demonstrations in the courtroom. The gun which the government contends is the murder weapon is demonstrative evidence. The insurance policy on which you are suing for recovery of death benefits in the face of a refusal by the insurance company is demonstrative evidence. Before such evidence can be marked as an exhibit, you must have some evidence that it is relevant and material to the issues being tried. It must at least "look like the gun" which the defendant was holding or which was found under his bed when the police arrested him after the shooting. At a minimum, the insurance policy on its face must name the deceased as the insured.

Mechanical devices which help the jury examine the document more readily (e. g., a wall or overhead projector) may be used if prior permission of the court is obtained. A human skeleton may be useful to a physician witness who wants to explain an anatomical part to the jury. However, the skeleton should not even be brought into the courtroom without prior permission of the court.

R. TELEPHONE CONVERSATION

It is not uncommon for counsel to ask a witness to relate a telephone conversation between himself and the opposing party. Such a conversation is admissible only after there is some basis for ruling that the voice on the other end of the telephone is that of the opposing party. Accordingly, it is essential to elicit from the witness the foundation for his familiarity with the other voice.[22] A close family relationship, a long term friendship or just a knowledge of his intonations based on earlier conversations—these should be in evidence before the conversation is admitted.

S. CUMULATIVE AND REPETITIOUS EVIDENCE

If your witness has testified fully and clearly as to the events which he witnessed, don't make him repeat his story. There is an unofficial presumption that the jury heard the witness the first time. Don't risk "turning off" the jury by repetition.

Similarly, if 15 people witnessed the accident, you need not feel constrained to call all these people. Make it clear through one or two witnesses that a formidable number of people saw the collision, but in the interest of saving everybody's time, you will not call the entire mob.[23] However, be careful to avoid the trap of failing to call an important witness and thereby allowing your opponent to comment on your failure to call. This omission may be an admission which will work to your embarrassment.

T. EVIDENCE FOR LIMITED PURPOSE

There will arise an occasion when you will find it necessary or desirable to offer evidence which at first blush appears inadmissible by your opponent. He will object and you will then be put to the task of satisfying the judge that you are offering it for a limited purpose and not on the merits of the principal issue of the case.[24] Credibility of a witness is an issue which may permit you to offer evidence which seems irrelevant at first, but which may be important in destroying the credibility of an important opposing witness. Two things are worth noting about this genre of evidence.

The trial judge has an abundance of discretion in ruling on the admissibility of this type of evidence. He must be satisfied that the jury on appropriate instructions will understand the purpose of the testimony. Accordingly, the party against whom such evidence is admitted should ask the court for an immediate instruction of the jury as to the purpose of the evidence. Second, the court should weigh the importance of such evidence against its possible prejudicial effect. For example, a witness whom you are cross-examining may have been guilty of a dastardly act for which he was not prosecuted. He denies the commission of it on the stand but you have the tools to prove that he

22. Fed.R.Evid. 901(5), (6).

23. Fed.R.Evid. 611(a).

24. Fed.R.Evid. 105; Cf. Fed.R.Evid. 407.

committed it. The court may rule against this type of evidence because the jury will be distracted from the main issue of the case in considering the morality, vel non, of what the witness did at an earlier time and under unrelated conditions.[25]

U. CHALKS AND DIAGRAMS

A drawing of the apartment in which the murder took place can be helpful to the jury. This drawing may be the product of an expert draftsman or a feeble effort on the blackboard by your first eye witness who funked drawing in high school. Don't call just anybody to make a drawing. Don't ask any witness to use a blackboard or to produce pre-dawn sketches without prior permission of the court.

When a question is asked which refers to the drawing, include reference to the drawing in your question; otherwise, the record on appeal will contain meaningless questions. Make sure that a reproduction of the drawing is included in the appellate record. Ask permission of the court to request the witness to leave the witness stand and to approach the blackboard.

The drawing is a chalk which should be given a letter or number for identification purposes in the record. A commonly accepted form of question in this connection is: "Now, Mrs. Jones, directing your attention to the diagram marked H for identification, point out with this crayon the exact spot where you found the dirty apple core."

V. USE OF INTERPRETER

If you know in advance of trial that a witness whom you will call cannot speak English, it is your task to provide an interpreter or to arrange for the services of a court-appointed interpreter. The interpreter is sworn by the clerk.[26] He is required to translate the question, await the answer in the witness's language and translate the answer into English. The answer should faithfully reproduce the statement of the witness without any contribution of the interpreter's frame of mind. Difficulties in expressing concepts familiar in English but foreign to the language of the witness will permit you some latitude in asking leading questions.

W-1. REDIRECT EXAMINATION—SCOPE

The universal rule limits the scope of redirect examination to matters touched in cross-examination. Redirect should not be used to insert matters forgotten on direct examination, if these matters were not explored on cross-examination. The court has discretion to

25. Fed.R.Evid. 608(b).

26. Fed.R.Evid. 604.

permit the exploration of new matters but it is seldom exercised in favor of allowing such a fresh start.

W-2. REDIRECT EXAMINATION—REHABILITATION

By far the most common purpose of redirect examination is the restoration of the witness's credibility after a devastating cross-examination. Not uncommonly, a witness will not be permitted to explain a damaging admission while he is being cross-examined. Accordingly, it is open to the re-examiner to ask the witness, "What did you mean when you said . . ., as you testified under cross-examination?" A skillful examiner can breathe new life into a witness who has been all but destroyed on cross-examination.

W-3. REDIRECT EXAMINATION—PRIOR CONSISTENT STATEMENTS

Generally, it is not open to you to demonstrate that a witness called by you has testified in a manner consistent with earlier statements made by him. However, this rule is subject to the exception that a witness whose credibility has been impugned on the basis of a suggestion of a recently contrived statement may be permitted to testify that on an earlier occasion, he made substantially the same statement. Under these circumstances, you may introduce the earlier statement to prove the consistency of the witness.

X. TAKING NOTES WHILE WITNESS TESTIFIES

Nobody can prescribe the best method for recalling what a witness says on the witness stand. Some lawyers are gifted with an extraordinary memory. They are endowed with instant recall. Perhaps, they have trained themselves to remember chapter and verse of everything that the witness said and the order in which he said it.

While you are examining a witness, you cannot conveniently take notes. If you are being assisted in the trial of a case by co-counsel, he or she may help in taking notes. When you have completed your direct examination, examine the notes to determine whether there is an item which requires more treatment.

While your opponent is examining a witness, take what notes you deem necessary for recall of the testimony. Some lawyers take down every word of the witness. Others capture only ideas by one or two words. Still others take no notes. They just stare at the witness. You will develop your own style.

EXERCISE 1

P and D have signed an agreement by which D agrees to pay P $500 per week if P acts as his bodyguard. P has performed these services for four weeks, but D has not paid him. P sues D.

Demonstrate the method by which you will introduce into evidence the employment agreement.

EXERCISE 2

Plaintiff sold a shipment of beef to the defendant on September 4, Yr.-1 for $1,000 in response to D's telephone order. P's driver delivered the beef to D's Shipping and Receiving Room, but the driver no longer works for P. D had always paid promptly in order to take advantage of P's discount. In this instance, D neither paid nor notified P of his reasons for not paying in spite of the many dunning letters from P. After six months of waiting and many demand letters, P sued D. D's only answer was denial of receipt of the shipment. The delivery slip had been prepared by the driver in duplicate. The original, which purportedly bears the initials of an employee of D's Shipping and Receiving Department, is among P's papers. The copy is given to the purchaser on delivery.

Demonstrate by questions and answers how you will jog the memory of P's driver to present evidence of delivery if you are counsel for P.

EXERCISE 3

Witness (W) saw a motor vehicle accident in which the plaintiff (P), a pedestrian, unsuccessfully negotiated a crossing in downtown Detroit in the face of signs in red saying "DON'T WALK." The defendant (D) entered the intersection at approximately 15 m.p.h. and struck P. It was raining heavily. The visibility was poor. W saw the collision at a distance of 8 to 10 feet while standing on the curb awaiting a favorable light for crossing.

W was an insurance adjuster on the job less than a month, though his employer had no connection with the parties involved in the accident. W gave his name to a police officer who had responded in an ambulance. W reached his home about two hours after the accident, following his customary rite of passage in "having a beer and a ball" at Charlie's, his favorite watering hole. W wrote a report at home in longhand, though he did not know the names of the parties.

The case came to trial four years after the accident. P calls W to the witness stand.

As trial counsel for P, demonstrate how you will elicit the contents of W's report.

EXERCISE 4

Mabel Finch has been the chief bookkeeper at Acme Co. for many years. During her tenure, Acme sold 10 cases of law books to Carter University Law School. Acme has never been paid. Mabel did not make the entry recording the sale. The accounts receivable clerk who entered the sale on Acme's books is married and living in the Carmel valley in California. Acme has sued Law School in Saint Paul, Minnesota.

As trial attorney for Acme, you have produced Mabel for testimony on the witness stand. Outline by question and answer how you will elicit evidence of the sale to Law School.

EXERCISE 5

A bystander who witnessed a rear-end collision in which P's motor vehicle was severely damaged is on the witness stand. The accident occurred in Yr.–5. You have photographs of the scene, including shots of your client's motor vehicle after the accident, the glass on the road and the front end damage to D's car. A professional photographer took the pictures but he has died since the accident.

Demonstrate the method by which you will introduce the photograph into evidence through this witness.

EXERCISE 6

A has worked for Bell Co. for several years as a purchasing agent. Tom Jones, the executive vice-president who hired A, orally authorized him to sign purchase contracts in behalf of Bell Co. Tom Jones is now deceased. Bell Co. has been sued by P on such a contract which was signed by A. One of the defenses interposed by Bell Co. is the absence of A's authority to sign the contract.

How will you prove A's authority to execute the contract and to bind Bell Co.? Demonstrate by questions and answers.

EXERCISE 7

Zeke signed an employment contract with Empire Co. He signed it in duplicate. One copy was retained by Empire, the other by him. After a short time, Empire discharged Zeke, who sued Empire. After Zeke had signed both copies, he made a Xerox copy. Zeke has lost his duplicate original copy. He has the Xerox copy.

Zeke is your first witness. How, if at all, is the Xerox copy admitted into evidence?

EXERCISE 8

Dr. Wimot Simpson is a thoracic surgeon whom you have called to testify as an expert for the plaintiff. He is prepared to give his opinion that the noxious fumes inhaled by the plaintiff during his working hours have caused irremediable lung disease. Your adversary, after you have elicited Dr. Simpson's name, address and occupation, stands and says: "To save time, I concede his qualifications."

What steps will you then take?

EXERCISE 9

A witness whose testimony is essential to your case has a criminal record. You are certain your adversary has a certified copy of the conviction and intends to use it to impeach his testimony.

In question and answer form, demonstrate how you will handle this matter.

EXERCISE 10

You represent Defendant (D). Jones is an important witness for D. He saw the plaintiff's (P) car come to rest after the accident. He heard P say that he was not injured. Jones observed no bruises or blood on P. He heard P say: "D, I feel worse for you than for myself. I've been in your shoes before. There was nothing that you could do to avoid hitting my car. C'est la vie."

A year or so after the accident, while discussing the accident with P's brother, Jones said: "Your poor brother. D was always a crazy driver. The night of the accident, D had run two red lights before hitting your brother."

You are aware that P knows of Jones's statements to his brother.

Demonstrate by question and answer how you will handle this matter.

EXERCISE 11

You are trial counsel for the plaintiff. A witness whose testimony is crucial to your case is biased against the defendant. He threatened, "I'll get you some day," two years before the accident which is the subject of the case. You are satisfied that he is telling the truth about his observation of the accident.

How will you conduct your direct examination of this witness in regard to his admitted bias against the defendant?

EXERCISE 12

One element in the case which you are trying to a jury is the fact that Sacramento was the capital of California on March 17, Yr.–3.

Describe how you will satisfy your burden of proof on this issue.

EXERCISE 13

A law in State X, one of the United States, imposes absolute liability on the operator of a motor vehicle who becomes involved in an accident while he is negotiating a left turn. The accident which occurred in State X is the subject matter of your case which is being tried to a jury in State Y. You represent the injured plaintiff who was a passenger in the motor vehicle which was proceeding in a straight away direction when struck by the defendant's car which was turning left.

Describe how you will use the law of State X.

EXERCISE 14

Your client was severely injured in a railroad grade crossing accident in which the train collided with your client's motor vehicle. The railroad was required to sound a bell alarm as it approached the crossing. You called the engineer as your witness because he was essential on many issues of your case in chief. He testified, inter alia, that he sounded the alarm. You have waiting in the wings three persons who were near the crossing and saw the accident but did not hear the alarm.

What steps will you take to introduce in evidence the testimony of these three persons regarding the failure of the alarm?

EXERCISE 15

You are defending a case in which it is essential for the plaintiff to prove that he was born in Chicago. You have had examined the records in the department of births, marriages and deaths of the City of Chicago and have found no record of his birth.

How, if at all, will you introduce evidence tending to show that the plaintiff was not born in Chicago?

EXERCISE 16

Stanley Gunz is a crucially important witness in the case for the plaintiff whom you represent. He saw the accident and talked at great length with the defendant after the accident. Gunz is recovering from major surgery performed the day before the trial commenced. He will not be available to testify for two months according to his doctor. Defense counsel took Stanley's deposition shortly after the case was entered. You have a copy.

How, if at all, will you be able to use this deposition?

EXERCISE 17

You and counsel for the defendant have reduced to writing the following stipulation: "The motor vehicle accident which is the subject matter of this action took place on September 7, Yr.-3 at the corner of Washington and Elm Streets, New Haven, Connecticut."

Describe how you will present this stipulation to the jury.

EXERCISE 18

You are the county prosecutor who is trying a murder case. The first police officer to arrive at the scene of the murder seized a gun which he has kept in his custody in his locker at the police station except for the short period of time during which the ballistician tested it. The officer has brought it to court for introduction into evidence. A witness whom you intend to call after the police officer will testify that the gun "looks an awful lot like the gun Jackie (defendant) was pointing at Bob (victim)."

Describe the steps which you will take to introduce the gun into evidence.

EXERCISE 19

Holophernes, the bookkeeper for Acme Co., answered the telephone when Bernie called to order 100 cases of Acme Special Lima Beans. When they were shipped, Bernie refused to accept them. In his telephone call, if Bernie made it, the price and quantity of beans were specified. On two earlier occasions, Holophernes had talked to Bernie on the telephone.

How will you introduce evidence of what Holophernes and Bernie said on the telephone?

ASSIGNMENT #6

ROLAND CHILD, p.p.a. et al. v. B & C REALTY, INC., LITTLEVALE POWER & LIGHT COMPANY, and CARDINAL WIRE AND CABLE CORP.

LAW FIRM #__1__. represents Ned Child and his son Roland.

LAW FIRM #__2__. represents B & C Realty, Inc., as defendant and as third party plaintiff.

LAW FIRM #__3__. represents Littlevale Power and Light Company, as defendant and as third party plaintiff.

LAW FIRM #__4__. represents Cardinal Wire and Cable Corp. as an original defendant and as a third party defendant.

PRELIMINARY FACTS

B & C Realty, Inc., a corporation with its principal place of business in Littlevale, has owned the premises at 1212 River Road, Littlevale, since Yr._15. The building consists of six apartments, two on each of the three floors. On January 1 of last year, Mr. and Mrs. Ned Child became tenants at will in Apartment 2A, which consisted of two bedrooms, bath, living room, kitchen and front and back porches. The tenants had three children, the youngest being Roland, age eight at the commencement of the tenancy.

Through the month of March last year, the porches were not used by the Child family, due to the cold and the snow.

When the building was erected in Yr.-16, its front, including porch rails, was directly above the property line separating the property from the public sidewalk. At that time, Littlevale Power & Light Company, a public utility liable for the negligence of its employees, erected two poles (one at each end of the building at 1212 River Road, each pole being located 9 feet, 3 inches from the building. They were the usual wooden "telephone type" poles, with two cross arms on each. The cross arms extended over the street and over the public sidewalk. Electric and telephone wires were accommodated by the cross arms. The electric wires, when installed on the cross arms, were at a height directly opposite the rail of the front porch of Apartment 2A. They were covered with an insulating material. The wires on the "sidewalk side" of the cross arms hung within four feet of the building front and porch rail.

The porch rail was attached to a wall at each end of the porch and was supported by verticle 1″ by 1″ wooden pieces, forty-eight inches high (from porch floor to underside of rail). A three inch gap existed between each two 1″ by 1″s.

On April 1 of last year, the weather in Littlevale was delightful. Mrs. Child opened the door to the front porch and allowed Roland to play there. He had some of his own toys with him. A broken television roof antenna was in one corner of the porch. One of its pieces was a tubular lightweight metal rod about five feet in length.

Mrs. Child was vacuuming the living room rug when she saw a bright flash through the windows. She rushed out to the porch. Her son was lying unconscious on the porch floor. She saw the tubular metal rod extending from the porch between two of the 1″ by 1″ uprights, touching the wire closest to the porch. She noticed an acrid odor, and blue smoke in the air. She grabbed her son by the feet, pulled him back into the living room, and 'phoned the police and the power and light company.

The police rushed Roland to the Littlevale Memorial Hospital where he came under the care of Doctor Karen Wefing. Dr. Wefing had been pediatrician for each of the Child children, and just happened to be at the hospital when Roland was brought in. She enlisted the assistance of two specialists, Dr. Robert Angelo (specialist in the treatment of burns) and Dr. Eugene Ek (specialist in internal medicine).

Roland had suffered third degree burns over 30% of his body surface. He spent a "stormy" three weeks in the Intensive Care Unit, then was transferred to the Children's Ward. He has been hospitalized since the incident and has undergone surgery on twelve separate occasions.

Since Yr.–20, the Revised By-Laws and Ordinances of the City of Littlevale have provided (R.BL & O., c. VII, § 20C) that no person, firm, public utility or other corporation shall cause to be placed or maintained a wire conducting electricity for light or power, over or under a public sidewalk or way, within nine feet of a residence, excepting so-called "service wiring" running to residences from overhead or underground wires.

In December of last year, Attorney J. R. Maxx (of the law firm representing plaintiff) brought an action in Superior Court. That action is entitled "Roland Child, a minor who brings this action by his father and next friend, Ned Child, and Ned Child vs. B & C Realty, Inc., and the Littlevale Power and Light Company." Attorneys for B & C Realty and for the Power and Light Company have each brought in Cardinal Wire and Cable Corporation as a third party defendant under the Rules of Civil Procedure. Plaintiff's attorneys have amended the Complaint, naming Cardinal Wire and Cable as a direct defendant also.

The Littlevale Police Department conducted an investigation of the incident, as did attorneys for each of the parties, and the Department of Public Utilities. The Police Department has in its possession photographs of the wires just opposite the Childs' porch. These show that about 50% of the insulating material was missing on the date of the incident. Dr. Wefing has had photographs taken of the burned areas of Roland's body, some on the date of admission, and others after each of the surgical procedures.

The action has been tried to a Master and is now being tried to a jury. The Master found for the plaintiffs and assessed substantial damages against all defendants.

PROBLEM

LAW FIRM FOR THE PLAINTIFFS: Attached hereto is a rough sketch, which was executed by Officer Norman Brice of Littlevale Police Department on the date of the incident. It is a portion of the records of the Department and was produced by reason of a subpoena duces tecum issued by the defendant, B & C Realty, Inc. You did not have such a subpoena served. Call the officer as a witness, and take the necessary steps to have him introduce the sketch as an exhibit, as well as reproduce it on the blackboard, and explain it.

POLICE DEPARTMENT
THE CITY OF LITTLEVALE

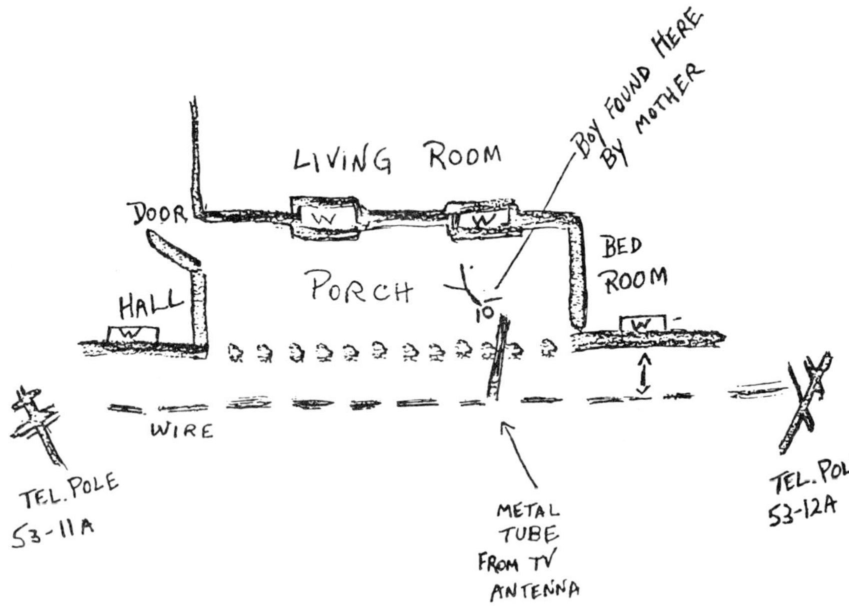

[C2008]

OVERHEAD VIEW—PORCH OF APT. 2A AT
1212 RIVER ROAD, LITTLEVALE,
APRIL 1, YR.–1.

Ptl. Norman Brice

LAW FIRM FOR THE LANDLORD PLAINTIFFS: (1) There is attached hereto a copy of Section 20C, c. VII, of Littlevale's Revised By-Laws and Ordinances. You have summonsed the City Clerk, Fred Anderson. He is prepared to testify that this section was passed by the City Council on June 3, Yr.–20 and signed that same date by the Mayor. He will state also that it has not been amended or repealed.

Call Mr. Anderson to the stand. Interrogate him to the extent necessary to offer the ordinance in evidence.

(2) Be prepared to explain to the class a procedure that you could have used, prior to trial, to establish the existence of the ordinance, and its application in this case.

LAW FIRM FOR CARDINAL WIRE AND CABLE CORP.: You were informed by the corporation's general manager that, subsequent to the incident in which the Child boy was injured, the Littlevale Power & Light Company removed the "suspect wire" which had been hung closest to the Child porch. Through the use of interrogatories and a request for production, you obtained a three foot long piece of the wire for inspection and testing. Counsel for the Childs and B & C Realty have done the same.

You turned over your piece of the wire to Dr. Duncan Harriman, chief of the Quality Control Division of your client. He is a recognized expert in the subject of wiring used for conducting electricity, and in insulating materials used thereon. He alone conducted tests on the wire and the insulation. He reported to you that he can testify that, without question, this wire was sold to Littlevale Power & Light in Yr.–17 for *interior use* only; that, when sold, it was wound on drums identical to those used for wiring manufactured for exterior all-weather use, but that the drums bore conspicuous legends warning buyers not to use it out of doors.

Call Dr. Harriman to the stand. Have him concede that after the tests were performed, the piece of wire was, somehow, lost or destroyed; that when he went this morning to retrieve it from his laboratory, it was not where he expected to find it. Then, attempt to have him testify concerning his testing of the wire and his conclusions.

Incidentally, Dr. Harriman informed you in a "corridor conference" just before coming into the courtroom that, four years ago, he was convicted of bribery of a State official after an attempt to obtain a State contract for Cardinal Wire and Cable [a felony] and paid a $10,000 fine, and that 20 years ago, he was convicted of driving negligently so as to endanger, and paid a $50 fine.

LAW FIRM FOR LITTLEVALE POWER & LIGHT. You had, by use of interrogatories, determined that Dr. Harriman would testify as an expert witness at trial for Cardinal Wire and Cable. You have obtained certified copies of the convictions of Dr. Harriman. Cross-examine the expert, if you wish, concerning these records, and if there is any objection by counsel for Cardinal Wire and Cable, be prepared to explain your offer at a side-bar conference.

CITY OF LITTLEVALE
REVISED BY–LAWS AND ORDINANCES

Adopted by the City Council by a vote of 12–0 on June 3, Yr.–20, and assigned on said date by his Honor, the Mayor of the City.

Excerpt

CHAPTER VII. PUBLIC SAFETY

. . . Section 20C. No person, firm, public utility or other corporation, shall cause to be placed or maintained a wire conducting electricity for light or power, over or under a public sidewalk or way, within nine (9) feet of a residence, excepting "service wiring" running to residences from overhead or underground wires or cables.

Whoever violates the provisions of this section shall be punished by a fine of not exceeding twenty dollars for each offense. . . .

Certificate

I, Fred Anderson, Clerk of the City of Littlevale, and the person in charge of its records, including the official copies of its By-Laws and Ordinances, certify that the foregoing is a true excerpt from the Revised By-Laws and Ordinances of this City; that said excerpted section has been in effect since its adoption June 3, Yr.–20, and that no amendment thereto has been adopted since said date.

/s/ FRED ANDERSON
Fred Anderson
City Clerk

ASSIGNMENT #7
STEVE'S PACKAGE STORE, INC. v. GOLDEN INDEMNITY COMPANY

THE LITIGATION

This is an action of contract to recover on a fidelity bond. The plaintiff corporation is the owner of a retail liquor store in the city of Land's End. In the Complaint, it is alleged that, since the opening of the store some six and a half years ago, the plaintiff corporation has purchased employee fidelity bonds on an annual basis; that, in exchange for stipulated premiums, the defendant promised to indemnify the plaintiff for losses suffered by reason of theft or embezzlement by named employees covered by the bonds; that, since the date of her employment one Margot Hayes was a named employee covered by the provisions of the bond; that said Margot Hayes had, over a period of more than two years, been stealing money from the plaintiff corporation by charging customers the full amount of their purchases, ringing up less than the full amount of purchase on the plaintiff's cash register and pocketing the difference; that the total amount of the defalcation of Margot Hayes was approximately $5,000, but that the defendant has, without right, refused to carry out the terms of its contract with plaintiff, and has refused to indemnify the plaintiff for its loss.

In its Answer, the defendant has conceded the execution of the bond and the payment of the annual premium by the plaintiff. It also admits that Margot Hayes, an employee of the plaintiff, was a person whose conduct was "covered" by the terms of the bond. It denies that Margot Hayes stole the amount of money claimed by the plaintiff; and leaves the plaintiff to its proof of the fact of theft, and the amount of money allegedly taken.

All pleadings are complete. Neither party has deposed Margot Hayes. The plaintiff corporation has entered into a written agreement with Margot Hayes to the effect that the plaintiff will not bring a civil suit against her if she will testify "to the truth" at the trial of this action against the defendant bonding company.

Both the plaintiff and the defendant are in possession of a transcript of an interview with Mrs. Hayes conducted July 6, Yr.–1 by Lieutenant Bloom of the Land's End Police Department.

No one has informed Mrs. Hayes that, if Golden Indemnity is found liable to Steve's Package Store, Inc., Golden would have the right to bring an action against Mrs. Hayes to recoup its loss. It is a fact that Mrs. Hayes, since being fired by Steve's Package Store, Inc., has been unable to keep up the mortgage payments on her home, and that the bank will probably foreclose in the near future, so that an action by the Company would probably be fruitless.

Mrs. Hayes has agreed to meet with the attorneys for the plaintiff, to prepare for her testimony at the trial of the action.

The transcript of her interview with the police lieutenant is attached hereto.

PROBLEM

LAW FIRM #__1__. Select one or more of your members to instruct Mrs. Hayes *generally* on the subject of testifying on *direct* examination. Discuss with her, among other subjects, the matters of dress, voice, and conduct on the stand. Decide for yourself whether you will discuss with her the possibility that, if the plaintiff prevails, the defendant may then bring an action against her to recoup its loss.

LAW FIRM #__2__. Select one or more of your members to CONDUCT the direct examination of this witness. (Both firms here supposedly are one, representing the plaintiff.)

MEMBERS OF BOTH FIRMS should be prepared, at the conclusion of the examination, to answer questions concerning (1) a duty, if any, to warn Mrs. Hayes of the possibility of an action against her by the Indemnity Company; (2) the necessity of her testifying, whether or not such an action may be brought; (3) the wisdom of seeking at trial a declaration by the Judge that she is a hostile witness.

THE CLASS should be prepared, at the conclusion of the assignment to discuss:

1. Techniques employed in the direct examination of a "personal injury plaintiff."
2. The direct examination of a party or non-party witness who has a record of prior convictions of crime.
3. Direct examination relating to pain and suffering of a party, by a non-party witness.

4. Direct examination of a witness testifying on the subject of "property damage."
5. Direct testimony on the diminution of earning capacity of (a) a salaried person, (b) a non-salaried self-employed person, (c) a non-employed person [housewife, child, retired person].
6. Testimony relating to life expectancy, and reduction to present value of future lost earnings.

TRANSCRIPTION OF INTERVIEW OF MRS. MARGOT HAYES TAKEN JULY 6, YR.–1 BY LIEUTENANT DENNIS BLOOM OF THE LAND'S END POLICE DEPARTMENT

Q. Mrs. Hayes, I have just read to you warnings required to be given by the *Miranda* decision of the U. S. Supreme Court. Do you understand each of these rights?

A. Yes.

Q. Are you confused at all about these rights? Do you have any questions you want to ask about them?

A. I know what you said.

Q. Remember, you can stop talking any time you want to, and refuse to answer any further. Also, you can confer with your lawyer who is here in the room any time you want. Clear?

A. What good will that do? He says that I may as well talk. He says the statement that I gave to Steve's private detective can be used against me in court. Is that true?

Q. I'm not a lawyer, lady, just a police officer. All I can say is that if you make a clean breast of it, it will probably go easier with you in Court. That's not a promise now—just a personal opinion. Do you want to answer my questions or not?

A. Go ahead. But most of what I told that b______ he forced out of me with threats.

Q. We'll get to that. Now, give me your full name and address.

A. Margot E. Hayes, 91 Horizon Road, Land's End.

Q. Are you married?

A. Married—to Victor Hayes.

Q. And you're how old?

A. Thirty-five tomorrow. Happy birthday to me.

Q. By whom are you employed?

A. Nobody, now.

Q. By whom were you employed up until yesterday?

A. Steve's Package Store, Inc.

Q. Who was your boss?

A. Steve Honig, the owner of the liquor store.

Q. What were your duties there?

A. It was a self-service store. I worked at the cash register.

Q. What days and what hours did you work?

A. Tuesday through Saturday, 9 to 5.

Q. And what was your weekly pay?

A. $150 a week.

Q. Mrs. Hayes, when a customer came to you with liquor that he wanted to purchase, how would you handle the sale?

A. We had little stickers on each bottle or other item in the store. I'd punch up the various items on the register, then ring the total, take his money and give him his change.

Q. Did you at any time charge the customer less than the full amount of his purchase? That is, did you let some bottles go through without ringing up the amount on the register?

A. I never gave any customer anything for nothing. Every customer paid full price for everything.

Q. All right, then. Did you ever charge the customer the full amount of his or her purchase, then take the full amount from the customer, but ring up only a part of the purchase, and pocket the money difference?

A. Well, yeah. Once in a great while.

Q. Explain to me how you did it, in your own words.

A. Do I have to tell him? (Question addressed to attorney, who responded: You'd better. If you won't, I'll drop out of your case.) Okay, then. Once in a while the customer wouldn't pay no attention to me ringing up the sale. If they bought three of the same items, I'd ring up two. I'd put all the money in the register; then, later on, hit the "No sale" key like you do when you make change, and take out the money for the third item, and put it in my pocketbook when nobody was around. That way, when the register tape and the cash were checked, they'd always tally.

Q. How often did you do this?

A. Not often.

Q. How many times a week?

A. Once—twice—maybe three times at the most.

Q. How long have you been doing it?

A. Some months.

Q. Mrs. Hayes, are you going to cooperate, or should I stop asking questions? Let's try it once more. How long have you been doing it? One month? Two months? A year?

A. I can't remember.

Q. O.K., Mrs. Hayes. I want you to know that Steve Honig claims that they inventory the store and check the inventory against the receipts and expenses, and they figure you took $5,000 to $10,000 during the last two years.

A. That's a lie. That bum takes stock from the store for his own home, and when one of his other stores runs short of an item, he ships from our store. That's probably the greatest part of the missing money.

Q. Mrs. Hayes, it's against the law for a retail store to transship to another retail store in the liquor business.

A. I know that, and Honig knows that, but now he has a patsy to blame for the missing inventory. He's playing it for all it's worth. And he ain't gonna lose a penny. My lawyer told me Honig will just make a claim on my employee fidelity bond, and the insurance company will have to pay every penny of the claim.

Q. That's not my business right now, Ma'am. I'll get to investigating that too, but for now, I want to know about the part you played. I want to know exactly how much you took from the store that didn't belong to you.

A. Look, Lieutenant. Anybody will tell you that my husband took a heart attack two years ago. I've got four kids. My husband used to earn $19,000 a year. Do you understand what it means to lose that income, try to keep the house, pay the mortgage, buy the food, clothe the kids? I didn't want to lose my house. I only took enough to barely get by, along with the lousy compensation payments that my husband gets.

Q. Please, Mrs. Hayes, the court will listen to all that. How much did you take and over what period of time?

A. I told you. I didn't take more than twenty-five bucks a week.

Q. For how long a time?

A. Since my husband took the heart attack.

Q. And that was two years ago?

A. Yeah, two years ago.

Q. Mrs. Hayes, that would make about $2,600 total. Now Honig's private detective says you admitted that you took over $5,000 during that time—or about $50 a week.

A. He threatened me, or I never would have said that. He forced me to say it, you understand?

Q. How did he threaten you? Did he twist your arm, or what?

A. Here's what happened. I'm at the register yesterday morning. Twice, I rung up the register short on customers. I figure to take out $14.98 when the store's empty of customers and Steve is out back. All of a sudden the second "customer" comes back into the store with the detective, Melvin—or whatever his name is. Then, they tell me the "customer" is really an employee of Melvin, that they've taken pictures of me, and know exactly what I've been doing. I begged them not to call you people. Melvin took me by the arm, Honig comes out of the back, and the two of them march me down cellar where a lot of the inventory is kept. They told me they'd see that I went to jail, and they'd sue me and take my house, and my husband and kids would wind up on welfare. Oh, they said terrible things. I really begged them not to do anything. They said they had to report the matter to the police, but they wouldn't sue me if I signed a statement for them, so I did it. Now that wouldn't hold up in court, would it?

Q. That's for your lawyer to answer Ma'am. In that statement, how much did you say you took?

A. Fifty dollars a week for over two years. But I didn't. I only took about twenty-five.

Q. All right. Are you willing to sign a transcript of this interview and swear under the penalties of perjury that it is true?

A. Yes, so help me God, I will.

The foregoing is a true verbatim transcript of an interview conducted by Lieutenant Bloom. It is true to the best of my knowledge and belief. Under the penalties of perjury.

/s/ Margot Hayes

Witness /s/ H. R. Reynolds,
Qualified and Certified Court Reporter

ASSIGNMENT #8

STATE v. STANLEY F. BENTON

BACKGROUND

Stanley Benton is charged in an indictment returned by the Grand Jury for Jefferson County with the murder of Nathan Saxe on February 2 of last year.

The case is on trial. Lieutenant Sean Martin has testified that at 1:55 a. m. on February 2, he was going off duty and leaving the Police Station, this city, when he had a conversation with the telephone operator at the switchboard near the front door. As a result of that conversation, he and Sergeant Ed Mazur took a cruiser and went to the corner of Depot and Callahan Streets. They form a "T" type of intersection. They approached the intersection travelling west on Callahan, and made a left or southerly turn on Depot Street. Parked about 35 feet from the corner on the right hand side of the street was a late model grey Ford. The driver's door was open. The interior overhead light was lit. The left leg of a man protruded through the open door. They parked the cruiser parallel to the Ford. They discovered the body of a man (later identified as Nathan Saxe) in the driver's position in the car, slumped toward the right. There was blood spattered on the steering wheel, the dash, the driver's door and part of the roof of the interior. They observed what appeared to be four bullet wounds in the face of the dead man. Sergeant Mazur had known Nathan Saxe, and knew that he lived in the multi-tenanted dwelling located on the southwest corner of the intersection of Callahan and Depot Streets (numbered 88 Callahan) on the second floor.

They placed radio calls to summon the medical examiner, a detective from the District Attorney's office, and the local police photographer and fingerprint expert.

Detective Sergeant Andy Illman of the Office of the District Attorney has also testified. He stated that as a result of a call, he went to the intersection of Depot and Callahan Streets, arriving there at about 2:48 a. m. He spoke to various officers and viewed the body and the vehicle in which it was located before the body and vehicle were removed from the scene. He walked from the "death car" north on Depot Street some 35 or 40 feet to the corner. He was now standing on the southwest corner of the intersection. He looked to the right, or to the east. Across Depot Street, on Callahan (on the south side of Callahan) there was an empty lot on the corner. About 100 feet from the corner was a church rectory. There was a tree in front of the rectory. Just east of the tree was a street light, and the light filtered through the tree branches (which were without leaves at that time). Across the street from the rectory were houses—the single family type. Between two houses was a driveway. This driveway was bordered on its sides by a hedge about four feet high, and the hedge was also located in front of both of those houses on the sidewalk line.

He looked to his left. On the south side of the street (where he was located) were all multi-tenanted wood frame dwellings. Each contained at least three apartments, one to each of three floors. If one walked in a westerly direction on Callahan Street, he would, in a few minutes, come to "Trolley Square" where an all-night coffee and doughnut shop were located.

Sergeant Illman spoke to the tenants on the first and third floors at 88 Callahan Street. Although he knocked for about five minutes at the door which provided entry to the second floor apartment, he received no response. Outside the front door to 88 Callahan Street, where the doorbells were located, there was a little card under one doorbell which had written on it: "2. N. Saxe. G. Morgan."

Sergeant Illman knew a Gene Morgan, and knew he lived in this area. After conversing with the first floor tenant a second time, the

Sergeant drove to the coffee shop in Trolley Square. He entered the shop and saw Gene Morgan seated at the counter drinking coffee. He spoke to Gene Morgan. Morgan would not speak a word. The Sergeant ordered Morgan out of the coffee shop and into the police car. Morgan did as ordered. In the car on the way to the station, Morgan said absolutely nothing.

Sergeant Illman and Morgan arrived at and entered the station at about 3:30 a. m. They were together in a room with three other officers until 6:10 a. m. before Morgan talked at all. A conversation was then held, and as a result of that conversation, Sergeant Illman and Lieutenant Martin obtained a warrant for the arrest of the defendant Stanley Benton.

Sergeant Illman and six other officers took the warrant and went to the Dowtowner Hotel in Millis Square, arriving there at 9:00 a. m. They notified the clerk at the desk of their purpose. They then went to the second floor and stationed themselves outside the door leading into Room 2C. Sergeant Illman rapped on the door. He heard "rustling sounds" inside the room, but no one responded. He called out loudly: "We are police. We have a warrant for the arrest of Stanley Benton. Open the door." There was no response. The Sergeant repeated the message in a loud voice. Again there was no response. The Sergeant then used a key given to him by the hotel clerk to open the door. He rushed inside, gun drawn, and the other police followed him. The entranceway was a corridor about five feet wide and four feet long. Once through that entranceway, the left wall continued on a straight line, but the right wall cut at a right angle to the right, and the room widened to about 15 feet. There was a double bed to the right. Beyond it was a clothes closet, where the door was ajar, and there were clothes hanging from the top of the door.

Stanley Benton was standing beyond the foot of the bed. He had shorts on and was pulling a T-shirt over his head. Still in the bed was Michele Nissen, age about 25, with a sheet and blanket covering her up to the neck. The Sergeant jumped on the bed with his gun pointed at the girl. He pulled the bed covers from her. She had no weapon. She was unclothed.

One of the other officers had his gun pointed at Benton, who finished putting on the T-shirt, then raised his hands. Benton was served with the arrest warrant, and was told that he was being placed under arrest for the murder of Nathan Saxe. "Miranda Rights" were read to him from a card.

Next to Benton on the floor of the room were men's socks, jeans, a tan colored "leather look" jacket and a pair of shoes. On the right sleeve of the jacket, the Sergeant saw what "appeared to me to be blood stains." Benton was permitted to dress, but the jacket was placed in a plastic bag obtained from one of the police cars. It was tagged appropriately by the Sergeant, and turned over to Officer Jane Richmond (evidence officer) when she arrived at the scene.

Sergeant Illman, at the request of the prosecutor, reproduced on a blackboard a sketch which he had executed and made a part of his official police report. The sketch depicted the area in the vicinity of the intersection of Callahan and Depot Streets. The Sergeant originally executed the sketch on the afternoon of February 2, the day on which Nathan Saxe met his death.

. . .

Gene Morgan, at the police station, on February 2, at about 6:10 a. m., talked to Sergeant Illman and Lieutenant Martin. The conversation was tape recorded, and a transcript (copy of which was supplied to defense counsel shortly after the return of the indictment) reads in part as follows:

MORGAN: I think I can talk now that you've taken a paraffin test. That will show that I didn't fire a gun.

MARTIN: Gene, why have you kept quiet this long? Don't you know it makes things look worse for you?

MORGAN: I knew you guys thought I did it, because I didn't call you right after it happened, I was scared. You watch one guy fire five or six times point blank at anothey guy, and you'd be scared too. I knew he'd kill me too if he could find me. I was scared, man. I didn't look in the car or nothin'. I knew Nathan was dead. All I wanted to do was run—even after Stan and Michele was gone.

MARTIN: Stan who? Michele who?

MORGAN: Stan Benton and his girl friend Michele. I don't know her last name. It was them that done it.

. . .

MORGAN: Last Wednesday. Nate and I were at the Silver Fox Lounge downtown. We left the place about 10:15 p. m. and headed for the parking lot across the street. We were feeling good—maybe staggering a bit and jostling each other in fun. Maybe we were slow crossing the street. I hear these tires squeal as an old Caddy stops at our left. Benton was in the passenger's seat. His girl Michele was driving. Benton lowers his window and yells: "O. K. odd couple. Outta the way." Nate takes nothin' from nobody. He knows Benton packs a gun. But Nate slams his fist on the Caddy hood. Benton got out and seemed to be reaching inside his leather jacket. Nate caught him a good one right on the jaw. I saw blood come from Benton's mouth. He got up off the ground and said: "You're dead. Both of you. You're dead." Nate laughed. We went to Nate's car and came home.

Last night we went to the Lounge again—late. Nate was really getting loaded. I asked him to cut out the drinking or he couldn't drive home. He laughed at me. I said: "To hell with you." I left by myself, and started walking home. It was cold. The air sort of sobered me up some. It's about a mile and a half from the Lounge to our house. I walked on the north sidewalk on Callahan Street. I remember crossing Jewel Street, when I heard a car coming from the rear of me. I looked back and all I saw was two headlights, but I had a funny feeling about that car. As it kept coming, I ducked into the driveway between 92 and 88 Callahan. There's a hedge outlining the driveway about four feet high. I sort of scrunched down, so I wouldn't be noticed.

The Caddy went by me. I recognized it. I couldn't see Benton's face, but I knew he was in it. I figured the girl was driving. The Caddy continued on until it got near to Trolley Square; then it did a U-turn. It came back on Callahan Street, past Depot, and parked under the tree in front of the rectory. Now I saw the people in the car. Benton and his girl. The car engine was kept running. I saw Benton get out of the car and walk down to our front steps at 88 Callahan. He didn't know I was watching from the hedge. Next thing I know, Nate's car goes by me slowly, and makes a left turn on Depot. Nate parked in his usual spot on Depot Street.

I saw Benton come from the steps, to the corner, around the back of Nate's car, and to the driver's door. He rapped on the window with his left hand. The car engine was turned off by Nate. I see the driver's door start to open; then Benton's hand, with an object in it, went inside the car. He fired twice. I could see the inside of the car light up as he fired each time. He pulled the door all the way open, put his left hand inside the car and took his left hand out again. Then, he fired some more—three or four times, I think.

Next, he leaves Nate's car, runs to the passenger's door of the Caddy, and they take off. I'm sick to my stomach, and shaking like a leaf. I just ran to get away—when I saw the lights on in the all-night doughnut shop, I went in. I just kept ordering coffee.

. . .

MORGAN: I'm sorry I ran. I'm ashamed I didn't go across the street to see if I could help Nate. I feel a little better now that I know I couldn't have done anything. But—I knew you cops knew about my record and would figure me for the killing right away.

PROBLEM

LAW FIRM # 1. You are the prosecutor. You will choose and prepare a person to play the role of Gene Morgan. You will conduct a direct examination. In the cousre of the examination you will make use of the chalk drawn upon the blackboard by Sergeant Illman to have Morgan illustrate his testimony. You will also introduce in evidence two photographs of Nathan Saxe's car.

LAW FIRM # 2. You represent the defendant. Make appropriate objections and be prepared to explain the bases for them.

ASSIGNMENT #9

NATALIE KAHN v. IVY SCHAEFFER AND IDLE HOURS LOUNGE

PROBLEM

The entire class is responsible for this assignment. The instructor may call on anyone to perform any portion of it.

ASSUME that evidence has been introduced which would warrant a jury in finding:

a. That on July 1, Yr.–2, Natalie Kahn was a passenger in the left rear seat of a four-door Pontiac sedan operated by her fiancé, Bill Sowar.

b. That the "plaintiff vehicle" was travelling north on a State Highway where the northbound lanes are separated from the southbound lanes only by a double white line.

c. That a Cadillac, operated by Ivy Schaeffer, headed south, crossed the double white line and collided left side to left side with the Pontiac, while both cars were travelling 55 m. p. h.

d. That Ivy Schaeffer, a 55 year old woman, had been drinking at the Idle Hours Lounge, just north of the accident scene; that she was served, after midnight, a total of six ounces of Scotch, and that the accident occurred at 1:00 a. m.

e. That the Idle Hours Lounge had, until June 1, been allowed by municipal permit to remain open and serve customers until 2:00 a. m., but that on June 1, the Licensing Board had revoked that portion of the permit allowing the Lounge to serve liquor after midnight.

f. That, subsequently to the accident, Ivy Schaeffer and Natalie Kahn were transported by the Police in the same ambulance to Memorial Hospital, a charitable hospital.

g. That a sample of Mrs. Schaeffer's blood was taken two hours after the accident, and forwarded to the State Police Chemistry Laboratory at 2008 Northern Boulevard. The result, a percentage of alcohol in the blood of .22 (which would give rise under G.L. c. 90, § 24 to a presumption that she was heavily under the influence).

h. That Natalie Kahn suffered a skull fracture, a crushing fracture of the left orbit of the eye, a comminuted fracture of the left cheekbone, a fracture of the right femur, and multiple pelvic fractures. Her left eye was enucleated surgically. An intramedullary rod was inserted in the right femur.

1. There has been introduced in evidence a poor quality 8″ x 10″ black and white photo showing the damage to the left side of the Pontiac.

Doctor Jeff Maleson is on the stand. You are to ask him a hypothetical question, using the exhibit, designed to show the causal relationship between the force of the accident and the injuries sustained by your client, Natalie Kahn.

2. You are Natalie Kahn's attorney, and you have in your possession an 8″ x 10″ black and white photo which was given to you by Doctor Maleson. It shows the right thigh of the young lady. During her hospitalization, Natalie's right femur fracture was reduced surgically and an intramedullary rod was inserted. The photo shows a lengthy scar and heavy cross stitch marks. You are to have the doctor identify the person, a portion of whose anatomy is shown in the picture. Conduct the interrogation necessary as a foundation for introduction of the photo in evidence.

3. Assume that you, Natalie's attorney, have another photo; that the young lady was fitted with a temporary artificial eye during her hospitalization; that the photo shows that the level of the artificial eye does not correspond with the level of the right eye. Assume that the effect is shocking! Would you want to introduce such a photo? Explain.

4. Please explain, chronologically, the steps you took in your preparation of the case, as Miss Kahn's attorney, to introduce in evidence the materials necessary to enable the jury to make the findings set forth in paragraph "e" on the first page of this assignment relative to the Idle Hours Lounge's permit and its partial revocation.

5. Assume that, after a month of hospitalization, Natalie Kahn died. Assume that this action was brought by the administratrix of her estate. You represent the plaintiff. Pose to Doctor Maleson a hypothetical question showing the "causal relationship" between the death and the injuries suffered in the accident. The remainder of the class will be prepared, on behalf of the defendants, to object to the question.

6. What steps would you take before and during trial, and what evidence would you introduce to prove that, at the time of the accident Mrs. Schaeffer was under the influence of liquor?

Chapter Eight

CROSS AND RECROSS EXAMINATION

A. CROSS–EXAMINATION—ITS PURPOSE

The purpose of cross-examination is two-fold: it should bring the spotlight to bear on the credibility of the witness, and it should elicit material in addition to that which has been brought out in direct examination. In most jurisdictions, the scope of cross-examination is limited to those topics touched in direct examination.[1]

B. THE DECISION NOT TO CROSS EXAMINE

Trial lawyers are by nature and training gladiators. They love combat. Although they may not admit it, the desire to destroy an opponent or a witness called by the opponent is strong. This witness is destroyed when he can be shown to be lying, mistaken, biased, fork-tongued or otherwise short on virtue. The battlefield is generally provided when the witness has completed his direct examination and stands helplessly ready for your withering cross-examination.

More difficult than exposing the witness to the jury's contempt or disbelief is the decision *not* to cross-examine. The impulse to launch into a lengthy cross-examination must be resisted at times.

If a witness has not hurt you, don't cross-examine him. If a witness has not hurt you and cannot help you, don't cross-examine him. If he has bruised but not mortally wounded your client, don't cross-examine him unless there is a reasonable likelihood that you can "shake him" or turn around his testimony to a point where it materially helps your case. The judgment required to know when *not* to cross-examine is always founded on a thorough grasp of the facts of the case.

C. THE ETIQUETTE OF CROSS–EXAMINATION

There is no Emily Post or Amy Vanderbilt handbook on the manners and mores of cross-examination. However, there is an irreducible minimum of precepts which every trial lawyer must observe. They are embarrassingly obvious but nonetheless vital. A violation of some may constitute unethical conduct.[2]

1. Fed.R.Evid. 611(b).

2. E. g. EC 7–25.

1. *Don't Shout at the Witness*

Neither judge nor jury will look kindly on you if you shout at the witness. The American spirit of fair play is offended when you yell or bark.

2. *Don't Turn Your Back on the Witness or on the Court*

When you are addressing the witness or the court, *never* turn your back. This is the height of incivility. Most judges will abruptly call you on this violation of good manners. It may appear "smart" to you to ask the witness a question while you are walking away from the witness. It is not smart because it is rude.

3. *Don't Sneer at the Witness*

If you have succeeded in exposing the witness to a blatant self-contradiction or to a ridiculous conclusion, pause for the jury to savor it and then proceed or sit down. Don't sneer.

4. *Never Be Vulgar*

From time to time, a witness will be called upon to testify as to the exact language used by someone. This language may contain vulgarity. Don't repeat this language unless it is absolutely necessary. Jurors may use vulgar language in their own conversations, but they do not expect it in a courtroom. They resent it as lese majesty on the part of a lawyer who is an officer of the court.

D. DANGER OF OVER-KILL

There is no substitute for a thorough knowledge of human nature in the successful trial of law suits. Human beings are the raw material of all cases. They are the instruments through which a case is proved and the triers of fact are also human beings, jurors or judges. If you seek success in the trial of a case, don't forget the simple conventions of polite society.

Once you have "scored" by exposing the witness as a liar or as one who is mistaken or by rendering his testimony beyond belief, stop. Don't bury the witness with further scorn. The jury will react sympathetically to the demolished witness. Once you have made your point, stop.

E. SCOPE OF CROSS-EXAMINATION

In most jurisdictions and in the Federal Court, cross-examination is limited to the subject matter of the direct examination and to matters touching the credibility of the witness.[3] A careful cross-examiner will not permit the witness to wander or to nail down those matters to which he has testified in direct examination. The cross-examiner

3. Fed.R.Evid. 611(b).

controls the scope of the interrogation because he is asking the questions. Accordingly, when you are cross-examining, narrow the inquiry to those matters which can be helpful to your case. Select your target with great care and shape the course of your cross-examination to pinpoint just those areas on which the witness has displayed vulnerability. Once you have struck successfully, don't linger in the area because the witness will try to "explain away" the admission.

F. LISTEN TO WITNESS'S ANSWER BEFORE ASKING NEXT QUESTION

Don't dismiss as puerile the admonition to listen carefully to the answer of the witness before asking the next question. The answer may be joltingly revealing. It may lead smoothly to the next question. It may also warn you not to ask a certain question.

There is a dispute among trial lawyers as to the efficacy of preparing questions in advance of cross-examination. It would seem almost impossible to prepare in detail a substantial number of questions because the cross-examiner cannot know what the answers to all his questions will be. Better to prepare *subjects* for coverage in cross-examination, leaving the fashioning of specific questions to the moment after you have received an answer.

Careful attention to the answer of the witness may provide a clue to a new and hitherto unthought of area for exploration in cross-examination.

G. THE ARGUMENTATIVE QUESTION

A question which is more informational than inquisitive is generally argumentative. "Do you mean to tell this court and jury that when you came upon the scene of this vicious crime at 9:30 P.M. at the corner of Drake and Paris Streets, you did not see Billie Chapman, slashing Lorretta Gump with a blood stained switch blade?" The cross-examiner is testifying in this case. He wants the jury to believe that Chapman slashed Lorretta with a switch blade. However, the cross-examiner is not under oath. He is not a witness. This is dirty pool and the trial judge may castigate the cross-examiner who has the cheek to try it.

An inoffensive and helpful form of question may start with, "Isn't it a fact that you were present when Chapman first spoke to Lorretta on the night about which we have been speaking during this trial?" Don't ask it if you are not sure that the witness was present. Limit the scope of the "Isn't it a fact . . ." type of question.

H. THE "WHY" QUESTION

There may be one isolated instance when it is not dangerous to ask "why" on examination, but it is difficult to think of it. Bear in mind that you are cross-examining a witness called by your adversary and you have elected to cross-examine him because he has harmed your cause in some way. You would not opt to cross-examine if you thought that you could not gain some ground or at least neutralize the ground gained by your opponent.

The question introduced by "why" is devastatingly broad. It permits the witness to explain more thoroughly than permitted on direct examination. He can testify to his inner thoughts and arcane motivations. Once you have asked the "why" question, you are helpless in shutting off the witness.

In that extraordinary instance when there is only one possible answer which the witness may give, you may chance the "why" question. However, the odds are against the possibility of this hypothesis.

I. DON'T REPEAT ANSWER AND NAME OF WITNESS BEFORE ASKING EVERY QUESTION

If your goal is to send the jury on a daydreaming enterprise, then continue to repeat the answer of the witness. Q. "Did you see Jack with his jacket on?" A. Ya, I did. Q. Now, you say that Jack was wearing a blue jacket, tell us whether it was buttoned or not." And on it goes until the judge and jury wish that they were anywhere but in the courtroom listening to you examine or cross-examine this witness.

Equally annoying is the habit of repeating the name of the witness every time a question is propounded to him. Perhaps there is warmth in mentioning the name of the witness before asking the *first* question, but don't overdo it. Q. Miss Gentile, are you aware that the defendant is deaf in one ear? Don't punctuate every question with, "Miss Gentile . . . ."

J. BLUNTING THE EFFECT OF THE EXPERT WITNESS

The expert appraiser called by your adversary has wounded your case. You will never be able to entice him into a contradiction or a denial of his opinion. His credentials are overpowering. His appearance is persuasive. However, an appeal to candor and fairness may be helpful. After all, real estate appraisal is not an exact science. Experts differ. A change in just one small factor which was used in arriving at the appraisal will change drastically the ultimate appraisal value. At least three of the ten constituent parts of the expert's opinion based on reproduction cost are variables about which experts differ. These and questions of like import tend to round the sharp edges of the expert's opinion. An expert appraiser who clings doggedly to every figure in his work-up may be seen as doctrinnaire by the jury. This impression is helpful to you.

Similarly, the medical doctor whose testimony has severely shaken your client's position that he was unable to return to work for 8 months may concede that his opinion is not cast in stone. After all, there have been reported cases of a period of disability extending beyond a year as a result of a trauma similar to the one suffered by your client. Of course, it is possible that the plaintiff's is one of those rare cases which do not respond speedily to the latest developments in antibiotics.

In a word, if your cross-examination can blunt the force of the expert's opinion, you have been successful. Don't try to lead him into a flat withdrawal or contradiction of his opinion testimony.

K. IMPEACHMENT—IN GENERAL

A person is said to be impeached when he is discredited or degraded. Credibility of a witness is essential in the trial of a case. When the testimony of a witness is demonstrated to be false, the trier of fact will not believe the witness. If the witness can be shown to be unreliable in one area, you may ask the jury during argument to believe him as to everything to which he has testified.

It does not follow, of course, that because a witness was mistaken in his testimony about part of the case, that he should be discredited in his testimony concerning an unrelated part of the case. The fact that a witness has difficulty seeing a distance of 200 yards does not translate into difficulty in hearing noises in the next room.

A witness may be impeached by showing a record of conviction for a crime,[4] by demonstrating bias or prejudice, by showing impairment of his sense faculties and by the introduction of prior inconsistent statements.[5]

L. IMPEACHMENT—CONVICTION OF CRIME

An adroit use of the discovery tools available to a lawyer before trial should reveal the name and address of any witness to be called by the opponent. If the jurisdiction in which the case is being tried maintains a central index of convicted criminals, a check of the index is in order. If you find that one of the persons to be called by your

4. Fed.R.Evid. 609.

5. Fed.R.Evid. 613.

opponent has a record of conviction, you may want to use it in cross-examination.[6] Care should be exercised. Not every conviction is helpful to you. For example, if public drunkenness is a crime in this state, you may not wish to use a conviction for this crime because of the sympathy which may be created for the witness in the minds and hearts of the jury. This judgment is especially true if such a conviction is isolated and remote in point of time. A conviction for a serious felony or for perjury, on the other hand, may prove to be just the devastating weapon that you need to demolish the testimony of this witness.

Statutes and rules vary as to the time periods within which a record is admissible.[7] The customary method for impeaching a witness, whether he be a party or not, is a form of questioning in which it becomes clear that the witness is the same person named in a certified record from which you are reading. After the witness acknowledges that he is the same John Smith who on July 30, Yr.–4 was found guilty of perjury in the Superior Court of Lakeside County and sentenced to 3 years in the state prison, you should offer into evidence the record itself. The witness is not permitted to comment on or explain the conviction. Many cross-examiners wait until the end of cross-examination to introduce the record. Others will lead off with it. The experts differ and your judgment may be as good as theirs in this regard.

M. IMPEACHMENT—BIAS OR PREJUDICE

It is open to you to show that a witness's testimony is false because he is particularly friendly with your opponent and that he would lie or distort the truth out of friendship. It is also within your competence to demonstrate that the witness has harbored a strong enmity for your client for many years. It follows, at least you so argue, that he will color the truth to hurt your client. Common experience points out the weakness of this method of impeachment. Antipathy for a person does not mean that perjury will follow, and friendship does not mean the end of truthfulness on the witness stand.

A common rhetorical question propounded under these circumstances is, "And, of course, Mr. Johnson, you want to do everything in this case to help your friend, Charles Plaintiff, don't you?" Such a question should not be used because the witness may very well rejoin that he would like to see his friend assisted, but that he would not, under any circumstances, commit perjury.

6. Fed.R.Evid. 609.

7. Fed.R.Evid. 609(b).

N. IMPEACHMENT—IMPAIRMENT OF PERCEPTIVE FACULTIES

The witness who is presented to you for cross-examination may have won medals for telling the truth in the past, but you may be able to demonstrate that his testimony should not be believed. He may respect the truth but suffer a handicap which makes it difficult or impossible for him to learn the truth. A person with blurred vision at a distance of 100 yards or more should not persuade the jury as to what occurred 300 yards from his vantage point. One who suffers hearing difficulties should not be permitted to leave the witness stand unchallenged after testifying to what he heard whispered at a distance from him.

A skillful cross-examiner may be able to demonstrate the effect of the witness's faulty memory. This strategy is accomplished by asking the witness a question about something which took place in court a few days before the day on which you are cross-examining him. The advantage of this method of impeachment is that the witness need not be disemboweled of his self respect and thereby become an object of the jury's sympathy. His testimony can be discredited without a character assassination.

O. IMPEACHMENT—PRIOR INCONSISTENT STATEMENT

The testimony of a witness may differ materially from statements which he has made on prior occasions. It is to your advantage to expose such inconsistency.

However, a word of caution. You must first set the stage by asking the witness whether he made a statement concerning this matter on a prior occasion, furnishing, where possible, the date, time and place of the statement. If he denies making such statement, you may offer extrinsic evidence of such statement through the testimony of another witness. It is wholly unethical to ask whether he made an earlier statement inconsistent with his testimony if you are satisfied that he did not make such statement. This is "dirty pool." [8] If you detect such a maneuver by your opponent, act immediately to demand an assurance that extrinsic evidence will be produced to prove the earlier inconsistent statement.

P. USE OF DEPOSITION

The deposition of a witness may be used in cross-examination to impeach or contradict the witness.[9] Fairness demands that the

8. EC 7-25.

9. Fed.R.Civ.P. 32(a)(1).

witness's testimony in the deposition not be taken out of context. Accordingly, if any part of a deposition is used, the adverse party may require you to introduce any other part which ought to be considered with the part introduced.[10]

Set the stage for the witness before introducing the deposition by asking him or her whether he or she remembers answering certain questions at a certain place on a certain occasion in the past. Remind him that he was accompanied by his attorney. Don't attempt to impeach him if his prior testimony at the deposition is not *materially* different from his testimony on the witness stand. The challenging and rather argumentative question, "Well you did not say that in your deposition," is not entirely fair if the witness was not asked that question when he was deposed.

Q. RESPONSES TO REQUESTS FOR ADMISSIONS

One discovery tool which is found in all jurisdictions is the request to admit or deny certain statements propounded by the party seeking the admissions.[11] It may be called a notice to admit facts or a request for admission of facts. The party to whom they are addressed—they may not be directed to a witness—is required to admit, deny or set forth reasons why such statement cannot be admitted or denied or object to the matter requested.

This device is commonly used to secure admissions as to the genuineness of signatures and documents. The failure to admit or deny or object or set forth reasons why an admission or denial is not possible results in an admission of the matter requested for purpose of the pending matter. This admission is conclusively binding on the party to whom the request is directed unless the court relieves the party for cause.

In cross-examining a party who has responded to requests for admission, be alert as to what he has already admitted or denied. You may find him contradicting himself. If you have occasion to use the responses, show them to the party-witness first, asking whether the signature appearing thereon is his and whether he remembers signing the document. Don't permit him to "explain" his responses.

These responses are worthless to you unless you read them into the record and make them part of the evidence in the case. Admissions (and denials) which are "in the papers" cannot be considered by the trier of fact nor are they of any value on appeal.

10. Fed.R.Civ.P. 32(a)(4); Fed.R.Crim.P. 15(e).

11. Fed.R.Civ.P. 36.

R. USE OF ANSWERS TO INTERROGATORIES

Unlike the responses to requests for admissions, answers to interrogatories [12] are not conclusively binding. Interrogatories and their answers may be explained by the party-witness (they may be propounded only to parties). Hence, unless you are satisfied that the witness cannot satisfactorily explain, don't give him the opportunity of rehabilitating himself after you have exposed a contradiction.

Before use is made of the answers to interrogatories, show them to the witness, pointing out his signature and asking him whether it is his signature. Permit the witness to read the particular interrogatory and answer before you propound the question concerning them. Fairness demands that you introduce all answers which are material to the particular answers which you seek.

Answers to interrogatories are not evidence until they are introduced into evidence. Accordingly, they should be read to the jury after the court grants permission.

S. ENDING ON HIGH NOTE

It is easy to state when cross-examination should end. It is difficult to practice it. The temptation to ask "just one more question" is sometimes irresistible and almost always devastating. After you have made your points, after you have "scored," resist with all your might the seduction of one more question.

If your cross-examination has been conducted properly, the ending should be natural. It should end on a triumphant note. There is no classical denouement to cross-examination—only a deliberate abruptness. If you are in doubt as to whether you should re-explore an area already examined, drop it unless you are reasonably certain that you can gain points with the jury by the renewed foray.

T. RECROSS–EXAMINATION

The parameters of recross examination are entirely discretionary. The scope is delimited by the matters covered in redirect examination. Recross-examination should not be attempted unless you are certain that you can gain a real advantage. If you succeed in "scoring," beware of the danger of over-kill. Limit your attack to a narrow area. If you must conduct recross, limit your thrust to the most vulnerable area of the witness's testimony.

12. Fed.R.Civ.P. 33.

EXERCISE 1

D's counsel has just completed his direct examination of Rocco, his most important witness. Rocco described in detail the unprovoked beating of D administered by P. D's defense to P's action for assault and battery is self defense. Rocco has a long criminal record. You have certified copies of all his convictions. You represent P.

What preliminary steps will you take? Describe how you will introduce these records.

EXERCISE 2

Herbie, an important witness for P, has just completed his description of the scene of the accident immediately after the collision of P's car and D's truck. He did not testify as to where he was when he viewed the scene. Your investigation reveals that he was on his front porch, 30 yards away. He had consumed a 6 pack of beer and a few glasses of muscatel.

Describe in question and answer form your method of impeaching Herbie.

EXERCISE 3

W has just testified on direct examination that D, your client, said when he packed a knife in his belt before leaving his apartment, "I'll get that bum (victim) tonight." D is indicted for assault and battery by means of a dangerous weapon, to wit, a knife on V to whom W referred in quoting D.

Three months after the stabbing, W told A, his friend, that on the night of the stabbing he met D for the first time in the bowling alley where the stabbing took place. W also told A that he (W) saw D grab V's knife and stab V after V had knocked him (D) to the ground.

Describe how you will impeach W with this information.

EXERCISE 4

Podlink has just completed his testimony for P. He has contradicted himself by testifying substantially differently from his testimony in a deposition taken by D.

How will you expose these contradictions?

EXERCISE 5

In a formal admission in response to a request for admission, D conceded that Jackson was acting within the scope of his authority when he signed the contract in behalf of D. On the witness stand during his direct examination, D said that Jackson had no authority to sign the contract.

You are trial counsel for P. How will you handle this?

EXERCISE 6

The plaintiff in response to interrogatories of D said that D's car was traveling 20 m. p. h. immediately before impact. On the witness stand, the plaintiff estimates D's speed to be 40 m. p. h.

Describe how you will impeach plaintiff.

ASSIGNMENT #10

NANCY MILLER v. ROBERT AUERMUELLER, D.M.D.

PROBLEM

This is a Superior Court trial with jury. The issue of liability is being tried separately. In the event of a finding for the plaintiff, there will be a subsequent proceeding before jury on the damages.

The plaintiff Nancy Miller has testified on direct examination. LAW FORM # 1. will conduct a cross-examination.

The plaintiff's expert, Dr. Nestor Broderick, has testified on direct examination. LAW FIRM # 2. will cross-examine him.

Miss Miller has testified on direct examination as follows: She resided until two years ago in the State of California. Prior to coming to this city, she had suffered a myocardial infarction. After her recovery and discharge from the hospital, she was told by her physician that, although she was "cured," since she was about to leave the state, she should notify any doctor who treated her thereafter, of the episode and treatment in California.

A month or so after her arrival in this city, she required a dental checkup and cleaning. She was accepted as a patient by Doctor Maxwell Sonnabend. She informed Doctor Sonnabend completely of her medical history.

About a year ago, she suffered pain and discomfort in the lower jaw while on a week's vacation. On her return home, she went to Doctor Sonnabend. He told her that she had a tooth in the lower jaw which had to be extracted, and stated that he wanted to refer her to Doctor Robert Auermueller, an oral surgeon. She agreed. Doctor Sonnabend, in her presence called Doctor Auermueller, and arranged an appointment for her.

On the appointed day at the appointed hour, Miss Miller appeared in Doctor Auermueller's office. The usual paper work having been done, the doctor examined the problem, and told Miss Miller that she had an "impacted second mandibular bicuspid with a dentigerous cyst around it." Upon receiving this information "I lapsed into unconsciousness." On awakening she saw by the clock on the wall that she had been "out" for three minutes.

Upon her recovery, the doctor told Miss Miller that there was no need for her to be apprehensive. He regretted that his use of technical language might have upset her, and said that her problem was not a serious one. The fact was, he said, that the tooth would have to be extracted, but the procedure would be a simple matter, and there was no real risk involved in it.

Miss Miller said that she was a "heart patient." The doctor replied that he knew of this. He had received copies of her records kept by Doctor Sonnabend. She protested at this point that she was terribly apprehensive about herself and dreaded any kind of contact with dental or medical physicians.

Miss Miller testified that Doctor Auermueller sent her home, to return three days later for the extraction. Before the procedure began, she said to the doctor: "Are you sure there's no danger, Doctor?" He patted her on the shoulder and said: "Now don't you worry. There's nothing to it. You'll be perfectly okay."

Five days after the procedure, Miss Miller still suffered from paresthesia of the lip and gum. She went to Doctor Auermueller's office, and he said: "Look, I make a mistake. I cut the mental nerve, and that's the source of your problem."

When she asked how long it would take before the situation corrected itself, he said: "It's permanent."

END OF EXCERPT OF DIRECT TESTIMONY
OF NANCY MILLER

. . .

Factual Background. Miss Miller visited her attorney. One month later he instituted this action seeking damages. In the pleadings filed in Court, Miss Miller contends that Doctor Auermueller failed to act with the care and skill to be expected of an oral surgeon practicing in this State, in that he negligently performed the procedure so that he cut the mental nerve. She also complains that he failed to inform his patient of a known danger inherent in such a procedure when obtaining the patient's consent.

. . .

EXCERPTS FROM PLAINTIFF'S ANSWERS TO INTERROGATORIES, SIGNED UNDER THE PENALTIES OF PERJURY.

Q. 3. On the occasion of your first visit to the defendant's office, did you inform him of the fact that you had, in the past, suffered a myocardial infarction?

A. 3. I told him that I was a heart patient.

Q. 4. If your answer to the preceding interrogatory is in the affirmative, recite in as much detail as possible, the precise words you used in informing the defendant that you had suffered a myocardian infarction.

A. 4. I told him that I was a heart patient.

. . .

Q. 8. Did you, in substance, state, at any time, to the defendant that you understood that the failure to remove the tooth in question would pose a very substantial risk to your health and well-being?

A. 8. Yes, but only after he told me there was no risk involved.

[Further answer required by the Court, on motion. The answer was stricken. The further answer was simply "Yes".]

Q. 9. On the occasion on which you "blacked out" or lost consciousness in the defendant's office, were you under the influence of alcohol, narcotic, or medication?

A. 9. I had Valium, but was not "under the influence".

Q. 10. Please recite as precisely as possible what, if anything the defendant said to you concerning any risk to the proposed extraction.

A. 10. He said that there was no risk involved at all. He said: Don't worry. There's nothing to it. I guarantee that you'll be okay. I guarantee it.

. . .

Q. 21. Are you the same Nancy Miller who, in the Superior Court for the County of Los Angeles, on January 11, Yr.__, pleaded guilty to possession of heroin with intent to sell, and received a suspended sentence of no less than 5 nor more than 10 years, with a probationary period of 6 years?

A. 21. Yes.

Q. 22. Did you, on November 22 of last year, file an application for a motor vehicle operator's license?

A. 22. Yes.

Q. 23. Did you answer the questions posed in that application, under the penalties of perjury, and sign your name to it?

A. 23. Yes.

Q. 24. If your answer to questions 22 and 23 are in the affirmative, what was your answer to the question: "Have you any physical or mental disability?"

A. 24. I assumed that the question referred to disabilities by reason of which a doctor had advised that a person should not drive, so I answered the question in the negative.

[Further answer required by the Court on motion. The answer was stricken, except for the words "I answered the question in the negative.]

SUMMARY OF TESTIMONY OF DOCTOR NESTOR BRODERICK ON DIRECT EXAMINATION.

The doctor testified that he practiced oral surgery in this state for almost forty years before retiring. He was asked to assume the truth of Miss Miller's testimony, which was recited by plaintiff counsel in great detail. Counsel concluded his hypothetical question as follows:

"Doctor, assuming the foregoing facts to be true, have you an opinion, based upon reasonable certainty, as to whether the conduct of Doctor Auermueller, when he cut the mental nerve in the course of the extraction, conformed to that degree of skill and care reasonably to be expected of an oral surgeon performing such a procedure in our dental community?"

The doctor answered that he did have an opinion, and when asked to give that opinion, was faced with an objection by defense counsel, to the effect that, since the doctor has retired, he is no longer qualified to testify as an expert witness. The Judge ruled that, since the doctor had testified that on the date of the extraction he was familiar with the standard of care expected to be exercised under the circumstances, his retirement is of no consequence. The doctor was permitted to answer. He stated:

"My opinion is that in all probability Doctor Auermueller was NOT negligent in performing the extraction."

Defense counsel exclaimed: "Well, thank you, Doctor!" This drew a prompt reprimand from the Judge. Plaintiff's counsel asked for the reasons behind the opinion, and the doctor replied: "The cutting of the mental nerve, in and of itself, is not proof that the doctor performed the extraction with anything but skill and care to be expected of him. The cutting of that nerve is always possible. We dentists all know that, and know that it can happen regardless of the amount of skill you possess and care that you exercise. I cannot say that the Doctor was negligent in performing the extraction, but he was guilty of another breach of duty to his patient."

Defense counsel moved that the last sentence be stricken as unresponsive to the question, and the motion was granted. The Judge instructed the Jury to disregard it.

Plaintiff counsel now asked: "Doctor, have you an opinion, based upon common accepted practice among dentists and particularly among oral surgeons as of the date that the extraction was done, whether there was *any* breach of duty by this doctor to his patient? Again, assuming the facts I outlined as being true." Upon receiving an affirmative response, counsel asked for the opinion.

The Doctor: "He failed to obtain consent properly from his patient." Another motion to strike was allowed.

Plaintiff counsel: "Doctor, have you an opinion as to whether good practice at that time required Doctor Auermueller, under the circumstances then existing, to have given any information to his patient concerning the procedure, before he began it?" This time there was no objection and the Doctor gave his opinion: "Good practice required that he tell his patient of the danger posed by this extraction; that the mental nerve was located somewhere in that area, and that there was a chance that it might be cut, resulting in paresthesia."

END OF EXCERPT OF DIRECT TESTIMONY
OF DOCTOR NESTOR BRODERICK

The defense law firm assigned to cross-examine the plaintiff's expert, Doctor Broderick, may assume:

(1) That, in answers to interrogatories, plaintiff had identified Dr. Broderick as the expert expected to testify at trial.

(2) That, upon receipt of the answers, an investigation was done of the doctor's background.

(3) That the investigator's report reveals that:

a. That doctor and the trial attorney for the plaintiff, a member of LAW FIRM # 3. are close personal friends. They golf together once a week, and both have invested in a realty trust with extensive holdings in a large condominium out of state.

b. In the comparatively short time since the doctor retired, he has testified in two other malpractice actions in which the same lawyer represented the plaintiff. You have obtained copies of the transcript of his testimony in those actions, but the transcripts have not provided any useful material for cross-examination purposes.

c. You have checked the State Medical Library, and have obtained a copy of an article published in the New Journal of Dental Medicine, authored by Doctor Broderick. The article is entitled "Malpractice and Dentistry," and at page 341 (Vol. XXI, No. 3) you have found the statement: ". . . The latest 'trend' is for plaintiffs to allege that the dentist failed to obtain 'informed consent' from the patient before performing the procedure. Such a claim is easily manufactured by unscrupulous patients who are bitterly disappointed with an unfortunate dental result, and should always be viewed with suspicion. . . ." At page 342 appeared the following: ". . . No dentist can be expected to explain to his patient every possible risk. Indeed, if one is dealing with a patient who is unduly apprehensive it becomes almost a duty on the part of the dentist not to mention the risk, for fear of aggravating the apprehension. This is certainly true when a risk is minimal. It seems to the author that the greater the danger created by the disclosure, the more the freedom of the doctor not to disclose. . . ."

PROBLEM

LAW FIRM # 3. will represent the plaintiff and will choose one of its members to register and argue objections during the cross-examination of Nancy Miller. Another member of the firm will register and argue objections during the cross-examination of Doctor Nestor Broderick.

ASSIGNMENT #11

MAURICE KING, ADMINISTRATOR v. TOWN GAS COMPANY

This is an action of tort, brought against the Town Gas Company, a corporation, by Maurice King, individually and as administrator of the estate of his late wife, Sonya King. The plaintiff seeks damages for his own personal injuries and property damage, and for the conscious suffering and death of his wife, allegedly sustained by reason of an explosion of gas in the King house on the first day of January, Yr._2. The action was brought in the Superior Court. Both parties claimed a trial by jury.

From the testimony introduced by the plaintiff, the jury would be warranted in finding the following facts:

The defendant's gas main, which ran by the plaintiff's home, was the source of the gas which exploded. The main was of two inch steel. It was laid in Yr._15. In January of Yr._4, when the plaintiff's home was built, a Skinner service saddle and gas cock were attached to the main three feet below street surface. A one inch house service pipe was run from the gas cock to the house. When the explosion occurred the main was carrying gas under 9 pounds of pressure per square inch. Within an hour after the explosion, vapor tests were taken in the earth over the saddle and cock and gave "100%" gas readings. Excavation showed that the main ran north and south; that the main was bowed down gradually for five feet on either side of the saddle and cock and that gas was escaping freely from the main where the saddle no longer clamped tightly about the main.

In Yr._4, when the service pipe was being installed, a trench had been excavated for the installation of a sewer by a local contractor. In this trench the gas main, for fifty feet on either side of the saddle and cock, had been exposed. To support the saddle and cock during this work, gas company employees had placed a vertical block of wood under it. When the trench was "backfilled," the vertical block was left in place.

Plaintiff called to the stand a retired gas company supervisor who, having qualified as an expert, testified that customary procedure followed by most gas companies at that time under such circumstances was to remove the vertical block when the backfilling was to be done; then to place horizontal pieces of wood under the saddle and cock, and at intervals of five feet under the gas main. The purpose of this procedure, said he, was to allow the main to settle gradually at all points, and to prevent bowing. He was of the opinion that, as a result of having left the vertical block in place, the saddle and cock were held in position while the main on either side of it sank; that this broke the "seal" of the saddle on the main, and allowed the gas to leak out.

On cross-examination by the defendant's attorney, plaintiff's expert admitted that he knew that when, after the explosion, the area was excavated, a rock weighing almost a ton had been found directly over the saddle and cock. He admitted that he had been told that the backfilling was done by the sewer contractor rather than by the gas company. He denied that the presence of the rock had anything to do with the gas leak, asserting that the rock could not have had anything to do with the bowing on either side of the connection.

Defendant's motion for a directed verdict at the close of the plaintiff's evidence was denied.

COUNSEL FOR THE DEFENDANT

You have engaged the services of Albert Chace, Ph. D., metallurgist and engineer. You have in your file his report to you, submitted after he concluded an experiment requested by you. It reads as follows:

Dear Attorney:

At your request I have familiarized myself with the facts concerning the explosion at the King home on January 1, Yr.–2, and the history of the main, service saddle and cock involved in it. In my opinion the Gas Company is not at fault, for the follwing reasons.

From your client I obtained a straight ten foot length of two inch steel main. I also obtained a new Skinner saddle and cock (identical to that which had been placed beneath the surface in front of the King home) and attached them to the main at its center in the same manner in which the original saddle and cock had been affixed. Both ends of the main and the cock were sealed off after gas had been introduced until it reached a pressure of 9 pounds per square inch. Now, by machine, in my presence and in my own laboratory, the main was bent downward on each side of the connection at the saddle. *No gas escaped* from this main until the bowing downward on each side of the connection was *twice* that found in the original main at the site. In my expert opinion, therefore, the bowing in the original main was NOT the cause of the gas leak.

As for the real cause, the blame lies with the sewer contractor. When the contractor did the backfilling he allowed a large rock to be placed directly above the saddle and cock. As time went by, with automobile traffic passing above the connection, and settlement of the earth taking place, the rock turned the saddle slightly on the main. This situation deteriorated until the seal was eventually completely broken.

For my usual fee, I am willing to testify to the foregoing effect in court.

One other matter is worthy of comment. I am informed that the plaintiff will advance the theory that the vertical blocking under the saddle and cock, and the absence of horizontal blocking, was the cause of the bowing of the main. Even if there were some logic to the claim, I was a consultant at that time to a number of gas companies. I am prepared to state that it *was* customary to leave vertical blocking in place. Ordinarily the wood rots quite quickly and does not affect the process of gradual and even settlement of the main. No gas company should be held to anticipate that piece of wood would last as long as this one did, beneath the surface of the street. Furthermore, even if it should have been anticipated that the wood would not rot, the bowing was not the cause of the leak, as explained hereinbefore.

PROBLEM

DEFENSE ATTORNEY. Call Mr. Chace to the stand. Qualify him as an expert. Conduct his direct examination.

PLAINTIFF ATTORNEY. Cross-examine the expert.

. . .

LAW FIRM #__2__. represents defendant.

LAW FIRM #__1__. represents plaintiff.

Chapter Nine

OBJECTIONS AND MOTIONS AT TRIAL

A. OBJECTIONS—IN GENERAL

The objections for discussion in this chapter are those addressed to evidence, or more accurately to what is offered as evidence. A knowledge of the rules of evidence, then, is important. Clearly, not everything which seems to be evidence qualifies as such.

It is crucial to this discussion to realize that a judge cannot rule on the admissibility of evidence in a vacuum. A question asked of a witness or an answer of a witness may be admissible for one limited purpose and inadmissible for all other purposes. It is impossible to determine admissibility without knowing the purpose for which the testimony or document is being offered. For example, classic hearsay consists of a statement offered in evidence in court but made by one outside of court when the statement is offered to prove its truth. The witness testifies: "Charlie Magoun whispered to me and Mike that Billie Plaintiff stole $5,000 from his boss over the last few months." It is perfectly clear that this statement is not admissible to prove that Billie Plaintiff stole from his boss. However, if the witness is testifying in an action of defamation brought by Billie Plaintiff against Charlie Magoun, the testimony is admissible. In this instance, when the court asks the question as to the purpose for which it is being offered, the plaintiff will reply: "To prove that the defendant, Charlie Magoun, said it." To this extent, it is admissible as something which the witness heard. The basis for its admissibility is the same as testimony as to what a witness saw at the intersection in a motor vehicle tort case. Hence, always identify the purpose for which the evidence is being offered.

B. OBJECTIONS—PURPOSE

In polite company, we don't abruptly interrupt a person who is speaking and say, "I object." We may not agree, but a fundamental canon of urbanity is to permit the person to talk before confronting him or her with our disagreement. While trial lawyers are enjoined to be polite, they should not be required to allow a witness to answer a question which offends the rules of evidence. If the question is inoffensive but the answer is a transgression, you have the obligation as an advocate for your client to move to strike the answer. Of course, you should make your objection politely but firmly.

The following are some good reasons for interposing objections.

1. Evidence which offends a rule of evidence may be considered fully by the trier of fact if no objection is made and sustained. Testimony which is blatantly hearsay is entitled to full probative force if left unchallenged.

2. If you are counsel for the defendant, you should be ever alert to the possibility of a directed verdict in your favor. If you succeed in excluding evidence which offends the rules, you may reduce the plaintiff's case to something less than prima facie. In this instance, you will be entitled to a directed verdict.

3. Some inadmissible evidence is highly prejudicial to your case. You don't want the jury to hear it. Accordingly, be ever ready with a seasonable objection. Don't wait until the objectionable matter has sunk into the jury's consciousness. Ask the court to instruct the jury to disregard it. You may also ask the court to warn your opponent about any future forays into the inadmissible area.

4. Though nobody wants to lose, it may be that your only hope is on appeal. If the trier of fact does not quite see the case as you think it should be viewed, the next best thing is to bring about a reversal of the judgment on appeal.

Your appellate rights to a review of questions of evidence are dependent on your preserving your rights. To preserve your rights to appellate review, you must object seasonably. In some jurisdictions, though not in the federal courts,[1] it is still necessary to claim an exception after the ruling on your objection has gone against your position.

C. OBJECTIONS—METHOD OF MAKING

As part of trial preparation, you should anticipate those sectors which will cause you or your opponent problems. If you are going to introduce evidence which may have borderline admissibility, prepare a short memorandum of law supporting its admissibility. Cite a case or statute which is on point or closely analogous. This is part of your function as a trial lawyer. You have an obligation to assist the trial judge. After discovery has been completed, you should have some ideas as to the problems of proof which face your opponent. Be prepared to argue against offers of evidence which you think are inadmissible.

As soon as the objectionable matter in the question becomes apparent, stand (you just never object from a sitting position if you want the court to hear you) and say "I object." Some lawyers prefer the more bombastic rhetoric, "I pray Your Honor's judgment."

1. Fed.R.Civ.P. 46.

Accompanying your objection should be the grounds which you tender as sufficient to sustain your objection. "I object on the ground that the question calls for a conclusion."

If your objection is to the question, it is untimely made if interposed when the witness is answering the question. If you object to the answer—more accurately, this calls for a motion to strike—make your motion before the next question is asked. Some leeway is permitted when faced with a whirlwind type witness whose speed leaves no time in which to attend to those technical rules of objecting. You are not out of order if you ask the court to slow the witness down in this case.

In those jurisdictions which still require the saving of an exception to preserve appellate rights, after your objection has been overruled, you must then ask, "Please note my exception," or, "Save my exception," or words of similar import.

D. OBJECTIONS—TRAPS TO AVOID WHEN MAKING

1. Do not make a general objection. An objection made without specifying the ground is a general objection. If the evidence sought to be introduced is admissible for *any* purpose or under *any* theory, your unspecified objection will be overruled. Further, when you select the ground, be careful to select the correct ground. If you specify an erroneous ground, your objection will be overruled though there existed a correct ground for exclusion.

2. Be firm but polite when interposing an objection. Don't be a wiseacre.

3. Don't carp. If the court should overrule your objection, note your exception (if this rubric is required in your jurisdiction). Don't argue with the judge.

4. Only a few words are required to preserve your rights in making an objection. This should not be the occasion for a speech or an argument. If the court invites argument on the point, then accept the invitation; otherwise, avoid oratory.

5. The objection is made to the court, not to your opponent. Don't argue with your opponent. Your remarks throughout the trial are directed to the witness, the court or the jury, never to opposing counsel.

E. OBJECTIONS—COMMON GROUNDS

1. *Hearsay*

The day seems fast approaching when only the poorest quality hearsay will be excluded—that hearsay which is twice or three times removed from the declarant. Until such day arrives—after all, we make some terribly important decisions in our life on no more than hearsay evidence to support them—we shall be required to know hearsay and, more importantly, we shall have to develop a "nose" for it.[2] When we hear it, we shall have to be able to detect it instantly. This attribute of perception presupposes that we know the exceptions to the rule against hearsay.[3] There is no shortcut; you must perspire in the learning process.

The recognition of and objection to it is a two-step process. First, is the witness's answer a statement of one made outside of court and presented in court to prove that it is true? Second, if it qualifies as hearsay, is there a pigeonhole or exception which makes it admissible? This mental exercise requires split second timing, but it is attainable. After you have tried a substantial number of cases, you will develop the "nose" for hearsay. You will spring to your feet almost by reflex when you perceive hearsay.

2. *Form of Question*

Form should not be permitted to triumph over substance, but a question in irregular or improper form is objectionable. Examples abound. A question which permits the witness to give a narrative, non-stop answer is in poor form. Similarly, a question which contains one or more other questions within it, an argumentative or a leading question—these are all subject to objection for form, though the substance of what is sought may be quite relevant and proper.

3. *"We've Been Over and Over This, Your Honor"*

If your opponent has enjoyed a triumph in some section of his examination or cross-examination, he may return to it even though it has been fully explored. This should evoke an objection from you on the ground of repetitiousness.

4. *Irrelevancy and Materiality*

There is a difference between these verbal Siamese twins. That is irrelevant which is not pertinent to the case. Materiality speaks to the question of whether the evidence has legally sufficient weight to prove the issues in the case.

A question is not relevant if its answer bears no logical relationship to any issue in the case.[4] The name of the breakfast cereal consumed by the defendant on the morning of the day on which he allegedly bludgeoned the butcher in a robbery attempt at closing time, 6 p. m., does not relate to any issue in the case. Hence, it is irrelevant.

Agreements made by the parties before committing their contract to writing are legally immaterial and under the parol evidence rule, they are not admissible to vary the terms of the written contract.

2. Fed.R.Evid. 801, 802.

3. Fed.R.Evid. 803.

4. Fed.R.Evid. 401, 402.

As a matter of law, such earlier agreements are immaterial because they cannot tend to prove the content of the written contract. Evidence of an employee's contributory negligence in a workmen's compensation case is immaterial because contributory negligence is not a defense in such a case.

5. *Question Calls for a Conclusion*

The witness who is not an expert generally is disabled from rendering an opinion on the witness stand. It is true that some matters of everyday life are within the competence of a lay witness.[5] If a person is familiar with the characteristics of another's handwriting, he may give an opinion as to whether the writing on a document is that of the other person. An experienced driver may be permitted to give an opinion as to the speed of a vehicle, other factors being equal. These are exceptions to the general rule that only an expert can competently render an opinion as a witness.[6] There are introductory tell-tale words which should alert you to the imminence of a nonqualified opinion. When the witness starts with, "I believe" or "It is my considered judgment that . . ." or "It is incredible to me that the defendant would venture into this trap . . .", you should be ready with an objection. This language is conclusory.

6. *Self-Serving Declarations*

There is a thin line between the vice of a conclusory answer and that of a self-serving declaration. Though not all conclusory statements are self-serving, most all self-serving statements are conclusory. "I did all that I possibly could do to avoid hitting the plaintiff." This is self-serving and conclusory. It is inadmissible. "Do you think that you were at all negligent in the operation of your motor vehicle?" is a question which is improper.

7. *Parol Evidence Rule*

The rule that the failure to object constitutes a waiver and permits the trier of fact to consider for its full probative force the objectionable evidence does *not* apply to evidence which offends the parol evidence rule. The reason is that this rule is one of substantive law and not of evidence. However, it is unwise not to register an objection when your opponent attempts to introduce evidence of prior oral agreements tending to modify the ultimate document which purportedly contains the entire agreement of the parties. Exceptions to the rule should be understood. These include a showing of fraud, conditional delivery, subsequent agreements and clarification in the face of an ambiguity.

8. *The Document Speaks for Itself*

If your opponent hands the witness a document which has been marked as an exhibit and asks the witness to explain what is meant

5. Fed.R.Evid. 701.

6. Fed.R.Evid. 702, 703.

by the first sentence of the third paragraph, you should object. The document is the evidence, not the gratuitous interpretation of it given by the witness.

There are unusual circumstances which might justify such a question. If the witness is a signatory to the document and if there appears on the document a clearly ambiguous term which means nothing standing alone, in his discretion, the judge may allow a party to explain the usage of the term in the trade or business and any discussion about the term between the parties before they signed the document. In this instance, the evidence is not introduced to contradict, to add to, to eliminate from, or to modify the written document. The sole purpose of this testimony is to explain.

On another occasion, the court may permit you to ask the witness to read a portion of the document. If you wish to examine or cross-examine the witness about some part of the document, it is helpful to the jury to hear the language about which you are desirous of examining the witness before your examination starts.

9. *Best Evidence Rule*

Most lawyers will not insist on the original document if satisfied that the copy which is being used is an exact copy of the original. True, the best evidence is the original.[7] True, you can insist on its production or an explanation as to where it is and why it has not been produced. True, you can require the court to make the preliminary findings which may or may not excuse the production of the original. However, it is generally better practice to examine the copy and in a burst of largesse which will not be lost on the jury say, "Let the copy go in."

10. *Hypothetical Question*

If your opponent has not given you a copy of the hypothetical question which he is going to propound to the expert witness, listen carefully to each hypothesis. Be alert to an assumption about which there has been no evidence. Be equally alert to those assumptions about which there has been disputed evidence. As to the latter, you will have the right to ask the witness whether his opinion would be the same if the evidence were as some of the evidence indicated, though not as the question was asked. If you discover a hypothesis in the question about which there has been no evidence, object before any answer is rendered but after the question has been completed. The expert will probably be asked first whether he has an opinion before he is asked what his opinion is. Object after the question is asked. It is in this precise area where instant recall of the evidence is a useful attribute.

7. Fed.R.Evid. 1001, 1002, 1003, 1004.

11. *Lay the Foundation*

In some jurisdictions, before a witness can be impeached by a showing of a prior inconsistent statement, the examiner is required to lay a foundation. The foundation consists of asking the witness whether he ever visited a certain place, whether he met a certain person there at a particular time on a specified date. Then he is asked whether he ever told such person whatever is inconsistent with his testimony on the witness stand in this case.[8]

A foundation is required if the admissibility of the evidence which you seek to introduce is dependent on preliminary findings by the court. Business entries and declarations of a deceased person are examples of evidence which require the court to make qualified findings. Ask the qualifying questions first. If you neglect, your opponent will object to the failure to lay the required foundation.

F. RESPONSE TO OBJECTIONS

If an objection is interposed to your question, you should be prepared to respond. If the court invites a response, make it short but to the issue raised. If the court rules adversely to you without asking for a comment from you, ask the court: "May I be heard, your honor?" Unless the question or issue is beyond dispute, the court will probably permit you to argue. However, don't argue before the jury. Ask for permission to go to the side bar with the court reporter. The court may insist that you argue from the counsel table. In this instance, you have no option.

You should not ask to be heard on every adverse ruling unless they are all plainly wrong. The jury may very well conclude that you are a "sore loser" or a captious critic. One signal quality of a good trial lawyer is his ability to rebound after several encounters with the court in which he emerges on the short end of the ruling. When you are permitted to argue your position on the evidential issue, don't be petulant. Set forth your arguments and await the court's ruling. If adverse, save your rights for appellate review and return to the interrogation of the witness.

G. OFFER OF PROOF

If you are conducting the direct examination of a witness and an objection to a question is sustained, you may want to indicate to the court what the witness would say if permitted to answer. This is an offer of proof.[9] It should be made at the side bar after permission is granted to approach the bench and to make the offer. Its purpose is to give the appellate court a basis for deciding whether the ruling was correct in the light of the expected answer. Also, if the ruling was

8. Cf. Fed.R.Evid. 613.

9. Fed.R.Evid. 103(a)(2).

erroneous, it permits the appellate court to determine whether any prejudice was suffered by its exclusion. It is not sufficient to demonstrate error on appeal. The error must be harmul and prejudicial. Without an offer as to what the witness's answer would have been, it is generally difficult if not impossible to demonstrate prejudice.

There are two methods for making an offer of proof. In one instance, you indicate at the side bar that if the witness were permitted to answer this question he would say thus and so. This is the more commonly accepted method. In the other mode, the jurors are excused and the witness is asked on voir dire to answer the question.

H. MAKING THE RECORD

It has been said that all good trial lawyers try their cases with one eye on the record and the other on the witness. Preserving a good record requires concentration.[10] When an adverse verdict is returned, all is not lost if you have preserved (or more accurately, made) a good record for appeal. Objections followed by exceptions (if the jurisdiction requires them) preserve your rights. Whenever possible, induce the judge to give reasons for his rulings (experienced judges probably will refuse) because in this way you may be able to demonstrate an erroneous ruling.

When examining a witness about an exhibit, refer to the exhibit's number and to the particular piece or line in the exhibit. This will permit the appellate court to focus on the precise material which you claim is the source of the error.

Ask the judge to permit the court reporter to record the conferences which you may have at the side bar or in the lobby.

I. WHEN NOT TO OBJECT

You will experience a measure of compulsion to stand and object every time you hear an objectionable question or answer. Train yourself to evaluate the question or answer before objecting. If your opponent is an inexperienced lawyer, you may find yourself objecting to every question. This may build sympathy for your adversary and for his client. If an answer to an objectionable question cannot possibly harm your case, let it go. Don't press at every turn.

When your opponent begins to ask a series of questions which are improper, ask for a bench conference. You have the right to request the judge to rule preliminarily on the line of inquiry and the type of questions which you suspect are in the offing at this juncture.

10. Fed.R.Evid. 103.

The court often will accommodate you and forbid your opponent to pursue this line of interrogation or this type of question. You may use this device to attack both the substantive area of his interrogation and the form of his questions.

If the witness continues to make unresponsive and objectionable answers, you may ask the court to instruct the witness to listen more carefully to the questions and to answer the precise questions asked without going on a frolic of his own making.

The question of when not to object is one of pure judgment. Some of this expertise is played by ear. Just keep in mind the possible hazards of over-objecting.

J. LIMITING INSTRUCTIONS

If your opponent has succeeded in persuading the court that a certain question is admissible for a limited purpose, it is your task to ask the court to give a limiting instruction. The jury should be told immediately that such evidence is offered only for the limited purpose of identification or for whatever purpose it qualifies. Don't make the mistake of letting such an instruction pass until the court gives its final instructions to the jury. It is too late then. The jury has already been influenced by the evidence.

K. MOTION FOR MISTRIAL

Misconduct on the part of a party, an attorney, the judge, a juror, a witness or a third person may bring about grounds for a mistrial. When the judge declares a mistrial, the case must be tried again unless, if it is a criminal case, protection from double jeopardy prevents its retrial. Not all mistrials are declared because of misconduct. Occasionally, circumstances beyond the control of all parties may cause a mistrial. Some examples of problems which may result in mistrial follow.

1. *Attorneys*

Instructions given by the court immediately after an improper remark by counsel or by a witness will generally be sufficient to cure any prejudice that may be caused. However, if an attorney makes inflammatory remarks during his opening, his examination of a witness or in his closing argument, a mistrial may be the only remedy. Of course, the court may consider a contempt action against the offending attorney, but that course of conduct does not remedy the harm done to the jury's consideration of the case. You should not be conspicuously sensitive in this area because the court is not prone to grant a mistrial unless it is the only remedy. It is a last resort. Many judges will censure you if you make the motion for mistrial within the hearing of the jury. Accordingly, if you deem it necessary to make such a motion, ask to approach the bench and spread it on the record out of the hearing of the jury.

2. *Witness*

A witness who is caught up in his examination or cross-examination may blurt out a remark which is exceptionally prejudicial. For example, he may disclose that one of the parties has an extensive criminal record. Such evidence is not admissible unless the party takes the witness stand and then only fairly current records are admissible within the discretion of the trial judge. He may not allow any record to be introduced. Hence, the disclosure by the witness is harmful beyond repair.

3. *Juror*

If a juror talks to a witness or a party during the trial, the court may find it necessary to declare a mistrial. The proper course for the judge is an interrogation of both the juror and the witness or party in the presence of all counsel. It may be that they discussed briefly only the weather.

If an attempt is made to reach a juror so as to influence his verdict, the trial judge will very probably declare a mistrial. The danger here is not so much an inclination on the part of the juror to find for the party whose interests were promoted by the approach. The juror probably will bend every effort to display how untouched he is and offend justice by requiring more cogent evidence before returning a verdict for the party whose interests were improperly promoted. Whichever course the juror may take, the judge should not allow the case to be decided by this jury.

Unfortunately, the demands of a free press occasionally collide with the right of a party to have his case decided by a tribunal which is uninfluenced by extraneous material. The evidence is the only basis for a verdict. If the jury has been exposed to media coverage, an inquiry must be made by the trial judge to determine what effect the exposure has had on the jury's capacity to return a true verdict—a verdict based on the evidence and on nothing else. Little or no harm is done if the newspaper carries only that part of the trial which the jury has already seen or heard. The trouble arises when the media splash across their pages information about the parties or the case which has not been exposed to the jury. A voir dire examination on a motion to suppress in a criminal case is on point. If the court has ruled that the evidence should be suppressed, the newspaper account may seriously affect the rights of the criminal defendant to a fair trial.

4. *Judge*

Regrettably, the fallen human nature of the judge occasionally will become all too evident. He will display his pique at counsel or a witness. At such times, he is not the model of the detached and impartial magistrate. He is a fallen angel. If his conduct is serious and highly likely to cause prejudice which cannot be removed by a curative instruction when he returns to himself and realizes his fault, you are required to make a motion for a mistrial. The danger is obvious. Your motion may exacerbate him the more, but you have no option beyond this motion in protecting your client from a verdict infected with prejudice. You will probably never feel more alone in your professional life than when you ask for a mistrial under these conditions.

5. *Third Persons*

A courtroom is a stage on which very serious drama is portrayed. It is real life. The stakes are quite high; sometimes, life itself is at stake. It should not shock you to learn that on such a stage, unpredictably, there are dramatic scenes. Spectators quarrel, men and women faint and family members of the parties are guilty of highly charged outbursts. When these occur, you must weigh the possibility of prejudice to the jury. You do not want to start again and retry the case if this is avoidable. If, however, it is your mature judgment that a true verdict is not likely because of these scenes, make the motion for a mistrial.

6. *Causes Beyond Control*

The illness of the judge, a juror, counsel or a key witness may require a mistrial. In the case of a juror who becomes ill, an attempt should be made to proceed with the trial with fewer than the customary number.[11]

If the jury cannot reach a verdict after a substantial period of deliberation, the court is required to declare a mistrial.

11. Fed.R.Civ.P. 48; Fed.R.Crim.P. 23 (b).

Chapter Ten

MOTIONS AT CLOSE OF EVIDENCE

A. MOTION TO AMEND PLEADINGS TO CONFORM TO EVIDENCE

Consistent with the modern largesse in the sector of amendments, the Federal Rules [1] and the laws and rules of most jurisdictions today permit a party to amend his pleadings after the trial has commenced and even after judgment when necessary. If you have offered evidence which does not touch an issue raised by the pleadings, the court may allow you to amend the pleadings at that point in the trial. If your opponent needs time to meet such evidence, the court may grant a short continuance for that purpose.

A convenient time to examine the pleadings, to be assured that there is no variance between the proof which you have adduced and the pleadings which you have drawn, is at the close of the plaintiff's evidence if you represent the plaintiff.

If you are counsel for the defendant, a valuable defense may have lately occurred to you. As early as the lightning strikes you should bring a motion to amend your answer to include such a defense. The plaintiff must be afforded the opportunity of meeting such a defense. The earlier the motion is presented, the less chance there is for prejudice to your opponent.

B. MOTION FOR DIRECTED VERDICT—CIVIL

The plaintiff is the party who bears the burden of proof though, as to some affirmative defenses, the defendant must carry the burden. Before the plaintiff knows whether he has met the burden, he must "get across the rail" by producing a prima facie case. This attainment consists of producing some evidence beyond a mere scintilla in support of every element in the case. It is not the judge's function to pass on the credibility of the evidence but only on its presence or absence for purposes of ruling on a motion for directed verdict [2] which is the device used to test the presence of a prima facie case.

The moving party shall set forth the grounds within the written motion. The filing of such a motion is not a waiver of the moving party's right to present evidence if the motion is not granted.

The trial judge should not grant a motion for directed verdict if he is in doubt. A more responsible course of action is a denial. The moving party may renew his efforts after the jury have spoken,

1. Fed.R.Civ.P. 15(b).

2. Fed.R.Civ.P. 50(a).

if then necessary, by a motion for judgment notwithstanding the evidence.[3]

There is no place in a case tried to a judge without a jury for a motion for directed verdict because a judge does not render a verdict. A judge makes findings. The jury alone renders a verdict. At the close of the plaintiff's evidence in a jury-waived civil case, counsel for the defendant should file a motion to dismiss, setting forth as grounds that " . . . upon the facts and the law the plaintiff has shown no right to relief." If the court does not allow his motion, the defendant is not precluded from offering evidence. The litmus is the same whether it is a motion for directed verdict or a motion to dismiss—has the party with the burden of proof introduced *some* evidence beyond a scintilla to support every element of his case? For example, in a medical malpractice trial, the plaintiff has not made out a prima facie case if he has introduced evidence only as to the physician's negligence in treating her and an injury. The gaping hole should have been filled with some evidence of the causal relationship between the negligence and the harm.

Long before the trial, you should have made a list of the elements to be proved. As some evidence is introduced on each element, check this element off the list. Make a short summary of the evidence given by each witness. When the time arrives for you to argue for or against a motion for directed verdict, this summary will be helpful.

Mechanically, the motion for directed verdict and its jury-waived counterpart is argued outside the presence of the jury. It is your opportunity to tell the court about the *law* of the case. Use the laundry list of elements of the tort or contract. Demonstrate by recalling the evidence whether some evidence has been introduced as to each such element.

C. MOTION FOR DIRECTED VERDICT—CRIMINAL

At the close of the government's case, you, as defense counsel, should file a motion for directed verdict if you are satisfied that the prosecution has failed to present a prima facie case. If there is any doubt about this question, resolve it by filing the motion. The concept is the same whether the case is civil or criminal. A prima facie case is one in which the government has introduced *some* evidence on every required element of the crimes for which the defendant is being tried, including those lesser crimes included within the crimes set forth in the indictment.

In the federal courts, the name of the pleading is motion for judgment of acquittal.[4] Under the criminal rules adopted in many

3. Fed.R.Civ.P. 50(b).

4. Fed.R.Crim.P. 29(a).

states, the defendant files a Motion for Required Finding of Not Guilty. These names do not describe anything different from the motion for directed verdict. If the case has been tried without a jury, a motion to dismiss or a motion for directed finding may be required, depending upon the name used in the particular jurisdiction.

It is essential for defense counsel to be alert to the evidence which the government has introduced. Check off the laundry list the evidence as to each required element. If there is an element at the close of the government's case which does not bear a check, reevaluate the case. This void may be exactly the basis which you need for a successful motion for directed verdict.

If you are the prosecutor, place the list of required elements in a prominent place in or on the folder. It is not enough to *have* evidence of every element in the case. It is your obligation to produce it in court. A short summary of the evidence elicited from each witness is helpful when you are called upon to resist a motion for directed verdict.

If the court has not allowed the motion, the defendant may then introduce evidence. At the close of his evidence, the motion should be renewed. A new argument may be presented, if the court allows further argument.

FORM

STATE OF ______

Yellowstone, ss.

Superior Court
No. 8765

PLAINTIFF v. DEFENDANT

MOTION FOR DIRECTED VERDICT

Now comes the defendant in the above-captioned case and moves the court to direct the jury to return a verdict for the defendant on the ground that there has been no evidence introduced tending to prove any causal relationship between the acts allegedly committed by the defendant and the injury suffered by the plaintiff.

Plaintiff,
By her attorney,

September 8, Yr.–0.

____

FORM

STATE OF ______

Bremen, ss.

Superior Court
No. 482–C

PLAINTIFF v. DEFENDANT

MOTION TO DISMISS—FAILURE TO PRESENT PRIMA FACIE CASE

Now comes the defendant in the above-entitled case and moves the court to dismiss the plaintiff's case on the ground that the plaintiff had failed to demonstrate on any view of the evidence a right to recover.

Defendant,
By his attorney,

September 8, Yr.–0.

____

FORM

STATE OF BLISS

Sunshine, ss.

Superior Court
No. 1234

STATE v. JOHN JONES

MOTION FOR DIRECTED VERDICT

Now comes the defendant in the above-captioned case in which the State has indicted him for robbery and moves the court to direct the jury to return a verdict of not guilty on the ground that there has been no evidence beyond a scintilla of either force or fear.

John Jones,
By his attorney,

September 8, Yr.–0.

____

ASSIGNMENT #12

RUTH SWEFINGER v. DAMIEN COLMAR

This is an action of tort for personal injury. The plaintiff is Ruth Swefinger, a widow, age 52 at the time of trial. She is represented by LAW FIRM # 1. who will choose a person to play the role.

The defendants are Damien Colmar, M.D. and his wife Jill. Each is age 35. They are represented by LAW FIRM #__2__. who will choose persons to play these roles. The defendant firm will also choose someone to pay the role of Courtney Colmar, who was four at the time of the incident, and is six at the time of trial.

The jury has been impanelled. The opening has been made by plaintiff, and a motion for a directed verdict on the opening statement, filed in writing by defendants, has been denied.

PROBLEM

PLAINTIFF FIRM: Call Ruth Swefinger as your witness. She MUST testify on direct examination in accordance with a statement that she has given to you, in writing, as follows:

I am Ruth Swefinger, now 50 years of age. I am a widow. I was married to Brent Swefinger. He died five years ago. He was an executive with an electronics firm. I receive benefits from his life insurance—approximately $8,000 a year which I will continue to get until I die. When Brent passed away, I obtained a job as an assistant librarian, working 30 hours a week at $3.50 an hour. I have also been a free-lance writer for more than 20 years—doing historical "fillers" for newspapers and magazines. A "filler" is a very short composition—ranging from a paragraph in a magazine to a partial column in a newspaper. I earn about $1,000 to $1,500 a year with this type of writing. I have submitted full-length articles on "historical" personalities to magazines like Reader's Digest (one or two a year) but have had only one accepted (the month before my injury). I was paid $250 for an eight-page article on Dolly Madison which appeared in a popular monthly magazine.

I enjoy bowling—candlepins. Every Tuesday and Thursday night I bowled in a "mixed" Church league, and averaged 102 per string.

My life, however, was lonely, and except for Tuesday and Thursday nights, I had a lot of free time. I love children, but never had any of my own. I'm a good cook, too. So—a couple of years ago I started advertising in a local newspaper for babysitting jobs. I specified that I was available weekends from 5 p. m. on Friday to midnight Sunday.

I was surprised at the response. Two weeks each month, on the average, I was engaged to babysit. Doctor and Mrs. Colmar had never called on me, however, until the doctor phoned me one Wednesday evening. He said he had seen my "ad" and asked if I'd be available Friday at 5 p. m. to Sunday at midnight. I said "Yes". He asked my charge and I said it depended on the number and ages of children. He said there were two: a son, Sean, age six, and Courtney, a daughter, age four. He told me they had a dog. I said I'd charge $40; that I would tend to the children and the dog, that I would cook and do just minor housekeeping chores. He said: "That's fine. My wife and I are going down the shore with a bird-watching group. I'll pick you up at 5 p. m. Friday at your apartment."

At 5 p. m. on the dot he appeared, and he drove me to his home. During the drive, he talked constantly about his medical practice. I couldn't get a word in edgewise. It was about a ten-minute drive. When we got to his home (a beautiful ranch-type house with a circular drive, and a tennis court, and a swimming pool), he rushed ahead of me to the front door. He rang and his wife opened the door. She was ready to leave. She said hello when I was introduced. Then she turned to Sean and said: "Don't you forget to feed the dog and the cockatoo." I said: "What's a cockatoo?" And she said: "Don't worry. It's just a bird. Its cage is in the dining room. Sean will feed it." Then she told her husband they'd better rush if they were going to beat the heavy traffic, and off they went.

That night went smoothly enough. The children showed me the house. I recall vaguely seeing a bird cage in the dining room, but I don't remember what the bird looked like except that it was in the cage.

I made fish cakes, which the children enjoyed very much. We ate in the kitchen. At 8:30 p. m., after watching some television, I put the children to bed. Each had their own room. I asked them what they wanted for breakfast next morning, and they said they always had bacon and eggs. I went to the living room to watch the TV. At about 9:30 p. m., I heard Courtney crying. I went to her room. She was just lonesome and said she wanted her mother. I lay on the bed with her, sang her a couple of songs, and soon she dropped off to sleep. I returned to the living room. I went to bed myself just as the "Tonight" show was coming on.

Next morning I awoke at seven. I was in the kitchen when the two children came in. I told them they'd have time to wash up before breakfast. Each of them went to their own bathroom. I finished the bacon and laid the strips out on a heavy brown paper. I kept some of the fat in the frying pan, and was frying the first three eggs. Suddenly I heard a fluttering sound to my left. I looked and saw a large bird coming directly at my head! It flew right at me. I was shocked. I turned by head to the right. The bird landed with its claws right on my eyeglass frames. I swung at it, but it seemed to be caught. I was so surprised I stepped backwards and fell—hard. The glasses fell off and the bird flew away.

I had terrible pain in my left hip and my left hand. I screamed for help. The children came. One of them—Sean—ran to a neighbor's house and in about 15 minutes the police arrived and I was taken to Cooperative Hospital.

While I was lying on the floor, I asked Courtney about the bird. She said the bird was allowed to fly around the house. When Sean came back, I asked him if this was true and he said: "Sure. All the time. Daddy is very proud of the bird. The bird flies onto people's heads and Daddy always gets a big laugh out of it. The bird never hurt anybody before."

I was in the hospital seven weeks. Being a part-time employee at the library, I don't get medical insurance or sick leave. I had to pay my own hospital bill. It took $4,000 of my savings. My doctor charged me over $2,500 because he had to "pin" the hip fracture and reduce the colles fracture in my wrist.

I'm left handed. I haven't been able to bowl since that bird knocked me over. I can type, and have been able to do so since six months after the accident. My hip troubles me in wet and cold weather. The doctor says I've developed traumatic arthritis.

Doctor Colmar visited me only once in the hospital. He said: "I'm sorry. It was stupid of me not to tell you about the bird flying about the house. I just forgot. Don't worry, though. We have $100,000 worth of liability coverage on our homeowner's insurance policy. We'll be able to settle this claim easily."

. . .

DEFENSE COUNSEL: Object to objectionable questions. Move to strike answers or portions of answers when the occasion requires. Then, CROSS-EXAMINE Mrs. Swefinger. Your investigator has turned up nothing but "good reports" about this lady.

. . .

PLAINTIFF COUNSEL will now call as a witness the six year old Courtney Colmar. DEFENDANT will object. The Judge will conduct a hearing on the competency of Courtney to testify. At its conclusion, both parties will be permitted to argue, briefly. The Judge will make his ruling.

If Courtney is permitted to testify, she will state on direct that she remembers Mrs. Swefinger. She is the "lady who fell in the kitchen and screamed." She will not have any memory of any conversation with Mrs. Swefinger. She will remember a bird, but won't know what kind it was, except that it had more than one color on it. She will recall that the bird used to land on her father's head, but nobody else's. She will describe the bird as being about the size of a pigeon. When asked "Where is the bird now?", she will remember that one day her brother left the kitchen door open and the bird flew out, and they haven't seen the bird since.

DEFENDANT will decline to cross-examine.

. . .

PLAINTIFF will introduce the hospital record and bill, with the assent of the defendant. It establishes that Mrs. Swefinger suffered a linear fracture of the head of the left femur and a colles fracture of the left wrist.

. . .

PLAINTIFF will now introduce the bill of the doctor. It gives the dates and places of treatment, the treatment rendered, itemized charges, and is executed in accordance with the statutory requirements.

PLAINTIFF will offer a copy of the written notice to the opposing party of intention to offer the bill at the trial. DEFENDANT will not object.

. . .

PLAINTIFF WILL NOW REST

. . .

DEFENDANT will offer a written MOTION FOR DIRECTED VERDICT at the close of plaintiff's evidence. The Judge will excuse the Jury and hear argument on the motion. Each side will be permitted no more than four minutes.

. . .

If the Judge denies the motion for directed verdict, DEFENDANT will call Doctor Damian Colmar to the stand.

When he is asked his name and address, the doctor will not only give the information requested, but will start to "rattle off" his medical qualifications. PLAINTIFF will take the appropriate steps to stop him. The doctor will then testify as follows:

He and his wife owned the home in question (free of mortgage, of course). Their children on the date of this incident were Courtney (now six) and Sean (now eight). Sean is away at a military school. Mrs. Colmar is presently keeping an appointment with her psychiatrist, but is expected in court at any time.

Yes, they owned the bird, but it was NOT a cockatoo. The bird on Baretta's program is a cockatoo, but "ours was a cockatiel, a much smaller bird, about the size of a large canary or a small pigeon." The bird was allowed to fly freely about the house, but never landed on "anybody's head but mine." This was a "one-man bird." He had never frightened anyone on any other occasion, and shouldn't have been frightening to Mrs. Swefinger. She was told about the bird. "Just as I and my frau were leaving the house, I heard Mrs. Colmar tell Mrs. Swefinger distinctly: "We have a cockatiel. It is free to fly in the house. If it bothers you, just tell Sean to lock the bird in his cage." I am positive these were the very words used by my wife.

Q. Doctor, do you know what "scienter" is?

A. Of course, it means "knowledge."

PLAINTIFF: Objection.

JUDGE: Your objection comes too late.

Q. Did you have any "scienter" of a propensity on the part of your bird to fly directly towards persons other than yourself?

[PLAINTIFF will NOT object.]

A. Absolutely not. He had never done it before.

PLAINTIFF: Motion to strike.

JUDGE: Denied.

PLAINTIFF: My objection to the ruling.

JUDGE: Noted.

The doctor will be asked if he visited Mrs. Swefinger at the hospital, and he'll answer that he dropped in "on several occasions." All he remembers of conversation is that he expressed sorrow over the lady's injuries. He will add, without another question being put to him: "Wait a minute. I do recall that I told Mrs. Swefinger I'd pay her medical bills if she wouldn't make a claim. I'd still do it if she'd drop this silly lawsuit."

END OF DIRECT EXAM

PLAINTIFF COUNSEL WILL NOW STATE: "I do not care to dignify this witness with cross-examination."

DEFENDANT will object and give the grounds for the objection at a side bar conference.

DEFENDANT will now look about the room, and see that Mrs. Colmar has just entered. He will request a five-minute recess to "speak to the witness". DEFENSE COUNSEL will state to the doctor: "That's my job sir. Your Honor, may I have five minutes?"

THE JUDGE: You may not. Put your witness on the stand, if you wish.

. . .

DEFENDANT WILL CALL MRS. COLMAR. She will identify herself as one of the owners of the house, but when asked if she owned a bird, she will state that she did not. She will then explain that the bird was bought by her husband, and the bird was strictly his.

She will be asked if she recalls Mrs. Swefinger, and will state that she does; that she recalls Mrs. Swefinger coming to the house on the Friday that she and her husband were going down to the shore, but she will state that she does not recall her conversation with Mrs. Swefinger. She just remembers that she had a conversation, and that it was about the children and the pets.

PLAINTIFF will decline to cross-examine.

. . .

DEFENDANT WILL REST

. . .

DEFENDANT will file another motion in writing—a motion for a directed verdict at the close of all the evidence.

THE JUDGE will excuse the jury.

COUNSEL FOR BOTH SIDES will file "Requests for Instructions to the Jury" (no more than six requests per party). The Judge will listen to brief argument on the Motion. If he denies the Motion, he will indicate the action he will take on each request. Any party aggrieved by the judge's action will take the steps necessary to protect rights on the record.

. . .

Chapter Eleven

CLOSING ARGUMENTS AND JURY INSTRUCTIONS

A. CLOSING ARGUMENT—PURPOSE

The last opportunity that you will have to persuade the jury directly is your summation. If you represent the defendant, you will argue first, unless the court for exceptional reasons permits the batting order to be changed.[1] As plaintiff's counsel, you will have the last advocate's word. The judge has the verbum ultimum because he instructs the jury in the law after the attorneys have given their summation.

The purpose of final argument is two-fold: first, to convince the jury that your client deserves to be given the verdict; second, to persuade them to render such a verdict. Appeals to reason and logic tend to convince, while persuasion works on the will.

A weak case can be won with an extraordinary closing argument, but don't look for miracles if your case is hopeless. Prepare well in advance for the closing argument.

B. CLOSING ARGUMENT—A FEW SUGGESTIONS

1. *A Pleasant Opening*

It is neither unethical nor insincere to thank the jury for their courtesy and attention during the trial. Some lawyers like to caution the jury about taking offense at the lawyers for objections interposed. "It is all part of the trial. It is our job to object when we detect what we think is an objectionable question or answer. Please don't take affront at our conduct." Such an admonition is helpful.

2. *"Your Memory Controls"*

Before you begin to recall the testimony of the many witnesses, tell the jury that if they find a disparity between what you recall and their memory, they should rely on their collective memory. You would never deliberately distort the testimony but, after all, you are only human and fallible.

3. *Opening Remarks Are Important*

Some lawyers incline towards an innocuous exordium. "Ladies and gentlemen of the jury, neither you nor I was at the Palladium on the night that Lispenard was shot. We were probably miles away.

1. Fed.R.Crim.P. 29.1.

We must rely on witnesses who were there or were nearby. Let's take a close look at these witnesses and the stories they tell."

4. *Examine the Testimony of Each Witness*

Under certain circumstances, it is good strategy to examine the testimony of each witness. Don't use this technique if any one witness was devastatingly adverse to your client's case. You cannot afford to recall only those witnesses whose testimony was helpful to your cause. If no witness demolished your case, take each one and "explain" the testimony. Be bold to ask the jury to draw inferences favorable to your client, wherever possible. If this cannot be accomplished, impeach those witnesses whose testimony or character permit impeachment.

5. *Comment on Opponent's Opening*

If you took notes during your opponent's opening statements to the jury, use those notes in the presence of the jury. It conveys the impression that you are not relying on your memory alone. Point out that your opponent said that he would prove such and so, but failed. "Where was the evidence of speed that he said he would present?" is a powerful rhetorical question. This strategy is especially cogent if you are the last attorney to address the jury.

6. *The Law of The Case is For the Judge, But . . .*

It is the judge's duty to instruct the jury in the law of the case. Some judges are especially sensitive about this duty and guard it jealously. In their sessions, lawyers are cautious to the extreme in avoiding all references to the law, concentrating instead on the facts of the case. However, where possible, tell the jury what the judge will later tell them in the words which the judge will probably use. The jury will be impressed that you and the judge think alike and use the same words. This task is made easier if you have had the opportunity to see the judge's charge in advance of your argument. Don't overdo this strategy. It falls to the court to charge the jury. Your foray into the "law part" of the case should be brief and only to the extent necessary to argue the facts.

7. *Use Exhibits and Chalks*

There is no precept which forbids the use of the contract or the gun if they are in evidence. Your final argument will mean more to the jury if you use these exhibits as props for your rhetoric. Point out those parts of the contract or insurance policy which are especially material to your case so that when the jury are in the deliberation room, they will turn to these sections. The diagram which has been used throughout the trial should be available to you in summation. If it is particularly important, ask the court to permit it to go into the jury room.

Don't eschew the blackboard in setting forth the special damages about which there has been testimony. The extent to which you may use the blackboard to demonstrate damages is entirely within the court's discretion. Whenever permitted, use it for all it is worth. What the jury *sees* at this critical stage of the trial is far more impressionable than what it heard two weeks earlier.

8. *Establish Eye Contact with Jury*

Make the most of the short time when you are addressing the jury. Don't speak "above" them. Look intently at them, individually. This posture tends to impress them with your sincerity. Don't ignore the entire panel in order to heap attention on a juror who, you think, is favorably disposed to your case. You may be wrong and in the course of wooing this juror, you may alienate those jurors who are leaning in your direction.

9. *Face up to Weaknesses in Your Case*

If there are gaping holes in your case, don't ignore them. Candor to a jury is refreshing. There is generally a plausible explanation for a weakness. You can ask the jury to draw an inference favorable to your case from a set or subset of facts which may appear to be dismally unfavorable to your position. If you represent the plaintiff, tell the jury that you are not required to eliminate all possible explanations for your client's injury except the defendant's negligence. If you have demonstrated that there is a greater likelihood that your client's broken arm was caused by the defendant's negligent operation of the motor vehicle than by any other cause, you have carried your burden.

10. *Refer to Voir Dire Questions in Appeal to Fairness*

It is appropriate to remind the jurors of the questions which were asked when the jury were impaneled. "Ladies and gentlemen, you can now understand why it was so important for me to ask those questions about your thoughts on racial discrimination in public housing. The plaintiff is not entitled to any special treatment because he is a non-English speaking Hispanic who is forced to live in public housing. However, he is entitled to no less than the fair treatment which you would accord another person who suffered the wrongs of which he has complained. We look only for fairness, not special treatment. We ask only that the language barrier and depressed economic plight of the plaintiff not be a hindrance to his recovery for these injuries." A word of caution is in order. Any blatantly emotional pitch based on racial consideration will backfire. Be cautious not to stir up a contrived racial battle. This strategy is transparent.

11. *In Criminal Case, Emphasize Heavy Burden on Prosecution*

In defending a criminal case, it is generally helpful to stress the heavy burden of proof which the government must carry. Proof beyond a reasonable doubt imposes on the prosecution the obligation of convincing the jury to a moral certainty. If a juror has a reasonable doubt, the defendant is entitled to it.

12. *If Defending, Anticipate Closing Argument of Opponent*

As a result of pre-trial discovery and your exposure to the evidence at trial, you should be in a position to know quite well the course which your opponent's argument will take. If you are defense counsel, anticipate the points which he will raise. Answer them. Tell the jury that when you complete your argument and sit, you will, without doubt, think of several matters which you should have addressed.[2]

13. *Summation After Bench Trial*

Too many lawyers waive argument after a trial without a jury. They seem to think that it is wasted effort. This is generally not true. A judge is human. He wants to be persuaded. You can assist your case immeasurably by an argument in which the facts are marshalled and an appeal to logic is made. Though emotional flurries are more fitting for a jury than for a judge, your argument to the court should not be wooden. Appeal to the court to draw those inferences which are favorable to your cause. While avoiding a detailed summary of the evidence, you should not hesitate to refresh the court's memory about the testimony of an important witness.

14. *Be As Brief As Possible*

Don't overrate the attention span of jurors. In most jurisdictions, there is a time limit on final arguments. In many states, the summation may not exceed thirty minutes without leave of court granted before the argument begins. You should not feel constrained to use every minute of the time allotment. Make the points of your summation and sit down with the satisfaction that you have done all that you can do. Your opening and closing remarks should be highly polished. Don't tax the jurors' patience by a long and arduous journey through the testimony of every witness. There is an art to inducing the jury to believe that they, not you, thought of an important item in the case. Plant the seed and watch it grow. Be brief.

C. CLOSING ARGUMENT—TRAPS TO AVOID

1. *Not All Witnesses Called by Your Opponent Are Liars*

You are generally in a better position with the jury to demonstrate that those witnesses who testified against your client are mistaken persons rather than liars. There is no limit to the extent to which you can demonstrate how mistaken they are. There is a limit to the amount of obloquy which you may tastefully pour on a witness without being damaged in your own cause.

2. *Your Personal Beliefs Have No Place in the Summation*

You are an advocate. The case is not yours in a proprietary sense. It is unethical for you to tell the jury your own beliefs or feelings about

2. Cf. Fed.R.Crim.P. 29.1.

the case. Appeal to their reason, to their common sense, perhaps obliquely to their heart, but don't reveal your own beliefs.[3] Criminal convictions in increasing numbers are being reversed because of the prosecutor's error of telling the jury that he believes the defendant guilty.

3. *Avoid Commenting on Matters Not in Evidence*

It is highly improper to refer to matters which are not in evidence. If a matter is in no way a part of the evidence of the case, you have no right to mention it or to ask the jury to draw therefrom an inference favorable to your client.

4. *Don't Appeal to Prejudice or Passion*

There is a danger that as you become "worked up" in your argument, you may slip into an appeal to passion or prejudice. This can be fatal. Every good trial lawyer has self-restraint. Don't permit your rhetorical repertoire to include such base considerations.

5. *Don't Read Your Argument*

It is difficult to think of anything that will destroy the force of your summation as readily as the reading of it. Take the time to memorize it if you fear that you will forget the important parts. After some experiences, you will learn to memorize topics in a logical order. The words will come to you as the topics surface in your memory. Like a good golf swing, your delivery will be fluid. If you are still frightened about a possible memory lapse, leave a paper with the important matters on the counsel table. Return to it for refreshment when you feel it necessary. Tell the jury that you don't want to forget anything and hence you have written a few notes to yourself.

Some lawyers very effectively read their notes of the testimony of an important witness to the jury. This gesture gives the impression that you consider it important and that your recall is accurate. After reading it, put down the paper.

D. CLOSING ARGUMENT—MAKING OBJECTION

If your adversary argues a matter impermissibly, you will have to decide whether to object or not. There are several schools of thought on this question. Some lawyers believe that you should stand and object immediately when an objectionable argument is made. Another segment of the bar will never object to anything said in opening or closing remarks to the jury. It seems that somewhere in the middle, a course of conduct can be carved out to protect your client and at the same time not alienate the jury.

3. DR 7-106(C)(4); EC 7-24.

If your adversary's argument reaches the outrageous outer limits, don't allow it to go unchallenged. However, the timing of your objection is important. In most jurisdictions, an objection to an argument is not untimely made if interposed immediately *after* the argument. Of course, if the summation is utterly flagrant, in disregard of all the rules of evidence and decency, you have no option. Interrupt by objecting.

If you wait until the end of the summation to object, ask the court for permission to approach the bench. For the record, set forth the specific parts to which you object. Ask the court to instruct the jury to disregard those remarks and to tell the jury why they should be disregarded.

If you argue last, you may be able to correct forcefully some of the errors of which your opponent is guilty. In fact, the impropriety of your adversary's argument may add just the correct amount of salt to your own argument. However, not all judges will permit you to fight fire with fire. Hence, you should keep your own summation within acceptable bounds.

E. JURY INSTRUCTIONS—THEIR PURPOSE

The jury are the triers of the facts. They find the facts and their fact findings are not appealable. However, in applying the law to the facts, the jury are required to take the law as the judge instructs them. They may not apply their own version of the law of contributory negligence or accord and satisfaction. The judge will instruct them in the law and instruct them as to their obligation to accept and apply the law as it is given to them by the judge. If the judge commits prejudicial error in his charge to the jury, the aggrieved party has a right to appeal such error.

The judge, in turn, is not free to instruct the jury in the law as he or she might like it to be, but rather, the law as it is. The judge should not express his disaffection for the law as it is. He should tell the jury that until the legislature or the appellate court changes the law, it is as he or she has instructed them. It must be applied whether the jury like it or not.

F. JURY INSTRUCTIONS—THE ATTORNEY'S ROLE

Some judges will prepare a draft of their charge and submit it to counsel for comments. If this should be your good fortune, use the opportunity to suggest changes favorable to your case. You should be scrupulous in conforming your suggestions to the law. It is a flagrant violation of ethics to propose to the judge an instruction knowing it to be incorrect. Your client will not thank you for causing a retrial when the error is discovered on appeal and the rescript orders a new trial.

You might suggest examples for inclusion in the charge which are favorable to your case. You might request the judge to include some legal principles which may be persuasive in their application to your case. In any event, use the golden opportunity if the judge permits you to make suggestions and to examine his proposed charge to the jury.

G. JURY INSTRUCTIONS—DRAWING REQUESTS

Whether you have had the opportunity to examine the judge's charge in advance or not, you should prepare and submit requests for instructions to the jury. In most jurisdictions, the requests shall be filed with the court at the close of the evidence, though the judge may, in his discretion, require an earlier filing.

The requests should be as specific as you can make them. They should incorporate the names of the parties in the case and the places which have figured in the evidence. In a word, they should be personalized and not wooden. There are a few boilerplate requests, such as those bearing on the presumption of innocence, the burden of proof, the definition of negligence and the need for a majority verdict in civil cases (and a unanimous verdict in criminal cases) and the like. However, even as to these routine matters, you may request an instruction in terms of the particular case.

The requests will depend upon the nature of the verdict sought. If the jury is asked for a special verdict [4] or a general verdict accompanied by answers to interrogatories,[5] your requests should be tailored to these verdicts. The broad-based instructions which are required in a general verdict case are out of place in these instances.

A judge is not obligated to give a requested instruction in the precise language of the request. However, if the request is proper, it is reversible error to fail to give the requested instruction in some form. Make it easy for the court by not filing an excessive number of requests and by phrasing them simply in language which is congruous with the judge's style.

H. JURY INSTRUCTIONS—MAKING OBJECTIONS

If the court should instruct the jury in incorrect principles of law, or if your requests are not allowed in some form, you should object at the close of the charge.[6] Ask to approach the bench and for the record call the court's attention to the precise language which you

4. Fed.R.Civ.P. 49(a).

5. Fed.R.Civ.P. 49(b).

6. Fed.R.Civ.P. 51.

deem offensive. The shotgun approach will save no appellate rights for you. You must be specific in your claim of error.

I. REQUESTS FOR RULINGS IN TRIAL WITHOUT JURY

In most jurisdictions, counsel are permitted to file requests for rulings of law with the court at the close of the evidence. These are legal principles which should be applied to the facts in the case. They are offered as an aid to the judge. Many lawyers use them as booby traps for the court. The judge is required to rule on them. In this way, the parties know whether the judge is applying the correct principles of law. The failure to allow a correct request for ruling and the denial of a proper request may be reversible error. In a jury case, the parties know the law which the jury apply because the judge instructs them in their presence. In a bench trial, the judge applies the law in pectore, leaving the parties without any idea whether correct legal rules were applied.

Request for rulings of law should not be mixed with requests for findings of fact, which, in most jurisdictions, may be ignored or, at least, not acted on by the trial judge.

FORM FOR REQUESTS FOR RULINGS

Now comes the plaintiff and requests the court to rule as follows:

1. The defendant has the burden of proving that he and the plaintiff entered into an accord and satisfaction.

2. If the plaintiff's negligence is found to be only 50% of the total negligence, he may recover 50% of the total damages assessed by the court.

3. The failure of the defendant to admit or deny in response to the plaintiff's request for admission that he was traveling 80 miles per hour through the red light at the corner of Elm and Seaver Streets one minute before the collision is an admission which is conclusively binding on the defendant pursuant to Rule 36.

The plaintiff,
By his attorney,

____

J. REQUESTS FOR FINDINGS OF FACT—TRIAL WITHOUT JURY

Unlike the obligation connected with requests for rulings of law, the court is generally not required to act on requests for findings of fact. However, in a bench trial, the court will find requests for findings of fact a handy device for recalling the testimony of witnesses. Their value is especially pronounced in a prolonged trial. A good lawyer can help his case immeasurably if he draws requests for findings of fact with care. He can guide the court at the very moment when the case is being decided. In a sense, requests for findings of fact are more important than a brief on the law of the case because presumably the law must be applied to the facts as the court finds the facts. The lazy judge, the overworked judge, the conscientious judge—they all welcome requests for findings of fact. The requests render his task of formulating his findings and rulings easier. In most jurisdictions, the judge in a bench trial is required to file written findings of fact and conclusions of law. Help him whenever possible by submitting requests for findings of fact.

FORM OF REQUESTS FOR FINDINGS OF FACT

The defendant requests the court to find the following facts:

1. The plaintiff was an unlicensed operator of the motor vehicle at the time of the accident.

2. The plaintiff was under the influence of liquor at the time of the accident.

3. The defendant did all that was humanly possible to avoid colliding with the plaintiff's motor vehicle.

4. The plaintiff was traveling the wrong way on Elm Street, a one-way street.

The Defendant,
By his attorney,

____

K. QUESTIONS FROM JURY AFTER DELIBERATIONS HAVE BEGUN

It is not uncommon for the jury to be perplexed by a question after they have launched into their deliberations. Regardless of how careful and thorough the judge has been in his instructions, the jury will frequently find some aspect of the case a stumbling block. At this point, they will tell the bailiff or court officer of their problem. He will instruct them to write the question and seal it in an envelope. He will deliver it to the judge who will call counsel into the courtroom or lobby and in their presence read the question. The judge may then tell the attorneys how he will answer it and he may invite suggestions. The jury is then brought to the courtroom where the judge in the presence of counsel will respond to the question. These proceedings should be recorded by the reporter because they are part of the trial and appellate rights may be saved to the answer given by the court.

ASSIGNMENT #13

CARYL MC CRACKEN, ADMINISTRATRIX v. TRIPLE T MANUFACTURING CORP.

This is an action of tort, brought against the Triple T Manufacturing Corp., a corporation, by Caryl McCracken, as administratrix of the estate of her late husband, Scott McCracken, for the use and benefit of herself and her three children. The plaintiff seeks compensatory damages for the pecuniary loss suffered by the "dependents" of Scott McCracken, reimbursement for reasonable funeral and burial expense, and punitive damages for alleged willful, wanton, reckless conduct or gross negligence on the part of the defendant. The theories of liability are: (1) a breach of warranty of merchantability with respect to a crane sold to Scott McCracken's employer and (2) negligence, willful, wanton or reckless conduct or gross negligence in the manufacture of the crane by the defendant. Scott McCracken was injured December 2, Yr.–2, and died the following February 2nd. The action is in the Superior Court, and has been tried to a jury.

From depositions read into evidence, the following facts appear clearly. The crane in question was purchased by Scott's employer, Hyatt Construction Company. On the order of Hyatt, Triple T constructed it for primary use as a power shovel, although it could be converted to other uses by removing the shovel bucket and equipping it with a different boom. The machine had two sets of brakes designed to hold the bucket in the air. One foot pedal, applied with pressure by the ball and toes of the right foot, was designed to hold the bucket only while pressure was applied (similar to the function of the foot brake on an automobile). Another pedal, when pressed by the heel of the right foot, was intended to cause a locking brake to engage, and to remain engaged until released by the use of a hand-release lever. This served a purpose similar to that of a parking brake on an automobile.

The crane was delivered to a construction site two weeks before the incident. Scott McCracken alone operated the machine on working days up to and including the date of the accident, December 2nd. On that day at about 11 a. m., Scott experienced a minor difficulty. During the preceding working days, he had been excavating a ditch to accomodate the foundation of a bridge abutment. He had been scooping gravel with the bucket, lifting it up, turning to the right, and dumping the gravel in trucks so that it could be carted to another location. When the bucket was over the truck, Scott pressed a button which caused a tongue to become disengaged from a lock, allowing the bottom of the bucket to open, and the gravel to fall into the waiting truck. He would then swing the crane to the left (as the "bucket door" closed when the button was released), lower the bucket, take another scoop of earth and go through the same procedure. At quitting time each day, Scott put the bucket down on the ground in the trench. Until the morning of December 2, he did not have one occasion on which to engage the locking or parking brake, with the bucket in the air. His assistant, Charlie Freed, the "oiler," who was with Scott during the entire period, has so testified. Charlie was then on a "work release" program from a nearby correctional institution where he was servng three to five years after conviction of a felony—assault and battery with a dangerous weapon (a knife). He conceded the conviction on cross-examination.

On December 2, Scott, while scooping gravel, struck a boulder with the bucket. This caused a burr to form on the metal tongue. When Scott pressed the button to disengage the tongue from the lock, the tongue could not pull out of the lock because of the burr. This had happened at other times, with different machines, and Scott employed the usual "remedy." He swung the boom back over the trench, and lowered the bucket so that the bottom of it was about two feet above the ground. He applied the "parking" brake with his heel. He then took an acetylene torch. He lay on the ground to the right of the suspended bucket, and began to burn the burr. Suddenly the brake let go, the bucket dropped downward and to the right, landing partly on Scott, causing him to suffer severe internal injuries. The "oiler" nearby jumped into the crane cab, lifted the bucket off Scott and he was rushed to a nearby hospital.

Counsel may assume that on the date of this accident, the Wrongful Death Statute was both "compensatory" and "penal" in nature. "Dependents" in such a case are entitled to recover damages for "pecuniary loss"—their loss in net income sustained by reason of the death. Recovery may also be had for reasonable funeral and burial expense. Finally, if a jury finds the defendant's conduct to have been willful, wanton, reckless or grossly negligent, it may award punitive damages in the minimum amount of $5,000.

Counsel may also assume that a statute in effect on the date of the incident and the date of the death provided that lack of privity should be no defense in an action brought against the manufacturer of a product to recover damages for breach of warranty "if the person injured was a person whom the manufacturer might expect to use, consume, or be affected by the goods."

Assume further that a statute also in effect at all pertinent times provided that in an action for personal injury or death, the plaintiff or plaintiff's decedent is presumed to have been in the exercise of due care; that the burden of proof of lack of due care rests on the defendant; and that the doctrine of comparative negligence applies—that recovery is barred only if the plaintiff's or decedent's causal negligence exceeds 50% of the total negligence attributable causally to the injury or death. The negligence, if any, of the plaintiff or plaintiff's decedent is to be compared to the negligence of all persons against whom the action was brought.

The physician who attended Scott McCracken in his last illness testified, in part, as follows:

. . .

A. My name is Michael J. Bottalico, a doctor of medicine licensed to practice in this state since my graduation from Harvard Medical School in Yr.–20. I served my internship at Mercy Memorial and a residency in internal medicine and cardiology at Washington Hospital in Alaska. I served in the Armed Forces as a captain, Medical Corps, for two years and have been practicing internal medicine here since. I am a diplomate of the American Board in Internal Medicine, belong to the usual medical societies and am on the teaching staff of two local medical schools.

. . .

A. Scott McCracken first came under my care six years ago. He had suffered a coronary and was brought to the Cooperative Hospital where I was on emergency duty. He accepted me as his physician. I tended him during his hospital stay, which lasted three weeks.

Q. What type of treatment did you give him on that occasion?

A. The usual treatment for a slight coronary: bed rest, medication and advice.

Q. When did you next see him?

A. May I check my notes for the date?

Q. Certainly.

A. December 2, Yr.–2, when he was brought to Cooperative Hospital after his accident. His wife called my office and I went right over. Doctor Smythe was caring for the internal injuries. I was concerned only with his heart condition and high blood pressure. I treated him conservatively.

Q. How often did you see him before he died?

A. Every morning.

Q. Did something happen on the morning of February 2nd?

A. Yes. As a result of a call, I went to Cooperative Hospital, to the hallway outside of Mr. McCracken's room.

Q. What did you find when you got there?

A. I found Mr. McCracken on the floor. Nurses were about.

Q. What observations did you make of him?

A. He was dead. I pronounced him to be so. It was I who executed the death certificate.

Q. Have you an opinion based on reasonable medical certainty as to the cause of his death?

A. I have.

Q. And what is your opinion?

A. In layman's terms, a heart attack. And that was confirmed by autopsy.

. . .

Q. Doctor, based upon the facts I have asked you to assume concerning Mr. McCracken's heart condition prior to the date of the incident on December 2, and assuming the facts concerning the incident to be true, and assuming the truth of the injuries received December 2 as I have recited them for you, and assuming further the course of his treatment as disclosed by the hospital record, and assuming the truth of the contents of the autopsy report which has been admitted in evidence, have you an opinion, based on reasonable medical certainty, as to whether the injuries suffered in the December 2 incident hastened his death to any degree?

Defense Counsel: Objection.

Court: Over-ruled. You may answer.

A. I have an opinion. His injuries hastened his death to some degree.

EXCERPTS FROM CROSS–EXAMINATION

Q. Doctor, on the first occasion that you saw Scott McCracken, he was brought to the hospital, having taken a coronary?

A. Yes.

Q. Where was he when he suffered that attack?

Plaintiff Counsel: Objection! May we be heard at the bench, your honor? (Counsel approach.) Your honor, *where* he took the attack is not material. It happens that McCracken was then in a jail cell, having been engaged in a fight in a local bar. My opponent simply wants to prejudice this poor widow's rights.

The Court: Objection sustained.

Defense Counsel: Offer of proof, your honor. That the witness would state McCracken was in jail when he suffered the attack.

Q. Doctor, have you an opinion as to the sobriety of Mr. McCracken when you first saw him?

Plaintiff Counsel: I object.

The Court: Come to the side.

Defense Counsel: I expect to prove, Judge, that McCracken's drinking habits also contributed to his death.

The Court: I'll allow the question.

Q. Doctor, will you now answer my question?

A. He was grossly inebriated.

Q. Did you take a history from Mr. McCracken?

A. Of course I did.

Q. Did he tell you that he was an alcoholic?

A. Yes he did.

Q. What advice did you give him, before discharging him from the hospital?

A. I warned him to give up drinking and told him to get a sedentary job rather than a laborious one.

Q. Doctor, when you found him in the hospital hallway, had he been drinking?

A. I don't know that from my own knowledge.

Q. But you assisted in the autopsy, didn't you?

A. Yes.

Q. And the autopsy report disclosed the level of alcohol by volume in the blood, didn't it?

A. Yes.

Q. And the level that was found—what did it indicate to you about Mr. McCracken's sobriety at the time of his death?

A. That he was grossly inebriated.

Q. You didn't see anyone bring liquor to him in the hospital, did you?

A. No, and I didn't give it to him.

Q. Now Doctor, if we assume that when you met Mr. McCracken for the first time he was inebriated, and that you advised him to stop drinking and take a sedentary job; and if we assume further that he kept his job as a crane operator and was inebriated when he died of a heart attack, *those* facts would *change* your opinion that his injuries hastened his death, wouldn't they?

A. No, sir. They would not.

Q. But his disobedience of your orders also hastened his death. Am I not right?

A. Yes, sir. Just as did his injuries.

EXCERPTS FROM CROSS–EXAMINATION OF THE PLAINTIFF, MRS. SCOTT McCRACKEN

Q. Mrs. McCracken, you are now 32 years of age?

A. Yes.

Q. And the mother of the three little girls sitting in the first row of spectators?

A. Yes.

Q. Did your lawyer tell you to bring those children to Court every day?

Plaintiff Counsel: Objection.

Defense Counsel: I'll withdraw the question.

Q. Mrs. McCracken, not that there's anything wrong with it, but you're keeping company with another man now, are you not?

Plaintiff Counsel: Objection, your Honor!

The Court: To the side, counsellors. Now, defense counsel, I'm ordering you not to pursue that line of questioning.

Defense Counsel: But Judge, I believe this attractive woman intends to marry again, and I want to show it to diminish the damages.

The Court: You know better than that. The cases hold she is entitled to receive as damages the loss occasioned to her by her husband's death—loss of the money she would have received from him had he lived. Those damages can't be "mitigated."

Defense Counsel: That question has not yet been determined in this state, your Honor. Let my objection to your ruling be noted.

Q. Mrs. McCracken, your girls are aged 3, 5 and 8?

A. Yes.

[Defense counsel requests a bench conference and asks the Judge to send the children from the Courtroom.]

The Court: For what reason?

Defense Counsel: Your Honor, the damages to be awarded to a child depend, for one thing, upon the number of years a child would live with the father had he not died. I intend to prove through the mother that the youngest child has leukemia and then bring in her doctor as part of my case to show the child's life expectancy is no more than four years.

Plaintiff Counsel: I will stipulate that Elaine suffers from leukemia and that if her doctor were here he would testify that in his opinion her life expectancy is no more than four years.

. . .

Q. Mrs. McCracken, in this suit you are asking for damages for the loss of the care, guidance and companionship of your husband. Right?

A. Right.

Q. Then I ask you if it isn't true that you and your husband were having trouble during the last year of his life?

A. He brought home his week's pay every Friday that we lived together. He never failed to support me and the kids.

Q. All right, Mrs. McCracken, but he drank heavily during that last year, didn't he?

A. Other men drink too.

Q. But you called the police to the house four times that year, didn't you?

A. He only hit me once. And then he said he was sorry for it. The other times he just threatened, and the police arrived before anything really happened.

PROBLEM

LAW FIRM # 1, representing defendant, will be allowed a total of 30 minutes for argument. Two members of the firm will be permitted to argue, 15 minutes each.

LAW FIRM # 2, for the plaintiff, will argue similarly.

Chapter Twelve

POST–TRIAL PROCEDURES

A. POLLING THE JURY

When the jury return from their deliberations, the clerk of court asks the foreman whether the jury have reached a verdict. When the foreman responds affirmatively, the clerk asks for the jury slips. He shows the verdict slips to the judge who will direct the clerk to read the verdict. In a criminal case, the clerk asks the foreman to announce the verdict.

There is no uniform rule as to the right to poll the jury. Under the Federal Rules of Criminal Procedure, the defendant in a criminal case has a right to have the jury polled.[1] On the court's own motion without a request from the defendant, the jury may be polled. If the verdict is not unanimous, the jury are directed to return to deliberations or they are discharged.

In civil cases, there is probably no right to poll the jury, though it may be permitted. The verdict in a civil case need not be unanimous.

B. MOTION FOR JUDGMENT NOTWITHSTANDING VERDICT

A device used by many judges in "close" cases is the judgment notwithstanding the verdict.[2] This option is preferable to a directed verdict because if the judge erroneously allows a motion for directed verdict, the case has to be tried again to determine damages. If the motion for judgment notwithstanding the verdict is erroneously allowed, no great harm or delay is suffered because the jury have already spoken to the issue of damages.

If your motion for directed verdict has been denied, you should renew it after the verdict is returned as a motion for judgment notwithstanding the verdict. The legal principles are the same as those governing the motion for directed verdict, i. e., there was a legal insufficiency of evidence to permit the party with the burden of proof to recover a verdict. The plaintiff failed to make out a prima facie case.[3]

The motion for judgment notwithstanding the verdict shall be filed within 10 days of entry of judgment or within whatever period is allowed by the rules and statutes of the forum.

1. Fed.R.Crim.P. 31(d).

2. Fed.R.Civ.P. 50(b), (c), (d).

3. As to motion for directed verdict see Chapter Ten, supra.

In some jurisdictions the motion for judgment notwithstanding the verdict bears the name of a motion for a verdict under leave reserved.

C. MOTION FOR NEW TRIAL

In addition to the motion for judgment notwithstanding the verdict, there is provision in all jurisdictions for a motion for new trial. Under the Federal rules,[4] a motion for new trial may be combined with a motion for judgment notwithstanding the verdict. It shall also be served not later than 10 days after entry of the judgment. Common grounds asserted in motions for new trials are that the verdict was against the weight of the evidence, that the verdict was against the law, and that there is newly discovered evidence which could not have been discovered prior to or at trial and which may make a material difference in the outcome. Grounds available after a jury trial may not be useful after a trial without a jury. Local practice governs.

D. MOTION FOR RELIEF FROM JUDGMENT

The name of the motion may differ from forum to forum. In some jurisdictions, it is called a motion to vacate a judgment. Under the federal rules and the rules practice of many jurisdictions, it is denominated a motion for relief from judgment.[5]

The following are grounds which may be urged in support of the motion: mistake, inadvertence, surprise, excusable neglect, newly discovered evidence which could not have been discovered in time for a motion for a new trial, fraud, misrepresentation or other misconduct of an adverse party.[6] A motion which sets forth any of the above reasons shall be made no later than one year after the judgment was entered. Additionally, a motion for relief from judgment will lie on grounds that the judgment was void, or that the judgment has been satisfied or vacated or for any other reason justifying relief from the judgment. There is no time constraint on the latter grounds.[7]

An independent action to set aside the judgment may also be brought in place of a motion for relief from judgment. In most jurisdictions, the old writ of audita querela, the writ or bill of review, the writ of supersedeas and the like have been abolished.[8]

A word of caution is in order. Don't wax optimistic to your client about the chances of success of a motion for relief from judgment.

4. Fed.R.Civ.P. 50(b)(c)(d); For criminal cases see Fed.R.Crim.P. 33.

5. Fed.R.Civ.P. 60.

6. Fed.R.Civ.P. 60(b).

7. Fed.R.Civ.P. 60(b).

8. Fed.R.Civ.P. 60(b).

Judges are slow to grant this relief. There has to be finality to court proceedings. There are appellate avenues open to you if you are satisfied that error has been committed.

E. MOTION TO AMEND FINDINGS

Under the federal rules, within 10 days after the entry of judgment in a case tried without jury, you may file a motion to amend or to make additional findings.[9] These devices may be important to you even though you have won the case. Their importance may not be felt until the case is argued on appeal, at which time you may need the additional findings to hold your judgment.

You should examine the findings of the judge in a jury-waived case with care. There may be "holes" in the findings or inconsistencies. The judge may have ignored a crucial element in the case. An appellate court will give you short shrift if you fail to exercise all your rights at the trial court level.

F. MOTION TO AMEND JUDGMENT

A judgment as drawn may be defective for a variety of reasons. You may have prevailed but to no avail if the appellate court sets aside a judgment which could have been corrected before appeal. Clerical errors may vitiate a judgment.[10] A judgment which calls for affirmative action on the part of one party should be clear as to what it demands. There can be no remedy by way of contempt if the mandate is not clear and unequivocal.

The remedy in all these instances is a motion to alter or amend the judgment.[11]

G. MOTION IN ARREST OF JUDGMENT

If the court is without jurisdiction of the offense or if the indictment or complaint fails to charge an offense, the court will entertain a motion in arrest of judgment. It is, in a sense, a belated motion to dismiss coming as it does after the judgment has been entered.[12]

H. STAY OF PROCEEDINGS

Local law plays an important role in this area of stays, but a few considerations may be helpful. If you have had the benefit of an in-

9. Fed.R.Civ.P. 52(b).

10. Fed.R.Civ.P. 60(a).

11. Cf. Fed.R.Civ.P. 59(e).

12. Fed.R.Crim.P. 34.

junction while the case was being tried, you may now lose its benefits if the judgment is adverse. Renew, where necessary, either in the trial court or in the appellate court your application for injunctive relief pending appeal. If you did not prevail in the action, you will probably be required to post a bond or other security as a condition of continued injunctive relief.[13]

I. THE EXECUTION

Once it becomes apparent that no appeal is to be taken, an execution will issue to the prevailing party. The execution is written evidence of the judgment. In every jurisdiction, there are statutory vehicles for use in enforcing a judgment. If an attachment has been made of real or personal property, levy is now available.[14] Supplementary process or, as it was called years ago, poor debtor proceedings, may be instituted. Victory to a plaintiff is receipt of the money or the performance of the acts required by the execution. Your engagement as a lawyer is not completed until your client has received what is his due under the execution or, at least, until you have expended your efforts to collect what belongs to your client pursuant to the execution.[15]

J. STAY OF EXECUTION—CRIMINAL CASE

When a defendant has been found guilty, he may appeal. If he elects to appeal, he may file a motion for stay of the sentence pending appeal.[16] The court may grant such stay. The trial court may increase the bail or may revoke the bail. The defendant may seek a stay from the appellate court. Generally, the defendant should demonstrate a likelihood of success in his appeal if he is to succeed in securing a stay.

K. HARMLESS ERROR

One of the most sobering considerations for a trial lawyer who has failed to win is the thought that it is not enough to demonstrate error on the part of the judge. Error by itself is not helpful. At every post trial stage, counsel who seeks relief must demonstrate that the error was prejudicial. Error is prejudicial if it affects the substantial rights of the parties.[17]

13. Fed.R.Civ.P. 62.

14. Cf. Fed.R.Civ.P. 64.

15. Fed.R.Civ.P. 69.

16. Cf. Fed.R.Crim.P. 38(a)(2), (3).

17. Fed.R.Civ.P. 61.

FORM

STATE OF ______

Suffolk, ss. Superior Court
No. 2468

PLAINTIFF v. DEFENDANT

MOTION FOR ENTRY OF JUDGMENT
NOTWITHSTANDING VERDICT

The defendant whose motion for directed verdict was filed and denied at the close of evidence now moves the court for entry of judgment notwithstanding the verdict on the ground that there was no evidence beyond a scintilla of any causal relationship between the defendant's acts and the ultimate injury to the plaintiff from which a jury could return a verdict for the plaintiff.

PLAINTIFF,
By his attorney,

____

FORM

MOTION FOR NEW TRIAL

In the United States District Court for the ______ District of ______,
______ Division

UNITED STATES OF AMERICA
v.
JOHN DOE
No. ______

The defendant moves the court to grant him a new trial for the following reasons:

1. The court erred in denying defendant's motion for acquittal made at the conclusion of the evidence.

2. The verdict is contrary to the weight of the evidence.

3. The verdict is not supported by substantial evidence.

4. The court erred in sustaining objections to questions addressed to the witness Richard Roe.

5. The court erred in admitting testimony of the witness Richard Roe to which objections were made.

6. The court erred in charging the jury and in refusing to charge the jury as requested.

7. The defendant was substantially prejudiced and deprived of a fair trial by reasons of the following circumstances: the attorney for the government stated in his argument that the defendant had not taken the witness stand and that the defendant had been convicted of the crime.

8. The court erred in denying the defendant's motion for a mistrial.

____

Attorney for Defendant

FORM

MOTION IN ARREST OF JUDGMENT

In the United States District Court for the ______ District of ______, ______ Division

UNITED STATES OF AMERICA
v.
JOHN DOE
} No. ______

The defendant moves the court to arrest the judgment for the following reasons:

1. The indictment does not state facts sufficient to constitute an offense against the United States.

2. This court is without jurisdiction of the offense, in that the offense if any was not committed in this district.

____

Attorney for Defendant

APPENDIX

STATE v. GOSSET

STATEMENT OF THE CASE

The defendant, Bruce Gosset, has been indicted for indecent assault and battery, carnal abuse and murder of a six year-old girl in the vicinity of Middle Brook Park, on April 26, Yr.–2. The state contends the defendant fled to Las Vegas shortly after the crime. The defendant's alibi is that on the date of the commission of the crimes, he went to a local lounge, attended a party, returned home and spent the remainder of the evening at another lounge. He says he went to work on April 27 and did not go to Las Vegas until April 29, Yr.–2.

LIST OF AVAILABLE WITNESSES

Bruce Gosset	Defendant
Sgt. Harold F. Johnson	Police officer—homicide unit
Gerald Farr	Brother of victim
Allen Farr	Brother of victim
Joyce McKay	Mother of victim
Dr. Mark I. Snow	Medical examiner
Sean Hackett	Police officer
Nils Billert	Police officer
David Wayne	Police officer

Detective's Report

(Prior Charge of Assault/Molestation of Child)

Victim: Marcia Clarke
Suspect: Bruce Gosset

Evidence and Facts

On Sunday February 8, Yr.–2 Marcia Clarke 8 yrs. of 281 Stone Road was accosted by a black male in front of Hill Grocery Store at Thomas Ave. and Center St. about 6 p.m. Described as 6–1 195 Blk with chin beard and a scar over his eye and walked funny. Black and gray hair, this man approached her and asked her to show him where Lynn Boulevard was, said he would give her a dime; she walked with the man down Thomas Ave. and somewhere in the middle of Thomas Ave. the man stated that he was going into a house to change his clothes. The little girl accompanied man into this house, when inside a second floor bedroom the man pulled a knife and forced the little girl to put his private in her mouth, after which he put adhesive tape over the girl's mouth and eyes and led her from the building and left her in the vicinity of Lynn and Thomas St.

As a result of investigation Det. Wygandt and Deke brought several pictures to the little girl's house and in the presence of Det.

Deke and the child's mother this little girl selected a picture of Bruce Gosset Picture #147–691 as the person who did this and Warrants were issued from the District Court. Later he was indicted and was arrested in Las Vegas and returned here for trial.

Report submitted by Kevin Wygandt
Det.
Division No. 86

POLICE REPORT

STATE

v.

Bruce Gosset

OFFENSE Unnatural act Confirming and putting in fear Assault by means Date on or about 2-8-YR-2

TO COMMANDING OFFICER.

From Det. Kevin Wygandt Div. No. Two

Court none Judge none Date of trial none

Arresting Officer Sgt. Johnson Prosecuting Officer none

Complainant Marcia Clarke Address 281 Stone Rd.

Defendant Bruce Gosset Address 90 Center St.

Description of Defendant Col Male 6-1 195 Chin Beard D.O.B. 9-16-YR-32

Charge when booked at station Never Booked at Station

Charge or charges when warrant issued Assault by Means Unnatural Act. Kidnapping

Disposition Appealed Held for Grand Jury Held

WITNESSES	ADDRESS
Bonnie Clarke	281 Stone Rd.
Marcia Clarke	281 Stone Rd.
Kevin Wygandt	District Two
Roland Deke	District Two
Harold Johnson	Homicide

OVER

Form 210 [C2009]

STATE OF ______

______ ss.

At the SUPERIOR COURT, begun and holden at the City of ______, within and for the County of ______, for the transaction of Criminal Business, on the first Monday of October, Yr.–1.

THE JURORS for the State of ______ on their oath present that

BRUCE GOSSET, otherwise known as BRUCE GOSSERT on the twenty-sixth day of April, Yr.–2, did assault and beat one Margaret Farr, with intent to murder her, and by such assault and beating did kill and murder the said Margaret Farr.

A TRUE BILL

William Retzer
Assistant District Attorney

Martin V. Paulsen
Foreman of the Grand Jury

October 12, Yr.–1.

Returned into said Superior Court by the Grand Jurors and ordered to be filed.

Attest: Paul E. Oliver, Clerk.

STATE OF ______

______ ss.

At the SUPERIOR COURT, begun and holden at the City of ______, within and for the County of ______, for the transaction of Criminal Business, on the first Monday of October, Yr.–1.

THE JURORS for the State of ______, on their oath present that

BRUCE GOSSET, otherwise known as BRUCE GOSSERT on the twenty-sixth day of April, Yr.–2 in and upon one Margaret Farr, a female child under the age of sixteen years, did make an assault, with the intent her, the said Margaret Farr, unlawfully and carnally to know and abuse; and her the said Margaret Farr, then and there did unlawfully and carnally know and abuse.

A TRUE BILL

William Retzer
Assistant District Attorney

Martin V. Paulsen
Foreman of the Grand Jury

October 12, Yr.–1.

Returned into said Superior Court by the Grand Jurors and ordered to be filed.

Attest: Paul E. Oliver, Clerk.

Department of Public Safety

CHEMICAL LABORATORY
126 Eastern Avenue

Date:	5/15/Yr.–2
Lab. No.:	32498
Medical No.:	CME 6753
Date Submitted:	4/29/Yr.–2
Name of Victim:	Margaret Farr
Submitted By:	Dr. Snow
Results:	Blood:
	Alcohol = Negative
	Blood Group:
	Blood decomposed.
	Results were inconclusive.

Report to: Dr. Snow
SAM:PC

Scott A. Miller
Chemist

City of North Las Vegas

Police Department

Sgt. Harold F. Johnson
Detective/Homicide Division
(City) Police Department

March 20, Yr.–0.

Dear Sgt. Johnson:

Enclosed you will find copies of the arrest report on subject Bruce Gosset, per our phone conversation this date. The following is a resume of my investigation of a local homicide and of the different conversations I had with Mr. Gosset in reference to statements he made to this officer about a homicide that occurred in your jurisdiction.

On 9–17–Yr.–2 at approximately 6:00 P.M., this officer was assigned to investigate a homicide occurring in the City of N. Las Vegas, Nevada. The victim had been left in the desert area nude and strangled with her bra. A missing person report had been filed on 9–12–Yr.–2 at approximately 8:30 a. m., after victim's vehicle had been located in a casino parking lot.

Victim was last seen on 9–10–Yr.–2 in the company of "Bruce" described as NMA 6′ 0″, balding, mustache, approximately 31 years.

On 9–18–Yr.–2 information was received that "Bruce" may be one Bruce Gosset, living at 58 Ventura. An attempt to contact this subject was made with negative results.

An ATL was broadcast and on 9–19–Yr.–2 at approximately 10:50 P.M., a vehicle was stopped with a subject fitting Gosset's description. However, the subject had no identification in his possession, except that of a Bank of America card in the name of Donald A. Bracken. A passenger in the vehicle was also identified as Donald A. Bracken.

This officer contacted #1 subject and advised him of his rights per Miranda. He identified himself as Bruce Gosset. He related the following information.

That on 9–19–Yr.–2, he was advised by friends that the FBI was looking for him for something to do with a problem with his wife. This officer advised Mr. Gosset that we were investigating a local homicide and that we found that he was the last known person to see the victim. A statement was taken from him in relation to the events of 9–10–Yr.–2. He was further advised that it was officers of this department that had been at his residence looking for him and not the FBI. There was not enough evidence at this time to hold Mr. Gosset.

During the next few weeks, this officer had occasion to talk again with Mr. Gosset and on each occasion Mr. Gosset was aware and advised of his rights. On one occasion this officer asked Mr. Gosset why he had left (City). He related that he had lived in (City) (not relating address), but that a young girl had been killed in his neighborhood; that he knew the girl as she also lived nearby and that he had seen her; that he had moved from this residence soon afterwards. He stated that one evening at approximately 10:00 P.M. some friends had contacted him and said the police were at your old house looking for you. He related that he knew it was about the little girl and that the police had previously tried to convict him of a similar crime. He said, "I borrowed some money from my brother and I was on the bus to Las Vegas at 5 minutes to 12 that night. I knew if they caught me they would beat a confession out of me. They (the police) lied before so they could convict me of a crime I didn't do."

(City) was contacted to see if any warrants were outstanding on 10–29–Yr.–2. This officer arrested Bruce Gosset on warrants from the other jurisdiction and also on circumstantial evidence, developed from our homicide. He was again advised of his rights. During subsequent interview, subject stated that he would rather go to prison in Nevada than return to (City). He again related "they will beat a confession from me or kill me."

Due to lack of physical evidence, the homicide charge was dropped. The subject, however, related to this officer that if he didn't get the death penalty in Nevada he would plead guilty. He wanted to know the penalties involved in this State. He was advised that if he pled guilty it would probably be for Second Degree Murder, with a penalty of ten (10) years to life. He further wanted to know if he pled guilty here would (City) still come after him. He indicated that he would plead guilty to Second Degree here if I would guarantee he wouldn't have to go to (City). I told him that was not within my authority.

Due to the fact that our homicide charge was dropped, Mr. Gosset was subsequently returned to the (City) area on their warrants.

Sincerely,

Chief of Police
By: ______________
Detective Sgt.

60311–12 Grand Jury, October 6, Yr.–1.

60342–43 ADA W. Retzer

STATE
v.
BRUCE GOSSET AKA
BRUCE GOSSERT

Murder–1.
Indecent A & B on child under 14.
Abuse of female child.

WITNESS SWORN

Q. Identify yourself.

A. Harold F. Johnson, Sgt., Homicide Unit.

Q. Will you outline the case with respect to the murder of Margaret Farr.

A. On April 26, Yr.–2, about 4:30 P.M., Margaret Farr with her two brothers went to a movie on Thomas Avenue.

Q. What day of the week was this?

A. A Sunday. They left the theatre about 4:30 P.M., and crossed Thomas Avenue to the other side and when they got to the other side a man was standing there and the man spoke to them and asked if they would get him a pack of cigarettes so the three children and the man crossed the street to the store and outside the store the man gave Gerald Farr some money and told him to buy him a pack of Pall Malls.

Q. Excuse me, was it Gerald or Allen?

A. I'm not sure—one of the brothers . . . and the two boys went into the store and the man and Margaret waited outside.

When the boys came out of the store, this man and Margaret were gone. The two boys went home and told their mother and grandmother and they made another search of the neighborhood but Margaret was nowhere to be found. At 7:00 A.M. the next morning Margaret's body was found in Middle Brook Park.

Q. What was the condition of the body?

A. She had been strangled.

Q. Was there any evidence of sexual assault?

A. Yes.

Q. Do you have in your possession a report from the Federal Bureau of Investigation with respect to examination of hairs taken from the defendant and compared with those found on the victim?

A. Yes.

Q. How old was the victim?

A. Six years.

Q. Will you summarize the report from the FBI?

A. We took a lot of hairs from her clothes, underclothes, and coat and we took hairs from the suspect, Bruce Gosset, and we found that seven hairs found on the body of the girl compared with head hairs of Gosset were the same. We found two hairs compared with the pubic hair taken from Gosset to be the same.

Q. Can you tell us what the defendant did following the murder—where he went?

A. The defendant left for Las Vegas at midnight.

Q. Midnight of April 26?

A. Yes.

Q. And did you interview the defendant in Las Vegas?

A. Yes I did.

Q. And did you give him the Miranda Warning?

A. Yes I did.

Q. And following the Miranda Warning did you talk to him and ask him some questions?

A. Yes I did.

Q. Tell us the substance of this conversation you had with the defendant.

A. He said he knew the girl and that he left the City that night because of his record.

Q. Did he indicate to you that he knew a little girl was murdered and that the police would be looking for him and others as well?

A. Yes he did.

Q. When was it first disclosed to the public that a little girl had been murdered?

A. The morning the body was discovered.

Q. Was there any disclosure made, to your knowledge, that a little girl was murdered prior to midnight of April 26?

A. No sir.

JQ. What made the police tie in the defendant?

A. We went through the neighborhood where the girl disappeared and talked with people and a party had a child that had been molested and this party picked out pictures of Bruce Gosset and also it fitted the description the boys had given us.

JQ. Have the boys seen the pictures?

A. No.

Q. Was Allen Farr confronted with the defendant in the lineup?

A. Yes.

Q. What did he do?

A. Allen didn't identify the defendant in the lineup.

Q. Did he tell his mother that he had seen him—when he came home from viewing the lineup?

A. Yes, he said he told his mother he saw the man in the lineup.

Q. Why didn't he pick him out of the lineup?

A. He was frightened.

Q. Did he indicate this man made any kind of a face at him?

A. He said the man stared at him.

Q. Any questions?

JQ. How old are the two boys?

A. Allen is 10, the other one is 8.

JQ. Did Gerald have anything to add?

A. Yes, he saw the same lineup and he said that looks like the man who took my sister.

JQ. How did the FBI acquire these hairs?

A. We sent them for analysis.

JQ. Is that the usual procedure?

A. It is.

JQ. Did he resist extradiction?

A. He was unwilling at first to return but then he decided to come back voluntarily.

Q. Do you have the death certificate?

A. Yes.

Q. Will you read it please.

A. Margaret Farr, date of death, April 27, Yr.–2, female, negro, single. Cause of death: Asphyxia, strangulation by ligature. Homicide. Signed . . . Dr. Mark I. Snow.

Q. Thank you.

WITNESS SWORN

Q. What is your name?

A. Joyce McKay.

Q. Where do you live?

A. 80 Sterling Boulevard.

Q. Where were you living April 26, Yr.–2?

A. 12 Mountain Road.

Q. Are you the mother of the victim, Margaret Farr?

A. Yes.

Q. When did you last see your daughter Margaret?

A. At approximately 1:00 P.M., April 26, Yr.–2.

Q. At that time did she go somewhere?

A. Yes, my husband had sent her and her two brothers to the movies.

Q. And the three children left for the movies at approximately one o'clock?

A. Yes.

Q. And that was the last time you saw her?

A. Yes.

Q. Did you see her body on the morning of April 27th?

A. No.

Q. You didn't view the body?

A. No.

Q. Sometime, many months after April 26th, did you and your two boys go to Police Headquarters to view a lineup to see whether or not Bruce Gosset was one of the men in that lineup?

A. Yes.

Q. Did both boys go down there?

A. Yes.

Q. Were you with them?

A. No, my husband went with them.

Q. Were you still living on Mountain Road at this time?

A. No.

Q. You had moved to Sterling Boulevard?

A. Yes.

Q. Did one or both boys tell you about the lineup?

A. Yes, Allen.

Q. Allen had something to say about it?

A. Yes.

Q. What did Allen say about it?

A. He said he identified the man he seen with Margaret on that Sunday.

Q. And did Gerald say anything to you about the lineup?

A. He said he seen him also.

Q. Did either or both tell you they didn't pick him out at the lineup itself?

A. No.

Q. Did you later learn that either or both of them did not identify him at the lineup because they were scared?

A. Yes I did.

Q. Can you tell us whether that was Allen or Gerald?

A. Allen.

Q. Did Allen tell you why he was scared?

A. Yes.

Q. What did he say?

A. He said he looked directly at the man and it frightened him to look at him.

Q. How old was Margaret?

A. Six.

Q. Any questions? Thank you.

WITNESS SWORN

Q. What is your name?

A. Allen Farr.

Q. Where do you live Allen?

A. 80 Sterling Boulevard.

Q. Was that your mother who just left here, Mrs. Joyce McKay?

A. Yes.

Q. And was Margaret Farr your sister?

A. Yes.

Q. Now Allen, going back to April 26, Yr.–2, sometime early in afternoon, did you go to the movies with your sister Margaret?

A. Yes.

Q. And when you left the movies, tell us what happened?

A. We come out of the movies and—

Q. Who was with you besides Margaret?

A. My brother Gerald.

Q. So the three of you came from the movies together?

A. Yes, we walked across the street, Thomas Avenue, and a man was leaning against the wall and—

Q. A man was leaning against the wall? What wall?

A. A wall in back of the housing project, and he asked us for a store I never heard of and then he asked if that was a store across the street and I said yes, and he asked me to go in and get him a pack of cigarettes and we all walked across the street and bought him the cigarettes.

Q. Who went in the store with you?

A. Me and my brother.

Q. Where was your sister?

A. I don't know.

Q. Did she go into the store with you?

A. I don't know.

Q. Did she cross the street with you?

A. Yes.

Q. Did the man cross the street?

A. Yes.

Q. But you didn't see her go into the store?

A. No.

Q. What did you do?

A. I bought the cigarettes and looked for my sister and couldn't find her and I went home first to my grandmother's house.

Q. Did your brother Gerald go with you?

A. Yes, and my Uncle Larry was there and we told him and he said go back and look for her.

Q. But you never found her?

A. No.

Q. Had you ever seen this man before?

A. Yes.

Q. Where did you see him before?

A. In the same store.

Q. Is that the Hill Grocery?

A. Yes.

Q. How many times had you seen him in that store prior to April 26th?

A. Every Sunday.

Q. Did he work in that store?

A. Yes, he put the papers together.

Q. You don't know whether he was an employee?

A. No.

Q. You saw him every Sunday?

A. Yes.

Q. You had seen him putting papers together?

A. Yes.

Q. How many times before April 26th, had you seen him putting papers together in this store, if you can recall?

A. No.

Q. But you say his face was familiar to you?

A. Yes.

Q. You didn't know his name?

A. No.

Q. At sometime, months after this happened, were you brought to Headquarters?

A. Yes.

Q. Did your father go with you?

A. Yes.

Q. And your brother Gerald go with you?

A. Yes.

Q. Were you asked to look at certain men in the lineup?

A. Yes.

Q. At that time did you see Bruce Gosset?

A. No.

Q. At any time in the lineup did you see Bruce Gosset?

A. No.

Q. You never saw him in the lineup?

A. No.

Q. Have you since learned the name of this man that you had seen in the store, the Hill Grocery, on prior Sundays?

A. Yes.

Q. What's his name?

A. Bruce Gosset.

Q. And Bruce Gosset is the man that was last seen with your sister?

A. Yes.

Q. Were you shown pictures of certain men and asked to pick out the man you saw with your sister?

A. Yes.

Q. And did you see a picture of Bruce Gosset among those pictures you were shown?

A. No.

Q. Was your brother Gerald with you at the lineup?

A. Yes.

Q. Did you have anything to say to your mother when you came home after the lineup?

A. Yes.

Q. What did you say to her?

A. That I identified the man.

Q. Had you identified the man?

A. No.

Q. Had you seen him?

A. No.

Q. You were there when your brother Gerald was at the lineup?

A. Yes.

Q. Did he identify a man in the lineup?

A. He said he thinks he did.

Q. Questions?

JQ. You said that after you bought the cigarettes for this man you looked for your sister but couldn't find her, is that right?

A. Yes.

JQ. Was the man still outside the store?

A. No.

JQ. This business of the lineup, when you saw all these men, did any —did you recognize any one at all in the lineup?

A. Yes, the tall man, kind of bald.

Q. Was that the man you saw with your sister?

A. I thought he was but he was clean-shaven then.

Q. In the lineup he was clean-shaven?

A. Yes.

Q. What about the time you saw him with your sister, was he clean-shaven?

A. No, he had a goatee.

Q. You say you thought it was the same man—I'm asking you today, do you think the man you saw in the lineup, now clean-shaven, was the man you last saw with your sister?

A. Yes.

JQ. Allen, when you got home did you tell your mother you thought you saw the man in the lineup?

A. Yes.

JQ. Why did you tell her that?

A. I was afraid.

JQ. Afraid of whom?

A. The man.

Q. Allen, let's go back to the lineup—you saw certain men walk by you or were they in a group?

A. In a line.

Q. Were they walking or standing still?

A. Standing still.

Q. I'm asking you now, at that time did you see the man who was last seen with your sister in that lineup?

A. Yes.

Q. At that time did you pick him out and tell the police who you thought was the man?

A. No.

Q. Why not?

A. I was afraid.

Q. When you came home did you tell your mother you saw the man in the lineup who was last seen with your sister?

A. Yes.

JQ. And you've since found out the man you saw in the lineup is Bruce Gosset?

A. Yes.

Q. Did you know, at any time when you saw this man putting papers together, his name?

A. No.

Q. Ever hear him called any name?

A. No.

Q. Any further questions? You may step out.

WITNESS SWORN

Q. What is your name?

A. Gerald Farr.

Q. Where do you live Gerald?

A. 80 Sterling Boulevard.

Q. Is Allen Farr your brother?

A. Yes.

Q. And your mother is Mrs. McKay?
A. Right.
Q. How old are you?
A. Ten.
Q. How old is Allen?
A. Eleven.
Q. What grade are you in?
A. Fourth.
Q. And Margaret Farr was your sister?
A. Yes.
Q. April 26, Yr.–2, Sunday afternoon, did you go to the movies?
A. Yes.
Q. Who went with you to the movies that afternoon?
A. My brother and sister.
Q. Your brother Allen and your sister Margaret?
A. Yes.
Q. What time did you get out of the movies, do you remember?
A. No.
Q. What did you do when you got out of the movies?
A. We were walking on the way home and seen this guy standing against the wall and he asked where was the store and he said—
Q. Gerald, speak up nice and loud so all these people can hear you.
A. I met a man and my brother told him where the store was and we walked across the street.
Q. Who walked across the street?
A. My brother and sister and this man, and he gave my brother the money and me and my brother—
Q. Did he tell you what to get in the store?
A. Pack of Pall Malls.
Q. Who went in the store?
A. Me and my brother.
Q. Did your sister Margaret go in the store?
A. No.
Q. Where was she?
A. Standing next to this man.
Q. Where—on the sidewalk?
A. Yes.
Q. And did you buy the cigarettes in the store?
A. Yes.

Q. And when you came out of the store what happened?

A. We didn't see my sister or the man.

Q. This man who asked you to get him the cigarettes, had you ever seen him before?

A. Yes.

Q. Where had you seen him before?

A. In the Hill Grocery.

Q. In the Hill Grocery? Is that the same store you went in to buy the cigarettes for this man?

A. Yes.

Q. How many times had you seen him before April 26th?

A. Every Sunday he was in the store.

Q. What would he be doing in the store?

A. I'd be getting the papers.

Q. What was he doing?

A. Cutting the wires on the papers, putting the papers together.

Q. You never saw your sister after that Sunday afternoon?

A. No.

Q. Some months after this were you taken down to Headquarters, by your father?

A. Yes.

Q. Who was with you?

A. My brother and I.

Q. And your father?

A. Yes.

Q. Tell us what went on in Headquarters?

A. We went to this room where a whole bunch of men were lined up and we went in and my brother went in and we identified the guy.

Q. Were you there when your brother identified the man?

A. He told me he did.

Q. What did he say?

A. He said he identified the guy.

Q. Did he use the word "identified"?

A. Yes.

Q. Were you brought in this room with your brother or alone?

A. Alone.

Q. Did you see certain men in that room?

A. Yes.

Q. Were they standing still or walking?

A. Standing still.

Q. Did you see the man in there that you had last seen with your sister?

A. Yes.

Q. And you identified him for the police? Did you tell the police that was the man?

A. Not really.

Q. Did you see the man in there you had last seen with your sister?

A. Yes.

Q. Did he look the same as he looked on April 26th?

A. No.

Q. What difference was there in his looks when you saw him at Headquarters, and on the day he asked you to buy him the cigarettes?

A. He was clean-shaven.

Q. He was clean-shaven—when, on April 26th? That was the day you went to the movies. You say he was clean-shaven that day?

A. No he wasn't.

Q. What was different about him?

A. He had a goatee.

Q. He had a goatee on April 26th, what's that?

A. It's like a beard—right here (witness indicates chin).

Q. And did he have that same goatee when you saw him in the line-up at Headquarters?

A. No.

Q. Did he have any kind of a growth of hair?

A. No.

Q. Did you say anything to your mother when you came home after seeing the lineup?

A. Yes.

Q. What did you say to her?

A. I told her I thought I seen the man.

Q. You didn't tell her you identified him?

A. Yes.

Q. Do you know what that means—identified?

A. Yes, it means I recognize.

Q. But you didn't say at the lineup, that's the man?

A. No.

Q. You told your mother?

A. Yes.

Q. What did you say?

A. I identified the man.

Q. And what you meant was you thought you saw the man?

A. Yes.

Q. Questions?

JQ. If you were shown a picture of this man today, could you identify him?

A. Yes.

JQ. Gerald, none of the people in here are policemen, don't be nervous; when you were going home with your brother Allen, after the lineup, did you talk this over with your brother and decide what you were going to tell your mother?

A. No.

JQ. Did your father say anything to you going home?

A. No.

JQ. Have the police ever shown you photos of this man, Bruce Gosset, and tried to convince you this is the man you saw with your sister?

A. No.

Q. Did anyone ever put any pressure on you to identify this man?

A. No.

Q. You may step out.

SGT. JOHNSON RECALLED

Q. Sergeant, do you have pictures of this man with you?

A. Yes.

Q. And have the pictures been shown to the children?

A. I've never shown them pictures.

Q. Do you know whether any other police officer has shown them pictures?

A. No, I told them I didn't want them looking at pictures.

JQ. Why is that?

A. Because it could fix it in their minds.

JQ. You have the photos there?

A. Yes.

JQ. Do you have a transcript of what went on at the lineup?

A. Yes . . . (reads transcript to G.J.). Allen did not identify anyone.

Q. Where was this girl last seen?

A. Near the Hill Grocery.

Q. What street?

A. Thomas, Abington and Center.

Q. And where was her body found?

A. In Middle Brook Park in a place called the Wilderness.

Q. Has the mother of these Farr boys seen these photos?

A. No.

ALLEN FARR RECALLED

Q. Allen, I'm going to show you a photo of two men and ask if either of the two men is the man you saw last with your sister?

A. (witness looks at photos)

COURT: For the record the witness is pointing to the man on the right.

JQ. Is that the man you saw in the lineup?

A. Yes.

JQ. Have you ever seen that picture before?

A. No.

Q. You may wait outside.

GERALD FARR RECALLED

Q. Gerald, I'm going to show you a picture and ask if either one of these men is the man you last saw with your sister (shows picture to witness).

COURT: For the record the witness is pointing to the man on the right.

Q. Did you see that man in the lineup?

A. Yes.

JG. Have you ever seen that picture before?

A. No.

Q. You may wait outside.

Grand Jury, October 8, Yr.–1.

ADA William Retzer

(cont'd from 10–6–Yr.–1).

WITNESS SWORN

Q. Identify yourself for the record.

A. Dr. Mark I. Snow.

Q. Your position?

A. Physician, pathologist, Medical Examiner.

Q. Doctor, did you examine the body of Margaret Farr?

A. I did.

Q. Will you tell us the results of that examination?

A. I found the body to be that of a well-developed, well-nourished girl who appeared to be the stated age of six years. She measured 43″ in length and was a normal appearing girl of six years —there was no malnutrition, and estimated weight would be 67 lbs., within the normal range. I went to the scene in Middle Brook Park and found the body fully clothed and had the body brought back to the Central Mortuary and on examination of the neck found a rope tightly knotted around the neck. I removed the rope and found a bruise in this area consistent with pressure on the skin in this area (indicating). There was also a bluish black area on one side of the neck, no abrasions, no scrapings of the skin but a bluish discoloration on one side.

Turning the body over I found a mark on the back of the body consistent with abrasion and scraping just to one side of the midline and this measured about 1″ by ¾″. Then, to complete the autopsy, I found that the scalp and skull had no fractures, brain was intact and on examination of the organs of the neck I found on the voice box, on that side (indicating) a hemorrhage, reddish-gray hemorrhagic area, that is, extravasation of blood going into tissues—the blood vessels were broken and there was blood going into the tissues.

On examination of the external genitalia, vulva and vagina, I found at the apex or top of the vagina, a small abrasion about ¼″ in diameter. I found no tearing of the vulva or vagina and there was no bleeding in the vagina or in the anus. However, on taking specimens of these two areas and sending them to the chemistry lab at 126 Eastern Avenue, these were analyzed for sperm and for acid-phosphate tests, and specimens from both the vagina and anus were positive for sperm. These were examined by me to confirm this. I then certified the case as: Asphyxia by strangulation. Homicide.

Q. It is your opinion that the girl was penetrated in both the vagina and the anus?

A. Yes.

JQ. Was this before or after strangulation?

A. In my opinion I'd say penetration was after unconsciousness at least, and probably after death, or in that area.

Q. Thank you Doctor.

POLICE DEPARTMENT

DIVISION No. Nine

REPORT OF MISSING PERSON

April 26, YR-2

FARR Margaret M. | 12 Mountain Rd.

Name of Missing Person | Home Address

Thomas Ave. & Center St. - last seen | 4/26/YR-2 | 3:30PM. : Student

unknown destination | unknown - cause of absence

PHYSICAL DESCRIPTION

SEX	NATIVITY	AGE	HEIGHT FEET	HEIGHT INCHES	WEIGHT	EYES COLOR	HAIR COLOR	MUSTACHE STYLE AND COLOR	BEARD STYLE AND COLOR	COMPLEX
Male Female X	U.S.	6	3	9	47	brown	lt. brown	-	-	brown skinned

COLOR	RELIGION	TEETH PECULIARITIES	CONDITION PHYSICAL	CONDITION MENTAL	PHOTO
White Black X	Protestant		good	good	Received Not Received

DEFORMITIES	SCARS	TATTOO MARKS
none	none	none

DESCRIPTION OF WEARING APPAREL

LAUNDRY MARKS	CLOTHES MADE BY	JEWELRY WORN	MONEY CARRIED

OVERCOAT	COAT Green lined	TROUSERS green tights
SUIT	VEST	SHOES black patent leather
DRESS	SHIRT	STOCKINGS
WAIST	COLLAR	GLOVES
SKIRT	NECKTIE	HAT

PERSON INTERESTED

Reported by	ADDRESS	TELEPHONE NUMBER	RELATIONSHIP
McKay Joyce LAST NAME FIRST NAME INITIAL	12 Mountain Rd.		mother

NOTE:—Report Progress and Disposition by Marking; Unfounded; not Located; Returned Home; Located by Police.

t.t. 6864 issued @ 6:27PM
Second Notice Sent out on TT#6964 at 9:38 A.M. Monday 4/27/YR-2

J. A. PETERSON
Investigating Officer
John A. Peterson

G. Mills
George Mills

[C2010]

ARREST REPORT 77487

Arrestee's Name	Booking Number(s)		
GOSSET, Bruce	NR-15266	Homicide/Fug.-Kidnap-AWDW-Rape-	Felony

Sex	Des.	Age	Divn. & Detl. Arr.	Location of First Contact	Rptg. Dist.	Date and Time Arrested
M	Neg.	30	Det.	2108 Paloma #5	L.V.	10-29-YR-2 3:45PM

Type	Date/Time Booked	Disposition of Arrestee's Vehicle	Other Property Booked
Fel.	10-29-RY-2 4:00 PM	none	personal

Birth Date	Birthplace	Residence Address	City	Employed By
	Greenwood, Miss.	2108 Paloma #5	L.V.	So.Nev.Mem.Hosp.

HT.	WT.	Hair		Visible Marks, Scars, Deformities	Occupation	Social Security Number
6-1	185	blk	brn	scar right eye 2 inch	kitchen help	

Nickname and/or Alias	Clothing Worn
none	blue green pants, pull over shirt, blue hat

License Number	State	Type	Vehicle Used (Year, make, body type, color, license number, identifying marks)
none			none

Driving Vehicle (Direction and name of street)	At or Between Streets
DNA	DNA

Location Crime Committed	Complaints or Evidence of Illness or Injury, and by Whom Treated
City of NLV	none

		Intox. No.	List Connecting Reports by Type and Identifying Number
			warrants per teletypes

Victim's Name (Firm name if business)	Residence Address (Business address if firm)	City	Residence Phone	X	Business Phone	X
STANTON, Elizabeth	5566 Belmont	L.V.				

Witnesses:	Residence Address	City	Residence Phone	X	Business Phone	X
1. Billert, Sgt.	NLVPD					
2. Wayne, Det.	NLVPD					
3.						

Parents or Guardian (Juvenile only)	Residence Address	City	Residence Phone	X	Business Phone	X
1. DNA						
2.						
3.						

Parents Notified By	Date	Time	Place Juvenile Detained	Was Juv. Fingerprinted?	Photographed?
				☐ Yes ☐ No	☐ Yes ☐ No

CIRCUMSTANCES OF ARREST:

On 10-29-YR-2 at approximately 3:45 P.M. this officer and Sgt. Billert and Det. Wayne contacted arrestee GOSSET, Bruce at his residence. These officers had knowledge of existing warrants for the arrest of suspect GOSSET, Bruce. Charges as follows: Kidnap, AWDW, Rape un-natural sex crimes, warrant #5195 #5196 #5197. Also that GOSSET was a suspect in a homicide case #77487 this jurisdiction. Due to similarity of M.O. and other information available to this officer, suspect was also charged with this homicide.

Certified copies of warrants are in route, also teletype confirmation. Suspect was arrested, transported to NLVPD, booked. In was immediately, at time of arrest advised of his rights and stated he understood them.

No other action taken. Investigation to be continued.

Date/Time Typed:	Division	Clerk	Arresting Officer(s)	Serial Number	Division—Detail	Vacation Dates
10-30-YR-2 3:34 AM	REC	AS	S/S/P.R. Hackett		Det.	
Supervisor Approving:	Serial Number					
S/S/PR. Hackett						

ARREST REPORT (C2011)

SAUNDERS v. ALBRECHT

STATEMENT OF THE CASE

The plaintiff, Jean Marie Saunders, sued the defendant, Dr. Michael A. Albrecht, a general practitioner, for injuries, pain and suffering, and mental anguish arising from defendant's negligent performance of a surgical procedure associated with the delivery of the plaintiff's first child on September 19, Yr.–6, which resulted in the plaintiff's developing a rectovaginal fistula. The plaintiff further alleges that the defendant unsuccessfully attempted to repair the fistula, leaving the plaintiff permanently injured. The plaintiff's husband, Walter F. Saunders, has sued the defendant for loss of consortium.

The defendant has denied all allegations of negligence and raises the affirmative defenses of assumption of risk and contributory negligence, and further claims that plaintiff's action is barred by the applicable statute of limitations. The defendant contends that any injuries sustained by the plaintiff were caused by persons for whose conduct defendant is not responsible.

LIST OF AVAILABLE WITNESSES AND COUNSEL

Jean Marie Saunders	Plaintiff
Walter F. Saunders	Plaintiff
Michael A. Albrecht	Defendant
Richard C. Fleming	Attorney for plaintiffs
Frank Needle	Attorney for defendant
Johanna Ross	Attorney for defendant
Dr. Leyden	Defendant's expert
Dr. Blake	Plaintiff's expert
Dr. Good	Plaintiff's expert
Dr. Longwood	Attending physician and surgeon
Dr. Percy	Radiologist
Dr. Post	Anaesthesiologist
Dr. Chapel	Anaesthesiologist
Dr. Kay	Attending physician—ob/gyn
Dr. Cameron	Attending physician—ob/gyn
Dr. Gordon	General practitioner
Dr. Oliver	General practitioner
Dr. Andrews	Associate of Dr. Longwood

STATE OF ______

______, ss.

Superior Court
No. 1587
Filed September 16, Yr.–3.

JEAN MARIE SAUNDERS and WALTER F. SAUNDERS,
Plaintiffs,
v.
MICHAEL A. ALBRECHT,
Defendant.

COMPLAINT

1. The Plaintiffs, Jean Marie Saunders and Walter F. Saunders, are husband and wife and the parents of Stephanie Saunders and Matthew Saunders.

2. The Defendant is a resident of ______, County of ______, ______, and on or about September 19, Yr.–6, held himself out to be a physician engaged in the general practice of medicine; that, in such capacity and for consideration, the Defendant undertook to treat

the Plaintiff, Jean Marie Saunders, during her pregnancy and to deliver the child she was bearing; that, at the time of the delivery, an episiotomy was made and was subsequently repaired by the Defendant in an inadequate manner. Due to the negligence and carelessness of the Defendant's repair, the Plaintiff, Jean Marie Saunders, developed a rectovaginal fistula resulting in injury, pain and mental anguish.

3. The Plaintiff, Jean Marie Saunders, says that on or about December 28, Yr.–5, the Defendant held himself out to be a physician engaged in the general practice of medicine; that, in such capacity and for consideration, the Defendant undertook to treat the Plaintiff, Jean Marie Saunders, during her second pregnancy and to deliver the child she was bearing; that, following said delivery, the Defendant undertook to repair the rectovaginal fistula which had occurred after the delivery of the first child. Due to the negligence and carelessness of the Defendant, said repairs were unsuccessful causing the Plaintiff, Jean Marie Saunders, severe injuries, pain and anguish in that she incurred further medical and hospital expenses and was incapacitated, permanently harmed and prevented from following her usual duties for a long period of time.

4. The Defendant is a resident of ______, County of ______, ______, and on or about September 19, Yr.–6, held himself out to be a physician engaged in the general practice of medicine; that, in such capacity and for consideration, the Defendant undertook to treat the Plaintiff, Jean Marie Saunders, during her pregnancy and to deliver the child she was bearing; that, at the time of the delivery, an episiotomy was made and was subsequently repaired by the Defendant in an inadequate manner. Due to the negligence and carelessness of the Defendant's repair, the Plaintiff Walter F. Saunders, incurred expenses for his wife, Plaintiff, Jean Marie Saunders, for which he is responsible.

5. The Plaintiff, Jean Marie Saunders, says that on or about December 28, Yr.–5, the Defendant held himself out to be a physician engaged in the general practice of medicine; that, in such capacity and for consideration, the Defendant undertook to treat the Plaintiff, Jean Marie Saunders, during her second pregnancy and to deliver the child she was bearing; that following said delivery, the Defendant undertook to repair the rectovaginal fistula which had occurred after the delivery of the first child. Due to the negligence and carelessness of the Defendant said repairs were unsuccessful causing the Plaintiff, Walter F. Saunders, expenses incurred for his wife, Jean Marie Saunders, for which he is responsible.

6. The Defendant is a resident of ______, County of ______, ______, and on or about September 19, Yr.–6, held himself out to be a physician engaged in the general practice of medicine; that on or about September 19, Yr.–6, the Plaintiff Jean Marie Saunders,

was a patient at Parker Memorial Hospital during the delivery of her child; that the Defendant undertook to treat the Plaintiff, Jean Marie Saunders, during her pregnancy and to deliver the child she was bearing; that, at the time of the delivery, an episiotomy was made and was subsequently repaired by the Defendant in an inadequate manner. Due to the negligence and carelessness of the Defendant's repair, the Plaintiff, Walter F. Saunders, says that he has suffered the loss of consortium of his said wife and has been deprived of her services, affection and society.

7. The Defendant is a resident of ______, County of ______, ______, and on or about December 28, Yr.–5, held himself out to be a physician engaged in the general practice of medicine; that on or about December 28, Yr.–5, the Plaintiff, Jean Marie Saunders, was a patient at Parker Memorial Hospital during the delivery of her child; that the Defendant undertook to treat the Plaintiff, Jean Marie Saunders, during her pregnancy and to deliver the child she was bearing; that, at the time of the delivery, an episiotomy was made in an inadequate manner. Due to the negligence and carelessness of the Defendant's repair, the Plaintiff, Walter F. Saunders, says that he has suffered the loss of consortium of his said wife and has been deprived of her services, affection and society.

WHEREFORE, the Plaintiffs demand judgment against the Defendant in the sum of Two Hundred Thousand ($200,000.00) Dollars with interest and costs.

The Plaintiffs claim a trial by jury.

JEAN MARIE SAUNDERS and
WALTER F. SAUNDERS
By their Attorney,

____

Richard C. Fleming
600 W. Broad Avenue

September 15, Yr.–3.

STATE OF ______

______, ss.

Superior Court
No. 1587

JEAN MARIE SAUNDERS and WALTER F. SAUNDERS v. MICHAEL A. ALBRECHT

ANSWER OF DEFENDANT MICHAEL A. ALBRECHT

Defendant, Michael A. Albrecht, answers the allegations in the numbered paragraphs of the plaintiffs' complaint as follows:

1. Admitted.

2. Defendant admits that he is a resident of ______, County of ______, State of ______, and on or about September 19, Yr.–6, held

himself out to be a physician engaged in the general practice of medicine; that, in such capacity and for consideration, he undertook to treat plaintiff, Jean Marie Saunders, during her pregnancy and to deliver the child she was bearing. He denies the remaining allegations of this paragraph.

3. Defendant admits that on or about December 28, Yr.–5, he held himself out to be a physician engaged in the general practice of medicine; that in such capacity and for consideration, he undertook to treat plaintiff, Jean Marie Saunders, during her second pregnancy and to deliver the child she was bearing, and that, at the time of the delivery, he undertook to repair the rectovaginal fistula which had occurred after the delivery of the first child. He denies the remaining allegations of this paragraph.

4. Defendant admits that he is a resident of ______, County of ______, State of ______, and on or about September 19, Yr.–6, held himself out to be a physician engaged in the general practice of medicine; that, in such capacity and for consideration, he undertook to treat plaintiff Jean Marie Saunders during her pregnancy and to deliver the child she was bearing. He denies the remaining allegations of this paragraph.

5. Defendant admits that on or about December 28, Yr.–5, he held himself out to be a physician engaged in the general practice of medicine; that in such capacity and for consideration, he undertook to treat plaintiff Jean Marie Saunders during her second pregnancy and to deliver the child she was bearing, and that, at the time of the delivery, he undertook to repair the rectovaginal fistula which had occurred after the delivery of the first child. He denies the remaining allegations of this paragraph.

6. Defendant admits that he is a resident of ______, County of ______, State of ______, and on or about September 19, Yr.–6, held himself out to be a physician engaged in the general practice of medicine. He admits that, on or about September 19, Yr.–6, plaintiff Jean Marie Saunders was a patient at Parker Memorial Hospital during the delivery of her child, and that he undertook to treat her during her pregnancy and to deliver the child she was bearing. He denies the remaining allegations of this paragraph.

7. Defendant admits that he is a resident of ______, County of ______, State of ______, and on or about December 28, Yr.–5, held himself out to be a physician engaged in the general practice of medicine. He admits that, on or about December 28, Yr.–5, plaintiff Jean Marie Saunders was a patient at Parker Memorial Hospital during the delivery of her child, and that he undertook to treat her during her pregnancy and to deliver the child she was bearing. He denies the remaining allegations of this paragraph.

Affirmative Defenses

1. If plaintiff Jean Marie Saunders was injured as alleged, she had assumed the risk of some or all of the injuries which she sustained.

2. If plaintiff Jean Marie Saunders was injured as alleged, her injuries were caused, in whole or in part, by her own negligence, and the plaintiffs may not recover therefor, or such recovery is subject to diminution.

3. If plaintiff Jean Marie Saunders was injured as alleged, her injuries were caused by a person or persons for whose conduct this defendant was not and is not responsible.

4. The plaintiffs' claims are barred, in whole or in part, by the provisions of the applicable statute of limitations.

WHEREFORE, defendant prays that the plaintiffs' complaint be dismissed with prejudice, that judgment be entered in his favor on the merits, and that he be awarded his costs.

Defendant demands a trial by jury in this action of all issues so triable.

By his Attorneys,

____
Frank Needle

____
Johanna Ross
Attorneys for defendant
Michael A. Albrecht
Simmons & Dabney
Suite 1180
45 Talmidge Street

October 20, Yr.–3.

STATE OF ______

_______, ss.

Superior Court
No. 1587

JEAN MARIE SAUNDERS and WALTER F. SAUNDERS v. MICHAEL A. ALBRECHT

DEFENDANT MICHAEL A. ALBRECHT'S REQUEST FOR PRODUCTION OF DOCUMENTS

Defendant Michael A. Albrecht, pursuant to Rules of Civil Procedure hereby requests that the plaintiffs, Jean Marie Saunders and Walter F. Saunders, produce the documents set forth below and permit such documents to be inspected and copied on behalf of defendant.

Defendant specifies that such inspection and copying take place at the offices of his attorneys, Simmons & Dabney, Suite 1180, 45

Talmidge Street, ______, on or before August 25, Yr.–2, during usual business hours.

The documents, including the originals and all copies thereof in the possession, custody or control of the plaintiffs, which defendant requests the plaintiffs to produce are the following:

1. All documents, including but not limited to letters, prescriptions, written instructions, notes and records, relating in any way to the plaintiff Jean Marie Saunders' health, physical condition, medical care, history, diagnosis, and/or treatment at any hospital and/or by defendant and/or any other medical practitioner at any time from September 1, Yr.–7 to the present.

2. All medical and hospital records, including but not limited to x-ray and/or EEG reports, progress notes, laboratory reports and consultations, from all medical facilities including but not limited to nursing and/or convalescent homes at which plaintiff Jean Marie Saunders was treated and/or confined at any time after September 1, Yr.–7.

3. All federal and state income tax returns and W–2 forms filed on behalf of plaintiffs Jean Marie Saunders and/or Walter F. Saunders whether individual, joint, partnership and/or corporate returns for any period commencing on or after January 1, Yr.–8.

4. All documents, including but not limited to bills, statements, checks and receipts, relating in any way to costs, losses, damages and/or expenses incurred on account of the occurrences alleged in the plaintiff's complaint in this action, whether for medical and/or hospital care; treatment and/or confinement; drugs and/or medications; testing, evaluation and/or therapy; and/or surgical and/or therapeutic devices and/or equipment.

5. All documents relating in any way to any claim which may have been made by or on behalf of plaintiff Jean Marie Saunders for social security, disability, compensation or other financial payments or benefits at any time after September 1, Yr.–7.

By his Attorneys,

____

Frank Needle

____

Johanna Ross

Attorneys for defendant,
Michael A. Albrecht
Simmons & Dabney
Suite 1180
45 Talmidge Street

July 26, Yr.–2.

STATE OF ______

______, ss.

Superior Court
No. 1587

JEAN MARIE SAUNDERS and WALTER F. SAUNDERS,
Plaintiffs,
v.
MICHAEL A. ALBRECHT,
Defendant.

PLAINTIFFS' JEAN MARIE SAUNDERS AND WALTER F. SAUNDERS RESPONSE TO DEFENDANT'S REQUEST FOR PRODUCTION OF DOCUMENTS

The Plaintiffs, Jean Marie Saunders and Walter F. Saunders, hereby respond to the Defendant's Request for Production of Documents in this case as follows:

1. The Plaintiffs, Jean Marie Saunders and Walter F. Saunders, object to Paragraph 1 of the Defendant's Request to the extent that it calls for them to produce documents which are beyond the scope of discovery permitted by Rules of Civil Procedure because they are protected by the attorney/client privilege and involve the work product of the Plaintiffs' attorneys. Moreover, documents requested were prepared in anticipation of litigation or for trial by the Plaintiffs' representative, including their attorney, medical consultants, or agents.

2. The Plaintiffs, Jean Marie Saunders and Walter F. Saunders, object to Paragraph 2 of the Defendant's Request in that all hospital and medical records including but not limited to x-ray and/or EEG reports, progress notes, laboratory reports and consultations, from all medical facilities including but not limited to nursing and/or convalescent homes at which the plaintiff, Jean Marie Saunders was treated and/or confined at any time after September 1, Yr.–7 are available to the Defendant upon petition to the Superior Court and the Plaintiffs further state that they are willing to sign releases to enable the Defendant to obtain the same.

3. The Plaintiffs, Jean Marie Saunders and Walter F. Saunders object to the documents requested in Paragraph 3 to the extent that they call for them to produce documents which are beyond the scope of discovery permitted by Rules of Civil Procedure because they are privileged information.

4. The Plaintiffs, Jean Marie Saunders and Walter F. Saunders object to Paragraph 4 of the Defendant's Request to the extent that

it is overly broad in that it does not limit or specify what documents they are requesting but provide herewith copies of all medical bills, hospital bills and doctors' bills in the possession of the Plaintiffs.

5. The Plaintiffs, Jean Marie Saunders and Walter F. Saunders, state that they have no documents relating in any way to any claim which may have been made by or on behalf of the Plaintiff, Jean Marie Saunders, for social security, disability, compensation or other financial payments or benefits at any time after September 1, Yr.–7.

By their Attorney,

____

Richard C. Fleming
600 W. Broad Avenue

Dated: September 8, Yr.–2.

STATE OF ______

______, ss. Superior Court
No. 1587

JEAN MARIE SAUNDERS and WALTER F. SAUNDERS v. MICHAEL A. ALBRECHT

ANSWERS OF DEFENDANT MICHAEL A. ALBRECHT TO INTERROGATORIES PROPOUNDED BY PLAINTIFF JEAN MARIE SAUNDERS

Interrogatory

1. State the name, address and field of claimed expertise of each person whom you have retained, consulted and/or specially employed as an expert in anticipation of this litigation and/or in preparation for trial herein, whether or not such person will be called as a witness at trial; and as to each person whom you expect to call as expert witness on your behalf at trial, state:
   (a) The subject matter on which he is expected to testify;
   (b) The substance of all facts and opinions to which he is expected to testify; and
   (c) A summary of the grounds and specific data upon which each such opinion will be based.

Answer

John Leyden, M.D., 4 Crown Street, obstetrics-gynecology.

(a) The witness is expected to testify that the medical care rendered by defendant to plaintiff Jean Marie Saunders was in accordance with the standards of good medical practice for physicians of his specialty.

(b) The witness will testify that Mrs. Saunders' fistula, first noted following her first pregnancy, should not have been repaired. Further, if the fistula existed, it would be so minimal that including the fistula in the episiotomy repair subsequently should have posed no problems.

He will further testify that Dr. Albrecht was not negligent in not obtaining a consultation with either an obstetrician-gynecologist or surgeon prior to Mrs. Saunders' second delivery.

Finally, the witness will testify that there was no medical indication for Mrs. Saunders to have a sterilization procedure performed at the time of her final operation for colostomy repair.

(c) The grounds of Dr. Leyden's opinions are that it is standard medical practice to wait at least six months for a repair of a fistula. The waiting period is necessary because the fistula may heal spontaneously and if it does not time is needed for infection or inflammation to subside. Further, Dr. Albrecht was unable to visualize the fistula on exam and Mrs. Saunders was not bothered by her symptoms to the extent that she made repeated attempts to contact Dr. Albrecht for relief.

The grounds of his further opinion are that a consultation with either an obstetrician-gynecologist or surgeon prior to the second delivery would not have altered the course of events or helped Mrs. Saunders.

Finally, Dr. Leyden finds nothing in Mrs. Saunders' chart to support her contention that she was advised to have a sterilization procedure performed because it was medically indicated nor does he know of any medical contraindication to future pregnancies. Dr. Leyden is of the opinion that Mrs. Saunders could safely have had future pregnancies without endangering the fistula repair.

Interrogatory

2. With respect to each such expert which the Defendant intends to call as an expert at the trial, please give a complete bibliography of books, treatises, articles and other works which each such witness regards as authoritative on the subject on which such person will testify.

Answer

This interrogatory is objected to on the ground that it is beyond the scope of discovery permitted by Rules of Civil Procedure. The Rules provide for discovery of only the identity of each person expected to be called as an expert witness, the substance of facts and opinions to which the expert is expected to testify and a summary of the grounds for each opinion. It does not provide for discovery of a complete bibliography of books, treatises, articles and other works which each witness regards as authoritative on the subject on which such person will testify.

Interrogatory

3. Please state the manner in which each expert became familiar with the facts of the case.

Answer

This interrogatory is objected to on the ground that it is beyond the scope of discovery permitted by Rules of Civil Procedure. The Rules provide for discovery of only the identity of each person expected to be called as an expert witness, the substance of facts and opinions to which the expert is expected to testify and a summary of the grounds for each opinion. It does not provide for discovery of the manner in which each expert became familiar with the facts of the case.

Interrogatory

4. With respect to each expert intended to be called at the trial, please state his or her:
   (a) educational background; and
   (b) experience with comparable or similar medical occurrences, injuries, illnesses or disabilities.

Answer

This interrogatory is objected to on the ground that it is beyond the scope of discovery permitted by Rules of Civil Procedure. The Rules provide for discovery of only the identity of each person expected to be called as an expert witness, the substance of facts and opinions to with the expert is expected to testify and a summary of the grounds for each opinion. It does not provide for discovery of an expert's educational background or experience with comparable or similar medical occurrences, injuries, illnesses or disabilities.

Interrogatory

5. Please state each expert's relationship with the Defendant, if any.

Answer

This interrogatory is objected to on the ground that it is beyond the scope of discovery permitted by Rules of Civil Procedure. The Rules provide for discovery of only the identity of each person expected to be called as an expert witness, the substance of facts and opinions to which the expert is expected to testify and a summary of the grounds for each opinion. It does not provide for discovery of each expert's relationship with the defendant, if any.

Signed under the pains and penalties of perjury this ______ day of ______, Yr.–1.

____
Michael A. Albrecht

The defendant objects to interrogatories nos. 2, 3, 4 and 5 on the grounds set forth in response thereto.

By his Attorneys,

____
Franklin Needle

____
Johanna Ross

Attorneys for defendant,
Michael A. Albrecht
45 Talmidge Street
Suite 1180

STATE OF ______

______, ss.

Superior Court
No. 1587

JEAN MARIE SAUNDERS and WALTER F. SAUNDERS,
Plaintiffs,
v.
MICHAEL A. ALBRECHT,
Defendant.

ANSWERS OF THE PLAINTIFF, JEAN MARIE SAUNDERS TO INTERROGATORIES PROPOUNDED BY THE DEFENDANT, MICHAEL A. ALBRECHT

1. Identify yourself fully, giving your full name, date of birth, residence, occupation, business address, marital status, and, if married, the name of your spouse.

Answer

Jean Marie Saunders, December 6, Yr.–29, 25 Mill Street, housewife, married, Walter F. Saunders.

2. State all addresses at which you lived within five years prior to the occurrences alleged in your complaint, giving the street and

number, town or city, and state, and the dates between which you lived at each such address.

Answer

208 Arby Drive, January, Yr.–7 to October, Yr.–5; 25 Mill Street, October, Yr.–5 to present.

3. Describe all injuries, ailments and pains you claim to have suffered or contracted as a result of the occurrences alleged in your complaint, giving physical injuries, including the parts of your body affected and outward signs of injury, any injuries, ailments or pains having no outward signs, and the severity and duration, giving dates, of each injury, ailment and pain.

Answer

September 21, Yr.–6 to December 31, Yr.–5—Rectal/vaginal fistula, no pain, passing of gas through vagina;

December 31, Yr.–5 to July 16, Yr.–4—Injury to rectal/vaginal fistula with feces passing through vagina. No control over bowel movements until April 10, Yr.–4;

April 10, Yr.–4—Colostomy operation, pain from incision and irritation around stoma, pain lasted about two weeks, irritation until closing of colostomy on July 16, Yr.–4;

May 7, Yr.–4—Surgery for repair of fistula, severe pain for one week from operation, continued pain in rectum and vagina for three months following, hemorrhaging following this operation which required an inpatient admission, pain during attempts of sexual intercourse for over one year following last surgery;

July 14, Yr.–4—Closing of colostomy, pain and suffering for weeks following. Pain caused from operation and bowel movements;

December 31, Yr.–5 to present—Pains in rectal area of varying intensity;

July 14, Yr.–4—Tubal ligation accompanying final surgery, permanent in nature.

4. State whether you were confined to bed as a result of any of the occurrences alleged in your complaint, and, if so, state the length of time and the dates between which you were so confined and describe the injuries, ailments and/or pains which caused such confinement.

Answer

Yes, I was so confined.

January 2, Yr.–4 to January 20, Yr.–4, approximately, hemorrhaging following delivery of second child;

April 10, Yr.–4 to May 1, Yr.–4, approximately, first surgical procedure and convalescent period at home following release from hospital.

5. State whether you were confined to your home as a result of any of the occurrences alleged in your complaint, and, if so, state the length of time and the dates between which you were so confined and describe the injuries, ailments and/or pains which caused such confinement.

Answer

Yes, I was so confined.

January 9, Yr.–4, approximately, Convalescent period following delivery and release from hospital following hemorrhaging;

April 17, Yr.–4 to May 7, Yr.–4, approximately, Convalescent period following first surgical procedure;

May 18, Yr.–4 to July 14, Yr–4, approximately, Convalescent period following second surgical procedure and hemorrhaging which followed it;

July 25, Yr.–4 to October 10, Yr.–4, approximately, Convalescent period following third surgical procedure.

6. State the length of time and the dates between which you suffered pain or inconvenience from any of the injuries or ailments you claim to have sustained or contracted as a result of the occurrences alleged in your complaint, and state which injuries or ailments caused such suffering.

Answer

December 27, Yr.–5 to October 19, Yr.–4—Pains and ailments as a result of surgical procedures and hemorrhaging;

December 27, Yr.–5 to May 7, Yr.–4—Passing of fecus uncontrollably making it necessary to wear protective devices in addition to the pain and mental suffering involved;

April 12, Yr.–4 to July 14, Yr.–4—Mental suffering as well as pain of having a colostomy;

December 27, Yr.–5 to present—Pain in rectum and vagina due to surgery and repairs;

December 27, Yr.–5 to present—Pain in vagina making sexual intercourse impossible for many months. Attempts at sexual intercourse were very painful for an extended period of time and sexual intercourse is presently painful and unpleasurable as a direct result of surgery.

December 27, Yr.–5 to present—Various aches and pains of the body continuing in varying degrees at the present time as a direct result of surgery;

December 27, Yr.–5 to October 10, Yr.–4—Inability for all practical purposes to care for children except for a few isolated periods for this entire period as a direct result of these problems;

Since April 10, Yr.–4—Permanent disfiguring, scars from surgery;

Since July 14, Yr.–4—Permanent sterility.

7. State whether, as a result of any of the occurrences alleged in your complaint, you lost any time from your occupation, employment or schooling or were incapacitated from any other activity, and, if so, state:

   (a) the name and address of your school and/or employer and/or other sources of income immediately before such occurrences;

   (b) all wages, salaries and other earnings and income you received during the year immediately before such occurrences, stating the source and amount of each item, how often wages and other payments were received, and the aggregate amount, if any, which you lost as a result of the occurrences alleged in your complaint;

   (c) the length of time, giving dates, which you lost from your occupation, employment or schooling and/or were so incapacitated;

   (d) a description of your responsibilities, duties and activities in your occupation, employment or schooling immediately before such occurrences; and

   (e) a description of the nature and extent of such incapacity and of the activities from which you were incapacitated.

Answer

Employed as a housewife, incapacitated as stated above. The duties as housewife from which I was prevented from performing including care and feeding of two small children, care of house, and of spouse and of all other duties usual and incidental to my occupation.

(a) 25 Mill Street.

(b) Not applicable.

(c) See Interrogatories Nos. 3, 4, 5, and 6.

(d) See introductory paragraph of this question.

(e) Basically full incapacity from December 27, Yr.–5 to October 10, Yr.–4, partial incapacity during a few isolated periods.

8. State whether you were treated and/or confined at any hospital, nursing home, sanatorium or other facility as a result of any of the occurrences alleged in your complaint, and, if so, state:
   (a) the name and address of each such facility;
   (b) the length of time and dates between which you were treated and/or confined at each such facility;
   (c) the injuries, ailments and/or pains which caused each such treatment and/or confinement;
   (d) the charges for each such treatment and/or confinement; and
   (e) a complete description of each such treatment and of the care and advice you received, including the nature of each test, examination, operation, medication and other diagnostic or therapeutic procedure performed or administered, the date thereof, and reasons therefor, and the identity of each person performing any function relating to such treatment, care or advice.

Answer

Yes, I was so confined and treated.

(a) Parker Memorial Hospital, Ford Road.

(b) Parker Memorial Hospital, January 4, Yr.–4 to January 9, Yr.–4; April 10, Yr.–4 to April 17, Yr.–4; May 7, Yr.–4 to May 18, Yr.–4; May 20, Yr.–4 to May 23, Yr.–4; July 14, Yr.–4 to July 25, Yr.–4.

(c) All injuries, ailments, and/or pains were caused by original injury, hemorrhaging, or surgery.

(d) Parker Memorial Hospital

1/4/Yr.–4 to 1/9/Yr.–4	$ 505.30
4/10/Yr.–4 to 4/17/Yr.–4	882.67
5/7/Yr.–4 to 5/18/Yr.–4	1,589.93
5/20/Yr.–4 to 5/23/Yr.–4	333.75
7/14/Yr.–4 to 7/25/Yr.–4	2,168.03

(e) January 4, Yr.–4 to January 9, Yr.–4—I was admitted to Parker Memorial Hospital for hemorrhaging after delivery of my child. Dr. Paul Oliver (covering for Dr. Michael Albrecht) examined me in the emergency room. He admitted me to the hospital for observation and I was given an intravenous solution. Dr. Joseph Gordon examined me one day and left me no instructions. Dr. Frank Post, an anaesthesiologist, examined me for neck, back, and chest pains which were severe at the time, and he was unable to determine the cause of the pain. Dr. Michael Albrecht examined me, ordered X-rays of the chest, sitz baths, and various medications.

April 10, Yr.–4 to April 17, Yr.–4—I was an inpatient at Parker Memorial Hospital for a colostomy operation. Dr. William Longwood, a surgeon, and Dr. R. Edward Bailey, a resident, at the hospital, also treated me. I received various medications including, but not limited to, seconal, and demerol and had a number of tests performed including, but not limited to, CBC, Urine, blood sugar, BUN, ECG, Chest X-rays.

May 7, Yr.–4 to May 18, Yr.–4—I was an inpatient at Parker Memorial Hospital for repair of a rectal/vaginal fistula. Dr. William Longwood was a surgeon and ordered various tests, blood, urine, X-ray, EKG, and various medications including iron, ampicillan, seconal, morphine, and prescribed sitz baths. I took various medications on discharge including emperin compound, codeine, tetracycline and continued the sitz baths. I returned to Dr. Longwood's office in two weeks where I was examined by Dr. Warren Andrews, an associate of Dr. Longwood's who made tests for pathology of vagina and perineal mucosa and prescribed further sitz baths.

May 20, Yr.–4 to May 23, Yr.–4—admitted to Parker Memorial Hospital for post-operative bleeding. Received medications including ampicillan, multivitamins, iron and so forth and discharged to my home for self-treatment.

July 14, Yr.–4 to July 25, Yr.–4—I was admitted to Parker Memorial Hospital for an operation to close my colostomy. Dr. William Longwood was the surgeon and Dr. A. West was the resident who treated me. In addition to the operation, I had various tests and medications and was discharged to my home and continued on medications and treatments at home.

9. State whether you were treated and/or examined by any physician, surgeon, nurse and/or other practitioner, and/or by any person acting on such person's behalf or at his request or direction, as a result of any of the occurrences alleged in your complaint, and, if so, state:

   (a) the name, address and occupation and/or specialty of each such person;

   (b) the date of each such treatment and/or examination and the name of each such person who treated you on each such occasion;

   (c) the charges for each such treatment and/or examination; and

   (d) a complete description of each such treatment and/or examination and of the care and advice you received, including the nature of each test, examination, operation, medication and other diagnostic or therapeutic procedure performed or administered, the date thereof, the reasons therefor, and the identity of each person performing any function relating to such treatment, care or advice.

Answer

Yes, I was so treated.

(a) Dr. Michael Albrecht, 70 Barrows Road, General Practitioner.

Dr. William Longwood, 105 Hilton Road, Surgeon.
Dr. Percy, 2077 Liberty Highway, Radiologist (X-Rays).
Dr. Post, Dr. Chapel and Dr. Gordon, Eastern Anaesthesiologists, Inc., Obstetrics and Gynecology.

Dr. Albert Kay, Obstetrics and Gynecology.

Dr. Gerald Cameron, Ford Road, Obstetrics and Gynecology.

Dr. Joseph Gordon, N. Filmore Street, General Practitioner.

Dr. Paul Oliver, 43 Ferry Landing Road, General Practitioner.

(b) Dr. Albrecht, January 4, Yr.–4 to January 9, Yr.–4, May 20, Yr.–4, July, Yr.–4 and October, Yr.–4, to the best of my knowledge.

Dr. Longwood, March, Yr.–4, April 11, Yr.–4 to April 17, Yr.–4, May 1, Yr.–4, May 8, Yr.–4 to May 18, Yr.–4, May 20, Yr.–4 to May 23, Yr.–4, July 14, Yr.–4 to July 25, Yr.–4, June 17, Yr.–4, September 25, Yr.–4, to the best of my knowledge.

Dr. Percy, each hospital stay for X-rays.

Dr. Gordon, Dr. Post, Dr. Chapel, anaesthesia each surgery.

Dr. Cameron, October or November, Yr.–4.

Dr. Oliver, January 4, Yr.–4.

(c)

Dr. Michael Albrecht	$ 110.00
Dr. Percy	54.00
Dr. William Longwood	1,605.00
Dr. Chapel	240.00
Dr. Albert Kay	30.00
Dr. Phillips and Dr. Cameron	10.00
Dr. Joseph Gordon	22.00

(d) I have indicated the date of treatment in part "b" of the question. Advice as outlined in 8 "e." Dr. Albrecht, treatments were for rectal/vaginal fistula and for hemorrhaging before my case was referred to Dr. Longwood.

Dr. Longwood performed all surgery and all care was related to it. Dr. Percy—X-rays before each surgery after hemorrhaging.

Dr. Post, Dr. Chapel and Dr. Gordon—anaesthesia before each surgery.

Dr. Cameron—evaluation following surgery.

Dr. Kay—evaluation following surgery.

Dr. Gordon—emergency room treatment while covering for Dr. Albrecht.

10. State whether you are presently suffering from any injury, ailment, or pain, or from any loss of time from your occupation, employment or schooling, or from any incapacity from any other activity, resulting from any of the occurrences alleged in your complaint, and, if so, describe the nature and extent of each such injury, ailment and pain and of each such loss and incapacity, including the expected duration thereof.

Answer

Yes, various aches and pains of body and rectal/vaginal area which are continuing at the present time. I don't know or have any expectations of the duration of my present pain.

11. State whether you claim that you will suffer permanently from any injury, ailment or pain, or from any loss of time from your occupation, employment or schooling, or from any incapacity from any other activity, resulting from any of the occurrences alleged in your complaint, and, if so, describe the nature and extent of each such injury, ailment and pain and of each such loss and incapacity.

Answer

Permanent disfiguring, scars and reproductive sterility.

12. State whether you claim that you are suffering and/or expect to suffer any loss of earnings and/or earning capacity as a result of any of the occurrences alleged in your complaint, and, if so, state all facts upon which you base such a claim, including the duration and amount of each such loss.

Answer

I have not nor do I expect to suffer loss of earnings or earning capacity.

13. Describe every illness, injury, disease, ailment or operation, not described elsewhere in your answers to these interrogatories, which you had suffered from within five years prior to the occurrences alleged in your complaint and/or at any time during or after the occurrences alleged in your complaint, giving the dates upon which each was had or suffered from and the name and address of each person by whom, and facility at which, you were treated therefor.

Answer

None prior to accident. None since except for usual colds and flu.

14. Describe your physical condition and the state of your health at the time you were first seen by this defendant and/or by any other person acting on his behalf or at his request or direction, and on each occasion thereafter when you were seen by this defendant and/or by any such other person, and identify each person who saw you on each such occasion.

Answer

Physical condition and health were excellent until the problems referred to in the complaint occurred.

15. With regard to each condition, illness, ailment or injury from which you claim you were suffering when you first saw this defendant and/or other person acting on his behalf, or at his direction or request, state:

    (a) how long you had suffered from it, giving dates;

    (b) the date and nature of each treatment you received for it; and

    (c) the name and address of each person by whom and/or facility at which you were treated for it.

Answer

(a) (b) (c) (d)

When I first saw Dr. Albrecht it was only for normal obstetrical care.

16. Describe every act and procedure performed and/or ordered by this defendant and/or by any other person acting on his behalf or at his direction or request, to examine or treat you, giving the date, place and nature of each examination and treatment, the identity of each person present at the time, the parts of your body examined and/or treated, the methods and instruments used, and all treatment, advice, therapy and medication given to or prescribed for you.

Answer

Dr. Albrecht ordered sitz baths after both deliveries, September 16, Yr.–6 and December 27, Yr.–5. Orders were for while I was in the hospital and for when I was home. No one else present to the best of my recollection.

17. State the date and place and describe the circumstances and content of each statement, communication and conversation between you and this defendant and/or any other person acting on his behalf or at his direction or request, and identify each person

present when each such statement, communication and conversation took place.

Answer

Conversations generally concerned treatment and home care of the various problems encountered, i. e. how many baths to take, when could children come home, etc.

After birth of Stephanie (our first child) I was instructed to take three sitz baths daily. These daily baths continued for months. No other special instructions were given. The original instructions were given in September Yr.–6. I told Dr. Albrecht about passing of gas through the vagina and I was told it would probably heal on its own. After a few months, I was told it would be fixed after the birth of our last child. The reason for this, it was explained, was that any child after that would have to be taken Caesarean so that the hole would not appear again.

December 31, Yr.–5 I told Dr. Albrecht in the presence of Mrs. Terry Morris (nurse) that I passed two bowel movements through my vagina. I believe Phyllis Dodge, a patient sharing my room at the time, was also present. Dr. Albrecht responded, "Don't ruin my day, it is too early to tell; you have to give it a chance to heal as there are a lot of stitches." I was released from the hospital and continued to pass feces uncontrollably through my vagina.

January 4, Yr.–4—Conversation with Dr. Albrecht in emergency room after minor hemorrhaging. When I asked why I was bleeding, he told me that he thought my uterus had moved or something of that nature. I was told to continue taking sitz baths and that it might heal.

Early February—About 1½ months after delivery of the baby, I was informed by Dr. Albrecht that he had contacted Dr. William Longwood and that I would have to have surgery to repair the fistula which was over 1½ inches long. I was told that I would need three operations.

March, Yr.–4—Discussed case with Dr. Longwood after an initial examination. Many conversations followed (daily while in the hospital) with Dr. Longwood until September or October of Yr.–4. Conversations generally concerned my condition and treatment as a result of my surgeries.

18. State the date and place and describe the circumstances and content of all advice or instructions given by this defendant and/or any other person acting on his behalf or at his direction or request, with regard to your medical condition and/or to your care and treatment, and identify each person who gave each such advice and instruction.

Answer

Fall Yr.–6—Dr. Albrecht told me to take three sitz baths daily in an effort to heal the problem on its own. *No* other advice or instructions were given to me.

January, Yr.–4—Similar instructions to take sitz baths in an effort to heal the fistula.

January, Yr.–4—to August, Yr.–4—Various instructions by Dr. Albrecht and Dr. Longwood to take iron supplements, sitz baths (at various times), and other things in connection with my treatment.

19. State whether you have incurred and/or expect to incur any loss, cost, damage or expense, not referred to in your answers to these interrogatories, as a result of any of the occurrences alleged in your complaint, and, if so, itemize and describe each such loss, cost, damage and expense, giving the reasons therefor and the amount and date thereof.

Answer

I do not know if there will be further expenses.

20. With respect to the allegations in your complaint that this defendant was negligent, careless and unskillful, state all facts upon which such allegations are based.

Answer

The defendant doctor was guilty of negligence by:

(a) failing to consult with an Obstetrician-Gynecologist upon originally diagnosing the rectal/vaginal fistula.

(b) failure to repair the fistula before another pregnancy.

(c) failure to consult with a surgeon or to have a surgeon perform the repairs he made of the fistula particularly in view of the fact that Dr. Albrecht, as a General Practitioner, attempted difficult and complicated surgical procedure by himself despite the fact that he had encountered only one other similar fistula during his entire medical career on a patient who was not his.

(d) not attempting repair of the fistula after delivery of the child to tissue that was traumatized by the delivery of a child.

(e) failure to inform the physicians who were covering for him of the complications I was suffering after the delivery of my second child when he went away on vacation.

21. State the name, address and field of claimed expertise of each person whom you have retained, consulted and/or specially employed as an expert in anticipation of this litigation and/or in preparation for trial herein, whether or not such person will

be called as a witness at trial; and as to each person whom you expect to be called as an expert witness on your behalf at trial, state:

(a) the subject matter on which he is expected to testify;

(b) the substance of all facts and opinions to which he is expected to testify; and

(c) a summary of the grounds upon which each such opinion will be based.

Answer

Marc L. Blake, 1954 Nelson Parkway, Obstetrician-Gynecologist, who I expect my attorneys will call as a witness at trial.

(a) Whether or not Dr. Albrecht was negligent and performed medical and surgical treatment consistent with good medical practice.

(b) 1. That Dr. Albrecht should have obtained a consultation from an expert when the rectal/vaginal fistula was expected after the birth of my first child.

2. The fistula should have been repaired before second pregnancy was initiated.

3. Dr. Albrecht should not have undertaken surgical repairs of the fistula as his training was not sufficient to preparing him for a procedure of such magnitude.

(c) Dr. Blake's qualifications and experience, his review of the medical records, and knowledge of my experiences, and his opinion based on the above as to what constitutes good medical practice.

Signed under the pains and penalties of perjury this ______ day of February, Yr.–2.

____

Jean Marie Saunders

STATE OF ______

______, ss.

Superior Court
No. 1587

JEAN MARIE SAUNDERS and WALTER F. SAUNDERS,
Plaintiffs,

v.

MICHAEL A. ALBRECHT,
Defendant.

PLAINTIFF, JEAN MARIE SAUNDERS', FURTHER ANSWERS TO INTERROGATORIES PROPOUNDED BY THE DEFENDANT, MICHAEL A. ALBRECHT

21. State the name, address and field of claimed expertise of each person whom you have retained, consulted and/or specially employed as an expert in anticipation of this litigation and/or in preparation for trial herein, whether or not such person will be called as a witness at trial; and as to each person whom you expect to be called as an expert witness on your behalf at trial, state:
    (a) the subject matter on which he is expected to testify;
    (b) the substance of all facts and opinions to which he is expected to testify; and
    (c) a summary of the grounds upon which each such opinion will be based.

FURTHER ANSWER

Melvin Good, M.D. 1–A Seller Avenue, Obstetrician and Gynecologist.

(a) The treatment of Jean Marie Saunders by Dr. Albrecht from September 19, Yr.–6 through December of Yr.–4.

(b) That from the time the fistula was first discovered until its final closure, Dr. Albrecht's management was not consistent with good standard medical practice in the management of rectovaginal fistulas.

(c) Acceptable medical practice would dictate that the fistula should have been closed prior to the second pregnancy between four and six months after the first delivery. The delivery of Jean Marie Saunder's second child before the fistula was closed should have been by Caesarean section. The attempt to close the fistula immediately after the delivery of the patient's second child was contraindicated because the cure rate is not good enough.

Signed under the pains and penalties of perjury this eighteenth day of April, Yr.–0.

____

Jean Marie Saunders

STATE OF ______

______, ss. Superior Court No. 1587

JEAN MARIE SAUNDERS and WALTER F. SAUNDERS,
Plaintiffs,
v.
MICHAEL A. ALBRECHT,
Defendant.

ANSWERS OF THE PLAINTIFF, WALTER F. SAUNDERS, TO INTERROGATORIES PROPOUNDED BY THE DEFENDANT, MICHAEL A. ALBRECHT

1. Identify yourself fully, giving your full name, date of birth, residence, occupation, business address, marital status, and, if married, the name of your spouse.

Answer

Walter F. Saunders, December 9, Yr.–31, 25 Mill Street, 1212 Shaw Lane, married, Jean Marie Saunders.

2. State all addresses at which you lived within five years prior to the occurrences alleged in your complaint, giving the street and number, town or city, and state, and the dates between which you lived at each such address.

Answer

208 Arby Drive, January, Yr.–7 to October, Yr.–5; 25 Mill Street, October, Yr.–5 to present.

3. State the date and place and describe the circumstances and content of each statement, communication and conversation between you and this defendant, or at his direction or request, and identify each person present when each such statement, communication and conversation took place.

Answer

December 27, Yr.–5—Conversation with Dr. Albrecht shortly after he had finished delivering our second child. No one else was present. He informed me that he had delivered baby and had made repairs and that everything went well.

Early January, Yr.–4—I brought my daughter Stephanie to Dr. Albrecht's office while my wife was in the hospital for one of her normal appointments. Conversation confined to my daughter. No one else present.

February, Yr.–4—My wife and I brought both children to Dr. Albrecht's office for an appointment. Both children were sick. Conversation concerned children and the tough times we were having. No, only wife present.

4. State the date and place and describe the circumstances and content of all advice or instructions given by this defendant, or at his direction or request, with regard to Jean Marie Saunders' medical condition and/or to her care and treatment, and identify each person who gave each such advice and instruction and each person to whom it was given.

Answer

Dr. Albrecht told my wife at the end of September, Yr.–6 to take sitz baths two or three times daily to help healing.

In January of Yr.–4, Dr. Albrecht instructed my wife that she would need surgery to correct the rectal/vaginal fistula and that the repairs should be done as soon as possible. Conversation occurred in his office.

March, Yr.–4 to October, Yr.–4—Dr. Longwood gave my wife numerous instructions in connection with her three surgical procedures. Instructions included what she should physically do at home as well as what medications she should take. Dr. Albrecht had referred my wife to Dr. Longwood.

November, Yr.–4—Dr. Albrecht requested my wife to come to his office to begin exercises to stretch her vagina. My wife went on one occasion. My wife had gone because our attempts at intercourse had been unsuccessful due to tremendous physical pain. No one else present to my knowledge.

5. State whether you claim damages for a loss of the consortium of Jean Marie Saunders, including her services, affection and society, as a result of the occurrences alleged in your complaint, and, if so, state all facts upon which such claim is based.

Answer

Yes, I claim damages for a loss of consortium including my wife's services, affection and society. Claims based on Dr. Albrecht's negligence which resulted in my wife hemorrhaging following the delivery of our second child as well as the breakdown of his repair work which required three surgical procedures to correct.

6. During the period of your marriage before the occurrences alleged in your complaint, how many hours per week did you spend in the presence of Jean Marie Saunders, excluding sleeping time, and how were those hours spent?

Answer

Hours varied depending on the time of year. Thirty hours is perhaps an overall average. Hours spent in leisure activities, home improvement, sporting events of various kinds.

7. State whether you claim that the alleged injuries to Jean Marie Saunders limited or restricted your leisure activities, and, if so, describe in detail the way in which such injuries limited or restricted your leisure activities.

Answer

Yes, complete elimination of leisure activities due to hospitalizations and lengthy periods of convalescence.

8. State whether you and Jean Marie Saunders have participated together in any charitable, social, athletic, educational, intellectual, spiritual, religious or any other type of joint activity for relaxation, pleasure or personal improvement, and, if so, for each such activity state:
   (a) a description of the activity;
   (b) how long you participated together in such activity and with what frequency;
   (c) the number of hours you participated together in the activity in each of the twelve months preceding the alleged injuries;
   (d) the number of hours you participated together in the activity in each month after her alleged injuries; and
   (e) whether you claim the alleged injuries restricted or terminated such joint participation, and, if so, state:
      (1) in what manner and to what extent; and
      (2) when you and your spouse will be able to resume such activity.

Answer

My wife and I did participate a great deal in joint activities at various times of the year but many of them do not fall into precise categories.

Social

(a) Activities would include visiting friends, relatives, going to the movies, or sporting events.

(b) Activities were participated in together since before our marriage. Perhaps we would average two social activities per week.

(c) An average of 20 hours per month.

(d) Zero hours.

(e) (1) Complete elimination.

(2) Activities resumed on a limited basis in approximately early November, Yr.–4.

Athletic

(a) My wife and I have played tennis, badminton, basketball, and golf together, in addition to swimming and boating.

(b) We would perhaps average four athletic activities per month. Our participation began even before our marriage.

(c) Average of ten hours per month.

(d) Zero hours.

(e) (1) Complete elimination.

(2) Activities resumed on a limited basis in the summer of Yr.–3.

Educational

None.

Intellectual

None so specifically designated.

Spiritual or Religious

(a) Attending church.

(b) Since before our marriage, approximately two times per year jointly as I am a Catholic and my wife Episcopalian.

(c) One hour approximately every six months.

(d) Zero hours.

(e) (1) Complete elimination.

(2) Activities resumed late Yr.–4 to the best of my recollection.

9. State whether there is any activity, not referred to above, in which you and Jean Marie Saunders participated together, which you claim has been limited or terminated because of the occurrences alleged in your complaint, and, if so, for each such activity, state:

(a) a description of the activity;

(b) the number of hours for each of the twelve months before the alleged injuries that you participated in the activity by yourself or with a person other than Jean Marie Saunders; and

(c) the number of hours in each month after the alleged injuries that you participated in the activity by yourself or with a person other than Jean Marie Saunders.

Answer

Care and Raising of our Family

(a) Includes care of children and other duties of parenthood.

(b) Approximately 12 hours per month by myself.

Approximately 60 hours with my wife per month.

(c) Approximately 120 hours per month.

Home Improvements

(a) Gardening, maintenance, various projects.

(b) Approximately 40 hours per month.

(c) Approximately 20 hours per month.

10. State whether you claim that the alleged injuries suffered by Jean Marie Saunders terminated or limited your sexual relations, and, if so, state in what manner the injuries terminated or limited such relations.

Answer

Yes, relations terminated due to physical impossibility to perform because of surgery. Following the surgery, relations terminated due to physical pain.

11. State whether you engaged in sexual relations with Jean Marie Saunders during the twelve-month period before her alleged injuries, and, if so, state the frequency of such relations over this period.

Answer

Yes, approximately three times weekly.

12. State whether you have engaged in sexual relations with Jean Marie Saunders since her alleged injuries, and, if so, state the frequency of such relations in each month since the alleged injuries.

Answer

Yes.

January to March, Yr.-4—None.

April, Yr.-4—Once.

May to September, Yr.-4—None.

October, Yr.-4—Once.

November, Yr.–4—Once.

December, Yr.–4—Twice.

January, Yr.–3—Three times.

February, Yr.–3—Three times.

March, Yr.–3 to January, Yr.–2—approximately four times per month to the best of my recollection.

13. If you have not engaged in sexual relations with Jean Marie Saunders since her alleged injuries, state:
    (a) whether this was caused by her alleged injuries, and, if so, in what manner, and
    (b) whether you will be able to resume such relations in the future, and, if so, when.

Answer

(a) Not applicable.

(b) Not applicable.

14. State whether there is any activity, not referred to above, in which you and Jean Marie Saunders participated together before her alleged injuries which you claim has been limited or terminated because of the occurrences alleged in your complaint, and, if so, for each such activity, state:
    (a) a description of the activity;
    (b) the injury which caused the termination or limitation;
    (c) the extent to which such activity is limited; and
    (d) whether Jean Marie Saunders will be able to resume such activity at a future time, and, if so, when.

Answer

(a) (b) (c) (d)

Although there is no specific activity not referred to above in which my wife and I participated together before her injuries, I was for a long period of time deprived of the quiet enjoyment of the presence and companionship and simple social intercourse with a healthy, happy, and loving wife, and our children were deprived of the loving maternal care and educational, social and emotional benefits of a healthy, happy, and loving mother all of which, although not fitting into a particular category or cubbyhole, was a great loss to myself, my children, and our family unit.

15. State whether you have incurred and/or expect to incur any loss, cost, damage or expense, not referred to in your other answers to these interrogatories, as a result of any of the occurrences alleged in your complaint, and, if so, itemize and describe each such loss, cost, damage and expense, giving the reasons therefor and the amount and date thereof.

Answer

I. *Hemorrhaging after delivery of baby*

	Inpatient	
Parker Memorial Hospital	1/4–1/9/Yr.–4	505.30
Dr. Michael A. Albrecht	1/4–1/9/Yr.–4	110.00
Dr. Percy (X-rays)	1/4/Yr.–4	21.00
Parker Memorial Hospital (Lab Tests)	1/22/Yr.–4	33.90

II. *First Surgery—Colostomy*

Parker Memorial Hospital	4/10–4/17/Yr.–4 Inpatient	882.67
Dr. William Longwood	4/11–4/17, 5/1/Yr.–4	425.00
Dr. Percy (X-rays)	4/10/Yr.–4	11.00

III. *Second Surgery—Repair*

Parker Memorial Hospital	5/7–5/18/Yr.–4	1,589.93
Dr. William Longwood	5/8–5/18/Yr.–4	285.00
Dr. Percy	5/7/Yr.–4	11.00
Dr. Chapel (Anaesthesia)	5/8/Yr.–4 No bill in records	140.00

IV. *Hemorrhaging after second operation*

Parker Memorial Hospital	5/20–5/23/Yr.–4	333.75
Dr. William Longwood	5/20–5/23/Yr.–4	55.00

V. *Third Surgery—Closing of Colostomy*

Parker Memorial Hospital	7/14–7/25/Yr.–4	2,168.03
Dr. William Longwood	7/14–7/25/Yr.–4	820.00
Dr. Percy (X-rays)	7/14/Yr.–4	11.00
Dr. Chapel (Anaesthesia)	7/14/Yr.–4	100.00

Miscellaneous

Dr. William Longwood	6/17, 9/25/Yr.–4	20.00
Dr. Albert Kay	12/12/Yr.–4	30.00
Dr. Phillips and Dr. Cameron	Fall, Yr.–4	10.00
Dr. Joseph Gordon		
Two emergency room calls for Dr. Albrecht	5/20, 7/Yr.–4	22.00

Medication, Prescriptions

Pain killers (Codeine, Darvon)		43.09
Valium, feosol (Iron), aspirin, colostomy products, etc.		25.00
	Total	$7,652.67

16. State whether you claim that you are suffering and/or expect to suffer any loss of Jean Marie Saunders' earnings and/or earning capacity as a result of any of the occurrences alleged in your complaint, and, if so, state all facts upon which you base such a claim, including the duration and amount of each such loss.

Answer

I am not suffering nor do I expect to suffer any loss due to any loss of my wife's earning capacity.

17. With respect to the allegations in your complaint that this defendant was negligent, careless and unskillful, state all facts upon which such allegations are based.

Answer

The Defendant doctor was guilty of negligence by:

(a) failing to consult with an Obstetrician-Gynecologist upon originally diagnosing the rectal/vaginal fistula.

(b) failure to repair the fistula before another pregnancy.

(c) failure to consult with a surgeon or to have a surgeon perform the repairs he made of the fistula particularly in view of the fact that Dr. Albrecht, as a General Practitioner, attempted difficult and complicated surgical procedure by himself despite the fact that he had encountered only one other similar fistula during his entire medical career on a patient who was not his.

(d) not attempting repair of the fistula after delivery of the child to tissue that was traumatized by the delivery of a child.

(e) failure to inform the physicians who were covering for him of the complications my wife was suffering after the delivery of her second child when he went away on vacation.

18. State the name, address and field of claimed expertise of each person whom you have retained, consulted and/or specially employed as an expert in anticipation of this litigation and/or in preparation for trial herein, whether or not such person will be called as a witness at trial; and as to each person expected to be called as an expert witness on your behalf at trial, state:

(a) the subject matter on which he is expected to testify;

(b) the substance of all facts and opinions to which he is expected to testify; and

(c) a summary of the grounds upon which each such opinion will be based.

Answer

Marc L. Blake, 1954 Nelson Parkway, Obstetrician-Gynecologist, whom I expect my attorneys will call as a witness at trial.

(a) Whether or not Dr. Albrecht was negligent and performed medical and surgical treatment consistent with good medical practice.

(b) (1) That Dr. Albrecht should have obtained a consultation from an expert when the rectal/vaginal fistula was expected after the birth of my wife's first child.

(2) The fistula should have been repaired before second pregnancy was initiated.

(3) Dr. Albrecht should not have undertaken surgical repairs of the fistula as his training was not sufficient to preparing him for a procedure of such magnitude.

(c) Dr. Blake's qualifications and experience, his review of the medical records, and knowledge of my wife's experiences, and his opinion based on the above as to what constitutes good medical practice.

Signed under the pains and penalties of perjury this ______ day of February, Yr.–2.

____
Walter F. Saunders

STATE OF ______

______, ss.

Superior Court
No. 1587

JEAN MARIE SAUNDERS and WALTER F. SAUNDERS,
Plaintiffs,

v.

MICHAEL A. ALBRECHT,
Defendant.

FURTHER ANSWERS OF THE PLAINTIFF, WALTER F. SAUNDERS, TO INTERROGATORIES PROPOUNDED BY THE DEFENDANT, MICHAEL A. ALBRECHT

5. State whether you claim damages for a loss of the consortium of Jean Marie Saunders, including her services, affection and society, as a result of the occurrences alleged in your complaint, and, if so, state all facts upon which such claim is based.

Further Answer

Yes, my wife was unable to perform her duties as a wife and mother in that she was unable to care for her children, for her house, and to a lesser extent, for herself for a considerable period of time. Our sexual relations were terminated for a considerable period of time and our social life together was greatly altered and curtailed.

14. State whether there is any activity, not referred to above, in which you and Jean Marie Saunders participated together before her alleged injuries which you claim has been limited or terminated because of the occurrences alleged in your complaint, and, if so, for each such activity, state:
   (a) a description of the activity;
   (b) the injury which caused the termination or limitation;
   (c) the extent to which such activity is limited; and
   (d) whether Jean Marie Saunders will be able to resume such activity at a future time, and, if so, when.

Further Answer

(a) None.
(b) Not applicable.
(c) Not applicable.
(d) Not applicable.

18. State the name, address and field of claimed expertise of each person whom you have retained, consulted and/or specially employed as an expert in anticipation of this litigation and/or in preparation for trial herein, whether or not such person will be called as a witness at trial; and as to each person expected to be called as an expert witness on your behalf at trial, state:
   (b) the substance of all facts and opinions to which he is expected to testify, and
   (c) a summary of the grounds upon which each such opinion will be based.

Further Answer

(b) (1) When complication of a rectal/vaginal fistula was expected after the first baby was born, a consultation was not obtained from an expert in the field.

(2) It would have been much easier and safer to have repaired the fistula before the second pregnancy was initiated, since the failure rate to correct such a defect carries a much greater risk during a pregnancy and likewise at the time of delivery.

(3) Dr. Albrecht's notes do not go into the meticulous details of layers of closure in the surgical repair of the patient, Jean Marie Saunders', lesions.

(c) (1) (Relates to (b) 1.) It was bad medical practice for Dr. Albrecht not to obtain a consultation at this time.

(2) (Relates to (b) 2.) The traumatic effect on the tissue because of the baby's head passing through the vagina, would cause further complications with regard to the fistula and had a successful repair been effected prior to the second pregnancy, delivery by Caesarean would have spared a breakdown of such repair, and it was bad medical practice not to do so.

(3) (Relates to (b) 3.) The notes of Dr. Albrecht's surgical repair should have contained meticulous details of the layers of closure and it is bad medical practice for them not to.

Signed under the pains and penalties of perjury this ______ day of July, Yr.–2.

____
Walter F. Saunders

THE ST. PAUL COMPANIES

Dr. Michael A. Albrecht
70 Barrows Road

December 13, Yr.–3.

Dear Dr. Albrecht:

Named Insured Michael A. Albrecht	Claim Number __________	Policy Number __________
Plaintiff Jean Marie Saunders	Date of Loss 11/01/Yr.–5.	Summons & Complaint No. 1587
Defendant Michael A. Albrecht		
Court ______ Superior Court	State of ______	Amount sued for $200,000.00

This will acknowledge receipt of the Summons and Complaint recently served upon you in this matter. We are referring the defense of this lawsuit to Simmons & Dabney, Suite 1180, 45 Talmidge Street, ______, who will protect your interests pursuant to the terms and conditions of the above insurance policy.

We wish to point out that the amount sued for is in excess of the limits of liability provided under this policy. This Company cannot be responsible for the payment of any amount in excess of these limits of liability in the settlement of any claim or satisfaction of any judgment which may be rendered. You may, therefore, be personally liable for such amount.

It is your privilege, if you so desire, to engage your own attorney at your own expense in the defense of your uninsured exposure in this suit. You should also immediately consult your own attorney or notify our office in writing if you have any intention of presenting a cross complaint or counterclaim to the action which has been brought against you. We assure you that our attorneys will cooperate to the fullest extent possible with any attorneys you may select.

Our attorneys will communicate with you in due course in the preparation of your defense. In the meantime we ask that you do not discuss this case with anyone except your own attorney, the above law firm or a representative of this Company.

Yours very truly,

____

Claims Supervisor

RE: Jean Marie Saunders & Walter F. Saunders v.
Michael A. Albrecht

EXPENSES

Filing Fee—Complaint—	Superior Court	$ 10.00
Deputy Sheriffs		
Summons to defendant		9.60
		$ 19.60
Photo Service—Medical Illustrations		33.60
Deposition of Defendant		138.00
Deposition of Jean Marie Saunders and Walter F. Saunders		105.00
Marc Blake, M.D.		
Review of Hospital Record, Consultations, and Testimony		2,000.00
Melvin Good, M.D.		
Rendering Opinion and Court Appearance		2,500.00
Kent Knapp, M.D.		
Written Report and Consultation		500.00
		$5,276.60

TOTAL EXPENSES

$ 19.60
5,276.60
$5,296.20

COMBINATION PROFESSIONAL POLICY

PHYSICIANS, SURGEONS AND DENTISTS

St. Paul Insurance Company

A Capital Stock Company

ITEM 1. Name of Insured and Business Address

Michael A. Albrecht, M.D.
70 Barrows Rd.

ITEM 2. Policy Period

From	To	
11/1/YR-1	11/1/YR-0	12:01 A.M., standard time at the

address of the Named Insured as stated herein.

COVERAGES	LIMITS OF LIABILITY		PREMIUMS
A. PROFESSIONAL LIABILTY	$ 100,000.	Each Claim	
	$ 300,000.	Annual Aggregate	$________
B. OFFICE PREMISES AND PERSONAL INJURY LIABILITY	$________	Each Occurrence	
	$________	Annual Aggregate	
			$________
C. OFFICE PREMISES MEDICAL PAYMENTS	$________	Each Person	
	$________	Each Accident	
D. DEFENDANTS REIMBURSEMENT COVERAGE	$ 200.	Daily Rate	
	$ 5,000.	Per Suit Liability	$________

[C2012]

MICHAEL A. ALBRECHT, M. D.

Name: Jean Marie Saunders .... Age: 22 .... Date: 3/8/YR-6 .... Insurance: BC/BS(Med)
Address: 208 Arby Dr. .... Husband: Walter .... Tel ....
Para: 0 .... Date of Last Period: Dec. 9 .... Date of Quickening .... Expected Date of Labor Delivery: 9/16/YR-6
Gravida: I .... Polio 1st .... 2nd .... 3rd 4th: 4/13/YR-6
Family History: neg .... Hermatological History: hct. 37.4 hgb. 13
.... Hinton: non reactive
Past History: neg .... Group: O .... Rh: Pos
.... Husb's group .... Rh ....
.... Anti-Rh agglutinins ....
Previous Pregnancies and Labors .... Absent: antibody screening test neg.
.... Present ....
.... Titres ....
Menstrual History .... Transfusions ....
Present Pregnancy ....
X-Ray Pelvimetry ....
Physical Examination ....
Pelvic Examination: Small gynecoid pelvis
Obstetrical and Medical Complications ....

WATCH FOR DYSTOCIA IF ANY SIZE BABY

3-8-YR-6	Blood tests ordered. Start vitamins depending on blood tests.
4-5-YR-6	Normal prenatal course. She has a pretty good cold but unless she runs a fever we will leave her alone.
5-4-YR-6	Normal prenatal course.
6-4-YR-6	Normal course. Weight gain
7-9-YR-6	Normal prenatal course
8-17-YR-6	Normal prenatal course
9-28-YR-6	Perineotins-sc-infected but looks o.k. (2 wks.)

8/31/YR-6 Cervix is thin. Vertex is mid. 10 days
9/11/YR-6 Two finger dilated. Delivery soon I'm sure.
10/12/YR-6 Re-checked the perineum. This thing is healing well, has a small hemorrhoid. will check again at 6 wk. ch.
11/8/YR-6 postpartum check. She says she is passing gas vaginally. I can't find it but it probably is there. Check again in 2 wks. Am terribly worried that she has a recto-vaginal fistula.

[C2013]

Date	3/8	4/5	5/4	6/4	[illegible]	8/17	[illegible]	9/[illegible]	11/3	11/26
Headache		+	|	|	|	off & on		occas		
Vision		+	|	|	|	|	—	|		
Nausea		+	|	heartburn	yes	|	|	|		
Vom.		—	|	|	|	|	|	|		
Pain		cramps +	side cramps	pressure	side cramps	back	back	[illegible] cramps		
Digestion		—	|	|	|	|	|	|		
Bowels		—	|	const.	|	irreg	occas	[illegible]		
Urine		—	freq	freq	|	|	|	|		
Bleeding		—	|	|	|	|	|	|		
Leuk.		—	sl.	sl	sl.	sl.	sl	sl.		
Sleep		poor	fair	|	better	fair	no	no		
Weight	108	110	117	125	128	135	139	139	115	
B. P.	110/62	118/58	110/58	102/58	100/[illegible]	108/58	114/78	120/7[illegible]	1[illegible]/72	
Pulse			80	68	88	84		76		
Edema			|	|	|	—	[illegible]	[illegible]		
Breasts			sore	sore	sore	sore	sore	sore		
Motion			yes	yes	yes	yes	yes	yes		
Fundus			[illegible]	|	|	[illegible]	|	|		
Fetal Heart						120				
Position						[illegible]				
Engagement						[illegible]				
Alb.	0	0	0	0					0	
Sug.	0	0	0	0					0	

[C2014]

MICHAEL A. ALBRECHT, M. D.

Name .. Jean Marie Saunders .. Age . 23 .. Date .... Insurance ......
Address .. 25 Mill Street .. Husband .. Walter ..... Tel ....
Para . I .... Date of Last Period . 4/3/YR-5 . Date of Quickening .... Expected Date of Labor . YR-4 1/10 . Delivery ....
Gravida .. II .... Polio 1st .... 2nd .... 3rd .... 4th ....
Family History . Grandparents diabetic ... Hematological History . hgh 12.6/hct 35.1
.... Hinton .. now reactive ....
Past History .. neg. .... Group .... 0 .... Rh .. positive .....
.... Husb's group .... Rh ....
.... Anti-Rh agglutinins ....
Previous Pregnancies and Labors .... Baby .... Absent ....
ut. 7-1 .... Present ....
Labor 4 hours .... Titres ....
....
Menstrual History .... Transfusions . antibody screening neg. ....
Present Pregnancy ....
....
X-Ray Pelvimetry ....
Physical Examination ....
....
....
Pelvic Examination ....
....
....
Obstetrical and Medical Complications ....
....
....

6-25-YR-5 Small gynecoid pelvis. Blood tests ordered. Vitamins deferred until we see her blood count. Concerned about her potential rectavaginal fistual here. Watch this near term.

8-12-YR-5 Normal Prenatal course.

9-13-YR-5 Normal prenatal course.

10-25-YR-5 Normal prenatal course.

11-26-YR-5 The vertex is in her pelvis. I don't think it is going to be too big a baby. 3 weeks internal.

12-19-YR-5 Is 2 fingers dialated. Vertex is mid. Posterior. See in 1 week. Induce at that time.

12-26-YR-5 Is 3 fingers dialated. Vertex is mix. Admit for tomorrow.

1-13-YR-4 Has a rectal vaginal fistula which did not heal with the repair. Her uterus is well diluted. She is on methagin for 1 more day. Stay on her iron until I see her in 6 weeks. At that time we will discuss repairing this mess.

[C2015]

Date	[illegible]	8/12	[illegible]	[illegible]	[illegible]	[illegible]	[illegible]	[illegible]	[illegible]	[illegible]
Headache	yes	|	yes	yes	+	—	+		[illegible]	
Vision	—	|					—			
Nausea	yes	|	—	—	yes	—	—			
Vom.	no	|	—	—	[illegible]	—				
Pain	[illegible]	[illegible]	[illegible]	[illegible]	[illegible]	[illegible]	[illegible]			
Digestion	[illegible]	[illegible]	[illegible]	|	—	—	—			
Bowels	—	|	—	|	—	—	—			
Urine	—	|	—	|	—	—	—			
Bleeding	—	|	—		—	+	+			
Leuk.	—	|	↑	↑	Sl.	↑	↑			
Sleep	no	fair		|	—	—	poor			
Weight	106	108	114	130	138	132	129½	112	112	
B. P.	108/[illegible]	110/66	100/60	[illegible]	[illegible]	[illegible]	[illegible]	[illegible]	[illegible]	
Pulse	/			—	—					
Edema	—		—	—	[illegible]					
Breasts	sore	N	sore	—	—					
Motion	no	+	yes	yes	yes					
Fundus		3/5	|	[illegible]	[illegible]					
Fetal Heart		—		120	130					
Position		—		[illegible]	[illegible]					
Engagement				0	+					
Alb.	0			0	0					
Sug.	0				0					

[C2016]

PARKER MEMORIAL HOSPITAL

Name	Admittance Date	Discharge Date	Hospital No.
Jean Marie Saunders	1/4/YR-4	1/9/YR-4	365018

Final Diagnosis:
Primary Diagnosis: 1. Postpartum hemorrhage
Probable recto-vaginal fistula

Procedures:
Operations:
Treatment:

Methergine
Parenteral fluids
Observation

Complications: None

Treatment of Complications: None

Result/Disposition: Improved

Narrative Summary (If Indicated):

This 24-year-old girl was admitted to the hospital approximately seven days postpartum with heavy bright red bleeding. In the course of her stay her blood level dropped to 9.5 gm. hemoglobin and she stabilized nicely there.

The uterus responded to Methergine therapy and at the time of discharge it was well involuted and with only a minimal flow. She was to be treated further on the outside with oral iron therapy. It should be noted that at the time of delivery a previous recto-vaginal fistula was encountered and an attempt was made to repair it by episiotomy but unfortunately the episiotomy had to practically go through this area. At the time of discharge whether this repair will hold remains doubtful and the patient and her husband were well aware of this complication.

Dictated 1.15 (Signature) Michael A. Albrecht
Michael A. Albrecht, M.D./pjn 1.15

[C2017]

PARKER MEMORIAL HOSPITAL

Name	Floor	Admittance Date	Hospital No.
Jean Marie Saunders	NI		365018

Chief Complaint:

Vaginal bleeding.

Present Illness: 24-year-old Gravida 2/Para 2, who is about seven days postpartum, is admitted to the hospital with bright red bleeding. Her delivery was without complication, with the exception of the trial to repair a previous rectovaginal fistula. It became apparent at the time of discharge and subsequently, in the following days, that the repair was not going to work out too well, and this has been a problem. On the day of admission, and one day earlier she had a heavy flow of blood Her blood count was taken in the Emergency Room two days prior to admission and it was normal. On the day of admission it still remains normal, but she is flowing heavily.

Past History: Since her delivery, it should be noted she is passing gas and fecal-colored material through her vagina as well as her rectum. She has been afebrile. She is nursing at the present time, and doing very well in that department.

Family History:

Not contributory.

Dictated 1.6.YR-4

(Signature) Michael A. Albrecht

Michael A. Albrecht, M.D./pmr
1.7
[C2018]

000443

OPERATIVE RECORD

PARKER MEMORIAL HOSPITAL

362904-0 411-1
SAUNDERS, JEAN M. 12 6
25 Mill St.
CX 032 38 4810 GROUP 90572
C 4 17 P DNA
Dr. William Longwood 8AK

SURGEON Dr. Longwood ASSISTANT Dr. Andrews

ANESTHETIST Dr. Fowler CIRCULATING NURSE J. Lennon, R. N.

NAME	LOCATION	DATE	HOSPITAL NO.
Jean Saunders		4/11/YR-4	

DICTATED: 4/11/YR-4

REPORT

Preoperative Diagnosis: Rectovaginal fistula.
Postoperative Diagnosis: Same.
Operation: Right transverse loop colostomy for alimentary tract diversion and preparation for repair of rectovaginal vistula.

Procedure: This 24 year old gravida 2, para 2, AB 0 woman has a rectovaginal fistula probably as early as 18 months ago at the time of her first pregnancy. It was very small and basically asymptomatic at that time; however, after her second pregnancy four months ago, the fistula became quite large. There was an attempted repair at the end of the pregnancy which was not successful. It was felt that the most reasonable attempt would be to divert her alimentary tract and several weeks later repair it primarily.

Procedure: Under general endotracheal anesthesia, the patient was prepped with Betadine and draped in the appropriate manner. A 2" transverse horitontal incision was made in the right upper quadrant. This extended down through the subcu fascia. The rectus muscle was then retracted medially revealing the posterior rectus fascia and peritoneum. This was entered without difficulty. Bleeders in the subcu were tied off with #3-0 plain catgut. We were able to identify the omentum and transverse colon. The transverse colon loop was then brought up without difficulty. There was very little omental and mesenteric fat. We were able to find an area that was relatively avascular in which we could place a finger loop around. A plastic bridge was then applied underneath. Omentum was then tacked back into the abdomen. Small tags of epiploic fat were then clamped with straight clamps and tied off with #3-0 plain catgut. The fascia on the medial side was then tightened using #3-0 chromic catgut interrupted sutures x3.

A few subcutaneous sutures were then also placed and three skin stitches were placed on the medial border using #3-0 Dermalon sutures. The bridge was also reinforced with the same sutures. Using Babcock retraction, a clamp was applied transversely over the bowel and a segment of bowel was shaved off. The clamp will be left on for approximately 48 hours when the patient will have her alimentary tract open through the colostomy. Adaptic sponge was placed over the bowel and a dry cotton sponge was wrapped around. Dry sterile dressings were applied. The sponge and needle count were correct. At the end of the procedure, the patient also had the rectovaginal fistula checked and on examination under anesthesia, it was found to be quite large. She recovered from the anesthesia well. She was extubated in the operating room, returned to the recovery room in good condition.

William Longwood, M.D., 4/10/YR-4

cc: Dr. Andrews - dictated

(C2019)

PARKER MEMORIAL HOSPITAL

NAME	FLOOR	ADMITTANCE DATE	HOSPITAL NO
Jean Saunders			367904-0

CHIEF COMPLAINT:

Rectovaginal fistula.

PRESENT ILLNESS:

This is the fourth Parker Memorial admission for this generally healthy 24 year old white female who is gravida 2, para 2, AB 0. At the time of her first delivery in September of YR-6 she had a tight low forceps delivery requiring a complete perineotomy which was repaired at that time, but following which the patient noted passing gas pervagina. At the time of her second delivery in December of YR-5 an attempt was made to repair her rectovaginal fistula. However, she noted passing gas pervagina postpartum and subsequently noted the passage of stool per vagina on occasion. She was readmitted in January of YR-4 one week postpartum, for post partum hemorrhage, which was treated with Methergine and iron. Following discharge from that admission, she again noted the passage of fecal matter from her vagina and was referred by Dr. Cochrane to Dr. Walker who confirmed the diagnosis of rectovaginal fistula and is admitting the patient on this occasion for an elective diverting right transverse colostomy prior to subsequent perineal repair. She has had no infectious process or fevers related to this complication, but does wear a peripad when she is out of the house because of occasional fecal staining coming from her vagina.

PAST HISTORY:

The patient has had no other operations except as stated above. No other hospitalizations or significant illnesses. Her only medication at this time is iron, although she stopped taking birth control pills just a week ago. No known allergies. She does not smoke or drink.

Review of Systems: Entirely negative otherwise.

FAMILY HISTORY:

Positive for carcinoma of the lung in a grandparent and for hypertension in her father. NO family history of coronary artery disease, cerebrovascular disease, renal disease, bleeding disorders or asthma. There is a family history of adult onset diabetes.

DICTATED: 4/11/YR-4

(SIGNATURE) H. R. Chace

H.R. Chace, M.D./cav 4/15/YR-4

[C2030]

PARKER MEMORIAL HOSPITAL

NAME	ADMITTANCE DATE	DISCHARGE DATE	HOSPITAL NO.
Jean Marie Saunders	4/10/YR-4	4/17/YR-4	367904-0

FINAL DIAGNOSIS:
PRIMARY DIAGNOSIS: 1. Rectovaginal fistula.

PROCEDURES:
OPERATIONS:
TREATMENT: Right upper quadrant loop transverse diverting colostomy.

COMPLICATIONS: None.

TREATMENT OF COMPLICATIONS: None.

RESULT/DISPOSITION: Discharged home, condition improved.

NARRATIVE SUMMARY (IF INDICATED):

This is a 24-year-old married lady who was admitted with a known rectovaginal fistula which occurred after a perineotomy in delivery She had two deliveries, the last one about four months ago. Her height, 5'4 weight, 116 lbs.; blood pressure, 130/82.

LABORATORY: Hematocrit was 43.3; hemoglobin, 16 grams; white blood count and differential, normal; blood sugar, 83; BUN,11; creatinine, 1.1; urine showed 25 to 30 red cells; blood type was O, Rh+; chest x-ray was normal. Electrocardiogram read by Dr. Springer was within normal limits.

Her operative procedure had been discussed with the patient and she is admitted at this time for elective right upper quadrant loop transverse diverting colostomy and the plan is to send her home and then readmit her for repair of her rectovaginal fistula and then two months so later, to close her colostomy. She was done the day after admission and was discharged home today, her 7th postoperative day. Her condition was good. Her colostomy is working fine. She is up and about and doing well. She is to return to my office in approximately 2 weeks.

DICTATED: 4/17/YR-4

(SIGNATURE) [signature]

William M. Longwood, M.D./mjc

[C2031]

PARKER MEMORIAL HOSPITAL

NAME	FLOOR	ADMITTANCE DATE	HOSPITAL NO.
Jean Saunders		5-7/YR-4	368678-9

CHIEF COMPLAINT:

Recto-vaginal fistula.

PRESENT ILLNESS:

This is the 4th Parker Memorial Admission for this 24-year-old white female, housewife, who enters for repair of her recto-vaginal fistula. At her first birth in Sept. YR-6 she was said to have had a normal vaginal delivery with a tight low forceps delivery and complete perineotomy with repair. After that time she noted that she passed foul smelling gas through her vagina but only occasionally when she had more gas than usual, in her abdomen. At the time of her second birth 12-27 YR-5 there was a median episiotomy through a previous recto-vaginal fistula and at that time he attempted to repair the previous recto-vaginal fistula. However, even before she left the Hospital, she realized that she was passing gas and occasional amounts of diarrheal stool through her vagina. . She was readmitted on 1/4/YR-4 for vaginal hemorrhage, this being 7 days postpartum. At that time she was passing gases and stool through her vagina. Hemorrhage at that time was controlled by Methergine which did cause her uterus to involute. While at home she did continue to pass large amounts of stool with each defectation through her vagina. She returned here approximately four weeks ago for a right transverse loop colostomy. The information from that admission is not now available. Since that

PAST HISTORY: time her colostomy has functioned well. The contents are becoming thicker, perhaps due to the iron medication. The stool through her vagina gradually ceased and none has been passed for the past two weeks. She has had a normal white, not foul smelling vaginal discharge. She has no urinary symptoms. For the past two weeks she has not passed any mucous or any kind of stool through her anus. She returned now for repair of the recto-vaginal fistula.

ast History: No previous hospitalizations. She does mention being sensitive to cigarette smoke but has no allergies. Medications include Enduron 1 po., q.d. and iron pills.

FAMILY HISTORY:

Negative for diabetes, tuberculosis and arteriosclerotic cardiovascular disease.

DICTATED: 5-7 -YR-4

(SIGNATURE) Paula McGrory, M.D./lc 5-8-YR-4

[C2032]

PARKER MEMORIAL HOSPITAL

SAUNDERS, JEAN M. 12 06
25 Mill Street
BC 032384810
5 7 H 5 18 COS
DR. Longwood
JMS

SURGEON Dr. Longwood ASSISTANT Dr. Andrews

ANESTHETIST Dr. Chapel CIRCULATING NURSE W. Quinn

JEAN SAUNDERS 5/8/YR-4

NAME LOCATION DATE HOSPITAL NO.

Dictated: 5/8/YR-4 REPORT

Preoperative Diagnosis: Rectovaginal fistula.
Postoperative Diagnosis: Same.
Operation: Repair of rectovaginal fistula.

Indications: This 24 year old gravida 2, para 2 woman 18 months ago had a pregnancy with a small rectovaginal fistula noted at that time. She completed a second pregnancy five months ago at which time the fistula became quite large. There was an attempted repair at the time of her delivery which failed. She now has a very large defect. She was admitted here one month ago at which time she had an elective transverse colostomy performed to bypass the lower tract and give a better chance for healing in her final procedure. She is now coming in for rectovaginal fistula repair.

Procedure: Under general endotracheal anesthesia, the patient first had her bladder evacuated. She was prepped with Betadine and draped in the usual manner. Examination of the perineum and rectum and vagina demonstrated approximately 3-4 cm. in length rectovaginal fistula extending from a small lip of perineum that did divide the vagina and rectum. There was less than 1/2 cm. in width extending up towards the cervix. Palpating up towards the cervix demonstrated that there was decent tissue between the rectum and the vagina, but had quite a high distance. Our first step was to divide our bridge of tissue. We then identified the site at the mid portion between vaginal and rectal mucosa. Using sharp dissection with a knife, we were able to separate these layers and finally find the plane of vaginal tissue. The vaginal mucosa was then dissected from and retracted superiorly over the urethra. This was continued all the way posterior toward where decent normal tissue was identified. We then proceeded to clean off the rectal area and try to identify sphinoter muscle.

[C2033]

JEAN SAUNDERS Continued.....

We could identify some sphincter posteriorly, but anterior seemed to be completely gone. There were some perineal bands extending from the lateral levator muscles and these were identified and carefully trimmed and retracted laterally. We completely cleaned off the area of perirectal tissue and finally came up with a large band of extension of levators on either side. We then used #0 chromic catgut to approximate our levators extending as high as possible. We brought our sutures up proximally first to help approximate our ends. The levator muscle was quite thick and in good condition. It came together quite easily. We then approximated the levators in interrupted type fashion, bringing them halfway down from the site of the previous fistula. We then crossed over our widened bands of fascia extending from the levators. The right band was placed superiorly and the inferior band was placed over the edge of the rectum. Once completed, we then used a #2 chromic in a running type fashion to close our posterior vaginal mucosa in a running type fashion. This was brought down all the way to the level of the rectum. We then used #2-0 chromic to approximate our rectal mucosa edge to our skin. At the end of the procedure, we could easily place one finger into the rectum and there was a good sphincter type tone. Two fingers could easily be placed in the vagina. There was at least a 1" thickness of levator muscle across and between. We next packed the vagina with a long length of 1" Iodoform gauze. A #16 Foley catheter was placed within the bladder and placed to Foley drainage. A peripad was placed. Sponge, needle and instrument count were correct. The patient awoke in the operating room, extubated and brought to the recovery room in good condition.

William Longwood, M.D., 5/8/YR-4

cc: Warren Andrews, M.D.
(dictated)

Michael Albrecht, M.D.

[C2034]

PARKER MEMORIAL HOSPITAL

NAME	ADMITTANCE DATE	DISCHARGE DATE	HOSPITAL NO.
Jean Saunders	5/7/YR-4	5/18/YR-4	368678-9

FINAL DIAGNOSIS:
PRIMARY DIAGNOSIS:

1. Rectovaginal fistula.
2. Status post quadrant loop transverse diverting colostomy.
3. Anemia secondary to repair of fistula.

PROCEDURES:
OPERATIONS:
TREATMENT:

Repair of rectovaginal fistula, Sitz baths and Ampicillin, iron.

COMPLICATIONS:

None.

TREATMENT OF COMPLICATIONS:

None.

RESULT/DISPOSITION: Improved. Discharged home.

NARRATIVE SUMMARY (IF INDICATED): This is a 24-year old married lady who is admitted for repair of a rectovaginal fistula. She had a previous right upper quadrant loop transverse diverting colostomy approximately a month ago and is now admitted for repair of the fistula.

Height 5'3", weight 112 lb., blood pressure 108/78. White blood count and differential were normal. Postoperative hematocrit dropped to 29.9 and she has been placed on iron. Admission urine showed some blood but she was having her period and after this repeat urine was normal. Urine colony count was less than 25,000 and blood type was O,Rh+. Electrocardiogram read by Dr. Springer was within normal limits and chest x-ray was normal. On the day after admission she had a repair of rectovaginal fistula.

She was fairly uncomfortable postoperatively, been on Sitz and she was started on some Ampicillin and she is discharged home today, her 10th postoperative day. Her temperature, pulse and respirations are normal and she is slowly improving. She is discharged home with some Empirin Compound ½ gr. Codeine and some Tetracycline 250 mg. 4 times a day for the next 10 days, to continue with Sitz baths and to return to my office in 2 weeks. The plan is to readmit her some time in the next 2 months for closure of her colostomy.

William Longwood, M.D., 5/19/YR-4

5/18/YR-4
cc: Dr. Albrecht

[C2035]

PARKER MEMORIAL HOSPITAL

NAME	ADMITTANCE DATE	DISCHARGE DATE	HOSPITAL NO.
Jean Saunders	5/20/YR-4	5/23/YR-4	369073-2

FINAL DIAGNOSIS:
PRIMARY DIAGNOSIS: 1.

Rectovaginal fistula, status postoperative.
Right upper quadrant ileal loop colostomy.
Secondary anemia.
Bleeding from perineal region.

PROCEDURES:
OPERATIONS:
TREATMENT:

Symptomatic	Ampicillin
Sitz baths	Multivitamins
Iron	Valium

COMPLICATIONS: None

TREATMENT OF COMPLICATIONS: None

RESULT/DISPOSITION: Improved

NARRATIVE SUMMARY (IF INDICATED):

This is a 24-year-old married lady who was just recently discharged from the hospital three days ago after repair of a rectovaginal fistula. She also has had a previous right upper quadrant loop transverse colostomy and began to have bleeding in the perineal region. She was seen in the Emergency Room for a checkup and it was thought that she may have had some blood staining around the wound but this was intact. It was felt that she may have had some clots in her rectum also. She was admitted for observation.

Hematocrit on admission was 33. Condition was stable. The patient's blood pressure was 110/70. Her most recent hematocrit was 30.4. She did some small amount of staining and also complained of some discomfort and a feeling that the rectum was full. On rectal examination a good sphincter tone with no clots palpable in the rectum. She was started on ambulation and sitz baths. Pelvic examination was not done. She was then placed on iron and multivitamins and was discharged home. The exact cause of this bleeding is not know; it is probably from her perineal wound where some of the sutures were re-absorbed and it may be she had a collection of blood which was then released.

She was discharged home on iron, Ampicillin, and multivitamins. She is to return to my office in ten days to two weeks for checkup.

cc: Dr. Albrecht
Dictated 5.23

William Longwood, M.D./Pat 5.29

[C2036]

PARKER MEMORIAL HOSPITAL

NAME	FLOOR	ADMITTANCE DATE	HOSPITAL NO.
Jean Saunders		5-20-YR-4	369073-2

CHIEF COMPLAINT:

Bleeding.

PRESENT ILLNESS:

This 24-year-old patient was just discharged from the hospital about 3 days ago after a rectal vaginal fistula repair on 5-8-YR-4She has been home about 3 days and this morning she noticed that she was having quite a bit of bleeding from her perineal area. She came to the Emergency Room for a check. In the Emergency Room she was found to have some blood staining around the wound which was intact but she did pass some clots from her rectum. She still felt like her rectum was full. Her hematocrit was 33 in the emergency room. She was stable. She was admitted for observation.

PAST HISTORY:

See old chart and recent admission. Basically she has been very healthy. Only medications has been Iron which she is taking now. She is not allergic to any medications. Previous operation, see old chart.

FAMILY HISTORY:

See old chart.

DICTATED: 5-20-YR-4

(SIGNATURE)

Alan Flint, m.D./lc 5-21-75

[C2037]

PARKER MEMORIAL HOSPITAL

NAME	FLOOR	ADMITTANCE DATE	HOSPITAL NO.
SAUNDERS, Jean			367904-0

CHIEF COMPLAINT:

This is the 7th admission for this 24-year old white female who comes in for closure of her colostomy.

Patient is a mother of two children. She does not drink. She is an occasional smoker.

PRESENT ILLNESS:

Her history dates back to two years ago when she first had her delivery and after a perineotomy in delivery she developed a rectovaginal fistula. The fistula did not heal and worsened after the second delivery. In April, YR-4, patient had a transverse colostomy and a month later a repair of her rectovaginal fistula. At present she notes still some discharges from the area but her colostomy is functioning very well. She is in now for closure of her colostomy.

PAST HISTORY:

She is not allergic to any medicine. She is not on any medications at present.

Review of systems: negative.

FAMILY HISTORY:

Negative.

(Signature) Francis Niven, MD/rm 7/16

[C2038]

PATHOLOGICAL REPORT

PARKER MEMORIAL HOSPITAL

Pathological No. S-75-1688 | Date July 16 YR-4 | Unit No. 370802-1

Name SAUNDERS, Jean M. | Age 24 | Ward PED-185-3

Doctor Longwood

Material: A. Rt. & Lt. fallopian tube segments (rt. tube with string)
B. Transverse colon

Clinical Diagnosis: Rectal-Vaginal fistula
Colostomy

Description of Specimen:

A. Specimen with attached black suture consists of soft pinkish gray 5 x 4 mm. fragment of tissue. This specimen is labeled A1.

Also received are 2 similar appearing segments respectively measuring 5 x 3 mm. and 8 x 3 mm. which is comprised of soft pale pinkish gray tissue. Section from this segment is labeled A2.

B. Specimen consists of an 8 x up to 3.5 cm. segment of large bowel presenting at one end around its lumen an irregular rim of firm white tissue. At this end a 1 x 0.5 cm. mucosal bulge is noted. The entire external surface shows irregular fibrous thickening. The lumen is widely patent throughout. The wall is somewhat edematous throughout. One half of the mucosal surface is deep crimson and approximately 1.3 cm. from the colostomy opening a 2.5 x 0.7 cm. longitudinal hyperplastic zone is seen to border a shallow crater, the middle of which presents a suture thread connecting the 2 borders surrounding the crater. Section from the colostomy end is labeled B1.

Diagnosis: (Microscopic) A1 and A2: Segments of oviducts.
B: Segment of large bowel consistent with revision of colostomy.

Examined by: Margaret T. Troy
Margaret T. Troy, M.D./pml

[C2039]

PARKER MEMORIAL HOSPITAL

Jean M. Saunders

Ped. 7/16/ YR-4 370802

We next proceeded to mobilize the already standing colostomy. This was done by excising the colostomy in a transverse manner and a bielliptical incision. Mobilization of this was done sharply with scissors and with blunt dissection and the transverse colon became quite mobile. We then trimmed the edges of the mucosa to allow it to roll back, having previously been turned outwards. As this was done we then proceeded to close the colon in a transverse manner with interrupted #4-0 silk sutures. After the colon had been satisfactorily closed, we then placed in our fingers to examine lumen patency. We were surprised to find that the lumen had been obliterated by the bogginess of the mucosa that had been turned in from the previous standing colostomy. We then proceeded to mobilize the distal and proximal areas of the transverse colon besides the previous colostomy and this was done. The mesentery was divided between individual Kelly clamps and ligated with 3 silk ligatures. We then cleaned off the borders of the colon where we had ripped places for the clamps to go and for the anastomosis to take place. At this time we then placed 2 clamps at the site for excision of the bowel, this being approximately 10 cm. away from the previous anastomosis on the bowel and excised the colostomy and the area generally surrounding same. After this had been done we then began a closed anastomosis placing interrupted #4-0 silk sutures radially around the closed bowel, between clamps. This having been done successfully we were also able to turn the bowel with good mobility. The clamps were removed and a very perfect circle was then created. Individual silks were tied down without any problem. The anastomosis at that time admitted a finger and a half in diameter and was much more satisfactory. We then closed the defect in the mesentery with #4-0 silk interrupted sutures. After copious irrigation with Saline Solution, we began closing the abdomen, at which time sponge count was correct. Closure of the abdomen was with chromic catgut in the peritoneum and in the fascia and in addition to subcutaneous tissue. Interrupted nylon sutures were placed in the skin for skin reapproximation. Estimated blood loss for this procedure was 125 cc. and fluids intraoperatively included 600 cc. of Dextrose, 5%, 1/4 Saline. The patient had no intraoperative problems, was extubated and returned to the Recovery Room without difficulty.

7/17 cc. Dr. West

William Longwood, M. D.

[C2040]

370802 1 PED 185 3
SAUNDERS, JEAN M. 12 06 50
25 Mill Street
BC-90572
7 14 W 7 21 COS

SURGEON Dr. Longwood ASSISTANT Dr. West

ANESTHETIST Dr. Fowler CIRCULATING NURSE R. Rizemann

Jean M. Saunders	Ped.	7/16/YR-4	370802
NAME	LOCATION	DATE	HOSPITAL NO.

Dictated: 7/17/YR-4

REPORT

Preoperative Diagnosis: Transverse colostomy for previous diversion from rectovaginal fistula secondary to childbirth.

Postoperative diagnosis: Same.

OPERATION: TRANSVERSE ABDOMINAL BILATERAL TUBAL LIGATION: CLOSING OF COLOSTOMY BY TRANSVERSE COLONIC RESECTION AND END-TO-END ANASTOMOSIS.

INDICATIONS: This 34-year-old lady, at the time of her last childbirth in the latter portion of last year, had some tearing of the vaginal posterior wall and had the development of a rectovaginal fistula. This was subsequently closed in late May and the patient has done extremely well.

PROCEDURE: With the patient in the lithotomy position, she had a rectal examination which showed the posterior vaginal wall to be intact in the vagina and there was no communication apparent from digital vaginal examination, nor visually from a rectovaginal fistula. Previous operations had obliterated this. At this time, a suction cup was put on the cervix uteri for mobility. The abdomen was prepped and draped and with the patient under good general anesthesia, a midline lower abdominal incisiion was made approximately 7 cm. in diameter. Upon entering the abdomen, with mobility of the uterus at our disposal from the suction, the left and right tubes were readily available. The right tube was isolated between Babcock clamps and the mesentery of same between hemostats. Using the scissors we divided and excised a piece of the right tube and ligated its stump with #5-0 silk. Silk was also used to ligate its mesentery which had also been mobilized. We proceeded to carry out the same procedure on the left side and hemostasis was made absolute after this. Closure of the abdomen was carried out using chromic catcut in the peritoncum in addition to the fascia and catgut also in the subcutaneous tissue. Plain catgut was placed in a subcuticular fashion for skin reapproximation. Suction was then removed from the uterus.

[C2041]

PARKER MEMORIAL HOSPITAL

NAME	ADMITTANCE DATE	DISCHARGE DATE	HOSPITAL NO.
Jean M. Saunders	7/14/YR-4	7/25/YR-4	370802-1

FINAL DIAGNOSIS:
PRIMARY DIAGNOSIS:

1. Status post rectovaginal fistula.
2. Right upper quadrant loop transverse colostomy.
3. Status post repair for vaginal fistula.

PROCEDURES:
OPERATIONS:
TREATMENT: Resection of transverse colon with end-to-end anastomosis.
Ancef.

COMPLICATIONS: None.

TREATMENT OF COMPLICATIONS: NOne.

RESULT/DISPOSITION: Improved.

NARRATIVE SUMMARY (IF INDICATED):

This is a 24-year old married lady who had a rectovaginal fistula in April and had a transverse colostomy and a month later had repair of rectovaginal fistula and is now admitted for closure of her colostomy. She is Para 2, Gravida 2. She is also admitted for an elective bilateral salpingectomy.

Weight 109 lb., blood pressure 100/60. Laboratory work- hematocrit 39.8, hemoglobin 13.8 gm., white count and differential were normal. Discharge hematocrit was 35.8, hemoglobin 12.6 gm. Blood type was O Rh+, RPR non-reactive and her urine was negative. Random blood sugar was 104, BUN 14, creatinine 1.1. Electrocardiogram read by Dr. Springer was within normal limits and chest x-ray was normal.

Patient was prepared for surgery and was started on Ancef and on her third hospital day the patient had a resection of a transverse colon with end-to-end anastomosis. She also had a bilateral partial salpingectomy with separate incision.

She has done well postoperatively. She started to have bouts of severe diarrhea for a day or two which had quieted down. She is now on a regular diet and moved her bowels once yesterday. Her temperature, pulse and respirations are normal. Her wound is clean. Discharged home her 9th postoperative day, condition good.

[C2042]

'27

PARKER MEMORIAL HOSPITAL

JEAN MARIE SAUNDERS

NURSE'S NOTES

XO-5Q

RS8VLL-1980
(pv)

Date & Hour	Diet	Urine	Stool	Treatment, Observations, Remarks	Signature
Jan. 4, YR-4 3:40 p.m.				24 yrs. female came to E.R states that she was hemorrhaging for the 2nd time after delivering baby on 12/27 YR-5. BP 118/80 – Stat blood work done. Vaginal exam done by Dr. Oliver many clots expelled – I.V.	
4:20 p.m.				started 1000 cc D5 N/Ringers c̄ #18 medicut c̄ 20u Pitocin	
4:30 p.m.				BP dropped 60/30 – Pt. pale cold c̄ clammy to touch Admit to [illegible] – Post Partum Hemmorrhage – Referred by Dr. Oliver for Dr. Albrecht	P. Trofford
5:00 p.m.				BP 84/60	
6:30 p.m.				1000 cc D5W Ringers Lactate c̄ 20 u Pitocin added, absorbed 1000 cc D5W Ringers Lactate c̄ 200 Syntocin added	Q. Wade
5 15				white female Admitted on stretcher color very pale IV infusing well T 98 P 88 R 20 wt. 120 Ht. 5'4" states she has no Allergies Also states she only takes ASP at Home Appears concerned About Ability to continue nursing BP 46-52 P 84-100 Had short period of crying PAD – mod. Amt. of Red staining & small-lg clots	J. Woodsum

4 [C2043]

'27

PARKER MEMORIAL HOSPITAL

JEAN MARIE SAUNDERS

NURSE'S NOTES

XO-5Q

RS8VLL-1980
(pv)

Date & Hour	Diet	Urine	Stool	Treatment, Observations, Remarks	Signature
3-11				instructed on how to use breast pump Shift care given Sips po urine 400cc IV 1550	K. North RN
1-5-YR-4 1 AM 1 AM					K. North RN
				1000 cc D5 in Ringers c̄ 20 u Syntocin finally absorbed	C. Wollenberg RN
12-6				IV infusing well Pt c/o ache in (R) upper arm - Pt. feels its due to IV Mod. amt. drainage on peri-pad Changed X2. Sm. clots present on first pad. BP 88/50, 98/50, 100/60 & P 72 & strong. Wants to be transferred to semi private rm. where she feels she would be able to sleep better	C. Chaffey RN
7-3 p.m.				Partial Am. care - Peri pads changed X3 - mod. amt's blood drng - no clots. Flow ↓ at this time Voiding well - Eating well c/o low back pain Breast pump used X2	M. Gulick RN
5:45 pm				Rx narc med given for c/o abd. pain	P. Hunt LPN
3-11:30				IV infusing well 1000 cc D 1/4 S c̄ 20 Pit Abs. 1000 cc D 1/4 S c̄ 20 Pit Absng - peri pad chg X II mod amt. sang drn c̄ 1 Sm clot c/o back pain Stated pain radiated to leg	

[C2044]

'27

PARKER MEMORIAL HOSPITAL

JEAN MARIE SAUNDERS

NURSE'S NOTES

XO-5Q

RS8VLL-1980
(pv)

Date & Hour	Diet	Urine	Stool	Treatment, Observations, Remarks	Signature
CON'T 3-11 30				& also upward & states shortness of breath. Dr. Fowler called & answered. back pain decreased in severity abd cramps cont. used breast pump X1 still appears very pale & apprehensive	K. North RN K. North RN
JAN. 6, YR-4 12 30 a.m.				RX (NARCAmed) given P. for abd. CRAMPS	B. Focile
10 15 a.m.				1000 D5 in 1/4 STR. saline ē 20 [illegible] absorbed	
				IV D/C	B. Focile
12 30 - 6 AM				Pt. APPEARED to have slept well p̄ med., peri PAD changed X1 - sm. amt. staining, voiding adeq.	B. Focile
7 - 9 30				A.M. Care - Breast pump used X1 - to be used now on pr R baby is now on formula at home Pad changed at 9 30 mod. amt. Red staining on peri pad	
9 30 - 11				Vaginal culture obtained & sent to lab - mod. am't bright red staining on peri pad Peri care done X 3	
11 - 3				c/o Backache & slight discomfort on inspiration - Dr. Albrecht notified. Refused to get up. States she feels very weak. Still appears pale.	S. Gustafson
3-11				[illegible] pain [illegible] back [illegible] cramps [illegible] mod amt. [illegible] pt. [illegible]	M. Reed

[C2045]

'27

PARKER MEMORIAL HOSPITAL

JEAN MARIE SAUNDERS

NURSE'S NOTES

XO-5Q

RS8VLL-1980 (pv)

Date & Hour	Diet	Urine	Stool	Treatment, Observations, Remarks	Signature
Jan 7, YR-4 12-6				Pt appeared to sleep well. No c/o. Small amt. red staining on peripad. Up to BR - voiding adequately.	AN
7-3:30 pm.				Self pm care. back care given. Taking diet and fluids well - peripad changed X 3. sm. dk red staining noted. Up + about - voiding adequately	Rodgers
3-11				Pt ambu in corridor x 1, tolerated fairly well. Peripad chain x 1 - mod. dark staining [illegible] large [illegible]. [illegible] backgown resting comfortably	Selcun
Jan 8, YR-4 12-6				Appeared to sleep well all noc. No c/o. Mod. amt light stain on peri-pad. sleeping quietly @ present	D.A.C.
9:00				Pt. up to shower in am Up + about ad lib Peri pad Changed X 3 c̄, mod amt of dk red staining. Offers no Complaints	Lilli
3-11		✓		ONE PAD USED, SM. AMT. LT. PINK DRAINAGE. AMBULATING, VOIDED 400 CC. PREPARED FOR NOC	JK
9:35 pm				[illegible] PO for headache	
Jan. 9, YR-4 12-6				Appeared to sleep well. Peripad not changed. Very sm. amt. light pink drainage present. Lump @ base of spine noted - pt states it does not hurt. No c/o. sleeping quietly @ present.	JR
8-1:30				Pt. up to shower in am. BC given. C/o "pain that goes from lower back up to my head." Up + about ad lib Peri-pad Changed X 3, c̄ mod amt of dark red staining.	Lilli
1:30				Pt. discharged via wheelchair.	

[C2046]

'27

PARKER MEMORIAL HOSPITAL

JEAN MARIE SAUNDERS

NURSE'S NOTES

XO-5Q

RS8VLL-1980 (pv)

Date & Hour	Diet	Urine	Stool	Treatment, Observations, Remarks	Signature
4/10/YR-4 2pm				White female admitted to Rm 411 admitting dx: Vaginal-rectal fistula. Referring Physician [illegible] T 47 4/3 P 130/82 P 72 R 20 No known allergies No dentures Pt is menstruating at present. Appears sl nervous. Pre op teaching done - Pt. comprehensive	Aruban
2⁴⁵pm				Prep done from nipple line to top of pubes. Pt. very inquisitive concerning surgery. As many questions answered as possible.	Aruban
3-11³⁰				Pt. pacing hall - very nervous appearance	T.R.
APR 11, YR-4					
12-6	NPO-OR			Appeared to sleep [illegible] well [illegible]	Michele Coccia
6 am				Prepared for surg	
7am				Pre-op Med Given IM as ordered	
8A	Surgery			#18 medicut in [illegible] hand	
				500 cc D5 1/4S started & running	
				[illegible] [illegible] [illegible] colostomy	
				To Recovery Room	P. Matei RN
10³⁰am	Recovery			500 D5 1/4 NSal [illegible] 500 D5 1/4 N. sal [illegible]	
1 [illegible]pm.				[illegible] for pain	
7-3 (error)					

[C2047]

'27

PARKER MEMORIAL HOSPITAL

JEAN MARIE SAUNDERS

NURSE'S NOTES

XO-5Q

RS8VLL-1980 (pv)

Date & Hour	Diet	Urine	Stool	Treatment, Observations, Remarks	Signature
11^{30}-3^{30}				Ret'd from RR alert - color good. drg c̄ staining - increased to fifty cent piece during, moving well, coughing c̄ prod.; OOB to chair to void - 100cc; voided x 2 on bedpan 75cc + 25cc; tol ice chips, per pad - mod dark red staining - changed x1, IV of D5 ¼ S 500cc abs, 1000cc of D5 ¼ S hung	JR
3-11^{30} PM				Comfortable evening. Douglas [illegible] vaginal - sleeping in naps all evening. Stg has some old staining - intact. IV running well. Voided.	Paulsen
APR. 12, YR-4 1^{20} 4"				1000 D5 ¼ S abs 1000 cc D5 ¼ [illegible] rd (nara) Demerol pain I.V running well - voiding	Arubon
12-6				sm amt new st on drg conf medicated IV infusing well voiding	
8:20 AM 7-3				Rx (Vistaril) Im for pain AM care. Backcare. No new staining noted. C/o some cramps. Taking small amt of clear liq. only sips. IV running well	N. M. East
11^{00}				1000cc D5 ¼ S abs. 1000 cc D5 ¼ S added. voiding well. amb x 2. did very well. No c/o @ present.	Traft

[C2048]

27

PARKER MEMORIAL HOSPITAL

JEAN MARIE SAUNDERS

NURSE'S NOTES

XO-5Q

RS8VLL-1980 (pv)

Date & Hour	Diet	Urine	Stool	Treatment, Observations, Remarks	Signature
3-11:30				Amb x 2 - Tol well	[illegible]
				Pt states pain med doesn't	
				hold her more than 2°	
				Dsg has ↑ sero - sang staining	
				on it. Tol flds poorly - c/o ↑ gas pains	
				IV infusing	
				Some colostomy teaching	
				alone. pt shown bag & given	
				booklet to read. Pt would like	
				to speak to a member of ostomy	
				club before discharge.	
				Pt appears receptive & cooperative.	
				Backcare	
9 PM				1000 D5 1/4 S abs'd	Daria
				1000 D5 1/4 S hung IV	
5:30 pm + 9 pm				Rx med (narc) IM given for incisional pain	
APR 13, YR-4					
12-7:30 AM				RX (NARC) FOR PAIN (STOMA REGION)	[illegible]
2:15 AM				STAT RX (NARC) GIVEN FOR	
				PERSISTANT STOMA PAIN.	
2-6				Sleeping comf ō stat med.	
				IV infusing well. voiding	
				[illegible] + old staining on dsg	
6 AM				Colostomy clamp removed by	
				Dr Andrews — [illegible]	
				flatus expelled. Passing liq feces.	
				[illegible] BM removed	
				from stoma by Dr Andrews	
				Colostomy bag in place	
6:30 AM				1000 cc D5 1/4 S abs 1000 cc D5 1/4 S hung	Noble

[C2049]

'27

PARKER MEMORIAL HOSPITAL

JEAN MARIE SAUNDERS

NURSE'S NOTES

XO-5Q

RS8VLL-1980 (pv)

Date & Hour	Diet	Urine	Stool	Treatment, Observations, Remarks	Signature
12 pm				500 cc D5 ¼ S c/o IV ∅	
				IV removed	Tell
2pm				RX (NARC) PO FOR PAIN	Severa
7-3				AM care. Backcare given. Ambulated	
				well in hallway twice. Taking fluids	
				fairly well. Colostomy bag emptied	
				c̄ some liquid stool. Colostomy	
				teaching started. Pt. emptied bag	
				by self + seems very interested.	
				Voided well. Good day	Malone
3-11[30]				Pt changed own colostomy bag.	
				Pt. somewhat teary-eyed this	
				pm. Up amb by self	
				c/o some incisinal pain	
				voiding q s. Tol po's well	
				Back CARE	Dubonnet
7[30] pm				Rx narc given pt for pain	
11[15] pm				Rx narc given hs for sleep	Sal
APR 14, YR-4					
12-6				Appeared to sleep well n/c.	
3[45] AM				Rx NARCOTIC GIVEN PT FOR PAIN —	
6 —				Colostomy bag emptied - sm. amt	
				brown liq. stool —	
8-2		✓		SELF AM CARE + BACK CARE GIVEN	B. DARIEN
				AMBULATED IN HALLWAY. TAKING DIET	
				FAIR PT CHANGED COLOSTOMY BAG BY SELF	
				+ IS INTERESTED IN DOING HER OWN CARE.	
				PT c/o FATIGUE + PAIN AROUND STOMA	
				NAPPED MOST OF PM	
1[15] pm				Rx narcotic given for pain (PO)	B. DARIEN
5[45] pm				Rx NARC given for pain (PO)	Traft

[C2060]

'27

PARKER MEMORIAL HOSPITAL

JEAN MARIE SAUNDERS

NURSE'S NOTES

XO-5Q
RS8VLL-1980
(pv)

Date & Hour	Diet	Urine	Stool	Treatment, Observations, Remarks	Signature
3-10	good	✓	✓	H.S. care. Colostomy draining liquid brown feces. Bag emptied x3 by pt. Expelling lge amt. flatulence. Mod. incisional pain relieved by med. Good appetite. No nausea, distention. Voiding q.s. Anatomy of colostomy and H.S. explained. Major concern is "odor."	Ambrose
APR 15, YR-4					
1^45 AM				Rx narcotic given po for discomfort	K.R.
2-6				Appeared to sleep well. passed m/c sm amt liq in colostomy bag.	
8am.				Rx (narc) po for pain	K.R.
12.05 p.m.				Rx (narc) po for pain	
8-2	good	✓	✓	self am care. ambulated in hallway x2. Taking diet well. Pt. taking care of colostomy by herself. seems concerned c̄ odor & the stoma. Pt. c/o fatigue & pain around stoma. sm amt. liquid (brown) drainage. Pt feels she'll need help at home p̄ disch. Voiding q.s.	K.R.
6PM				Rx (narc) p.o. for incisional pain.	Kraft
				H.S. care. Colostomy draining liquid brown feces. Bag emptied by pt. lge. amt. flatulence expelled through colostomy. Mod. incisional pain relieved by med. No nausea, distention or complaints. Good appetite.	

[C2051]

'27

PARKER MEMORIAL HOSPITAL

JEAN MARIE SAUNDERS

NURSE'S NOTES

XO-5Q

RS8VLL-1980

(pv)

Date & Hour	Diet	Urine	Stool	Treatment, Observations, Remarks	Signature
				Voiding q.s. Amb. ad lib.	Traft
APR 16, YR-4					
2^30 am				c/o pain - Rx narcotic given po.	Aruban
12-6 am				Slept well thru noc. No voiced discomforts noted	
7^40 am				Rx (narc) po for pain.	
11^15 am				Rx (narc) po for pain.	
7-3 pm				Showered early this am. Colostomy care done by self. Appears depressed worried about caring for herself and family when she is discharged. States she feels very tired. Saline enema ordered for rectum. Unable to give because saline drains through fistula and out vagina. Very upsetting to pt. Irrigation through colostomy done by Dr. ________ M.D. Amt. black fecal returns c black liq returns. Appetite fair.	Goulda
3-1130				Up & about in Rm. Appears in good spirits. Own colostomy care done. n/c offered	Goulda
10 pm				Rx med po given for pain	[illegible]
April 17, YR-4					
12-6				Appeared to sleep well n/c	
7^30 am				Rx (med) po for pain	
				NUTRITION: Gave pt. list of gas forming foods which she should avoid. Pt seemed to understand & had no questions	Dolly

[C2062]

PARKER MEMORIAL HOSPITAL

JEAN MARIE SAUNDERS

NURSE'S NOTES

XO-5Q

RS8VLL-1980 (pv)

Date & Hour	Diet	Urine	Stool	Treatment, Observations, Remarks	Signature
8/7/YR-4 7-11³⁰AM				AM care - up + about colostomy care by self - discharge 11³⁰AM	AEW
2:30 pm.				pt. admitted to EW III 375 BP. 108/78 T 98⁶ P88 R 20 allergic to cigarette smoke. Has a colostomy & states post op right upper quadrant loop transverse colostomy	
3:05				Pubic Perineal Prep done.	
3-11³⁰				Saline enema given c clear returns. pt. couldn't hold any of water in. BP 120/78. Appear apprehensive. Appetite good. No complaints offered.	Raintree
MAY 8, YR-4 12-6 AM				Slept well NPO for surgery Urine spec to lab. Prepared for OR T 97⁶ P-92 R 20 BP Ring in safe. pre-op	P.O.
6⁰⁰ AM				Pre op antibiotic given	
6⁴⁵ AM				Pre op med given	
7³⁰ AM				called to OR	Tina Curry
8⁰⁰ AM	Surgery			#18 Medicut in lt arm 500 cc D5W c 1/4 sc STARTED. FULLY absorbed IV 250 cc D5W c Abs med. started second dos SD/c 500 cc D5W STARTED Repair of Rectal Vaginal Fistula Iodoform Gauze Packing #16 Foley c 5cc bag inserted & connected to [illegible] To Recovery Room	S. Blake
11	Recovery			500cc D5W abst 1000cc D5 1/4 sc / hung	Wendell
11/10	"			Rx narc. 10 ✓ rectal pain	Wendell

[C2053]

'27

JEAN MARIE SAUNDERS

PARKER MEMORIAL HOSPITAL

NURSE'S NOTES

XO-5Q

RS8VLL-1980
(pv)

Date & Hour	Diet	Urine	Stool	Treatment, Observations, Remarks	Signature
				Returned to unit BP 90/60 - Pulse 76 -	
				Pink staining to pad.	DR
1-3^30 pm				c/o incisional pain BP 112/70.	
				Very restless	
3PM				Rx (narc) given IM - abd pain	
6^20 pm				Rx (narc) med. spld. pain.	
8^00 pm				1000 cc D5 1/4 S absorbed	Diina Roy
				1000 cc D5 1/4 S hung.	
3-11 pm.				Drowsy c/o extreme pain on movement Medic	
				x2 c relief. IV infusing, NPO, peri-pad	
				chgd x1 - Mod. amt bright red drainage	
				PT is oriented - no restraint jacket on	Arubar
				AM care.	
9^50 AM				Rx (narc) IM for abd. pain	T.A.C.
May 9, YR-4	12^50 pm			med c Morphine Sq 8mg IM for vaginal-	
				rectal discomfort. Scant drg on Peri pad.	
				Foley drg 700cc T-100 po	Gilroy
MAY 9, YR-4	3^35 pm			crying c discomfort in rectal vagina	
				med c Morphine SQ 8 mg IM	
				skin - warm flushed - Foley drg	
				clear urine 150 cc @ 4 PM	
				T-100° po much difficulty c moving	
				& turning. scant drg on peri pad.	
				Alert & oriented.	Gilroy
	6^30 pm			1,000 cc D5 1/4 S absorbed	Nichols
				1,000 cc D5 1/4 S hung	
8^00-2^30	Reg.			BP 102/58 5 110/60 Changed ... colostomy	
				bag. Perineal x2 c ...	
				Peri changed x2 c Mod amt. red	
				drainage. When stood up @ 11^30 pt c/o	
				dizziness and "flushed" feel. Put to	
				bed & regained senses. BP 110/50 T 100 -	
				104-34. Seen by Dr. Longwood	O'Kiin

[C2054]

'27

PARKER MEMORIAL HOSPITAL

JEAN MARIE SAUNDERS

N U R S E ' S N O T E S

XO-5Q

RS8VLL-1980

(pv)

Date & Hour	Diet	Urine	Stool	Treatment, Observations, Remarks	Signature
				pain med changed as pt c/o itchiness.	
				Stated pt could ambulate when "she	Curtin
				felt like it. Med. for pain	
7^{45} am				Rx (narc) IM for pain	Curtin
11:05 am				Rx (narc) IM for pain	Curtin
2^{30} pm.				Rx (narc) IM for pain.	Curtin
6^{05} pm.				Rx med. (narc) IM for pain	JAMES
9^{40} pm				1000cc D_5 1/4S absorbed and IV D/c.	JAMES
				as pt took over 1500 cc po.	
3-11^{30}				Pt resting comf. pain when she turns	perone
				BC prepared for sleep period...	perone
10 PM				Rx (NARC) IM FOR PAIN	TRAFT
12m				med (narc) IM for pain	[illegible]
4pm				med (narc) IM for pain	[illegible]
12-6AM				Generally comf. but sleeping only in short naps	
				c/o vaginal pain. Med relieves pain in 1 1/2	
				[illegible] - no back care. Foley draining	
				[illegible]	
				pain [illegible] changed x2 [illegible] and old	
				bloody drainage	
				Col.-clean	[illegible]
7 am				med (narc) for pain	
10^{15} AM				Rx (narc) po for headache	Elaine
7-3				APPETITE FAIR. FOLEY DRAINING	TERRY
				CLEAR. URINE SMALL AMOUNT DK	
				RED STAINING ON PERI-PAD.	
				REFUSED SITZ BATH.	
				COLOSTOMY CARE DONE. STOOD BY	
				SIDE OF BED FOR A FEW MIN. -	
				UNTIL SHE BEGAN TO FEEL FAINT.	
				BACK CARE	

[C2055]

27

PARKER MEMORIAL HOSPITAL

JEAN MARIE SAUNDERS

NURSE'S NOTES

XO-5Q

RS8VLL-1980

(pv)

Date & Hour	Diet	Urine	Stool	Treatment, Observations, Remarks	Signature
9 pm				Rx narc po for pain	
3-11 PM				Up in w/c in corridor x1	
				ambulated c̄ help to BR	
				sitzbath given - tol well.	
				sm amt dk red staining on peri	
				pad; Colostomy draining large	
				amount loose brown BM x1. Appears	
				in good spirits. No c/o @ present	Hooper
7 PM				Rx (narc) po for pain	Hooper
11 PM				Rx (narc) po for pain	Hooper
MAY 11, YR-4 2[45] pm				med (narc) po pain	Angie
12-6 AM				[illegible] c̄ pain, med po Foley	
				draining clear urine. peripad changed - sm	
				amt. old bloody drainage. sm amt feces in	
				colostomy. [illegible] much better [illegible]	
6[50] PM				med (narc) po pain	Angie
7-3				AM Care C + B x 2	
				Sitz Bath much more	
				comf day colostomy	
				Changed by pt. sm amt dry	
				on peripad. Foley 450cc	Pauline
12 noon				Rx (narc) po for pain	
5[45] pm				Rx (narc) po for, [illegible] pain	Pauline
3-11 PM				Sitzbath x1 seems to tol only	
				fairly. Still unsteady on feet	
				gets dizzy. Sm amt dk red staining	
				on peripad. Dr. Farne in	
				@ 10[30] pm - removed vaginal packing.	
				Colostomy draining dk brown, soft	
				feces. Foley draining.	D'Ambrose

[C2056]

27

PARKER MEMORIAL HOSPITAL

JEAN MARIE SAUNDERS

NURSE'S NOTES

XO-5Q

RS8VLL-1980

(pv)

Date & Hour	Diet	Urine	Stool	Treatment, Observations, Remarks	Signature
5/11 945/pm				Rx (NARC) po for pain	Pauline
1030/pm				Rx (NARC) po for sleep as	
				ordered	
5/12/YR-4					Meloney
12-2 am				Seemed to sleep well c̄ no comp.	
2 am				Colostomy [illegible] x1 mostly [illegible]	
				[illegible] of stomach black stool	
				Small amt of pink staining on peripad.	
4 25 am				Rx (narc) given po for pain	
5-6 am				Seems comf. this time	
11 45 am.				Percodan given per pain	MC
8-12				a.m. care c̄ assist, taking [illegible] fluid well	
				urine spec for c+s taken, colostomy,	
				[illegible] x1 - [illegible] - [illegible] black stool, c/o gas	
				pains, passing lge amt gas, sitz bath x1	
				25 min, [illegible] x2, [illegible] amt drainage	
				amb to bathroom - tolerated fairly well	Q. R.
				c/o pain in side ([illegible])	
7 40/pm				Rx (NARC) PO FOR PAIN	
10 25/pm				Rx (NARC) PO FOR PAIN	
3-11 pm				SITZ BATH FOR 2 MIN. ONLY -	TANYA
				AMB. IN HALL SHORT WAY -	
				Foley DRG WELL - TAKING	
				FLUIDS WELL - SOMEWHAT DEPRESSED -	
				NO ST ON PERI-PAD -	
				PREP FOR [illegible] - C/O ALOT PAIN	
5/13/YR-4					
12 am				Rx (narc) given po for gas pain	[illegible]
6 am				Rx (narc) given po for gas pain	
12 noon				[illegible] refuses to have colostomy	
				[illegible] because she feels [illegible]	

[C2057]

27

PARKER MEMORIAL HOSPITAL

JEAN MARIE SAUNDERS

NURSE'S NOTES

XO-5Q

RS8VLL-1980

Date & Hour	Diet	Urine	Stool	Treatment, Observations, Remarks	Signature
MAY 13, YR-4					
12 [illegible]				Seemed depressed at times [illegible]	C.C.
				[illegible]	
10⁰⁰ AM				Rx (narc) given for pain	C.C.
1¹⁰ pm				Rx (narc) for pain administered	C.C.
8-2				tub bath taken, tolerated well, sitz bath	
				x2. (10-15 min in pm) peri - coughing [illegible]	
				[illegible], passing gas, ambulated	
				in hall, [illegible] for short period,	
				voided - good [illegible], C + S	
				taken - sent to lab, colostomy [illegible] x1 -	
				soft stool, taking [illegible] fluid well.	[illegible]
				forced fluids	
5³⁰ PM				Rx (NARC) PO FOR [illegible] PAIN	C.C.
9³⁰ PM				Rx (NARC) PO FOR [illegible] PAIN	C.C.
3-11pm.				Amb. in hall ̄c assist. tolerated fairly	
				well passing flatus and lg [illegible]	
				odorous black formed stool thru	
				Colostomy. Voiding, sitz bath for	
				5 min x 2 [illegible] red drag on	
				peri pad. Back care refused, appears	
				to be in much pain.	[illegible]
May 14, YR-4					
12 AM				Rx (narc) given p.o for vaginal pain	
				Up to [illegible] ̄c help [illegible] fairly well but	
				weak - seems discouraged, depressed	
				[illegible] much gas -	
				colostomy has some stool output [illegible]	
				[illegible] care later in am. slept in long	
				naps - no staining on pad.	
6 AM				Rx (narc) given po for vaginal pain	
10 AM				Rx (narc) given po for vaginal	
				discomfort.	[illegible]

[C2068]

27

PARKER MEMORIAL HOSPITAL

JEAN MARIE SAUNDERS

NURSE'S NOTES

XO-5Q

RS8VLL-1980

(pv)

Date & Hour	Diet	Urine	Stool	Treatment, Observations, Remarks	Signature
MAY 13, YR-4					
12-6 am				[illegible] depressed [illegible]	[illegible]
				[illegible]	
10[00] am				Rx (narc) given for pain	C.C.
1[10] p.m.				Rx (narc) for pain administered.	C.C.
8-2				tub bath taken, tolerated well, sitz bath	
				x2, (10-15 min in pm) peri-area [illegible], [illegible] amt	
				discharge on pad, passing gas, ambulated	
				in hall x1, up in chair for short period,	
				voided - good [illegible] - foley removed	
				[illegible] taken [illegible] to lib, colostomy [illegible]	
				x1 - soft stool, taking [illegible] fluids	
				well, [illegible] fluids	[illegible]
5[30] pm				Rx (narc) PO FOR INCIS. PAIN	Young
				Rx (narc) PO FOR INCIS. PAIN	
3-11 pm				Amb. in hall [illegible] assist - tolerated fairly	
				well. Passing flatus and lg. amt. [illegible]	
				black formed stool thru colostomy. Voiding	
				Sitz bath for 5 min x2 Sm amt. Red drkg	
				on peri-pad. Back care refused	
				appears to be in much pain.	Cecily
May 14, YR-4					
12 AM				Rx (narc) given p.o for vaginal pain	
				Pt up to BR c help [illegible] fairly well but weak -	
				seems discouraged + depressed - c/o much	
				gas - colostomy has some stool but pt	
				wants to do care later in am [illegible] in long	
				[illegible] - [illegible] staining on pads	
6 AM				Rx (narc) given PO for vaginal pain	
10 AM				Rx (narc) given po for vaginal	
				discomfort.	
10[40]				Pt states there was some relieve	
				of pain p med was given	D'Arnot

[C2059]

27

PARKER MEMORIAL HOSPITAL

JEAN MARIE SAUNDERS

NURSE'S NOTES

XO-5Q

RSSVLL-1980

Date & Hour	Diet	Urine	Stool	Treatment, Observations, Remarks	Signature
10^{40}				Pt. states there was some relief of pain	
				p med was given	
8-2	Bland II			sitz bath given 15 mins	
				tolerated well. Self colostomy care	
				done ambulated x2 in hall. Pt.	
				c/o vaginal pain also pt. seemed	
				quite fatigued p bath. Pt slept	
				well p med (narc) was given for	
				pain appetite good voiding	
				adeq. Slept for short time in	
				afternoon.	Welburne
3pm				Rx (narc) po for pain	Peters
6PM				RX (NARC) PO FOR PAIN	Peters
3-11pm				Ambulated in corridor, sitz bath done	
				as ordered, very small amt staining,	
				colostomy change by self	A.
10PM				Rx (NARC) PO FOR INCIS PAIN.	C.C.
5/15 YR-4					
4^{45} am				med (narc) po pain	
12-8 am				Relatively comf. rest ē med. Up to BR. Perineal pad changed	
				x1 - scant bloody drainage. Says fluid in col.	
				bag - pt. did not want to change it at this time	
				to fluids. depressed + unhappy.	
8-2				Tub bath x2 tol well Colostomy bag	
				changed x2 in a.m. same fluid. Also Peri	
				pad changed x2 ē a.m. amt lt red	
				staining. Appetite good. Voiding q.s.	
				Very drowsy. Sleeping in naps	Falconi
8pm				Rx (narc) po for pain	
4^{30} pm				Rx (NARC) PO FOR PAIN	
9^{40} pm				Rx (NARC) PO FOR PAIN	F.
3-11^{30}				Pt had a sitz bath in tub	
				colostomy had a q amt. of soft + formed	
				+ real soft [illegible] prepared for sleep [illegible]	

[C2060]

27

PARKER MEMORIAL HOSPITAL

JEAN MARIE SAUNDERS

NURSE'S NOTES

XO-5Q

RS8VLL-1980

Date & Hour	Diet	Urine	Stool	Treatment, Observations, Remarks	Signature
				staining peri pant	
5/16	YR-4				
	2:30			Med. po narc pain vag.	
	5:45			Med po narc. pain vag.	[illegible]
12-6 AM				Slept between med. Self peri care by t. PR. Cont.	
				to have vag. pain	[illegible]
8-12				tub bath x1 Pt. refused Valium	
				@ 9 stating it's making her too	
				drowsy. Appetite fair. Ambu	
				much better. Colostomy bag	
				changed x1—area itchy and	
				reddened around stoma taking	
				sitz in BR [illegible]	O.L.
9am				Rx (med) po refused by pt.	C.C.
9:30 AM				Rx (narc) po for pain	C.C.
12-3:30 pm				Amb in corridor. Seems to be	
				doing well. Tub bath x1. Seemed	
				more comfortable.	C.C.
[illegible]				Rx (narc) po for pain	[illegible]
3-10 PM				[illegible] sm amt. staining	
				on peripad. colostomy care by self	
				Prep. for sleep.	E. [illegible]
11 PM				c/o SOB & crying states has had a	
				"funny feeling in chest" all day—	
				BP 96/70 P 58 R 24	
				Dr. Tuckman notified	Perond
10:10 pm				Rx (narc) po for pain	
5/17	YR-4			Cough & breathing diff. [illegible] EKG	
				ordered.	
12-2				Restless [illegible] c/o pain in [illegible] area	
2:35				Rx (narc) po for pain	
3-5				Slept	
5:35				[illegible] pain [illegible] of stitches Rx (narc) po for pain.	
6:35				Rx (narc) given po inc. [illegible] pain	Regina

[C2061]

27

PARKER MEMORIAL HOSPITAL

JEAN MARIE SAUNDERS

NURSE'S NOTES

XO-5Q

RS8VLL-1980

Date & Hour	Diet	Urine	Stool	Treatment, Observations, Remarks	Signature
7-3				Took sitz bath in am tol. well	
				Had sm. sitz bath in BR this PM.	
				Still having lg. amt vaginal pain	
				No c/o pain today. Looking forward	
				to discharge.	Larkin
5/17, YR-4					
1^{30} pm.				Rx (narc) given for incision pain	C.C.
6^{50} pm				Rx (NARC) PO FOR INCIS. PAIN	
9^{30} pm				Rx (NARC) PO. FOR INCIS. PAIN	
3-11 pm				CP IN ROOM - SITZ BATH X2 -	
				DEPRESSED; DISCOURAGED ABOUT COND. -	
				FEELS SHE IS NOT READY FOR	
				DISCHARGE BECAUSE OF SEVERE	
				SORENESS - VOIDING - EATING	
				WELL - REFUSED B.C.	Delina
May 18, YR-4					
12-3				Restless - depressed - does not	
				feel she is strong enough to go	
				home.	
				Complaining of severe soreness	
				in area of suturing.	
3-				Rx (narc) given p.o. for pain	
3^{30}-5				Sleeping in short naps	
5^{30}				Rx (narc) given for pain	[illegible]
7-12				Up & about & took tub bath	
				Sm amt pink vaginal drainage	
				Still c/o vaginal pain.	
12				Discharged home.	McC

[C2062]

27

PARKER MEMORIAL HOSPITAL

JEAN MARIE SAUNDERS

NURSE'S NOTES

XO-5Q

RS8VLL-1980

Date & Hour	Diet	Urine	Stool	Treatment, Observations, Remarks	Signature
5-20-YR-4	9[45] AM			White female admit to ER C/O	
				bleeding from rectum - to bed upon	
				admission V.S. 110/70 P 100	
				T 90. Exam by Dr.	Dolly
	10 [15] am			Lg clot c approx 150 cc - 200 cc bld	
				passed via rectum -	
				Exam Dr. I.V. 1100 D5 1/4 S/E	
				20 meq KCl started (R) hand -	
				Admit to hospital	Dolly
	10[30]			116/60 - P 80	
	11[30]			110/64 - P 80	
	11:30			Admitted to E w N room 263	
				via stretcher (T) 48 P 80 R 22	
				PT. had a small amount	
				red staining on peri pad	
				IV infusing well. PT appears	
				To be fairly comfortable	LPN - Millet
	11:45			BP 116/[illegible] analgesic to pain med.	
	1:45			Med. c Demerol 50 mg PO at 1:45 for headache	
				pt. stated was very painful	[illegible]
	11:30 - 3:30			Pt resting in bed. Pt com-	
				plained of severe headache	
				this PM PT complained of	
				lower abdominal discomfort	
				and rectal pain this PM.	giles
	3[30]	✓		Mod. amt bright staining c small clots	
				appears to be coming from the vagina	giles
7 P				[illegible] po for pain	
3-11 P				Pericare [illegible] staining [illegible]	Miller
				[illegible] IV infusing well.	
				c/o headache - soreness in perineal area	
				Relief c medication	

[C2083]

27

PARKER MEMORIAL HOSPITAL JEAN MARIE SAUNDERS

NURSE'S NOTES

XO-5Q

RSSVLL-1980

Date & Hour	Diet	Urine	Stool	Treatment, Observations, Remarks	Signature
5/20 YR-4 3-11				[illegible] greenish black stool via	
				colostomy. Neg. for O.B. H.O. called c̄	
				8PM Hct + Hgb.	
				Pt. c/o weakness. voided x1.	Webber, R.N.
5/21 YR-4					
12[illegible]				1000 cc D5 1/4 str saline c̄ 20 KCL abs	
				IV and 1000 cc D5 1/4 str saline c̄ 20	
				mg KCL hung.	Halloran
12^{30}				T 98^2 peri pad chg. Sm amt of red stg. —	
				sero-[illegible] dcg.	[illegible]
12-6				Slept most of noc. [illegible]	
				amt of pink stg. on peri pad	
				IV [illegible]	[illegible]
9[illegible]PM				600cc D5 1/4 S c̄ 20 meq KCL	
				absorbed [illegible] & D/c.	
[illegible]				Rx (name) po for pain [illegible] - vag. area	[illegible]
7-3PM				c/o pain in rectal vag area	
				Colostomy draining small amt. green	
				brown liquid	
				Sitz bath for 30" [illegible]	
				Tol [illegible] Peri Pad changed x2	
				scant → small [illegible] pink staining	
				Taking PO'S c̄ urging	
				Slept in short naps	Sullivan
6[illegible]				Rx (name) po for pain	C.C.
10p				Rx (name) po for pain	C.C.
7-11				Sitz bath taken x1. PT changed	
				own colostomy. Peri Pad count done	
				as ordered. Appetite much better	
				[illegible] in better spirits.	[illegible]
5-22 YR-4					
6AM				[illegible] for pain	
12-7[illegible]				sm amt of lt. pink stg. on peri pad	
				[illegible] slept well — taking fluids well.	[illegible]

[C2064]

27

PARKER MEMORIAL HOSPITAL

JEAN MARIE SAUNDERS

NURSE'S NOTES

XO-5Q

RS8VLL-1980

Date & Hour	Diet	Urine	Stool	Treatment, Observations, Remarks	Signature
8-12 pm	Reg	II	Colostomy	Self am care self colostomy care. Bar care given. Colostomy drainage brown & mushy consistency. Voiding q.s. adequately sm. amt pinkish red staining on peri pad. Sitz bath given 2x states "Soothing while in tub but once out aches just as much as before." Taking fluids well. Appetite fair. States "very uncomfortable & sore." Resting in napping.	[illegible]
10 pm				Rectal examination done by [illegible]	
12:00-3:30				Pt resting in bed. Appears to be comfortable. No complaints offered.	[illegible], RN
4:15 am				Rx med (narc) given po for pain.	
3:30-11:30				up ad lib. self colostomy care done. Voiding adeq. – peri pad changed by pt. c scant amt pinkish staining. sitz bath x1 tol well. c/o pain in early PM – prep for [illegible]	[illegible]
10:05 pm				Rx med (narc) given po for pain.	[illegible]
5-23 YR-4					
12-6 AM				Appeared to sleep well. No complaints offered.	
8 AM-10 PM	reg		Colostomy	Self am care self colostomy care. Taking food & fluids well. Sitz bath given 1x tolerated well. Up & walking in hall. Pt upset & crying @ the idea of going home. Stated "I'm afraid something else will happen and I'll have to come back."	
10 PM				Appears more relaxed now, packing to go home.	[illegible] RN

[C2065]

27

PARKER MEMORIAL HOSPITAL

JEAN MARIE SAUNDERS

NURSE'S NOTES

XO-5Q

RS8VLL-1980

Date & Hour	Diet	Urine	Stool	Treatment, Observations, Remarks	Signature
5-23 YR-4 (Cont)					
10:20 AM				Discharged to home	
July 14, YR-4				White female pt. adm. to ped. 185[3]	
				T. 98[6] P. 96. R. 18	
				Ht WT. 109 lbs BP 100/60	
				ALLERGIES: SMOKE - ? morphine	
				MEDS:	
				DENTURES:	
				dx Rectal Vaginal fistula	Short
				Referred by	
6-11 pm		✓		Routine evening care To x-ray	
				clear liq. diet	Castile
7-15, YR-4					
12-6 AM	NPO			N.P.O for FBS	
				slept in naps	Castile
7-9				naps up to BR. Sleeping	
8[45]				Transferred to SE via w/chair	
9-3				Prep done checked by D.	
				Saline enema given - Some	
				liquid (brown) thru Colostomy	
				Sitz bath by pt.	
5				Visited by [illegible] nurse re procedure	
				explained	
3-11[30] pm				B.P. 78/50 - Sitz Bath done	
				Ambulated PM Care	
JULY 16, YR-4					
12-6 AM				Slept fairly well	
6 AM				Prepared for surg. showered,	
				pt. refused to take [illegible]	
				not know anything about [illegible].	[illegible]

[C2066]

"27

PARKER MEMORIAL HOSPITAL

JEAN MARIE SAUNDERS

NURSE'S NOTES

XO-5Q

RS8VLL-1980

Date & Hour	Diet	Urine	Stool	Treatment, Observations, Remarks	Signature
JULY 16	YR-4		(cont)	Pt. stated that she is [illegible] allergic	
				to morphine.	
6⁴⁵ pm				Dr. notified about NG	
				NG to be inserted in OR	
				Dr. changed pre op order [illegible]	
7 pm				Pre op meds given & charted	
7³⁰ pm				called to OR – gowns & [illegible]	
				sent ā pt.	Choate
8⁰⁰ pm	Surgery			#18 Medicut inserted – Lt hand	
				500cc D5W/¼ SS started [illegible] abs. IV	
				1000cc D5W/¼ SS started –	
				#18 Saline Sump N/G Tube inserted –	
				Closure of Colostomy – Bilateral Tubal	
				Ligation (Bowel Resection)	
				To Recovery Room	MARIE
11¹⁵ am				50 D5W ā Ancef + 5m [illegible] abs IV.	E.
11⁴⁵	RK			Rx (narcotic) [illegible] pain	[illegible]
1⁴⁵ pm				RETURNED FROM RR B/P 100/60	
				P-80 R-20. SKIN-WARM-DRY, COLOR-PINK	
				NOT ON PINK STAINING ON UPPER ABD. dsg,	
				IV APPEARS TO BE INFUSING WELL. GAMCO	
				SUCTION DRAINING WELL, C/O CHEST +	
				INCISION a/PAIN, APPEARS TO BE ALERT	Przblrzeskei, R.N.
2-5³⁰ PM				VS. seem stable BP 114/64 P 82 +	
				Reg. + R 24 – Color seems pale	
				Dsgs. intact ē no further	
				staining noted IV infusing well –	
				c/o "Chest pain" in mid sternal area	
				& difficulty in breathing + reported	
				to Dr. Longwood	
2⁴⁵				rx narcotic for post op pain	
2⁴⁵-3⁵ PM				States has relief pain medication	
				has not voided yet – N.G. tube	
				drained 150cc [illegible] drainage	TRA

[C2087]

1-27

PARKER MEMORIAL HOSPITAL

JEAN MARIE SAUNDERS

NURSE'S NOTES

XO-5Q

RS8VLL-1980

Date & Hour	Diet	Urine	Stool	Treatment, Observations, Remarks	Signature
				c̄ some brown [illegible] noted-	
				seems to be resting comfortably [illegible]	TRA
7/20 YR-4 (cont)					
4pm				1000 cc D5¼ NS absorbed [illegible] 1000cc D5¼	
				NS added to IV.	[illegible]
6 pm				150 cc [illegible] absorbed IV med	
3-11 30 pm				Special [illegible] care - turned c̄	
				C & D. B [illegible] - Sump tube	
				irrigated - draining well	
				dressing dry intact -	
				Slight vaginal red staining	
				voided 8pm 160 cc - c/o pain-	
				IV running -	[illegible]
9 15 pm				Rx med (narc) IM / pain c̄ some relief	
5 55 pm				RV (narc IM for pain) given	
July 17 YR-4					
[illegible] 40				100 cc 5% D/W with IV med absorbed	
12 15		200		Rx med (narc) given for pain	
				[illegible] dry & intact BP 1[illegible]/[illegible]	
				[illegible] well. [illegible]	
				[illegible]	
				[illegible] at 1 : 5 c̄ 15 cc saline	
				Backcare x 2	
				[illegible] [illegible] fairly well.	
				IV running well	DD, LPN
3 45 am				Rx med given for pain BP 1[illegible]/[illegible] [illegible]-30	
8 05 am				Rx (NARC) given IM for pain R-18	
5 30 am		200		1000 cc D5¼ NS absorbed	
				1000 cc D5¼ NS added	
				100 cc 5% D/W with IV med absorbed	
				[illegible] staining noted	
				dsd's dry & intact	
				Appears apprehensive & in	
6 30 pm				great deal of pain even c̄ med.	[illegible]

[C2068]

C27

PARKER MEMORIAL HOSPITAL

JEAN MARIE SAUNDERS

NURSE'S NOTES

XO-5Q

RS8VLL-1980

Date & Hour	Diet	Urine	Stool	Treatment, Observations, Remarks	Signature
10 AM		250		150 cc drainage clear fld c	
				mucous shreds in [illegible]	
				drainage. Voiding well	[illegible]
12 N				Rx (Narc) given IM for pain R-20	
2 P				15 mEq KCL + [illegible] added to	
				[illegible] IV at 50 cc	Janis
3 P		✓	0	Bed bath c assist. turning fairly well,	
				deep breathing but not coughing [illegible]	
				staying on upper dsg. IV's infusing	
				well. [illegible] drainingwell -	
				50 cc c sm. specks of blood.	D [illegible]
7/12				N/G tube irrigated c .5 cc saline	
				x2 - [illegible] c difficulty	
				~~100 cc D5W absorbed c IV [illegible]~~	
				~~[illegible]~~	[illegible]
3-11					
4:30 PM				Rx narcotic IM for pain	[illegible]
5 PM				1000 cc D5 1/4 saline out absorbed	
				1000 cc D5 1/4 Saline c no [illegible]	
6 PM				100 cc D5W c med absorbed [illegible]	M. - R.N.
7:15 PM				Rx narcotic IM for pain	
		-		Resting quietly - taking	
				ice chips IV infusing	
				well. Encouraged to cough	
				+ deep breathing Turning	
				well in bed. Back care	[illegible]
JULY 18 YR-4					
12 mid				100 cc D5W c med absorbed	
12:10 AM				Rx (narc) IM for incisional pain	[illegible]
				Rx (med) given [illegible] for [illegible]	
12:10 - 4:45 AM				Slept fairly @ med, no further [illegible]	
				[illegible] NG irrigated x2	
				drained 400 cc. IV infusing well	[illegible]

[C2069]

'27

PARKER MEMORIAL HOSPITAL JEAN MARIE SAUNDERS

NURSE'S NOTES

XO-5Q

RS8VLL-1980

Date & Hour	Diet	Urine	Stool	Treatment, Observations, Remarks	Signature
4 45 am				Rx (narc) given IM for incisional pain.	
4 45 - 6 am				Slept, relaxed c̄ med.	Dana
5 20				1000 cc D5 1/4 c̄ 30 KCl [illegible]	
				1000 cc D5 1/4 c̄ 30 KCl [illegible]	
9 am				300 cc D5 1/4 c̄ 30 KCl [illegible]	
				1000 cc [illegible] 30 KCl [illegible]	[illegible]
10 am				Rx (narc) given IM for incisional pain	
12 noon				100 cc D5W absorbed c̄ IV Bolus Med	
1 45 PM				Rx (narc) given IM for incisional pain	[illegible] LVN
7-3 30				assisted c̄ bath - C & B x 2.	
				did fairly well - ambulated x 2	
				before getting up - IV infusing	
				well - refuses sips of H_2O for	
				ice chips - lips [illegible] -	
				cold cream applied - [illegible]	
				draining [illegible] well - [illegible] green	
				liquid - [illegible] x 2 - [illegible]	
				[illegible] pt noticed blood upon [illegible]	
				herself - seems to be [illegible]	
				not [illegible] - [illegible]	
				[illegible] with [illegible].	Annie
4 38 pm				Rx (narc) given for incisional pain	
6 pm				IV Bolus 100 cc D5W c̄ med hung	
8 pm				Rx (narc) given IM for incisional pain	
				IV Bolus 100 cc D5W c̄ med absorbed	D.
3-11 pm.		✓		TAKING CHIPS. VOIDING ADEQ. NO	
				FURTHER STAINING NOTED ON	
				PERI-PAD DSGS DRY & INTACT	
				IV INFUSING WELL	
				BACK CARE PREP FOR NOC	
				N/G TUBE IRRIGATED x 2 c̄ 15 cc N.S.	C. Fakhe

[C2070]

'27

PARKER MEMORIAL HOSPITAL

JEAN MARIE SAUNDERS

NURSE'S NOTES

XO-5Q

RS8VLL-1980

Date & Hour	Diet	Urine	Stool	Treatment, Observations, Remarks	Signature
8:30				1000 cc Normosol M D5W c̄ meds absorbed.	
				c̄ 1 amp MVI & 1/2 amp Berocca Chung	Bernie
JULY 19, YR-4 11:30p				Rx (none) given IM for pain	
12 A				100cc D5W c̄ med. absorbed	
5AM				Rx (none) given IM for pain c̄ effect	
6AM				100 cc D5W c̄ med absorbed	D.B., L.P.N.
12-6 AM				Slept in naps, no further staining on drg. NG irrigated x2 - drained 250 cc. IV infusing well w/o drg.	DB
JULY 19, YR-4 (continued)					
12-6 AM (cont)				Pt. stated that she had shakes, + sob, probably due to Demerol refused Demerol in pm but c/o pain, resident notified.	O'Brien
9:25 PM				Rx (none) given I.M. for pain	
12 PM				100 cc D5W c̄ med absorbed	
12:25 PM				Rx (none) given I.M. for pain.	Tanya
7-3:00 pm				assisted c̄ bath - [illegible] x2 c̄ [illegible] - pt believes this new med made pt nauseous & SOB - states she felt sick - but couldn't [illegible] why - also [illegible] a walk [illegible] clean & dry, [illegible] did very well. but did not want to get up this afternoon, [illegible] well [illegible] - [illegible] during [illegible] time but now [illegible]	[illegible]
5-45				Rx (none) IM for pain	
6				100 cc D5W c̄ [illegible] med. [illegible] abs	
8 pm				1000 cc D5/4 c̄ 20 mEq KCl absorbed IV.	
				1000 cc D5/4NS + 20 mEq KCl [illegible] added	
				IV [illegible] —	[illegible]

[C2071]

'27

PARKER MEMORIAL HOSPITAL

JEAN MARIE SAUNDERS

NURSE'S NOTES

XO-50

RS8VLL-1980

Date & Hour	Diet	Urine	Stool	Treatment, Observations, Remarks	Signature
3-11 30 pm				Ng tube draining well	
				IV running C+Bx1	
				Pt care [illegible]	
				[illegible]	
				[illegible] c/o [illegible]	Malone
7-19-YR-4					
11 20				Rx (narc) IM for pain	J.K.R., LPN
JULY 20, YR-4					
	12-6 AM			Slept in long naps. Fairly comf c meds [illegible]	
				clean dsg dry voiding [illegible] draining IV	
				inf well. No other difficulties	[illegible]
8 15 AM				Rx (narc) given I.M. for pain	
12 PM				100 cc D5W c med. absorbed	
12 15 PM				Rx (narc) given IM for pain	
1 PM				Rx med given IM - [illegible]	JR.
7-3 30 pm				Pain day - would not get up this	
				am did very well getting up	
				this am [illegible]	
				[illegible] still [illegible]	
				of [illegible]	
				[illegible] x 2 for pain + x, for	
				[illegible]	
				[illegible] drainage	[illegible]
4 pm				1000 cc D5 ½ NS c 20 [illegible]	I.V.
				1000 cc D5 ½ NS + 20 [illegible]	[illegible]
4 05 pm				Rx med (narc) IM / pain	
6 pm				100 cc D5W absorbed IV c med	
8 40 pm				Rx med (narc) [illegible] pain relief	
3-11 20 pm				IV running Ng draining	
				well [illegible] - tol well	
				PM care - incision line dry -	
				c/o pain -	[illegible]

[C2072]

27

PARKER MEMORIAL HOSPITAL

JEAN MARIE SAUNDERS

NURSE'S NOTES

XO-5Q

RS8VLL-1980

Date & Hour	Diet	Urine	Stool	Treatment, Observations, Remarks	Signature
JULY 21, YR-4					
12[illegible]				Rx (narc) IM for abd. pain	
4[illegible]				Rx (narc) IM for abd. pain	
3:30				1000 D5 1/2 NS c 20 meq KCL + 1/2 Amp	
				MVI abs IV and D5 1/2 NS c 20 meq	
				KCL hung.	[illegible]
12-6				Incont. of brownish liq stool 3x [illegible].	
				[illegible] - 200cc Passing flatus - NG	
				tube irrig well - drg. lt yellow.	
				Drg. [illegible] and intact.	[illegible]
July 21, YR-4					
10 am				50cc SPA 12.5 [illegible] hung	
10:45 am				50cc SPA 12.5 [illegible] abs	[illegible]
7-11:30 pm				Did most of own care. Still cannot	
				tell when she has to have B.M.	
				Voiding in [illegible] = [illegible] amts. IV	
				infusing well. C+B for 1/2° [illegible] well	
				NG tube removed by Dr Longwood	
				[illegible] nausea + op site pain.	V.V.
2pm				1000cc D5 1/2 S c 20 meq KCl absorbed	
				1000 cc D5 1/4 NS c 30 meq KCl + 1 Amp	
				MVI hung	[illegible]
9:30 pm				Rx (narc) given IM for incisional	
				pain	[illegible]
11:30 3				Pt voiding adeq. liquid BM light	
				brown. No c/o of nausea	
				received SPA 12 AM B+B -	
				seen by Dr Longwood	
				I.V. infusing well -	
5 pm				[illegible] IV	
6 pm				succ SPA absorbed IV	Paula

[C2073]

'27

PARKER MEMORIAL HOSPITAL

JEAN MARIE SAUNDERS

NURSE'S NOTES

XO-5Q

RS8VLL-1980

Date & Hour	Diet	Urine	Stool	Treatment, Observations, Remarks	Signature
3-21				Pt's care c/o passing feces through vagina seems very upset & scared by [illegible] ate poorly c/o also having discharge (loose stool) on & off bedpan several x's c+B for short while c/o pain. Amt. to Bed well. Back care given.	P.T.
11PM				Pt has large and watery feces	Marie
7/21 YR-4					
9am				Rx med IM/apprehensive c some relief	MC
JULY 22 YR-4					
12-6				Pt had best night sleep since she'd been here. Stated she feels much better p Rx med. IV infusing well. Loose stool seemed to have cleared since L/med given	[illegible]
2[10] AM				1000cc D5 1/4 NS + 30 meq KCl + 1 amp.	
2[10] PM				[illegible] absorbed	Angela
				1000cc D5 1/4NS + 30 meq KCl hanging	
2[15] PM				Rx (narc) given po for incisional pain	Angela
7-3[30] pm				good day today up x3 c-B & to BR loose watery stools x2 - incision line clean, taking fluids well. In good spirits today - [illegible] to get up & get going	[illegible]
9[30] pm				1000cc D5 1/4 & 30 KCl absorbed	[illegible]
				1000 cc 5% D5 1/4 c KCl/[illegible] hung & [illegible]	
2[30]				[illegible]	[illegible]
6[45] pm				Rx narc given po for pain	[illegible]

[C2074]

1-27

PARKER MEMORIAL HOSPITAL

JEAN MARIE SAUNDERS

NURSE'S NOTES

XO-5Q

RS8VLL-1980

Date & Hour	Diet	Urine	Stool	Treatment, Observations, Remarks	Signature
3-11				Pt c+b for supper. [illegible] well. [illegible]	
				[illegible]	
				good. [illegible]	
				[illegible] applied to [illegible]	
				+? [illegible]	Nardone
JUL 23 YR-4					
12 noon				Pt. complaining of itchiness in perineal	
				area. area washed soap & [illegible]	Pibher, L.P.N.
2:00				c/o of incision pain, Med c̄ Percodan tabs Ia	
6 AM				slept well good [illegible]	
9 AM				Rx (narc) given p.o. for pain	
1 PM				Rx (narc) given p.o. for pain	AP
7-3:30				good day showered [illegible]	
				[illegible] in hall-	
				[illegible] - states	
				she [illegible] - states	
				she is [illegible]	
				[illegible] when [illegible]	
				[illegible]	
				incision pain [illegible]	Sally
9 pm				Rx narc given PO for pain	
3-11				[illegible]	
				[illegible]	
				[illegible] care given	Nardone
JUL 24 YR-4					
2:30 am				comp. of pain, Med c̄ Percodan tabs ī P.O	
12-6 a.m.				slept in med naps [illegible]-225cc	
				[illegible] of pain during noc	
12:30 pm				Rx (narc) given p.o. for pain	[illegible]

[C2075]

'27

PARKER MEMORIAL HOSPITAL

JEAN MARIE SAUNDERS

NURSE'S NOTES

XO-5Q

RS8VLL-1980

Date & Hour	Diet	Urine	Stool	Treatment, Observations, Remarks	Signature
7-3:30 pm				showered & bathed - states she got dizzy leaning back but that it felt real good - up & about - [illegible] today. [illegible] relief - [illegible] [illegible]	J. Michel, R.N.
4:45 pm				Rx med ([illegible]) po/incisional pain ō relief	
8:45 pm				Rx'd (same) po/incisional pain & relief	
3-11				PM care. No c/o. up about ate well. Prep. for NOC	Micci
JUL 25 YR-4					
12-4				Comp. of feeling dizzy when leaning forward in bed. Appears to have slept well	
6 am				No complaints; sleeping	T. By CPN
7-12:30 pm				bathed in tub - ate fair d/c	
12:30 p				disch home c̄ [illegible]	Nora

(C2076)

PARKER MEMORIAL HOSPITAL

JEAN MARIE SAUNDERS

PHYSICIAN'S ORDERS

DIAGNOSIS

DRUG ALLERGIES

XO-5Q
RS8VLL-1980pv

INSTRUCTIONS:
1. IMPRINT SET BEFORE PLACING IN CHART.
2. DETACH FIRST COPY BELOW ORIGINAL AND SEND TO PHARMACY EACH TIME PHYSICIAN WRITES A SET OF ORDERS.
3. INDICATE COPY REMOVED BY PLACING INITIALS IN COLUMN OPPOSITE PHYSICIAN'S SIGNATURE.
4. THE SIGNATURE OF A PHYSICIAN MUST ACCOMPANY EACH SET OF ORDERS.

USE BALL POINT PEN & PRESS FIRMLY.

DATE	TIME	PHYSICIAN'S ORDERS	INITIAL WH COPY REMOV
	8/15 PM	NPO ā MN	
		Phenergan 10 mg) IM	
		Atropine 0.4 mg) 7am MN	
		[illegible signature]	[initials]
Apr	11, YR	Post op orders	
		- Procedure: Transverse Colostomy	
		- Anesthesia: [illegible]	
		- Allergies: None	
		- Condition: Good	
		- VS BP per [illegible] q 4° on floor - [illegible] Temps only	
		- Diet: NPO - [illegible] / ice chips OK	
		- IV: D5 1/4 S - Run at 100cc/hr.	
		- Due to void in 8 hrs → (5pm) No cath needed	
		- Activity: Dangle + Walk tonight x1	
		OOB - walk ad lib tomorrow	
		Oxygen, swabs to mouth	
		- Cough + Deep Breathing - [illegible]	
		- Meds - Demerol 50-75 mg IM q 3-4 pm	
		pain - [illegible] tomorrow	
		- Nembutal 100 mg po q hs.	
		- Compazine 10 mg IM q 6° prn N+V	
		- (If vomits [illegible] call [illegible] for	
		[illegible] order.)	
		(Labs) None	

[C2077]

PARKER MEMORIAL HOSPITAL

PHYSICIAN'S ORDERS

JEAN MARIE SAUNDERS

DIAGNOSIS

DRUG ALLERGIES

XO-5Q
RS8VLL-1980pv

INSTRUCTIONS:
1. IMPRINT SET BEFORE PLACING IN CHART.
2. DETACH FIRST COPY BELOW ORIGINAL AND SEND TO PHARMACY EACH TIME PHYSICIAN WRITES A SET OF ORDERS.
3. INDICATE COPY REMOVED BY PLACING INITIALS IN COLUMN OPPOSITE PHYSICIAN'S SIGNATURE.
4. THE SIGNATURE OF A PHYSICIAN MUST ACCOMPANY EACH SET OF ORDERS.

USE BALL POINT PEN & PRESS FIRMLY.

DATE	TIME	PHYSICIAN'S ORDERS	INITIAL IF COPY REMOVED
4/11/YR-4	10 AM	1/RR → floor	
		[illegible]	
4-12 YR-4		IV:	
		D5 1/4S run at 100cc /HR + run continuous	
		clears at max of 30cc / Hr – sips + chips avg.	
		Call Ho-d [illegible]	
		excessive	
		No dig today	
		OOB walking today	
		Ho will remove clamp tommorrow AM – have bags available by then	
		OOB walking today.	
4-13 YR-4	2:15 pm	Demerol 50 mg IM-STAT.	
		OOB walking today to Dr. [illegible] → [illegible] today.	
		Get good fitin [illegible] – shots open	
		DC: D5 1/4S run at 100 cc/HR – D/C this noon if po's go well.	

[C2078]

PARKER MEMORIAL HOSPITAL

PHYSICIAN'S ORDERS

JEAN MARIE SAUNDERS

DIAGNOSIS Rectal-Vaginal Fistula

DRUG ALLERGIES

XO-5Q
RS8VLL-1980pv

INSTRUCTIONS:
1. IMPRINT SET BEFORE PLACING IN CHART.
2. DETACH FIRST COPY BELOW ORIGINAL AND SEND TO PHARMACY EACH TIME PHYSICIAN WRITES A SET OF ORDERS.
3. INDICATE COPY REMOVED BY PLACING INITIALS IN COLUMN OPPOSITE PHYSICIAN'S SIGNATURE.
4. THE SIGNATURE OF A PHYSICIAN MUST ACCOMPANY EACH SET OF ORDERS.

USE BALL POINT PEN & PRESS FIRMLY.

DATE	TIME	PHYSICIAN'S ORDERS	INITIAL WHEN COPY REMOVED
4-13 YR-4	[illegible]	Post push diet Push PO fluids [illegible]	
April 14, YR-4	[illegible]	Cont house diet Use pt [illegible] to retain Air in [illegible] when it is free of AIR.	
April 15, YR-4	10:30 am	Saline enema tomorrow am ([illegible]) Possible discharge in [illegible]. will need home care ([illegible] already checked [illegible])	
April 16, YR-4	11:30	Anaprox 50-75 mg PO q 3-4 prn pain FeSO4 300 mg PO BID [illegible] Try Darvocet N 100 mg po q 3 [illegible]	

[C2079]

PARKER MEMORIAL HOSPITAL

PHYSICIAN'S ORDERS

JEAN MARIE SAUNDERS

XO-5Q
RS8VLL-1980pv

DIAGNOSIS: Status post op rt upper [illegible] loop transverse colostomy

DRUG ALLERGIES:

INSTRUCTIONS:
1. IMPRINT SET BEFORE PLACING IN CHART.
2. DETACH FIRST COPY BELOW ORIGINAL AND SEND TO PHARMACY EACH TIME PHYSICIAN WRITES A SET OF ORDERS.
3. INDICATE COPY REMOVED BY PLACING INITIALS IN COLUMN OPPOSITE PHYSICIAN'S SIGNATURE.
4. THE SIGNATURE OF A PHYSICIAN MUST ACCOMPANY EACH SET OF ORDERS.

USE BALL POINT PEN & PRESS FIRMLY.

DATE	TIME	PHYSICIAN'S ORDERS	INITIAL & COPY REMOVED
4-17 YR-4		(1) WNO (2) D [illegible] today [illegible]	
7 May YR-4	7:30 P	(1) Phenobarb (.30 mgm p.o. Stat (2) h.s. med as ordered plus one repeat (3) old chart (of one month ago) to Surgery with pt. (4) N.P.O. after midnight (5) Nembutal 100 mgm IM. 6.45 Atrop 0.4 mgm IM.	
May 8, YR-4		Post oper Plans: Procedure: Repair of Recto vaginal Fistula Anesthesia: Gen endotrach. Allergies: [illegible] VS As per RR - [illegible] on floor Diet: NPO [illegible] clear as tolerated this pm IV: D5 1/4 S run at 100 cc/hr. Foley to gravity & call Ho if out put ≤ than 100cc in 4 hrs. Perineal over vagina - call Ho if excessive bleeding. Note (There is a [illegible] pack in vagina + pt is also having her period) call Ho if > the 5 pads soaked Perineal care [illegible]	

[C2080]

PARKER MEMORIAL HOSPITAL

JEAN MARIE SAUNDERS

PHYSICIAN'S ORDERS

DIAGNOSIS

DRUG ALLERGIES

XO-5Q
RS8VLL-1980pv

INSTRUCTIONS:
1. IMPRINT SET BEFORE PLACING IN CHART.
2. DETACH FIRST COPY BELOW ORIGINAL AND SEND TO PHARMACY EACH TIME PHYSICIAN WRITES A SET OF ORDERS.
3. INDICATE COPY REMOVED BY PLACING INITIALS IN COLUMN OPPOSITE PHYSICIAN'S SIGNATURE.
4. THE SIGNATURE OF A PHYSICIAN MUST ACCOMPANY EACH SET OF ORDERS.
USE BALL POINT PEN & PRESS FIRMLY.

DATE	TIME	PHYSICIAN'S ORDERS	INITIAL & COPY REMOVED
		Urge Cough + Deep BREATHING	
		Activity: Bed Rest : Dangle x 2	
		TONIGHT: TOMORROW OOB + WALK x 3.	
		ROUTINE COLOSTOMY CARE:	
2AM		meds'!	
		MS 4-8mg IM/SQ q 3-4° prn pain.	
		(will most likely need med q 3°)	
		Nembutal 100mg IM/po q hs prn sleep	
		Compazine 10mg IM q 6 prn N+V.	
		LABS: CBC in AM.	
	11	Narcan 5mg IO stat To	
		RR → Floor To	
May 9 YR-4			
		↑ MS To 10mg IM q 3-4° prn pain. q 3°	
		straight if needed	
		Diet clears → house TODAY AS Tolerated	
		IV D5 1/4 S Run AT 80cc/HR —	
8AM		Urge Cough + Deep BREATHING!	
		Activity: OOB — chair + walk today + 3.	
		Cont Foley + careful peri CARE.	
		C/S + UA TODAY.	
		Call Ho if routine CBC report THIS AM.	

[C2081]

PARKER MEMORIAL HOSPITAL

PHYSICIAN'S ORDERS

JEAN MARIE SAUNDERS

XO-5Q
RS8VLL-1980pv

DIAGNOSIS

Status post opt. lt. upper [illegible]

DRUG ALLERGIES

INSTRUCTIONS:
1. IMPRINT SET BEFORE PLACING IN CHART.
2. DETACH FIRST COPY BELOW ORIGINAL AND SEND TO PHARMACY EACH TIME PHYSICIAN WRITES A SET OF ORDERS.
3. INDICATE COPY REMOVED BY PLACING INITIALS IN COLUMN OPPOSITE PHYSICIAN'S SIGNATURE.
4. THE SIGNATURE OF A PHYSICIAN MUST ACCOMPANY EACH SET OF ORDERS.

USE BALL POINT PEN & PRESS FIRMLY.

DATE	TIME	PHYSICIAN'S ORDERS	INITIAL WHEN COPY REMOVED
5/9	8AM	IV po's go well (e tonight – ? then (1300 cc) – will D/C IV tonight	
		Will start SITZ BATHS (T) TOMMORROW	
		① D.C. [illegible]	
		② [illegible] 1–1.5 mg [illegible]	
		③ [illegible]	
5/10	YR-4	FeSO4 300 mg PO BID	
		Percodan 1–2 tab PO q 4° PAIN (if no shots desired)	
		If still wants shots for pain can have Percodan 1 tab po 1½ hr after pain shot.	
		✓ Call HO Temp > 101[6] po.	
		✓ START SITZ BATHS TID TODAY	
		✓ CBC c diff THIS AM.	
5.10	YR-4	① [illegible] 5 mg p o q.d.	
5/11-YR-4	10 PM	May use 5-10 mg Valium po 4 id	
		Percodan 2 [illegible] q 2 3° pm	
		Pt may refuse Valium if she wishes	
		Percodan 2-3 po q 2-3° pm	

[C2082]

PARKER MEMORIAL HOSPITAL

PHYSICIAN'S ORDERS

JEAN MARIE SAUNDERS

DIAGNOSIS Repair of fistula–recto-vaginal (Colostomy)

DRUG ALLERGIES none known

XO-5Q
RS8VLL-1980pv

INSTRUCTIONS:
1. IMPRINT SET BEFORE PLACING IN CHART.
2. DETACH FIRST COPY BELOW ORIGINAL AND SEND TO PHARMACY EACH TIME PHYSICIAN WRITES A SET OF ORDERS.
3. INDICATE COPY REMOVED BY PLACING INITIALS IN COLUMN OPPOSITE PHYSICIAN'S SIGNATURE.
4. THE SIGNATURE OF A PHYSICIAN MUST ACCOMPANY EACH SET OF ORDERS.

USE BALL POINT PEN & PRESS FIRMLY.

DATE	TIME	PHYSICIAN'S ORDERS	INITIAL & COPY REM'D
	10 25 pm	Chloral hydrate 1.0 gm po tonight	
5/12 YR-4	9 pm	✓(Denied) Wrong...	
		✓ REOS + UA Today	
5/13		✓ Dambutol 100 mg po q hs prn sleep	
		CAN REPEAT X1 ĉ 80mg?	
		✓ D/C Foley THIS AM	
		✓ SITZ BATH q 4 hr after Foley out – AS	
		✓ much as possible	
	9 am	✓ C&S before Foley out	
		✓ CBC, diff Today	
		✓ Call MD Temp > 101 po	
		✓ Push po fluids	
		✓ Due To VOID by 5:00 pm	
		✓ Cath q 2° after 1:00 pm	
5/14 YR-4		① [illegible]	
5/15 YR-4		✓ Renew Narcotic	
		✓ BATH Tab or SITZ BATH minimum of	
		✓ TID (AS much AS possible)	
	8 pm	✓ R/O Zinium WASHES ĉ [illegible]	
		✓ qid	
		✓ CBC Removed AM	

[C2083]

PARKER MEMORIAL HOSPITAL

PHYSICIAN'S ORDERS

JEAN MARIE SAUNDERS

DIAGNOSIS

DRUG ALLERGIES

XO-5Q
RS8VLL-1980pv

INSTRUCTIONS:
1. IMPRINT SET BEFORE PLACING IN CHART.
2. DETACH FIRST COPY BELOW ORIGINAL AND SEND TO PHARMACY EACH TIME PHYSICIAN WRITES A SET OF ORDERS.
3. INDICATE COPY REMOVED BY PLACING INITIALS IN COLUMN OPPOSITE PHYSICIAN'S SIGNATURE.
4. THE SIGNATURE OF A PHYSICIAN MUST ACCOMPANY EACH SET OF ORDERS.

USE BALL POINT PEN & PRESS FIRMLY.

DATE	TIME	PHYSICIAN'S ORDERS	INITIAL WHEN COPY REMOVED
May 16 YR-4		Karaya powder (or any type of drying powder) about colostomy Bag site for itching red irritated area. Cont. Request As much as possible BATHS + perineum WASHES.	
	2PM	(1) ✓ Ferrous sulfate 0.3 gr po q.i.d. Cancel; ✓ [illegible] po [illegible]; (2) Ampicillin 500 mg po tid	
	11PM	EKG now	
5/17 YR-4	1PM	[crossed out] Cont BATHS AS much AS possible.	
May 18 YR-4	9:45PM	Renew Narcotic - (1) [illegible]	

[C2084]

PARKER MEMORIAL HOSPITAL

JEAN MARIE SAUNDERS

PHYSICIAN'S ORDERS

DIAGNOSIS: Post-op bleeding

DRUG ALLERGIES

XO-5Q
RS8VLL-1980pv

INSTRUCTIONS:
1. IMPRINT SET BEFORE PLACING IN CHART.
2. DETACH FIRST COPY BELOW ORIGINAL AND SEND TO PHARMACY EACH TIME PHYSICIAN WRITES A SET OF ORDERS.
3. INDICATE COPY REMOVED BY PLACING INITIALS IN COLUMN OPPOSITE PHYSICIAN'S SIGNATURE.
4. THE SIGNATURE OF A PHYSICIAN MUST ACCOMPANY EACH SET OF ORDERS.

USE BALL POINT PEN & PRESS FIRMLY.

DATE	TIME	PHYSICIAN'S ORDERS	INITIAL WHEN COPY REMOVED
5/20	YR-4	① Admit	
	✓	② Dx: s/p retrograde ... bleeding ...	
	✓	③ Cond: good	
	✓	④ Allergies: ∅	
	✓	⑤ Clears	
	✓	⑥ Complete bed rest	
	✓	⑦ Period of	
	✓	⑧ V.S. Q1H	
	✓	⑨ I+O	
		⑩ Lab: - Urinalysis	
	✓	Hct STAT, at 2PM, 8PM, today — crossmatch	
	✓	- CBC ... AM	
	✓	- Clot to BB → type +	
	✓	Xmatch 2 u B WB	
		⑪ IV's —	
		D5 1/4 NS c̄ 20 mEq KCl/liter at	
		75 cc QH, START 10:20 AM	
	✓	MEDS: Amoral 50 mg IM/po q 3-4 ° prn pain	
2 PM	✗	Fe SO4 300 mg po BID	
	✗	Multivit 1 tab po qd.	
	✗	... 250 mg po qid.	
	✗	Valium 5 mg po ...	
5/20	✓ 10:00	BP Q4°	

[C2085]

PARKER MEMORIAL HOSPITAL

JEAN MARIE SAUNDERS

PHYSICIAN'S ORDERS

DIAGNOSIS Post-op Bleeding

DRUG ALLERGIES

XO-5Q
RS8VLL-1980pv

INSTRUCTIONS:
1. IMPRINT SET BEFORE PLACING IN CHART.
2. DETACH FIRST COPY BELOW ORIGINAL AND SEND TO PHARMACY EACH TIME PHYSICIAN WRITES A SET OF ORDERS.
3. INDICATE COPY REMOVED BY PLACING INITIALS IN COLUMN OPPOSITE PHYSICIAN'S SIGNATURE.
4. THE SIGNATURE OF A PHYSICIAN MUST ACCOMPANY EACH SET OF ORDERS.

USE BALL POINT PEN & PRESS FIRMLY.

DATE	TIME	PHYSICIAN'S ORDERS	INITIAL WHEN COPY REMOVED
5-31-YR-4	10:30 PM	✓ DC IV	
		✓ OOB today + start Sitz Bath in Bath Tub as much as possible (at least TID)	
		✓ Δ VS to q 4°	
		✓ RN Pad count — cont.	
		✓ CBC tommorrow AM	
	2:30	✓ D int [illegible]	
May 22 YR-4	8:30 AM	✓ DC Peri pad count	
		✓ Sitz Bath qid if possible today	
		✓ Please get some [illegible]	
		✓ [illegible] ointment at bedside	
		✓ For HO or DR to do an exam today.	
5/23 YR-4		✓ Renew Narcotic	
	10 PM	✓ May be discharged [illegible]	

[C2086]

PARKER MEMORIAL HOSPITAL

JEAN MARIE SAUNDERS

PHYSICIAN'S ORDERS

DIAGNOSIS

DRUG ALLERGIES

XO-5Q
RS8VLL-1980pv

INSTRUCTIONS:
1. IMPRINT SET BEFORE PLACING IN CHART.
2. DETACH FIRST COPY BELOW ORIGINAL AND SEND TO PHARMACY EACH TIME PHYSICIAN WRITES A SET OF ORDERS.
3. INDICATE COPY REMOVED BY PLACING INITIALS IN COLUMN OPPOSITE PHYSICIAN'S SIGNATURE.
4. THE SIGNATURE OF A PHYSICIAN MUST ACCOMPANY EACH SET OF ORDERS.

USE BALL POINT PEN & PRESS FIRMLY.

DATE	TIME	PHYSICIAN'S ORDERS	INITIAL & COPY REMO.
7-15-YR-4	9 AM	SITZ baths TID	
		[illegible]	
		NPO p MN	
	6 PM	Morphine 10 mg / Atropine 0.4 mg } IM Mix 7 AM	
7/16	6 45 AM	NG to be inserted in OR	
	6 45 AM	Pre op meds - Demerol 100 mg / Atropine 0.4 mg } IM Mix 7 AM	
		previous pre op orders	
July 16 YR-4	10 AM	1) Op: Bilateral transabdominal tubal ligation, Celiotomy closure by retention [illegible]	
		2) [illegible] as per [illegible] 4 hrs on [illegible]	
		3) Fluids: D5 1/4 NS; [illegible] 75 cc/hr.	
		4) N/B to [illegible]	
		5) [illegible] to void by 8 pm, call Res if [illegible]	
		6. Meds:	

[C2087]

PARKER MEMORIAL HOSPITAL

PHYSICIAN'S ORDERS

JEAN MARIE SAUNDERS

XO-5Q
RS8VLL-1980pv

DIAGNOSIS

DRUG ALLERGIES

INSTRUCTIONS:
1. IMPRINT SET BEFORE PLACING IN CHART.
2. DETACH FIRST COPY BELOW ORIGINAL AND SEND TO PHARMACY EACH TIME PHYSICIAN WRITES A SET OF ORDERS.
3. INDICATE COPY REMOVED BY PLACING INITIALS IN COLUMN OPPOSITE PHYSICIAN'S SIGNATURE.
4. THE SIGNATURE OF A PHYSICIAN MUST ACCOMPANY EACH SET OF ORDERS.

USE BALL POINT PEN & PRESS FIRMLY.

DATE	TIME	PHYSICIAN'S ORDERS	INITIAL & COPY REMOVED
		Ancef 1 gm IV now to	
		Ancef 1 gm IV q 6 hrs.	
		~~[illegible]~~	
		Compazine 10 mg IM q 4 hrs prn N+V.	
		7) Lab: CBC in AM	
		8) Irrigate N/G c̄ 15cc NS q 4 hr + prn	
		9) Demerol 50 mg IM q 4 hr prn pain	
	1:35 pm	RR → FLOOR – IV.	
	2:55 PM	change Demerol to Demerol 50 mg IM q 3-4° prn	
		Demerol to 75 mg IM q 3-4 prn	
July 17	YR-4	1) Fluids:	
		D5 ½ NS c̄ 30 mEq KCl	
		Add 1 amp MVI per 1000 cc	
		Run at 80 cc per hour	
		2) Ice chips po only	
		3) Stockings	
	10 PM	4) Meds:	
		Restoril 90 mg PO h.s. prn sleep	
		Demerol 75 mg IM q 3-4 hr prn pain	
		5) Cough, Deep breathe	

[C2088]

PARKER MEMORIAL HOSPITAL

JEAN MARIE SAUNDERS

PHYSICIAN'S ORDERS

DIAGNOSIS

DRUG ALLERGIES

XO-5Q
RS8VLL-1980pv

INSTRUCTIONS:

1. IMPRINT SET BEFORE PLACING IN CHART.
2. DETACH FIRST COPY BELOW ORIGINAL AND SEND TO PHARMACY EACH TIME PHYSICIAN WRITES A SET OF ORDERS.
3. INDICATE COPY REMOVED BY PLACING INITIALS IN COLUMN OPPOSITE PHYSICIAN'S SIGNATURE.
4. THE SIGNATURE OF A PHYSICIAN MUST ACCOMPANY EACH SET OF ORDERS.

USE BALL POINT PEN & PRESS FIRMLY.

DATE	TIME	PHYSICIAN'S ORDERS	INITIAL WH COPY REMD
July 18, YR-4	8²⁰ pm	(1) Normosol M + 3 [illegible] mg KCl per liter Add 1 Amp MVI ē 1 Amp Berocca C [illegible] (2) Bed [illegible] (medicate before)	
	6¹⁵	① Sips [illegible]	
7-19 YR-4	5 AM	Codeine 30 mg IM q 3-4° prn dc Demerol 75 mg	
July 19	9³⁰ AM	① [illegible] 1 mg [illegible] q 3-4 [illegible] ② Valium 5 mg [illegible] q 4-6 hr [illegible] ③ IV. 5% D- ½ [illegible] ē 20 mg KCl [illegible] [illegible] @ [illegible]	
7-20 YR-4	2 pm	IV: D5/½ NS + 20 mg KCl/liter at 100 cc/hr. MVI in every other bottle Abdominal Binder stat	

[C2089]

PARKER MEMORIAL HOSPITAL

PHYSICIAN'S ORDERS

JEAN MARIE SAUNDERS

DIAGNOSIS

DRUG ALLERGIES

XO-5Q
RS8VLL-1980pv

INSTRUCTIONS:
1. IMPRINT SET BEFORE PLACING IN CHART.
2. DETACH FIRST COPY BELOW ORIGINAL AND SEND TO PHARMACY EACH TIME PHYSICIAN WRITES A SET OF ORDERS.
3. INDICATE COPY REMOVED BY PLACING INITIALS IN COLUMN OPPOSITE PHYSICIAN'S SIGNATURE.
4. THE SIGNATURE OF A PHYSICIAN MUST ACCOMPANY EACH SET OF ORDERS.
USE BALL POINT PEN & PRESS FIRMLY.

DATE	TIME	PHYSICIAN'S ORDERS	INITIAL WHEN COPY REMOVED
9-21		1) Fluids:	
		D5 ½ NS + 30 mg KCl	
		✓ Add 1 amp MVI in every other bottle	
		Run at 80 cc/h.	
		2) [illegible] 12 gm now [illegible]	
		✓ 5 gm [illegible] over 1 hr	
		✓ 3) [illegible] po — clear to	
9 1/21 [illegible]		✓ full liquids 50 – 60 cc/hr	
		✓ 4) Lytes, CBC + [illegible] am	
7/21	12 40 AM	D/C Ancef IV	
		[illegible]	
		[illegible]	
		1) [illegible]	
		[illegible]	
		2) [illegible] cream for	
		peri-rectal [illegible]	
		Apply q 6 h.	
7/22, [illegible]	12 30 AM 12 25 AM	Rectal [illegible] be used	
		tonight	

[C2090]

PARKER MEMORIAL HOSPITAL

JEAN MARIE SAUNDERS

PHYSICIAN'S ORDERS

DIAGNOSIS

DRUG ALLERGIES

XO-5Q
RS8VLL-1980pv

INSTRUCTIONS:
1. IMPRINT SET BEFORE PLACING IN CHART.
2. DETACH FIRST COPY BELOW ORIGINAL AND SEND TO PHARMACY EACH TIME PHYSICIAN WRITES A SET OF ORDERS.
3. INDICATE COPY REMOVED BY PLACING INITIALS IN COLUMN OPPOSITE PHYSICIAN'S SIGNATURE.
4. THE SIGNATURE OF A PHYSICIAN MUST ACCOMPANY EACH SET OF ORDERS.

USE BALL POINT PEN & PRESS FIRMLY.

DATE	TIME	PHYSICIAN'S ORDERS	INITIAL OF COPY REM'D
	9 PM	1) Fluids: D5 1/4 NS + 30 mg KCl / litre. Add 1 amp MVI to litre. Run at 125 cc/hr × 6 hrs. Then D/C I.V. 2) Push PO's 3) D/C + I/O record 4) Rectal Medical Unguent + S peri-rectal area and cruel.	
	3 PM	1) Ambulate in order 2) B.R.P.	
	2 PM	Percodan tab i po q4° prn	
	7[10] PM	D/C Dem. Injection	
	10[15] PM	Nembutal 100 mg P.O. per hs.	
July 23, YR-4	9[55] AM	1) May take shower 2) House diet	
July 24, YR-4		1) D/C Percodan 2) Codeine 15 mg po q 4 hr per prn	
	10[05] AM	1) May have tub	
July 25, YR-4	12[30] pm	1) D/C meds today	

[C2091]

STATE v. CARTER P. MALONE

STATEMENT OF THE CASE

The defendant, Carter P. Malone, has been indicted on two counts of assault with intent to rob; 6 counts of assault with intent to murder; and one count of unlawfully carrying a firearm. These charges arise from an armed robbery which occurred at Cookie's Restaurant and Bakery, Sunnyside Avenue, on August 28, Yr.–1. His accomplices were Nelson Plummer and Mitchell Lyman, who were also similarly charged. The defendant's alibi is that he was in the vicinity of the City Power Plant at the time of the crimes alleged.

LIST OF AVAILABLE WITNESSES AND COUNSEL

Carter P. Malone	Defendant
Drew Hagen	Defendant's attorney
Nelson Plummer	Co-defendant
Alton Scully	Attorney for Nelson Plummer
Carla Raintree	Wife of Nelson Plummer
Mitchell Lyman	Co-defendant
Natalie Shelton	Co-owner of Cookie's Restaurant & Bakery
Raymond Shelton	Co-owner of Cookie's Restaurant & Bakery
Brian McGregor	Employee of Cookie's Restaurant & Bakery
Sam Prince	Private investigator for prosecutor
Chip Olsen	Mitchell Lyman's stepson
Richard Hillman	Head of local prisoners union
Barry Kenner	Police officer
Mason Bates	Police officer
Tony Fielding	Police officer
Randy Breck	Police officer
Carl DeAngelo	Police officer
Wayne Kolter	Police officer
Simon Dobbs	Police detective

CHARGE: *Assault to Rob—Armed*

Being armed with a certain dangerous weapon; to wit a revolver did assault Brian McGregor with intent to rob him.

DATE: 8/27/Yr.–1.

CHARGE: *Assault to Rob—Armed*

Being armed with a certain dangerous weapon; to wit a revolver did assault Natalie Shelton with intent to rob her.

DATE: 8/27/Yr.–1.

CHARGE: *Assault to Murder—Armed*

Being armed with a certain dangerous weapon; to wit a revolver did assault Barry Kenner with intent to murder him.

DATE: 8/27/Yr.-1.

CHARGE: *Assault to Murder—Armed*

Being armed with a certain dangerous weapon; to wit revolver did assault Mason Bates with intent to murder him.

DATE: 8/27/Yr.-1.

CHARGE: *Assault to Murder—Armed*

Being armed with a certain dangerous weapon; to wit revolver did assault Tony Fielding with intent to murder him.

DATE: 8/27/Yr.-1.

CHARGE: *Assault to Murder—Armed*

Being armed with a certain dangerous weapon; to wit a revolver did assault Randy Breck with intent to murder him.

DATE: 8/27/Yr.-1.

CHARGE: *Assault to Murder—Armed*

Being armed with a certain dangerous weapon; to wit a revolver did assault Carl DeAngelo with intent to murder him.

DATE: 8/27/Yr.-1.

CHARGE: *Assault to Murder—Armed*

Being armed with a certain dangerous weapon; to wit a revolver did assault Wayne Kolter with intent to murder him.

DATE: 8/27/Yr.-1.

CHARGE: *Unlawfully Carrying Firearm on Person (Handgun)*

Not having permission under the General Laws of this State, did unlawfully carry on his person a certain firearm, to wit: a revolver from which a bullet could be discharged the length of the barrel of said firearm being less than 16″.

DATE: 8/27/Yr.-1.

WITNESSES: Brian McGregor, 1 General Lee Drive
Natalie Shelton, 42 Merit Way
Wayne Kolter, District #11
Carl DeAngelo, District 11
Randy Breck, District 11
Tony Fielding, District 11
Mason Bates, District 11
Barry Kenner, District 11

MEMORANDUM

TO: Christopher West, Assistant District Attorney

FROM: Sam Prince, Investigator

SUBJECT: State v. Malone

DATE: July 9, Yr.–0.

On Monday, July 9, Yr.–0, Carla Raintree, AKA Marlo Friederick, girlfriend of Nelson Plummer, contacted Sam Prince and related that she had been telephonically contacted at 588 Appleton Terrace, regarding the *Malone* trial.

At approximately 11:30 a.m., Raintree received a call from an unindentified white male who stated the following:

"Is Marlo there?"

"No, who is this?"

"A friend of Nelson's. Will she be back?"

"Late."

"I'll call back."

At approximately 2:15 p.m., Raintree received another call from an unidentified white male, who she speculates to be the same as above:

"Is Marlo there?"

"This is she, who is this?"

"A friend of Nelson's. He is wondering if you have been in touch with your friend?"

"No."

"Nelson's wondering if you could talk to him. He has turned state's evidence. Talk to him for Nelson and get him to change his mind."

"I'm not in touch with him."

"Well talk to him. Remember, you don't know Nelson."

"If Nelson wants to talk to me, have him call me but I'll be away for awhile."

"Nelson can't call you."

"He has before."

Raintree related that the second call was made on a pay telephone but that no background noise nor voice traits were distinguishable.

Raintree is employed as a dancer, nights, at the Bird of Paradise Lounge, 8765 Toro Street.

Raintree also resides at 51–A Beachaven Cottages; no telephone number available.

021330–56 Grand Jury, September 12, Yr.–1. ADA Jon Merrill

STATE v. CARTER P. MALONE
NELSON PLUMMER
MITCHELL LYMAN

Unlawfully carrying firearm 3 cts
Assault w/i to murder armed 18 cts
Assault w/i to rob 9 cts armed

WITNESS SWORN

Q. Identify yourself.

A. Brian McGregor.

Q. Where do you live?

A. 20 Firebrand Place.

Q. Are you employed?

A. At Cookie's Restaurant & Bakery.

Q. Where is that located?

A. 11–19 Sunnyside Avenue.

Q. Directing your attention to August 28 this year Yr.–1 were you working at Cookie's that day?

A. I was.

Q. What hours were you working?

A. 3 to 11 to close.

Q. What is your job at the restaurant?

A. Cook.

Q. Were you in the kitchen at that time?

A. I was.

Q. Directing your attention to about 10:40 that evening did something happen in the kitchen of the restaurant?

A. Yes.

Q. Tell us what happened.

A. Okay, a man with a white coat had no mask came in. Billy was leaving the kitchen.

Q. Tell us what you observed.

A. Billy was walking out back. He saw the man with the gun. He ran down front. The man with the gun ran after him told him hold it right there don't move get back over to the kitchen. He went back, another man came out with a nylon stocking over his head said everybody get out and get in the bakery and on the floor.

Q. Did you agree to?

A. Yes, he pulled us out from behind the kitchen one at a time, called us a few names and punks also put the gun to Billy's head. After Billy ran he said he would kill him if he pulled any more stuff like that.

Q. You mean run.

A. Yes.

Q. What did he do to you or say to you?

A. I was the last one out of the kitchen. He grabbed my shirt put the gun in my stomach said don't pull anything he would kill me pushed me in the bakery.

Q. What happened?

A. I went in the bakery sat on the floor two other men in front of me Ray and Pete.

Q. Employees of the restaurant?

A. Yes, Pete started to walk out headed toward the back door, another man in the bakery leaning against the freezer and table with a gun on him said get on the floor. He fell to the floor. I sat against another refrigerator on the floor until the dish washer came in sat next to me with the waitress.

Q. Were you in a position when sitting on the floor where you could see what was going on in the kitchen?

A. Just the part headed toward the kitchen, there was a table in front of me. I was between the table and refrigerator. I was sitting down.

Q. After sitting on the floor what did you observe happen?

A. The waitress and bus boy came in sat down, two more waitresses came in sat on the floor. The dish washer and man that cleaned the floors were all lined up all laying on the floor, waitresses on this side (indicating) cooks laying on the floor too.

Q. Did you hear anything after that?

A. After they made everybody get on the floor they were looking for the man, meanwhile when they came the manager's wife came upstairs. They asked her where the manager was. I saw them put the gun to her head.

Q. Mrs. Shelton?

A. Yes, all she knew he was out front, he came asked me and the dish washer next to me where the manager was. I did not say nothing. The dish washer next to me said he is out front.

Q. Was the restaurant closed?

A. Yes.

Q. What time did it close?

A. 10.

Q. You were cleaning up.

A. Yes.

Q. Did you hear anything after that conversation?

A. One of the men was out front in the dining room. He came back said the police were all around the place. I don't know who it was. The one in the blue coat Malone he said we better get out of here.

Q. He said it to the other two men.

A. Yes, they headed out the back door then shooting started.

Q. When they headed out the back door were the masks removed from their faces?

A. Okay, Lyman he had a red bandana on his face sitting on his neck the nylon stocking off Malone and Plummer had no mask.

Q. Before each left you were able to see their faces.

A. Yes.

Q. Did you later identify them as the three men?

A. Yes.

Q. Plummer, Malone, Lyman.

A. Yes.

Q. At some point during the time you and the other employees were on the floor did they ask you where the safe was or what the combination of the safe was?

A. No.

Q. At any time did they say anything to you that indicated they were talking to you and others concerning where the safe was and questions to that effect?

A. No, because they had already been over to the safe and they took one of the bakers and asked him to open it. He did not have the combination or anything.

Q. Any questions?

JQ. Did you ever see any of these people before in that restaurant?

A. No.

JQ. They were never customers before?

A. No. After the shooting started one man came back which was Malone. He did not have the mask on. He had a slight limp going out the bakery door. He went out in thirty seconds to a minute two police came in, by then I was already standing up. I said he just went out the bakery door he could be out front or the dining room. They went after him.

Q. The police?

A. Yes.

Q. Did they follow him out the door?

A. They went down, I went out behind the policeman. They had guns drawn. I got the keys and let the police in the door. They said get everybody in the bakery don't move. We rounded everybody up. They followed the pool of blood.

WITNESS SWORN

Q. Identify yourself.

A. Natalie Shelton.

Q. Where do you live?

A. 42 Merit Way.

Q. Mrs. Shelton are you employed?

A. Yes.

Q. Where do you work?

A. Cookie's.

Q. Directing your attention to August 27 this year were you working that day?

A. Yes.

Q. More specifically directing your attention to 10:45 that evening were you working in the restaurant?

A. Yes.

Q. Had the restaurant closed?

A. Yes.

Q. Where were you?

A. Down in the office.

Q. Doing bookkeeping?

A. Yes.

Q. At some time did you come to the kitchen of the restaurant?

A. About 10:45.

Q. What happened when you came upstairs to the kitchen?

A. I came upstairs rounded the corner and saw some of the bakers and cooks on the floor and a man in front of me with a gun. He told me lay down on the floor and I would not get hurt and I did. He put the gun to my head asked me where the manager was. I said I left him upstairs in the dining room. He asked my manager's name. I told him his name was Roy. He again asked me where is he. I said I did not know I left him upstairs.

Q. Upstairs?

A. In the dining room somewhere. While I was downstairs he called me a liar then did not say anything else to me.

Q. Any conversation about a safe?

A. No.

Q. Did he ask you anything about a safe?

A. No.

Q. What else happened?

A. I remained on the floor a few minutes later heard gunshots. I did not get up again until police officers came in said it was all right we could all get up.

Q. Approximately how long was that from the time you saw the man with the gun until the police told you it was all right?

A. Within ten minutes.

Q. Did you subsequently identify the man that pointed the gun at you?

A. Yes.

Q. What was his name?

A. Plummer.

Q. Did you see any other man with a gun?

A. Another man with a stocking mask on blue jacket with a gun.

Q. You did not see him without the mask on?

A. No.

WITNESS SWORN

Q. Identify yourself.

A. Raymond Shelton.

Q. Where do you live?

A. 42 Merit Way.

Q. Are you employed?

A. Yes, I am the owner.

Q. Are you the owner of the restaurant?

A. Yes.

Q. What is the name of the restaurant?

A. Cookie's.

Q. Where is that located?

A. 11–19 Sunnyside Avenue.

Q. August 27 this year were you working in the restaurant that night?

A. Yes.

Q. Approximately 10:45 did something happen in the restaurant?

A. I was in the middle of the dining room and saw Plummer.

Q. Tell us now what you observed.

A. I saw one of my cooks run the full length of the kitchen, it is visible from the dining room. It made me look up. I saw a stranger in the kitchen with a white jacket, white pants. I did not see a gun yet. I started walking toward him to see what he was doing there. At that time he had pushed Billy, pushed him back to the back of the kitchen. I saw the second gunman with a stocking mask. He had a gun out. He was fairly short. The gun was high up, I could see the gun. I was with one of my night managers Chad Lawry. He yelled to me they have guns, at that time I saw the second gun with a fellow dressed in white. I was approximately at that time 20 to 25 feet too hard for them to see out from inside the kitchen. It is not one way glass, we were so bright in the kitchen, the lights low in the dining room, it is mirrored effect unless you walk to the glass and look through it from the dining room you can see everything in the kitchen. At that time we realized they had guns about forty feet to go out the front door, we almost made it without him seeing me except for the last eight feet he opened the kitchen door put the gun out. I was already running. I kept going right out the door. There was one waitress, she was on the pay phone grabbed her pulled her with me, three of use got out the front door and hit the fire alarm at the corner across the street. There was an off duty waitress that lives two houses away outside with her boyfriend. I yelled to her call 911, the police answered the call within 2½ minutes, the building was surrounded within 4 to 5 minutes.

Q. Before leaving the restaurant did you make observations of the man at the cash register or near the cash register?

A. After hitting the fire alarm the waitress went to the second house to call 911. I stayed in front of the building the front parking lot. I went to the window. I saw I believe Malone dressed in blue with a stocking mask. I could see him leaning over the register. It is a computer register if you hit the wrong register it jams. All I could see was a red light. I could see him playing with the keys trying to open it.

Q. The cash register?

A. Yes.

Q. Did you later identify any of the men you saw?

A. Plummer, he was the only one without a mask.

Q. Was he the man at the register?

A. No, Malone.

Q. Did you later identify the man at the register as Malone?

A. Yes.

Q. What happened after that?

A. The first cruiser came it must have been 2½ to 3 minutes came down Sunnyside Avenue. I was in the middle of Sunnyside Avenue. They pulled beside me with guns drawn. I said 2 to 3, I only saw 2 they were still in there. I told them there was quite a few people in there, 20 people employees still there then 2 to 3 other cruisers came right behind. I took Carl DeAngelo . . .

Q. A police officer.

A. Yes and his partner Wayne Kolter, I took them to the back street Everett Avenue. I took them up the street, one fire door the fire door was visible. I could see that it is right at the corner, second one hidden by a cedar fence really could not see. I knew that was padlocked, two padlocked, the third one is where they came out at the dumpster, they have to climb the dumpster to the fence then they would be on Everett Avenue.

Q. Did you later see either of the men you saw in the restaurant?

A. Plummer.

Q. Where?

A. On the driveway shot 3 to 4 times.

Q. Is he the only one you saw that was in the restaurant?

A. Yes.

Q. At some time did you have conversation with the employees in your restaurant after this shooting had stopped?

A. We were all gathered in front of the retail bakery after they were out in the parking lot, some had already gone home. There was about 15 left.

Q. Did you have conversation?

A. Each one telling their side told it to the police.

Q. Did anyone tell you about conversation they had with any of the gunmen about the safe or combination of the safe?

A. 2 to 3, one of the bakers on duty they asked him for the combination.

Q. Of the safe?

A. Yes, they put a gun to his back, he said I only work here I don't have the keys.

Q. His name?

A. Brian McGregor.

Q. Any questions of the jurors?

WITNESS SWORN

Q. Identify yourself.

A. Officer Randy Breck.

Q. What is your occupation?

A. Police officer.

Q. How long have you been a police officer?

A. 8 years.

Q. In this city?

A. Yes.

Q. Directing your attention to August 27 this year tell us were you on duty that day?

A. I was.

Q. What shift were you working?

A. 5 to 12:45 a. m.

Q. At approximately 10:30 that evening did you get a call at some time?

A. Yes.

Q. What was the call?

A. Armed robbery at Cookie's bakery at the corner of Towne Road and Sunnyside Avenue.

Q. Did you respond to the call?

A. Yes.

Q. Who was with you?

A. Ptl. Owen Sanger.

Q. Can you describe what you observed when you arrived at Cookie's that night?

A. When I arrived at the scene I parked my vehicle to the side of the bakery so as to not make ourselves obvious, somebody informed me that the three suspects were still inside the bakery armed with weapons. I did not know who told me at the time, we treated it as a real call.

Q. What did you do?

A. Once I found that out I ran to the front of the bakery took cover behind a parked motor vehicle, just as I did this I heard somebody say the holdup men were now exiting the bakery as I was facing the bakery coming out to the right side exit, at this time I ran to the location. I observed two males standing on top of a cement wall. I heard one of my brother officers say to halt and drop the weapons.

Q. Both carrying weapons?

A. Yes at the time I saw they were weapons.

Q. Hand guns?

A. Yes, so they disregarded the command by the police, one fellow in a white jacket later identified by name as Plummer turned and fired at me at which time I returned fire. I saw him drop. I saw the other guy who was with him. I saw he was apprehended also I left that location went to the front door of the bakery took cover again. I did not know if they were all out of there or what. In a few seconds I saw a gentleman a white male coming to the doors where I was located. I was still under cover, I was taking cover. I saw the fellow try the door. I did not know if he was an employee or what. He tried the doors they were locked. He turned around. I saw he was carrying a black automatic. I commanded him to freeze and drop the weapon. He disregarded it and hopped behind a wooden barrier. I called for more help, one was still in there, the doors were locked, by the time we got in there he was wounded. We tracked blood to the rear of the restaurant a dining area. He apparently made his exit through the fire exit at the rear of the restaurant. We checked the ladies room, mens room.

Q. Did you later identify him?

A. Yes.

Q. As who?

A. Malone, when things quieted down I was later assigned to search the area around there behind the restaurant for possible vehicles, my partner and I did this, in the rear directly behind the fire door found a vehicle with Oklahoma plates and a key in the ignition.

Q. Who was it registered to?

A. Checked it for stolen through NCIC locally, no stolen record, later found it was registered to Plummer, that is all I did that night.

Q. The man you observed that exited through the side door you said was bleeding, did you actually see him bleeding?

A. Not at the time I saw the blood.

JQ. What were the lighting conditions that made it so easy to identify them?

A. This guy was about thirty feet from me, well lighted inside and outside lights on the building and street lights.

WITNESS SWORN

Q. Identify yourself.

A. Officer Mason Bates, district 11.

Q. How long have you been a police officer?

A. 8 years.

Q. Directing your attention to August 27 this year Yr.–1 tell us were you on duty that day?

A. That evening assigned to the Harry 3–11 unit with Tom Pilcher.

Q. What shift were your working?

A. Same shift 5:30 to 1.

Q. Directing your attention to about 10:30 that night did you receive a call that night?

A. In the station at the time district 11 heard a call come over the radio holdup in progress at Cookie's.

Q. Did you proceed there?

A. As a result of that went to the car drove down Sunnyside Avenue a few blocks away, I pulled to the corner of the restaurant at Sunnyside Avenue and the access road parallel to Towne Road. I believe we were the third car.

Q. Who were the other officers there?

A. I could see officer Carl DeAngelo and Wayne Kolter in the front officer Tony Fielding, Barry Kenner the previous witness Randy Breck and officer Sanger were on the scene. After I got out of the cruiser took up a position along with officer Fielding, Kenner and Breck in front of the restaurant while waiting for other officers to circle behind. I worked my way down the front to the northeast corner at which point I was able to look in make further observations of people in the restaurant. I could see a night cleaner in there, he was polishing the floor not aware what was going on. Twenty seconds later I was at the northeast most corner of the restaurant. Officer Kenner to my right said they are going back out the back door words to that effect. I could see a white male later identified as Nelson Plummer, he was scaling an eight foot wall ran between 90 Everett Avenue on top of the wall was a three foot chain link fence, since I could observe him going over the fence as he got over the fence I again heard Kenner yell halt I am a police officer. I saw Plummer fire to his right to the Everett Avenue side. I could hear fire from another direction. Plummer turned to myself Kenner and Fielding and fired a round directly at us. At this point I fired three rounds at Plummer. He disappeared below the wall in the alley would have given him a foot to 18″ to cover. I ran to the northeast most corner of the parking lot behind a parked vehicle to further observe as he tried to make an escape through the back yard my partner Pilcher was still going over the wall. Officer Fielding had taken a position below the wall, as I saw Fielding there I saw an arm come up and over in his direction. I cannot identify the arm and fire a round directly at him.

Q. At officer Fielding?

A. Yes.

Q. The arm was not in uniform?

A. No, it was definitely not an officer; we were in uniform at the time.

Q. Were you able to subsequently identify the arm?

A. I cannot say at this time. I saw the arm come over saw the muzzle flash. I fired another round in the direction of the person that shot at officer Fielding, that person dropped out of sight again I was not able to determine because of the chaotic conditions whether I had struck him or not. I cannot tell if I hit Plummer or not. I stayed in my position until I saw DeAngelo appear at the top of the wall and to hold our fire. He placed the people up there in custody. I went with Fielding to the front door of the restaurant trying to gain entrance unable to moved to the second set of doors at which point some of the employees came and let us in. We gathered all employees in one central area saw blood on the floor followed it back through the restaurant two aisles worked our way down to the mens room to the ladies room, observed bloodstains leading to the fire exit on Everett Avenue. We felt sure whoever left bloodstains made good their escape. We were given instruction by the sergeant in charge of the scene down there.

WITNESS SWORN

Q. Identify yourself.

A. Carl DeAngelo, district 11.

Q. How long have you been a police officer?

A. 8 years.

Q. Directing your attention to August 27, Yr.–1 were you on duty that day?

A. I was.

Q. Did you have occasion to go to Cookie's Restaurant?

A. Yes.

Q. As a result of a call?

A. Yes.

Q. Other officers testified briefly; tell us what you did at the time you arrived.

A. I came down Sunnyside Avenue. I stopped at the corner of Everett and Sunnyside, observed officers out in front of the restaurant. I saw the owner Raymond Shelton at the corner of Everett and Sunnyside. He yelled to my partner and myself they can go out the rear door. We ran up Everett to the rear of the restaurant at 90 Everett a driveway saw two white males climbing over a fence both armed with hand guns. My partner said halt police. The fellow in front fired as they came over, the fellow in front later identified as Nelson Plummer.

Q. At whom did he fire?

A. Shot fired I felt in our direction.

Q. Yourself and your partner.

A. Yes, out to the street there, Lyman ran to the rear of the building. We fired at him. We ran behind a car in the rear lot. My partner said give it up throw it up. He was either on the ground or going down. He fired again, we fired again. He was flat on the ground. We ran to him, my partner kicked the gun from his hand. I went down the driveway. I could see Lyman his leg sticking out from the porch. I said for him to come out. He made a motion. I fired a shot. He said I have had enough. He was hiding under the porch. He had a 38 snub nose revolver in his hand and a red bandana on his neck.

Q. He was identified.

A. As Mitchell Lyman.

Q. The first man identified.

A. As Nelson Plummer.

Q. Can you describe the weapon you took from him?

A. He was armed with a 38 caliber revolver Bull barrel I believe a Diamond Back revolver.

JQ. About how many shots were fired?

A. Two shots fired from Plummer's gun.

Q. Did you retrieve any weapon?

A. Retrieved weapons Plummer and Lyman had.

WITNESS SWORN

Q. Identify yourself.

A. Officer Wayne Kolter, district 11.

Q. How long have you been an officer?

A. 10 years.

Q. Directing your attention to August 27 this year were you on duty that day?

A. I was.

Q. More specifically about 10:30 that evening did you have occasion to go to Cookie's Restaurant?

A. Yes.

Q. Your brother officers testified on much of the detail, briefly tell the Grand Jury what you observed at the time you arrived at the restaurant.

A. On the date in question officer DeAngelo and myself responded to a radio call of a holdup in progress at Cookie's. Approximately 10:36 p. m. upon arrival going down to the restaurant another radio call that the three suspects are in there and are armed. We immediately go down Sunnyside Avenue observed many police cars in front of the building. Officer DeAngelo and myself parked at the corner of Everett and Sunnyside. We alighted from the vehicle and ran to the street to secure the rear of the building. I observed two shadows at the rear of the building near a dumpster adjacent to the alleyway at the right of 90 Everett, they just jumped over the fence. At that time I did not know whether they were possible hostages that escaped or employees that managed to get away. I yelled halt police, as soon as I did one of the defendants Plummer fired one shot.

Q. At you and officer DeAngelo?

A. Yes, at that time we returned fire. I believe my bullet or his bullet knocked him to the ground. We went behind a parked car loaded our service revolvers. We started approaching the defendant. He was down lying down with the gun still in his hand. I was not sure if he was dead or not. I thought maybe we could arrest him, as we approached him he raised his revolver fired another shot. We returned fire managed to subdue him. Officer DeAngelo arrested the defendant Lyman hiding under a porch in the alleyway in the rear of the alley.

Q. How did you subdue Plummer?

A. I kicked the gun out of his hand.

Q. Did you recover the gun?

A. I did.

Q. What kind of a gun?

A. 38 revolver Bull barrel had a copper jacket supervelle bullet, two shots fired from the chamber of the revolver, that revolver run through NCIC stolen 2/10/Yr.–1 in Oklahoma City from a sporting goods store.

JQ. Were guns submitted to ballistics?

A. Yes.

JQ. Were they found capable of firing?

A. As far as I know, we have not received a report yet.

Q. The guns you took from the men were the same guns that were fired at you?

A. No question about it the one Plummer had in his hand.

Q. He was in view until you took the gun from him?

A. Right sir.

WITNESS SWORN

Q. Identify yourself.

A. Det. Sgt. Simon Dobbs, Metropolitan police headquarters.

Q. How long have you been a Metropolitan officer?

A. 22 years.

Q. August 27 of this year were you on duty that night?

A. I was.

Q. Were you aware of a robbery at Cookie's Restaurant some time during the evening?

A. Yes.

Q. How did you become aware of the robbery?

A. Over the police radio it said police were investigating the robbery of Cookie's.

Q. Were you aware one suspect escaped from the holdup?

A. Yes.

Q. Did you get any description of the suspect?

A. Yes.

Q. What was the description?

A. Man about 40 years, blue shirt, brown pants with grey hair was the original description I received.

Q. Did you subsequently talk to the police about the description?

A. Yes.

Q. Did you get a further description?

A. It changed from grey hair to brown other than that the same.

Q. Some time around 11:30 that night did you have occasion to observe the man while performing your duties?

A. About 12:30 observed a man of the description given walking in a parking lot of the gas station on Towne Road directly across from Cookie's. I was approaching the individual from the opposite direction. He walked toward me. I drove into the parking lot of the gas station and through it. He crossed through the parking lot on the service road was now at the parking lot of the Chatterbox. I approached him from the rear my automobile lights shone on him there appeared to be blood on the leg of his trousers.

Q. Was he walking?

A. He was walking away from me. I alighted from the cruiser drew my service revolver told him stop. He did. I told him to lay on his face, he did, handcuffed him, asked where he was shot, he said in the foot. I called for an ambulance and back up.

Q. Did you later identify him?

A. Yes sir I did.

Q. Who did you identify?

A. Carter P. Malone.

Q. When you observed him was he limping?

A. No.

Q. Where was he shot?

A. Right through the ankle bone, after apprehending him I asked him if he wanted to remain in the position he was in or stand up, he said he would like to stand up. A fellow came from the

Chatterbox identified himself as an EMT from the City Health and Hospitals offered to examine the man's wound. Malone agreed. He had an entrance and exit hole through his ankle.

STATE OF ______

______, ss. Superior Court

STATE
v.
CARTER P. MALONE

MOTION TO SUPPRESS ALL IDENTIFICATION TESTIMONY

Defendant moves this Court to suppress all in-court and out-of-court identification testimony regarding the defendant, Carter P. Malone, offered by police officers and/or civilian witnesses at trial.

As grounds for this Motion the defendant says that the identification procedures used for out-of-court identification were impermissibly suggestive and will taint all future identifications of him by such witnesses, in deprivation of his rights to due process, effective assistance of counsel and to not incriminate himself.

Defendant further moves this Court for leave to file this motion late.

By his Attorney,

____

Drew Hagen

AFFIDAVIT OF COUNSEL

Drew Hagen, deposes and says as follows in support of Motion to Suppress All Identification Testimony:

1. I am counsel to the defendant, Carter P. Malone.

2. At the last court appearance on these indictments, November 16, Yr.–1, the Commonwealth revealed to me that the identification of the defendant was made as follows:

(a) police witnesses—The police officers who identify Mr. Malone participated in a one to one show-up more than an hour after the alleged incidents while Mr. Malone was in custody and accused and/or suspected of committing the crimes alleged.

(b) civilian witnesses—The civilian witnesses who identify Mr. Malone in the minutes of the Grand Jury were told by the police who was who and were instructed as to who the defendant was. No other identification procedures were used.

Signed under the penalties of perjury this 20th day of November, Yr.–1.

____

Drew Hagen

STATE OF ______

______, ss. Superior Court

STATE
v.
CARTER P. MALONE

RESPONSE TO STATE'S MOTION FOR DISCOVERY

In response to the State's Motion for Discovery, the defendant, by and through counsel states:

1. The defendant is prepared and plans, at this point in the defense preparation, to present evidence in the nature of an alibi.

2. Said evidence will place the defendant in the vicinity of the City Power Plant at the time of the crimes alleged in these indictments.

3. The prospective alibi witness is Richard Hillman, date of birth: March 1, Yr.–39; residence: 20 Ocean Avenue.

The defendant will supply information on any other prospective alibi witness who is located as soon as such information is received.

December 19, Yr.–1.

By his Attorney,

____

Drew Hagen

STATE OF ______

______, ss. Superior Court

STATE
v.
CARTER P. MALONE

DEFENDANT'S MOTION IN LIMINE

Carter P. Malone moves this Court to rule upon two matters which it is anticipated will arise during the trial of these indictments, before the commencement. Mr. Malone believes that the interests of a fair trial require an advance ruling on these matters.

1. Mr. Malone intends to present witnesses establishing an alibi. However, he is concerned that if he presents such evidence this Court might instruct the jury that an alibi is the last refuge of the guilty, or words to that effect. If such is the intention of this Court, Mr. Malone would re-evaluate presenting alibi evidence.

2. At least one prospective defense witness has been incarcerated in the past. Mr. Malone realizes that past convictions may be proper

impeachment methods for the prosecution to use, with the Court's permission. However, Mr. Malone is concerned that questions regarding the incarceration of a defense witness could tend to imply that Mr. Malone was acquainted with a witness because he (Malone) had also been incarcerated for a crime.

Since Mr. Malone does not intend to testify, any implication that he has been convicted in the past is impermissible and would greatly prejudice him.

WHEREFORE, Carter P. Malone prays this Court rule on these matters as follows:

1. That no separate instruction on alibi witnesses will be given to the jury, or, alternatively that this Court specify in advance what instruction on alibi witnesses and/or evidence will be given by the Court to the jury.

2. That any questions to any witness which could by its terms or answer lead to the inference that Mr. Malone has past convictions or has been incarcerated in the past are impermissible, and that the Assistant District Attorney be instructed to avoid such questions.

By his Attorney,

____

Drew Hagen

STATE OF ______

______, ss. Superior Court

STATE
v.
CARTER P. MALONE

MOTION FOR EXCULPATORY EVIDENCE REGARDING WITNESS NELSON PLUMMER

Carter P. Malone moves this Court to direct the State to furnish him with evidence tending to impeach the testimony of Nelson Plummer, specifically

1. A statement of all rewards and/or inducements offered to him in exchange for his testimony and/or mentioned to him directly or indirectly by any agent of the State directly or through his attorney.

2. The name and address of the agent of the State who had conversations with Plummer wherein his testimony was discussed and/or rewards and/or inducements were discussed.

3. A statement of the substance of the discussions between Plummer and the State's agent or agents.

In support of this motion Mr. Malone states that his attorney has been informed that the State intends to call Plummer as a rebuttal witness and has been informed that negotiations may have taken place to induce Plummer to testify as a State witness.

By his Attorney,

____

Drew Hagen

AFFIDAVIT OF COUNSEL

Drew Hagen deposes and says as follows in support of Motion for Exculpatory Evidence Regarding Witness Nelson Plummer:

1. I am counsel to Carter P. Malone by appointment of this Court under Rules of the Superior Court.

2. Nelson Plummer is charged with crimes arising out of the same incident that generated the indictments against Mr. Malone. Some months ago Plummer entered a plea of guilty and his sentencing was delayed until after the trial of Carter Malone.

3. I have been informed by the Assistant District Attorney prosecuting this case that he intends to call Plummer as a rebuttal witness in Mr. Malone's trial.

4. On June 13, Yr.–0 and again on June 14, Yr.–0 I had telephone conversations with Plummer's attorney, Alton Scully, during which I requested his permission to interview Plummer.

5. Attorney Scully informed me that he believed that Plummer had agreed to testify for the State to "shave a few years off the recommendation" that the State would make to the Court at the time of Plummer's sentencing. Mr. Scully also informed me that he believed that an agent of the State had spoken to Plummer relative to these arrangements, but he did not believe that these conversations had been reduced to writing.

6. The information sought in this motion will be exculpatory or will, potentially, lead to exculpatory evidence that will tend to impeach the testimony of Plummer.

Signed under the pains and penalties of perjury this 14th day of June, Yr.–0.

____

Drew Hagen

January 20, Yr.–0, approximately 9:40 a. m., at the Gray Grove Jail. Sam Prince with Attorney Alton Scully, representing Nelson Plummer for his alleged criminal acts on August 27, Yr.–1, an armed robbery and hold up of Cookie's Restaurant.

Q. (By Sam Prince) Mr. Plummer, are you aware that the information that you are giving me today may be used in a court case?

A. Yes, I do.

Q. You've been advised of your rights. You know that you don't have to speak to me.

A. Yes, sir, I do.

Q. You know your attorney can interrupt at any time.

A. Yes, I do.

Q. You can terminate this at any time you want.

A. Yes, sir, I do.

Q. Are you aware of the attorney-client privileges?

A. Yes, sir.

Q. Essentially that means that what is between you and your attorney is strictly the privilege of the attorney to know. I have no right to know what's going on. And by talking to me now, and with tape recorder going, you're aware that the tape is going, too?

A. Yes, sir.

Q. OK. You know you're waiving this attorney-client privilege?

A. Yes sir, I do.

Q. And with the subsequent action, the information that we intend to use with the subsequent court case that may be resulting from this, that the attorney-client privilege will be waived at that time, too?

A. Yes, sir, I know.

Q. No one's forced you to come here today? No one's forced you to talk to me in any way, have they?

A. No, sir.

Q. No threats or anything like that?

A. No, sir.

Q. Any promises been made by any law enforcement officials?

A. None whatsoever.

Q. No one from the DA's office came and spoke to you before?

A. No, sir.

Q. Other members of law enforcement, for instance, Alcohol, Tobacco and Firearms, they, no one promised you anything there?

A. No, sir.

Q. Drug Enforcement Administration?

A. No, sir.

Q. You've had prior dealings with them, correct?

A. Yes, sir.

Q. Now tell me the story about Hagen? How many times has he been to see you?

A. Three times, once in the hospital and twice since I've been here in jail.

Q. The latest time being when?

A. Last week.

Q. Last week, ok. How long did he stay last week?

A. About 10 minutes.

Q. Start from the very beginning and tell me essentially how this came to be? Right after you were arrested, right to the present time—how the story concerning Hagen's soliciting you to commit perjury came to be?

A. I was in the hospital when Hagen first came down and he asked me if there was anything I needed and what have you. And that was basically the entire conversation there as what my needs were. Later on, Hagen came down here to the jail and we discussed Carter's case and how it looked and how my case looked, Mitchell's case looked and what have you. And I told him at that time that I would be in agreement to testify for Carter if we could get Carter off and I believe that Mitchell would too. Then it was left at that. And then later on, just about two or three weeks ago, Carter called my wife from the penitentiary.

Q. OK. And your wife's name is?

A. Carla Raintree.

Q. She also has a nickname?

A. "Marlo."

Q. And she is, where is she now?

A. She's in the House of Correction on a 60 day sentence.

Q. And what's that charge?

A. It's a Mann Act charge.

Q. Now when he called Carla, what did he say to Carla?

A. He told Carla that they had a deal set up and that he wanted her to try to get down there so that she could relay it to me and he wanted her to come in under a phony I.D., not under her own name. Carla told him that she didn't know if she was going to be able to get this I.D., that she'd try. She couldn't get the I.D., so a friend of Carter's called—a girl—called and told her that she was going down to see Carter and Carla told her, "Well find out what Carter wants and tell me everything that he wants." So the girl went down and saw Carter and then called Carla that night and told Carla everything that Carter said which was that we were going to use Joe Friend as the third principal party in this robbery and that Drew would be contacting me and get me a picture of Friend so that I would know what he looked like and I was to testify that it was me and Mitchell and this Joe Friend and not Carter that was involved and that some people from Friends of Family were to testify that Carter was someplace else when that all happened and they also had a story concocted in regards to the shooting.

Q. When you say Drew, who do you mean?

A. Sir?

Q. You said Drew?

A. Yes. Drew Hagen.

Q. Drew Hagen is who?

A. Carter's attorney.

Q. So you say, just to recap it a bit, that Carter called Carla. Carter called her and told her the story? Correct?

A. Yes, sir.

Q. OK. And review the story one more time.

A. The story was that I was to testify that Joe Friend was the third party involved in this robbery. Some people at the State Pen, which I had omitted the first time when I told you the story, some people at the State Pen who have killed this Joe Friend, have told Carter that his body cannot be found and law enforcement officials have not been able to find him. He's been on the lam since Yr.–7 and they haven't found his body since then. And this was the reason that we were using Joe Friend. And that Drew Hagen was to contact me and to get me a picture of Joe Friend so I would know what he looked like. And basically that was the conversation.

Q. OK. Joe Friend and Carter Malone were friends while at the State Pen?

A. No, no.

Q. How were they acquainted?

A. I believe he knew him at the State Pen, but they were not friends. This Joe Friend was killed for being an informer by underworld characters. And I doubt very seriously if they were friends at the State Pen.

Q. Were you ever acquainted with Joe Friend?

A. No.

Q. Did you ever meet him?

A. No, I haven't.

Q. Ever see him?

A. No.

Q. OK. So essentially what we have is that Drew Hagen coming down and speaking to you a couple of weeks ago.

A. Yes, sir.

Q. Going over the story about Joe Friend, how did he leave it with you? Did he say he was coming back?

A. No. When Drew came in and talked to me this last time, he asked me if I would still testify for Carter and I told him that I would. He asked me where my case was at and I told him I don't know. The only time I see my attorney is when I go to court. And a couple of times he's been down. I said, "I don't know where my case is at right now." He says, "Well, how do you feel about still testifying for Carter?" And I told him, "I'll testify for him." He said, "Well, this is what we want you to say," and then he lined out the same thing that Carter had explained to Carla. And I told him that well I was under the impression from the conversation that Carla had with Carter, that you had a picture of Joe Friend and he said, "Yeah. I'm trying to get one." He says, "I don't have one right now, but I'll try to get you one before the court day." Then he explained to me how my testimony would be used . . . that I would give it to an investigator, and that the investigator would take down my statement. And he told me at this time, this was a quote on his part, "Be very careful what you say to this investigator because we're doing a number on him." "He's a straight shooter and he doesn't know what we're doing." He says, "So be extremely careful what you tell him." And I told him, "All right." That I would. Then we just briefly capped what my testimony would be and how he would use it. He said if my case was still up in the air and I hadn't plead guilty at that time, then he would put me on the stand and I would merely take the Fifth Amendment privilege—self-incrimination—and refuse to testify and at that time the investigator can be put on the stand and my statement could be used. Or if I had already plead guilty than I could take the stand and testify in Carter's behalf. But either way, the statement would probably be used and the investigator would probably be used. At this time, he asked me if my attorney, Alton Scully, knew anything of Carter's involvement in the robbery and what have you and I told him, "No." And he said, "Well, good, keep him in the dark." And he asked me how much I had talked to Alton about the case and I told him, "Very little because we are negotiating a guilty plea." And he said, "Well, let him, don't let him know anything more than possible." And that was about the conversation. And then he said he would contact Alton Scully and see where my case was at in regards to my statement. If it was all right as far as Alton was concerned about using it. And that was just basically it.

Q. OK. When the investigator came down to speak to you, he took a statement from you and he wrote it down in front of you?

A. Right.

Q. Did you sign that statement?

A. No, sir, I didn't. The investigator told me after he got through taking the statement, he said, "I work for Drew Hagen, but I must be truthful with you, he says, in your own best interest."

He said, "I would suggest that you talk to your attorney before you sign this statement. This statement is extremely incriminating, and I don't think it would be in your best interest to sign this statement until you talk to your attorney." He said, "You can do anything you please, but if I were you . . ." and then he said, "In my opinion," he says, "Drew Hagen is going to stir a lot of shit with this statement." He says, "I strongly suggest that you talk to your attorney about it." So I told him that I would.

Q. The statement you gave Drew Hagen's investigator?

A. Right.

Q. Was that true or false?

A. That was a false statement.

Q. A false statement. And that story was given to you by whom?

A. It's the story that Carter related to Carla. I merely put Joe Friend in the position that Carter was in in that statement.

Q. It was also the statement that Drew Hagen related to you, too?

A. Right.

Q. Drew Hagen told you essentially to say that, to say the statement that you gave the investigator?

A. Right.

Q. Have you had any contact with Malone or Lyman?

A. Just when I go to court. Basically not much has been said there because Malone wants to present the image that . . . to court officials . . . that he and I don't know each other. So very little has been said in court.

Q. Do you have any idea if Drew Hagen approached Mitchell Lyman? If he's part of this scheme which would exclude Carter Malone from the deal and include Joe Friend in his place?

A. Yes, sir, I do. Mr. Hagen told me that he had contacted Mitchell Lyman and that Mitchell Lyman was going to testify the same way that I did and that he would use my statement . . . testify exactly to what my statement said.

Q. When did Hagen tell you that Lyman was going to say the same thing?

A. This was the last time he visited me . . . last week.

Q. Do you have any other contacts in the jail? Is there anyone in this jail now that is related to any of the other defendants?

A. Yes. Chip Olsen.

Q. Has he approached with any kind of information at all? Has he approached you the same type of story?

A. No, sir, he hasn't.

Q. And how is Olsen related to this whole deal?

A. He's Mitchell Lyman's stepson. He's merely a contact between me and Drew Hagen, but Drew Hagen had relayed nothing in between Olsen except to tell Olsen when he'd be down to see me.

Q. Tell me about Richard Hillman.

A. Richard Hillman heads the chapter of Friends and Families, which is on the same order of National Prisoners Union but on a smaller scale here in this state, and I headed the local chapter of the Prisoners Union in Oklahoma City. I met Hillman through my contacts within the Prisoners Union when I arrived here, which was about July 1st . . . ..

Q. Yr.–1?

A. Yes, sir, Yr.–1. And Hillman put me on and introduced me to Malone and Lyman as two individuals to work with. And when I say work I mean armed robberies. And that was how I met Malone and Lyman. Malone was living at Drew Hagen's house and I was there at his house several times visiting with Carter Malone. And Mitchell was living in another town at the time. The first meeting took place, though, at a safe house that Hillman had set up just for the purpose of underworld characters conducting business. I guess dope transactions, gun transactions, what have you.

Q. Where is that located?

A. I'm not sure of the exact address, he no longer has it. It's somewhere around Spivac Square, but I'm not sure of what the address was.

Q. You said you know that Malone and Hagen, his attorney, were living together?

A. Yes, sir. I knew that Carter was living in Hagen's house.

Q. And you had visited Malone up there several times?

A. Yes, sir. I have.

Q. Will you describe the house?

A. Yes, sir. When you walk in, downstairs, the living room area, there's a large living room. The dinette and the living room are attached. It's an old three story structure. They were doing a lot of work on the plumbing fixtures at that time. Down in the basement they had a shower set up. On the second or third floor, there's another shower and rest room area where they were doing a lot of work at. Carter lived on the top floor. I believe this was a three story structure. I may have been . . . yes, it was, it was a three story structure. Carter lived on the third floor towards that, which way is that direction here?

Q. South.

A. South. The far south bedroom. There was one phone in the house with an extremely long extension cord. About 50 feet.

Q. How did you say that Malone and Hagen met? How were they friendly? How did they come to live together?

A. They . . . well that's bad news. That's the only reason he came in here. Richard Hillman set it up. Drew Hagen is the lawyer for the Friends and Family Organization and Hillman set that up when Carter got out of prison for a place for him to stay.

Q. How would you describe Hagen? Would you describe him as a radical in the way that . . . in the term that radical would mean, such . . . ?

A. A left-winged politician. Yes, sir. He's a radical in that way.

Q. And how is his involvement in Friends and Family?

A. He . . . they had a neighborhood law firm there and he is their attorney. He handles their law suits and what have you. And he had a lot of contact down there with the prisoners and with the Friends and Family headquarters also.

Q. To your knowledge, has he ever lived with any other ex-convicts? Anyone of the nature that Malone would be hanging around with?

A. No.

Q. No?

A. You mean has any other ex-convicts ever lived? Not to my knowledge. I don't know. They could have. I just don't know.

Q. This house, now, where is it located?

A. It's about a block from Spivac Square. It sets up on the hill there. It's about a block from Spivac Square.

Q. What color is it? Do you remember?

A. No. I don't remember. I don't remember.

Q. Now let's talk about the incident over at Cookie's. From the very beginning, can you tell me when it was planned?

A. We were called in . . . I was called by Carter Malone. I was at Carla's house and he wanted me to meet him.

Q. Where, do you know?

A. Teddy's.

Q. Teddy's on the beach?

A. Right.

Q. OK.

A. Now Malone wanted me to pick him up at his house and we were to meet Mitch over there. So that's what I did. Carla and I picked up Carter at his house, Drew's house. We drove over and we met Mitch. When we met Mitch, a couple robberies were discussed and Carter mentioned this restaurant. They had been out all week. This restaurant wasn't planned. Out of all the robberies they had set up, this was the only one that wasn't planned. But Carter thought it might go down for a quick 10 grand and it didn't look that hard to do. And so it was decided that we would go there and do it.

Q. When was this decided now? If the robbery took place on August 27, Yr.–1?

A. August 27, Yr.–1.

Q. In the afternoon, morning?

A. No, it was night just prior to us going over there and doing it. It was late when we got over there.

Q. Did you have the guns with you at that time?

A. Yeah. We did.

Q. Who had the guns? Did one guy have the gun or did they each have their own gun?

A. Everybody had their own gun. I had to drive back and get mine, which was one of the reasons we were so late getting over there. I didn't have my gun with me. And I had to drive back down and get mine.

Q. What kind of gun did you have?

A. .38 diamond back and I had left it with Carla.

Q. Where did you get that gun?

A. I got it in Oklahoma in a burglary there.

Q. Did you do the burglary yourself?

A. No. No. Some people there did the whole thing and various select number of people had access to those guns and I was one of them that they let have one.

Q. Was it given to you or did you buy it?

A. It was given to me, two of them given to me, a 380 and that .38.

Q. What did Carter Malone have for a gun?

A. .38 snub nose.

Q. Where did he get his gun?

A. I don't know. I never asked him.

Q. Mitchell Lyman, how about his gun?

A. It was either a .32 or a .38 snub nose, also.

Q. Were you aware of where he got this gun?

A. I'm aware since the ATF people told me where his gun came from. I take it for granted that Carter's came from the same place. It came from some sort of burglary or robbery down in Georgia, somewhere around there, Kentucky, somewhere.

Q. OK. So just prior to going over to Cookie's you planned the robbery? It was Carter's idea?

A. His idea, I don't know. It was his idea to go over there and do that robbery. Now the way the robbery came down and how it was handled was Mitch's idea after we got over there and he looked at it, Mitch decided how we were going to do it and I told him, "hey, that's crazy." That place I could see from the outside was too big to be running in the back door and trying to gather up all those people. He thought . . . Mitch had already had five or six drinks at that time, I don't think he was thinking . . . anyway we went ahead and did it his way and the end result was half the people got away and a shoot-out with the police department and what have you.

Q. Do you remember what you were wearing that night?

A. I was wearing a three-piece suit and I changed in the car. I took off my suit jacket and put on a white windbreaker.

Q. A white windbreaker?

A. Yeah.

Q. How about Carter? What was he wearing?

A. He was wearing a dark jacket, dark slacks and a hose, nylon stocking.

Q. Nylon stocking. Were you wearing a mask?

A. No, I wasn't.

Q. Was Mitchell Lyman?

A. Yeah. He was wearing a bandana, red and white bandana.

Q. What was he wearing for clothes, do you remember?

A. No, I don't. It was all dark, too.

Q. OK. So tell me how you got in the restaurant?

A. Mitch tried to get in the side door and he couldn't jimmie the side door and he went through the back door and checked it out. That's the one leading to the bakery. Then he came back and he told us that's the way he thought we should enter and that's when I told him he was crazy.

Q. Now getting back, just to recap it. It was said that Mitchell cased the place, you went in the back door into the bakery, because Mitchell thought it was going to be the best way in.

A. Right.

Q. From there, tell me what happened?

A. All three of us went through that back door there. While they were rounding up the people inside the place, I'm speaking of the bakery and kitchen area there, I was trying to determine who had the combination to the safe, where he was at and I was told by a cook there that the manager had it. And I went up front to look for the manager and it took me a while to find the front, the eating area up there, and by the time I found it, the manager had gotten away. I told Carter this at that time and we went up there and found two girls hiding underneath a table and I looked out the window and I saw police officers were sneaking up on the place there. I told Carter then that they already ridden down on us and we'd better get away. One thing that had been discussed before that is that if the situation ever came down like that, all of us agreed that we wouldn't take any hostages and we'd just do our best to get out of there without involving any hostages or anyone else but ourselves. And that's why we elected the way we went out. Mitch and I hit the back wall there and Carter gave us covering fire until we got to the wall. We hit the wall. Mitch's gun wouldn't fire. He ran back behind me and I gave Mitch covering fire until he tried to get around the corner there and they shot me three times.

Q. Where were you shot?

A. Twice in this leg and once in this leg.

Q. How many times did you fire at the police?

A. Twice.

Q. Did Mitchell fire at all?

A. No. Mitch's gun wouldn't fire.

Q. How many times did Carter fire at the police?

A. I don't know. He said he unloaded on them. It was what he told me at the hospital. He said he unloaded them all.

Q. He told you that in the hospital.

A. Yeah. I don't know how many times he fired. I really don't know. He said he got hit right outside that back door there. When he got hit in the ankle and of course it severed an artery and that's why he didn't get any further than he got.

Q. Did he tell you how he got away?

A. No, he didn't. He said he went out a side door there. And, he did say that he walked right through all the police that were outside and he got on down the street. Someplace near a filling station or something. At that time he was trying to call Rich Hillman. Trying to get somewhere he could call Rich Hillman to come and pick him up.

Q. Are you aware that he was captured right across the street?

A. Yes, I am.

Q. Are you aware that he was captured right across the street?

A. He told me a couple of blocks away. I wasn't aware that he was captured right across the street.

Q. Did he say why he went back there?

A. No. He didn't. He just said that he was bleeding to death.
Q. What was the split going to be from the robbery?
A. Three ways.
Q. Three ways equal?
A. Yeah.
Q. How did you get there in the first place?
A. Equal. It was always understood that we kick Rich so much, 10% off of the robbery, that's Rich Hillman of Friends and Family, to keep that organization running.
Q. Was he in any part?
A. Not any planning part.
Q. Was he aware that you were going to rob somewhere?
A. Right. That's why he put us together.
Q. He was. So he organized you for that fact?
A. Right.
Q. Do you remember when he organized you?
A. When I contacted him. They had been working someone else and they needed a third person because they had a Brinks job going with an inside man on Brinks, who had been setting up these scores with this one particular guy for a period of years. This guy hadn't been working as good as he had in the past and he was beginning to lose his heart as far as doing bank robberies. And he backed off. This one score took too long to go down. It was in the . . . the town right next to Cookie's there.
Q. Middletown?
A. Name another one and I'll tell you?
Q. Chester?
A. Chester. Chester Circle. The National Bank that sits right there at that circle. They had set on it for so long that the information that the Brink's driver gave them was no longer any good. They had changed the way that they were delivering it. They had split that bundle up. At that time it was something around $80,000. They had split that up into three different shipments, therefore, it wasn't coming in at the same time. And so they had to back off. The Brink's driver was mad about, or whoever worked for Brinks, their inside contact, was mad that they had layed on it for so long. It was two weeks. And the reason that they had done that was this third person that was involved, through no fault of Carter or Mitch, 'cuz they wanted to do it after they looked at it for two days.
Q. So Richard Hillman was aware that he had put you people together for criminal activity?

A. Right.

Q. Had you been involved with Mitchell or Carter in any other criminal acts?

A. No, I haven't.

Q. This is the only type that you've ever tried? How did you get from where the meeting took place when you discussed these robberies, these potential robberies, how did you get from there to Cookie's?

A. I used my car to go pick up Carter and then go on down . . . I mean, yeah. Carla and I went down and picked up Carter.

Q. What kind of car do you use?

A. I have a Dodge.

Q. Is that local license plate?

A. No. It has Oklahoma plates on it.

Q. Do you remember the number?

A. No, sir, I don't.

Q. Could you tell me a little bit . . . you mentioned a couple drop cars?

A. We had two drop cars lined up for another robbery. A bigger robbery that was supposed to come down the next week. They thought that it might go down Monday. And a lot of equipment that we could use. One of the drop cars was already near Cookie's. It was a Ford.

Q. Was it stolen car?

A. Right. Galaxy. And it was one that Mitch had stolen. Right it was a Galaxy. There was some equipment left in it. I don't know if the equipment was ever taken out. By equipment I'm speaking of a dent-puller and some screwdrivers and things. When we got there it was decided that we didn't have enough time to go pick up the scanner and what have you and so we used my car and didn't bother going to pick up the drop car or line anything else up. It was just a spur of the moment robbery that Carter felt would go down pretty easy.

Q. Do you have any more guns?

A. Yes. I had a 380 and a commander sub machine gun, which we didn't use in that robbery also.

Q. How about any other equipment?

A. I had a scanner, I had a CB pickup. I had a CB itself. I had earphones with the selector switch on the CB programmer, like if we wanted to work off Channel 7, the guy could take this receiver and put it in his pocket, put the earphone in his ear and another person could transmit to him from the car. I had one of those and, of course, the scanner. And that was about it.

Q. And you were going to use those to avoid police surveillance?

A. Right.

Q. Back to Drew Hagen, the attorney for Malone, how have you left it with him? Are you going to call him or is he going to drop down to see you?

A. I left it with him that I would give that statement to the investigator, however, I told the investigator that the next time that I saw Hagen, I would sign that statement. To tell Drew that I would sign that statement, and I expected to see him Friday in court. And then when we didn't go to court Friday, I don't know how everything is left up at this point right now.

Q. Are you aware, as I told you before, that the information that you've given me today may be used against the lawyer, if, in fact, this fact pattern pans out?

A. Yes, sir, I am.

Q. OK. You are. Would you consent to cooperating with the District Attorney's Office?

A. Yes, sir I would.

Q. In that this conversation could be used as information for action against the attorney.

A. Yes, sir, I would, and so would my wife, Carla Raintree.

Q. She would, OK, fine. Again, I'm asking you. Has anything been promised you?

A. No, sir, nothing's been promised me.

Q. Nothing at all. Nothing in the way of money, rewards . . . ?

A. Nothing.

Q. Nothing. Any reduction in sentence, nothing's been mentioned about that?

A. None.

Q. How about promises made to you by Hagen. Did he make any promises to you? What is your end of this deal?

A. The only promise that was made to me and wasn't made through Hagen, it was made through Rich Hillman, is that wherever I went within the prison system, Carter would break me out if I testified for Carter.

Q. When you say break you out, is that a physical breakout, or does that mean he would arrange for you to be transferred to another prison?

A. No. That means physical breakout.

Q. I see. Does Carter Malone have the capacity to and the equipment to break you out of the State Pen?

A. I don't know if he has the capacity. He's got the equipment. I don't know if he could take me out of the State Pen. I've looked at the North Prison, he's capable of getting me out of North. I don't know if he could get me out of the State Pen or not on a strongarm. Of course, I don't think he would try a strongarm on the State Pen. He would probably have me moved to a hospital or someplace where he could do it from there.

Q. And how did he relay this information that he was going to break you out of the State Penitentiary? Did he do it through the attorney Drew Hagen?

A. No. Carter told me while we were in the hospital that if he beat this, wherever I went, he'd come and get me and Mitch. He'd break us both out.

Q. Why does Carter want to get out of this so bad?

A. Carter's got a life sentence, two life sentences I understand that revoked his parole and he has no hope of getting back on the streets if he doesn't beat this. Here's one other thing I didn't relate to you. My wife was threatened very discreetly by Rich Hillman. They don't want her in that courtroom. They're afraid that this whole thing is going to blow up even if she appears in court. And the DA just decided to subpoena her right then and find out how much she knows. Which she knows quite a little bit. She sat in on some bank robberies that was planned and what have you before she left the room and didn't want to know more than possible. But they don't want her down there. Hillman told her and he left this impression in her mind, so she asked about a van that Rich had been using, and he said I had to get rid of it because there was too much blood on it. And she asked what he meant by that and he made some kind of statement about somebody talking too much and that . . . that statement was made directly to intimidate her. That's how she took it and that's how I'd take it.

Q. Going back, a few steps back, you said that if this robbery of Cookie's had panned out and you got the money, 10%—Rich Hillman was afforded 10% of the money.

A. Right.

Q. Had in the past any money been given to him from your criminal enterprises with Malone?

A. Yes, it had.

Q. How much? Do you remember?

A. About a grand.

Q. About a grand. Is that one lump sum?

A. Yeah.

Q. How many times had you paid him?

A. One time.

Q. One time a $1,000.

A. Then another time I fronted some money for they were holding a vigilance up at the North Prison and they had a bunch of people up there and they wanted to put on a picnic and what have you and they were calling around town trying to get things together. We chipped in and gave them the money they needed $400 or $500, whatever it took.

Q. Can you think of anything else you'd like to tell me?

A. No. I think that just about covers everything right there.

Q. When this case comes to court against Carter Malone and you with this information you've just given me, when they put you on the stand, what do you intend to say? Are you going to tell the truth?

A. No. I plan to do what Drew Hagen . . . I talked it over with my attorney. My attorney doesn't know what to do at this point. He asked me . . . he was extremely upset that Drew Hagen was doing this. And because he is an attorney and what have you because Drew's an attorney, with his involvement in this whole thing and that he feels it is extremely unethical and asked me if, how I felt.

Q. If you get on the stand in view of the fact that you just gave me this testimony, OK, you're telling me the right story, the one that you feel is the right story.

A. Yes, sir.

Q. When they ask you a question, how are you going to answer in court?

A. Under oath, I'll answer truthfully. I thought that you were referring to whether I would be on the stand and take the Fifth Amendment privilege of self-incrimination.

Q. I just want to know if you're going to tell the truth when you get on the stand?

A. Yes, sir.

Q. Is the story that Carter Malone is part of the robbery team with you and Mr. Lyman that night, is that true?

A. Yes, sir. That's correct.

Q. The story that Joe Friend was part of the robbery team, was that story dreamed up by Carter Malone and related to you by Drew Hagen, his attorney, is that true?

A. Yes, sir, that's true.

Q. That's true?

A. Yes, sir.

Q. That he was part of the robbery team or . . . ..

A. No. That it was concocted by Carter Malone.

Q. Do you have anything else you'd like to say?

A. I can't think of anything else.

Q. Thanks.

TENANT ADM. v. ODYSSEY CORP.

STATEMENT OF THE CASE

This is a product liability action arising out of a fire in a motor home which overturned while being driven on a major artery on June 8, Yr.–5, in which four persons, including this plaintiff's decedent, were killed. Miles R. Tenant, Administrator of the Estate of Kent Tenant, sues both the manufacturer and the retail distributor of the motor home. The manufacturer has impleaded the maker of component parts as a third party defendant.

LIST OF AVAILABLE WITNESSES AND COUNSEL

Miles R. Tenant, Jr.	Plaintiff, Administrator of the Estate of Kent Tenant
Grant Edsel	Eyewitness
Paul Dover	Eyewitness
Frank Brummer	Accident investigator, Department of Motor Vehicles
Matthew Dupres	President of Defendant corporation, Discovery Trailers, Inc.
Sy Felcham	Owner of motor home
Robert Sica	Past employee of Defendant corporation, Odyssey Corporation
Jeffrey Terrio	Chief engineer of Defendant corporation, Odyssey Corporation
David Cochin	Employee of Defendant corporation, Magnum Motors Corporation
Jack M. Leavitt	Attorney for Plaintiff
Brian Wayne	Attorney for Defendant, Magnum Motors Corporation
Ted Vreeland	Attorney for Defendant, Odyssey Corporation
Ramsey Moreman	Attorney for Defendant, Odyssey Corporation

STATE OF ______

______, ss. Superior Court

MILES R. TENANT, ADMINISTRATOR OF THE GOODS AND ESTATE OF KENT TENANT, **Plaintiff,** **v.** **ODYSSEY CORPORATION AND DISCOVERY TRAILERS INC.,** **Defendant.**	COMPLAINT

COUNT I

1. The Plaintiff, Miles R. Tenant, is a resident of N. Edgeton, County of ______, ______, and is the duly appointed Administrator of the Goods and Estate of Kent Tenant, deceased.
2. The Defendant Odyssey Corporation is a corporation organized under the laws of a state other than the State of ______ with a usual place of business in ______.
3. The Defendant, Discovery Trailers, Inc., is a corporation organized under the laws of the State of ______ with a usual place of business in ______, County of ______.
4. At all times material hereto, the Defendant Odyssey Corporation, through its Odyssey Recreation Division, was in the business of manufacturing and selling, for distribution to the public, motor vehicles known as mobile homes or campers.
5. The Defendant, Discovery Trailers, Inc. at all times material hereto, was in the business of selling, at retail, to the public such vehicles.
6. Prior to June 8, Yr.–5, the Defendant Discovery Trailers, Inc. sold a motor vehicle, known as a motor home or camper.
7. In the sale of said vehicle the Defendant Discovery Trailers, Inc. was negligent, careless and unskillful in that it failed to give adequate warnings and instructions of hazards attendant upon its use, of which it knew, or which it had reason to know.
8. On or about June 8, Yr.–5, the Plaintiff's decedent, Kent Tenant, was a passenger, and in the exercise of reasonable care, in said camper or motor home.
9. As a result of the aforesaid negligence of the Defendant, Discovery Trailers, Inc., the Plaintiff's decedent was caused to sustain excruciatingly painful injuries, which resulted in his death, on June 8, Yr.–5.

This action is brought pursuant to General Laws Chapter 229, Section 2 for the benefit of the statutory beneficiaries named herein.

WHEREFORE, the Plaintiff demands judgment in the sum of One Million Dollars ($1,000,000.00), exclusive of costs and interest.

COUNT II

Paragraphs 1 through 8 of Count I are hereby incorporated by reference, and made Paragraphs 1 through 8 of this Count II.

9. As a result of the aforesaid negligence of the Defendant Discovery Trailers, Inc., the Plaintiff's decedent sustained excruciatingly painful burns from which he suffered consciously until his death.

WHEREFORE, the Plaintiff demands judgment in the sum of Two Hundred Thousand Dollars ($200,000.00), exclusive of costs and interest.

COUNT III

Paragraphs 1 through 4 of Count I are hereby incorporated by reference and made Paragraphs 1 through 4 of this Count III.

5. The Defendant Odyssey Corporation manufactured a certain camper or motor home which it sold and distributed to the public through the Defendant Discovery Trailers, Inc.

6. The Defendant Odyssey Corporation was negligent and grossly negligent in the manufacture, construction and design of said motor vehicle, and was further negligent and grossly negligent in its failure to give warnings and instructions concerning the hazards attendant upon its use, of which hazards it had actual knowledge, or in the exercise of reasonable care, should have had knowledge.

7. As a result of the aforesaid negligence, both gross and ordinary, the Plaintiff's intestate, while a passenger in said motor vehicle on June 8, Yr.–5, was caused to sustain personal injuries from which she died.

This action is brought pursuant to General Laws Chapter 229, Section 2, for the benefit of the statutory beneficiaries named herein.

WHEREFORE, the Plaintiff demands judgment in the sum of One Million Dollars ($1,000,000.00), exclusive of costs and interest.

COUNT IV

Paragraphs 1 through 6 of Count III are hereby incorporated by reference and made Paragraphs 1 through 6 of this Count IV.

7. As a result of the aforesaid negligence, both gross and ordinary, of the Defendant Odyssey Corporation, the Plaintiff's intestate, while a passenger in said motor vehicle on June 8, Yr.–5, was caused to sustain excruciatingly painful burns from which he suffered consciously until his death.

WHEREFORE, the Plaintiff demands judgment in the sum of Two Hundred Thousand Dollars ($200,000.00), exclusive of costs and interest.

COUNT V

Paragraphs 1 through 5 of Count I are hereby incorporated by reference and made Paragraphs 1 through 5 of this Count V.

6. Prior to June 8, Yr.–5, the Defendant Discovery Trailers, Inc. sold a certain camper or motor home manufactured by the Defendant Odyssey Corporation, and in doing so made certain implied warranties of merchantability and fitness for a particular purpose.
7. Said warranties were breached because said motor home was not of merchantable quality or of fitness for a particular purpose, but, in fact, was defective and hazardous.
8. As a result of said breach of warranty, the Plaintiff's intestate, on June 8, Yr.–5, was caused to sustain personal injuries from which he died.

Due notice has been given to the Defendant Discovery Trailers, Inc. of the Plaintiff's intention to bring suit for said injuries.

WHEREFORE, the Plaintiff demands judgment in the sum of One Million Dollars ($1,000,000.00), exclusive of costs and interest.

COUNT VI

Paragraphs 1 through 7 of Count V are hereby incorporated by reference and made Paragraphs 1 through 7 of this Count VI.

8. As a result of said breach of warranty, the Plaintiff's intestate, on June 8, Yr.–5, was caused to sustain excruciatingly painful burns from which he suffered consciously until his death.

WHEREFORE, the Plaintiff demands judgment in the sum of Two Hundred Thousand Dollars ($200,000.00), exclusive of costs and interest.

COUNT VII

Paragraphs 1 through 5 of Count I are hereby incorporated by reference and made Paragraphs 1 through 5 of this Count VII.

6. Prior to June 8, Yr.–5, the Defendant Odyssey Corporation, through its Odyssey Recreation Division, manufactured and sold motor vehicles known as motor homes or campers, and in doing so made certain implied warranties of merchantability and fitness for a particular purpose.
7. Said warranties were breached because said motor home was not of merchantable quality or of fitness for a particular purpose, but, in fact, was defective and hazardous.

8. As a result of said breach of warranty, the Plaintiff's intestate, on June 8, Yr.–5, was caused to sustain personal injuries from which he died.

Due notice has been given to the Defendant Odyssey Corporation of the Plaintiff's intention to bring suit for said injuries.

WHEREFORE, the Plaintiff demands judgment in the sum of One Million Dollars ($1,000,000.00), exclusive of costs and interest.

COUNT VIII

Paragraphs 1 through 7 of Count VII are hereby incorporated by reference and made Paragraphs 1 through 7 of this Count VIII.

8. As a result of said breach of warranty, the Plaintiff's intestate, on June 8, Yr.–5, was caused to sustained excruciatingly painful burns from which he suffered consciously until his death.

WHEREFORE, the Plaintiff demands judgment in the sum of Two Hundred Thousand Dollars ($200,000.00), exclusive of costs and interest.

PLAINTIFF CLAIMS TRIAL BY JURY.

By his Attorneys,
PORTNOY & LEAVITT

____

JACK M. LEAVITT
18–20 Professional Plaza

STATE OF ______

_______, ss. Superior Court

MILES R. TENANT, ADMR., Plaintiff, **v.** **ODYSSEY CORPORATION, et al., Defendant.**	PLAINTIFF'S STATEMENT UNDER RULE 29

This is an action of tort wherein the Plaintiff, Miles R. Tenant, Administrator of the Estate of Kent Tenant, seeks to recover damages for the injuries sustained by his decedent, Kent Tenant, as a result of the negligence of the Defendants, on or about June 8, Yr.–5.

As a result of the aforesaid negligence, the Plaintiff's decedent was caused to sustain excruciatingly painful burns, from which he slowly burned to death. The loss to the statutory beneficiaries, because of his death, exceeds the sum of Four Thousand ($4,000.00) Dollars.

The Plaintiff reserves the right to introduce further evidence at the time of trial, not herein specified.

The Plaintiff respectfully believes that there is a reasonable likelihood of a recovery in excess of Four Thousand ($4,000.00) Dollars.

By his Attorneys,
PORTNOY & LEAVITT, P.C.

____

JACK M. LEAVITT

STATE OF ______

______, ss. Superior Court

MILES R. TENANT, ADMR., Plaintiff, v. ODYSSEY CORPORATION, et al., Defendants.	MOTION OF THE DEFENDANT, ODYSSEY CORPORATION, TO ENLARGE TIME TO ANSWER PLAINTIFF'S COMPLAINT

The defendant, Odyssey Corporation moves that the time in which to answer plaintiff's complaint be enlarged up to and including November 4, Yr.–5.

By its attorneys,
MACMILLAN, MOSCONE & JONES

____

TED VREELAND
Metropolitan Oval

Assented to:

____

JACK M. LEAVITT
PORTNOY & LEAVITT
18–20 Professional Plaza

STATE OF ______

______, ss. Superior Court

MILES R. TENANT, ADMR., Plaintiff, **v.** **ODYSSEY CORPORATION, et al., Defendants.**	ANSWER OF DEFENDANT ODYSSEY CORPORATION

The defendant, Odyssey Corporation, makes this its answer to the plaintiff's complaint:

COUNT III

1. The defendant is without knowledge or information sufficient to form a belief as to the truth of the allegations contained in paragraph 1 and calls upon the plaintiff to prove the same.
2. The defendant admits the allegations contained in paragraph 2.
3. The defendant is without knowledge or information sufficient to form a belief as to the truth of the allegations contained in paragraph 3 and calls upon the plaintiff to prove the same.
4. The defendant admits the allegations contained in paragraph 4.
5. The defendant admits the allegations contained in paragraph 5.
6. The defendant denies the allegations contained in paragraph 6.
7. The defendant denies the allegations contained in paragraph 7.

The defendant is without knowledge or information sufficient to form a belief as to the truth of the allegation of the existence of next of kin and calls upon the plaintiff to prove the same.

The defendant denies that the plaintiff is entitled to judgment.

COUNT IV

The defendant reiterates its answer to paragraphs 1–6 of Count III.

7. The defendant denies the allegations contained in paragraph 7.

The defendant denies that the plaintiff is entitled to judgment.

COUNT VII

1. The defendant is without knowledge or information sufficient to form a belief as to the truth of the allegations contained in paragraph 1 and calls upon the plaintiff to prove the same.
2. The defendant admits the allegations contained in paragraph 2.

3. The defendant is without knowledge or information sufficient to form a belief as to the truth of the allegations contained in paragraph 3 and calls upon the plaintiff to prove the same.
4. The defendant admits the allegations contained in paragraph 4.
5. The defendant is without knowledge or information sufficient to form a belief as to the truth of the allegations contained in paragraph 5 and calls upon the plaintiff to prove the same.
6. The defendant denies the allegations contained in paragraph 6.
7. The defendant denies the allegations contained in paragraph 7.
8. The defendant denies the allegations contained in paragraph 8.

The defendant denies that due notice was given the defendant by the plaintiff.

The defendant denies that the plaintiff is entitled to judgment.

COUNT VIII

The defendant reiterates its answer to paragraphs 1–7 of Count VII.

8. The defendant denies the allegations contained in paragraph 8.

The defendant denies that the plaintiff is entitled to judgment.

FIRST DEFENSE

And further answering, the defendant says the injury or damage complained of was caused in whole or in part by the negligence of the plaintiff.

SECOND DEFENSE

And further answering, the defendant says that if the plaintiff was injured or damaged as alleged, the plaintiff assumed the risk of such injuries or damage.

THIRD DEFENSE

And further answering, the defendant says the cause of action is barred by reason of the Statute of Limitations.

THE DEFENDANT CLAIMS A TRIAL BY JURY.

By its attorneys
MACMILLAN, MOSCONE & JONES

____

TED VREELAND

STATE OF ______

MILES R. TENANT, ADMR., **Plaintiff,** **v.** **DISCOVERY TRAILERS, INC.,** **Defendant, and** **THE ODYSSEY CORPORATION,** **Defendant and Third-Party Plaintiff,** **v.** **MAGNUM MOTORS CORPORATION,** **Third-Party Defendant.**	______, ss. Superior Court MOTION OF DEFENDANT ODYSSEY CORPORATION FOR LEAVE TO CAUSE A THIRD-PARTY SUMMONS AND COMPLAINT TO BE SERVED UPON MAGNUM MOTORS CORPORATION

Now comes defendant Odyssey Corporation in the above-named action and moves for leave to cause a third-party summons and a copy of a third-party complaint (the original of which is filed herewith) to be served upon Magnum Motors Corporation, a party which is or may be liable to the defendant for all or part of the plaintiff's claim against the defendant.

As grounds for its motion the defendant says the following:

1. This is a product liability action arising out of a fire in a motor home on June 8, Yr.–5, in which four persons were killed.
2. Part of the plaintiff's claim against the defendant is that the right front wheel and tire of the motor home were defective, and that the gasoline tank was negligently positioned on the vehicle so as to be vulnerable to side impacts.
3. The defendant purchased the entire frame, motor and underbody of the motor home from Magnum Motors Corporation (Magnum). Included on the unit were all the wheels and tires. Magnum also manufactured the gasoline tank and installed it on the Magnum frame.

WHEREFORE, the defendant submits that its motion should be allowed.

By its attorneys,
MACMILLAN, MOSCONE & JONES

____

TED VREELAND
Metropolitan Oval

STATE OF ______

______, ss. Superior Court

MILES R. TENANT, ADMR., Plaintiff, v. **DISCOVERY TRAILERS, INC. Defendant, and THE ODYSSEY CORPORATION, Defendant and Third-Party Plaintiff,** v. **MAGNUM MOTORS CORPORATION, Third-Party Defendant.**	THIRD-PARTY COMPLAINT AND JURY CLAIM OF THE ODYSSEY CORPORATION AGAINST MAGNUM MOTORS CORPORATION

COUNT I

(COMMON LAW INDEMNITY)

1. Defendant and third-party plaintiff The Odyssey Corporation is a Delaware corporation with a usual place of business in ______, ______.
2. Third-party defendant Magnum Motors Corporation is a Delaware corporation with a usual place of business in ______.
3. The third-party defendant is duly qualified to do business in this state.
4. The plaintiff in this action filed and served a Complaint against the defendant and third-party plaintiff. The Complaint is attached hereto as Appendix A and is incorporated herein by reference. The third-party defendant is or may be liable to the defendant and third-party plaintiff for all or part of the plaintiff's claim against the defendant and third-party plaintiff.
5. The plaintiff in this action alleges in the Complaint that the defendant and third-party plaintiff is liable to the plaintiff for the following conduct which was allegedly the proximate cause of an accident which occurred on or about June 8, Yr.–5:
   (a) The defendant and third-party plaintiff was negligent in the sale or manufacture of certain motor homes, hereinafter referred to as "the product."
   (b) The defendant and third-party plaintiff breached certain express and implied warranties which it owed to persons using the product and to the general public.

6. The defendant and third-party plaintiff says that if the defendant and third-party plaintiff in fact sold or manufactured the product which was allegedly involved in the accident, which the defendant and third-party plaintiff denies, then the third-party defendant initiated and participated in the sale and manufacture of the product as follows: The third-party defendant sold the entire chassis for the motor home as an integrated and complete unit to the defendant and third-party plaintiff. The chassis included, among many other component parts, the motor, steering assembly, wheels and tires, frame and gasoline tank. The third-party defendant decided where the gasoline tank would be located on the frame, and mounted it on the frame. The plaintiffs in this and four related actions pending in Superior Court claim that the aforesaid component parts of the product were defective and that the gasoline tank was negligently mounted and located on the frame.

7. If the product or any component part of the product or any product warnings or instructions were defective, which the defendant and third-party plaintiff denies, then the third-party defendant was negligent with respect to the plaintiff and to the defendant and third-party plaintiff in the following respects: the product or its component parts were negligently and carelessly developed, designed, manufactured, assembled, inspected, tested, packaged, distributed, sold, advertised, marketed and provided with warnings and instructions by the third-party defendant.

8. As the direct and proximate result of the third-party defendant's said negligence the plaintiff suffered injuries and damages and the defendant and third-party plaintiff was exposed to derivative or vicarious liability to the plaintiff. The defendant and third-party plaintiff was not *in pari delicto* with the third-party defendant and did not participate in the negligence of the third-party defendant. The negligence of the defendant and third-party plaintiff, if any, was constructive, while the negligence of the third-party defendant was actual. The defendant and third-party plaintiff is therefore entitled to be indemnified in full by the third-party defendant.

9. WHEREFORE, the defendant and third-party plaintiff demands judgment against the third-party defendant in the full amount of any sums it pays or is ordered to pay to the plaintiff, together with interest, costs and attorneys' fees incurred both in defending the original action and in prosecuting this third-party action.

COUNT II

(CONTRIBUTION)

10. The defendant and third-party plaintiff incorporates herein by reference paragraphs 1 through 7, supra.
11. The plaintiff's injuries and damages were the direct and proximate result of the third-party defendant's said negligence. If the defendant and third-party plaintiff is liable in tort to the plaintiff, which the defendant and third-party plaintiff denies, then the third-party defendant is jointly liable in tort for the same injury. The defendant and third-party plaintiff is therefore entitled to contribution from the third-party defendant pursuant to the provisons of General Laws Chapter 231B.
12. WHEREFORE, the defendant and third-party plaintiff demands judgment against the third-party defendant in the full amount of the third-party defendant's pro rata share of the entire liability to the plaintiff, together with interest and costs.

COUNT III

(BREACHES OF WARRANTIES)

13. The defendant and third-party plaintiff incorporates herein by reference paragraphs 1 through 6, supra.
14. The third-party defendant expressly and impliedly warranted to the defendant and third-party plaintiff that the product or its component parts were merchantable, safe and fit for a particular purpose. The third-party defendant was a merchant with respect to goods of the kind involved in the accident. The third-party defendant had reason to know the particular purpose for which the goods were required and that the defendant and third-party plaintiff was relying on the third-party defendant's skill and judgment to select and furnish suitable goods. If the product or any component part of the product was in any way defective, which the defendant and third-party plaintiff denies, then the said product or component part was not in fact merchantable, safe and fit as warranted by the third-party defendant. The third-party defendant therefore breached its warranties to the defendant and third-party plaintiff. The third-party defendant was notified of its breaches within a reasonable time after discovery of the breaches.
15. As the direct and proximate result of the third-party defendant's breaches of warranties the plaintiff suffered injuries and damages and the defendant and third-party plaintiff was exposed to derivative or vicarious liability to the plaintiff.

16. WHEREFORE, the defendant and third-party plaintiff demands judgment against the third-party defendant in the full amount of any sums it pays or is ordered to pay to the plaintiff, together with interest, costs and attorneys' fees incurred both in defending the original action and in prosecuting this third-party action.

COUNT IV

(STRICT LIABILITY)

17. The defendant and third-party plaintiff incorporates herein by reference paragraphs 1 through 6, supra.

18. If the product or any component part of the product was in any way defective, which the defendant and third-party plaintiff denies, then the said product or component part was sold by the third-party defendant in a defective condition unreasonably dangerous to the plaintiff and to the defendant and third-party plaintiff. The third-party defendant is engaged in the business of selling such a product or component part, and the said product or component part was expected to and did reach the defendant and third-party plaintiff without substantial change in the condition in which it was sold.

19. As the direct and proximate result of the third-party defendant's sale of a defective product or component part, the plaintiff suffered injuries and damages and the defendant and third-party plaintiff was exposed to derivative or vicarious liability to the plaintiff. The third-party defendant is therefore strictly liable to the defendant and third-party plaintiff and the defendant and third-party plaintiff is entitled to be indemnified in full by the third-party defendant.

20. WHEREFORE, the defendant and third-party plaintiff demands judgment against the third-party defendant in the full amount of any sums it pays or is ordered to pay to the plaintiff, together with interest, costs and attorneys' fees incurred both in defending the original action and in prosecuting this third-party action.

JURY CLAIM

21. The defendant and third-party plaintiff claims a trial by jury of each claim asserted or to be asserted by the defendant and third-party plaintiff and of each defense asserted or to be asserted by any third-party defendant.

By its attorneys,
MACMILLAN, MOSCONE & JONES

____

TED VREELAND
Metropolitan Oval

STATE OF _____

________, ss. Superior Court

MILES R. TENANT, ADMR., Plaintiff, v. **THE ODYSSEY CORPORATION, Defendant and Third-Party Plaintiff,** v. **MAGNUM MOTORS CORPORATION, Third-Party Defendant.**	ANSWER OF THIRD-PARTY DEFENDANT MAGNUM MOTORS CORPORATION

COUNT I

1. Neither admit nor deny, due to lack of sufficient information.
2. Admit it was, but has since been dissolved.
3. Denied.
4. Admit the first sentence of this paragraph. Admit that a copy of the plaintiff's complaint is attached. Deny the balance of the allegations in this paragraph and those incorporated therein.
5. Admit that such has been alleged.
6. Denied.
7. Denied.
8. Denied.
9. No answer required as this is a prayer for judgment.

COUNT II

10. Paragraphs 1 through 7 supra of the third-party defendant's answer are incorporated herein.
11. Denied.
12. No answer required since this is a prayer for judgment.

COUNT III

13. Paragraphs 1 through 6, supra, of the third-party defendant's answer are incorporated herein.
14. Denied.
15. Denied.
16. No answer required since this is a prayer for judgment.

COUNT IV

17. Paragraphs 1 through 6, supra, of the third-party defendant's answer are incorporated herein.
18. Denied.
19. Denied.
20. No answer required as this is a prayer for judgment.
21. No answer required.

FIRST AFFIRMATIVE DEFENSE

And for further answer, the third-party defendant says that the injuries and damage complained of was caused in whole or in part by the negligence of the third-party plaintiff, which negligence was equal to or greater than that of the defendant, if any, which is expressly denied, whereby third-party plaintiff is barred from recovery from the third-party defendant.

SECOND DEFENSE

If the third-party plaintiff was the recipient of any warranties as alleged, which is denied, the third-party plaintiff failed to seasonably notify the defendant of any alleged breach of warranty as required by law, wherefore, the third-party plaintiff is not entitled to recover.

By its attorney,

____

BRIAN WAYNE
52 Ashe Street

STATE OF ______

______, ss. Superior Court

MILES R. TENANT, ADMR., Plaintiff, **v.** **DISCOVERY TRAILERS, INC., Defendant, and** **THE ODYSSEY CORPORATION, Defendant and Third-Party Plaintiff,** **v.** **MAGNUM MOTORS CORPORATION, Third-Party Defendant.**	MOTION OF DEFENDANT AND THIRD-PARTY PLAINTIFF THE ODYSSEY CORPORATION (1) FOR AN ORDER ADDING A THIRD-PARTY DEFENDANT, (2) FOR LEAVE TO AMEND ITS THIRD-PARTY COMPLAINT BY ADDING COUNTS, AND (3) FOR LEAVE TO CAUSE A SUMMONS AND COMPLAINT TO BE SERVED UPON A THIRD-PARTY DEFENDANT

Now comes defendant and third-party plaintiff The Odyssey Corporation (Odyssey) in the above-named action and moves:

(1) pursuant to Rule 21, Rules of Civil Procedure, an order adding Magnum Corporation (Magnum) as a third-party defendant, since Magnum is or may be liable to Odyssey for all or part of the plaintiff's claim against Odyssey; and,

(2) for leave to amend its third-party complaint by adding thereto the attached Counts against Magnum; and

(3) for leave to cause a summons and a copy of the third-party complaint, as amended, to be served upon Magnum.

As grounds for its motion Odyssey says that the chassis of the motor home which was allegedly defective and gave rise to the plaintiff's action was manufactured by Magnum. The chassis was manufactured by Magnum Corporation and immediately upon completion was acquired by third-party defendant Magnum Motors Corporation, which sold it to Odyssey. Until Magnum Motors Corporation answered interrogatories on May 10, Yr.–3. Odyssey believed that the chassis was manufactured as well as sold by Magnum Motors Corporation.

By its attorneys,
MACMILLAN, MOSCONE & JONES

____

TED VREELAND
Metropolitan Oval

STATE OF ______

______, ss. Superior Court

MILES R. TENANT, ADMINISTRATOR OF THE GOODS AND ESTATE OF KENT TENANT, **Plaintiff,** **v.** **DISCOVERY TRAILERS, INC.,** **Defendant, and** **THE ODYSSEY CORPORATION,** **Defendant and Third-Party Plaintiff,** **v.** **MAGNUM MOTORS CORPORATION AND MAGNUM CORPORATION,** **Third-Party Defendants.**	ADDITIONAL COUNTS TO THE THIRD–PARTY COMPLAINT AND JURY CLAIM OF THE ODYSSEY CORPORATION AGAINST MAGNUM CORPORATION

COUNT V

(COMMON LAW INDEMNITY)

22. Defendant and third-party plaintiff the Odyssey Corporation is a Delaware corporation with an usual place of business in ______, ______.
23. Third-party defendant Magnum Corporation is a Delaware corporation with an usual place of business in ______, ______.
24. The third-party defendant is duly qualified to do business in this state.
25. The plaintiff in this action filed and served a Complaint against the defendant and third-party plaintiff. The Complaint is attached hereto as Appendix A and is incorporated herein by reference. The third-party defendant is or may be liable to the defendant and third-party plaintiff for all or part of the plaintiff's claim against the defendant and third-party plaintiff.
26. The plaintiff in this action alleges in the Complaint that the defendant and third-party plaintiff is liable to the plaintiff for the following conduct which was allegedly the proximate cause of an accident which occurred on or about June 8, Yr.–5:

(a) The defendant and third-party plaintiff was negligent in the sale or manufacture of a certain motor home, hereinafter referred to as "the product."

(b) The defendant and third-party plaintiff breached certain express and implied warranties which it owed to persons using the product and to the general public.

27. The defendant and third-party plaintiff says that if the defendant and third-party plaintiff in fact sold or manufactured the product which was allegedly involved in the accident, which the defendant and third-party plaintiff denies, then the third-party defendant initiated and participated in the sale and manufacture of the product as follows: The third-party defendant manufactured the entire chassis for the motor home as an integrated and complete unit and it was sold by third-party defendant Magnum Motors Corporation to the defendant and third-party plaintiff. The chassis included, among many other component parts, the motor, steering assembly, wheels and tires, frame and gasoline tank. The third-party defendant decided where the gasoline tank would be located on the frame, and mounted it on the frame. The plaintiffs in this and five related actions pending in Superior Court claim that the aforesaid component parts of the product were defective and that the gasoline tank was negligently mounted and located on the frame.

28. If the product or any component part of the product or any product warnings or instructions were defective, which the defendant and third-party plaintiff denies, then the third-party defendant was negligent with respect to the plaintiff and to the defendant and third-party plaintiff in the following respects: the product or its component parts were negligently and carelessly developed, designed, manufactured, assembled, inspected, tested, packaged, distributed, sold, advertised, marketed and provided with warnings and instructions by the third-party defendant.

29. As the direct and proximate result of the third-party defendant's said negligence the plaintiff suffered injuries and damages and the defendant and third-party plaintiff was exposed to derivative or vicarious liability to the plaintiff. The defendant and third-party plaintiff was not *in pari delicto* with the third-party defendant and did not participate in the negligence of the third-party defendant. The negligence of the defendant and third-party plaintiff, if any, was constructive, while the negligence of the third-party defendant was actual. The defendant and third-party plaintiff is therefore entitled to be indemnified in full by the third-party defendant.

30. WHEREFORE, the defendant and third-party plaintiff demands judgment against third-party defendant Magnum Corporation

in the full amount of any sums it pays or is ordered to pay to the plaintiff, together with interest, costs and attorneys' fees incurred both in defending the original action and in prosecuting this third-party action.

COUNT VI

(CONTRIBUTION)

31. The defendant and third-party plaintiff incorporates herein by reference paragraphs 22 through 28, supra.

32. The plaintiff's injuries and damages were the direct and proximate result of the third-party defendant's said negligence. If the defendant and third-party plaintiff is liable in tort to the plaintiff, which the defendant and third-party plaintiff denies, then the third-party defendant is jointly liable in tort for the same injury. The defendant and third-party plaintiff is therefore entitled to contribution from the third-party defendant pursuant to the provisions of General Laws, Chapter 231B.

33. WHEREFORE, the defendant and third-party plaintiff demands judgment against third-party defendant Magnum Corporation in the full amount of the third-party defendant's pro rata share of the entire liability to the plaintiff, together with interest and costs.

COUNT VII

(BREACHES OF WARRANTIES)

34. The defendant and third-party plaintiff incorporates herein by reference paragraphs 22 through 27, supra.

35. The third-party defendant expressly and impliedly warranted to the defendant and third-party plaintiff that the product or its component parts were merchantable, safe and fit for a particular purpose. The third-party defendant was a merchant with respect to goods of the kind involved in the accident. The third-party defendant had reason to know the particular purpose for which the goods were required and that the defendant and third-party plaintiff was relying on the third-party defendant's skill and judgment to select and furnish suitable goods. If the product or any component part of the product was in any way defective, which the defendant and third-party plaintiff denies, then the said product or component part was not in fact merchantable, safe and fit as warranted by the third-party defendant. The third-party defendant therefore breached its warranties to the defendant and third-party plaintiff. The third-party defendant was notified of its breaches within a reasonable time after discovery of the breaches.

36. As the direct and proximate result of the third-party defendant's breaches of warranties the plaintiff suffered injuries and damages and the defendant and third-party plaintiff was exposed to derivative or vicarious liability to the plaintiff.

37. WHEREFORE, the defendant and third-party plaintiff demands judgment against the third-party defendant Magnum Corporation in the full amount of any sums it pays or is ordered to pay to the plaintiff, together with interest, costs and attorneys' fees incurred both in defending the original action and in prosecuting this third-party action.

COUNT VIII

(STRICT LIABILITY)

38. The defendant and third-party plaintiff incorporates herein by reference paragraphs 22 through 27, supra.

39. If the product or any component part of the product was in any way defective, which the defendant and third-party plaintiff denies, then the said product or component part was sold by the third-party defendant in a defective condition unreasonably dangerous to the plaintiff and to the defendant and third-party plaintiff. The third-party defendant is engaged in the business of selling such a product or component part, and the said product or component part was expected to and did reach the defendant and third-party plaintiff without substantial change in the condition in which it was sold.

40. As the direct and proximate result of the third-party defendant's sale of a defective product or component part, the plaintiff suffered injuries and damages and the defendant and third-party plaintiff was exposed to derivative or vicarious liability to the plaintiff. The third-party defendant is therefore strictly liable to the defendant and third-party plaintiff and the defendant and third-party plaintiff is entitled to be indemnified in full by the third-party defendant.

41. WHEREFORE, the defendant and third-party plaintiff demands judgment against third-party defendant Magnum Corporation in the full amount of any sums it pays or is ordered to pay to the plaintiff, together with interest, costs and attorneys' fees incurred both in defending the original action and in prosecuting this third-party action.

JURY CLAIM

42. The defendant and third-party plaintiff claims a trial by jury of each claim asserted or to be asserted by the defendant and third-

party plaintiff and of each defense asserted or to be asserted by any third-party defendant.

By its attorneys,
MACMILLAN, MOSCONE & JONES

____

TED VREELAND
Metropolitan Oval

STATE OF ______

______, ss. Superior Court

MILES R. TENANT, ADMINISTRATOR OF THE GOODS AND ESTATE OF KENT TENANT
v.
THE ODYSSEY CORPORATION
v.
MAGNUM CORPORATION

ANSWER OF THIRD-PARTY DEFENDANT
MAGNUM CORPORATION

The third-party defendant Magnum Corporation, in response to the amended complaint of third-party Plaintiff replies to the serially numbered paragraphs of the complaint, pertaining to Magnum Corporation, as follows:

COUNT V

22. Admit.
23. Admit.
24. Admit.
25. Admits that the Plaintiff filed and served the complaint. Deny the balance of this paragraph.
26. Admit that such is alleged. Deny the allegations.
27. Denied.
28. Denied.
29. Denied.
30. No answer required as this is a demand for judgment.

COUNT VI

31. The answer to paragraphs 22–28, supra, are incorporated by reference herein.

32. Denied.

33. No answer required as this is a demand for judgment.

COUNT VII

34. The answers to paragraphs 22–27, supra, are incorporated by reference herein.

35. Admit it was a merchant with respect to a portion of the goods involved in the accident. Deny all other allegations in this paragraph.

36. Denied.

37. No answer required as this is a demand for judgment.

COUNT VIII

38. The answers to paragraphs 22–27, supra, are hereby incorporated herein.

39. Denied.

40. Denied.

41. No answer required as this is a demand for judgment.

42. No answer required.

FIRST AFFIRMATIVE DEFENSE

The third-party defendant says that the injuries and damage complained of was caused in whole or in part by the negligence of the third-party plaintiff, which negligence was equal to or greater than that, if any, of third-party defendant Magnum Corporation, which is expressly denied, whereby third-party plaintiff is barred from recovery from third-party defendant.

SECOND AFFIRMATIVE DEFENSE

If the third-party plaintiff was the recipient of any warranties as alleged, which is denied, the third-party plaintiff failed to seasonably notify the third-party defendant of any alleged breach as required by law, wherefore third-party plaintiff is not entitled to recover.

THIRD AFFIRMATIVE DEFENSE

Third-party defendant Magnum Corporation says that if the third-party plaintiff is found to be negligent, it may not have indemnity against third-party defendant Magnum Corporation.

By its Attorney,

____

Brian Wayne
52 Ashe Street

STATE OF ______

______, ss. Superior Court

MILES R. TENANT, ADMINISTRATOR OF THE GOODS AND ESTATE OF KENT TENANT
v.
THE ODYSSEY CORPORATION, et al.

THIRD-PARTY DEFENDANT MAGNUM CORPORATION'S MOTION FOR COMMISSION TO TAKE ORAL DEPOSITION OF WITNESS OUTSIDE OF STATE

Third-party defendant Magnum Corporation says that Grant Edsel is a witness to the events involved in the above action. Grant Edsel is a citizen of Maine with a resident in either Gorham or Buxton, Maine. It has not become necessary for Magnum Corporation to obtain the testimony upon oral deposition of Mr. Grant Edsel.

WHEREFORE, Magnum Corporation moves that the Court issue a commission to take the oral deposition of said Grant Edsel before a person authorized by the law of the State of Maine to administer oaths at the offices of Bradford & Moisan, 1 Sanford Street, Bangor, Maine.

By its Attorney,
MERLE & WAYNE

By: ______________
Brian Wayne
52 Ashe Street

STATE OF ______

______, ss. Superior Court

MILES R. TENANT, ADMINISTRATOR OF THE GOODS AND ESTATE OF KENT TENANT, **Plaintiff,** **v.** **DISCOVERY TRAILERS, INC.,** **Defendant, and** **THE ODYSSEY CORPORATION,** **Defendant/Third-Party Plaintiff,** **v.** **MAGNUM MOTORS CORPORATION AND MAGNUM CORPORATION,** **Third-Party Defendants.**	ANSWERS OF DEFENDANT THE ODYSSEY CORPORATION TO INTERROGATORIES OF THE PLAINTIFF (FIRST SET)

1. QUESTION: Kindly state your name, your address and your position with the Defendant, Odyssey.

   ANSWER: Curt Younger, Box 11–K, Pauling, Indiana, Manager-Financial Services.

2. QUESTION: For each of the components listed on the internal memorandum to Curt Younger from Joel Mazur, which is attached to these Interrogatories, kindly state: the name of each product, its model number, brand name, and other identifying legend used by the vendor for identification, and used by the Defendant for purposes of ordering same.

3. QUESTION: For each item on Exhibit A attached hereto, kindly set out in full, to the extent known by the Defendant, the specifications of each.

   ANSWER FOR INTERROGATORY 2 and 3: Attached as Appendix A is a list of the identifying legends for the component parts of the motor homes. These are the best product descriptions that the defendant is capable of giving.

   The defendant does not draft the specifications for these component parts. The defendant purchases the parts from industry suppliers who represent that the parts conform with industry codes and standards, and the defendant uses the parts in conformance with industry codes and standards, such as NFPA 501C and ANSIA 119.2.

Signed under the pains and penalties of perjury this 30th day of September, Yr.–3.

____
Curt Younger

EXHIBIT "A"

Panel	Pan American Gyro-Tex Co. 6 Lexington Park Drive Elkhart, IN 46514 48x78-84-90-96, Vinyle Woodgrain
Carpet	Nagy E. J. & Associates, Inc. 2600 Nagy Drive Elkhart, IN 46514 Sweetwater Carpet, Style 991, 895, 208 - green tweed
Cushions	Kinder Manufacturing Inc. 2323 South 17th Street Elkhart, IN 46514 TR1018FP-5 Sewn with Fire-guard fabric with plastic
Window & Frames	Adams & Westlake Company 1025 North Michigan Street Elkhart, IN 46514 #7300 model windows
Seats	Freedman Seating Company 2021 Lee Stree P. O. Box 1250 Evanston, IL 60204 #7000 Hi Rider
Fiberglas	We make our own parts fabricated from standard raw Owen-Corning
Alum Under Belly	Alum A Form, Division of Elixir Industries 2040 Toledo Road Elkhart, IN 46514 90" Belly Pan
Alum Exterior	Alum A Form, Division of Elixir Industries 2040 Toledo Road Elkhart, IN 46514 .024 PreFormed metal
Paints	Rollie Williams 1179 Kent Street Elkhart, IN 46514 Shop rags and miscellaneous cleaners
	Maurer Industrial Supply, Inc. 820 North Ward Elkhart, IN 46514 Shop supplies

[C2092]

EXHIBIT "A" (Continued)

Caulking	Elixir Corporation 2040 Industrial Parkway Elkhart, IN 46514 Extruded sealant tape
LP Gas Storage	Brunner Engineering P. O. Box 569 Bedford, IN 14x40 S-2157, ample gas tank or 14x24 S-2158
Bath Fixtures	Ultra Glass Corporation Industrial Park Lakeville, IN 46536 Fiberglas bath tub
Moulding & Trim	Digiorgio Corporation Service Center Division P. O. Box 3380, Main Office Fullerton, CA 92634
Local:	D & G Shelter Products County Road 12 Elkhart, IN 46514 Interior moulding
Screens	Adams & Westlake Company 1025 North Michigan Street Elkhart, IN 46514 Windshields and side windows
Curtains & Drapes	Draperies by Jackie 123 South Elkhart Street Wakarusa, IN 46573 Drapes
	D & M Draperies P. O. Box 144 Edwardsburg, MI 49112 Drapes
Shades	Joanna Wester Mills Company 2141 South Jefferson Street Chicago, IL 60616 Shades

[C2093]

EXHIBIT "A" (Continued)

Interior Lights	Triangle Home Products 2111 Industrial Parkway Elkhart, IN 46514 Interior Lights #45541-11 12 Volt, Flourescent #45521-11 Double QV Flourescent
Side Wall Material in Bath (Tile Board)	U. S. Plywood 14000 McKinley Highway Mishawaka, IN Bathroom Wall Board
Wood 5/8 Underlayment 1/4 Utility Lavan	Robert Weed Plywood Corporation P. O. Box 487 Bristol, IN Flooring Material
Ceiling Material	Jim Upson Corporation 14000 McKinley Highway Mishawaka, IN Vinyl Laminated Ceiling Material
5/8" Underlayment	U. S. Plywood 14000 McKinley Highway Mishawaka, IN Flooring Material
Interior Wood Door	Creative Woodworkers P. O. Box 767 Sturgis, MI 49091 Interior Cabinet Framed Doors
Wood Construction Lumber	Cook County Lumber 200 West Chicago, IL Dimensional Lumber
Wood Reg. Lumber	Lumber Specialties, Inc. 50415 Herbert Granger, IN 46530 Pre-Cut Side Wall Studs & Roof Rafters

[C2094]

EXHIBIT "A" (Continued)

Laminate	Midwest Laminated Plastic Products, Inc. 1926 West Lusher Avenue Elkhart, IN 46514 Counter-top Material 24x96 or 36x96 Kidd
Metal Roofing	Winbro Division of Phillips 2030 South Main Street Elkhart, IN 46514 Galvanized Roof Material
Rubber Hose & LP Regulator	S. H. Leggitt Company, Inc. Waco, TX L. P. Hoses
Aux. Gas Tanks	Bock Products, Inc. 1901 West Hively Avenue Elkhart, IN 46514 Gasoline Tanks
Escape Hatch	Strawsine Mfg. Company 435 West Harrison Elkhart, IN 46514 Ceiling Escape Hatch #135 - #3 Garnish
Folding Doors	American Door Company, Inc. 2424 Home Street Mishawaka, IN Interior Divider Doors
	Elkhart Door, Inc. 1601 Fieldhouse Avenue Elkhart, IN 46514 Interior Divider Doors
Sky Lights Luma Domes	Ventline, Inc. State Road 15 South Bristol, In Ceiling Vents #V2001, V2026, #V20125, 1100 Down Vent

[C2095]

EXHIBIT "A" (Continued)

Plastic Trim Covers	Pierce Tool & Die Company, Inc. 3362 South Main Elkhart, IN 46514 Exterior Screw Covêr
	Conroth Company P. O. Box 515 St. Joe Street Bristol, IN Plastic Vinyle Insert
Insulation	Inland Distributors of Elkhart, Inc. 1741 Conant Street Elkhart, IN 46514 R #4, Fiberglas

[C2096]

STATE OF ______

______, ss. Superior Court

MILES R. TENANT, ADMINISTRATOR OF THE GOODS AND ESTATE OF KENT TENANT, **Plaintiff,** v. **ODYSSEY CORPORATION, et al.** **Defendant, Third-Party Plaintiff,** v. **MAGNUM CORPORATION, et al.** **Third-Party Defendants.**	ANSWERS OF THIRD–PARTY DEFENDANT MAGNUM CORPORATION TO INTERROGATORIES OF THE PLAINTIFF

Int. 1. State the name and present address of each person whom the third-party defendant expects may be called by it as an expert witness at the trial of this action.

Ans. 1. (a) J. Genza and/or F. Currier, both of 21 Sterling, Santa Monica, California.

(b) Possibly Dana Ives and/or Jeff Bell, both of the Department of Economics, Brown University, Providence, Rhode Island.

(c) Possibly Frank Brummer, Dane Moran and Edward Dearborn, all employed by accident investigation unit, Registry of Motor Vehicles.

(d) Dr. Hans Eisemann, Medical Examiner, St. Potain Street, may be called.

(e) Possibly Elliott Faber, State Police.

(f) David Cochin and possibly Robert Ewing and Carey Vicar, all of Magnum Corporation, Detroit, Michigan.

Int. 2. Describe in detail the subject matter on which each may be expected to testify.

Ans. 2. (a) J. Genza and/or F. Currier will testify as to their accident reconstruction, and opinions held concerning the accident vehicle, components thereof, its course, direction, and possibly its approximate speed, the possible causes of the accident, the fence or I-beam supporting cables which was struck, and its design, and effect upon the accident vehicle, and probable causes of explosion(s) after the vehicle came to rest.

(b) Dr. Dana Ives and/or Jeff Bell, if called, may be expected to testify concerning calculations made by Dr. O'Connor. Since the exact basis of Dr. O'Connor's calculations and his assumptions are unknown, we can only surmise that these men will testify concerning inflation, discount rate, increases in productivity, income taxes, prospects for marriage, affects of marriage, all relating to future earnings of the various decedents.

(c) Frank Brummer, Dane Moran and Edward Dearborn are expected to testify on the subjects covered in their depositions or reports.

(d) Dr. Eisemann, if called, is expected to testify concerning identities he established, of remains, post-accident.

(e) Trooper Faber, if called, is expected to testify as to matters referred to in his reports.

(f) Mr. Cochin is expected to testify on the subjects referred to in his deposition. Robert Ewing and Carey Vicar are expected to testify concerning the RM350 chassis and development of its interfacing with the body installed by Odyssey. They may testify as to the evaluation of said interfacing. One or both of them may testify on the subject of power steering and/or braking.

Int. 3. State in detail the substance of all facts and opinions about which each expert may be expected to testify at the trial of this action.

Ans. 3. (a) Mr. Genza and/or Mr. Currier are expected to testify that the accident vehicle traveled at least 50 and probably 100 feet in the breakdown lane with the right wheels off the pavement, on the gravel shoulder; the motor home then reached a series of vertical steel posts that, starting with the second post, had been installed to support three horizontal steel cables. The right front wheel snagged the first rigid I-beam post which initiated ramping of the right front; subsequent contact forced the motor home to rotate clockwise to develop a left broadside slide to a roll onto its left side. A fire started and subsequently during rescue efforts, an explosion reportedly occurred which made it necessary to discontinue rescue, owing to a marked increase in rate of burning.

This accident occurred because of gross inattentiveness or inexperience of the driver; the injury exposure from the double collision with the steel posts and the ramped airborne and subsequent fall of the vehicle onto its left side may have caused critical injuries for unrestrained occupants but not necessarily for all four occupants. The subsequent stages of the fire were of course non-survivable.

The steel posts placed at the side of the road represent a crude and dangerous substitution for a guard rail and are likely to introduce more danger to an errant vehicle than the contoured slope beyond. The rail lacks the usual approach-end anchorage safety design features and presents to the vehicle a series of dangerous harpoon-like structures likely to snag and gore, rather than to uneventfully deflect a vehicle under the varying circumstances of off-pavement incidences. This I-beam cable structure has design properties enabling it to rip open any under-body fuel system regardless of where it is positioned. Directly opposite the defective I-beam structure was installed the safe, nationally accepted, W-section guard rail having a design based on findings from full scale collision research conducted by Mr. James Genza and other researchers.

The right front wheel snagged the first dangerously positioned vertical steel post, then impacted the cable turnbuckle with the right front tire. The unramped right side slammed down onto vertical steel posts causing the destruction to the posts as they applied force against the forward end of the side-mounted fuel tank. This force deflected the tank rearward pulling it from its anchorages, as it rotated to become wedged against the forward surfaces of the right duals. Inspection of this tank would be necessary to provide a detailed accounting of fuel release; however, even without possible openings generated by the dangerous geometry and exposure of the steel posts, fuel loss will occur from feed and vent line disruptions. The rate of burning for fuel line detachment alone is initially slow with several minutes required before the rate of burning would exclude further rescue efforts. Tests which Mr. Genza has conducted indicate that fuel tanks can dump their contents just as rapidly when fitted with liners and filled with foam as tanks without these devices. The state of art in Yr.–6 precluded the use of liners and/or fillers as measures toward improving fuel tank integrity.

The L.P. gas storage tank is located at the left side ahead of the dual wheels, the side onto which the vehicle fell and slid before coming to rest. In order for an explosion to have occurred, L.P. gas had to be released within the vehicle. Disruption of one or a combination of the feed lines to the hot water heater, furnace or stove because of one or both collisions would serve to develop an open L.P. gas line within the vehicle. However, the explosion which reportedly stopped rescue efforts at the windshield area would not have occurred if the driver had followed the standard operating procedure of turning to "off" the L.P. gas supply valve at the tank. Subsequent heating of the L.P. gas tank will activate the pressure relief and overfill valve allowing gradual controlled venting of the L.P. gas at the tank outside the vehicle. This produces a local burn-out of the tank and will not result in an explosion. Thermal expansion of gasoline will force it out via the cap or fittings and as it escapes it burns at the tank outside the vehicle, but will not explode.

There are three principal fuel storage systems for this motor home:

(1) A 14½ by 18 by 38¼ inch side-mounted gasoline rectangular tank located 9 feet behind the front bumper, which places it behind the entrance steps, well forward of the rear duals and 9 inches inboard of the right side of the vehicle.

(2) A 10 by 9 by 32 inch rectangular rear-mounted gasoline tank centrally located between and below the frame rails, 18⅜ inches forward the rear bumper.

(3) A cylindrical liquid petroleum gas cylinder with semi-spherical ends 38 inches long by 13 inches diameter mounted 34 inches forward of the left rear duals and 11 inches inboard of the left side panel.

Fuel lines from these storage systems are routed as follows:

(1) *Side tank*—A steel line from the side tank courses inboard of the right frame rail and forward to the fuel tank selector valve and from that valve forward to the engine. A steel fuel line from the side tank transfers fuel rearward to the right rear position of the motor generator.

(2) *Rear tank*—A steel line from the top of the rear tank courses forward along the inboard concavity of the right frame to the fuel tank selector valve mounted inboard of the right frame and forward of the right side fuel tank. The fuel selector valve

is operated by a flex-sheathed control wire connected to the fuel selector at the driver's compartment.

(3) *L.P.G. tank*—The L.P. gas tank at the mid-left side has a feed line that courses rearward from the tank and at a location about one foot aft of the tank, branches to three lines that course vertically through floor ports to the respective locations of the water heater, cooking stove and forced air heater.

Detailed observations were made concerning the three fuel storage systems, the manner of attachment, fuel system piping, flex coupling, recessing, road clearances and similar features. The side-mounted gasoline tank appears to follow established practices and procedures common to the industry.

An examination of a similar motor home was made on March 1, Yr.–2. There are two separate multiple wire connectors at the steering column; the blue plastic connector when disconnected stopped operation of the turn indicator, emergency flashers and horn from operating. The engine could be started and stopped in a normal manner and accessory features including the radio continued to operate until additionally the white plastic multiple connector was separated. With the blue and white multiple wire connectors disconnected, the ignition was rendered inoperative along with the starter, power to ignition and accessory equipment such as radio and heater blower. Consequently, the reported sound of music coming from the motor home following the roll-over establishes that the ignition switch continued to be functional throughout the accident.

This Yr.–6 Odyssey 23-foot motor home was driven on a test track for purposes of evaluating its performance under various hypothetical emergency conditions. These included off-road recovery attended with loss of power steering as well as verification of the standby power inherent with power brake systems. These tests established that a driver of average skill operating this vehicle in a normally attentive manner could be confronted with sudden full loss of power assist and manage directional control and safe braking to a stop without need for excessive steering or braking force. The off-road recovery test included all right wheels fully off the pavement onto a mud-soft and partially glassy surface. Notwithstanding the approximately one inch drop from the edge of the pavement and the 1 to 1½ inch depression into the off-pavement shoulder, steering back onto the pavement at speeds ranging from 10 to 40 m. p. h. were made with uneventful ease. Tests also showed that loss of ignition would not eliminate power assist steering, since the rear wheels via the transmission provided power assist.

This motor home collision developed a low volume initial fuel system leak with subsequent ignition. Based on the eye witness description of events, the initial disruption of the right side gasoline tank from snagging by the steel I-beams was promptly followed by a slow leak of the L.P.G. system inside the vehicle, apparently following steel post-induced upset with attending impact disruption of one or more of the in-cabin L.P.G. supplied accessories. This in-cabin leakage is possible only if someone failed to shut off the main supply valve at the L.P.G. tank before the vehicle was allowed to move. The danger from the L.P.G. leakage would be dependent on an ignition source inside the vehicle such as a pilot light or cigarette, unless the outside cabin fire continued long enough to burn through, thus providing an ignition source.

This accident occurred because of inattentiveness or inexperience of the driver; injuries would be produced because of the severe impact exposure occasioned by crashing into a dangerous cluster of steel posts. Any motor home exposed to the steel post ramping, snagging collision upset to which this motor home was exposed or to comparable exposures of the same basic nature would sustain a post-crash fire. Complications could ensue if occupants were not belted to protect them from the impact trauma; if traveling without closing off the L.P.G. service valve, a critical thermal exposure could occur before escape or rescue was accomplished.

The dangerously defective steel posts intended for, but in no manner provided a guard rail protective function.

(b) Uncertain, and dependent upon the calculations, factors, figures and statistics used by Dr. O'Connor.

(c) Brummer, Moran, Dearborn are expected to testify as to facts and opinions contained in their reports and/or depositions. Beyond this, we are not able to state.

(d) Dr. Eisemann is expected to testify as to his identification of remains via dental records or information. Beyond this, we are not able to state.

(e) Trooper Faber is expected to testify according to his reports. Beyond this, we are not able to state.

(f) Mr. Cochin is expected to testify substantially in accordance with his deposition. Mr. R. Ewing and/or Carey Vicar are expected to testify that power steering assist would be present, while the vehicle is in gear and in motion.

Int. 4. State in detail a summary of the grounds for each such opinion listed in your Answer to Interrogatory No. 3, and state in detail the substance of all facts upon which such opinions are based.

Ans. 4. (a) The basis for Mr. Genza or Mr. Currier's opinions are an actual examination of the accident chassis, and accident scene, photographs of both, his examination of a similar motor home, and discovery in the case, his tests or evaluations referred to previously, his education, experience in vehicle handling and crash tests, his research, background, and related experience concerning highway design, accident scene collision induced fires, fuel system design, occupant kinematics, and guard rail design.

(b) Opinions of Messrs. Ives and Bell will be based upon their background, education and experience, coupled with facts which may be learned during the conduct of trial.

(c) These gentlemen's exact qualifications are unknown. We expect to learn that they may have taken courses, and that they have had experience in accident reconstruction.

(d) We expect Dr. Eisemann to qualify based on his education and experience.

(e) These gentlemen's exact qualifications are unknown. We expect to learn that they may have taken courses, and that they have had experience in accident reconstruction.

(f) Mr. Cochin's qualifications and experience are stated in his deposition. Mr. Vicar and Mr. Ewing are expected to qualify from their experience.

STATE OF ______

______, ss. Superior Court

MILES R. TENANT, ADMINISTRATOR OF THE GOODS AND ESTATE OF KENT TENANT **v.** **DISCOVERY TRAILERS, INC. et al.** **v.** **MAGNUM MOTORS CORPORATION**	REQUEST OF THIRD–PARTY DEFENDANT, TO THIRD-PARTY PLAINTIFF DISCOVERY TRAILERS, INC. FOR PRODUCTION PURSUANT TO RULE 34

The third-party defendant Magnum Motors, pursuant to Rule 34, requests that the third-party plaintiff, Discovery Trailers, Inc., produce for inspection and copying the items described and enumerated below:

1. Any and all invoices, bills of sale and related documents concerning the sale of a Swinger, 22′ Squire model, motor home, and more particular Serial No. S101–386.
2. All documents and writings showing the date of sale referred to in No. 1, and the identity and address of the purchaser.
3. All writing and documents showing, and those tending to show the mileage indicated on the odometer, at the time of the sale referred to in No. 1.
4. Any and all pre-delivery inspection sheets relating to the vehicle and referred to in No. 1 above.
5. Any and all work orders, of any type and description, concerning or relating to the vehicle referred to in No. 1 above.
6. Any and all warranty repair orders concerning the vehicle referred to in No. 1 above.
7. Any and all service and maintenance work orders concerning or relating to the vehicle referred to in No. 1.
8. Any and all writings showing, stating or reflecting complaints concerning the vehicle referred to in No. 1 above.

Production of the documents called for is to be made on or before February 2, Yr.–4, at the offices of Merle & Wayne, 52 Ashe Street.

Compliance with this request, at the option of the third-party plaintiff Discovery Trailers, Inc, may be accomplished by production of copies of the documents described.

By its attorney,

____

Brian Wayne
52 Ashe Street

STATE OF ______

______, ss. Superior Court
Civil Action

MILES R. TENANT, ADMINISTRATOR OF THE GOODS AND ESTATE OF KENT TENANT, **Plaintiff,** v. **THE ODYSSEY CORPORATION,** **Defendant/Third-Party Plaintiff,** v. **MAGNUM CORP., et al.,** **Third-Party Defendants.**	PLAINTIFF'S REQUEST FOR PRODUCTION TO THIRD-PARTY DEFENDANT, MAGNUM CORPORATION

Pursuant to Rule 34 of the Rules of Civil Procedure, the Plaintiff makes the following Requests for Production, to be answered in accordance with the following definitions and instructions.

DEFINITIONS:

A. The word "documents" includes, but is not necessarily limited to, all memoranda, written statements, periodicals, books, circulars, and written material of every type and every description, however produced or reproduced, including, but not limited to, policy or other manuals, memoranda, correspondence, reports, financial statements, newspaper clippings, notations of conferences or telephone conversations, interoffice memoranda or communications, drawings of any kind, tracings, shop drawings, blueprints, including complete history of revisions, sketches, flow diagrams, photographs, notebooks, instructions, invoices, bills, receipts, specifications, and any other written, printed, or drawn materials. If more than one copy of the documents is in existence, and any copies bear notations, whether handwritten or otherwise, which do not appear on all copies, each such annotated copy shall be separately identified and the substance of the notations given in addition to the substantive contents of the documents, with the notations, shall be furnished.

B. The word "Chassis" shall mean the chassis, including the fuel system and gas tank of the vehicle which is the subject vehicle of the Complaint, including the chassis from which the subject chassis was developed.

C. The word "Defendant" shall mean the defendant Magnum Corporation and/or Magnum Motors Corporation, unless the contrary appears.

INSTRUCTIONS:

The Plaintiff specifies as a reasonable time, place and means of making the production under Rule 34 of the Rules of Civil Procedure, that legible copies of all items reproducible by the Defendant be made at the expense of Plaintiff's counsel, and mailed or delivered to Plaintiff's counsel's office at 18–20 Professional Plaza, within thirty (30) days of service of this Request for Production. In the alternative, the Defendant may, at the time of service of its Responses, notify counsel for the Plaintiff when and where the originals of said documents will be given to a messenger for removal, copying and returning forthwith. As for items not copyable, said items are to be made available for inspection at a time and place mutually convenient to counsel for the parties, but in no event later than thirty (30) days after this Request.

REQUEST FOR PRODUCTION

The Defendant is requested to produce all documents relating to the chassis dealing with, pertaining or relating to any study, test, analysis, report, advertising or promotion which relate to:

1. The environment of use for which the chassis was or was to be designed.

2. The performance specifications.

3. Design objectives.

4. Quality assurance (the determination of whether the chassis did comply with the design objectives).

5. Market analysis.

The Plaintiffs,
By their Attorneys,
PORTNOY & LEAVITT

____

JACK M. LEAVITT
18–20 Professional Plaza

STATE OF ______

______, ss.

Superior Court
Civil Action

MILES R. TENANT, ADMINISTRATOR OF THE GOODS AND ESTATE OF KENT TENANT **v.** **ODYSSEY CORPORATION, et al.** **v.** **MAGNUM CORPORATION, et al.**	PLAINTIFF'S COMPLAINT AGAINST THE THIRD–DEFENDANT, MAGNUM CORPORATION

COUNT I

1.

The Magnum Corporation has been impleaded by the Defendant, third-party plaintiff, Odyssey Corporation, and the Plaintiff herein asserts his claims against the Magnum Corporation pursuant to Rule 14A of the Rules of Civil Procedure.

2.

At all times material hereto, the third-party defendant, Magnum Corporation, was in the business of manufacturing and distributing truck chassis, including the fuel system, for use as chassis in motor homes, otherwise known as recreational vehicles.

3.

Prior to June 8, Yr.–5, the third-party defendant, Magnum Corporation, sold a truck chassis, together with its fuel system, to the Defendant, third-party plaintiff, Odyssey Corporation, for use in the manufacture of a recreational vehicle known as a Swinger.

4.

On or about June 8, Yr.–5, the Plaintiff's decedent was, while in the exercise of due care, a passenger in a recreational vehicle whose chassis and fuel system were manufactured by the third-party defendant, Magnum Corporation.

5.

The third-party defendant, Magnum Corporation, was negligent, careless and unskillful in its design, construction, manufacture, choice of materials and distribution of said chassis.

6.

As a result of the aforesaid negligence of the third-party defendant, Magnum Corporation, the Plaintiff's decedent was caused to sustain excruciatingly painful injuries which resulted in his death of June 8, Yr.–5.

This action is brought pursuant to General Laws, Chapter 229, Section 2, for the benefit of the statutory beneficiaries named therein.

WHEREFORE, the Plaintiff demands judgment in the sum of One Million ($1,000,000.00) Dollars, exclusive of costs and interest.

COUNT II

1.

Paragraphs 1 through 5 of Count I are hereby incorporated by reference and made Paragraphs 1 through 5 of this Count II.

6.

As a result of the aforesaid negligence of the third-party defendant, Magnum Corporation, the Plaintiff's decedent sustained excruciatingly painful burns from which she suffered consciously until her death.

WHEREFORE, the Plaintiff demands judgment in the sum of Two Hundred Thousand ($200,000.00) Dollars, exclusive of costs and interest.

COUNT III

1.

Paragraphs 1 through 4 of Count I are hereby incorporated by reference and make Paragraphs 1 through 4 of this Count III.

5.

Prior to June 8, Yr.–5, the third-party defendant, Magnum Corporation, in selling said chassis, together with its fuel system, made certain implied warranties of merchantability and fitness for a particular purpose.

6.

Said warranties were breached because said motor home was not of merchantable quality or fitness for a particular purpose, but, in fact, was defective and hazardous.

7.

As a result of said breaches of warranties, the Plaintiff's intestate, on June 8, Yr.–5, was caused to sustain excruciatingly painful personal injuries, from which he died.

This action is brought pursuant to General Laws, Chapter 229, Section 2, for the benefit of the statutory beneficiaries named therein.

The third-party defendant, Magnum Corporation, has been given due notice of the aforesaid claims.

WHEREFORE, the Plaintiff demands judgment in the sum of One Million ($1,000,000.00) Dollars, exclusive of costs and interest.

COUNT IV

1.

Paragraphs 1 through 6 of Count III are hereby incorporated by reference and made paragraphs 1 through 6 of this Count IV.

7.

As a result of said breaches of warranties, the Plaintiff's intestate, on June 8, Yr.–5, was caused to sustain excruciatingly painful personal injuries from which he suffered consciously until his death.

WHEREFORE, the Plaintiff demands judgment in the sum of Two Hundred Thousand ($200,000.00) Dollars, exclusive of costs and interest.

THE PLAINTIFF DEMANDS TRIAL BY JURY.

The Plaintiff,

By his Attorneys,

PORTNEY & LEAVITT

By: ____________________

JACK M. LEAVITT
18–20 Professional Plaza

STATE OF ______

______, ss. Superior Court

MILES R. TENANT, ADMINISTRATOR OF THE GOODS AND ESTATE OF KENT TENANT **v.** **ODYSSEY CORPORATION, et al.** **v.** **MAGNUM MOTOR CORPORATION, et al.**	ANSWER OF MAGNUM CORPORATION TO PLAINTIFF'S COMPLAINT

COUNT I

1. No answer required.
2. Admit.
3. Denied.
4. Admit that Plaintiff's decedent was a passenger. Deny the balance of the paragraph.
5. Denied.
6. Denied.

COUNT II

1. Paragraphs 1–5 of the answer to Count I are incorporated by reference herein, and made paragraphs 1–5 of the answer to Count II.
6. Denied.

COUNT III

1. Paragraphs 1–4 of the answer to Count I are incorporated by reference herein, and made paragraphs 1–4 of the answer to Count III.
5. Denied.
6. Denied.
7. Denied.

COUNT IV

1. Paragraph 1 through 6 of the answer to Count III are incorporated by reference herein, and made paragraphs 1–6 of this Count IV.
7. Denied.

By its Attorney,

____

Brian Wayne
52 Ashe Street

STATE OF ______

______, ss. Superior Court

MILES R. TENANT, ADMINISTRATOR OF THE GOODS AND ESTATE OF KENT TENANT

v.

ODYSSEY CORPORATION, et al.

ANSWERS OF THE PLAINTIFF TO INTERROGATORIES OF THE DEFENDANT, ODYSSEY CORPORATION

QUESTION NO. 1

Please give your full name, residence, business address and occupation.

ANSWER NO. 1

Miles R. Tenant, 20 Star Avenue, North Arby, teacher.

QUESTION NO. 2

Please give the full name, date of birth, the late residence, business address and occupation of the deceased.

ANSWER NO. 2

Kent Tenant; 18 years, six months, 44 Ted Road, Greengrove, none, student.

QUESTION NO. 3

Please state the date on which you were appointed personal representative of the deceased including the identity of the Court.

ANSWER NO. 3

September 9, Yr.–5, in the County Probate Court.

QUESTION NO. 4

Please describe in detail the injuries to the deceased as a result of the alleged accident.

ANSWER NO. 4

Third degree burns; carbon monoxide asphyxiation.

QUESTION NO. 5

Please state how long a period of time elapsed from the time of the accident until the time the deceased passed away.

ANSWER NO. 5

It is believed that a period of ten to fifteen minutes elapsed.

QUESTION NO. 6

If you allege that the decedent suffered consciously, please state what manifestations of conscious suffering were shown, at what time and during what period such manifestations were shown.

ANSWER NO. 6

He was heard to scream for help and cry out in pain.

QUESTION NO. 7

Please give in detail an itemized account of all expenses incurred by you as a result of deceased's alleged accident.

ANSWER NO. 7

Funeral Expense	$1,800.00
Memorial Stone	675.00
Cemetery Lot	300.00

These are the immediate costs only.

QUESTION NO. 8

If the decedent was employed at the time of the alleged accident, please give:

(a) the name and address of any person or company by which the decedent was then employed;

(b) the occupation and average weekly income of the decedent.

ANSWER NO. 8

(a) Town of Greengrove, Cemetery Department, Centre Street, Greengrove.

(b) Summer job at which he earned money for college. He earned $120.00 per week.

QUESTION NO. 9

Please estimate as nearly as you are able the total amount of financial loss suffered by the deceased's estate as a result of the alleged accident.

ANSWER NO. 9

Three Hundred Thousand ($300,000.00) Dollars.

QUESTION NO. 10

Please state the names, addresses and ages of all next-of-kin left by the decedent.

ANSWER NO. 10

Miles R. Tenant, Sr., father, 56 years of age;

Janet Tenant, mother, 56 years of age;

Holly Tenant, sister, 32 years of age;

Miles R. Tenant, brother, 29 years of age.

QUESTION NO. 11

Please describe fully and in complete detail how the alleged accident happened, stating what happened in the order in which events took place.

ANSWER NO. 11

The deceased was a passenger in the camper manufactured by the Defendant. The right front tire of the vehicle sustained a sudden loss of air, possibly a blowout. The driver apparently pulled over, or the camper veered to the right and struck the guard rail, causing the gasoline tank, known as the saddle tank, to rupture and ignite. The vehicle thereupon turned over on its side in flames. The Plaintiff's decedent and his companions burned to death.

QUESTION NO. 12

Please state fully and in complete detail all that the defendant did or failed to do which in any way caused or contributed to cause the accident alleged in your complaint.

ANSWER NO. 12

The Defendant designed and manufactured the camper in a manner inconsistent with sound and safe engineering practices, among which were the location of the center of gravity at a place that was too high for reasonable stability, the location of a gas tank in a place where it was foreseeable that in a side impact it was likely to ignite and break loose from its attachments; its failure to properly isolate the gasoline tank and the LP gas tanks from the passenger compartment; the failure to have adequate and proper escape routes in case the main door should become unusable; the failure to use proper materials in the manufacture of the body of the camper; improper design of the wheels. As discovery progresses, the claims of the Plaintiff may be either enlarged or reduced.

QUESTION NO. 13

Please state when, in what form and the substance of any notice you claim you gave the defendant with regard to your alleged accident.

ANSWER NO. 13

See attached letter sent by certified mail.

QUESTION NO. 14

Please describe fully and in complete detail in what manner the mobile home camper was not suitable for the purpose for which it was intended and the manner in which it was defective and hazardous as alleged in your complaint.

ANSWER NO. 14

The matter is covered in our answer to Interrogatory No. 12.

QUESTION NO. 15

With respect to each examination, inspection and testing of the mobile motor camper home and any of its component parts including tires for the purpose of ascertaining or determining the particular part or parts that caused injury and death to the decedent as alleged in your complaint, please state:

(a) the identity by name and address of each person or firm who made such an examination, inspection and test;

(b) the date(s) and place of each such examination, inspection and test;

(c) in as much detail as possible the findings made as a result of each such examination, inspection and test;

(d) when and where the attorneys for the defendant may examine a copy of the report of each such examination, inspection and test or attach a copy(s) to your answers hereto.

ANSWER NO. 15

(a) Mr. Todd Sikorsky, 202 Stone Road, Bellevale; Leonard Ernst, 8 Longview, North Arby.

(b) Approximately July 30, Yr.–5, in Pelham.

(c) The Plaintiff declines to answer this interrogatory on the advice of counsel, on the grounds that it seeks material beyond the scope of material which may be discovered under Rule 26(B)(4) of the Rules of Civil Procedure.

(d) The report is not yet completed, but, in any event, will not be made available to Defendant's counsel, since Rule 26(B)(4) does not require that reports of expert witnesses or experts called for consultation shall be submitted to the adverse party.

QUESTION NO. 16

If you intend to make use of one or more experts at trial, please state:

(a) the identity and address of each prospective expert witness;

(b) the subject matter on which he is expected to testify;

(c) the facts, opinions and grounds therefor as to which the expert is expected to testify;

(d) the courts in which each such person has qualified as an expert in his field, the name and docket number of the case in which he has so appeared and the date upon which each such person has appeared as an expert witness.

ANSWER NO. 16

Discovery and investigation are not sufficiently complete so that the Plaintiff is able to answer this interrogatory at the present time. An appropriate answer will be filed, pursuant to the guidelines of Rule 26(B)(4) of the Rules of Civil Procedure and Rule 26(E) of the Rules of Civil Procedure, just as soon as enough material has been assembled to provide an intelligent answer to this interrogatory.

QUESTION NO. 17

Please specify how the defendant was negligent in each of the following areas: in the manufacture, production, design, development, testing, inspection, marketing and distributing the mobile home camper described in your complaint.

ANSWER NO. 17

At the present time the Plaintiff is unable to answer only to the extent covered by the answer to Interrogatory No. 12.

QUESTION NO. 18

Do you or your attorneys claim that the mobile home camper described in your complaint failed to comply with or pass any industry or trade test or standard? If so, please identify the test or standard and in what precise manner there was failure to comply.

ANSWER NO. 18

This answer cannot be given now since the Plaintiff has engaged in no discovery. It will be supplemented pursuant to Rule 26(E) of the Rules of Civil Procedure.

QUESTION NO. 19

Please identify all non-expert witnesses you expect to call at the trial of this action.

ANSWER NO. 19

No decisions, even tentatively, have been made with respect to the non-expert witnesses we expect to call. This answer will be supplemented in accordance with Rule 26(E) of the Rules of Civil Procedure.

Signed under the pains and penalties of perjury this fifth day of March, Yr.–4.

____

MILES R. TENANT

STATE OF ______

_______, ss. Superior Court

MILES R. TENANT, ADMINISTRATOR OF THE GOODS AND ESTATE OF KENT TENANT v. **ODYSSEY CORPORATION, et al.** v. **MAGNUM CORPORATION**	ANSWERS OF THE PLAINTIFF, MILES R. TENANT, ADMINISTRATOR, TO ADDITIONAL INTERROGATORIES OF THE DEFENDANT, ODYSSEY CORPORATION

QUESTION NO. 1

Please state the date of promulgation of and please transcribe each oral, written, printed or graphic representation, statement, document, advertisement, catalogue, circular and brochure uttered or propounded by or on behalf of the defendant which relates to the virtues, qualities, characteristics, capabilities or capacity of the product or to the dangers, limitations or propensities of the product and of which the plaintiff and the plaintiff's decedent and the persons who purchased the product were aware prior to the time of the accident.

ANSWER NO. 1

I do not know what representations, statements, documents, advertisements, catalogues, circulars and brochures referred to in Interrogatory No. 1 were seen by the person who purchased the product involved, or of which he or she was aware. So far as I am aware, the Plaintiff's decedent was aware of no such documents or advertisements, and I was not.

QUESTION NO. 2

Please identify fully and transcribe every written or printed document and statement and please describe every illustration which accompanied the product when it was purchased, including in your answer (by way of illustration but not by way of limitation) the exact contents of any statements or illustration on the product itself and the exact contents of each pamphlet, set of directions or instructions, owner's or operator's manual, leaflet and booklet of any kind which accompanied the product when it was purchased. If any such document is now unavailable and you are unable to remember or reconstruct the exact wording of any such document, please state as fully as you now are able the substance of each statement contained in each such document.

ANSWER NO. 2

I do not know.

Signed under the pains and penalties of perjury this ______ day of ______, Yr.–3.

____
MILES R. TENANT

STATE OF ______

______, ss. Superior Court

MILES R. TENANT, ADMINISTRATOR OF THE GOODS AND ESTATE OF KENT TENANT v. ODYSSEY CORPORATION, et al. v. MAGNUM MOTORS CORPORATION	(PORTION OF) ANSWERS OF THE PLAINTIFF TO INTERROGATORIES PROPOUNDED BY THE THIRD-PARTY DEFENDANT

QUESTION NO. 4

Was your intestate's health or physical condition in any way impaired just prior to the time of this accident, and if so, please state how it was so impaired.

ANSWER NO. 4

No.

QUESTION NO. 5

During the ten years prior to death, had your intestate consulted, been treated or examined by a doctor, and if so, please give the name and address of the doctor and the reason for each treatment, consultation or examination.

ANSWER NO. 5

Dr. Penta at the Greengrove Medical Center, Greengrove; routine physical required for employment by the Town of Greengrove.

QUESTION NO. 6

During the ten years prior to his death, had your intestate undergone any surgical operation; if your answer is affirmative, please give the name and address of the operating physician and the reason for the operation.

ANSWER NO. 6

No.

QUESTION NO. 7

During the ten years prior to his death, had your intestate ever been hospitalized; if your answer is affirmative, please state the name, and address of the hospital, the dates of hospitalization, and the cause for the hospitalization.

ANSWER NO. 7

No.

QUESTION NO. 8

Please give the name and address of any physician who routinely treated your intestate and your family.

ANSWER NO. 8

Dr. Penta and Dr. Wekman at the Greengrove Medical Center, Greengrove.

QUESTION NO. 9

Please state each and every school, including colleges and universities, which your intestate attended, give the dates of attendance at each, the date of graduation from each, and any degrees which he may have received.

ANSWER NO. 9

Kent was in the Greengrove school system for 12 years, graduating from high school in June, Yr.–6. He attended the Oxham School of Agriculture at the State University for one year, from September, Yr.–6 to May, Yr.–5.

QUESTION NO. 10

Please state the name and address of every employer of your intestate, and state every position which your intestate held with each employer.

ANSWER NO. 10

Greengrove Cinema, Greengrove Mall, Greengrove; he was an usher; he had worked for the Town of Greengrove for two weeks prior to his death.

QUESTION NO. 11

If your intestate was planning to pursue a specific career, please state what the career was and describe the preparation and education he had received for this career.

ANSWER NO. 11

Kent had decided to be a veterinarian, and was working toward this goal at the Oxham School of Agriculture at the State University, where he was majoring in animal science.

QUESTION NO. 15

If your intestate was treated by any doctor between the time of the fire and the time of his death please describe all such treatment and give the name and address of said doctor.

ANSWER NO. 15

He was not treated by any doctor, as there was no doctor at the scene of the accident, where he died.

QUESTION NO. 16

Please state the name and address of any person who heard your intestate make any utterance or observed him make any movement between the time of the accident and the time of his death.

ANSWER NO. 16

Paul Dover of Tonawanda, New York and Grant Edsel of Gorham, Maine.

QUESTION NO. 17

As to each person listed in your answers to interrogatory #15, please state exactly what that person heard or observed.

ANSWER NO. 17

Not applicable.

QUESTION NO. 18

Please identify by name and address each person whom you expect to call as an expert witness at trial.

ANSWER NO. 18

The information requested in this Interrogatory is not known at this time, and will be supplemented pursuant to Rule 26(e) of the Rules of Civil Procedure.

QUESTION NO. 19

Please state the subject matter on which each of the above named is expected to testify.

ANSWER NO. 19

See Answer to Interrogatory No. 18.

QUESTION NO. 20

Please state the substance of the facts and opinions to which the expert is expected to testify.

ANSWER NO. 20

See Answer to Interrogatory No. 18.

QUESTION NO. 21

Please state a summary of the grounds for each opinion described above.

ANSWER NO. 21

See Answer to Interrogatory No. 18.

. . .

QUESTION NO. 24

Please state all facts upon which you base your allegation that defendant Discovery Trailers, Inc. was negligent.

ANSWER NO. 24

To the extent that the information sought is discoverable, this interrogatory will be supplemented prior to trial.

QUESTION NO. 25

Please state all facts upon which you base your allegation that defendant Discovery Trailers, Inc. breached certain warranties to your intestate.

ANSWER NO. 25

See Answer to Interrogatory No. 24.

QUESTION NO. 26

If you allege or will allege that Magnum Corporation breached certain warranties to your intestate, please state all facts upon which you base this allegation.

ANSWER NO. 26

The information requested in this Interrogatory is unknown at this time.

ANSWER NO. 27

If you allege that any of the defendants or third-party defendants failed to comply with any state or federal statute, code or regulation in the design, manufacture, construction or assembly of the motor home involved in this accident, please designate completely each such statute or regulation.

ANSWER NO. 28

This Interrogatory is objected to on the grounds that it seeks the work product of plaintiff's counsel concerning theories of laws.

SIGNED under the pains and penalties of perjury this ______ day of ______, Yr.–3.

____
MILES R. TENANT

Deposition of Matthew Dupres

DIRECT EXAMINATION

Q. (By Mr. Aspen) What is your name, please?

A. Matthew Dupres.

Q. What is your occupation?

A. I am a home builder. Builder.

Q. And as a builder, what kind of things do you build?

A. House, homes.

Q. What connection, if at all, did you have with a certain organization known as Discovery Trailers, Inc. at any time?

A. Two different positions. At one time I was the vice president. And after my brother left, I became the president.

Q. Brother's name?

A. Richard Dupres.

Q. What was the business of Discovery Trailers?

A. Selling recreational vehicles, trailer homes.

Q. About when did it commence business?

A. About Yr.–7, I believe.

Q. Is it still in business?

A. No, it's not.

Q. When did it stop doing business?

A. We, more or less, went out of business officially somewhere around Yr.–5.

Q. Did the company have any facilities for service on recreational vehicles or was it strictly sales?

A. No, we did some service on the thing. If it was a motor vehicle, it was sent to a Dodge dealer.

Q. Pardon?

A. We would service like our own trailers or a part of the direct vehicle, like if there was a refrigeration problem or something like that. If it was a motor vehicle problem, we would send it to a Magnum dealer because it was all Dodge parts.

Q. Were all of your types of equipment on Magnum chassis?

A. Yes.

Q. What brands or makes of recreational vehicles did you sell? And I am talking about the body itself as distinguished from the chassis and engine.

A. A Swinger.

Q. Made by whom?

A. Odyssey Corporation.

Q. Did you have a franchise?

A. Yes.

Q. Was it in writing?

A. That I wouldn't know because, like I say, my brother was the one that started the business and when he left the state, I more or less inherited getting rid of the business.

Q. About when did he leave?

A. He left in, I believe it was the middle of Yr.–6.

Q. And then you took over?

A. Right.

Q. Did you have any mechanical repair facilities to handle the body of these vehicles as distinguished from chassis and engine?

A. No. What we did is: we just had a part-time fellow that we called to come in if we had any problems. It was not a big agency.

Q. Did you have any salesmen after you took over?

A. No.

Q. Did you have any employees after you took over?

A. No.

Q. Were there any employees other than the part-time mechanic?

A. No.

Q. We are interested in a certain 22-foot Swinger, Squire model motor home with a serial number which is named under summons or notice of deposition that was served on you. Do you understand that?

A. Yes, I do.

Q. With respect to vehicles of the type described, where would you get them from, how would you get them?

A. Well, the only vehicles we handled—we only handled two models. One was Swinger and the other was Blazer on trailers, and they both came out of Indiana. And they would both be shipped via the factory to our place.

The motor homes would be driven, and the trailers would be towed on the trailer truck. So a vehicle such as the motor home that would hit our place, it would have probably, I believe it was about 1,000 miles from here to Indiana, whatever the trip was because it would have been driven out.

Q. So that if this has to come before a jury, so they will know what we are talking about, what is the difference between the motor home that you sold and the trailer that you sold?

A. Well, the motor home travels under its own power and the trailer is something you tow behind your car or a truck.

Q. In other words, the motor home had some sort of living quarters which were a part of the chassis, is that true?

A. Part of the chassis, right.

Q. And the trailers had some sort of living quarters that would be towed behind another vehicle?

A. Exactly.

Q. How were the trailers, if I can use that word, meaning a motor home that was towed, how were they brought to you? In other words, what kind of a vehicle would bring them to you?

A. I believe it was a company-owned—By Company-owned, I am talking about Blazer. I believe they own their own trucks and trailers, and they would load two or three at once on a trailer and haul them out that way. In other words, they wouldn't tow them individually whereas the motor home was driven.

Q. Which company made the motor home which was already on the chassis?

A. That is Odyssey. Odyssey was the name of the manufacturer I believe, but they called the motor home the Swinger.

Q. And the other company furnished you with what?

A. Just travel trailers.

Q. How much, if any, contact did you have with Discovery Trailers before your brother left and you took over?

A. Well, it was a business that was running—run out of the same property that I worked on so I was there all the time. Actual contact with it, very little, to be truthful.

Q. When you say out of the same property you worked on, what do you mean?

A. At that time I was in the swimming pool business and I owned the building that the trailer business was run out of. So it was—Actually I was there all the time even though I wasn't directly involved with the trailer business.

Q. Then is it a fair statement to say that at the same location you ran a swimming pool business and your brother ran Discovery Trailers?

A. Yes, it is.

Q. Were you an officer of Discovery when your brother was running it?

A. Yes, I was.

Q. And what position?

A. If I remember correctly, I was vice president.

Q. With respect to the Swinger, Squire model referred to in the notice of deposition, was that sold while you were running the company or while your brother was?

A. While I was.

Q. What, if any, inspection or alteration or service did your company make on Swingers of the type involved in this case upon receipt?

A. Well, you inspected it upon receipt for any damages that were done that you might want to hold the company liable for in shipping.

Q. What kind of damage?

A. Oh, broken doors or glass or drawers that might have fallen out in shipment or whatever. It was also that we would put a secondary check on all the lines such as the gas lines. I am talking about the propane gas lines now.

Q. What kind of a check did that amount to?

A. It would amount to—It would be done with pressure valves and air, and you build up so many pounds of pressure in the lines, and you have to let it set like an hour to make sure it wouldn't drop below, I think it might have been 90 pounds, I don't know. The mechanic would have to answer that.

You put so many pounds of pressure in your lines, and the same as in the water lines, and if it held for an hour, whatever the standard time was, then a test of that sort.

Q. Was that done both with the propane and the water lines?

A. Yes, both.

Q. Any other inspection, except obvious physical damage?

A. No, that would be about it.

Q. To whom was the Swinger referred to in this deposition sold and what documentation do you have showing that?

A. It was sold to Sy Felcham, and that's his bill of sale to me, and the finance contract with the bank below it.

Q. Were you the person who made the sales to the buyer of this?

A. Yes, I was.

Q. When this vehicle was received by Discovery Trailers, Inc., was there any documentation that exhibited the pre-delivery inspection that you described, such as checking the pressures, of leakages, or was it just a matter of course?

A. It was just a matter of course on our end. That was also done at the factory too, though.

And I know at the time I had gone out with my brother, we went through the factory, they had check lists on each vehicle as it went along the assembly line.

Q. By the factory, what do you mean?

A. Odyssey—Swinger, I should say.

Q. Was there more than one gas tank on the final Swinger?

A. On the one I sold?

Q. Yes, sir.

A. Because if there was, it was an option. Yes, an auxiliary 25-gallon gas tank. Yes.

Q. And where was that located?

A. I believe there would be one at the rear of the vehicle and one in the middle of the vehicle, both usually on the same side so when you pulled in, you could fill them both at one time.

Q. Can you be a little more definite on that?

A. I know on the one I owned. I just don't want to answer the wrong thing on this 22-footer because I never owned or drove it.

The one I owned, there was one, if I recall correctly, in the left rear of the motor home and one halfway down on the left-hand side of the motor home. And it would have a cover on it like that (indicating).

Q. I am showing you a document entitled, Swinger Motor Home Owner's Manual. Was that the type of owner's manual which accompanied the Swinger model which we are concerned with?

A. Yes, it is.

Q. Where was it in the motor home? In other words, was it in some compartment or did you have it independently?

A. No. These are things that we would have handed them directly along with the other papers. Otherwise, if you left it in the motor home, it would disappear. So it would have been something that he got handed at the time of purchase.

Q. Do you have any definite memory of having handed Felcham this type of book?

A. I believe I gave him one, yes, sir.

Q. Now let's get back to the gas tanks. How many filling accesses were there to the gasoline supply?

A. Well, on this one, according to my bill of sale, there would be two.

Q. And where were the access fillers?

A. The standard filler would be in the rear of the bus on the left-hand side.

Q. Excuse me. By rear, do you mean the extreme rear or are you talking about the rear part of the side?

A. The auxiliary tank would be halfway down the side of the bus, at the low part of the bus.

Q. Is this on the side?

A. On the side.

Q. Was it visible from the outside?

A. Yes, and there would be a thing marking Gas.

Now the other one, I take it back. I said it was at the rear left. On the rear of the bus there would be a spare tire, and that's where the other gas tank was. That's where the standard one was. The tire would swing down, and you put your gas directly into the bus.

I said to the side; I take it back.

Q. You are talking about the exact rear of the middle of the bus?

A. The exact rear middle.

Q. So the auxiliary tank would be on the left side visible to a person looking at the left side, is that true?

A. Yes.

Q. And would the filler be at the tank?

A. Yes.

Q. The regular gas tank would be at the rear end of the bus?

A. Right.

Q. Behind the spare tire?

A. Behind the spare in the middle, right.

Q. Now at the factory, the Odyssey factory, do you know whether the auxiliary tanks, if any, were installed at the Odyssey factory, or did they come under—

A. No, it would have been at the Odyssey factory.

Q. That it would be installed, right?

A. Well, according to my invoice, that's where it was installed.

Q. Right. Was this Swinger with which we are concerned a special order or was it on your lot?

A. It was on my lot.

Q. All right. So, in other words, it came with the auxiliary tank already on it.

A. Yes, it did.

Q. Were there any other tanks on the vehicle, except gas tanks?

A. There would be at least one water tank.

Q. Do you remember where this was located?

A. About two-thirds to the rear of the vehicle.

Q. On which side?

A. I don't really—See, there were so many different models on this particular one, I really don't remember. There would also be an 80-pound L.P. gas tank.

Q. Do you remember where that was located?

A. I believe they were more or less about halfway to the back and under the vehicle.

Q. Visible from the outside?

A. No.

Q. Was the water tank visible from the outside of the vehicle?

A. No, only the filler spout, that's all, where you would connect to fill it. But it would be under a cabinet inside.

There would also be a holding tank for sewerage.

Q. What is a holding tank?

A. Well, with the air flow from the toilet or from your shower would run into it, and you would go to a dumping station to get rid of it. That would probably be a 50-gallon tank.

Q. And where was that?

A. Again, it depends on the layout of that particular unit. If I recall, it probably was about in the middle, but it depends on the layout of the 22-footer.

Q. Do you remember which side?

A. No, I don't.

It says in my invoice here, it had a rear lounge cocktail table. So with that in mind, then, the toilets would have been in the center of the bus and the holding tank was always under the toilet, so it would have been around the center of the bus.

Q. Following the sale of this vehicle, did your company do any work on it?

A. Following—After he took it, you mean?

Q. Yes, sir.

A. I think he came back because it was running lousy, and it could have been because it had sat for a while. It was delivered in May and by the time he bought it—and I believe he took it to Dodge at the time, and they fixed whatever it was, tuned it up, did something.

Q. Was that something he told you?

A. Well, he came back to me because it was running poorly, and I sent him to the Dodge dealer, which was a practice. We didn't get involved with the motor home at all.

Q. Did you have any more talk with him after he had been to Dodge?

A. None other than the fact they fixed it, he was satisfied.

Q. He told you that he had taken it to the Dodge, had he?

A. Yes.

Q. And later on he told you that they had fixed it?

A. Right.

Q. Okay. Did your company itself do any work or maintenance on it?

A. After he took it, I don't believe so. I think he was a fairly satisfied customer, to my knowledge.

Q. Was the only complaint that you received from the buyer the fact that it wasn't running right, as a result of which you sent him to a Dodge dealer?

A. A Dodge dealer, right.

Q. That's all?

A. Right

Q. Do you now have a memory as to whether the auxiliary gas tank was on the left or the right side? And by left or right, I am speaking from the driver's position.

A. I really couldn't answer that, to be truthful. Again, it was Yr.–6 and it was probably the furthest thought from my mind, which side it was on.

Q. Had you noticed auxiliary gas tanks on other Swingers, or was this the only one you ever had close contact with?

A. No, because I owned a 28-footer myself so I should remember which side it was on, but again, it was three years ago, and I really don't exactly recall now which side it was on.

I thought it was on the left, but this gentleman said it was on the right. I am not too sure, to be truthful. I am sure the main filler was in the back, that much I remember.

Again, I don't want to reconstruct the Swinger, but I think which side it was on might have had something to do with the inside floor plan layout because wherever the toilet went, that other tank had to be under it as a rule.

Q. By other tank, you mean what?

A. The holding tank for the sewerage.

Q. I notice in the owner's manual there is an item describing an escape hatch vent, optional on all 18-foot model, standard on all other models.

Did this Swinger with which we are concerned have an escape hatch?

A. I believe it was standard. It doesn't show it as an option or an extra in the thing here.

Q. And still on that same page, does the printing accurately describe how it should operate.

A. Yes, cranked up. Right.

Deposition of Sy Felcham

EXAMINATION BY MR. MOREMAN

Q. Would you state your name, please?

A. Sy Felcham.

Q. Do you have a business address, sir?

A. Yes, Greengrove Police Station, Greengrove.

Q. What is your occupation?

A. Police officer.

Q. And your rank is what?

A. K–9 Handler.

Q. What is your education, sir?

A. High school.

Q. Which high school and what year?

A. Greengrove High School in Yr.–14.

Q. Any training at all beyond high school?

A. No.

Q. When did you go with the Greengrove Police Force?

A. June of Yr.–9.

Q. And you went on the force as what position?

A. Patrolman.

Q. And from that, you progressed to what?

A. K–9 Handler.

Q. When did you become that?

A. October of Yr.–5.

Q. Before the police, what did you do for work?

A. Heavy equipment assistant.

Q. For whom?

A. Local 4, heavy equipment operators.

Q. How long were you a heavy equipment operator?

A. I believe three or four years. I don't recall.

Q. What type of heavy equipment did you handle?

A. Gradeall, tower cranes, cranes, all kinds of heavy equipment.

Q. Any trucks?

A. No.

Q. Are these types of equipment all off-the-road vehicles?

A. No. Gradeall, and cranes, and truck cranes, I suppose, are part of trucks.

Q. But you never were a truck driver?

A. No.

Q. Before you did heavy equipment work, what did you do?

A. I was in the navy.

Q. How many years?

A. One year, six months, and 27 days.

Q. So you went from the navy to heavy equipment to the police force?

A. Yes.

Q. You owned the vehicle which was involved in this accident?

A. Yes.

Q. When did you acquire it?

A. October of Yr.–6, the 23rd, I believe.

Q. Who did you buy the vehicle from?

A. Discovery Trailers, Inc.

Q. Did you know the people up there before you bought it?

A. Yes. I did.

Q. Who did you know?

A. Matt Dupres.

Q. How did you know him?

A. I worked with him through high school. He used to have a gas station and pool company—swim pools.

Q. How did you happen to come to him to purchase the vehicle? Did you tell him about it? Did you tell him you were in the market for one?

A. Yes.

Q. When did that occur?

A. A couple of weeks before I purchased it.

Q. You went up to his location?

A. Yes.

Q. And you looked at units that were on the lot?

A. Yes.

Q. And the unit that you ultimately purchased, was that up there on the lot when you went up there on that occasion?

A. Yes. It was.

Q. And this was about two weeks before you actually purchased it?

A. Yes. It was.

Q. Now, was Discovery Trailers at that time going out of business?

A. Yes. They were.

Q. And Matt Dupres had told you that?

A. Yes.

Q. Now, how many different units did you look at when you got up there that day?

A. Probably five or six different ones.

Q. And you decided on this particular unit?

A. Yes.

Q. Did you take it for a test drive?

A. Yes. I did.

Q. How long a test drive did you take it for?

A. Probably two or three hours.

Q. Where did you go?

A. Picked up my family and we went for a ride. You know, just went for a ride.

Q. On highways?

A. Yes.

Q. When did you decide to buy it, that same day that you took it, for a test drive?

A. No.

Q. When did you decide?

A. Probably three days before this date—three or four days before that date that I did buy it.

Q. Three or four days before the 23rd of October?

A. Yes.

Q. Did you go back to Matt Dupres?

A. Yes.

Q. Did he show you around the unit when you first saw the unit?

A. Yes. He did.

Q. Tell me what he pointed out to you?

A. All the features and how to operate the features.

Q. And what features are we talking about?

A. The stove, the heat, tape deck, air conditioning, and whatnot.

Q. Did he show you the escape hatch?

A. Yes. He did.

Q. And that was on the ceiling inside the unit?

A. Yes. It was.

Q. And he operated that and showed you how to do it?

A. Yes.

Q. And it was after that time that you purchased it?

A. After I purchased the unit?

Q. That was on your first visit up with your family to view the unit?

A. On my first visit, no.

Q. Subsequently?

A. Yes.

Q. Was it the day that you picked it up, the 23rd day of October, Yr.–6?

A. Yes.

Q. And you took it from there to your home?

A. Yes.

Q. Where was it usually garaged?

A. At my home.

Q. Do you have a garage there?

A. No.

Q. Parked outside all the time?

A. Yes.

Q. Now, between—tell me what use you put the unit to that fall of Yr.–6?

A. I went to Lake Luzcerne, New York with my family. I think that was a month after I purchased it and returned home. After that, I had some horses down the shore.

Q. For the winter?

A. For a couple of months, I had it down the shore probably the beginning of Yr.–5.

Q. Was that one camping trip to New York the primary use of the vehicle in Yr.–6?

A. Yes.

Q. And after you came home—when was that in Yr.–6, do you recall what month?

A. I believe it was November. I think it was the following month that I purchased it.

Q. Then, in early Yr.–5, you brought it down the shore?

A. Yes.

Q. And it stayed there for approximately what months?

A. I think it was the month of February.

Q. So it was down there about a month?

A. Yes.

Q. And your best estimate is February, Yr.–5?

A. Yes.

Q. And it wasn't used for that month?

A. Yes. It was.

Q. It was?

A. I used to travel down there and stay in it over the weekends on my days off.

Q. Now, going back to the fall of Yr.–6, the trip to Lake Luzcerne. Did you have any problems with the unit?

A. No. I didn't.

Q. Did you have any problems up to the time you took it down the shore?

A. No.

Q. Did you ever have it back to Discovery or anybody for repairs or maintenance?

A. No. I didn't.

Q. Now, how often did you spend the night down the shore during February of Yr.–5?

A. Every day that I had off.

Q. About how many was that?

A. Probably ten or twelve days.

Q. And the unit would remain stationary?

A. Yes.

Q. And you just slept in it?

A. Yes.

Q. Any problems of any kind with it during that period?

A. No.

Q. Now, what was done with the unit after February of Yr.–5? What use did you put it to?

A. I brought it home, parked it until the summer of Yr.–5?

Q. Did you ever use it on the road during that period?

A. Yes.

Q. Where did you go?

A. On short trips here and there, you know, down to the shore—not often, but back down to the shore a couple of times. You know, just day trips.

Q. When was your first big trip with the vehicle in the summer of Yr.–5?

A. I didn't have any.

Q. From February of Yr.–5 to the beginning of the summer, you used it a few times for short trips?

A. No.

Q. Any problems in that time during that use?

A. No.

Q. Ever have it in for repairs or maintenance of any kind?

A. No.

Q. Tell me who used it first in the spring or summer of Yr.–5?

A. Me.

Q. What did you use it for?

A. Just the short trips—the day trips that I was going on.

Q. When was the first long trip it took in Yr.–5?

A. When I gave it to Kent Tenant.

Q. Had you known Mr. Tenant before he took it?

A. Yes.

Q. When did you first meet Kent Tenant?

A. Probably Yr.–17 or Yr.–16. I don't recall exactly.

Q. You were several years older than him?

A. Yes.

Q. What was the occasion of your meeting him in Yr.–17 or Yr.–16?

A. His brother was a very good friend of mine.

Q. And the brother's name was what?

A. Miles Tenant.

Q. Did you know Kent as a friend from that time up until the time of the accident?

A. How would you classify friend? I knew him, and we weren't friendly until later on, until he got older.

Q. When would you estimate that was?

A. Probably Yr.–17 or Yr.–18.

Q. Now, would you see Kent on a fairly regular basis up until the time of the accident?

A. After he was out of the service, yes.

Q. Now, up until the time of the accident, how often would you see Kent Tenant?

A. I don't know. I'd see the family quite often. I don't know—a couple of times a week—three times a week.

Q. Was he often there when you saw the family?

A. Yes.

Q. Were you a social acquaintance of Kent Tenant?

A. No.

Q. Would you ever go out in groups with him?

A. No.

Q. Would you go out with his brother, Miles?

A. Yes.

Q. You would describe him, Miles, as a social acquaintance of yours?

A. Yes.

Q. Now, how did it happen that you gave or turned the vehicle over to Kent Tenant on the weekend of this accident?

A. He asked me to use the vehicle to go—to go up to visit some friends of his. I told him I'd let him know in a couple of days. Then, I was working down at a garage that was owned by Miles and his father—on my own car I was working—he came down and asked me if he could use it. I said that he could. That's how he got to use it.

Q. There was apparently a couple of days delay when he first asked if he could use it and when you finally made up your mind?

A. Yes.

Q. Why was that?

A. I was reluctant to let him use it. I didn't want anybody to use it. He was the first one to ask me if he could use it.

Q. Had he ever seen the vehicle before this?

A. Yes.

Q. When was that?

A. I guess he'd seen me drive it around or whatever.

Q. Had he ever been over to your house when the vehicle was at your property?

A. I don't recall if he was or not. I believe he was.

Q. On a social occasion?

A. Yes.

Q. Was that shortly after you had purchased it?

A. Yes.

Q. Where was the vehicle parked at that time, in your driveway?

A. Yes.

Q. Did he take the occasion to go out and look at it?

A. I believe so.

Q. And you showed him around the vehicle?

A. Yes.

Q. Did you go inside the vehicle on that occasion?

A. Yes.

Q. And if you can recapture for me, the best you can, the conversation you had with him inside the vehicle.

A. He just said it was pretty nice. At that time, he just said it was pretty nice and that was basically the thing. I showed him around and that was all.

Q. Did you show him some of the features of the vehicle?

A. I don't recall at that time. No.

Q. But, in any event, the two of you stepped into the vehicle?

A. Yes.

Q. This was shortly after you got it in October of Yr.–6?

A. I couldn't say that close, probably six months after I got it. It was a couple of months before he took it.

Q. Now, did you know any of the other people who were in the vehicle when the accident took place?

A. No. I don't.

Q. Now, did you ever give Kent Tenant a ride in the vehicle at any time?

A. Yes.

Q. When was that, sir?

A. It was the day before he took it or two days before he took it—the day he came down to the garage, and he asked me if he could use it, and I said yes. I took him into the vehicle and showed him around. I showed him how to operate the heater and the stove because it was still pretty cold nights then—showed him how to operate the bathroom, and we both got in it. I let him drive. We went down the street, we gassed up, and we returned back to his father's garage.

Q. Well, when was this, the second time he discussed with you—

A. When he came down to the garage.

Q. And that is the garage owned by Kent Tenant's father?

A. Both his father and his brother.

Q. On that occasion, you said he could borrow it?

A. Yes.

Q. Now, where did you take it to get gassed up, do you remember the name of the station?

A. I believe it was Frank's Sunoco.

Q. And the address would be what?

A. It's on Cambridge Street in Greengrove. I don't know the number.

Q. Now, when he came down to see you at his brother's and father's garage, I take it the unit was back at your house?

A. No. It was at the garage.

Q. It was at the garage?

A. Yes.

Q. Had you driven it down there?

A. Yes.

Q. For what purpose?

A. I was working on a Corvette there, and it was my only means of transportation at the time.

Q. Now, to repeat an earlier question, up to this day, had you had any problems at all with the unit?

A. No.

Q. Never had it in for maintenance or repair of any kind?

A. No.

Q. Same tires that were on it originally?

A. Yes.

Q. Any tuning up on the engine or anything like that?

A. No.

Q. So you came to the garage, you got in the unit, and you took it for a ride?

A. Yes.

Q. Who was driving when you first got in?

A. Kent Tenant.

Q. Did you go directly down to Frank's Sunoco?

A. Yes.

Q. What was the distance from where you were to Frank's Sunoco?

A. Probably a quarter of a mile.

Q. Why did you have Tenant driving?

A. Well, I was interested to see if he knew how to operate it.

Q. How did he do?

A. Good.

Q. Do you recall, and this is a picky question—do you recall if you charged gas at Frank's Sunoco or paid cash?

A. Paid cash; paid cash. He was the one who was going to use it, so he bought the gas.

Q. Did you fill the vehicle?

A. Yes. I believe he did.

Q. Now, as I recall, there are two gas tanks on the vehicle?

A. Yes.

Q. Do you know what one—

A. They were both filled, I believe. One was filled; he filled the other one.

Q. On the day that you went down to Frank's Sunoco, which one did he fill?

A. He filled the regular tank.

Q. He didn't put anything into the reserve tank?

A. No. He didn't.

Q. Do you recall specifically if there was anything in the reserve tank?

A. I believe the reserve tank was full.

Q. When had that been filled, if you recall?

A. I don't recall.

Q. On that day that you went down to Frank's Sunoco, did you get out and check to see if the reserve tank was filled?

A. No. I didn't.

Q. And you can't recall, as you sit here today, when it was filled?

A. Probably a couple of weeks prior to that, to the best of my memory.

Q. You don't have any specific recollection of the occasion?

A. No.

Q. When you say probably a couple of weeks, you're guessing?

A. Yes.

Q. Did you have a regular or usual gas station where you filled it up?

A. No.

Q. Did you use charge cards?

A. Occasionally.

Q. What kind of charge cards?

A. Texaco charge.

Q. That's your only one?

A. Yes.

Q. Is there a Texaco station near your home?

A. Yes. There is.

Q. What's the name of that?

A. I don't know. It's changed hands several times.

Q. What street is it on?

A. Cambridge Street.

Q. At Frank's that day, did you check the oil or anything else?

A. No.

Q. You just put gas in?

A. Yes.

Q. Now—

A. We checked the oil back at the garage.

Q. You had already done that?

A. When we returned.

Q. After you left Frank's, did you take it for a test drive of any kind?

A. Yes.

Q. Where did you go?

A. We just drove up Cambridge Street, possibly a couple of miles, and returned—turned around and returned to the garage.

Q. Who was driving?

A. Kent Tenant.

Q. How did he do?

A. Good.

Q. Did he state to you that he had had any experience in driving vehicles of this nature?

A. No.

Q. Now, you came back to the garage and what did you do there?

A. Just checked the oil. I showed him how to operate everything, asked him if he had any questions. He had no questions. That was it.

Q. Did you show him where the instruction manual was kept?

A. Yes.

Q. Where was that?

A. In the glove box—not a glove box but there was a panel there where the instructions were.

Q. And that's about a 50-page booklet of instructions?

A. I don't believe so. I don't recall to tell you the truth.

Q. Now, sir, that is a Xeroxed copy, so it doesn't have the physical lay-out that the manual would have. Does that appear to be it?

A. That would appear to be similar. Yes.

Q. Did you take that out of the glove compartment?

A. Did I take it out?

Q. Yes.

A. What do you mean, take it out?

Q. You showed him where it was?

A. Yes.

Q. Did anyone at that time take it out to look at it?

A. I took all the papers out. There was some other papers there. I took all the papers out.

Q. And you showed Mr. Tenant what they were?

A. Yes.

Q. Did you take them out of the envelope?

A. Yes.

Q. Did you go through them with Mr. Tenant?

A. No. I just said that if he had any questions, you know, about how to operate everything, just look through the manual and they'll tell you. All the other instructions were there, too.

Q. Did he, at that time, leaf through the instruction manual?

A. I don't believe so.

Q. Now, did you show him how to operate the various features and appliances of the unit?

A. Yes.

Q. Did you point out the escape hatch to him?

A. Yes.

Q. Did you show him how it worked?

A. Yes.

Q. Did you operate it once or twice?

A. Yes.

Q. Did you show him how the various appliances worked?

A. Yes.

Q. Which appliances did you go through?

A. The stove, auxiliary power, the heater, and generator, and what-not.

Q. Did all these seem to be in order?

A. Yes.

Q. Did you test operate some of the other ones besides the escape hatch?

A. Yes. I lit the stove.

Q. Was that working?

A. Yes. And I showed him how to light the heater.

Q. Was that working?

A. Yes.

Q. Did the escape hatch work normally?

A. Yes.

Q. No problems with it?

A. No.

Q. When did that vehicle leave your possession that day?

A. That day.

Q. Do you have a date?

A. No. It was either the day before—I believe it was the day before. It might have been the day—two days before.

Q. Did you see it between that time and the time of the accident?

A. No.

Q. Did you hear anything about it between that time and the time of the accident?

A. No.

Q. Did Kent Tenant call you up with any further questions about it?

A. No.

Q. The next thing you heard was the happening of the accident itself?

A. Yes.

Q. Do you know from the time that the vehicle left your premises until the time of the accident—do you know where it was kept?

A. No. I don't.

Q. Where did Kent Tenant live?

A. Greengrove.

Q. And that's near your house?

A. A little distance away.

Q. But between the time you let the vehicle go and the time of the accident, you had no correspondence or communication with Kent Tenant or with anyone about the vehicle?

A. No.

Q. When did you hear about the accident?

A. It was two o'clock in the morning. It was a Saturday morning about 3:30.

Q. Did you go out to look at the camper thereafter?

A. Yes. I did.

Q. Where was it located when you went out to look at it?

A. It was in a towing yard. I don't believe it was a junk yard.

Q. When you first saw the vehicle, was it no longer attached to towing apparatus?

A. I believe it wasn't. No.

Q. It was just sitting on the ground?

A. Yes. It was.

Q. It had been dropped off?

A. I believe so.

Q. And this is during the day—on the day after the accident?

A. I believe it was the following day.

CROSS EXAMINATION BY MR. ASPEN

Q. The propane gas tank was on the left side of the vehicle, wasn't it?

A. Yes. It was.

Q. About how far back from the front?

A. Probably in the middle.

Q. It was an upright sort of roundish tank, wasn't it?

A. No. It was laying on its side.

Q. And from one end of it, there was a pipe that came off and went somewhere, wasn't it?

A. I believe it was from the center.

Q. From the center?

A. I believe so. I don't know. I believe it was from the center.

Q. Was there a shut-off on the tank?

A. Yes. There was.

Q. And was there one pipe or more than one pipe that led off the tank?

A. Just one, I believe.

Q. And about how far did that pipe start away from the side of the vehicle, or was it under the vehicle?

A. It was under the vehicle. It was a compartment like a trap door that you opened from the side. You reached in and turned the gas on or off and have it filled or whatnot.

Q. From the tank, where did the pipe go?

A. It went inside the vehicle.

Q. And about how long was the pipe before it went inside the vehicle?

A. I couldn't tell you.

Q. Are you talking about two feet or two inches?

A. Between a foot or two, I believe.

Q. Did it go inside the vehicle from underneath or straight through?

A. I couldn't tell you. I really don't recall.

Q. Well, then, there was a control and a gauge. Where were these controls located?

A. This was on the tank. This was all on the tank.

Q. After the accident when you saw the vehicle, did you notice that some pipes of the propane system had been ripped out?

A. I don't believe there were any pipes left on the tank, but the tank was intact.

Q. The second part only that feed to the stove and heater had been ripped out?

A. Yes.

Q. What did you mean by ripped out?

A. They were missing.

Q. Nothing there?

A. No. Just the tank.

Q. Did the gauge show empty, or was that burned?

A. I don't know. I didn't read the gauge. I couldn't tell you if the gauge was still there.

Q. Do you know, when the operator took the home, whether the gas was turned on at the tank or off at the tank?

A. Turned off at the tank.

CROSS EXAMINATION BY MR. LEAVITT

Q. Could you just explain to us how the escape hatch worked—what did you have to do to open it?

A. There was a screen inside; there was a plastic cap, and there was a crank on it to roll up.

Q. Did you have to take the screen off?

A. You have to remove the screen, I believe.

Q. Then, in order to crank it open—

A. You could crank it open.

Q. How would you remove the screen?

A. I believe the screen just pushed out.

Q. Where was the crank located?

A. In the center of the door—center of the hatch like.

Q. Do you recall approximately how many turns one would have to make on the crank to open it?

A. Several times.

Deposition of Paul Dover

EXAMINATION BY MR. LEAVITT

Q. Mr. Dover, would you tell us, please, for the record your name?

A. Paul Dover.

Q. What is your occupation, sir?

A. Long-distance truck driver.

Q. And for whom do you drive a truck?

A. Consolidated Freightways.

Q. How long have you been driving a truck?

A. Thirty-five years, give or take a little.

Q. Now, on June 7, Yr.–5, did you have occasion to be driving in this state?

A. Yes, sir, I did.

Q. Now, where were you driving in the evening of that day?

A. On the Turnpike towards New York.

Q. Now, as you drove on the Turnpike, did you have occasion to see a recreational vehicle known as a Swinger?

A. Yes, I did.

Q. At some time that evening, did you come upon an accident involving that Swinger?

A. Yes. Yes, I did.

Q. Where on the Turnpike did you first see the Swinger?

A. I observed this vehicle at about the 68 mile post on the Turnpike first.

Q. Tell us what you observed about the Swinger at the time you first saw it.

A. Well, it was parked on the shoulder of the road which is the breakdown lane of the Turnpike—just parked there.

Q. Did you notice anything unusual about it?

A. No, I did not—nothing unusual about it.

Q. When did you next see this vehicle?

A. Well, the next time I saw it, it passed me I would say maybe a couple of miles before the scene of the accident.

Q. And how far from the place where you first saw it stopped on the breakdown lane did it pass you?

A. About 42 miles—40–42 miles.

Q. Were you able to form a judgment of approximately how fast you were going when the camper passed you?

A. 45 miles an hour.

Q. And were you able to form a judgment as to the speed of the camper?

A. 50 miles an hour.

Q. Now, tell us what, if anything you noticed about the camper as it passed you?

A. Well, the only thing that I noticed about it was that I had been thinking about buying one of these campers myself, and I just happened to notice this one when it passed me about what a good-appearing vehicle it seemed to be, and I thought to myself, I wouldn't mind having one of them myself.

Q. What happened after it passed you?

A. It pulled back into the driving lane and—

Q. What happened next?

A. Well, like I say, it went up the road and out of my sight, and the next thing that I saw, my headlights picked up an overturned vehicle on the shoulder of the road.

Q. When you say the shoulder again, do you mean—

A. The breakdown lane—partly in the breakdown lane and partly in the driving lane.

Q. What did you notice about the vehicle when you first saw it overturned?

A. Well, when I first saw it, it was just—the vehicle was just turned over on its side and of course the thing—the first thing you see is all the wheels and the undercarriage facing you, and that was just—it just laid there in that position.

Q. What happened next?

A. Well, within—oh, I'd say five seconds or so after I saw the vehicle, it just burst into flames.

Q. What did you do?

A. Well, of course my first thought was to get up to it and try and get the people out of it if they hadn't already gotten out which they hadn't, so I pulled by truck up as close to the camper—I parked it at a safe distance away and got out of the truck, ran up to the vehicle—the burning vehicle, and of course you couldn't get near the bottom or the top—which was the top then, the side which was up. The flames were burning, and so I ran around the vehicle, and of course the first thing I did was look in the windshield, and you couldn't see nothing in there because it was completely black like the smoke had seared the windshield over and sort of—like black smoke had formed on the glass and you couldn't see nothing in there—you couldn't see a thing.

Q. When you went around to the windshield, did you hear any sound from the interior of the vehicle?

A. Yes.

Q. Tell us what you heard.

A. Well, I could hear a number of people in there hollering and screaming, "Help. Get us out of here."

Q. What did you do?

A. Well, I tried to kick in the windshield.

Q. Did you have any success?

A. No, I did not.

Q. Then what happened?

A. Then I tried to look around for a rock or something to break the windshield, and there wasn't any right there available.

Q. And did the screaming continue while you were looking—

A. Yes, sir.

Q. Go ahead.

A. And then I knew I had a heavy tire iron in the cab of my truck. So I ran back to get that, and then in the meantime, this other trucking unit—the Old Colony Transportation unit driven by Grant Edsel stopped. He had parked his truck alongside of mine. He was just getting out of his cab with his fire extinguisher, and I told him that the people were still in there hollering and screaming to get out.

Q. Did the two of you then do something?

A. Yes, I told him I had to have a bar to break the windshield, and he reached in his cab and got the bar and handed it to me, and then we both ran up to the vehicle and around to the front in the area of the windshield, and I proceeded to try to break the windshield out with this bar.

Q. While you were doing this, did you hear any sounds from the interior?

A. Yes, the people were still hollering and screaming—Help, let them out.

Q. How long did you work at trying to break the windshield with this bar?

A. Well, maybe a couple of minutes.

Q. Were you able to make any headway with the windshield?

A. Yes, I had a hole started through the windshield, not a very big one but I did get a hole started through it.

Q. Then what happened?

A. Then there was another terrific explosion.

Q. When you say another, had there been an explosion before this?

A. Well, there was—there was quite a few explosions before this which turned out I guess from the tires which were burning and exploding—something I found out afterwards. Like I say, this explosion came, and it blew me and Mr. Edsel back up against the guardrails sort of—well, on top of each other.

Q. After this explosion, did you hear anything else from—did you hear anything else from—did you hear the people screaming?

A. No, I did not. After this explosion there was no more sounds.

Q. Can you tell us about how much time elapsed from the time that you first came upon the camper overturned to the time of this last explosion?

A. Five to six minutes.

Q. After the last explosion, what happened?

A. Well, after the explosion knocked us down, we got back up again, and you couldn't get near the burning vehicle because the heat was so great that there was just no possible chance to get back to it, and about that time the emergency vehicle from the Turnpike had pulled up there, and I asked the operator if he had a long bar figuring if he had a long bar that I could get back and reach this windshield again and get it battered out of there, but even with a long bar you couldn't get near it.

Q. So what happened next?

A. Well, in the meantime, the State Police had gotten there, and them and the emergency truck and a number of other truckers had gotten their fire extinguishers out of course, and were using them on this burning vehicle trying to put the fire out but it was no use; it was just beyond the point of putting it out with that kind of equipment. The State Police called from the emergency vehicle and radioed out for the fire equipment that takes care of the Turnpike situation.

Q. Were you able to get the windshield off eventually?

A. Not really off. The heat and I suppose the explosion—the windshield sort of melted and sort of rolled—

Q. Blew out?

A. . . . out and one body badly burned of course just rolled out with the windshield.

Q. This latter—Can you tell us where this last explosion originated from? Was it inside or outside the vehicle the one that knocked you and Mr. Edsel . . ..

A. It must have originated from the inside of the vehicle.

Q. When you say it must have, is that something based on your observations?

A. My own opinion, yes.

Q. Opinion is a tricky word with us lawyers. Let me put the question this way: Were you able to observe the origin of that explosion, either visually or with your ears?

A. No.

CROSS EXAMINATION BY MR. WAYNE

Q. I think you said you first saw this motor home when it was pulled off to the side of the road, and you passed it, is that right?

A. That's right.

Q. And you saw it a second time when it proceeded to pass you on the Turnpike?

A. That's right.

Q. How much time elapsed between the time it passed you and the time that you came upon the accident scene?

A. You mean the first time I saw the vehicle or . . . . .

Q. Well, you said that at some point after you had first seen it pulled off on the shoulder of the road, it later passed you and pulled back into the driving lane and then went out of your view I think, is that right?

A. Right.

Q. How much time elapsed between the point it left your view until the point when you saw it again turned over on its side?

A. Well, it passed me I would say about two miles from the point of the accident and whatever time it takes to travel two miles at 40 or 45 miles an hour.

Q. Now, when you ran up to the motor home, you said you heard voices inside, is that right?

A. That's right.

Q. How many voices did you hear?

A. I would just say a number of voices.

Q. How do you know it was a number instead of just one voice?

A. Well, there seemed to be a difference, you know, in voices like maybe some male and some female.

Q. Did you hear a male voice and a female voice?

A. I would say, yes. I'm not positive but I would say, yes.

Q. Did you ever see any movement at all inside that camper?

A. No.

CROSS EXAMINATION BY MR. VREELAND

Q. You told us that you first saw the camper when it was parked along the right shoulder of the Turnpike at approximately the 68 mile post, is that correct?

A. That's right.

Q. How do you recall that it was the 68 mile post?

A. Well, I drive that road every day, and I observed on the next trips through where this vehicle was sitting, and it is the area of the 68 mile post.

Q. It was at night time, is that correct?

A. Yes.

Q. Was there anything particular about the location of the vehicle that enabled you to pinpoint it later on when you came through?

A. Yes, in a way. It is on a downhill area which was quite a steep hill there I would say. It was part way down the hill.

Q. If we went out there this afternoon, do you think you could pinpoint the exact same spot again?

A. Yes.

Q. You saw the camper next when it passed you, is that correct?

A. Yes.

Q. And you estimated that at 40 to 42 miles later, is that correct?

A. That's right.

Q. Would you tell us how you were able to identify that distance as 40 to 42 miles?

A. Well, the point of the accident was the 24 mile post, and I saw the vehicle a couple of miles before that; so you subtract 26 from 68, and you get 42–40, somewhere in that area.

Q. Now, when the vehicle passed you, were you able to positively identify it as being the same vehicle you had seen earlier on the side of the road?

A. Well, only the fact that like I say, I admired the vehicle when I first saw it, and when it passed me again, why I took particular notice of the fact that this was the same type vehicle.

Q. But you didn't notice the license plate for instance, did you?

A. No—well, no.

Q. Did you notice anything else that distinquished this particular camper from another camper of the same type?

A. Yes, in a way because this camper is made under a Swinger name which you don't see a lot of them. There is quite a few but they are not as popular as some other vehicle, and this was a very attractive, nice-appearing vehicle that I thought that I would like to own one like that myself.

Q. When you first saw the vehicle parked on the side of the road, were you able to identify it was a Swinger vehicle?

A. Well, yes, that name on the side of it.

Q. You know that yourself at that time?

A. Yes, I was observant—I was quite observant about this camper motor home type vehicle because I was very interested in purchasing one myself.

Q. And when it passed you later on, you saw that it was a Swinger again, is that right?

A. That's right.

Q. Was there anything about the vehicle other than the fact that it was a Swinger which led you to the conclusion that it was the same vehicle that you had seen earlier parked by the side of the road?

A. Well, no, other than the fact that it was the same make, same model, and it looked like the same one that passed me before.

Q. You mean which you had passed before?

A. Yes, I passed it when it was sitting on the side of the road.

Q. Did you notice any other traffic around you at the time the camper passed you?

A. No, I did not. There wasn't any other traffic.

Q. There was no other traffic directly behind you?

A. Not close. I suppose there was traffic. It was Friday night, and traffic is quite heavy. Of course by midnight, it slows down considerably but there was traffic probably behind me.

Q. But you don't recall seeing it?

A. Not particularly.

Q. And when you came upon the camper after it had turned over, was there any traffic behind you that you noticed then?

A. If there was, I didn't notice because my thoughts were to get the truck parked at a safe distance away and get out of it and get up to this camper. I wasn't concerned about traffic.

Q. Did any vehicles pass you as you were pulling over to park?

A. No.

Q. How much time elapsed between the time you first parked your vehicle and the time that the Old Colony truck arrived?

A. I would say three to four minutes.

Q. Did any other vehicles arrive between those two times?

A. No, they didn't.

Q. So the Old Colony truck was the first to arrive after yours, is that right?

A. Yes.

Q. Did you talk to Mr. Leavitt prior to your deposition today?

A. Yes, I did.

Q. And did you discuss with him your testimony?

A. Yes.

Deposition of Frank Brummer

EXAMINATION BY MR. MOREMAN

Q. Would you state your name, please.

A. My name is Frank Brummer.

Q. By whom are you employed?

A. The Registry of Motor Vehicles.

Q. What is your rank or position with the Registry?

A. I am a temporary investigator.

Q. And how long have you been with the Registry?

A. Since Yr.–10.

Q. And you are in the Accident Investigation section?

A. Correct.

Q. When did you go into the Accident Investigation section?

A. June, Yr.–7.

Q. Have you been in that section since then?

A. Yes, I have.

Q. And your title is temporary investigator. What is meant by temporary?

A. A temporary is that you are appointed because there are no permanent openings. I came off a competitive list, and there was no permanent opening; so they appointed me as a temporary.

Q. And you have been a temporary investigator since June of Yr.–7?

A. No, I have been a temporary investigator since April of Yr.–3.

Q. What were you before then?

A. An examiner.

Q. What does an examiner do?

A. Well, they issue licenses, learner's permits; we do investigations on dealer repairs; we do investigation of fatal accidents; we do investigating of accidents. There is eye screening, file reports; there is many other duties.

Q. Now, were you connected in any way with the investigation which is referred to in the subpoena?

A. Yes, I was.

Q. What in general terms was your role in the investigation of this accident, and include in your answer the times that you responded to the scene or that you examined the scene, et cetera.

A. Can I refer back to my notes on that?

Q. Sure. What I am looking for at the outset is this: Generally what was your job with respect to this accident?

A. My job was to respond to the location of the accident, the area of the accident, make observations, inspect the vehicle involved and try to obtain witnesses and try to determine the cause of the accident.

Q. What is the first thing you did when you got on the job?

A. We stopped at the scene, the Turnpike, between mile marker 24 and 25.

Q. Did you have a photographer with you?

A. No.

Q. Did you have cameras with you?

A. Yes.

Q. Who was taking the pictures?

A. I was.

Q. What did you do at the scene of the accident?

A. Took measurements, made observations of the roadway—the area in general.

Q. How long did you spend at the scene of the accident?

A. Well, we went back to the scene a couple of times—I would say a couple of hours all told.

Q. Well, let's talk about the first time you were at the scene of the accident. How much time did you spend?

A. I would say approximately an hour.

Q. After you left the scene of the accident that first time, what did you do?

A. We went to the Registry of Motor Vehicles.

Q. Who did you talk to?

A. The supervisor I believe he was. The name I don't know. I would have to look it up to see his name.

Q. What did you say to him, and what did he say to you?

A. Just general specifics. We wanted basic information, and we were looking for Dearborn, the inspector. I don't believe he was there when we first arrived, but he did arrive after that.

Q. Why were you looking for Dearborn?

A. For him to give us the initial information which he obtained shortly after the accident. That is the following day anyway minimum.

Q. Do you know if Dearborn was out there while the camper was still on the roadway?

A. I don't think so, no.

Q. And how long did you talk with the supervisor?

A. About a half hour.

Q. From there where did you go?

A. I believe we went to the garage, the towing garage where the vehicle was.

Q. Was that all you did with respect to the accident on that first day you were out there?

A. No.

Q. What else did you do?

A. Went to the dump.

Q. What did you do at the dump?

A. Tried to locate the gas tank that was missing from the vehicle.

Q. Who told you that it was at the dump?

A. I don't remember who it was.

Q. But someone did tell you to go down the dump to look for it?

A. Yes, evidently. I would guess it was the man at the garage. We were asking for the remaining parts of the vehicle. The information we had was it was not totally burned as in the photographs. I believe the left side was still sort of in place, but it had, in towing and so forth, disintegrated, and the remains that were taken from the scene were scraped up and taken to the dump. So we responded to the dump.

Q. In other words the chassis was towed in by somebody?

A. Yes.

Q. And that left some parts and some junk out on the roadway?

A. Correct.

Q. And that was scraped up and taken to the dump?

A. Yes.

Q. Do you know by whom?

A. No, I don't. I believe it was the Turnpike Authority.

Q. Did you find any remains at all of the vehicle at the dump?

A. No.

Q. Did you talk with someone at the dump?

Q. Now, on that first day of investigation, after you left the dump, where did you go?

A. I believe I might have went back to the scene. I can't be certain of the exact sequence of events. I would say we went back to the scene again for more observations.

Q. How long were you at the scene as you recall?

A. I would approximate another hour.

Q. What did you do at the scene during that hour?

A. Made more observations.

Q. You made notes?

A. Made notes.

Q. Did you take pictures?

A. I think we did, yes.

Q. What did you do after that?

A. I believe we returned home after that.

Q. Now, did you look for parts of the vehicle at the scene of the accident on those two visits?

A. Yes.

Q. Did you find anything?

A. Not that I recall, no, except for a few pieces of plastic—metal which may or may not have pertained to the vehicle.

Q. You walked down to the tree line, and I take it you must have walked east and west of the actual accident scene?

A. Yes.

Q. Approximately how far east did you walk and approximately how far west?

A. East I probably walked back five or six hundred feet and west maybe one hundred or two hundred feet.

Q. And you looked for that whole distance between the tree line and the Turnpike for any evidence you might find?

A. Yes.

Q. And you located nothing in that rectangle?

A. Nothing. I wouldn't say nothing—there was some evidence on the roadway.

Q. What I am concerned with, were there any parts of the vehicle other than the plastic that you have mentioned?

A. No.

Q. Did you ever see the bumper at any time?

A. The bumper?

Q. Either bumper.

A. I believe, yes.

Q. Which one did you see?

A. The front mainly.

Q. Where did you see that?

A. On the wreck—the remains of the vehicle. I would have to review the photographs to be certain of that. I'll have to strike that. No, I didn't see the bumper.

Q. Did you ever see a tire print or mark on the shoulder or a wheel print or a mark on the shoulder?

A. No.

Q. Did you look for that when you went out to investigate?

A. Yes.

Q. And you did not see anything that would constitute an impression of a wheel or a tire on the dirt coming up to the guardrail?

A. On the dirt, no.

Q. Did you see an impression or tire mark anywhere?

A. Yes, I did.

Q. Where did you see it?

A. I seen an impression on the vertical upright of the guardrail and also a burning impression, charring impression on the asphalt surface of the roadway itself.

Q. Any skid marks or tire marks anywhere or wheel marks anywhere leading up to the guardrail?

A. No.

Q. And again you went back in an easterly direction from the scene about 600 feet?

A. Yes.

Q. Now, how did you learn that it was a Yr.–6 Dodge motor home, 22-foot Swinger model?

A. I believe it was through the registration.

Q. Now, there is a conclusion in your report that says, "Possible fatigue or inattention of driver," and that was the Registry's conclusion as to what precipitated the accident?

A. That was the Chief Inspector's conclusion, yes.

Q. There is a statement again on Page 1: "Road surface is of bituminous concrete with no contributable defects." Apparently the road surface was examined?

A. Yes.

Q. When you were out at the scene of the accident, did you examine the road surface?

A. Yes.

Q. Were you looking to see if there were any defects in it?

A. Yes.

Q. Did you find any?

A. No.

Q. How would you describe the condition of the road surface that you observed?

A. Except as resulted from the accident, the road surface was good.

Q. Now, there is a statement that in the westerly direction, the roadway is 39 feet wide. Who made that measurement?

A. I believe I did.

Q. You mention a site distance of approximately 500 feet east of the accident site.

A. Yes.

Q. What is meant by that term?

A. If you stand at the accident site and you look east, you see approximately 500 feet eastbound.

Q. At which point the road curves?

A. It is a grade curve anyway—it is approximately 500 feet.

Q. Was that stepped out or estimated?

A. Estimated.

Q. Who made the estimate?

A. Me.

Q. In the upper right-hand corner there is a ¾-one-inch bolt impression. Is that in your handwriting?

A. Yes.

Q. What does that refer to?

A. I believe that is the impression that was on the guardrail, ¾ inch to an inch bolt impression.

Q. And when you use the word guardrail in that sentence, you were referring to one of the vertical I-beams?

A. Yes.

Q. Which of the vertical I-beams?

A. I believe it was the first one. I'm not certain—either the first or the one with the anchored cable. We will have to check the photographs to be sure of that one.

Q. What did the impression on the I-beam look like?

A. Well, there is about three closely knot vertical lines imprinted right on the I-beam post.

Q. And what was that—what kind of a piece of metal or item was that consistent with?

A. It appeared to me to be a threaded bolt.

Q. Did you find on the vehicle anywhere a threaded bolt?

A. Yes.

Q. Where did you find it?

A. On the front axle going through the spindle—right front.

Q. On Page 3 there is a statement that the vehicle had become airborne on the right side and came down striking and bending the third, fourth and fifth steel I-beam rail posts. Was that your opinion having investigated this accident?

A. Yes.

Q. Why did you come to the conclusion that the vehicle was airborne?

A. Because the mile marker post—the first and second posts were disrupted, one was untouched and the other two or three following were removed or destroyed or bent over.

Q. Which indicates to you that the vehicle cleared at least one or two posts before it came down again?

A. I don't think it steered around it.

Q. The answer to that question is Yes?

A. Yes.

Q. Did you see burn marks in the area, sir?

A. Yes, I did.

Q. And could you describe to me where you saw them?

A. They were in the roadway. One was approximately eight feet ten inches out from the edge of the roadway and the other was practically in line with the edge or maybe a little out.

Q. You saw two burn areas?

A. Yes, among others.

Q. What were the others?

A. Well, there was—all the way across was singed—burned; the general area was burned.

Q. At the bottom there is a statement that there was no evidence of alcohol. From what did you derive that information?

A. Well, talking to Inspector Dearborn, talking to whoever was involved.

Q. Did Dearborn look through the wreck for evidence of alcohol?

A. I couldn't tell you.

Q. Did you ever talk about that?

A. Just briefly.

Q. What did he tell you?

A. He didn't have any evidence of alcohol.

Q. Did he tell you he made a search for that through the remains of the camper?

A. Yes. We generally always do, but there was nothing to search there.

Q. Because everything was burned up?

A. Yes.

Q. At some point in your file here there was a notation that the axle was actually bent. Did you personally observe that?

A. Yes, I did.

Q. What portion of the front axle?

A. I could be wrong, but I believe it was bent—the whole axle was sort of bent from the middle out along the right side back.

Q. So on the right-hand extreme of the axle?

A. From the right side of the axle, the front axle, was bent to the rear, and it appeared to be bending in the middle.

Deposition of Robert Sica

EXAMINATION BY MR. LEAVITT

Q. What is your name?

A. My name is Bob Sica.

Q. What is your present occupation, sir?

A. My present occupation is general manager of a recreational vehicle company.

Q. What is the name of that company?

A. Weekend Traveler, Incorporated.

Q. At some time, sir, were you associated with Odyssey Corporation?

A. Yes.

Q. What were your dates of association with Odyssey?

A. June of Yr.–10 through November of Yr.–6.

Q. What was your position with Odyssey?

A. My first position was senior vice president of Monitor Coach and director of manufacturing for the Odyssey Recreational Vehicle Division.

Q. How long were you director of manufacturing, sir?

A. Until December 31st of Yr.–9.

Q. What was your next position?

A. As general manager of the Swinger Recreational Division of Odyssey Recreational Vehicle Division.

Q. The years that you were general manager of the Odyssey Recreational Division was from—

A. December 31, Yr.–0 until November 12, Yr.–6.

Q. What was Monitor Coach?

A. Monitor Coach was another part of the Odyssey Recreational Vehicle Division.

Q. What were your duties as director of manufacturing of the Monitor Coach?

A. To manage the manufacturing areas at our plants.

Q. What were your duties as manager of the Odyssey Recreational Division?

A. My duties were to manage the Swinger complex, coordinate the efforts with the recreational division, develop budgets, establish objectives for the company, hire the necessary people and day-to-day management.

Q. What do you mean by establish objectives?

A. Determine the future course of the company in connection with the recreational vehicle division which was headed up by another individual and my superior.

Q. Now, what kind of objectives was it your duty to try to establish?

A. Sales objectives and an improved product.

Q. As part of your duties as the general manager, did the people who were responsible for designing the Swingers, were they your subordinates?

A. Not entirely. We hired an outside consulting firm to help develop the initial plan of the new products.

Q. Who was the outside consulting firm?

A. Severin from Chicago.

Q. What kind of consulting did Severin do for Odyssey?

A. Design.

Q. When you say design, in what areas of design was Severin concerned with?

A. The exterior apperances, the aesthetics of the products and the interior color coordination.

Q. Essentially they were concerned in the cosmetic design so to speak?

A. It was more than cosmetics; it was visual. The window openings —it was more than cosmetics. It was some functional.

Q. And the functional aspect of their work involved the designing of windows and positioning of the driver and that kind of thing?

A. We had discussions with them. They sat in at all of our products meetings. They sat in all of them.

Q. Did they provide engineering services to Odyssey?

A. Not manufacturing engineering.

Q. What kind of engineering did they provide?

A. Design as far as the general appearances and the location of people or the coach relating to people, and so on.

Q. Did they provide consulting advice with respect to choice of materials and the location of portions of the power train, for example?

A. Which question are you asking me? There is two there.

Q. Both.

A. I don't think I can answer them.

Q. To what extent, if at all, did Severin provide consulting services with respect to choice of materials?

A. They provided advice to us on what is generally accepted in the industry and in the country as being acceptable to the consumer as far as convenience, comfort.

Q. And did they provide any consulting services with respect to safety design or design of safety factors I should say?

A. Yes.

Q. In what respect?

A. In our discussions. These people are very knowledgeable of the industry and aware of all the industry regulations, federal regulations, and so their effort was coordinated with ours to give every consideration to that.

Q. What kind of safety considerations did their work deal with?

A. Obviously the 302 flammability in Yr.–7 was a proposed regulation, and so this was given every consideration.

Q. Anything else?

A. I don't recall all the discussions that we had on the product. It's been many years ago.

Q. Was there anything else that you can recall?

A. It was in the developing of this particular product—they sat in on all products meetings. Everything that was discussed was discussed with them, and they participated in the discussions.

Q. Let me ask you this: Were you present at these product development discussions?

A. Always.

Q. Was anything discussed at these product development meetings with respect to protecting the integrity of the fuel system?

A. Every bit of that coach was discussed. We went through it thoroughly with their engineering staff, and this was a meeting of all the people involved, all the responsible people involved in the company with the Severin staff. We discussed all parts of this unit.

Q. Was the problem of protecting the integrity of the fuel system specifically discussed?

A. I don't recall the discussions on that. I do recall discussing every part of the product at one time or another at these product meetings.

Q. Do you have any recollection of any discussion at all concerning protecting the integrity of the fuel system?

A. Let us define the integrity of the fuel system.

Q. By the fuel system I refer to the system of the vehicle beginning at the filler neck of the gas tank through the gas tank fuel and the fuel lines up to and including the carburetor.

A. Yes. Our discussion and our decision was to not change the location or relocate the Dodge gas tank and to use the Dodge Body Builders as our guide.

Q. Do I understand you to say, and if not, please set us right, that the only aspect of the fuel system as I defined it previously that was discussed was the question of whether or not to relocate the main gas tank?

A. No. Obviously we put on an auxiliary tank. So this was discussed. The systems were discussed. I will tell you that the ground rules that we started out with, that everything we did, would be in complete compliance with Dodge's recommendation with their Body Builders Book, with the federal standards and our own industry-established standards. These are the ground rules we started with.

Q. Was any consideration in these discussions given to protecting the main gas tank by means of any structural member?

A. If you mean some extra supports, we did with the perimeter frame, the steel perimeter frame that we put around this unit, gives it added protection, and the purpose of the frame was for several purposes but the perimeter steel frame was put around there to give it added protection.

Q. Now, the steel perimeter frame you are referring to are the metal members that support the floor?

A. Yes.

Q. And that, of course, was above the gas tank as it came from Dodge, was it not?

A. It was right on top of the chassis frame.

Q. That is above the gas tank?

A. Right on top of the frame.

Q. That put it above the gas tank, did it not?

A. Yes.

Q. So was any consideration given to protecting the gas tank from front or side impacts by means of anything other than wooden members to which the outer skin was attached?

A. All of our considerations were governed by the need to build this unit within the federal standards with the least amount of weight you can put on this unit.

Q. What considerations were given?

A. A steel perimeter frame around the outside of that coach plus two layers of 3/16ths plywood which makes 3/8ths on the side wall construction—there is a welded step in front of it, and this is standard—above standard practice for the industry. The Swinger structure was above the standard established by our competitors.

Q. Was any consideration given to putting a metal protective guard of some sort around the side of the tank to protect it from side impact?

A. The metal frame—the perimeter frame did protect it from side impact. This was on the outside. It wasn't as low as the tank, agreed, but it was there for that purpose, for a side protection.

Q. Well, the tank was on the same—portions of it were on the same level as the bumper of the vehicle, is that so?

A. It seems reasonable that it would be.

Q. And the bumper on this vehicle was approximately the same level as the ordinary bumpers found on other motor vehicles?

A. That's true.

Q. Were you aware at the time of the height of the bumpers of most motor vehicles on the road?

A. Yes.

Q. And was any thought given to protecting the vehicles' main fuel tank from side impact at that height?

A. We considered every possibility when we built this product.

Q. And what means were considered to protect the gas tank from side impact other than the frame which holds the wooden floor which you told us about?

A. The side wall, itself, had structural strength. The metal frame that backs it up, and this side wall extended well below the egress to the gas tank, was recessed below the bottom of the side wall. The wood frame with the two layers of plywood securely fastened to the metal frame protected this area.

Q. Was consideration given to any additional side protection?

A. I am sure we considered every consideration in the development of this product. The exact details of the conversations I don't remember.

Q. Are you aware now of any specific decision not to put a metal protective structure around the side of the tank other than the metal which holds up the floor?

A. No, I don't remember the decision-making process on this. I do know that it was a state of the art, the industry-accepted practice to go with the Dodge tank where it was and not relocate it as recommended by the Dodge people. We felt if an additional shield were necessary that Dodge engineers would have recognized it.

Q. Do I understand you to say that essentially you gave no independent consideration to an additional shield because Dodge did not recommend the additional—

A. We gave consideration to all of these areas; no additional shield was put on.

Q. I am sorry. Are you telling us that no additional—that the decision not to put on an additional shield was made because Dodge did not recommend an additional shield?

A. This is one of the considerations. The other considerations are the weight.

Q. What weight would an additional shield have added to this—

A. It would depend upon the shield.

Q. Are you telling us then that you never got in the design—in the handling of this particular problem of protecting the fuel tank, you never got to the point of considering different types of shields and their affects on the overall weight of the vehicle?

A. In our consideration for protection, we shielded it from the outside with the frame and the heavy side wall that we put on. Additional shields in our product—we discussed all parts of this product, but it wasn't decided that shields in addition to the Magnum-provided ones were essential, were necessary.

Q. Did you consider specifically the possibility of shielding the gas tank in addition to the shielding that you have told us about for the outside wooden structure and skin?

A. I don't recall the discussions. I know that we discussed this—we discussed the auxiliary tank, the propane tank—

Q. What I am trying to find out, Mr. Sica, is whether or not additional shielding was—additional to what you told us about, that is the wooden members and the skin and the metal flooring supports were ever considered?

A. I am not sure. We discussed all parts of this product. I want to make that part absolutely clear, and—

Q. What I am trying to get to is when you were discussing the integrity of the fuel system, did you consider as a design possibility the installation of a shield around the gas tank underneath the metal floor supports?

A. I am not sure if we discussed that part or not. We discussed shielding it and did shield it. We discussed the weight limitations established by the federal government.

Q. Is it your testimony that you do not recall any discussion concerning additional shielding about the gas tank?

A. I don't recall the nature of our discussion about additional shielding.

Q. Do you recall whether or not there was discussion concerning the feasibility of additional shielding?

A. I think that was discussed with the Dodge people.

Q. Well, did Odyssey have any crash tests done on the Swinger vehicles?

A. No.

Q. Specifically were any type of destructive tests done on the Odyssey Swinger vehicles to determine the integrity of the fuel tank under impact conditions?

A. No.

Q. What was your understanding of the tests that Dodge performed on the Odyssey Swingers at their proving grounds?

A. To test the systems and make the total road test of the product and to rate our product by their standards, whether we were building it and marrying our product really to theirs in an acceptable manner.

Q. And how did you gain that understanding of what their tests were?

A. Conversation with the Dodge representatives.

Q. At any time, to your knowledge, was the desirability of Dodge crash testing with the Swinger recreational vehicle ever discussed?

A. Yes.

Q. When did this discussion take place, and who participated in it?

A. I have served on the Standards Committee of the Recreational Vehicle Institute and now the RVA in Yr.–12. These discussions came up in our industry meetings. As a result we each went back to our own companies and asked ourselves can be have a total destruction test or destroy our products in the magnitude of the testing procedures.

Q. By magnitude you mean the costs?

A. The testing sites, the costs; the measuring devices were not available within our industry.

Q. Well, were you aware that the Magnum Corporation did have facilities to do crash testing?

A. Yes.

Q. Did you ever ask Magnum to do any crash testing for your products?

A. No.

Q. Was the feasibility or the desirability of asking Magnum to do crash testing ever discussed among management to your knowledge?

A. Within our own group we discussed the possibility of doing crash tests.

Q. Within your group meaning at Odyssey?

A. And within our industry.

Q. Let's stick with Odyssey for the moment. In the course of these discussions, was the desirability of asking Magnum to do these crash tests ever raised?

A. I am not sure whether it was discussed that Magnum might do the tests or not.

Q. Do you have any memory of anyone making such a suggestion?

A. No.

Q. To your knowledge Magnum was never asked to do such tests, is that true?

A. We did not ask Magnum to do a total destruction test of our product.

Q. Was that because of the costs involved?

A. That would have been one of the considerations.

Q. Was that the major consideration?

A. No.

Q. Tell me if you will your other considerations—

A. The other consideration is the number of vehicles that would have to be crashed from different angles, different ways—roll-over, front end—that just hadn't been done in our industry by any of the companies to my knowledge.

Q. So the number of tests that you felt that would be done was a factor because of the costs, is that correct?

A. It was one of the considerations.

Q. And the other consideration was that—

A. The facilities, the amount of products, the amount of people that it would take to do this and monitor it correctly.

Q. Magnum had the facilities?

A. They had the test track. Whether they had facilities to measure motor home destruction, I don't know.

Q. Well, in any event your people never inquired about it, is that correct?

A. I am not sure whether they inquired or not. They were in constant communication with the Dodge people.

Q. If there had been any inquiries about Magnum doing crash testing for Odyssey, would you have been the person who would have initiated that inquiry?

A. Not necessarily, no.

Q. Who would have?

A. It would have been one of our engineers.

Q. That is one of your subordinates?

A. Yes.

Q. Did you ever direct one of your subordinates to initiate an inquiry as to whether or not it would be feasible to have Magnum do any crash testing for Odyssey?

A. I don't believe so. I know that we discussed this thoroughly at our Industry Standards meeting.

Q. Were you aware that there are various laboratories around the country such as Cornell that, in fact, did so crash testing of vehicles?

A. Yes.

Q. Did anyone at Odyssey ever initiate an inquiry to any one of these laboratories as to whether or not they could do crash testing for Odyssey?

A. Not directly to them, but we discussed them at our industry meetings.

Q. Now, the recreational vehicle industry has a trade association, does it not?

A. It does.

Q. And are all the major manufacturers of recreational vehicles a member of this trade association?

A. Yes.

Q. What is the name of the trade association?

A. RVIA—Recreational Vehicle Industry Association.

Q. Is one of the major functions of this trade association to represent the interests of the industry before governmental bodies on matters that affect the industry?

A. To represent the industry but not the individual companies.

Q. And it has represented the interests of the industry in rule-making hearings by the Department of Transportation, has it not?

A. Yes.

Q. And is it fair to say that the industry association has generally tried to persuade the Department of Transportation not to pass regulations which it regarded as unduly burdensome on the industry?

A. No, I think to the contrary. I think they have asked for interpretations and time elements, but I can't speak for the industry. However, I think that they have—to the contrary—they have encouraged federal standards.

Q. What standards do you think have been made tougher as a result of the association's work for the Department of Transportation?

A. I think that areas of lighting and visibility, windshield clearance, loading. I can't speak for the industry, but I know that their attitude is one of complete cooperation as our company has been.

Q. To your knowledge has the issue of crash testing recreational vehicles been discussed at the association meetings?

A. Yes, it has been.

Q. And I take it that the position of the association has been to oppose mandatory regulations requiring crash testing of recreational vehicles?

A. I am not sure of their official position. I have been out of it for three years.

Q. During the time you were there?

A. There was some early talk at that time prior to my leaving—leaving in Yr.–6, and the concern is of proper sites, how many models each person had, the mechanics of getting it done, and as I recall, they were asking for some time, and what is between now and then I haven't followed it that close.

Q. Was it generally accepted on the standards—the Standards Committee that crash testing of recreational vehicles was desirable with the proper equipment?

A. I think they recognized many problems connected with this: The different models, the different tests that would be necessary, total destructive tests and the testing equipment being available to properly monitor this to get some meaningful data back that would lead to a better product perhaps. The facilities were not available and the testing equipment for all of that.

Q. When you say not available, you mean that the manufacturers of recreational vehicles did not generally have them?

A. That's right.

Q. But technologically crash testing was feasible, was it not?

A. Crash testing has been done in the automobile industry for a long time, I am sure.

Q. Is it fair to say that the reason that your own company did not invest in the necessary equipment to do crash testing was because of the cost?

A. It was one of the considerations—the number of units that would have to be destroyed, and it isn't like 1 out of 800,000 automobiles; it is maybe 6 motor homes out of 500.

Q. And the reason, I take it, that the number of vehicles that would have to be crash tested is significant because of the costs, is that a correct statement?

A. It is not the only consideration. The industry—the largest companies or the smaller ones did not crash test their vehicles. Our company was not different than the rest.

Q. Let me ask you this question: Let me go back to the original question which I asked you. Did the members of the Standards Committee of the recreational—Strike that out.

Getting back to the question that I asked you earlier, Mr. Sica, was it generally felt among the members of the Standards Committee of the Recreational Vehicle Manufacturers Association when you were on the Standards Committee that crash testing, speaking generally, was worthwhile?

A. It wasn't clear how the tests would be performed or how they would be monitored and what data would be the end result of this to go by information on this particular product opposed to other moving vehicles. The discussions were held on how to get the job done.

Q. Was it the consensus while you were there that if test procedures were properly set up that crash testing would provide useful safety information with respect to recreational vehicles?

A. Yes, I felt that we all recognized that all the testing that could be done would be beneficial to our industry.

Q. When you were giving us reasons why Odyssey did not do crash testing, in addition to reasons which related to costs, you said nobody else in the industry was doing it, is that correct?

A. To the best of my knowledge.

Q. Well, I have stated your testimony correctly?

A. Yes.

Q. And what relevance, to your understanding, was it that nobody else in the industry was doing it?

A. The type tests was not determined—it was not determined what type tests would be the most meaningful and how many products would have to be destroyed, and the facilities were not available within our industry.

Q. Was any work done at Odyssey, to your knowledge, to develop an appropriate set of procedures for crash testing of recreational vehicles?

A. Our engineers discussed it several times. I don't know the exact result of these discussions.

Q. At any time to your knowledge did management at Odyssey instruct its engineers to try to develop a useful crash testing program?

A. No, they were not instructed to develop a crash testing program.

Q. At any time while you were at Odyssey did management engage any independent engineers or laboratories or consulting firms to develop a procedure for crash testing recreational vehicles?

A. No.

Q. Did Odyssey manufacture and sell a vehicle substantially similar to the 23-foot Swinger in the years prior to the Yr.–6 model year?

A. It was similar in floor plan and chassis and in many respects. However, there were some changes in the Yr.–6 model year.

Q. What was the nature of the Yr.–6 model year change?

A. An improved appearance, improved quality coach, more steel, less wood, a steel cage over the front end of the coach that protected the front end that wasn't there before; the steel perimeter frame, fiber glass front and rear. These are the major changes.

Q. What years did those changes—Those changes all came in the Yr.–6 model year?

A. Those came in the Yr.–6 model year.

Q. Was the vehicle substantially the same for years prior to the Yr.–7 model year then?

A. Yes.

Q. Over how many years was it substantially the same?

A. With minor changes, it had been the same since Yr.–11 to the best of my knowledge. There was another major change in the Yr.–6 model year: The silhouette was lower than three inches, the unit became three inches closer to the ground than the previous years' model.

Q. What was the reason?

A. To make it lower than most of our competitors, to lower the center of gravity, to make it a safer unit and bring the weight down.

Q. How was the reduction in height attained?

A. Two inches was taken out of the floor by taking out a 2 x 2 inch wood floor frame and one inch out of the ceiling.

Q. How much did this change lower the center of gravity?

A. I am not sure of the center of gravity, but it lowered the coach and lowered the—testing wasn't done on the center of gravity.

Q. Were any tests done, to your knowledge, at Odyssey on any of the 23-foot Swinger models from Yr.–11 through the model year of Yr.–6 to determine where the vertical center of gravity of the vehicle was?

A. No.

Q. Were any tests done to determine at what angle from the horizontal the vehicle could be raised before it rolled over?

A. No, unless it was done by Dodge at the proving ground, and my memory doesn't tell me what all was in that report.

Q. Did you or anybody in management at Odyssey ask Dodge to do such a roll-over test?

A. No. They decided what was going to be tested, to the best of my knowledge.

Q. Now, who decided on the design of the escape hatch in the 23-foot Swinger for the Yr.–6 model year or the previous years which used the same escape hatch?

A. That decision, to the best of my knowledge, was made before I got there, and it was kept within the product.

Q. Were you familiar with the design of the escape hatch, sir?

A. I was.

Q. During the product development discussions that you told us about, whether they included the Severin people or not, was the adequacy of the escape hatch ever discussed?

A. We discussed the fact that it wasn't required in this unit, but it was our plan to put in every safety feature we could, whether it was required or not, and put it in a location that was acceptable, and it turned out to be the location that was acceptable at a later date when it did become necessary.

Q. So it was decided to put in an escape hatch as a safety measure?

A. It was decided to leave the escape hatch. It had always been in the Swinger products.

Q. Was the design of the escape hatch reviewed at this time?

A. Yes.

Q. When was the design of the escape hatch reviewed?

A. It would have been reviewed in our product meetings in early Yr.–7 as we went over all components of this vehicle.

Q. Now, was any consideration given to using a larger escape hatch?

A. The windows provide a larger escape hatch. We increased the size of the windows which make an escape hatch in a sense, but the size was standard for industry; it was a purchased item not provided by ourselves.

MR. LEAVITT: I move to strike the whole answer as not responsive.

Repeat the question back to Mr. Sica. Try to answer it directly, as directly as you can.

(Question read.)

A. I don't recall.

Q. Were any engineers—Did anybody evaluate the adequacy of the escape hatch for Odyssey?

A. Yes.

Q. Who, please?

A. Our engineering staff. They would have reviewed it and reported back to our product meeting that this was the standard escape hatch in the industry, and it was an acceptable one.

Q. And you recall that they did make this report back?

A. They reported back on every part of this coach as we went through it from one end to the other.

Q. Do you specifically remember them reporting about the escape hatch?

A. I recall them reporting about all parts of this product, and this would not have been excluded.

Q. What was the basis for their conclusion that the escape hatch was adequate?

A. That it was the escape hatch reported by our industry for all the major manufacturers including ourselves, and it was larger than the minimum requirements established later for an escape hatch which was 20 inches by 13, and this was one in excess of that.

Q. Now, in the course of the various product development discussions as you have called them, was there any discussion concerning the labeling of the alternate means of egress otherwise known as an escape hatch?

A. These were always marked with an exit.

Q. Can you describe for us, if you will, what the exit—what the labeling for the escape hatch was in the Yr.–6 Swinger?

A. I can't describe that to you.

Q. Do you recall whether or not there was any discussion concerning changing the means of identifying this so-called alternate means of egress or escape hatch as we have been calling it in this deposition?

A. No. They were marked by the supplier, and we put an exit sign there.

Q. When you say you put an exit sign there, you mean on the escape hatch?

A. Yes.

Q. And you don't recall what that exit sign looked like?

A. No, I don't.

Q. Now, was there interior lighting in the Yr.–6 Swinger?

A. Yes.

Q. How was that controlled?

A. There is a 12-volt lighting system controlled by a 35 amp. converter.

Q. Did this take its power off the automotive battery or off the recreational battery?

A. Off the recreational battery. However, they were generally hooked up in tandem so both of them could be charged, but it took the power from the recreational battery.

Q. And the switch to turn on the interior light was located where?

A. At the lights.

Q. What was the lighting?

A. They were 12-volt lights.

Q. How many bulbs, that kind of thing, and where were the bulbs located?

A. I can't tell you where they were all—

Q. Was there any discussion of providing an illuminated identification for the escape hatch that was independent of the automotive or recreational battery?

A. No.

Q. Do you recall what the type paint was that the exit sign was made of?

A. I recall it being red and white.

Q. It was not fluorescent?

A. I'm not sure.

Q. Who decided—Strike that out. The interior materials such as the 3/16ths plywood paneling and the carpeting and plastic covering on the tables and galleys, I take it were rated for flame propagation?

A. Yes.

Q. What was their rating, sir?

A. I would say they conformed to 302, and we had asked our suppliers prior to the mandatory date at this time to supply all material that would conform to 302 which was a proposed standard at that time.

Q. If I suggest to you that the rating was Class C, does that refresh your memory as to what the rating was?

A. I can't identify what the Class C—

Q. Was any consideration given to making the interior materials more flame retardant or resistant than the proposed standard 302, at Odyssey that is?

A. Yes, every consideration was given to us, and we bought from our suppliers the material that would provide the greatest resistance to flame available to us, and whether it exceeded in every case 302, I am not sure, but at least equally—

Q. Are you aware of the different classifications that are given to materials based on flame spread?

A. No.

Q. Do you recall what the flame spread classification was in numerical value in the Yr.–6?

A. I don't recall.

Q. Was it 200?

A. I don't recall.

Q. Well, if I suggest to you that the Yr.–5 NFPA standard 501–C, standard for recreational vehicles provided that interior surfaces shall be made of materials whose flame spread classification shall not exceed 200 when tested by the standard method of test for surface burning characteristics of building materials, does that refresh your memory as to the standard of the interior materials of the Yr.–6?

A. I wasn't in the industry at that time.

Q. What efforts, if any, were made by Odyssey to obtain interior materials that exceeded the standards proposed in the standard 302? Let me put the question this way: Were any efforts, to your knowledge, made by Odyssey to obtain materials for the interior surface whose flame-resistant characteristics exceeded the proposed standard 302?

A. Our suppliers were instructed, and we asked them to certify and label all materials to equal or exceed the standard.

Q. And is that the extent of the efforts made to obtain materials whose flame-resistant characteristics—have you now told us everything that was done by Odyssey in its attempt to obtain materials whose flame-resistant characteristics exceeded the proposed standard 302?

A. Our engineers ran tests of their own to confirm the manufacturer's certification.

Q. Have you now told us everything that was done by Odyssey to obtain interior materials that were flame resistant?

A. To the best of my knowledge.

Q. Was any research done at Odyssey to determine whether or not materials more flame resistant were available on the market than those actually ordered and used in the Yr.–6 Swinger?

A. Our engineers run tests. To what length they sort out other materials, I don't recall. Our instructions were to equal or exceed the standard, and I am not sure of their efforts in this area.

Q. Well, you would be the one who would have been familiar with what efforts were made to determine the availability of materials more flame resistant than those that would meet 302, is that true?

A. I was not familiar with all things that our people were doing at all times. I was familiar with the end result of the product and the general instructions came from me.

Q. Are you saying to me then that you were the one who determined that the interior materials should meet proposed standard 302?

A. That's correct. This was our group—one of the criterion for developing the product.

Q. Are you familiar with the terms Class A, Class B and Class C building materials?

A. No.

Q. Was any consideration given by you or to your knowledge by anyone at Odyssey using interior materials that would have met either Class B and Class A flame propagation—

A. No answer.

Q. You don't know?

A. That's correct. I answered previously.

Q. Who was responsible for the design of the bumper, the front bumper in the manner in which it was attached to the Swinger?

A. I don't recall by name. It was an engineering function.

Q. And were any tests done to determine the adequacy of the bumper?

A. Not to my knowledge.

Q. Were any tests done to determine the impact resistance of that portion of the vehicle which extended over the side of the main gas tank; that is the skin and the wooden framing?

A. Will you rephrase that question?

Q. I think before you told us that on the completed Swinger, the side of the gas tank was covered by wooden framing and the outside skin of the Swinger.

A. That's correct.

Q. Now, was any testing done to determine the impact resistance of that portion of the vehicle which covered the side of the gas tank?

A. No.

Q. Why not?

A. To test that side would have meant to test all sides, because we had four sides to the vehicle. Certainly the front and back are prime considerations for testing. The road side is generally considered by the industry to be the side most likely to be involved in an accident. So it would have meant testing all products at all sides.

Q. Was the impact resistance of that portion of the vehicle that covered the side gas tank ever determined by calculation based on the materials used and their strength?

A. No.

Q. It would have been technically feasible to calculate to a reasonably close approximation the impact resistance of that portion of the vehicle, wouldn't it?

A. I don't know if it would or not.

Q. Did you ever ask any of your engineers to attempt such a calculation?

A. No.

Deposition of Jeffrey Terrio

EXAMINATION BY MR. LEAVITT

Q. May we have your name?

A. Jeffrey Terrio.

Q. What is your occupation, Mr. Terrio?

A. I am chief engineer for the Swinger Corporation.

Q. Swinger is a division or subsidiary of the Odyssey Corporation?

A. Yes.

Q. And you are here as the supervisory employee of the defendant, Odyssey Corporation, who has the most knowledge concerning the design, manufacturing procedures and of the materials used in its mobile home vehicle designated by the trade name Swinger?

A. Yes.

Q. How old are you, sir?

A. Twenty-eight.

Q. What is your educational and professional background—education and training?

A. I went to the Acme Institute of Technology for tool and die design.

Q. What is the nature of that institution?

A. It is tool and die design.

Q. Is it post-high school or instead of high school or post-college?

A. It is a technical institute after high school.

Q. How long did you go to the Acme Institute?

A. Three years.

Q. And did you obtain some sort of a degree?

A. It is a certificate; yes.

Q. Thereafter did you attend any other educational institution on a regular basis?

A. No.

Q. So you graduated from the Acme Institute then in what year?

A. Yr.–9, I believe.

Q. In Yr.–9 did you go to work?

A. Yes.

Q. For whom, please?

A. Holiday Rambler Corporation.

Q. What is the nature of that corporation, and where is it located?

A. They build recreational vehicles, and it is located in Indiana.

Q. What was your work with Holiday recreational vehicles?

A. I worked in the engineering department.

Q. As what?

A. As a draftsman.

Q. How long did you work for Holiday?

A. Approximately two years.

Q. In Yr.–7 then, you went to work where?

A. I went to work for Cobra Industries, Incorporated.

Q. Is Cobra Industries also a manufacturer of recreational vehicles?

A. Yes.

Q. What was your work there?

A. I was—I started out as a chief engineer—excuse me, a chief draftsman in the engineering department.

Q. How long did you work for Cobra Industries?

A. Approximately two years.

Q. To Yr.–5?

A. Yes.

Q. When did you go to work for the Odyssey Corporation?

A. July of Yr.–5.

Q. Are you familiar with the Yr.–6 model year line of Swingers?

A. Yes.

Q. Are you familiar with the design process for the Yr.–6 model year?

A. Yes.

Q. How did you become familiar with the design process?

A. That vehicle was in production—the same style of vehicle was in production when I started, and I took over the design of that vehicle, and by the drawings and records that we had there, it was obvious as to how it was laid out and designed.

Q. How long has Odyssey, to your knowledge, been in the business of manufacturing motor homes?

A. I don't know the date when they started.

Q. How many people performing engineering functions are employed by Odyssey who are involved in the manufacturing and designing of the Swinger recreational vehicles?

A. At this time?

Q. Yes.

A. Three.

Q. Do any of them have engineering degrees?

A. No.

Q. To your knowledge at the time I think in Yr.–7 when the Swinger Yr.–6 model would be designed, were any of the people in the engineering department involved in the Swinger's design holders of engineering degrees?

A. To the best of my knowledge, I don't know.

Q. Just for reference, Mr. Terrio, unless I specify otherwise, we will be talking from here on in of the Yr.–6 model year. Describe the manufacturing process for the 22-foot Squire using the Dodge RM–350 chassis. You might start with how the chassis is delivered.

A. The chassis is delivered with no body on it as such.

Q. It consists of the frame, the wheels, the fuel system, the transmission and the engine?

A. Exhaust system, yes.

Q. And the steering mechanism?

A. Yes.

Q. And then what happens to it?

A. The chassis goes into a chassis prep stage where there is a plastic seat on it; some brackets to hold parts on that are removed. We do not use them.

The parts package is removed from the chassis, and then it goes into the welding stage where a steel floor and a pilot floor which is up at the driver's compartment is welded to the chassis.

Q. You say there is a steel floor under the driver's compartment?

A. Yes.

Q. What is the gauge of that steel?

A. Eleven gauge. There are thicker gauges of steel in different areas. The gauges do vary.

Q. Go ahead.

A. In this stage of production, the LP gas tank is installed. The auxiliary fuel tank is installed. The auxiliary fuel tank is an option. It is installed between the rails in the rear on this particular model that we are discussing, the 22-foot Squire.

Q. Is there any particular reason why it is installed within the rails?

A. Basically just—there is a hold there, and there is only so many places you can put it. The—we call it recreational vehicle batteries—they are installed.

Q. Where are they installed?

A. On this vehicle they were installed above the transmission.

Q. So that they would end up inside the passenger compartment?

A. They are accessible from the inside, yes. They are sealed off to the inside.

Q. How are they sealed off?

A. There is a hinge plate that goes over the top that you remove your engine cover and tilt the plate back to get to it. It leaves that stage and goes into a rough plumbing station where the water tank is set on the chassis; the bathroom in parts is set on the chassis.

There are some water lines installed and some drainage lines installed. Then all the low floor drainage lines are completed at that stage. And then it goes to the next production stage where the side walls are placed on the vehicle.

Q. How is that done?

A. The side walls are built in a fixture and set on the vehicle and screwed with tek screws into the steel, the steel floor that was put on back in the welding shop. Then it would go to the next stage.

Q. What is the next stage?

A. The next stage is cabinet setting.

Q. What are your walls made out of?

A. 2 x 2 dadoed wood on 16-inch centers.

Q. What is dadoed wood?

A. It is dadoed. It is interlocking.

Q. What is it? Is it plywood?

A. It is spruce.

Q. What thickness?

A. It is 2 x 2—the actual dimension of the wood is an inch and a half square.

Q. Is that the frame you are talking about now?

A. That is the structure of the side walls. There are belt rails—what we call belt rails which run longitudinal through the dadoes in the side wall studs. There are three of those on each side.

Q. As I get your picture, this is the framing you are talking about for the walls?

A. Yes.

Q. What are the walls, themselves, made out of?

A. The interior walls?

Q. Yes.

A. That is three-sixteenths lauan paneling.

Q. Is any of this wood treated with any fire retardants?

A. Yes.

Q. Which wood?

A. All—the three-sixteenths paneling is treated with fire retardants.

Q. What kind of fire retardants.

A. It is treated to pass the Federal Motor Vehicle Safety Standard No. 302 which is a Class C rating.

Q. It is a Class C rating?

A. Yes.

Q. That means flame propagates—

A. 200 feet per minute. In the cabinet setting stage, all interior partitions—all dinettes, cabinets, overheads are placed in the vehicle. Then the roof is put on in the same stage.

The roof is preassembled on a fixture table. It is set on top and fastened to the side walls. Then it leaves that stage and goes into a rough wiring stage where the 110 volt wires are installed and some partial 12 volt wires are installed, and then it goes to the next stage which is a—like a finishing wiring stage where all lights are installed—all the wires that were installed previously are now hooked up, receptacles are put in; everything is terminated—all the wires are terminated where they belong in other words.

Then it goes to the next stage where the cabinet doors are put on the cabinets, hinges; the doorknobs are all preassembled. In this stage they fasten them to the cabinets and interior trim work is completed—molding out all the exposed rough edges, the corners, and so forth.

It goes to the next station where the fiber glass and insulation is installed in the walls and roof. Then the outside plating which is three-sixteenth lauan is installed. That covers the entire exterior of the vehicle. The two side walls, roof—the roof metal is installed here.

Q. What is the roof metal?

A. At that time it was 30 gauge galvanized—.030 galvanized.

Q. That is thinner than the steel which you say is on the floor?

A. Yes. The front and back fiber glass caps are installed here. Then it leaves that station and goes to another station.

In this station the exterior metal is installed, top and bottom wraps. All exterior molding is put on here. At some of these other stations in the final electrical station, the dash is installed, and in the plating station, all roof domes—Aluma-domes—in this case the escape hatch is installed there. Should the vehicle require an air conditioner, it is installed in that station. Then it goes to the metal station.

Q. Let me ask you this question: Is the lauan paneling treated at the Odyssey plant?

A. No.

Q. You buy that from another supplier?

A. Yes.

Q. And that supplier tells you that it meets a Class C fire propagation rating?

A. Yes.

Q. You don't know what is done to that paneling, if anything, to make it meet that rating, do you?

A. Each sheet is stamped on the back that it passes the required regulation.

Q. But you won't know if that is treated with a fire retardant or whether a Class C rating is just a natural property of that particular type of paneling; isn't that so?

A. I personally know it is treated.

Q. With what is it treated?

A. It is treated with a chemical.

Q. What chemical?

A. That I don't know.

Q. How do you know it is treated with a chemical?

A. From working with these suppliers.

Q. Have you seen them make it?

A. No, I have not.

Q. Who was the supplier at that time for the lauan paneling used?

A. I do not know.

Q. Do you have records at the plant that would tell you that?

A. Yes.

Q. What material were the overhead and rear cabinets made of?

A. The structure was spruce wood.

Q. The framing was spruce?

A. Yes.

Q. That is Class C material?

A. Yes. And the plating or the facing material was three-sixteenths paneling.

Q. That is the lauan paneling?

A. Yes.

Q. Now, in the Answers to Interrogatories, the company indicated that it was unable to determine or had no documents which indicated where the center of gravity of the 22-foot Squire was located with respect to three axes. Are you familiar with that question and answer? Have you seen it?

A. No.

Q. Let me put this question to you: Do you know or do you have any documents which locate the center of gravity of the 22-foot Squire for the Yr.–6 model year?

A. No.

Q. Do you know where the center of gravity of this vehicle is?

A. No.

Q. Do you know what angle from the vertical the vehicle can be tilted just before it will rollover?

A. No.

Q. Will you agree with me that in designing a recreational vehicle one of the primary considerations must be the safety of the occupants?

A. Yes.

Q. Will you also agree that emergency situations have to be considered in the design of the recreational vehicle?

A. Emergencies like what?

Q. In general, will you agree that certainly some emergency situations must be considered? Is that correct?

A. Yes.

Q. Based on your knowledge that you have gained that you have told us about from examining the various documents, drawings and specifications concerning the 22-foot Squire for the Yr.–6 model year and what you have learned from talking to your predecessor and others working at the company, what emergencies were considered in designing this particular Squire?

MR. LEAVITT. Objection. If you do anything that is going to give the witness a tipoff, there is going to be some real problems.

A. By the term emergency as you stated it, I would take that to mean like an exit other than the entrance door. I know they did because on our documents it shows the location of the emergency exit hatch.

Q. Is that the only emergency situation that you are aware of from the knowledge you have gained as head of the engineering department for Odyssey?

A. The word emergency covers a broad range.

Q. Intentionally so.

A. I would say there are other areas which they carefully control which would be weight distribution.

Q. Anything else?

A. The number and location of seat belts.

Q. Anything else?

A. Dashboard illumination, visibility. There are many more small areas that have to be taken into consideration when you are—

Q. What were they based on from your knowledge derived from your work at Odyssey?

A. The operation and location of all defroster—windshield defrost mechanisms; heat—interior heating location. Just the basic operability of the vehicle.

Q. I note that you have not named as one of the emergencies fire. Is that because so far as you can tell from examination of the documents relating to the design and manufacture of the 22-foot Squire, that fire emergencies were not considered?

A. No; that was taken into consideration.

Q. What was done in the design of this vehicle to reduce the hazard of injury or death to the occupants from fire?

A. All materials on the interior of the vehicle is treated to pass the Federal Motor Vehicle Safety Standard No. 302.

Q. What you are saying is that all materials in the vehicle are rated Class C on it for flame propagation rate, is that correct?

A. No.

Q. Is that the thing in the design that was done to reduce the risk of injury to the occupants by fire?

A. No.

Q. What else was done?

A. The electrical system, the 110 volt electrical system. We install breakers to prevent electrical shorts. It does not really prevent electrical shorts; it is to prohibit them from causing damage.

We install fuses in our 12 volt wires. Should a short occur, it will stop the chance of a fire.

Wall connections on our LP gas lines are in areas where they would not be considered as a compartment where gas should accumulate should a leak develop. In other words all connections are below the floor so that gas is dissipated in the air in the outside atmosphere.

Q. Now, have you exhausted—have you told us everything that was done by Odyssey in the design of the 22-foot Squire to reduce the risk of injury by fire?

A. No. All the installation of all appliances—the recommended manufacturer's installation instructions were followed to maintain all clearances for heat-producing appliances. The clearances —for instance above the range to the nearest combustible material were adhered to.

Q. Have you now finished telling us what was done in the design and manufacture of this vehicle to reduce the risk of fire—risk of injury by fire?

A. That is all the major items, yes.

Q. On drawing number—on print number 3733850 entitled RM–350 in Exhibit 4 for Identification which is the Yr.–6 Dodge Motor Home Body Builder's Book there is a location indicated labeled 40 gallon F tank which I take means fuel tank, optional location, 12 inches forward, 159 wheel base only.

What does that mean?

A. There are holes drilled in the chassis rail of the chassis which would allow us to completely disconnect the fuel tank and slide it forward 12 inches for an optional location.

Q. On the 22-foot Squire covered by Exhibit 1, was this optional location used for the gas tank or was it not?

A. I don't know.

Q. What was the capacity of that gas tank—this gas tank that we have been talking about, the so-called primary gas tank?

A. Yes, it is what we call the main gas tank.

Q. Now, what was the capacity of that gas tank?

A. Forty gallon—

Q. Of what material is that gas tank made?

A. The basic material is steel.

Q. And what gauge?

A. I do not know.

Q. How is that gas tank attached to the chassis?

A. There are straps. To the best of my knowledge there are two straps around the tank, completely around the tank, and it sits on a formed hat channel.

Q. Is it made up of two brackets?

A. That makes up the two brackets, yes. The brackets are an L-shaped bracket, and those are bolted to the frame.

Q. And the gas tank is secured by two metal straps that are wrapped around it and then attached to the brackets?

A. Yes.

Q. And that is the extent of the attachment of this gas tank to the chassis, is that correct?

A. Yes.

Q. Now, how is the fill neck attached to the gas tank? Is there a rubber grommet, or is it soldered to weld it on, or is it secured in some other manner?

A. On that particular vehicle, I don't know.

Q. In the gasoline distribution system, the fuel lines, are any of the fuel line attachments or connections or the fuel lines, themselves, made up of rubber or plastic or other non-metallic material?

A. To the best of my knowledge it is a metal fuel line.

Q. There are no non-metallic attachments as far as you know?

A. No, I believe there are some rubber attachments.

Q. Where are these rubber attachments?

A. Right at the connection to the gasoline tank. And also right where the gas line attaches to the fuel pump rubber is used.

Q. I notice that when you were telling us about the manufacturing process, you didn't mention any inspection procedures. Is that inadvertent or are there no—

A. Yes, there are several.

Q. Would you describe fully the inspection procedures followed during the manufacture of the 22-foot Swinger from the time the chassis arrives to the time that the completed product leaves the plant?

A. When the chassis arrives, before we even sign for the chassis, it is visually inspected for any damage, missing parts, anything of this nature; that is it, and it is noted, and we are reimbursed for them by the manufacturer of the chassis. The department—the individual department foreman in charge of each station or each group of stations, they are divided up in the plant, visually inspects all the work done at his station to see that it is done correctly.

Q. On each piece or randomly or—

A. No, each one. It is not—

Q. It is a hundred percent inspection?

A. He doesn't inspect each bolt. It is a visual inspection to see that all the material that was supposed to be installed in that station was indeed installed and just a—it is a visual inspection that he agrees that it was installed correctly.

Then as the—as the chassis proceeds down the production line, the LP gas system, once all the lines are installed and all the fittings are tightened, is subjected to a pressure test which tells us if there is a fitting either loose, not connected or perhaps even a defective fitting somewhere, and if there shows a leak, it is traced down and found and sealed and retested until it will pass that test, and then it proceeds on down the production line. As it reaches the final electrical stage—no, excuse me, the plating stage, a buzzer—it is a horn, an interplant horn, is hooked to the electrical system of the vehicle, and while the people are installing the exterior plating, the roof, the fiber glass caps, and so on, should a staple, a screw, a nail, anything penetrate a wire, that buzzer will go off. When that happens, everybody stops, backs out the last staple or screw, whatever they put in, until the horn stops, and then they tear apart—find the wire that was pierced, repair it and then go on.

Then the vehicle goes down to the—what would be the final finish area, and it is subjected to a plumbing test where the holding tanks are filled to capacity. The water—after the holding tanks are full, the water is continued into the system until it reaches the top of the stool, and then it is watched and monitored for any leakage.

They check all drainage lines for leakage. If they find it, it is repaired, and then it goes on. At that same station, they also do a water system check of the water lines. They subject it to a pressure, and should a leak occur, they trace it down, repair it, and it must maintain a pressure for 15 minutes, constant pressure, and also at the same station they dielectric test the 12 volt wires and the 110 volt wires of the vehicle. In that test they subject it to a range of four different voltages, the maximum being over a thousand volts. 1,080 volts. Also in the same station we do another LP gas test. That is a lower pressure test than the previous one which tests all the connections to the appliances, themselves.

In the last station of the production line, there is a person who is in charge of quality control to quality inspect the coach. In other words to see that all parts are there, that everything was done in a quality manner, that all trim work is in, all the draperies are there, et cetera. This person also checks to see that all tests were performed on the vehicle. As each person performs the test, they initial what we call a hard copy that follows the vehicle down the production line stating that he did complete that test.

Q. Now, have you completed the description of the testing inspection of the testing inspection procedures?

A. Yes.

Q. Was any testing done as part of the design process to determine the stability of this vehicle on the road?

A. Each new model was weighed—

Q. And that is the test that was done?

A. Yes.

Q. Was there any shielding of any kind placed around the gasoline tank, the primary gasoline tank, or the main gasoline tank on the 22-foot Squire?

A. The side wall extends down below—what we would call the frame structure, our frame structure that is bolted to the top of the chassis. That extends down to very near the bottom of the gas tank.

Q. It does not go underneath it?

A. No.

Q. And this consists of aluminum siding?

A. Wood.

Q. What is the thickness of that wood?

A. It is 2 x 2—2 x 2 wood.

Q. There is a solid wall of 2 x 2 wood extending down?

A. Oh, on 16-inch centers.

Q. So you have got a frame of 2 x 2 wood along the side?

A. Yes.

Q. And that is covered by the aluminum siding?

A. Yes.

Q. And that aluminum siding is what gauge did you say?

A. .024.

Q. And how many members extend down over the side of the gas tank?

A. Wood members?

Q. Yes.

A. In the area of the tank?

Q. Yes.

A. Approximately four.

Q. It is true that after you—after the front axle, the bottom of this gas tank is the lowest item on the chassis?

A. Yes.

Q. And there is no protection underneath the gas tank?

A. The only protection there would be the brackets that actually hold the gas tank.

Q. Now, has Odyssey carried out any crash tests to determine under what conditions the fuel system on any of its Swingers will maintain its integrity?

A. No.

Q. To your knowledge has Magnum conducted any such tests with respect to the chassis used on the 22–foot Squire?

A. I do not know.

Q. Are there any records at Odyssey that you have seen which indicate whether or not Odyssey has made inquiry of Magnum Corporation if Magnum has made such tests?

A. To my knowledge, there is no such document.

Q. Has the gas tank used as the main gas tank on the 22-foot Squire ever been subjected to any kind of stress or impact tests by anybody at Odyssey or on behalf of Odyssey to your knowledge?

A. To my knowledge, no.

Q. Did any documents that you have seen indicate whether or not such tests were ever requested by anyone at Odyssey?

A. No.

Q. Are there any records which would indicate whether or not the vendor was asked to treat this three-quarter inch plywood with any flame retardants?

A. I don't know.

Q. Was Odyssey given any guarantees by any of the vendors concerning the flammability characteristics of the three-quarter inch plywood used in the floor?

A. I don't know.

Q. Have you ever seen such guarantees?

A. Not on the plywood, no.

Q. What kind of carpeting was used on the 22-foot Squire covered by Exhibit 1?

A. You are asking me what the supplier's name is?

Q. Well, what kind, first of all, by material?

A. I don't know.

Q. Did Odyssey ever conduct any flammability tests on the carpeting used in the 22-foot Squire?

A. No.

Q. Did Odyssey obtain any guarantees concerning the flammability of the carpeting from its vendors?

A. I don't know.

Q. What is the flame spread rating of the carpeting?

A. Class C.

Q. Has any testing been done by Odyssey or in Odyssey's behalf to determine the effect of extreme heat aside from flame on the carpeting used on the flooring?

A. No.

Q. Do you know what gases, if any, are released when that carpeting is subjected to high levels of heat?

A. No.

Q. To your knowledge has anybody at Odyssey bothered to find out?

A. No.

Q. Now, this lauan paneling, can you tell us what it consists of?

A. It is plywood is what it is.

Q. And has Odyssey ever subjected it to any tests to determine its flammability or the rate of flame propagation?

A. Not to my knowledge, no.

Q. Has the manufacturer or any of the vendors of this paneling given any written guarantees to Odyssey concerning the flammability characteristics of the paneling?

A. I can't answer that. I don't know.

Q. You don't know?

A. No.

Q. What windows have drapes on the 22-foot Squire, Yr.–6 model?

A. All of them have drapes.

Q. What are the drapes made out of?

A. I don't know at that time what the material was.

Q. Now, according to the brochure, Exhibit 2 for Identification, it has laminate counters and table tops. What are laminate counters and table tops?

A. In that instance it is called laminant. It is five-eighths thick particle board with a .028—I am going to use a technical term —Formica top. That is a brand name but we didn't necessarily use Formica.

Q. Is that a plastic?

A. Yes, it is a vinyl—I don't know.

Q. Who is your vendor for the laminate?

A. I don't know.

Q. Do you know what kind of plastic is was?

A. No.

Q. Was it polyurethane?

A. No, definitely not.

Q. Polystyrene?

A. No.

Q. Polyvinyl chloride?

A. No.

Q. And what was the particle board made out of?

A. The particle board is a compressed board made up of adhesive and wood shavings.

Q. What kind of adhesive was used?

A. I don't know.

Q. Was it flammable?

A. Yes.

Q. According to the brochure, the cushions—there were cushions with—high-density foam cushions. Did that apply to the 22-foot Swinger we are talking about?

A. Yes.

Q. What was the foam made out of?

A. I can't think of what it was. I can't say for sure. I know it but I can't think of what it is now.

Q. Was that foam flammable?

A. I don't know. I would assume it would be.

Q. Was it some sort of a plastic compound, is that right?

A. I think so—a poly something.

Q. Now, there was 2 inches of fiber glass insulation in the walls of the Swinger, is that right?

A. Yes.

Q. What kind of fiber glass was it? Was it on rolls or—

A. It is on rolls.

Q. What was its backing made out of?

A. There was no backing.

Q. Just the plain fiber glass?

A. Yes.

Q. Was it true fiber glass, or was it some substitute?

A. No, it was fiber glass.

Q. Who was the vendor, do you know?

A. I don't know for sure. Like I said there are different vendors again so—the one that was purchased at that time, I don't know.

Q. You have told us earlier that all the interior materials on the Swinger complied with Federal Standard 302, is that right?

A. Yes.

Q. Have you seen any documents at Odyssey that indicates that any of these interior materials were tested according to the test procedure prescribed in Federal Standard 302?

A. Yes.

Q. Please identify then these documents that you have seen.

A. There were letters of certification from suppliers to us on the ones that I have seen on draperies, on both units, bath components such as the stool and a tub. I have seen it on an accordian door, on ABS plastic material. I have seen it on vinyl.

That is about all I can remember right now.

Q. Now, what type of resin was used in the fiber glass for the exterior, the front and rear ends?

A. I don't know.

Q. Was it treated with flame retardants?

A. To the best of my knowledge, no, it was not.

Q. You have shown me Page 24 of the Swinger Motor Home Owner's Manual which has been previously supplied in Answers to Interrogatories, and you indicated to me a photograph with the legend, "Escape hatch vent" which states "Optional on 18 foot models, standard on all other models. To operate, turn crank one turn, pull latch and push up complete hatch. Refer to instructions labeled on the hatch, itself."

Now, what I have asked for is the documents which will tell us what the instruction on the hatch, itself, says. Do you have those?

A. No.

Q. Are there any documents which will tell us what the label says?

A. I don't have any, no.

Q. Have you a copy of the label?

A. No.

Q. Is there a copy of the label in existence at Odyssey?

A. Yes.

Q. Who has a copy of that label?

A. They come in right on the escape hatch. The supplier puts the label on.

Q. What does the label say?

A. I don't know the exact terminology.

Q. Could you explain to me why there is no picture of the label in the instruction manual on Page 24?

A. No, I don't know.

Q. Were there insect screens on this hatch?

A. Yes.

Q. And how were they attached?

A. They are just part of the hatch.

Q. In order to get out, you have to somehow remove the insect screen, do you not?

A. No, that all goes with it. When you open the exit hatch, the screen and everything goes with it. It is all in one operation.

Q. And what are the dimensions of this exit hatch?

A. Approximately 22 inches square.

Q. Who is the vendor?

A. I don't know.

Q. Can you tell us what the considerations were in determining the size hatch that would be installed in this camper?

A. To the best of my knowledge that was the only size escape hatch available to the industry at that time.

Q. Was this hatch designed specifically for the recreational vehicle industry, or did it have other uses?

A. I would assume it was designed for the recreational vehicle industry.

Q. But you don't know?

A. I do not know, no.

Q. Was any consideration given by anyone at Odyssey to Odyssey making its own hatch?

A. No.

Q. Why not?

A. There is no money in making it. It is cheaper to buy it than to make it. We don't have the facilities—

Q. So the decision to use this kind of a hatch rather than to make one that would be larger was based entirely on an economic consideration?

A. No.

Q. What other consideration other than economic?

A. We did not have the technology or the ability to make the hatch. It is a molded lid which is—we don't have the equipment to do that.

Q. And the reason the equipment wasn't purchased was because it would be too expensive, is that right?

A. I don't know.

Q. Was any consideration ever given so far as you know from your examination of the documents relating to the design of the Swinger—was any consideration given to purchasing the equipment to make the hatch?

A. To my knowledge, no.

Q. Was any attempt made so far as you can tell from the examination of the documents to have a larger hatch made for Odyssey?

A. No.

Q. Now, sir, you say there was a label on these hatches with instructions to use them—how to use them, is that right?

A. Yes.

Q. How large was the label?

A. Approximately 1½ inches high x 4–4½ inches long.

Q. And how large was the lettering? An eighth of an inch high, a quarter inch high?

A. To my knowledge it is approaching a half an inch.

Q. And what color was the writing?

A. Silver.

Q. And where on the hatch was it located?

A. Right next to the handle—right next to the exit handle, itself.

Q. Is the exit handle shown in this picture on Page 24 of the Motor Home Owner's Manual?

A. Yes, you can just barely see it. See it? Right here (Indicating).

Q. What angle with the roof is the label? Is it parallel to the—

A. Perpendicular to it.

Q. It is perpendicular to the roof?

A. Yes.

Q. Now, do all the windows on the 22-foot Squire open?

A. No.

Q. Which windows do open?

A. It is not an easy question to answer. There is a window over the dinette behind the passenger that opens.

Q. And in its fully open position, what are the dimensions of the opening?

A. I don't know.

Q. Were the windows made by Odyssey or were they purchased from another—

A. They were purchased.

Q. Who was the vendor?

A. Adams West Lake.

Q. Are there documents in the possession of Odyssey which would indicate the dimensions of these windows when opened?

A. Not to my knowledge, no.

Q. Would you agree that this window is not suitable as an emergency escape opening? The window that you just described is not intended to be used as a means of emergency egress, is it?

A. No.

Q. That is because the opening is too small to be adequate for such a purpose, is that so?

A. No.

Q. Why is it not intended to be used?

A. It is intended for ventilation. That is what it was put there for.

Q. And it is not suitable because of its size and shape for use as an escape—means of escape, isn't that so?

A. To the best of my knowledge that window is large enough for emergency exit.

Q. How large is it?

A. The total window opening—the total window area is 22 x 58.

Q. 22 inches high by 58 inches long?

A. Yes.

Q. And when open?

A. I believe at that time on those windows half of that area was exposed.

Q. So it would be 22 by about 29, is that right?

A. Yes.

Q. And is this window opened by sliding?

A. Yes.

Q. What other windows open?

A. The driver and passenger side windows open.

Q. What were their opened dimensions?

A. The height is 34 inches by approximately 18 to 20 inches.

Q. And these open by sliding?

A. Yes.

Q. Now, were there any other labels or decals other than the one you have told us about by the escape hatch which indicated the location of the escape hatch?

A. No.

Q. If in the course of an emergency the electrical system failed, what means of illumination—emergency illumination was provided, if any, in the 22-foot Swinger, Yr.–6 model?

A. None.

Q. Was any consideration ever given to an emergency illumination system for the escape hatches?

A. To my knowledge, no.

Q. Are you familiar at all with the principles of so-called human engineering?

A. The size of the human body.

Q. The size and the function of the operator as it relates to the design of a machine or product.

A. I am to a limited degree, yes.

Q. And do you agree that one of the principles that have to be followed in proper design is the recognition that some operators at all times and most operators under sufficient stress will fall short of their potential for proper operation of the equipment?

A. I would imagine, yes.

Q. And therefore you would agree that proper design of escape mechanisms in any vehicle must have plenty of margin of safety so that people who are operating under stress can use it effectively, isn't that true?

A. Yes.

Q. From your examination of the corporate documents that relate to the design of the 22-foot Swinger, can you tell us whether or not any consideration was given to assisting persons to find the escape hatch when in darkness?

A. To the best of my knowledge, no.

Q. Certainly it would have been feasible to have a battery-operated light indicating the location of the emergency exit to be designed to actuate if the electrical system failed, isn't that true?

A. You are referring to a power system that is adhered only to the escape hatch?

Q. Yes.

A. It is possible.

Q. Now, have you brought with you any drawings or other documents which show the construction of the door frame?

A. Of the entrance door, itself?

Q. Yes.

A. I have drawings showing the rough opening we built for the door.

Q. And you can tell us what that material is made out of, what the frame is made out of?

A. For the cutout opening in the side wall, it was wood, 2 x 3 wood.

Q. 2 x 3 wood?

A. Yes.

Q. What about the door frame, itself? What was that?

A. Aluminum.

Q. Was that screwed onto the wood?

A. Yes.

Q. Now, was any consideration given to putting a second door or second means of emergency egress in the rear of this 22-foot Swinger on the Yr.–6 model?

A. I don't know.

Q. At least the documents you have seen that relate to the designing of this vehicle don't indicate that any consideration was given to putting an escape hatch or means of egress in the rear, is that a fair statement?

A. The drawings show that there were no other emergency exits that were planned as emergency exits other than the escape hatch in the roof.

Q. Was any consideration given to putting a door or escape hatch in the rear of the vehicle from what you can tell by looking at the documents?

A. I don't know.

Q. Have you ever worked in the mobile home industry?

A. I worked—I built one mobile home for Odyssey in the space of about two months. That is my only experience in the mobile home industry.

Q. When you say you built one, you made one or designed one?

A. It was a special program. It was a complete prototype, brand-new construction, and so forth.

Q. You designed it?

A. Yes, I designed the mobile home as such. I did not design the technology that went into it.

Q. In the course of your work and experience in the recreational vehicle industry and whatever experience you had, things you had to learn in making this mobile home, did you become familiar with the various fire problems, fire risks in mobile homes?

A. Yes. I think maybe I better explain what I did to this mobile home. It was a project sponsored by another company, completely paid by that company, and we set up in our research and development building the necessary equipment to build this mobile home. It underwent very, very rigorous testing both by ourselves, by several other independent testing laboratories such as structural strengths and fire resistance.

One was built, and that was it. It was never put into production.

Q. Now, one of the fire hazards in mobile homes is that fire tends to spread very quickly and burn very intensely in them, isn't that so?

A. From the tests I saw, yes.

Q. And that is primarily because materials that are used are flammable, light weight, and the space in which the fire burns is confined?

A. I don't know the reasons why the fire burns as fast as what it appears to.

Q. Do you agree that with respect to the rapidity of burning and the heat, that the risks and hazards in a mobile home are substantially the same as in a recreational vehicle?

A. No.

Q. In what respect are they different?

A. The layout of the floor plan is probably one of the biggest reasons.

Q. Why is that?

A. In a mobile home you have a long hallway which creates a tunnel which will feed the fire; in a motor home there is no—you have a hallway but it is broken up by cabinets, and the flames can't just shoot down the hallway.

Q. Is that the only difference?

A. That I know of, yes.

Q. Are you aware of any tests that have been done with respect to the fire hazards in recreational vehicles?

A. No.

Q. So your answer that the hazard isn't as great because of the lack of the hallway is essentially a theoretical answer, isn't that true?

A. It is my opinion based on the test results that I saw from the fire tests ran on the mobile home.

Q. You have never seen any comparable tests run on recreational vehicle bodies, have you?

A. No.

Q. Essentially you use the same methods of construction at Odyssey that are used in mobile homes, isn't that true?

A. The mobile home that I built is a totally new structure to this industry; it is not related at all to what we do now or what we did then in the Yr.–6—

Q. In the absence of a long, unbroken hallway in a recreational vehicle, in what respects are the fire risks different than in a mobile home?

A. I don't know.

Q. One respect that they are different is that the recreational vehicle may carry from 25 to 65 gallons of gasoline, isn't that so?

A. Yes, definitely. It carries its own fuel supply.

Q. Which the mobile home and trailer does not, isn't that so?

A. That's right.

Q. And in order to prevent this fuel supply from being a fire hazard, it is important that it be designed in such a way that it will maintain its integrity insofar as it's feasible in a collision or an accident, isn't that true?

A. Yes.

Q. It is also important when designing a recreational home so as to eliminate the fire caused by the gasoline to protect or insulate the passenger compartment from gasoline should the tank rupture, isn't that true?

A. Yes.

Q. It is important that any spilled gasoline be kept away from the passengers, isn't that so? That is true, also?

A. Yes.

Q. In order to do that, the partition that separates the gasoline system from the passengers must be strong enough to withstand tearing or disruption or puncturing and must also be able to withstand, for a sufficient period of time, heat generated by burning gasoline, isn't that true?

A. Yes.

Q. And it is also true that the alumium sheeting and the plywood and the nylon rug on the 22-foot Swinger will not withstand burning gas—the fire from burning gasoline, isn't that so?

A. That would depend how close it is from the driver.

Q. Well, from gasoline to the tank—

A. It would depend on the ventiliation from the area. If it is laying on its side, the wind can be blowing the heat away from it. There are many things that could enter into it.

Q. That aluminum sheeting was not designed or was not chosen to withstand the temperatures from a gasoline fire, isn't that true?

A. Yes.

Q. And except in fortuitous circumstances where the wind might blow the flame away from that aluminum sheeting, the gasoline fire is going to melt that very rapidly, isn't it?

A. Yes.

Q. Are you familiar with the LP gas system that was located in this vehicle?

A. I am familiar with LP gas systems.

Q. Are you familiar with the design of this particular LP gas system?

A. Through the drawings, yes.

Q. And was there a pressure relief valve as part of this system?

A. Yes, there was.

Q. Describe how that valve worked.

A. The valve works on the fact that if an excess amount of pressure builds up in the tank, it will at a rate that is—the safest rate as possible relieve that pressure.

Q. By letting the gas escape?

A. Yes.

Q. Now, in the owner's manual, you are familiar with the owner's manual for the Yr.–6 model, are you not?

A. I have seen it, yes.

Q. In the description of the transmission control quadrant, it states, relating to first gear, "Warning. To prevent excessive engine speed do not exceed 25 miles per hour in this range."

Now, what would the effect be if a driver were to drive in excess of 25 miles per hour in first gear?

A. To my knowledge it would damage the transmission.

Q. What sounds would the driver hear?

A. I don't know.

Q. Would he be aware that something was wrong if he inadvertently were driving at speeds faster than 25 miles per hour?

A. I would believe through sheer engine noise he would.

Q. So you would expect that an experienced driver, even if he had not been experienced in this particular vehicle, would know there was something wrong if he was driving in excess of 25 miles per hour in first gear, isn't that so?

A. I would assume so, yes.

Q. Was the fire extinguisher supplied as standard equipment?

A. Yes.

Q. And where was it located?

A. Next to the exterior door, the entrance door to the vehicle.

Q. Next to the entrance door to the vehicle?

A. Yes.

Q. On the inside or the outside?

A. Inside.

Q. What kind of fire extinguisher was it?

A. To the best of my knowledge it was a 5BC. I think they call it a 5 pound for B and C fires.

Q. I notice that in one of the diagrams that has been marked or blueprints that have been marked as an exhibit, there was a notation of a roll bar on the Swinger. Is there such a roll bar on the Swinger that is involved in this case?

A. As far as I know there was, yes.

Q. Now, these roll bars are on the sides, are they?

A. They are on the sides and across the roof.

Q. And what weight are they designed to withstand on a roll over?

A. I don't know.

Q. Have they ever been tested?

A. To my knowledge, no.

Q. Has the ability of the escape hatch to maintain its integrity in case the vehicle turns over on its side ever been tested?

A. To my knowledge, no.

Q. If the escape hatch frame does not maintain its integrity, it is likely to jam and be difficult, if not impossible, to open, isn't that so?

A. It would be my opinion but I would say that should it be jammed, it would pop open automatically.

Q. Why?

A. Because of the way it is designed.

Q. What is there about the design that would permit it to pop open rather than—

A. It sets inside a channel that has no grooves coming in, and it is all aluminum construction. If it should jam, the whole hatch, itself, would merely come together and pop the lid off it.

Q. Is there a way of blocking it from the inside?

A. The mechanism that opens the hatch also holds it shut.

Q. And that is a cranking device?

A. I don't know. I think it is a sliding device, isn't it? It slides.

Q. It slides?

A. Yes. You mean like a sliding bolt, is that what you mean?

Q. When you say it is a sliding device, what do you mean?

A. Yes, it is like a bolt—like a sliding bolt only it doesn't lock. In other words it doesn't—you know how a bolt—you would rotate it; this does not rotate.

Q. What does the crank do?

A. That simply opens the top and leaves the insect screen in a stationary position so it is just for ventilation.

Q. And in order to get the screen out, what do you have to do?

A. Slide—pull the slide mechanism, and it goes up automatically, or when you push it up.

Q. And then there are other hatches for ventilation on the roof of the Swinger?

A. Yes.

Q. And what are their inside dimensions?

A. They are approximately 14 inches square.

Q. You said the inside dimension of the escape hatch, so-called, was about 20—

A. 22 inches square.

Q. Now, there was a switch which permitted the driver to switch over from the main gas tank to the auxiliary gas tank.

A. Yes.

Q. And that is located where?

A. It was located at the driver's left hand.

Q. By the steering column?

A. Yes.

Deposition of David Cochin

EXAMINATION BY MR. MOREMAN

Q. Sir, would you please state your name?

A. David Cochin.

Q. Where do you work, sir?

A. Magnum Corporation, Detroit.

Q. How long have you worked for Magnum?

A. Twenty-one years.

Q. Have you always worked for that corporate entity?

A. Yes.

Q. When you started for Magnum, what was your position, sir?

A. I started in what is known as a Test and Development Engineer.

Q. What were your job duties as a person in that capacity?

A. Well, I started in the Advance Truck Engineering Department design engineering. My responsibilities were those of an incoming new engineer.

Q. You were right out of school?

A. Almost.

Q. Describe for me what the duties of a new incoming engineer would be.

A. Well, they would be performing theoretical analyses, stress calculations of brackets and parts, things that would be given to somebody that was technically trained but didn't have any experience in engineering.

Q. You were doing drafting, were you?

A. No, I was an engineer.

Q. So you were responsible for the design calculations, stress calculations, that kind of thing?

A. Yes.

Q. What division of Magnum Corporation did you come into 21 years ago?

A. I came into the Engineering Division. The department that I worked in was that of Truck Engineering.

Q. As a practical matter, what does that mean, the fact that you came into the Truck Engineering?

A. Our activity was limited to engineering as related to the truck products line as opposed to any other line such as passenger cars or anything.

Q. That's where you devoted most of your energies, is to trucks?

A. All of our energies.

Q. How long were you engaged in that capacity at that job?

A. 6 years.

Q. All facets of trucks, or limited to chassis at that time?

A. Limited to chassis.

Q. So right from the beginning of your experience with Magnum through Yr.–16 you were working on truck chassis?

A. Yes. Do you understand what chassis is?

Q. No.

A. Maybe I ought to qualify this a little bit. Chassis is the part that's below the body, if you like, which could be an engine. It could be a frame. It could be brakes. It could be axles.

Q. Could be all of those?

A. Any of those parts.

Q. Okay. It wouldn't include, for example, the cab?

A. It does not include the cab, sheet metal, fenders and such.

Q. Is a truck chassis a drivable unit?

A. Well, hardly. Yes, you can do it but you wouldn't like it.

Q. It's got the motor on it?

A. It's a prime mover, but you need a place to sit and operate it.

Q. It's got a transmission, engine, wheels?

A. Yes.

Q. Everything you need to move?

A. Yes.

Q. That's a truck chassis?

A. Yes.

Q. We'll use that definition for the rest of the Deposition, if that's all right with you.

Now, from Yr.–16 did you change positions?

A. Yes. In January of Yr.–16 I was made a Supervisor of Powertrain.

Q. Going back for a minute from the period Yr.–22 to Yr.–16, what did your job duties in that period consist of? What did you do on a day-to-day basis?

A. My responsibilities the latter part of that period were responsibilities which included the engine. So my job would have been to make sure that the engine that went into the truck and configured to do the job for that particular vehicle, whatever it took to do that.

Q. How about the earlier part of that period?

A. In the earlier part I handled frames, fuel systems—there is a number of areas. Oh, engine mounts, exhaust systems, front axles, some suspension work, possibly others.

Q. To the ones you have listed, are those the principal areas of responsibility?

A. Yes.

Q. What would doing the engineering work for a frame consist of? Would you put that in layman's terms?

A. All right. It would include the determination of the stresses in a frame for a given type of vehicle under a given load condition under all types of operation and the determination of suitable cross section in the frame side rail or the need for reinforcements; the section of the cross members; theoretical analysis of all of the components that go into make up the truck frame. The frame area would be very heavy on stress analysis.

Q. Now, tell me with respect to fuel systems what you mean by you handled fuel systems?

A. Handling of fuel systems would be the determination of the needs of the product for fuel capacity and then the design of a suitable fuel system to provide that fuel capacity within the vehicle configuration.

Q. What are the factors that go into designing a fuel system of a truck?

A. The factors that go into the designing of a fuel system would include the location of the tank on the vehicle, the selection of a location, the size of the tank, the type of the tank, the method of filling, venting the tank, the mounting, compliance with regulations and also achieve adequate product offering.

Q. What do you mean by an adequate product offering?

A. An adequate product offering would be whether there is enough range in the offering of tanks so that we've got a standard tank and we have perhaps one or more options without encumbering ourselves with an extensive number of options.

Q. So that the fuel system can be used on a bunch of different trucks; is that what you're saying?

A. It might be. It might be a standardization of parts from one vehicle to another. It might be just getting an adequate capacity on a given line of trucks.

Q. So with respect to the corporation, we're talking about, I suppose, the economy of being able to use these tanks in various products?

A. Economy wasn't a factor there. It was a question of not having four tanks when three tanks would meet all of the requirements.

Q. To get back to factors that go into the design of fuel tanks and fuel systems, you mentioned location of the tank on the vehicle. That's a factor apparently that's important to you?

A. Yes.

Q. For what reason?

A. Well, for many reasons. It's important from a standpoint of space available, from a compatibility with other components on the vehicle, from the ability to feed fuel to the engine from the selected location, and in some cases we have to return fuel to the tank from the engine, and last but not least, safety.

Q. All right. Why is that last category important?

A. Well, I think it's self-evident. I think it is a very important category. The selection of the location of a fuel tank is always done in regard to safety.

Q. That's always been true of your work on fuel systems?

A. Yes.

Q. You consider, as a motor vehicle designer, you consider that to be an important criteria?

A. Oh, yes.

Q. That is, safety of the location and configuration of a fuel system is something that would come within your expertise?

A. I would say so.

Q. That particular topic is something which you would consider to be within your expertise?

A. Yes.

Q. When did you get design responsibility?

A. Yr.–8.

Q. What does that mean here at Magnum, to get design responsibility?

A. I had the responsibility for the design and engineering of the powertrain.

Q. For all Magnum truck chassis?

A. Yes.

Q. How many truck chassis a year are we talking about back in Yr.–8?

A. Well, it would be a guess on my part.

Q. I want your best approximation.

A. 150,000 to 200,000.

Q. What has been your job description from Yr.–8 to the present?

A. That's my current job.

Q. Do you have a title?

A. Manager Chassis Engineering and Design.

Q. Again in layman's terms, what has your job over the last, let's say, two years consisted of on a day-to-day basis? What do you do?

A. Supervise the activities of the department.

Q. And those are the people who are designing chassis?

A. Yes, designing and engineering those portions of the chassis which come under powertrain.

Q. What other parts of the chassis are there besides powertrain?

A. There is the frame, suspension, steering, the brakes, wheels, hubs, drums, tires.

Q. Does the fuel system come under your supervision?

A. Yes.

Q. You're the top man right now in that area of chassis engineering for the powertrain?

A. In powertrain, yes.

Q. In the years subsequent to Yr.–8, roughly how many truck chassis a year is Magnum putting out?

A. Well, currently we're going to build between 450,000 and 500,000 units this year.

Q. How about for Yr.–6?

A. Well, again I don't know. It would be somewhere between the number that I gave you previously, which was 150,000 to 200,000 and the number which we just talked about, a half a million. It's been a fairly rapid climb through these years.

Q. For what reason, sir, do you know?

A. The success in certain markets.

Q. Such as?

A. Motor home is one. The B-Model van and wagons is another.

Q. Those are the two principal successful markets?

A. Yes, I would say so.

Q. In your opinion, those two areas are what we can contribute the increase in production to?

A. No, I don't think so. The whole market, our whole penetration has changed and I don't really know the figures. I know our conventional trucks have gone up. They just haven't shown as dramatic an increase as the B-Model vans and wagons.

Q. How about motor homes?

A. They've been dramatic.

Q. Now, when did they start to become dramatic?

A. Yr.–11. In Yr.–12 I was given responsibility to design the M-Model motor home chassis.

Q. That's the chassis we're talking about in this case?

A. We're talking in this case about a later version of that chassis.

Q. Essentially the same chassis?

A. Essentially similar.

Q. In other words, you designed a product that was going to be used for that specific task of carrying a motor home?

A. Yes.

Q. Did all final approvals, design concepts in the finished product have to be made by you?

A. Yes.

Q. I assume at some point they did that for the M-Model chassis?

A. Yes.

Q. Do you remember when that was when you gave it the final stamp of approval?

A. From the design standpoint?

Q. Yes.

A. It was approximately Yr.–12 that we completed the design. We built prototypes, tested the prototypes and made whatever changes were necessary. So it was probably the first of Yr.–11 when the final design approval was given.

Q. Was given by you?

A. Well, it was a collective program. You asked who was in charge of the design program. I was in charge of that. It wasn't solely my approval of the overall product.

Q. You approved the design configuration of the chassis?

A. I approved the design for release at that point based on the testing that had been done.

Q. What was the testing, by the way?

A. Prototype vehicles were built and tested by the proving grounds. I don't recall the number of vehicles.

Q. What kind of tests were done?

A. Well, one comes to mind. We make a steering compliance test. When you design a suspension and you design the steering for it, you work on the basis of theoretical points. When you build a prototype, you move the front axle through its full travel and compare what you did on paper with what happens in the iron. The report came back on that one that it was the closest compliance they had ever seen.

Q. Were there any crash tests?

A. No.

Q. Don't you usually do those on Magnum motor vehicles, passenger vehicles?

A. Present or past?

Q. Present?

A. Yes.

Q. You did them in Yr.–6?

A. Yes, I guess we were crashing in Yr.–6.

Q. But in any event, getting back to this M-chassis, no crash tests were done on that chassis?

A. That is correct.

Q. Did you ever test a chassis with a motor home built on top of it?

A. That's what we tested. A prototype was sent out and a body put on and the test was a complete unit.

Q. Did you see the body that was put on top of the chassis?

A. Yes, I saw that.

Q. Where was the door on that?

A. Right side behind the front axle.

Q. So between the two wheels on the right side?

A. Yes.

Q. Between the front axle and the back axle?

A. Yes.

Q. Where in relation to that location was the gasoline tank?

A. You mean how many feet apart was it?

Q. Yes, just describe as best you can.

A. On that installation it was probably ten feet—more than that, perhaps.

Q. Where was the gasoline tank?

A. On that one it was on the rear.

Q. Between the frame rails?

A. Yes.

Q. Was it over the rear axle or behind the rear axle?

A. Behind.

Q. Now, at the back of the vehicle is there a cross member going from one beam to the other?

A. Oh, yes.

Q. There is? All right. So there was a frame member rearward of the gasoline tank on that particular vehicle?

A. Yes.

Q. Did that prototype ever go into production?

A. Yes.

Q. With the gasoline tank in that place?

A. Yes.

Q. How many did you produce?

A. I couldn't tell you.

Q. Why was the gasoline tank placed there?

A. Because that's where it had been on the special equipment conversion.

Q. Why was it placed there on the special equipment conversions?

A. I don't have that information. We evaluated the location. It was a satisfactory location and we continued it in that position on the M-400.

Q. When you evaluated it, you used the factors we've already talked about today in the design and engineering of a fuel system?

A. Yes.

Q. One of those factors, and I think your words were "Last, but not least," one of those factors was safety?

A. Yes.

Q. You certainly applied that standard in your analysis of the rear placement of that gasoline tank?

A. Yes.

Q. What did you determine when you made that analysis?

A. It was a good location.

Q. From a safety standpoint?

A. Yes.

Q. Why was that?

A. It was under the body. It was protected by the body. The space was available for the tank in that location. The overhang was quite long on that particular vehicle, so that there was quite a bit of body behind it also.

Q. That adds safety?

A. Well, I think that subjectively it does.

Q. In fact it does?

A. I can't say that.

Q. All right. You say it was protected by the body. What parts of the body protected it, in your safety analysis?

A. Well, whatever body was around it.

Q. What body was around it? Did you have frame rails around it?

A. That's not the body.

Q. Okay. Tell me what portions.

A. It was under the vehicle. It wasn't exposed.

Q. It was not exposed?

A. That is right.

Q. By "exposed," what do you mean? Exposed to what?

A. You couldn't walk up to the gas tank. You couldn't walk up to the vehicle and touch the gas tank.

Q. It certainly didn't extend below the plane of the underside of the vehicle?

A. It did. Yes, it did.

Q. How far?

A. Oh, I don't know the dimension. That's one of the vulnerable points of that location.

Q. Is what?

A. The fact that it does extend below. It can be damaged from the rear. It's not a panacea by any means. These are all in balance, really. If a car were to hit a vehicle in the rear, it would go under and then contact the gas tank.

Q. But I think you said there was a lot of overhang in this M-400?

A. That is right. That's what I said when I said we evaluated it and said it was a satisfactory location, because it is further in.

Q. Provides shock absorption, right?

A. No, just further away.

Q. In the event of a rear end collision, it adds safety?

A. Yes.

Q. Now, it's between the frame rails on that M-400?

A. Yes.

Q. They add protection to it?

A. I would say they add some.

Q. In the event of a side impact, they would add—the frame rails would add some protection?

A. In the event of a frontal, it would be better yet, because it's at the other end. It just depends where you're coming from.

Q. I understand that. But in the event of a side impact, the frame rails add a measure of protection to the gas tank?

A. Again it depends how you attack the tank.

Q. Straight side impact?

A. How high? Something could go underneath the vehicle.

Q. Height of a motor vehicle? Height of a passenger car?

A. I don't know how the heights compare. I think the body affords more protection than the frame.

Q. Tell me all the directions the frame provides protection to the gas tank on the M-400.

A. Well, simply stated it would be anything that was coming from a direction that included the frame.

Q. And the frame was on three sides, right?

A. The frame was on two sides.

Q. And there was a cross member behind it?

A. Yes. But what I just said was that any direction that included the frame in its path. You see, it could be from inside the unit.

Q. It could be from outside, too?

A. Well, if you get outside, then you start to get below the tank. See, the tank is exposed from the side below the frame.

Q. Below the frame?

A. Yes.

Q. How much are you talking about? How much is exposed?

A. I can't recall the dimension.

Q. Is it inches we're talking about or feet?

A. Oh, yes.

Q. Not feet?

A. No.

Q. Number of inches?

A. Maybe eight inches.

Q. What is the overall height of—what was the overall height of the fuel tank on the M-400?

A. I couldn't tell you.

Q. Are you talking about inches or feet?

A. Well, it's not feet. It's a foot or less, perhaps.

Q. It's less than 12 inches, the height of the fuel tank?

A. I think it was.

Q. What's the width of the frame?

A. Thirty-four inches outside.

Q. What's the dimension of each frame rail?

A. I'd say it was about six inches deep with two and a half inch flanges, C-section.

Q. What are the dimensions of the cross piece that is in back of the gasoline tank on the M-400?

A. I don't know the dimensions. What I do remember is that the cross member behind the tank was not a heavy structural member.

Q. It was steel?

A. Yes, but it had a large hole in it because of the fill pipe coming through.

Q. Filled from the rear?

A. Yes.

Q. What was it there for? What was that piece there for, support?

A. To tie the end of the frame together.

Q. It's a structural member?

A. Yes. But the loads back there are greatly diminished.

Q. Now, in the M-400 the gasoline tank, was the top of it level with the top of the frame rails?

A. No.

Q. Below them?

A. Yes.

Q. By how much?

A. Perhaps an inch and a half.

Q. So the gasoline tank started about an inch and a half below the top frame rails?

A. Yes.

Q. We've already said that the frame rails were six and a half inches high?

A. I think I said six.

Q. So four and a half inches of the gasoline tank was between the frame rails, four and a half inches of the height of the gas tank?

A. If my estimates are accurate, that would be true.

Q. Now, at sometime the gasoline tank on this product was moved to the exterior of the frame rail on the curb side of the chassis, correct?

A. No.

Q. You're familiar with some of the specifics of this litigation. You know what the claims being made are?

A. I am somewhat familiar with it.

Q. It involved a vehicle identification number R49CG3S129038. Do you have to review that number or do you have something you can refer to?

A. Yes.

Q. Who manufactured that chassis? What corporation?

A. Magnum Corporation.

Q. Do you know when it was manufactured?

A. Early Yr.–6.

Q. Now, with respect to the ultimate use of these motor vehicle chassis, Magnum Corporation has recommended practices, does it not, for what a motor home manufacturer should do or should not do with the product that you make?

A. Magnum has recommended practices for an adaptation of a body to the chassis as it affects the chassis.

Q. And these are standards which the corporation suggests that manufacturers follow?

A. Yes.

Q. They're recommended practices with respect to the placement of the gasoline tank on your product, right?

A. Well, not exactly. We placed the fuel tank on the product.

Q. All right. You pick the best place for it?

A. That is right.

Q. You make recommendations to the companies that put motor home bodies on top of your chassis not to move the gasoline tank?

A. Yes.

Q. There are reasons that purchasers of the chassis are not supposed to move the gasoline tank, right?

A. Yes.

Q. One of them that you recommend—or one of the reasons for your recommendation is that moving the gasoline tank may impair the integrity of the gasoline tank?

A. That is right.

Q. One of the other bases for your recommended practice is that it might impair the mounting integrity of the gasoline tank to the vehicle?

A. That is right.

Q. You make those recommendations—by "you" I mean Magnum Corporation made those recommendations to the Odyssey Corporation?

A. I don't know that we did that. We make recommendations.

Q. To people who purchase your product?

A. We make recommendations to give to the sales department that they in turn will disseminate to the field.

Q. Your goal is to tell everybody?

A. That is right.

Q. Odyssey Corporation is a name you have heard before?

A. Yes.

Q. In other words, on the motor home the person who buys it from Magnum is recommended not to move the gas tank?

A. That is correct.

Q. That applies across the board to all models?

A. Yes.

Q. Including the vehicle that's involved in this accident?

A. That is correct.

Q. If that had been moved, would certain warranties be impaired, certain Magnum warranties?

A. They could be. If the fuel tank were moved and relocated elsewhere on the frame and additional holes were drilled in the frame in such a manner that it would contribute to a frame failure by lining up like toilet paper has holes in it and it failed at that point, then the warranty would be voided for that failure.

Q. On the RM–350, do you know whose decision it was to locate the gasoline tank on the side, on the curb side?

A. No.

Q. You approved the design?

A. Yes.

Q. You had final approval of the design with respect to the drive train aspect?

A. To the design, yes.

Q. And one of the facets of that was approving the location of the gasoline tank?

A. In part, yes.

Q. So you had the final say on the location of the gasoline tank?

A. I didn't say that.

Q. Did you have the final say on the location of the gasoline tank?

A. No, I wouldn't have the final say in the location. If somebody higher in management wanted it somewhere else, obviously they would have a higher say.

Q. At your level of management your say was final?

A. In my department.

Q. Okay. You could have been overturned by someone else.

A. Yes.

Q. But it wasn't?

A. That is right.

Q. And you approved of the location of the gasoline tank on the RM–350 where it was?

A. That is right.

Q. Now, was it your—and by "your" I mean you personally—was it your idea to put it where it was?

A. No.

Q. Whose idea was it?

A. I don't know.

Q. That's the way it came to you?

A. By tradition it had been there.

Q. There was no design reevaluation for gas tank location when the RM–350 was developed?

A. There was a design reevaluation at about that time. It was not later than—it was either in coincidence with or earlier than where we again reviewed the location.

Q. Of the gasoline tank?

A. Yes.

Q. For the RM–350?

A. I'm saying it was in coincidence with or preceded it.

Q. Were there then any written documents produced as a result of that reeevaluation?

A. I don't know of any.

Q. Were reports made?

A. No.

Q. Any memoranda of any kind?

A. None that I know of.

Q. You participated in that rethinking?

A. Yes.

Q. And apparently the decision was to leave it where it was?

A. Well, what I'm talking about was a change in the capacity of the tank to increase it. So when we increased the capacity, we again examined all of the parameters relative to the fuel tank.

Q. Which includes where it is on the vehicle?

A. Which includes where it is on the vehicle and we came to the same conclusion.

Q. To leave it there?

A. Yes.

Q. You participated in that rethinking?

A. Yes.

Q. And who participated in it?

A. Well, everybody that was involved with the fuel system at that time.

Q. Now, at that time were any tests performed on the vehicle to determine the best place to put the gas tank?

A. Was there any testing done when?

Q. Yr.–7. That's the time I'm talking about.

A. Well, we tested the new tanks.

Q. What did the testing consist of?

A. I don't recall. I'm not sure I ever knew.

Q. Were any crash tests performed?

A. No.

Q. Apparently you considered other locations at that time for the gasoline tank?

A. Yes.

Q. What other locations did you consider?

A. We looked at the rear of the frame.

Q. Why did you look there?

A. To standardize on the fuel tanks.

Q. What do you mean by that?

A. Well, we had—at the time we reconsidered the fuel tank offerings on these vehicles, some four, I think it was, arrangements; that is the M-chassis had, I think, four arrangements of fuel tanks.

Q. The first place you looked apparently was the rear of the frame?

A. I don't know if it was the first.

Q. You wanted to standardize the RM–350 with something else, with some other chassis that had it at the rear?

A. We were trying to arrive at one common fuel tank for all motor home chassis.

Q. In other words, the physical tank itself you wanted to standardize?

A. Yes.

Q. Was that the object of your analysis at that time?

A. Well, it was one of the factors that we considered at the time.

Q. What did your analysis of a rear location tell you?

A. There wasn't room.

Q. So you couldn't put it there?

A. That is right.

Q. Why wasn't there room?

A. There wasn't room because the frame overhang was too short.

Q. By frame overhang, what do you mean?

A. We term the frame behind the rear axle as frame overhang.

Q. Now, it would have been possible for you to design or redesign a tank that would fit into that space?

A. No.

Q. What is the reason for that?

A. Well, there is a cross member in that space. There is also an axle in that space.

Q. So that the primary problem of putting the tank in that location, I take it, was this cross member?

A. This cross member and there is a tailpipe in there also.

Q. But those two factors are really the major problems to putting it in there?

A. Yes.

Q. Now, alternative frame members could have been designed, could they not, that would replace this cross piece and yet allow room for the gasoline tank?

A. No. You have to have a cross member at that location because it reacts to the spring input, keeping the rails in place. You cannot obviate the need for that cross member.

Q. It could have been incorporated into a tank, could it not?

A. No.

Q. Why is that?

A. There is no technology for such an animal.

Q. Would you summarize again, please, the reasons—the principal reasons why you decided not to put it at the rear at that time?

A. Lack of capacity.

Q. Lack of space?

A. Fuel capacity, which is another way of saying lack of space.

Q. You could have put a smaller tank in?

A. Yes.

Q. What size tank could be put in there?

A. I don't recall.

Q. You could have designed a tank to fit in that space?

A. It would have been a different shape tank.

Q. But it could have been done?

A. Yes.

Q. Technically there is no problem with that?

A. Okay, it could be done.

Q. No insurmountable problem?

A. Okay.

Q. What capacity would the tank have been?

A. I still don't know.

Q. Now, where else did you consider putting the gasoline tank?

A. Well, we looked at putting it inside the frame.

Q. Middle of the vehicle?

A. In the middle of the vehicle.

Q. Where you didn't have the problem of cross members?

A. We have cross member problems.

Q. What did you find when you analyzed putting it in the middle of the vehicle?

A. It's a similar problem, there isn't enough space to get capacity.

Q. Is there a cross member problem?

A. There is a cross member, prop shaft, two brake boosters and the cross members vary from wheel base to wheel base.

Q. What was the largest capacity that you found that you could put in that part of the vehicle?

A. I don't recall.

Q. Now, where else did you consider putting the gas tank?

A. I don't know of any other places.

Q. Those are the only two places?

A. That's all I can recall. I'm sorry, I just remembered that we looked at the left side of the vehicle, too.

Q. Where it was on the vehicle involved in this accident?

A. No, it's on the right side.

Q. I'm sorry, the left side you looked at?

A. Yes.

Q. What did you find?

A. Well, the reason we didn't put it on the left side is because of the safety implication.

Q. What are they?

A. Well, it's based on some old experience with the school buses. It has been apparently felt in the industry and by the legislatures for some time that the left side is less safe than the right side because of the exposure of oncoming traffic. So given a preference, we would prefer to put it on the right side.

Q. What is the danger that is presented by putting it on the left side?

A. Well, the comments that I have heard are that it's exposed to another vehicle in a sideswipe-type accident.

Q. That presents a danger?

A. Well, that was the reason given.

Q. Certainly it would be exposed on the right side if there were a sideswipe-type accident?

A. Well, the velocities are less on the right as compared to the left.

Q. Same exposure?

A. But the velocities are less.

Q. But the same physical exposure?

A. But not to moving vehicles.

Q. In a sideswiping situation, what is there to hit? Put the tank on the left-hand side. What is there to protect the tank?

A. Well, the tank is protected by the body of the vehicle.

Q. There is no protection from the frame?

A. No.

Q. Now, did you get your gas tank from someone else?

A. Yes.

Q. From whom?

A. We buy them from various suppliers.

Q. Do you know who supplied the gas tanks for the RM–350 back in Yr.–6?

A. I'm told it was Brisken Company that supplied this tank.

Q. This was a 40 gallon volume tank?

A. Yes.

Q. Who designed the tank?

A. Chrysler.

Q. You submitted specifications to Brisken?

A. We submitted a design.

Q. And they executed the design?

A. Yes.

Q. Now, since June of Yr.–5, has any rethinking gone on about location of gasoline tanks on your motor home chassis?

A. Yes.

Q. Tell me what rethinking has been done.

A. Increased the capacity.

Q. How about location of fuel tanks?

A. This was always a part of any consideration, to make a change in the fuel system.

Q. When did this take place?

A. I don't recall.

Q. It's sometime since this accident took place that we're involved with in this lawsuit?

A. Perhaps it's about that time.

Q. Did you consider relocating fuel tanks at that time?

A. Oh, yes.

Q. What locations did you consider?

A. It's the same situation all over again, same alternate locations and what we could do.

Q. Did you come to the same conclusions?

A. Yes.

Q. Did you have any paperwork at all on that reevaluation process?

A. No.

Q. Nothing in writing?

A. Nothing that I could find.

Q. Today where are the fuel tanks located on the motor home chassis that you manufacture?

A. Same place.

Q. Mr. Cochin, what degrees do you have?

A. Bachelor of Science, Mechanical Engineering.

Q. From where?

A. Carnegie Institute of Technology.

Q. Is that it?

A. That's all.

Q. Now, when the RM–350 chassis is sent out to the body manufacturer, how many fuel tanks does it have on it?

A. One.

Q. That is the so-called sidesaddle tank?

A. It's not a saddle tank. It's side mounted.

Q. If an auxiliary tank is to be placed on the motor home, that is done by the body builder?

A. Yes.

Q. Does Magnum put on the chassis the valve switch to switch from one tank to the other?

A. No.

Q. That is also done by the manufacturer?

A. By the body builder.

Q. Yes, I'm sorry. Now, what is the material, both as to the material type and thickness or gauge that the fuel tank is made of on the RM–350?

A. It's made of what we call terneplate steel, which is a base lead coating on steel, .054 inches thick.

Q. How does the thickness of this tank compare to the thickness of fuel tanks on motor vehicles, on automobiles, if you know?

A. It's heavier.

Q. By how much?

A. As much as double.

Q. Now, at some point I think you told us that the volume of the tank on the predecessor of RM–350 had been changed from 25 gallons to 40 gallons?

A. Yes.

Q. How did the shape of the tank at 25 gallons compare to the shape at 40 gallons?

A. I believe it was exactly the same cross section. It was simply lengthened.

Q. Now, what were the design considerations which dictated the geometry of the 40 gallon tank?

A. The space available.

Q. And that's it?

A. Yes.

Q. So it's fair to say that in the design of the chassis, the tank was designed to fit available space rather than available space designed to fit the existing design of the tank; is that correct?

A. Not totally.

Q. In what way is it not correct?

A. Well, the location was selected for other reasons. But once the location was selected, then the tank was designed to fit the space available.

Q. Well, I understood your testimony to be that when this tank was redesigned upward from 25 to 40 gallons, the areas, other areas other than the side or other locations other than the sides that were considered, were rejected because you could not get a tank in there with the 40 gallon capacity?

A. I don't think I said that. I never made reference to the fact that we couldn't get a 40 gallon tank in any particular location. I think what I did say was we couldn't get adequate capacity in some locations.

Q. Well, by "adequate capacity," what do you mean?

A. Well, adequate in this case would be something approaching 40 gallons of fuel.

Q. Well, isn't the standard for determining adequate fuel capacity a capacity sufficient to permit cruising at highway speeds from four to six hours?

A. There is no standard.

Q. Well, isn't that a commonly accepted criteria for determining adequate capacity for fuel tanks?

A. No. I don't think I've ever heard it expressed in those terms.

Q. Well, how have you heard it expressed?

A. Well, the way this fuel tank size was arrived at was on experience. We had previously a 25 gallon fuel tank, which for this type of vehicle and this type of service was felt to give inadequate cruising range, whatever that is.

Q. Who made the determination that the cruising range of 25 gallons was not adequate?

A. This probably came from the body builders back to the Sales Department to the product planners to us.

Q. Was any effort—engineering effort made to redesign the chassis itself to fit around a larger gas tank?

A. As I said, we did try to redesign the chassis. We talked about the rear cross member.

Q. Was any attempt made to lengthen or further widen the dimension of the frame?

A. That's not possible.

Q. Why is that not possible?

A. Because your legal limits on your vehicle preclude your getting out beyond so many inches. If you'll work in from the tires and the spring, that's where your frame will be.

Q. You're saying the RM–350 is as wide as legal limits permit?

A. It's right at the limit. If it's not precisely there, it's very close to it.

Q. Now, did Magnum make any tests to determine the strength of the fuel tanks for the RM–350?

A. Yes.

Q. What were the nature of those tests?

A. It would be an endurance-type test.

Q. What does the endurance test consist of?

A. It would be run on the vehicle to see if there was any sign of leakage or fatiguing of the fuel tank.

Q. Were any drop tests done with the tank?

A. No.

Q. What is a drop test?

A. A drop test is a test where a fuel tank is filled with water to a certain percent of its volume and dropped first from 30 feet on its corner and 10 feet on its fill pipe.

Q. What is the purpose of a drop test?

A. It's to conform with the Federal Standards.

Q. What is the drop test supposed to tell us about the tank that's being dropped?

A. Whether or not it conforms with that standard or not.

Q. That standard relates to what?

A. Well, its resistance to impact.

Q. In Yr.–11 the drop test was a test which was known to automotive engineers, wasn't it?

A. Yes.

Q. The purpose of the drop test is to determine strength of a tank in a crash-type situation; isn't that so?

A. No, I don't think that's necessarily so. It's to determine the strength relative to that particular performance test.

Q. Well, the test, the performance test is done in order to give the engineer some idea of the tank's ability to withstand stresses in a crash; isn't that true?

A. It's to measure the stresses in a drop. You have to come back to that.

Q. Well, ordinarily, sir, in the foreseeable using of gas tanks in vehicles, they're not dropped, are they?

A. No.

Q. So the purpose of a drop test is something more than to determine the resistance of a tank when it's being dropped; isn't that so?

A. No, because it defines the condition. It has to pass a test under certain conditions where the tank is dropped onto concrete. It's a blunt surface that it meets.

Q. Isn't the purpose of the drop test to permit an engineer to extrapolate the results of a drop test to real life situations?

A. No.

Q. Is it important for an automotive engineer to know the strength of gasoline tanks in the vehicles he designs?

A. What do you mean when you say "strength?"

Q. Resistance to crushing, tearing, breaking, shearing, puncturing.

A. Yes.

Q. It's important to know the strength of the gas tank to those kinds of forces in order to make a determination as to whether or not the design of that gas tank is reasonably safe for its intended use; isn't that so?

A. A test is always a test to conform with a particular set of parameters. These may be determined by somebody to be representative of something in the real world, or again they may not be.

Q. The parameters that are set up for the drop test are set up so that it can be determined whether or not a tank is sufficiently strong so that it can be safely used in a motor vehicle; isn't that so?

A. No.

Q. What do you understand the purposes of the drop test to be?

A. Well, you're inferring that if a tank doesn't pass a drop test, it's unsafe for use in a vehicle. That's what you've said. That's not the case. The drop test is to establish a certain degree of strength in a tank to conform with a particular standard.

Q. The particular standard is set up for a purpose, isn't it?

A. I don't know what the purpose of the standard was originally set up for.

Q. The standard relating to the drop test was set up by whom?

A. ICC originally, to my knowledge.

Q. It was set up by the ICC for some purpose, wasn't it?

A. I presume so.

Q. What is your understanding, as an engineer, of the purpose of the standard?

A. The standard was set up to give a comparative base such that one could measure whether a tank had a certain level of performance or not.

Q. What was the purpose of trying to, as you understood it as an engineer, of determining whether or not a tank had a certain level of performance?

A. Well, I don't know what the original purpose of the standard was.

Q. Well, does the standard still exist?

A. It's under the BMCS now.

Q. Do you understand, as an engineer, what its purpose is now?

A. Well, I can't answer that question directly, because you see they set up two sets of standards and they define which applies to what type of tank. They have standards which we conform to and they tell the industry what the application of each of the standards is.

Q. And the purpose of these standards is to determine whether— in the last analysis, whether or not a tank is strong enough so that it can be safely used in whatever the application it is going to be used for; isn't that fair to say?

A. I think it's probably a safe assumption.

Q. And you, as an engineer, could determine from the results of a drop test whether or not in your judgment the tank was strong enough to withstand various types of crashes that vehicles are involved in in the real world; isn't that so?

A. No, I couldn't do that.

Q. There are engineers who could; isn't that right?

A. I don't believe so.

Q. In any event, were any tests done by Magnum or by anyone on Magnum's behalf to determine the strength of the gas tank used in the RM–350?

A. Relative to the BMCS standards?

Q. Relative to any standards at all, whether governmental, private, standards of the S.A.E., any standards at all?

A. Well, we examined our conformance to the BMCS standards.

Q. Were the tests done on the gas tanks used in the RM–350 to determine their strength?

A. As I said before, yes.

Q. What tests, please?

A. Durability test.

Q. Is that the only test?

A. I don't know of any others.

Q. You, sir, are the one who was produced here by your employer as the person with the most knowledge of the RM–350 chassis.

A. I don't know how I was defined.

Q. Well, if there were other tests done on the gas tanks, sir, you would know about them, wouldn't you?

A. Not necessarily.

Q. If such a test were done, would you not have seen test results?

A. Normally I would.

Q. You have seen none other than the durability test?

A. I don't know of any others that were run.

Q. You have seen none?

A. That is right.

Q. Now, sir, how is the fill pipe on this gas tank attached to it?

A. It's connected by a rubber hose and pair of clamps.

Q. Have any tests been done to determine the resistance of this connection to shear forces?

A. Not to my knowledge.

Q. Will you describe the anchorage for the gas tank on the RM–350 chassis?

A. There is a pair of L-shaped brackets mounted to the frame that the tank rests on; had two straps affixing it to those brackets.

Q. What kind of straps?

A. They are steel straps.

Q. Has any test been done by Magnum or anyone on its behalf, to determine the strength of this anchoring system to various forces applied against the tank?

A. The durability test.

Q. That is, there have been no type of tests to determine how much force is required to remove the tank from its anchorage?

A. I'm not aware of any.

Q. And again, if such tests were done, you would probably be aware that such a test was done; isn't that so?

A. It would be reasonable to assume that, I think.

Q. Now, when the RM–350 chassis leave Magnum Corporation, I take it the only shielding, from what you said earlier, and correct me if I'm mistaken, the only shielding of the gas tank that is placed on there by Magnum is a heat shield; is that correct?

A. I believe there was a heat shield on the tank.

Q. That is on the inboard—that's inboard on the tank; isn't that so?

A. Right.

Q. That's designed to keep the—to protect it to some degree from the heat generated by the engine and the exhaust?

A. Only the muffler.

Q. There was no shielding placed in or around the gas tank by Magnum to protect it from impact; is that so?

A. That's so.

Q. Now, how far inboard of the right front wheel, if it was inboard of it at all, was the tank on the RM–350 chassis?

A. It was inboard. I don't know the dimension. 3.67 inches.

Q. Now, from an engineering point of view, it would have been feasible to place a frame around the gas tank in its location on the RM–350; isn't that so?

A. No, I don't think it's practical.

Q. Why do you say it is not practical?

A. I say it is not practical because I don't feel there is a need for the additional piece.

Q. Is that the only reason, sir?

A. Well, based on standards which are in effect, based on experience, based on the protection the body affords, I think that the fuel tank is protected adequately without the need for some other device coming around it.

Q. Sir, a frame could be placed around the gas tank in the RM–350, could it not?

A. Certainly.

Q. What lines were attached other than the filler pipe to the fuel tank on the RM–350 by Chrysler?

A. We had a fuel line going to the fuel pump. We had an ECS line going to the canister.

Q. How was the line to the fuel pump attached to the tank?

A. I believe it was by rubber hose.

Q. And a clamp?

A. Oh, definitely.

Q. And the line to the ECS, how was that connected to the tank?

A. That is by hose and clamp.

Q. Rubber hose?

A. Rubber hose.

Q. Now, as part of the work that you do, particularly with respect to designing and engineering here at Magnum, do you familiarize yourself with the product lines of your competitors?

A. Yes.

Q. Mr. Cochin, to your knowledge at any time did General Motors design a motor home with the gas tank located within the frame?

A. I believe their current motor home has the fuel tank located inside the frame.

Q. When, to your knowledge, did General Motors first manufacture a motor home with the gas tank located within the frames?

A. You're talking about the tandem axle rear unit?

Q. Yes.

A. With that one, whenever that was introduced.

Q. What engineering device or technique did they use to get the fuel tank within the frames of that chassis?

A. Well, the only thing I can say is that they have designed the entire vehicle, body and chassis, so it's an entirely different problem. They still produce this unit.

Q. My question is: By what engineering—what engineering technique did they use so that they were able to get a gasoline tank within the frame of that chassis?

A. Other than, as I say, it's a different problem, because you've got the total vehicle. It's a different problem from what we're faced with in the sale of a chassis.

Q. What is the problem that you are faced with in the sale of a chassis that prevented your company from placing a gas tank within the frame of the chassis?

A. The problem that I cited earlier. There is no space.

Q. Well, how is it that General Motors is able to find the space in its chassis and Magnum cannot?

A. General Motors doesn't on their chassis. They do on their complete unit, which is a different problem.

Q. How do they manage it in their complete unit?

A. Well, I don't know, because it's entirely a different problem. I don't have that problem, or flexibility, if you want to term it that way.

Q. What is it in their design problems that gives them more flexibility than you have here at Magnum?

A. I'd have to know what their construction is, which I don't know.

Q. I take it from your answer you have never examined one of the GMC complete motor homes?

A. No. We have looked at them with interest, but not on a comparison. Because we are not in competition with the same type of unit, just as they are not in competition with that unit that they built.

Q. When you say you've looked at them with interest, what do you mean by that?

A. We've driven them and looked at them from a user's standpoint.

Q. Have you examined the drawings of that unit?

A. No, there aren't any, to my knowledge. We don't have any.

Q. Do you, or anybody in your department, know where and how the gas tank in the GMC motor home was located?

A. My fuel tank engineer has looked at it.

Q. Have you discussed the design of the fuel tank location in the GMC complete motor home with him?

A. No.

Q. How do you know he looked at it?

A. Because I asked him.

Q. So you had some discussion with him about it?

A. I asked him if he had seen it.

Q. And he told you he had?

A. Yes.

Q. That ended the conversation?

A. No. It was really relevant to another point. I asked him if he had seen it, how many tanks they had, and what kind of valving they used.

Q. I take it you never tried to find out how they engineered the location of their gas tank; that is, General Motors?

A. On the complete unit?

Q. Yes.

A. That is right.

Q. Now, sir, if you wanted to design a motor home chassis with a wheel base of about 159 inches of the same width that your RM–350 has, you wanted to design it so that the fuel tank would be within the frame members, could you do it?

A. What size?

Q. Twenty-five gallon or better?

A. 159 wheel base?

Q. Yes.

A. Well, if I started with the design like the GMC, I'm sure I could, because I don't have a prop shaft.

Q. When you say you don't have a prop shaft, you mean—

A. If I had a GMC arrangement, which is front wheel drive, there is no prop shaft to occupy the space that we were occupying in this kind of vehicle.

Q. So are you saying then, sir, that it is the prop shaft in the RM–350 which effectively prevents you from placing a gas tank of adequate volume within the frame members?

A. I've said that's one of the factors.

Q. Is that the prime factor?

A. I haven't assigned values as to which was the most important.

Q. Well, if you didn't have the prop shaft, what else would prevent the installation of a fuel tank within the frame members on a motor home chassis of the same wheel base and width as the RM–350?

A. Let me try and answer it this way. If I have the total responsibility for the body and the chassis, I have one set of parameters. I can place my components and I can locate my storage compartments, my brakes, my exhaust system with complete freedom because I've got the total package. If I don't have the total package, if I have simply a chassis, then I have to provide for a hand-off to somebody else to pick up and be able to do his thing. It's not always the same person or the same customer. That's wherein the difficulty lies.

Q. Sir, previously you told us that GMC could get its gas tank within the frame because it has a front wheel drive and no prop shaft as you have.

A. That's not what I said.

Q. Now, Mr. Cochin, what else other than the prop shaft in the RM–350 occupies space within the frame members that prevents you from placing a gas tank of adequate volume, as you have defined it, within the frame members of that chassis?

A. The combination of the exhaust system, the brake boosters, the prop shaft and the cross members all occupy space within the frame side rails.

Q. If you wanted to, sir, you could redesign the geometry of all of these items to accommodate a gas tank within the frame members, couldn't you?

A. I don't understand the question.

Q. Aside from the prop shaft, you could redesign the location configuration of the other items which you have mentioned previously that are within the frame of the RM–350 chassis so that they could accommodate the gas tank of adequate volume within the frame members, now couldn't you?

A. Without making a design investigation I couldn't answer your question.

Q. Is it fair to say, sir, that you and your department have never made such a design investigation?

A. To do what?

Q. To determine whether or not by redesigning the type of drive from rear to front wheel and by redesigning the location and configuration of the various items you have mentioned that are located within the frame of the RM–350 chassis to find out whether or not you could accommodate a gas tank of adequate volume within the frame members of the RM–350 chassis?

A. Yes.

Q. You haven't done investigation to determine whether or not by redesigning these other items in any way, whether in or out of the frame, you could make room within the frame for a gas tank of adequate volume?

A. No, we—

Q. Isn't that so?

A. No, we did do that.

Q. Do you mean to say—do I understand you to say that you did investigate the possibility of going from a rear wheel to front wheel drive on the RM–350?

A. You just said maintain these things within the frame. That we did study. We tried to put a tank inside the frame while maintaining these things inside the frame and we were unsuccessful.

Q. And these things included the drive shaft?

A. Yes.

Q. Are you telling me that you could not place all of these other items, other than of course the cross members, in, say some way inside the frame and have a gas tank in the frame if you didn't have a prop shaft to contend with?

A. The question now is "Remove the prop shaft and leave everything else in?"

Q. Yes.

A. That I haven't done.

Q. Now, earlier in the course of the Direct Examination you mentioned that the location of the gas tank was an important design consideration. Do you recall that?

A. Yes.

Q. And the engineering considerations that you mentioned were space available, compatibility with the other components, the ability to feed fuel or take it back and then you said, last but not least, safety; is that right?

A. Yes.

Q. Would you agree that a sound and accepted engineering practice would require that safety would be the most important consideration?

A. That requires a qualified answer. That's not a yes or no.

Q. Well, give me your qualified answer then.

A. Well, safety is not at any cost, as evidenced by the work that's been done in Washington. There has to be a cost effectiveness to safety. Who is to say what that is? But, regardless, there is some balance between the effectiveness of what it is that someone is proposing and what it costs. The safety cars perhaps are an example of that. They cost $1 million apiece, but they are obviously safer than a standard automobile. But they are not cost effective. None of us would have a car.

Q. As an engineer, how do you determine the cost effectiveness of a particular design with respect to safety?

A. Well, we keep safety uppermost in our mind. On a design such as this, we consider all of the parameters relative to this application; the selection of the location of the tank, the BMCS standards that we talked about earlier. We conform basically with those standards in the selection of this location, because they say that this is a protected location and by their definition it's an other than outside mounted fuel tank, which we essentially comply with.

Q. My question to you again is: How do you determine whether or not a design with respect to safety is cost effective?

A. That's what I'm saying. We compare it to the known standards, the industry practice.

Q. Do you not take into account the risks to human beings using the vehicle and compare the risks to the cost of a particular design?

A. We don't establish the cost. When we engineer a product, we try to engineer a product that meets all the objectives, including safety.

Q. My question to you is: In determining what the—when evaluating a particular design with respect to safety, do you consider the risks involved in that particular design as compared to another design?

A. Yes.

Q. Then do you also compare the costs of one particular design with the alternative design?

A. We might.

Q. What are the hazards with respect to the location of the gas tank that your department considered in designing the RM–350?

A. I don't know what you mean when you say "hazards."

Q. You said one of the factors that you considered was safety.

A. Yes.

Q. The issue of safety implies that there are some hazards to be guarded against; isn't that so?

A. Well, perhaps. Not necessarily, though.

Q. When you considered safety with the location of the gas tank, you had some hazards to users in mind, didn't you?

A. Well, let me answer it this way: We look at this location of the fuel tank. That's a sheltered location. It's been used in the industry for a lot of years and the experience in the industry has been good here. It's where the Government recommends and insists that you put it on a school bus.

Q. When you, as an engineer, talk about safety, you are talking about protecting people from some hazard; isn't that so?

A. Yes.

Q. The hazard that one should consider in the practice of automotive engineering with respect to the design and location of a gas tank is primarily the hazards of fires in a collision; isn't that so?

A. It may be. It may be something else, too.

Q. Well, that certainly would be one of the hazards you might consider?

A. It would be one of them.

Q. And it would be an important hazard to consider, wouldn't it?

A. It would be important.

Q. One of the reasons it would be important is because gasoline has an extremely high energy density; isn't that so?

A. Yes.

Q. Well, as you considered the design of the fuel tank and its location, did you familiarize yourself with the mechanisms by which collision and post-collision fires become started and how they behave?

A. That's not a simple question to answer.

Q. It's fair to say then that you were at least familiar with the mechanisms of collision fires?

A. I don't understand the question, mechanisms of collision fires?

Q. You are familiar with how post-collision fires in motor vehicles get started, how they behave; is that so?

A. I'm aware of circumstances that contribute to fires.

Q. You would agree that it was well known that the biggest hazard—biggest fire hazard in a collision is fuel spillage; isn't that so?

A. I don't know that.

Q. Well, would you agree as an engineer that that certainly is a significant cause of collision fires?

A. I would think it would be.

Q. And fuel spillage in collisions occur in part because of the crushing or tearing or shearing or puncturing of the fuel tank; isn't that so?

A. Usually.

Q. And another cause of the fuel spillage is the separation of the gas tank from the connection of the various lines, such as the filler pipe, the vents and the fuel feed lines; isn't that so?

A. Well, it wouldn't necessarily result in fuel spillage. It could.

Q. You were also aware, were you not, that if parts of a vehicle drag on a road at speeds as low as five miles per hour, sparks as high as 1,470 degrees Fahrenheit can be produced; isn't that true?

A. I haven't the slightest idea.

Q. Have you ever done, or had anybody in your department, investigate the sources of ignition of fuel spillage in motor vehicle collisions?

A. We have investigated what possible causes of ignition might occur.

Q. One of the well-known causes are sparks produced by friction between the automobile or the motor vehicle and other objects on or along the road; isn't that so?

A. That is true.

Q. Those sparks can be produced at low speeds as well as high speeds; isn't that true?

A. I would agree with that.

Q. Now, would it be fair to say that there are design objectives in the elimination of fire hazards resulting from motor vehicle crashes?

A. Well, I think that really comes under the category of concept of objectives.

Q. One such objective is to try to prevent the release of fuel during a collision; isn't that so?

A. Not necessarily.

Q. I say that's one of them?

A. No. The concept objective could be to locate the tank where history has shown it to be relatively sheltered from damage.

Q. And the purpose of locating the tank in such a place is to prevent the release of fuel during or immediately after a collision; isn't that right?

A. Yes, or the prevention of something from getting to it.

Q. Which would cause the release of fuel, right?

A. That or other—

Q. And another design objective would be to isolate the occupants from the heat and the flame, so that they have a fair chance of being rescued; isn't that so?

A. Well, I can't speak to that end.

Q. Well, you know, as an engineer, that one of the reasons, for example, in motor vehicles that the gas tank is separated from the passenger compartment by a metal partition is to keep flames out of the passenger compartment as much as possible; isn't that so?

A. The reason I said I can't speak to that end is because we don't provide the body which contains the people.

Q. I understand that. I'm now asking you this question as an engineer.

A. That isn't always true in the case of a car where there is a metal panel between the tank and the occupants.

Q. What isn't always true?

A. That there is a metal panel.

Q. But I say that is the reason or one of the reasons there is such a metal panel?

A. But all cars don't have that.

Q. In cars that do, one of the reasons for it is to separate the passengers from any flame from gasoline spillage; isn't that so?

A. It may separate them from the flame, but it doesn't necessarily separate them from the fire. See, fire outside of a metal panel will ignite something inside of the panel.

Q. Certainly you would agree that it's a better design from a safety point of view to separate the gas tank from people by metal than by a piece of plywood?

A. Well, you're taking this totally out of context. It's rather abstract, just to say that—

Q. Well, what's the answer?

A. I don't know what the answer is. If you're saying steel is fireproof and wood isn't; I would agree with that.

Q. Can we agree that it's sound engineering practice in designing a motor vehicle that one of the design objectives is to try to create a design that will isolate the occupants from the heat and fire of a post-collision fire insofar as it is reasonably practical to do so?

MR. WAYNE: I instruct him not to do so. If you want to ask him anything about truck chassis, fine. But if you want to go about asking him expert questions relating to motor vehicles and more specially motor vehicles with bodies on top of them, I think you are getting beyond his ken.

MR. LEAVITT: I don't think you should instruct him not to answer. If he can't answer, he will say so.

MR. WAYNE: You're not limiting him to truck chassis, one, and you're getting pretty far afield.

MR. LEAVITT: All right.

Q. To the extent that the design of a motor home should be such to isolate the occupants of it from the fact of a post-collision, that would be—at least with respect to the motor home used in the RM–350 chassis, that would be the responsibility of the body builder rather than your responsibility; is that so?

A. Again I think it's a qualified answer. From a chassis standpoint, we would select a sheltered location. From the latter standpoint, it would fall to the body builder.

Q. Are you familiar with the various design alternatives available to body builders for isolating occupants from possible post-collision and collision fires?

A. No.

Q. Now, in a collision when a gas tank is subject to crushing stresses, the internal pressure within the gas tank increases, does it not?

A. Only if the liquid uses up all the volume inside the tank, neglecting the compression of the volume there.

Q. Even in the absence of crushing forces on a gas tank, at least with respect to the gas tank in the RM–350, there is internal pressure caused by the gasoline vapors; isn't that so?

A. Normally there is none. Normally it's atmospheric.

Q. When you say "Normally," what do you mean "Normally?"

A. Short of malfunction, under normal operating conditions, the tank is operating at atmospheric pressure.

Q. This gas tank on the RM–350 was equipped with a pressure vacuum filler cap; isn't that so?

A. That is correct?

Q. That is to relieve internal pressure?

A. No, to limit internal positive or negative pressure.

Q. And ordinarily that is why you say that the pressure in the tank is at atmospheric pressure?

A. Not because of the cap. The tank is vented through the charcoal canister to the atmosphere. The only reason the pressure cap is on there is in the event that line would get pinched or restricted, that the pressure wouldn't build up in the tank. The cap will relieve any pressure in excess of 1½ PSI positive and PSI negative.

Q. Now, in order to prevent the spillage of fuel in a collision, one of the engineering approaches is to protect the gas tank by its location; isn't that so? That's one approach?

A. All right.

Q. And another approach that can be taken is to shield the gas tank from impact; isn't that so?

A. Okay.

Q. And another approach that can be taken is to strengthen the gas tank itself; isn't that so?

A. Okay. There are other alternatives, also.

Q. What other alternatives do you suggest?

A. I didn't suggest any.

Q. What do you suggest are other alternatives?

A. Well, in World War II they made aircraft fuel tanks that were foam filled. They also made aircraft fuel tanks that were bladder lined, so that they would seal up on being hit.

Q. What reason are foam filled and bladder lined tanks not used in the automotive industry?

A. I don't know. I guess it's just because there hasn't shown to be a need for it.

Q. Certainly such a tank is technically feasible; isn't that so?

A. No, I wouldn't say that.

Q. You don't think they are technically feasible?

A. I didn't say that either. I don't know. I'm sure there would be many problems.

Q. Has Magnum, to your knowledge, ever explored the technical feasibility of either foam filled or bladder lined fuel tanks?

A. Yes.

Q. When was that?

A. Some years ago.

Q. Was that exploration viewed at using them in motor vehicles?

A. Yes.

Q. Was that done in your department?

A. We had examined them.

Q. What were the results of that study?

A. Well, we had looked at the bladder, for example, as an alternative for passing the barrier tests. It was found unnecessary.

Q. By the barrier test, you're referring to the crash barrier test?

A. Yes.

Q. Was that the reason that it was not used?

A. Yes, it wasn't necessary.

Q. Was it economically feasible?

A. No.

Q. How much more would the use of a bladder lined 40 gallon tank have added to the cost of the RM–350 chassis?

A. I don't know. Except in the case that we examined, it was about $120 penalty.

Q. It would cost $100 more?

A. Yes. If it could be made.

Q. Well, such tanks were made for aircraft in World War II; isn't that so?

A. Yes.

Q. And certainly the technology in the country with respect to fuel tanks hasn't gotten worse since World War II, has it?

A. I hope not. But there is a difference between building a military aircraft and building a commercial vehicle.

Q. The best protection for a gas tank from impact damage would be to place it behind the strongest part of the vehicle; isn't that so?

A. Yes.

Q. Is it fair to say that the strongest part of the chassis are the outside frame members?

A. No.

Q. What is the strongest part?

A. I don't know what it is, because I know in some cases we have examined alternative locations and where we're able to resist certain types of attack in one case, we fail on another. It's all trade up. Also, frequency of event enters into that, too. How often does it get attacked from what direction?

Q. Fairly common impact with any motor vehicle is an impact to its side; isn't that so?

A. No. I think you find normally or more frequently the attack is frontal or rear.

Q. Well, you certainly have intersection accidents?

A. Yes.

Q. They are often attacks from the side, are they not?

A. Yes. But you'll find that this type of vehicle here is even less exposed to that, because it's principally a highway vehicle.

Q. And vehicles do get sideswiped, that's a side attack, isn't it?

A. Yes.

Q. Now, isn't it true that a gas tank placed within the frame of a chassis is in the least vulnerable position from attack from the exterior?

A. No, it isn't. As I said before, it depends upon the direction of attack.

Q. Well, if it's—the tank, if it's inside the frame of the vehicle, it's surrounded on all four sides by the heavy metal frame of the chassis; isn't that so?

A. No, not necessarily.

Q. Well, it is surrounded if it's within the four members, it's surrounded by the four members; isn't it, by definition?

A. But it is exposed on the bottom side, isn't it? It's also subject to attack from inside.

Q. You mean if one of the occupants goes after it with a can opener?

A. No. If you had a tank, for example, where the brake boosters were and you ran into a wall, the engine is driven back and the prop shaft buckles and it wipes out a fuel tank.

Q. So if you locate it in such a position to deal with that eventuality, you'd have to shield—you'd have to shield it from underneath, wouldn't you?

A. No. That would be an internal attack, that wouldn't be from the bottom.

Q. I thought you said—

A. I suggested two possibilities, a frontal attack and internal attack. The frequency of occurrences are at the front and rear rather than from any other directions.

Q. Are you saying then that the location of the gas tank within the frame of the chassis is a less safe position than a location of a tank on the outside of the chassis?

A. What I said was it's a judgment of where the attacks are coming from.

Q. Are you saying, given the alternatives, that it is less safe to place a gas tank within the frames of a chassis than to place it on the side, outside the frame?

A. No, I didn't say that.

Q. Is it more safe?

A. Well, it's a judgment as to where the tank can go, and if it doesn't fit inside the frame, then it's going—it's not a fair question.

Q. My question is: If you could make it fit in the frame, is it more safe to be within the frame or without the frame?

A. Again, it depends where in the frame, where is the attack coming from? If it's at the back, it's not as safe on a vehicle that's going to be attacked at the back.

Q. From a design engineer's perspective, is it more safe in general or less safe design to have the gas tank on the inside of the frame as compared to the outside?

A. That's what I have been answering, I think. It depends where the attack comes from and what frequency.

Q. Let's back up. Are you familiar in a general way with the frequency of different types of attack to fuel system integrity that motor homes are most likely to be subjected to?

A. In a general sense.

Q. Having in mind your knowledge of the frequency and type of attack to the integrity of the fuel system, do you say in your judgment it is more safe or less safe to locate the tank within the frame or without the frame?

A. Where in the frame?

Q. What is your view, or your judgment, with respect to the location of the gas tank within the frame towards the rear?

A. Exposure here is higher with a higher frequency than it is in the center or on the side.

Q. Sir, Magnum places the gas tank in the RM–400 chassis at the rear within the frame?

A. Yes.

Q. Is that a less safe or more safe application than if your company placed the gas tank on that chassis on the side, outside the frame?

A. Again, that's a different category. That has a much longer overhang on the vehicle.

Q. Isn't it true that even as early as Yr.–10 it was known among automotive engineers that trucks had a higher crash fire frequency than passenger vehicles?

A. I still don't know that to date.

Q. Sir, have you ever read the Fairchild-Hiller study entitled Investigation of Motor Vehicle Performance Standards for Fuel Tank Protection published by the Department of Transportation?

A. No.

Q. Isn't it considered proper practice in engineering to keep abreast of scientific developments in the field?

A. Yes.

Q. And part of the way an engineer keeps abreast of scientific developments in the field is to read the literature; isn't that so?

A. Yes.

Q. And one of the better sources of such literature, in fact, is the Department of Transportation; isn't that so?

MR. WAYNE: Objection. I instruct him not to answer.

THE WITNESS: Thank you.

Q. Do you, from time to time, read the engineering publications from the Department of Transportation?

A. I don't know what the engineering publications are that you refer to in the D.O.T.

Q. Have you ever read any of them?

A. I've read a lot of their material.

Q. Why do you read a lot of their material?

A. Because I must do that in the course of my job.

Q. The reason you must do that is that it not only keeps you abreast of governmental standards, but keeps you abreast of new developments in the field?

A. I don't really see that it's new developments that we're seeing from D.O.T.

Q. You certainly do read the publications of the Society of Automotive Engineers?

A. Yes.

Q. The reason you do that is to keep abreast of scientific developments in the field?

A. That other people are doing, yes.

Q. Have you attended various conferences that deal with problems of automotive safety?

A. I've been involved with some on occasions.

Q. Have you attended the STAPP, S-T-A-P-P, Car Crash Conferences?

A. No.

Q. Has anybody in your department attended such conferences?

A. No.

Q. Have you ever delivered any papers concerning fuel systems at any conference or seminar or other gathering of engineers?

A. No.

Q. Have you published anything?

A. No.

Q. Has anybody in your department delivered any papers at such a gathering with respect to fuel systems?

A. No.

Q. Has anybody in your department delivered any papers at such a journals any articles or studies concerning fuel systems?

A. I'm not sure.

Q. Before we mentioned sparks as the cause of ignition of spilled gasoline in crashes. Are there other sources of ignition of the gasoline?

A. Yes.

Q. What are they, sir?

A. There could be heat of compression.

Q. Of what? Compression of what?

A. Of the fuel.

Q. You mean from the crunching of the tank?

A. Possible.

Q. What else?

A. Electrical sparks.

Q. What else? Gasoline dripping on the exhaust pipe or the manifold?

A. That's very unlikely.

Q. Does not the exhaust pipe get hotter than the flash point of gasoline?

A. No, not in the area back here. Very doubtful we could get 1,200 degrees even on a manifold. That's not likely.

RE-EXAMINATION BY MR. MOREMAN

Q. Has it ever come to your attention from any source, Federal Government, SAE, anybody, have any complaints ever come to your attention about the location of the fuel tank in motor home chassis?

A. Not to my knowledge.

Q. Are you aware of any customer complaints?

A. For the location of the fuel tank?

Q. Yes, sir.

A. Our customer is the body builder. Yes, we get some of those. But they say, "It's in the way of the shower. Can't you put it somewhere else?"

Q. Nothing from the Federal Government?

A. No.

Q. Any state governments?

A. No.

Q. There are standards—were there standards before June 8th of Yr.–5 relating to fuel systems for under 10,000 pounds?

A. For recreational vehicles?

Q. Yes, sir.

A. No.

Q. Vans?

A. No.

Q. Passenger cars?

A. You said recreational vehicles. You said vans. I thought you meant recreational vehicles. Are you saying any kind of van?

Q. Yes.

A. The BMC regulates the operation of a vehicle. If you haul dynamite, I think it is you come under their jurisdiction. But it doesn't really matter what you're driving. It's not the vehicle they qualify, it's the service.

Q. What is the BMC?

A. Bureau of Motor Carrier Safety Regulations.

Q. Let me get this straight. Are there presently any standards which would be effective today?

A. For any recreational vehicles to date?

Q. Yes.

A. Yes.

Q. That standard apparently doesn't apply to over 10,000 pounds?

A. That is correct.

Q. Are there motor homes under 10,000 pounds?

A. Could be.

Q. Do some of your chassis that we talked about today fit motor homes under 10,000 pounds?

A. No.

Q. What's the smallest chassis?

A. It's 11,000 or 12,000 pounds, I'm not sure which.

Q. Do you know the designation of the standard?

A. The standard on fuel systems?

Q. Yes.

A. FMVSS 301.

Q. Is there an SAE equivalent standard?

A. No.

Q. Or recommended practice?

A. I think the SAE simply says that recommended practice is "secure", something that simple.

Q. Now, that standard sets up a crash test, barrier test, does it not?

A. Yes.

Q. It requires that you run the vehicle into the barrier and then measure the leakage from the tank?

A. Yes.

Q. Magnum does that for under 10,000 pound vehicles?

A. Yes.

Q. Is it all vehicles under 10,000 pounds?

A. Yes.

Q. What are the other parameters of that standard?

A. The essence of the standard is that a vehicle was run into a fixed barrier at 30 miles an hour.

Q. What do you then do, measure something?

A. Measure the loss of fuel and you can't lose more than an ounce, I think it is, in five minutes.

Q. When did that standard come into force?

A. It became effective 9–1 Yr.–3.

Q. Now, have you ever tested—has Magnum ever tested any vehicles over 10,000 pounds to see if they complied with the standard?

A. No.

Q. Sir, you stated with respect to placing a frame member around gasoline tanks on the RM–350, you said in your opinion it wasn't necessary?

A. Yes.

Q. It could be done?

A. It could be done.

Q. If it were to be done, the logical person to do it would be Magnum? You have the technology?

A. Well, it's not a question of technology. When you talk about the logical person, I could envision the body builder, when he builds his bird cage, building the frame around the fuel tank.

Q. If you were to put a frame around the fuel tank, you would have to attach it to the frame rails?

A. Not necessarily. It's really contingent as to how much bird cage—the more structure in the body, the less bird cage around the tank. Conversely, the less structure in the body, the more around the fuel tank.

Q. Magnum could have built some kind of frame around the fuel tank?

A. Possibly.

Q. In your opinion, that's not necessary?

A. That is right.

RE-EXAMINATION BY MR. LEAVITT

Q. You indicated that the body manufacturer would be just as logical a person in the chain of production to protect the side mounted fuel tank?

A. In our hypothet, the question was "Should we have one," and if the answer is "Yes," then the question is "Where is the more logical place to put it in." Well, it may be more logical for the body manufacturer to put it in because the amount of addition is dependent upon what he's got to begin with.

Q. So that the body manufacturer could provide outside impact shielding with his body construction, provided he used—he covered the gas tank, so to speak, with material of adequate strength to provide shielding; is that so?

A. Yes.

Q. From an engineering perspective, that in your opinion is equally feasible to Magnum building a metal frame around the outside of the tank as an impact shield; is that so?

A. It would be conceivable that we could supply a bird cage around the fuel tank.

Q. In part the reason for your opinion that an impact shield, that it was not necessary for Magnum to put an impact shield around the gas tank, was that the body manufacturer could do it just as easily?

A. No. We were on a hypothetical.

Q. Yes.

A. Now it sounds as though you're suggesting to me there should have been one there.

Q. All I'm saying is that was one of the reasons that you feel that there was no need for one by Magnum, was that if one should be put on, the body manufacturer could do it just as easily?

Q. Let me put this question to you: Without suggesting that the RM–350 chassis is or is not adequate for its intended purposes, my question to you is: Is it not feasible from an engineering point of view to have designed a chassis for motor homes with the wheel base of aproximately 159 inches with the longitudinal frame members ten inches wider than the—ten inches further apart than the distance between the longitudinal frame members on the RM–350 chassis?

A. Well, as I said earlier, if we were to move those frame rails out, we would go over the legal width of the dual tires, because that vehicle has larger tires.

Q. So in order to increase the distance between the longitudinal frame members, you would have to make other engineering adjustments in the design of the chassis, wouldn't you?

A. It sounds that we would have to make a change in the law.

Q. Well, are you telling me that you could not make a chassis with a 159 inch wheel base with the frame ten inches wider than the frame on the RM–350?

A. Not with dual tires.

Q. Well, without dual tires?

A. Then you could gain the width of each tire you take off.

Q. What would that width be?

A. I figured it before and it was roughly eight some inches.

Q. So such a chassis could be designed, couldn't it?

A. It's possible.

Q. Not only is it possible, but it would be feasible from an engineering point of view, wouldn't it?

A. No.

Q. Why do you say it would not be feasible?

A. Because we can't carry the load on a single tire.

Q. You could carry the load by having two axles with single tires each, couldn't you?

A. Yes, that's possible.

Deposition of Alex Thaler

EXAMINATION BY MR. LEAVITT

Q. Please identify yourself by giving us your name and your position with the Defendant, Odyssey.

A. My name is Alex Thaler. I am a service manager for the Odyssey Corporation, Swinger Division.

Q. How long have you been service manager for Odyssey?

A. I have been service manager since February of Yr.–4.

Q. Now, what are your duties as service manager?

A. My duties as service manager are to handle all warranty claims sent in by our dealers and handle all service work to be done in our service department.

Q. Now, Mr. Thaler, please tell us what your role in the design of the 22–foot Swinger for the Yr.–6 model was?

A. My role in the design—I had no role in the design, itself. Mine was in production. Mine was in the production end of it.

Q. Were you ever consulted by the designer with respect to what designs would be best for production?

A. I would say, yes, in some meetings that we had I was consulted.

Q. So your participation in the design of this vehicle was really the participation of a consultant, so to speak, is that right?

A. Right.

Q. Were there meetings at which you were present which the design of the vehicle as a whole was discussed?

A. No, I was not present except for a couple of meetings.

Q. Yes, but at some of these meetings, was the design as a whole discussed?

A. No, not as a whole.

Q. What aspects in design was discussed at the meetings which you were present?

A. The type of pumps, water pumps, that we used and some of the materials—colors of plywood, materials like this.

Q. So you did at least discuss from a design point of view the selection of materials to be used in the vehicle, is that correct?

A. I would say only the colors of materials.

Q. What is it about the colors of materials that is of particular interest to the production aspect of the manufacture of the vehicle?

A. The colors don't relate to production. I would say it relates to the sale of the product.

Q. But you were in production, not in sales, isn't that so?

A. This is true.

Q. Didn't you ever discuss the choice of the types of paneling to be used, the thickness of the material?

A. No, we didn't.

Q. You indicated the choice of materials for this vehicle was made by the sales manager, is that correct?

A. Correct.

Q. Was he an engineer?

A. I don't know.

Q. At any of the discussions relating to design which you were present, was the question of safety in design ever discussed?

A. I don't know.

Q. You don't remember?

A. I don't remember.

Q. Well, was the question—were questions of fire hazards with respect to design ever discussed in your presence concerning this vehicle?

A. I don't recall.

Q. Did you, yourself, ever raise any questions concerning the relationship of the materials selected and any possible fire hazards?

A. No, I didn't.

Q. Did anyone discuss with you the feasibility from the point of view of production of using materials different from the materials that went into the Yr.–6 model 22-foot Squire?

A. No.

Q. Did anyone discuss with you the production—the feasibility as far as production was concerned of changing the means whereby the occupants of one of these vehicles would be insulated or protected from any possible gasoline leakage from the fuel system?

A. No.

Q. Are you familiar with this Technical Report, Exhibit 27 for Identification?

A. I have seen it. I am not completely familiar with it.

Q. Can you tell us the circumstances under which this report was made?

A. Yes.

Q. What are the circumstances?

A. Magnum sent us a letter stating that they have a proving ground that we were able to accept. If we want to, we can send a unit to them for evaluation which we accepted.

Q. Now, in the Technical Report there are various recommendations for changes in the practice followed by Odyssey in the manufacture of the particular vehicle that was evaluated, are there not?

A. Yes.

Q. Were these recommendations of the Magnum Corporation followed?

A. I would have to say, yes, to the best of my ability they were.

Q. Well, what does to the best of your ability mean?

A. Well, some of those which—I am not familiar with the report, but I do know that Magnum had asked for some things to be changed that were our design we could not do.

Q. In other words you could not follow the recommendations without a change in your design, is that correct?

A. Right.

Q. Now, with respect to the fuel and emission system on the 20-foot Sportster covered in the Exhibit 27, is the system in that vehicle the same as the fuel and emission system in the 22-foot Squire for the Yr.–6 model year?

A. Yes, depending on the chassis that was used.

Q. If we assume a Dodge chassis, are the fuel and emission systems the same for each—between the 20-foot Sportster and the 22-foot Squire all built on a Dodge chassis?

A. If they were the same size chassis, yes.

Q. Did both the 20-foot Sportster and 22-foot Squire both use the RM–350 Dodge chassis?

A. I am not sure at that time there was an optional chassis used which we used on the 23-foot model which was not used on the 21.

Q. But if the optional chassis was not selected, both the 20-foot Sportster and the 22-foot Squire would both use the RM–350 Dodge chassis?

A. At present I am not sure what the RM–350 was, whether that is optional chassis or whether that is the standard chassis that we used.

Q. What documents would assist you in answering that question?

A. Our unit file.

Q. Would you look at the unit file which is Exhibit 28 and use that to refresh your recollection and tell us?

A. It is a standard chassis.

Q. So that we are all clear, the 20-foot Sportster covered by the report in Exhibit 27 and the 22-foot Squire shown on your unit file Exhibit 28, used identical chassis, is that correct?

A. Correct.

Q. And therefore their fuel and emission systems would be identical, is that correct?

A. Yes.

Q. Now, under Group F of this report entitled Fuel and Emission System, item Number 1 under the column Recommended Practice, it states, "Relocation of fuel tanks, brackets and heat shields is not recommended." Then it gives the reasons for the recommended practice, and then the evaluation says—it says, "Meets recommended practice, yes." Under the Comments column in handwritten pencil it says, "25-foot Senator relocated forward. See other notes." Now, can you tell us who made that notation?

A. No, I can't.

Q. Was that made by an employee of Odyssey or an employee of Magnum, if you know?

A. I do not know.

Q. What are the other notes to which that pencilled note refers?

A. I do not know.

Q. What does the note mean, if you know?

A. To the best of my knowledge, it means that the 25-foot Senator fuel tank had been relocated forward.

Q. By Odyssey?

A. Yes.

Q. Now, to your knowledge had there been any discussion by any employee of Odyssey with any employee of Magnum Corporation concerning the feasibility of relocating the gas tank on the RM–350 chassis?

A. I don't know.

Q. Had the feasibility of relocating the gas tank from a production point of view or from any other point of view ever been discussed with you by any employee of Odyssey?

A. No.

Q. Was any discussion—Did you have any discussion with anybody concerning the feasibility of providing better protection for the gas tank, itself, than was designed into the vehicle?

A. No.

Q. Based on your personal knowledge or the knowledge you have derived from being familiar with engineering documents at Odyssey, was any Swinger vehicle of any model year, Yr.–6 or earlier, ever given any crash test of any kind?

A. No.

Q. Have you seen any reports from any source of any crash or puncture tests or any other tests to test the structural strength of the gas tank?

A. No.

Q. To your knowledge has Odyssey ever requested any person or corporation to do such tests with respect to the gas tank?

A. No.

Q. Has Odyssey ever asked for an evaluation from a safety point of view of the location of the gas tank on the RM–350 chassis when used as a chassis for an Odyssey recreational vehicle?

A. To my knowledge, no.

Q. Have you seen any documents which indicate that such an evaluation was ever made for Odyssey?

A. No.

Q. Has Odyssey ever requested any person or corporation to evaluate the Swinger with respect to a fire hazard of any nature?

A. No.

Q. To your knowledge as quality control manager, have there been any complaints of any nature from any person with respect to the operation of the escape hatch on the 22-foot Swinger—

A. No, not as far as operation.

[*Exhibit 30, Advertising literature, marked for Identification.*]

Q. Mr. Thaler, looking at Exhibit 30 for Identification, it says in smaller type under the green type, "Swinger caps this year's good looks with custom-built fiberglass front and back ends painstakingly made in Swinger's own manufacturing facilities." Isn't it true that the fiberglass front and back ends were made for Swinger by someone else?

A. No, not at that time.

Q. They were made at the Swinger plant?

A. Right.

Q. And are you familiar with the method by which they were made?

A. I would have to answer that as partially.

Q. Are you familiar with the type of resins used in the fiberglass?

A. No.

Q. Was any fire retardant added to the resins?

A. I do not know.

Q. Now, it then says, "Where possible and practical, Swinger craftsmen build the component parts of their motor homes, themselves." Is it true that all the work done on the Swingers is done by unskilled laborers?

A. Component parts consist of appliances, I would say, and we have nothing to do with them; we purchase them from an outside supplier, and as far as your second question on unskilled labor, I would say our people are skilled in our product.

Q. What do you understand the term unskilled laborer to mean?

A. It is a person not knowing the product that he is building.

Q. Are the men who work on the assembly line at Swinger, were they given any training?

A. Yes.

Q. What kind of training?

A. On-the-line training by supervisors who have knowledge of the units.

Q. Were any of the materials used on the interior of the Swingers, to your knowledge, ever tested with respect to the behavior under thermal stress? Do you understand what I mean by thermal stress?

A. Not completely.

Q. I mean what happens to them when they are heated to very high temperatures and exposed to fire?

A. No, not to my knowledge.

Q. What durability tests were given to the Swingers or to the prototype models?

A. None.

Q. What durability tests were the component parts subjected to?

A. Through tests in our R & D department to see how long they would last, how long they would operate prior to using the materials in the unit.

Q. And so the R & D department did durability tests for the component parts for recreational vehicles?

A. Yes.

Q. What component parts were tested by R & D?

A. The batteries have been tested.

Q. For durability?

A. I would say durability to see how long they last. I would say that is a durability test. You are talking probably in the case of damage or something like this—no, we didn't perform a test on it to see how much strength it would take before the battery would fall apart or crush or anything like this.

Q. Now, describe any other durability tests on any other components that you are personally familiar with.

A. Water pumps. We hooked a battery to that, ran a water supply tank into it which would run the water through the pump, recirculated it back, and we let it run continuously, and I cannot tell you how long, just to see if the water pump would withstand the pressure.

Q. Anything else?

A. That's the only ones I'm familiar with.

Q. Now, I neglected to ask you, Mr. Thaler, but what is your training, education and experience in your field?

A. My only training is the School of Hard Knocks. I started in the business in Yr.–19 on the line.

Q. You are a high school graduate?

A. I am a high school graduate.

Q. Have you taken any technical courses?

A. No, I haven't.

Q. In Yr.–6, to your knowledge, did Odyssey have any licensed registered engineer who had responsibilities either in manufacturing, production or design for the Swingers?

A. I do not know any engineering degrees of what the personnel had at that time. I am not familiar with them.

Q. Are you familiar with the properties of the aluminum sheet that was placed on the underbody of the Swinger?

A. No.

Q. You do know, however, that aluminum is a very good conductor of heat, isn't that so?

A. I am not familiar with it.

Q. I noticed in Exhibit 27 for Identification under Group M in the document entitled Miscellaneous, Page 28, Item 2, it says, "Engine cover material. The engine cover should be impervious to fuel or fuel vapors or have an impervious barrier on the underside". The reason stated here is to prevent fuel and fuel vapors being soaked up and thereby providing a possible fire hazard, and under the column, meets recommended practice:, it says, "No." Photo Number 12 comments, "Painted plywood is very inadequate for fuel or oil repulsion." My question to you is: was the engine cover material changed as a result of this recommendation?

A. It has been changed.

Q. And what was it changed to?

A. We are using a foam insulation barrier, rubber. I don't know the technical name of the material.

Q. What is ABS?

A. ABS is a type of plastic, to my knowledge.

Q. Here the comment is, "Needs insulation F/G or ABS, 11/73." F/G I take it means fiberglass.

A. Yes.

Q. Do you know who put that comment in?

A. No, I don't know.

Q. Was any kind of sound deadening material or undercoat placed on the bottom of the 22-foot Squire in the Yr.–6 model year?

A. There was undercoating placed under the unit.

Q. Under the whole unit?

A. No, around wheel wells, engine cover, fire wall. There was an aluminum underbelly put under it that helped for deadening or insulation.

Q. In other words the purpose of the aluminum undersheet was to act essentially as a water vapor barrier, is that correct?

A. Correct.

Q. It was not intended to provide fire protection to the occupants, isn't that so?

A. That is true.

CROSS EXAMINATION BY MR. MOREMAN

Q. Mr. Thaler, you were asked on direct examination by Mr. Leavitt about the standards of quality which were followed by your company with respect to the production of the product which gives rise to this litigation. Would it also be fair to say that one of the standards of quality which was followed by your company was adherence to the various federal and industry standards which applied to recreational vehicles of this type?

A. Yes.

Q. Isn't it fair to say that one of the goals, one of the quality goals and criteria at your company was to make certain that your products, all of them, complied with all of the various federal and industrial and trade standards which were then applicable?

A. Yes.

Q. And included among those standards of quality which were adopted and followed by your company, isn't it fair to say we can count the Federal Motor Vehicle Safety Standard?

A. Yes.

Q. And can we also count among those standards the ANSI standards which have been produced here at this deposition?

A. Yes.

Q. Can we also count among those standards at least some publications of the Society of Automotive Engineers which have been produced at this deposition?

A. Yes.

Q. Isn't it also a fair statement to say that another quality standard adhered to by your company was overseeing and making certain that you received from your vendors some kind of indication that they complied with the various laws and standards which were then applicable with respect to safety and flammability?

A. Yes.

Q. And specifically with respect to flammability, isn't it fair to say that one of the standards of quality followed by your company was to ascertain from your vendors an assurance or obtain from your vendors an assurance that they had complied with the various regulations having to do with flammability of materials in recreational vehicles?

A. Yes.

REDIRECT EXAMINATION BY MR. LEAVITT

Q. Have you seen written assurances from the vendors that the items that they supplied to Odyssey did, in fact, comply with any standards?

A. No.

Q. So your answers concerning the assurances which were obtained by Odyssey was made entirely on—What is it based on or what are they based on?

A. Based on the fact that we follow these codes which are the ANSI codes, SAE codes and items of this nature.

Q. Your assumption that your product complies with the various flammability standards Mr. Moreman had reference to depends on the assumption that the component parts and materials by Odyssey's vendors comply with the applicable standards, isn't that true?

A. I would say, yes.

Q. And you have no personal knowledge based on any testing that you have done that, in fact, any of those components comply with any of those standards, do you?

A. No.

Q. And you have told us you have never seen any reports of any tests with respect to flammability done on any of the materials or components, isn't that true?

A. Yes.

Q. Before this lawsuit started, did anybody at Odyssey tell you that any of the materials or component parts used by Odyssey in its Swinger recreational vehicles were, in fact, tested to determine whether or not they comply with the applicable standards governing flammability?

A. Yes.

Q. Who told you that?

A. Different people in the organization.

Q. Name them.

A. Jeffrey Terrio; numerous people.

Q. Well, Mr. Terrio, we learned, didn't come to the company until almost the close of the Yr.–5 model year, isn't that true?

A. That is correct.

RECROSS EXAMINATION BY MR. MOREMAN

Q. Mr. Thaler, with respect to the federal standards having to do with the flammability of materials in recreational vehicles, isn't it fair to say that at some point you became aware that such a standard had gone into force?

A. Yes.

Q. And is it also fair to say that after that standard went into force, no products were built or put into the channels of commerce by your company which did not comply with that standard?

A. Yes, to the best of my knowledge.

Q. And so far as you know, isn't it fair to say that approximately the time that these standards went into force, you became aware by word of mouth from other employees of your employer that the vendors from whom your company purchased component parts were given assurances of compliance with this federal standard regarding flammability?

A. Yes.

Q. So you heard from your co-workers, and it is fair to say that it was a general conversation among the people of the plant and general knowledge that the vendors of the various component parts of your products were complying with the federal standard I have referred to?

A. Yes.

Q. And also were indicating to your company some form of assurance that the component parts so complied?

A. To the best of my knowledge.

REDIRECT EXAMINATION BY MR. LEAVITT

Q. And all this shop talk and conversations of which you learned of the existence of Federal Standard 302 and the assurances given—the assurances of compliance given by vendors occurred for the model year Yr.–4, is that right?

A. No.

Q. For Yr.–5?

A. This word of mouth was back in—prior to September of Yr.–7.

Q. And your knowledge of compliance with the federal standards is based entirely on this general conversation word of mouth, isn't it?

A. Partially. That plus the fact that the plywood we were getting in was stamped on the back of it which said it met code which I cannot really say that it did because I did not see tests, but it was stamped.

Q. And did it say what code it complied with on the stamp?

A. Yes.

Q. What code?

A. Class C code, fire—

Q. Of the National Fire Protection Association?

A. I would say, yes.

Q. And you understand that the code of the National Fire Protection Association relating to Class C is not the same as the regulations promulgated by the Department of Transportation of the United States, isn't that so?

A. I don't know.

Q. Well, you know that the National Fire Protection Association classifications of materials that stamp relates to deals with the classification for materials used in building construction, isn't that so?

A. I don't know.

Q. You don't know what it relates to, do you?

A. Not specifically, no.

Q. And you don't even know whether it has any relationship to use in recreational vehicles, multiple unit dwellings, high rise apartments or single residences, do you?

A. No.

Q. In fact, you have never read any of the National Fire Protection Association codes, have you?

A. No, I haven't.

INDEX

References are to Pages

References are to Pages

References are to Pages

†